Lamentations
FAITH IN A TURBULENT WORLD

Yeshivat Har Etzion ישיבת הר עציון

MAGGID

Yael Ziegler

LAMENTATIONS

FAITH IN A TURBULENT WORLD

Matan
Yeshivat Har Etzion
Maggid Books

Lamentations
Faith in a Turbulent World

First Edition, 2021

Maggid Books
An imprint of Koren Publishers Jerusalem Ltd.

POB 8531, New Milford, CT 06776-8531, USA
& POB 4044, Jerusalem 9104001, Israel
www.maggidbooks.com

Cover Image: *The Starry Night*, by Vincent van Gogh (1889)
Museum of Modern Art, New York, USA/Bridgeman Images

The publication of this book was made possible
through the generous support of *The Jewish Book Trust*.

ISBN 978-1-59264-555-8, *hardcover*

Printed and bound in the United States

In loving memory of our parents

Samuel and Yvette Levene
Dr Joss Leigh and Sheila

כִּי יְדַעְתִּיו לְמַעַן אֲשֶׁר יְצַוֶּה אֶת בָּנָיו וְאֶת בֵּיתוֹ אַחֲרָיו
וְשָׁמְרוּ דֶּרֶךְ ה׳ לַעֲשׂוֹת צְדָקָה וּמִשְׁפָּט

לעילוי נשמות

יצחק בן חיים צבי שווארץ ז״ל
Nicholas Schwartz

נלב״ע י״ג שבט תשע״א

שבע שיינדל בת דוד שווארץ ז״ל
Sondra Schwartz

נלב״ע י״ג שבט תשע״ח

נסים יפרח בן רחל ז״ל
Nisim Yifrach

נלב״ע י״ד טבת תשנ״ט

שרה גודמן-טווערסקי בת מאיר הכהן ז״ל
Sarah Goodman-Twersky

נלב״ע י״ז טבת תשנ״ג

Dedicated by the ones who loved them … and always will.

Contents

Introduction to Eikha

GOALS AND FOCUS

Writing a commentary on Eikha, the book of Lamentations, involves
a completely different set of challenges than writing a commentary
on Ruth.[1] In Ruth, I focused on the themes that emerged from an
examination of the plot and characters. Eikha, how ever, lacks plot and
characters. Thus, this commentary focuses instead on the themes and
ideas that arise from the poetic language so intrinsic to Eikha. With
masterful use of language, Eikha grapples with profound grief and
theological inquiry.

I will examine the book's broad themes, such as theodicy, Israel's
relationship with God, the fall of Jerusalem, and the effects of human
suffering, but I will also engage in a close reading of the text. This
presents a particular challenge, inasmuch as I must first contend with
the difficult words, the ellipses, and the deliberate ambiguities strewn
throughout biblical poetry. Interpreting Hebrew poetry in translation
presents another difficulty. In spite of the technical challenges, I hope
that this reading will yield a profound understanding of the book itself
and, more generally, that it will illustrate the depths of biblical poetry
and how it works to shape textual meaning.

This book employs an intertextual approach, examining the
relationship between Eikha and other books of Tanakh. Eikha's relationship with various prophetic books is of particular interest and

---

1. *Ruth: From Alienation to Monarchy* (Jerusalem: Maggid, 2015).

significance. Prophecies of rebuke and warning offer important background to the punitive and calamitous events, explaining the nature of the sins that led to Jerusalem's fall. Of no less interest are the prophecies of consolation that offer relief for Eikha's misery. Prophets often transmute language from Eikha, inverting its message from despair to hope.

While drawing on academic sources and methodology (to which I am indebted and appreciative), in this commentary I remain chiefly devoted to the religious quest. My interpretative framework is rooted in the world of Torah learning, in both its resources and goals. In the final analysis, I hope and pray that this encounter with Eikha moves people to strengthen and deepen their religious experience.

In the following introduction, I will discuss the technical questions that arise with respect to the book of Eikha. The book's title, its author, its cohesion, and its date of composition are all subject to discussion. After presenting a brief overview of various approaches to each of these issues, I will explain the approach that I adopt in this book.

TITLE OF THE BOOK

For the sake of consistency with the Maggid Studies in Tanakh series, this volume is entitled *Lamentations*, but throughout the commentary I will refer to the biblical book by its evocative Hebrew name, Eikha. The word "*Eikha*" opens the book (as well as chapters 2 and 4) with a rhetorical question, an elongated form of the word *eikh*, meaning "How?" This form seems to affix a sigh to the terse query, powerfully conveying the nation's bewildered pain.

Although the biblical book is popularly knowns as Eikha, this is not its official title. *Ḥazal* refer to it by the name *Kinot*, which parallels the English title Lamentations.[2] A *kina* is a lament used for the public mourning of an individual (II Sam. 1:17–27; 3:33–34). As a rhetorical device, prophets sometimes utter a *kina* for the nation,[3] or for the city

---

2. See, for example, Ḥagiga 5b; Bava Batra 14b; Y. Shabbat 16. The Greek and Latin names for the book, *Threnoi* or *Threni*, are a translation of the rabbinic title, *Kinot*.
3. See Ezekiel 19:1; Amos 5:1–2.

that represents the nation.[4] Jeremiah (9:9–10), for example, declares that he will engage in mourning rituals, including a *kina*, in advance of the impending destruction of Jerusalem and the cities of Judah. By calling this book *Kinot*, *Ḥazal* note that Eikha expresses grief for Judah's apparent demise, a seemingly irrevocable tragedy that threatens the continued spiritual and physical existence of the nation.

Fortunately, the Tanakh does not conclude with the exile and its ensuing lamentations. Several biblical books describe the return from the Babylonian exile to the land of Israel, illustrating the continuation of Israel's story and the nation's ability to rebuild following calamity.

AUTHORSHIP

While the book does not identify its author, there is a strong tradition that the prophet Jeremiah composed Eikha. The Talmud (Bava Batra 15a) states this as fact, and midrashim tend to cite verses from Eikha in Jeremiah's name.[5] Various translations (Greek Septuagint, Syriac Peshitta, Aramaic *Targum*, Latin Vulgate) open the book with an additional verse or a superscription that attributes authorship to Jeremiah.[6] Moreover, the Septuagint's placement of Eikha immediately after the book of Jeremiah (with some traditions regarding them as one continuous book) lends further support to this tradition.

Jeremiah prophesies before, during, and after the calamitous events that give rise to Eikha. Unsurprisingly, shared themes link Jeremiah's book to Eikha. These include the destruction of Jerusalem

---

4. A *kina* for the destruction of a city is a literary trope, in which the text likens the loss of a city to the death of an individual.

5. For a sampling of this prevalent practice, see Eikha Rabba 1:23, 51; 2:23; 4:18.

6. For example, the Greek translation (the Septuagint) prefixes this verse to the first chapter: "And it came to pass, after Israel was taken captive and Jerusalem made desolate, that Jeremiah sat weeping and lamented with this lamentation over Jerusalem, and said." An Aramaic *Targum*'s ascription is more concise and is affixed to the first verse of the book: "Jeremiah, the prophet and high priest, said." Although Jeremiah 1:1 does ascribe priesthood to Jeremiah, according to this targumic tradition Jeremiah was the high priest, a tradition not found elsewhere. This tradition may derive from the notion that Jeremiah's father, Ḥilkiya, should be identified as the high priest who functioned during the time of Josiah (see, e.g., Radak, Jer. 1:1, citing his father; and Malbim ad loc.).

and the Temple, the direct connection between sins and suffering, God's relationship to the events, the accountability of the false prophets, the futility of reliance upon political alliances, the terrible famine that causes maternal cannibalism, and the ultimate defeat of the enemies.

Similar phrases, shared vocabulary, and stylistic similarities further cement the connection between Jeremiah and Eikha.[7] Prophetic laments scattered throughout Jeremiah invoke a style and spirit similar to Eikha's laments. Compare Jeremiah's plaintive cry to those expressed in Eikha:

> How I wish my head were water and my eye a spring of tears; I would cry day and night for the fallen of the daughter of my nation! (Jer. 8:23)

> Their hearts cried out to the Lord, wall of the daughter of Zion. Let your tears flow like a stream day and night! Do not let yourself cease! Do not stop up your eyes! Get up! Cry out in the night at the top of each watch. Pour out your heart like water before the face of the Lord! (Eikha 2:18–19)

> Streams of water flow from my eye over the brokenness of the daughter of my nation. My eye flows and does not stop, refusing to cease. (Eikha 3:47–48)

Several biblical narratives associated with Jeremiah lend support to his authorship of Eikha. In II Chronicles 35:25, Jeremiah composes (or chants) lamentations on the occasion of Josiah's death, which are then inscribed in a "*sefer hakinot*," or book of lamentations. Some biblical interpreters adduce this verse as support for Jeremiah's authorship of

---

7. Some notable examples include the phrases "*betulat bat Zion*" and "*megurai misaviv*." Language strongly evocative of Eikha appears in Jeremiah 13:17, 22, 26; 14:17; 15:17; 20:7; 48:43. This partial list proffers some striking examples. For more on this, see G. H. Cohn, *Textual Tapestries: Explorations of the Five Megillot* (Jerusalem: Maggid, 2016), 217–29, and his references on p. 223, footnote 5.

Eikha, maintaining that some of these lamentations appear in Eikha, especially in chapter 4.[8] At the very least, this verse establishes Jeremiah's inclination and ability to compose lamentations.

In another biblical episode associated with Jeremiah's authorship of Eikha, he sends a scroll to the sinful Judean king, Jehoakim (Jer. 36). The scroll (referred to as *"megillat sefer"*) contains "all of the words that [God] said to [Jeremiah] regarding Israel, Judah, and all the nations from the day that [God] spoke to [Jeremiah], from the days of Josiah until today" (Jer. 36:2). Intended to galvanize the nation to repent, the scroll describes the catastrophic punishment that God plans to dispense (Jer. 36:3). Moreover, it testifies to the imminent arrival of the Babylonian king and the impending destruction of the land (Jer. 36:29).

This scroll frightens the king's officers (Jer. 36:16), but the king himself remains impassive (Jer. 36:24). Jehoakim feeds Jeremiah's scroll into the fireplace, a brash display of the king's disdain for prophetic counsel (Jer. 36:22–23). Following this episode, God instructs Jeremiah to rewrite the destroyed scroll, which Jeremiah does, supplementing it with new details (Jer. 36:32).

Some rabbinic sources identify the burnt scroll as the book of Eikha.[9] Ibn Ezra (in the introduction to his commentary on Eikha) disagrees, noting that Eikha contains none of Jeremiah's prophecies of doom and mentions neither specific events nor people from Jehoakim's time. Still, for some sources, the incident with the scroll lends credence to the idea that Jeremiah wrote Eikha.

Some modern scholars assert that Jeremiah did not write this book. They provide a variety of reasons, one of which is that Eikha does not name

---

8. See Eikha Rabba 4:1; Rashi, Eikha 4:1. In particular, Eikha 4:20 may allude to Josiah's death (see *Targum* on Eikha 1:18 and 4:20).

9. See *Midrash Tanḥuma, Parashat Shemini* 9; *Moed Katan* 26a; Rashi, Jeremiah 36:23, 32; Rashi, Eikha 1:1; Rashbam, Introduction to Eikha. There is some debate as to which parts of Eikha the king burned and what exactly Jeremiah added later (in accordance with Jer. 36:32). Rashi (Eikha 1:1; Jer. 36:32) maintains that chapters 1, 2, and 4 were written at God's initial command (Jer. 36:1), while chapter 3 was added later. A midrash (Eikha Rabba *Petiḥta* 28) discusses the issue, suggesting that only chapter 1 was in the original scroll. See also Radak, Jeremiah 36:30, who cites the debate.

Jeremiah, a known figure in Jerusalem.[10] However, this does not establish that Jeremiah is not the author; it only indicates that the author chose to remain anonymous. There could be a very good reason for Jeremiah to write Eikha without attaching his name. After all, he was a well-known prophet of rebuke. Coming from Jeremiah, the book would sound like a reprimand; worse, it could appear to be a justification of his prophetic exhortations. As we will see, this book is neither reproof nor vindication of prophetic reliability. Its tone is not that of an irate or pacified prophet, but rather of an anguished witness, a suffering member of a downtrodden nation.

In any case, Eikha deliberately obscures the identity of its author, deeming him non-essential and perhaps distracting. Moreover, the absence of an author is a statement in its own right. Anonymity enables the author to identify with his subject and share in the nation's grief. This intimacy would be difficult to achieve if the book attributed authorship to a renowned castigator. By choosing not to name its author, the book

---

10. Some scholars maintain that there are theological and ideological differences between the books. Among several examples, S. R. Driver, *An Introduction to the Literature of the Old Testament* (New York: Charles Scribner's Sons, reprinted 1914), 463, doubts that the author of Jeremiah would state that prophetic vision has ceased (Eikha 2:10) or would promote a favorable view of King Zedekiah (whom Driver assumes is the subject of Eikha 4:20). R. Gordis, *The Song of Songs and Lamentations* (New York: Ktav, reprinted 1974), 125, observes that Jeremiah's negative view of Israel's behavior in the Temple (which he describes as a den of thieves in Jer. 7:10) does not match the obvious regard for the Temple in the book of Eikha (e.g., 2:1, 6). D. R. Hillers, *Lamentations* (Anchor Bible; Garden City: Doubleday, 1972), xxi–xxii, opines that some of the first-person content of the book contradicts Jeremiah's own prophecies (as an example, he cites Eikha 4:17 and Jer. 2:18). Hillers further argues (p. xxii) that Eikha suggests an author "more closely identified with the common hopes and fears of the people than it was possible for Jeremiah to be."

Many of these arguments are dependent upon interpretation of the text. Moreover, these arguments tend to adopt a rather one-dimensional view of the prophet; they assume that Jeremiah could not hold more than one opinion or approach in his lifetime, notwithstanding changing circumstances. This type of evidence is at best inconclusive, and at worst unconvincing; it offers a poor assessment of the diversity of human character and the complexity of the positions people can hold. Furthermore, these arguments are compelling only if we assume that Jeremiah wrote this book from a personal, rather than a national (or religious-prophetic) perspective. In fact, Eikha and Jeremiah have very different aims, such that even if they have the same author, one expects to find different viewpoints in each.

remains the story of Everyman, a human tale of catastrophe that blurs any distinction among individuals.

While the question of authorship will not impact this book greatly, I will pay attention to the way Eikha intersects with the two additional books that *Ḥazal* attribute to Jeremiah in Bava Batra 15a, namely Kings and Jeremiah. According to rabbinic tradition, Jeremiah wrote three books, each of which expresses a different viewpoint on the catastrophic exile and destruction. The book of Kings provides the history of Jerusalem's fall and the book of Jeremiah the theological perspective, while Eikha supplies the emotional response.

We will not limit ourselves to understanding the book only within the context of Jeremiah's authorship. I intend to examine this book at face value – as the work of an anonymous representative of the nation. I will also search for interactions between Eikha and books not ascribed to Jeremiah. Indeed, we will see that several biblical books maintain strong linguistic connections with Eikha. The intersection between Eikha and the prophecies of consolation in Isaiah will prove to be especially rewarding, and I have devoted a separate chapter to this topic.

COHESION OF THE BOOK

Does the book of Eikha have a consistent narrative flow and progression, or is it an anthology of five independent laments? Some scholars assert that there is an absence of logical development in the book, and they therefore attempt to establish that the chapters are made up of distinct poems.[11] The absence of a plot that moves forward or characters that develop makes it difficult to establish that Eikha has a conscious or cohesive construction. Nevertheless, some scholars adduce the unity of form (such as alphabetic construction), thematic and verbal correspondences,

---

11. For example, A. Berlin, *Lamentations* (The Old Testament Library; Louisville: Westminster John Knox Press, 2004), 6, maintains that Eikha originally consisted of five separate poems. Gordis, 117, supports this view with the claim that each chapter sustains a different literary genre. (Since many of the studies cited in this book are best abbreviated as *Lamentations*, henceforth they will be cited by author name alone, e.g., Gordis, 117.)

and the lyric style as evidence of narrative cohesiveness.[12] Others have noted the way in which the book as a whole progresses and weaves together themes, ideas, and theological considerations.[13]

It seems evident that each chapter constitutes its own singular poetic composition. After all, each chapter (aside from the last) has its own complete acrostic form. For this reason, I will examine each chapter as a distinctive unit. At the conclusion of each chapter, I will summarize its themes, tone, structure, and trajectory. Nevertheless, I will also strongly advocate a reading of the book of Eikha as a unified construct, rather than as an anthology of separate lamentations. Only by viewing Eikha as a unified book can we discern the way it subtly, but magnificently, weaves its themes into a meaningful poetic arrangement. I will illustrate this in the final chapter of this book, where I seek to extract the book's theological approach from its structure.

DATE OF COMPOSITION

Although Eikha offers no specific date of composition, it presents itself as an eyewitness account of the events of 586 BCE. The book intertwines the siege, destruction, and exile of Jerusalem along with the nation's emotional and theological response. Many modern scholars accept the book's date at face value,[14] while some adduce linguistic evidence to support a date close to the destruction.[15] The book's lack of hope in the future and the rawness of the suffering may suggest the author's

---

12. See, for example, F. W. Dobbs-Allsopp, *Lamentations* (Interpretation; Louisville: Westminster John Knox Press, 2002), 5, 23; D. Grossberg, *Centripetal and Centrifugal Structures in Biblical Poetry* (SBL Monograph Series; Atlanta: Scholars Press, 1989), 83–104.

13. Y. Kaufmann, *Toldot HaEmuna HaYisraelit*, vol. 7 (Jerusalem: Bialik, 1964), 584–90, sees a poetic unity in the five chapters of the book. See also Grossberg, *Centripetal*, 95; J. Middlemas, "The Violent Storm in Lamentations," *JSOT* 29 (2004), 12.

14. See Hillers, xviii–xix; Dobbs-Allsopp, 4–5; J. Renkema, *Lamentations: Historical Commentary on the Old Testament*, trans. B. Doyle (Leuven: Peeters, 1998), 54; Berlin, 33. Gordis, 126, accepts this dating with regard to chapters 2 and 4, which graphically describe Jerusalem's fall. For a brief overview of the range of dates that scholars have proposed, see I. Provan, *Lamentations* (NCBC; Grand Rapids: Eerdmans, 1991), 10–11.

15. See Dobbs-Allsopp, "Linguistic Evidence for the Date of Lamentations," *Journal of the Near Eastern Society of Columbia University* 26 (1998), 8–9. Provan, 12.

proximity to the events. Nevertheless, as Berlin points out, a skilled author would have little trouble conjuring up the depth of feeling for these events, even if he lived long after.[16]

As I have noted, some rabbinic sources regard the composition of parts of Eikha as a response to several events that took place quite a bit earlier than Jerusalem's fall in 586 BCE (such as Josiah's death in 609 BCE). In my view, the question of when exactly the book was written remains less important than its ongoing relevance. The events leading up to and following the destruction of Jerusalem in 586 BCE constitute Eikha's historical context. Nevertheless, interpretive tradition does not limit Eikha's significance to its historical context. Instead, Eikha functions as a paradigm of national catastrophe; it is a blueprint for contending with suffering and all manner of analogous human experience. Rabbinic commentary tends to interpret Eikha in relation to its own contemporary national tragedies (including, but not limited to, the destruction of the Second Temple).[17] Thus, Eikha conveys a meaning that stretches beyond the events of 586 BCE. Rabbinic interpretation transforms Eikha into a book that transcends its calamitous era, enabling this catastrophe to offer meaning to other periods in Jewish history.

The answers to the questions raised in this chapter (title, authorship, cohesion, and date) remain inconclusive. I have attempted to offer the reasons for my approach to each of these issues. In the upcoming introductory chapters, I will examine the book's historical background, its theology, and its poetic features.

---

16. Berlin, 33.

17. I will examine this further in the chapter "Eikha Rabba: Filling Eikha's Void."

Historical Background

HISTORY AND THE TANAKH

The Tanakh is not primarily a history book; its purpose is theological, moral, and didactic, the tale of the history of the relationship between God and humans. There is no attempt to offer a complete historical account,[1] nor is there any notion of objectivity.[2] Instead, the Tanakh constructs partial narratives, designed to illustrate a particular theological understanding of historical events for an edifying purpose.

---

1. Many examples indicate this. Consider, for example, the book of Joshua's account of the conquest of the land, which depicts only four wars (Josh. 6–11), although it lists thirty-one kings killed (Josh. 12). Joshua does not claim that the war stories represent a comprehensive account of the conquest. Although it is beyond the scope of this study to examine the topic fully, these four wars appear to be arranged as a literary construct that offers a theological approach to the conquest of the land. Another example in which the biblical account deviates from a historical account may be observed in the story of Ahab. The biblical account devotes most of the story to the king's sins and Elijah's bid to induce his repentance. Ahab's building achievements are concentrated into just one verse (I Kings 22:39). His military power, as indicated by contemporary historical records (on the Black Obelisk, Ahab is said to have donated 2,000 chariots to the alliance against Shalmaneser III), is not fully described. A historical account of Ahab would surely have focused attention upon these significant facts of his reign.
2. The Tanakh recounts its historical narratives from a theological perspective. Righteous kings are likely to prosper, while evil kings receive their just desserts. Exceptions to this sometimes elicit explanations (see, for example, the explanation of Jeroboam II's unlikely success in II Kings 14:25–27, or the attempt to explain Josiah's death in II Kings 23:25–27).

The narrative events recorded in the Tanakh do take place within a geographical and historical context. The primary setting of the Tanakh is Israel and its northern and southern neighbors, the river valleys of Mesopotamia and Egypt. These fertile valleys were home to great civilizations and shifting patterns of empires and alliances, which often collided with Israel.

Archaeology has thus far produced little evidence to corroborate early biblical history. It is only beginning in the mid-ninth century BCE (during the period of Omri) that archaeological artifacts begin to relate directly to biblical characters and events. I will not list these texts here, but I will instead refer to them as they become relevant to the historical examination.

HISTORY AND THE BOOK OF EIKHA

Eikha is by no means a historical account of events, as it lacks narrative, dates, and identified persons. It does not attempt to relate a prose account of Jerusalem's fall or Babylonia's conquest. Nevertheless, to contextualize and understand the book, we must address its historical background. Eikha, after all, commemorates the climactic calamity of the Tanakh: the destruction of the First Temple and Jerusalem in 586 BCE, often referred to as the *ḥurban* (destruction).

Beginning with Abraham's initial journey to the land, Israel's national goals revolve around the land of Israel. Babylonia's conquest of Jerusalem and the exile of its population mark both a conclusion and a turning point for biblical history. Political, religious, economic, and social repercussions follow these catastrophic events, constituting the setting of the book.

We will briefly review the major historical events that lead to the *ḥurban*, as recorded both in the Tanakh and in external sources, pausing to examine three events that impact deeply upon Judah, Jerusalem, and the book of Eikha. These events are the exile of the Northern Kingdom in 722 BCE,[3] Sennacherib's failed military campaign to conquer Jerusalem in 701 BCE, and King Josiah's shocking death in 609 BCE. Each of these

---

3. *Ḥazal* often refer to this as the exile of the ten tribes (e.g., Megilla 14b; Sanhedrin 110b).

events has significant theological implications that affect the Judean kingdom. Together, they represent the historical-theological backdrop of the book of Eikha.

THE EXILE OF THE NORTHERN KINGDOM

Assyria had been a significant Mesopotamian kingdom from at least the third millennium BCE, its influence rising and falling alongside the fluctuating power patterns of the surrounding nations. During the Neo-Assyrian period (900–600 BCE), with which we are concerned, the Assyrians constructed the largest and most powerful empire ever known in the region. Sweeping through the ancient Near East, Assyria conquered cities, relocated large portions of the population to other regions, and replaced the indigenous kings with Assyrian governors. The Assyrians absorbed the conquered territories into their empire as provinces, eventually creating one enormous empire.

The Bible first mentions the Neo-Assyrian empire during the reign of Tiglath Pileser III (745–727 BCE), referred to also as Pul (II Kings 15:19). His military success affected the kings of both Israel[4] and Judah: Menachem ben Gadi of Israel offered tribute to keep him at bay (II Kings 15:19–20), while Ahaz of Judah allies himself with Tiglath Pileser III, bribing the Assyrian king to deflect his primary enemies, Israel and Aram (II Kings 16:7–8). The Judean kingdom still regarded the voracious Assyrians as an abiding threat, despite the alliance and substantial bribe, and the Judean king Ahaz took precautions in case the Assyrians attacked (II Kings 16:17–18).[5]

Tiglath Pileser eventually dismantled large portions of the Israelite kingdom, conquering parts of the Galilee (II Kings 15:29) and Transjordan (I Chr. 5:26). His son, Shalmaneser V (727–722 BCE),

---

4. While I will often use the term Israel to refer to the Northern Kingdom (and Judah to refer to the Southern Kingdom), I will also use the term in its more colloquial sense, to refer to the entire nation of Israel. Though this is a bit confusing, I have tried to distinguish between these usages.

5. See also II Chronicles 28:20–21, which asserts that Tiglath Pileser troubled Ahaz the king of Judah. It remains unclear as to whether this alludes to a direct assault (which seems unlikely), to an Assyrian betrayal of the alliance, or to the unwitting religious harm caused by Ahaz's enthusiasm for the Assyrians.

eventually besieged Israel's capital city, Samaria, in response to the rebellion of the Israelite king Hosea. After three years, Assyria conquered Samaria, deported its inhabitants, and repopulated the city with captives from the northern lands (II Kings 17:4–6).

The defeat and exile of the Northern Kingdom in 722 BCE was a devastating and unprecedented event. The nation had remained firmly rooted in its land since the conquest of Joshua. The mass exile of Israelites from the Promised Land raised theological questions as well as practical ones. How could the nation of Israel continue to maintain its national identity once a large percentage of its population had been scattered? Would they return to their land and reassume hegemony? Had God rejected the Israelite kingdom and selected the Judean kingdom as His chosen nation? Could this type of disaster befall the Judean kingdom, which contained the Temple? Assyria's ruthlessness and success produced an additional theological quandary: Is God just? If so, why do the wicked prosper? How is it possible that the evil Assyrians thrive, even as they oppress others so cruelly?

In the upcoming chapter, "Theology and Suffering," I will grapple with the way Eikha treats these troubling theological questions within the context of its own disaster. For now, I will simply note one point of certainty. Prophets such as Hosea and Amos provide ample warning for the impending disaster, informing the Northern Kingdom repeatedly and in advance that God will exile them if they continue to sin.[6] After the fact, the Tanakh affirms that Israel's sins functioned as the primary catalyst for the cataclysmic events.[7]

The Bible does not record Judah's response to Israel's exile.[8] Several biblical passages adduce Israel's calamity in order to warn Judah of its own vulnerability stemming from its sinfulness. While describing

---

6. Alongside their attempt to prevent the exile, these prophets offer tools to cope with it. One of the catalysts for classical prophecy (which begins with Hosea) is likely the need to prepare Israel for the challenges of exile.

7. See, for example, the lengthy enumeration of the sins of the Northern Kingdom in II Kings 17:7–23.

8. We may hear strains of Judah's attitude toward Israel's exile in Ezekiel 11:15 (see Rashi there). We will examine this verse later in this chapter.

the theological reason for Israel's exile, II Kings pauses to reflect ominously on Judah's sins: [9]

> And the Lord was greatly wrathful at Israel, and He removed them from Him. No one remains, except only the tribe of Judah. Judah also did not observe the commandments of the Lord their God, and they went in the ways of Israel, doing that which they did. (II Kings 17:18–19)

If God exiled one part of His nation as a result of their sins, why should a sinful Judah feel immune to this same punishment?[10]

The prophet Micah likewise regards Israel's exile as a warning for Judah. He opens his book by castigating both Israel and Judah for their sins (Mic. 1:5), asserting that God intends to wreak judgment upon both kingdoms. Describing God's annihilation of Samaria (Mic. 1:6–9), Micah then portrays the Assyrian destruction of much of Judah up to, but not including, Jerusalem (Mic. 1:9–15, especially verses 9 and 12). Nevertheless, Micah makes it plain that it was not because of her righteousness that God spared Jerusalem. Flinging accusations of sinfulness at Judah, Micah asserts that the sins of Israel abound within Judean cities as well:

> Harness your chariots to your horses, inhabitants of Lachish![11] She is the beginning of sin for Bat Zion. For in you the transgressions of Israel have been found. (Mic. 1:13)

Micah bluntly warns that God will not spare Jerusalem if she continues to sin. Following a lengthy description of Judah's transgressions, Micah

---

9. See also II Kings 17:13, which describes prophets warning both Israel and Judah.
10. The answer from the Judean perspective is that they believe that the Temple's presence in the Southern Kingdom offers them divine immunity, irrespective of the sins committed in the holy city.
11. Biblical exegetes (Ibn Ezra and Radak, Mic. 1:13) explain that the sins of the Northern Kingdom first penetrate Lachish, an important city in the lowlands of Judah. From there they spread to the rest of Judah.

utters a devastating (and unprecedented) prophecy.[12] In language that recalls the description of the ruins of Samaria in Micah 1:5, Micah foretells the impending devastation of Jerusalem, which will surely fall victim to God's wrath:[13]

> Therefore, because of you, Zion will be a plowed-up field, and Jerusalem will be in ruins, and the Temple Mount will be a shrine in the forest. (Mic. 3:12)

Jeremiah later cites Micah's prophecy, explaining that King Hezekiah and the Judeans heeded Micah's warning and repented, precipitating God's forgiveness and the suspension of His decree against Jerusalem:[14]

> Micah the Morashite who prophesied in the days of Hezekiah the king of Judah said to all the nation in Judah, "So says the Lord of hosts: Zion will be plowed up like a field and Jerusalem will be in ruins and the Temple Mount will be like a shrine in a forest." Did Hezekiah the king of Judah and all the Judeans kill him? Did they not fear the Lord and pray to the Lord, and the Lord regretted the evil that He had planned to do to them? (Jer. 26:18–19)

Judah's repentance is brief, and both Jeremiah (Jer. 3:6–10) and Ezekiel (Ezek. 23:1–49) castigate Judah for failing to internalize the lessons of Israel's punishment. Judeans seem to believe that the Israelite exile

---

12. While this is the first time that a prophet has explicitly prophesied of Jerusalem's destruction, God informed King Solomon from the outset that if the nation (and its kings) sin, God would destroy the Temple (I Kings 9:6–9).

13. Micah 6:9–16 compares "the city's" sins to those of Omri and Ahab, two of Israel's most sinful kings. While it is unclear whether he is describing the city of Samaria or Jerusalem (see Radak, Mic. 6:9), some exegetes assume that Micah is describing Jerusalem (see Metzudat David, Mic. 6:9). If Jerusalem's sins are like the sins of Israelite kings, we can expect that they will suffer the same fate as the Northern Kingdom.

14. The chronology of these events remains unclear. According to the source in Jeremiah 26:19, it seems that Micah's prophecy (3:12) *preceded* the miraculous deliverance of Jerusalem, while the book of Micah appears to indicate that his prophecy of devastation followed that event (see Mic. 1:9, 12 and 3:11–12).

has no bearing on Jerusalem's future. After all, the Temple resides in Jerusalem, distinguishing the consecrated Southern Kingdom from the Northern one.[15] Moreover, Judeans may erroneously assume that God safeguarded Jerusalem from the Assyrians because of their own righteousness. There is a prevailing notion that those who remain in the land represent the elect, chosen by God to continue Israel's legacy. Ezekiel disapprovingly refers to this attitude, prevalent among the inhabitants of Jerusalem:[16]

> Your brothers, your brothers … and all of the totality of the house of Israel, those to whom the inhabitants of Jerusalem said, "*They* have distanced themselves from the Lord and to *us* the land has been given as a heritage." (Ezek. 11:15)

The Judeans' attitude compounds the scope of the disaster following their own destruction and exile. They must now contend with the shattering of their beliefs alongside the catastrophe. The fact that the northern tribes have remained mostly in exile illustrates the difficulty of restoration. The possibility that their fate might be like that of the northern tribes deepens Judean dismay and confusion. Is Judah condemned to oblivion in exile? Has God rejected His entire nation?

SENNACHERIB'S FAILURE TO CONQUER JERUSALEM

Following the exile of the ten tribes in 722 BCE, Assyria's expansionist appetite grows. Sennacherib (705–681 BCE) wages several military campaigns, often against vassals who have rebelled. Hezekiah, king of Judah, rebels against Assyria (II Kings 18:7), prompting Sennacherib to demolish much of the Judean kingdom, including

---

15. Jeremiah 7:3–11 recalls how the Temple's presence in Jerusalem generates an attitude of complacency among the Judeans. See also Mic. 3:10. I will examine these prophecies in the continuation of this chapter.
16. The verse does not clarify specifically whom the inhabitants of Jerusalem were referring to. Rashi suggests that the Jerusalemites assumed this about all members of the nation of Israel previously exiled from the land, including the Northern Kingdom in 722 BCE and those exiled from Jerusalem during the exile of Jehoakhin in 597 BCE.

many fortified cities (II Kings 18:13).[17] The biblical account parallels for the most part Sennacherib's own account, recorded in the Prism of Sennacherib:

> I laid siege to forty-six of [Hezekiah's] strong cities, walled forts and to the countless small villages in their vicinity, and conquered (them) by means of well-stamped earth-ramps and battering-rams brought (thus) near (to the walls) (combined with) the attack by foot soldiers (using) mines, breeches as well as sapper work. I drove out (of them) 200,150 people, young and old, male and female, horses, mules, donkeys, camels, big and small cattle, and considered (them) booty... His towns, which I had plundered, I took away from his country and gave them to Mitinti, king of Ashdod, Padi, king of Ekron, and Sillibel, king of Gaza. Thus, I reduced his country, but I still increased his tribute... beyond his former tribute to be delivered to me annually.[18]

Sennacherib eventually turns his attention to Hezekiah's capital city, Jerusalem. It is a testimony to the importance of this story that three different biblical books record Sennacherib's siege of Jerusalem at length: II Kings 18:17–19:37, Isaiah 36–37, and II Chronicles 32:1–23.[19] The most striking feature of this episode is its stunning failure. Sennacherib's buoyant confidence in his own power resounds throughout the biblical account; note how Sennacherib's steward scornfully dismisses Hezekiah's trust in God's salvation:

---

17. Hezekiah allies with other Assyrian vassals following the death of Sargon and the perceived weakening of the Assyrian Empire. To read the Assyrian texts that describe the events of Sennacherib's reign that relate to biblical accounts, see M. Cogan, *The Raging Torrent: Historical Inscriptions from Assyria and Babylonia Relating to Ancient Israel* (Jerusalem: Carta, 2015), 120–43.

18. J. B. Pritchard, *The Ancient Near East: An Anthology of Texts and Pictures*, vol. 1 (Princeton: Princeton University Press, 1953, reprinted 1973), 200. Parentheses indicate Pritchard's interpolations for better understanding of the translation.

19. As we will see below, other biblical passages refer to this event as well, rendering it a central biblical event.

Did the gods of the nations save each one his land from the hands of the king of Assyria? Where are the gods of Hamath and Arpad? Where are the gods of Sepharvayim, Hena and Ivva? Did they [the gods] save Samaria from me? Who, among all the gods in the lands, saved their lands from my hands? Will the Lord save Jerusalem from me? (II Kings 18:33–35)

Sennacherib's boasting is well earned – Assyria has indeed barreled through the ancient Near East, defeating the rebellious nations with extraordinary ease (II Kings 18:34–35; 19:11–13). Why indeed should Judah succeed where other, much stronger, nations failed?

Nevertheless, Isaiah sends a reassuring prophecy to Hezekiah, announcing that Assyria's campaign will fail, and Jerusalem will emerge unscathed from the Assyrian assault:

So says the Lord, "Do not be afraid of the things that you have heard, in which the young men of the king of Assyria mocked Me. Behold…he will hear a rumor and return to his land and I will make him fall by sword in his land." (II Kings 19:6–7)

Isaiah sends another message to Hezekiah informing him that Assyria will not even launch a battle against Jerusalem:

Therefore, so says the Lord to the king of Assyria, "He will not enter this city, nor will he shoot there an arrow, nor advance against it with a shield, nor pour against it a siege mound." (II Kings 19:32)

That same night, according to II Kings 19:35, an angel of God strikes the camp of Assyria, killing 185,000 troops.[20] Isaiah's prophecy is meticulously fulfilled; Sennacherib returns to his land without

---

20. The order of events within the three biblical stories is somewhat inconsistent and does not fully concur with Assyrian annals. I have presented a simplified version of the story, without delving into its details or historical intricacies.

conquering Jerusalem and is assassinated (II Chr. 32:21; II Kings 19:36–37).[21] Unsurprisingly, Sennacherib's chronicle does not describe his failure to conquer Jerusalem. Nevertheless, in an unprecedented omission, Sennacherib neglects to boast of his conquest of Jerusalem, instead exultantly describing his siege of the capital city:

> As to Hezekiah, the Judean, he did not submit to my yoke, I laid siege to forty-six of his strong cities … Him I made a prisoner in Jerusalem, his royal residence, like a bird in a cage. I surrounded him with earthwork in order to molest those who were leaving his city's gate.[22]

Sennacherib's account appears designed to obscure his failure to conquer Jerusalem. The miraculous salvation of Jerusalem is certainly grounds for triumphant thanksgiving to God. Not only does the Bible explicitly describe this event three times, but Isaiah continuously refers to it in his prophecies.[23] This salvation of Jerusalem may also be the backdrop for several celebratory chapters in Psalms.[24] Consider the awe-filled description of Jerusalem's impenetrability and of God's special protection of the city in Psalms 46 and 48:

---

21. While the biblical accounts record Sennacherib's assassination immediately following his failure to capture Jerusalem (II Kings 19:36–37), historical evidence suggests that Sennacherib is assassinated several years later. Family tensions appear to have been present throughout Sennacherib's reign: Sennacherib's name in Akkadian alludes to dead brothers, thereby implying that he receives his throne name after the death of brothers (M. Cogan and H. Tadmor, *II Kings* [Anchor Bible; Garden City: Doubleday, 1988], 228).

22. Pritchard, *Ancient Near East*, 200.

23. This is a defining event for Isaiah; see, for example, Isaiah 10:24–34; 31:4–9. Particularly noteworthy is Isaiah's description of God protecting Jerusalem "like hovering birds" (Is. 31:5). This image clashes with Sennacherib's boastful claim that he made Hezekiah "like a bird in a cage."

24. Ibn Ezra raises this possibility (and rejects it) in his commentary on Psalms 46:1. Some scholars, however, do adopt this position. See, for example, C. A. Briggs, *The Book of Psalms* (ICC. Edinburgh: T & T Clark, 1906), 402; A. Cohen, *The Psalms* (London: Soncino, 1945), 150. The Malbim suggests that this is the historical background for Psalms 76. However, any attempt to deduce a precise historical context for these psalms remains speculative.

God is a shelter and a strength for us, His help during troubles is very present... A river with joyful streams is the city of God, the holy dwelling place of the most high. God in her midst shall never waver; God will help [the city] as the day breaks. (Ps. 46:2, 5–6)

Great is the Lord and very praiseworthy in the city of our God, the mountain of His holiness... God in [the city's] palaces became known as a shelter. For the Kings joined to pass through [the city] together. They saw and they were truly amazed, they became frightened and startled... "Just as we heard, so we have seen, in the city of the Lord of hosts, in the city of our God; God shall establish her for eternity!" (Ps. 48:2, 4–6, 9)

These psalms focus on the exultant declaration that God's city is inviolable, sheltering its residents. Foreign kings are moved to proclaim their belief in God and in the eternity of His city. While we cannot pinpoint the exact episode that motivates the composition of these psalms, Jerusalem's miraculous salvation from Sennacherib coheres well with their tone and content.

Ḥazal note disapprovingly that Hezekiah never sings a song of thanksgiving following this miraculous event. In fact, a gemara maintains that it is for this reason that Hezekiah, who was designated to become the Messiah, does not assume this role.[25] Is Hezekiah, like so many other kings, guilty of the sin of hubris, of failing to recall the source of his salvation? That is one possible explanation, but I would like to suggest that Hezekiah has a good reason not to sing a song of thanksgiving.

Although Jerusalem remains intact, the kingdom of Judah has been devastated and reduced to a mere fraction of its former size and power. Isaiah offers an incisive description of the situation:[26]

---

25. See Sanhedrin 94a.
26. See Radak on Isaiah 1:8 and Malbim on Isaiah 1:7–8. Also note Isaiah's metaphoric description of Assyria as a powerful river that overwhelms Judah but does not completely submerge it, reaching only its neck (Is. 8:7–8).

> Your land is desolate, your cities scorched by fire, your land before your eyes is devoured by foreigners; it is desolate, as it is overthrown by strangers. The daughter of Zion remains like a hut in a vineyard, like a lodge in a cucumber field, like a city besieged. Had not the Lord left us with a small remnant, we would be like Sodom, we would be akin to Gomorrah. (Is. 1:7–9)

Far from celebrating a national triumph, Hezekiah is contending with a national catastrophe. It seems more appropriate for him to be mourning the death, exile, and pillage of most of his kingdom, rather than singing a song of thanksgiving for the salvation of Jerusalem.

There is another reason to be cautious following this episode. Divine deliverance of the holy city allows people to draw an erroneous conclusion. They infer that God extends unconditional protection over the city that houses the holy Temple. After all, they reason, Jerusalem is God's dwelling place; God *needs* it to remain standing no less than its earthly inhabitants do!

Echoes of this assumption resound in various biblical contexts. Consider, for example, a prophecy of Micah. Following his scathing critique of Jerusalem's leaders, Micah cites them expressing misplaced confidence in the city's immutability.

> [Jerusalem's] leaders judge with bribery, her priests offer instructions for a price, her prophets offer divination for silver, and they rely on the Lord, saying, "Is not the Lord in our midst? No harm shall come to us!" (Mic. 3:11)

Micah rages against the sins of Jerusalem's political and religious leaders. Of particular concern is their blindness to any future repercussions for their depravity. The faulty assumption of Jerusalem's sacred immunity will prove to have fatal consequences. It is this erroneous belief that prompts Micah's prophecy of the destruction of Jerusalem and the Temple Mount.

A similar ideological clash between Jerusalem's confident populace and an outraged prophet resonates in Jeremiah's prophecy:

So says the Lord of hosts, God of Israel, "Improve your ways and your deeds and I will allow you to dwell in this place. Do not rely upon the false words in which they say, '[It is] the Lord's Sanctuary, the Lord's Sanctuary, the Lord's Sanctuary!' For, if you improve your ways and deeds…then I will settle you in this place, in the land that I gave to your forefathers, forever and until eternity. However, you rely upon those false words to no avail… And now because you have done all of these things, says the Lord, and I spoke to you every morning and you did not listen, and I called you and you did not answer, I will [destroy] this house that bears my name and that you rely upon…just as I did to Shiloh. And I will cast you out of My presence, just as I cast out your brethren, the seed of Ephraim." (Jer. 7:3–15)

Jerusalem's inhabitants consider its destruction to be theologically inconceivable. When Jeremiah prophesies the imminent destruction of both Jerusalem and the Temple, he is seized by the religious establishment (prophets and priests) and by the people and sentenced to death (Jer. 26:6–11)! Jeremiah's detractors maintain that his prophecy is blasphemous and false, yet it turns out to be devastatingly precise. Forced to rethink its assumptions, the nation of Israel must also contend with the astonishment of outsiders, who believed similarly that Jerusalem's sanctified status granted it protection.[27]

The deliverance of Jerusalem from the Assyrian army forms an important historical backdrop to the book of Eikha. An episode that began as an inspiring manifestation of divine intervention pivots in a catastrophic direction, leaving a bewildered nation to contend with Jerusalem's unexpected collapse.

JOSIAH'S DEATH

The reign of Ashurbanipal (669–627 BCE), the last powerful king of the mighty Assyrian Empire, marks both the pinnacle of the Assyrian Empire's power and the beginning of its decline. The fall of Assyria's capital city Nineveh to Babylonia in 612 BCE represents the final blow.

---

27. See Psalms 48:5–9 and its echoes in Eikha 2:15. See also Eikha 4:12.

Prior to its collapse, the Assyrian Empire is weakened by rebellions, shifting alliances, and loss of tributes, creating a power vacuum. Various nations, most notably Babylonia, seek to fill that vacuum.

Josiah reigns as king of Judah during the period of Assyria's deterioration and collapse (640–609 BCE). The power vacuum works to Josiah's advantage, enabling him to extend his rule over the region of the former Northern Kingdom of Israel. Biblical accounts describing Josiah's reign focus primarily on his religious reforms,[28] suggesting that the king's political success is a result of his piety. The confluence of political and religious success during Josiah's reign marks it as a period of unique optimism. To understand its significance, we will examine both Josiah's extraordinary success and his shocking death.

Josiah begins his reign as king at the age of eight after the assassination of his father Amon, who ruled for just two years. At this stage, Josiah's advisors likely rule the kingdom, adhering closely to the sinful policies of Josiah's predecessors, and especially his powerful grandfather, Manasseh. Manasseh ruled for an exceptionally long fifty-five years, and his was a corrupt period in which idolatry became entrenched and bloodshed prevailed.[29]

In the eighth year of Josiah's reign, when he is sixteen years old, he begins to seek God (II Chr. 34:3). Four years later, Josiah institutes a nationwide reform. He sweeps through Jerusalem and Judah, purging the land of idolatry. Yet Josiah's energetic campaign does not end there. The young king expands his campaign outside the borders of Judah, in the area of the former Northern Kingdom. Josiah boldly advances northward into the cities of Ephraim, Manasseh, and Naphtali, breaking altars, crushing idols, demolishing incense stands, and eliminating all forms of idolatry (II Chr. 34:6–7).

How does Josiah succeed in extending his authority over the Northern Kingdom when the Assyrian empire conquered it in 722

---

28. See II Kings 21 and II Chronicles 34.
29. Several biblical passages (e.g., II Kings 23:26; Jer. 15:4) state that God decrees destruction against Judah following Manasseh's reign. Manasseh's idolatrous policies prevailed for sixty-nine years (fifty-five of Manasseh, two of Amon, twelve of Josiah), which explains the decree of seventy years of punishment upon the nation (Jer. 25:11–12; Zech. 1:12; II Chr. 36:21).

BCE? Josiah's northward incursion is possible only due to the waning of Assyrian hegemony. In all likelihood, Josiah launches his northern campaign after Ashurbanipal's death (in approximately 627 BCE, the thirteenth year of Josiah's reign) and the subsequent rapid decline of the Assyrian Empire. This makes Josiah the first king since Rehoboam, the son of Solomon, to exercise control over the area of the united kingdom.[30] Josiah continues to implement his religious plans and aspirations. In the eighteenth year of his reign, at the age of twenty-six, he collects money for renovations of the Temple. During these renovations, the high priest finds a Torah scroll (II Kings 22:8). For reasons unclear in the text, the discovery elicits a strong reaction from the young king, who tears his clothes and sends messengers to Huldah the prophet for a divine oracle.[31] She confirms his fears and issues a devastating prophecy of doom for Jerusalem (II Kings 22:16–17). Nevertheless, Josiah does not despair, nor does he cease his relentless pursuit of pious reform. Gathering Judeans and Jerusalemites to the Temple, Josiah reaffirms the covenant between the nation and God (II Kings 23:1–3). He then intensifies the reform, doubling down on his bid to remove idolatry from the land (II Kings 23:4–20). Finally, Josiah gathers the nation together to celebrate

---

30. Previously, I observed that the nation had to contend with the fact that the northern exiles never return to reassert hegemony over their former land. Josiah's dominion over the northern area offers a positive spin on the exile of the Northern Kingdom. This exile allows the Davidic dynasty to take control over the entire territory of Israel, unifying the nation of Israel under one king. In his prophecy, Hosea recognizes this advantage in the otherwise calamitous exile of the Northern Kingdom (Hos. 2:2; 3:5).

31. Biblical interpreters offer various explanations as to why the discovery of the Torah elicits such a frightened response. Some suggest that the discovery implied that the sinful policies of previous kings (Ahaz or Manasseh) had led to the neglect, and perhaps even destruction, of the Torah (e.g., Radak, II Kings 22:8). Reading the Torah for the first time in a long while reminds them that the Torah warns against the very sins that are now prevalent. Alternatively, some suggest that the Torah scroll is positioned at Deuteronomy 28, the section known as the *Tokheha*, which delineates the punishments for protracted sinfulness (see Yoma 52b and Metzudat David, II Kings 22:8). The verse that particularly alarms the king and his officers includes the threat that God will exile the king along with his people as punishment (Deut. 28:36).

Passover, a mass event intended to reignite the nation's religious commitment (II Kings 23:21–25).

Josiah is one of the most devout of biblical kings.[32] His exhilarating reforms and unceasing energy spur a religious revolution. In biblical narratives, religious success tends to intersect with success in other spheres, indicating that God rewards the righteous. Indeed, at first, Josiah's reforms appear to generate unprecedented results.

Extending his reign to the Northern Kingdom, Josiah reunites the two kingdoms geographically and subsumes the remnants of the northern tribes under Judean reign.[33] The exiles begin to trickle home, suggesting the reversal of God's punishment.[34] The people may conclude that Josiah is that scion of the Davidic dynasty described by Isaiah (Is. 11:1–10), whose wisdom and piety would lead to the ingathering of the exiles (Is. 11:11–12, 16), the cessation of rivalry between the kingdoms (Is. 11:13), and the restoration of a Davidic king over a united kingdom. Israel's hopes and future rest upon the success of this pious king.

The impression of Josiah's extraordinary success is rivalled only by the disappointment that follows his death. In the thirty-first year of Josiah's reign, he goes to battle with Pharaoh Necho, who is on his way to assist the weakened Assyrians in battling the rising Babylonian empire. Necho attempts to avoid a war with Josiah, maintaining that he harbors no hostile intentions against him. He simply needs to use the Jezreel Valley as a thoroughfare (II Chr. 35:21). Josiah refuses Necho passage, possibly because he recognizes that his newfound hegemony over the northern territory remains precarious.[35] Moreover, Josiah may assume that God supports him and will hand him a victory (Taanit 22b). Despite his piety, Josiah dies in battle at age thirty-nine.

It is difficult to overestimate the impact of Josiah's death on the nation. A midrashic name derivation encapsulates its significance:

---

32. Note the sweeping praise of Josiah in II Kings 23:25.
33. II Chronicles 34:5–6, 9 indicates that at the time of Josiah's reign, some members of the exiled tribes resided in the north of Israel. It is unclear whether they had been there since the exile (see Rashi and Metzudat David on II Chr. 34:6) or whether they are among the exiles who returned during the weakening of the Assyrian Empire.
34. This is indicated in Jeremiah 3:11–12 (see also Megilla 14b).
35. See Radak, II Kings 23:29.

Why was he called Yoshiyahu [Josiah]? Because when he died, [the nation of] Israel despaired (*nityaashu*) of the kingship, and the righteous ones understood that the Temple is irredeemable. (*Batei Midrashot Bet*, Genesis)

Name etymologies endeavor to capture the essence of a person, his primary contribution and accomplishments. Astoundingly, this midrash suggests that Josiah's legacy is the terrible despair following his death.

Responses to Josiah's untimely death reverberate throughout biblical passages, merging and rising in a swell of mixed emotions: grief, despair, anger, and confusion. Initially, the public laments in an official display of anguish (II Chr. 35:25). Jeremiah acknowledges the difficulty of recovering from Josiah's death and advises the king's son to refrain from excessive mourning (Jer. 22:10). According to many exegetes, echoes of this anguish may reappear in Eikha 4:21:[36]

The breath of our nostrils, anointed of the Lord, was captured in their traps, about [whom] we said, "Under his shadow, we will live among the nations." (Eikha 4:21)

Confusion may even trump grief, as the problem of theodicy – an attempt to understand how God's goodness exists alongside evil – overshadows the experience of mourning Josiah. In the aftermath of the king's death, several prophets express their confusion at God's treatment of the wicked and the righteous. Jeremiah asks why the wicked prosper (Jer. 12:1–3). Habakkuk questions why evil people triumph over the righteous (Hab. 1:4, 13).[37] According to some biblical interpreters, several of Isaiah's prophecies also relate to this inexplicable event. Rashi and Radak both interpret the following verse within the context of Josiah's death:

---

36. See, for example, *Targum Eikha* 4:21; Taanit 22b.
37. We cannot know when exactly Jeremiah and Habakkuk uttered these prophecies. Both were prophesying at the time of Josiah's death (Habakkuk prophesied about the arrival of the Chaldeans, which takes place a mere five years after Josiah's death), and their prophecies expressing bewilderment at God's workings may stem from Josiah's death.

The righteous person is lost, and no person takes it to heart; people of virtue perish, and no one understands. Because of evil, the righteous perish. (Is. 57:1)[38]

Likewise, Abravanel suggests that the servant who suffers without cause in Isaiah 52:13–53:12 may refer to Josiah:

And his grave was placed with evildoers...though he had done no violence and there was no deceit in his mouth. (Is. 53:9)

Though none of these verses explicitly name Josiah, taken together, they suggest that prophets are perplexed about God's ways following Josiah's death.

Nevertheless, alongside this confusion, another muted response emerges, one that balances and mitigates the unrelenting current of baffled grief. Faint echoes of it lie buried in Jeremiah's prophecies, which repeatedly question the genuineness of the nation's repentance during Josiah's reform.[39] If the people have deceived Josiah, then perhaps they do not deserve his righteous leadership; his death is a justified punishment *for the nation.*[40]

An expression of faith in God's righteous judgments appears in the final chapter of Zephaniah, who prophesies during the reign of Josiah. After describing the sins of Jerusalem and her leaders, Zephaniah asserts:

The Lord is righteous in her midst; He does not commit perversions. Morning after morning He brings His justice to light; it is never lacking. But those who pervert [justice] know no shame. (Zeph. 3:5)

---

38. Rashi and Radak both regard this as an explanation for Josiah's premature death, which prevents him from experiencing the destruction of Jerusalem, as Huldah had prophesied (II Kings 22:20). Alternatively, the verse may simply indicate unresolved bewilderment at the death of the pious Josiah.
39. See Jeremiah 3:6–18, especially verse 10 (and Rashi and Radak there). See also Jeremiah 4:3 and Radak's explanation, and Jeremiah 8:4–12.
40. This coheres with Abravanel's reading of Josiah as the servant who suffers because of the sins of others, as described in Isaiah 53:4–9.

This assertion of unwavering belief in God's righteousness may represent another manner of approaching Josiah's death.[41] In fact, Zephaniah 3:5 is echoed in Eikha:

> *The Lord is righteous,* for I have rebelled against His mouth!
> (Eikha 1:19)

Rabbinic sources attribute these words to Josiah, who utters them as he lies dying from mortal wounds received in battle.[42] According to this reading, Josiah's staunch faith in God's justice stands in stark contrast to the incomprehension expressed in some prophetic passages.

These two contradictory approaches to comprehending Josiah's death (helpless confusion vs. confident faith) represent different ways in which humans contend with an incomprehensible world. Eikha strikes a similarly balanced posture in its approach to the problem of God's justice. On the one hand, Eikha articulates intense anger at God, generated by acute awareness of the capriciousness of death, the triumph of evildoers, and the suffering of the innocent. However, Eikha also assumes a measured pose, allowing a second approach to emerge from the turmoil, one that concludes that God remains just, even if events suggest otherwise.

Rabbinic sources maintain that the kernel of the book of Eikha begins to emerge in the aftermath of Josiah's death.[43] In a sense, Josiah's death sets in motion the impending catastrophe. After Josiah, no righteous king sits on the Davidic throne, and events rapidly spiral out of control. More significantly, Josiah's death marks the beginning of the nation's theological crisis, spawning the initial attempts to struggle with the complex questions that arise in the wake of the *ḥurban*.

---

41. Jeremiah likewise opens his query of why the evil prosper by asserting, "You are righteous, Lord" (Jer. 12:1).
42. Eikha Rabba 1:53; Taanit 22b.
43. Eikha Rabba 4:1; Rashi, Eikha 4:1. As I noted, some sources associate specific verses in Eikha with Josiah's death, especially in chapter 4 (but also 1:18).

CONCLUDING HISTORICAL EVENTS

A mere twenty-two years after Josiah's death, Babylonia besieges Jerusalem. The siege of Jerusalem lasts a year and a half. Jerusalem's inhabitants suffer terrible starvation and disease, followed by Babylonian conquest of the city and its feeble populace. Babylonian troops capture King Zedekiah, slaughter his sons, and blind him, taking the Judean king in chains to Babylonia (II Kings 25:5–7). The Babylonians raze the city and the Temple, destroying Jerusalem and exiling nearly all her surviving populace.

Biblical history would appear to terminate at this point. Jerusalem's fall represents the conclusion of the continuous narrative that begins in Genesis and concludes in the book of Kings. God's promises to the forefathers seem to have expired;[44] God brought their descendants to the Promised Land, and now He expels them. Successive deportations have steadily weakened Judah, resulting in a nation devoid of its economic infrastructure as well as its national pride.[45] The Davidic dynasty collapses, its capital is demolished, and God's holy Temple is desecrated. The usual means of religious expression disappear; priests no longer function, and daily sacrifice is no longer an option. The nation loses its political independence; deprived of its monarchy and leadership, it flails about in exile, struggling to contend with the tragic circumstances.

We will conclude this overview by again noting that Eikha is not an account of historical events. Eikha evokes the emotional and theological difficulties with which the nation must grapple. The result is a work of literary art, an astonishing and vivid portrayal of the painful human struggle with God.

---

44. *Ḥazal* debate when the merit of the forefathers ceases to function effectively on Israel's behalf. Most opinions concur that it occurs in conjunction with the exile of the Northern Kingdom, likely after II Kings 13:23. See Shabbat 55a and Leviticus Rabba 36:6.

45. Prior to the events of 586 BCE, Babylonia had already besieged Jerusalem in 597 (during the reign of Jehoakhin). This siege ended when Babylonia dethroned Jehoakhin, taking him into exile along with the rest of the royal family, officers, military, craftsman, and other notables (II Kings 24:10–16).

Theology and Suffering

God's punitive measures provoke a range of emotions within the nation. Reeling from grief, bewilderment, shame, and outrage, the nation grapples with God in the book of Eikha. This is to be expected. Long-held beliefs have been shattered and Israel's world lies in ruins. The nation had assumed that the holy city of Jerusalem enjoyed God's special protection, but He allowed cruel enemies to destroy it. The national calamity affects both adults and children; the innocent and the righteous suffer alongside sinners. God's incomprehensible conduct raises the frightening possibility of an irrevocable fissure in Israel's relationship with Him.

Eikha portrays God in a variety of ways, at times going so far as to depict Him as indifferent or hostile to Israel – even as Israel's enemy. Before examining Eikha's view of God, we must ask: To what extent does Jewish tradition regard such harsh depictions of God as legitimate? Does reverence preclude the possibility of reacting negatively to God's deeds, of questioning His inscrutable designs?

Philosophers of religion and rabbinic sources have developed a number of approaches to the problem of why a just God permits human suffering.[1] However, one thing is clear: piety does not inhibit biblical figures from questioning God's ways, often in a less than measured manner.

---

1. For a good overview, see Byron L. Sherwin, "Theodicy," in *Contemporary Jewish Religious Thought*, ed. Arthur A. Cohen and Paul Mendes-Flohr (New York: The Free Press, 1987), 959–70.

Consider Abraham's heated challenge of God's decision to destroy the cities of the plain: "Will the Judge of the world not do justice?" (Gen. 18:25). Or Moses, who confronts God in a similar tone, asking: "Why have You done evil to this nation; why have You sent me?" (Ex. 5:22). Isaiah boldly thrusts a measure of responsibility upon God for Israel's errant ways: "Why, God, do You make us stray from Your ways; why do You harden our hearts from revering You?" (Is. 63:17). Habakkuk digs in his heels, asserting his intention to "stand on my watch" until God "will reply to my complaint" (Hab. 2:1).[2] Job expresses his inability to understand God's ways: "Why did You place me as a target for You?… Why do You not bear my sins? (Job 7:20–21). Several notable chapters of Psalms fling a litany of complaints against God, cataloguing and questioning the myriad ways in which God has grieved humans: "Until when, Lord; will You forget me for eternity? Until when will You hide Your face from me? Until when will I have cares in my soul, daily anguish in my heart? Until when will my enemies rise against me?" (Ps. 13:2–3).[3]

The great religious personalities ask these questions because they believe in God's justice, because they wish to probe and understand the great mystery that underlies the relationship between God and humans. They hold firm to a faith in a God who allows questions, and in a religious quest that is genuine and fraught, an apt reflection of life.

Nevertheless, some readers still find these biblical complaints uncomfortable, and even theologically inappropriate. Who are we to question God's ways? Perhaps we must simply accept them and remain silent while God implements His impenetrable, but undoubtedly righteous, plans. In his commentary to Psalms 89:1, Ibn Ezra recounts a

---

2. In a well-known talmudic incident (Taanit 23a), Ḥoni HaMe'agel imitates Habakkuk when he draws a circle and asserts that he will not move until God sends the people rain. There is some opposition to Ḥoni's audacious demands. However, incidents such as this indicate that human boldness before God was not confined to the biblical period and continued to assert itself in later Jewish literature.

3. As a unique book that allows humans to use a full range of emotional experiences to express their relationship with God, Psalms contains many such examples of humans who probe God's ways, asking difficult questions. See, for example, Psalms 74:1, 10–11; 79:5; 80:5.

story of his encounter with a wise and pious man from Spain who refused to read Psalms 89 because of its harsh treatment of God.[4] In a response to Ibn Ezra, Radak (Ps. 89:39) disagrees with the anonymous detractor, maintaining that it is illegitimate to reject passages from the Tanakh. Tradition regards all of Tanakh as divinely inspired. It appears that God approves of human questioning when it emerges from an honest and mature attempt to grapple with one's relationship with God and His world.

It is undeniable that Eikha presents God as behaving like an enemy of Israel (Eikha 2:4–5). Instead of questioning this depiction, I will endeavor to understand its meaning. I will scrutinize how the book presents God and His various roles in Israel's calamity.[5] In doing so my goal is not, God forbid, to lessen reverence or love for God, but rather to mine Eikha for its approach to these preeminent questions of theology. We live in a world fraught with human suffering. It is my hope that our exploration of Eikha's candid confrontation with multiple dimensions of the divine-human relationship will afford readers an opportunity to consider more deeply their own relationships with God.

---

4. In his commentary, Ibn Ezra sometimes refers explicitly to R. Yehuda Halevi as a wise man from Spain. Based on this, some identify this anonymous man as the famed author of the *Kuzari*. See N. Elyakim, "Connections between R. Yehuda Halevi and R. A. Ibn Ezra in Interpretations of the Bible," *Shemaatin* 133–34 (1998), 88 [Hebrew].

5. Scholars continue to dispute whether Eikha is a book of theodicy, one that endeavors to defend God's benevolence. See, for example, J. Renkema, "Theodicy in Lamentations?" in A. Laato and J. C. de Moor, eds., *Theodicy in the World of the Bible* (Leiden, 2003), 415–28; F. W. Dobbs-Allsopp, *Lamentations* (IBC; Louisville, 2002), 27–33. Like Dobbs-Allsopp, I believe that the book contains both theodic and anti-theodic strains, vacillating on the issue of God's goodness from one chapter to the next. In doing so, Eikha shies away from a clear theodicy, instead constructing a polyvalent portrait of the nation's perception of God in the wake of the exile. I will attempt to establish and illustrate this fluctuation throughout this study. In the final chapter of this book, I propose to make sense of the book's various approaches to God's justness, by illustrating how the book's structure reflects its theological complexity.

EIKHA'S ELUSIVE THEOLOGY

The destruction and exile of the Judean kingdom, the fall of Jerusalem, and the burning of the Temple seem to mark the end of Israel's national aspirations. Predictably, the calamity raises questions in their minds regarding God's nature, omnipotence, and goodness. They are also forced to contemplate the nation's role in the tragedy: How are they to understand Israel's chosen status, her sins, and the measure of her culpability? Has Israel been disciplined justly for its behavior? A third set of questions revolves around the relationship between God and His nation. Is this relationship eternal, as God had promised? Is it immutable? What does it mean for Israel that God appears to have abandoned His city? Why would God allow the rise of a ferocious enemy that subjugates His nation?

Eikha's theology is not straightforward or organized.[6] Glaringly absent are an explicit inventory of Israel's sins, a consistent portrayal of God's nature, and a clear notion of how to explain the catastrophic events. God's voice is notably missing from Eikha, along with the customary biblical themes that commonly indicate His enduring relationship with Israel: God's covenant with the forefathers, His role as deliverer of Israel from Egypt, His parental affection for Israel, and His eternal pledge to the Davidic dynasty. The book also does not offer clear instructions to help the nation repair their traumatized relationship with God and restore communication with Him.

Although the book lacks a clear-cut theology, theological topics arise, claiming the reader's attention, even as we remain focused on the misery of the events. At its center (3:21–39), Eikha offers its sole lengthy reflection upon God's essence, ongoing graciousness, and fidelity.[7] This pivotal section illustrates the manner in which humans

---

6. Some scholars maintain that the book lacks a systematic theology because it is written simply to describe human suffering. See, for example, M. S. Moore, "Human Suffering in *Lamentations*," *Revue Biblique* 90 (1983), 534–55; Berlin, 17–18; C. Westermann, *Lamentations: Issues and Interpretations* (Minneapolis: Fortress Press, 1993), 76–81. Other scholars, however, argue for an existing theology in the book, though it may be woven subtly into the text; see, for example, Gottwald, 47–111; B. Albrektson, *Studies in the Text and Theology of the Book of Lamentations,* in *Studia Theologica Lundensia* 21 (Gleerup: Lund, 1963), 214–39.

7. See also the brief reflection in Eikha 5:19–20.

maintain a deep core of faith in God's enduring goodness, despite the ever-present suffering.

Nevertheless, for most of the book, the theological grappling offers a more complicated picture. The book acknowledges Israel's sinfulness, but also presents God's excessive punishments, enmity, and fierce anger. Jerusalem addresses God directly, expressing various shades of shame, defiance, and hope for reconciliation. God's silence clashes with Israel's vocal proclamations of faith, cries of despair, and angry accusations. The theological clarity that appears at the core of the book conflicts with the tension and uncertainty that dominate the surrounding portrait of the relationship.

I will present three approaches to address the elusive theology in the book. They are complementary, but not necessarily cohesive; each one charts its own path. The first explanation suggests that the book of Eikha does not focus on theology, but rather on emotions. The second proposes that the lack of systematic theology stems from the complexity of attempting to understand God's mysterious ways, and the third searches for a clear-cut theology in the literary artistry of the book.

A Book of Emotions

The first approach explains that Eikha is not interested in theology. Eikha is, rather, a book that focuses upon human ordeals.[8] Instead of offering solutions, the book aims to portray an emotional experience, suggesting that the raw, human response to suffering is itself a religious affair, one that builds and shapes character.

Eikha's seemingly inconsistent and rapidly changing attitudes toward God may be explained by the fact that emotions lie at its core. Is God just or not? An intellectual consideration of the matter approaches the question systematically, offering coherent, logical arguments. However, when humans address the same events through an emotional lens, contradictions abound. God is both just and unjust. Humans are

---

8. See, for example, K. O'Conner, "Lamentations," in *The New Interpreter's Bible*, vol. 6 (Nashville: Abington, 2001), 1024: "The book functions as a witness to pain, a testimony of survival, and an artistic transformation of dehumanizing suffering into exquisite literature."

simultaneously baffled, abashed, angered, and comforted by God. The ebb and flow of human emotions and the way they shift and converge, collide and contradict, can account for the rapid swing between different perspectives in Eikha. This represents the emotional condition of humans, offering a realistic and multifaceted portrait of how humans cope with God's role in their tragedy.

This can also explain the inconclusive nature of the book. Eikha offers little in the way of consolation. Emotions do not provide closure; they tend to be cyclical and unpredictable, often surfacing unexpectedly. It should not surprise us that Eikha does not progress in a linear fashion, nor that it does not conclude with a resolution; by their very nature, emotions, especially strong ones, remain turbulent.

An Inscrutable World

The second approach posits that, although Eikha is not a Job-like theological treatise on the meaning of suffering, it still contains theological reflection. Yet this reflection is complex and discordant.

As noted, God is portrayed in an inconsistent manner, fluctuating between a just deity ("The Lord is righteous," 1:18) wronged by a sinful nation ("Jerusalem has surely sinned," 1:8), and a God who has wrapped Himself in anger ("You cloaked Yourself in anger," 3:43), acted capriciously, and wantonly spewed His wrath upon innocent victims ("Look Lord and see, to whom have You done this?" 2:20).

Eikha's depiction of human responsibility is likewise contradictory. While the notion of human accountability can be found in Eikha, the book resists a one-dimensional rendering of the disaster, refusing to thrust responsibility solely upon human sinfulness. Eikha is not a book of confessions. Often, expressions of anger or confusion overshadow a previous admission of guilt. The intense, graphic description of Jerusalem's travails stuns the reader, leaving an indelible impression of raw and irredeemable suffering. Most poignantly, the repeated mention of children implies the agony of innocents. The lack of specificity with regard to the sins shifts the emphasis away from the nation's presumed evil, allowing the reader to focus on the enormity of the human suffering. In this context, Israel can hurl accusations at God, whose excessive punishments seem disproportionate to their actions.

This complex portrait may be the best we can do to make sense of the human condition. Without a simple solution for the problem of human suffering, the book does not deny that injustice abounds. However, at the same time, Eikha declines to surrender the idea that God runs the world with justice and that human beings must take responsibility for their deeds. This complex portrayal accurately reflects the theological paradox of a divinely controlled world saturated with injustice.

In a talmudic discourse, R. Meir maintains that God denied Moses's bid to understand why the righteous suffer and the evil prosper. This question lies beyond of the realm of human knowledge:

> R. Yoḥanan said in the name of R. Yosi: Three things Moses requested from God and they were granted him … [Moses's third question] was to know the ways of God, and this was granted him, as it says, "Show me Your ways" (Ex. 33:13). He said to Him, "Master of the universe! Why is there a righteous person who experiences good and a righteous person who experiences evil? [Why is there a] wicked person who experiences evil and a wicked person who experiences good?" …R. Meir disagreed with [R. Yosi], for R. Meir said: Two were granted to [Moses] and one [request] was not. As it says, "And I will be gracious to whom I will be gracious" (Ex. 33:19), even if he is not worthy. "And I will show mercy on whom I will show mercy" (ibid.), even if he is not worthy. (Berakhot 7a)

How is it possible to maintain a relationship with God given such a disquieting paradox? This ability to navigate an inscrutable world depends upon one's willingness to live with complexity, as well as faith in God. Lacking a satisfying answer, Eikha's presentation of this complexity produces a jarring but magnificent portrait of humans who struggle mightily to balance fidelity to God with candid recognition of an unjust world.

The chiastic structure of the book reflects its theological complexity.[9] The peripheral chapters (1 and 5) conclude with the nation's

---

9. As we will see in the next chapter, "Biblical Poetry and the Book of Eikha," Eikha's broad design maintains a concentric chiastic structure, in which parallel chapters revolve around a central axis (A B C B' A').

assumption of responsibility for the calamity. Chapters 2 and 4 reflect accusation and anger, protesting against a God who wields His anger indiscriminately, even against innocent children. Chapter 3, the pivotal center of the book, touches at the heart of human experience, expressing hope and faith in God's enduring compassion. At the conclusion of this study, I will closely examine this structure. For the present, it is sufficient to note that it reflects the idea that the divine-human relationship remains a complex affair, filled with backward and forward movements. Yet at its core, we find commitment, conviction, and optimism.

Deuteronomy 28 and the Literary Artistry of the Book

The third approach stems from the conviction that Eikha could not leave glaring theological questions so flagrantly unanswered. The decline and fall of the Judean kingdom, along with the apparent abrogation of God's promise to David of an eternal dynasty, must have meaning within a retributive context. Only this approach corresponds to our belief in divine goodness; human sinfulness results in human suffering. Nevertheless, as noted, the severity of the sin (and the absence of specific sins) does not appear to correspond to the degree of Israel's suffering, leaving open the question of the justice of these events.[10]

To the extent that Eikha provides an explanation for the events, we can discern it in the literary artistry of the book. Eikha contains numerous linguistic parallels to Deuteronomy 28, a chapter that establishes a covenant between God and His nation.[11] According to its tenets, Israel obligates itself to obey God and observe His commandments. If Israel fulfills its commitment, God promises a myriad of blessings. Disobedience brings punishments in its wake, which Deuteronomy 28:15–68 enumerates in frightening detail.[12]

---

10. Although Eikha refrains from enumerating specific sins, the book does make direct reference to sin. These appear especially in chapter 1, which repeatedly mentions Jerusalem's sins and rebellion (Eikha 1:5, 8, 14, 18, 20, 22).

11. Many have noted these allusions. See, for example, Albrektson, *Studies*, 231–37; Cohn, *Textual Tapestries*, 243–46.

12. Deuteronomy 28 is often termed a "*Tokheḥa*," which literally means "rebuke." This appellation appears to focus on the second half of the chapter (Deut. 28:15–68),

Eikha subtly weaves linguistic references to these punishments into its fabric, indicating that the fall of Jerusalem, the exile, and the accompanying catastrophe are the anticipated consequences of Israel's failure to live up to its obligations. In fact, Eikha implies that none of these events should come as a surprise; Israel had been warned that their sins would bring these very punishments.

Linguistic parallels between Eikha and Deuteronomy 28 appear in the following chart:

The Punishment	Eikha	Deuteronomy 28
Israel will not have respite (*mano'aḥ*).	לֹא מָצְאָה מָנוֹחַ (א׳, ג׳)	וְלֹא יִהְיֶה מָנוֹחַ לְכַף רַגְלֶךָ (כ״ח, ס״ה)
Enemies will pursue (*radaf*) and overtake Israel (*haseg*).	כָּל רֹדְפֶיהָ הִשִּׂיגוּהָ בֵּין הַמְּצָרִים (א׳, ג׳)	וּרְדָפוּךָ וְהִשִּׂיגוּךָ עַד הִשָּׁמְדָךְ (כ״ח, מ״ה)
The enemy will be at the head (*lerosh*).	הָיוּ צָרֶיהָ לְרֹאשׁ אֹיְבֶיהָ שָׁלוּ (א׳, ה׳)	הוּא יִהְיֶה לְרֹאשׁ וְאַתָּה תִּהְיֶה לְזָנָב (כ״ח, מ״ד)
Israel's children will go into captivity (*halakh shevi*).	עוֹלָלֶיהָ הָלְכוּ שְׁבִי לִפְנֵי צָר (א׳, ה׳) בְּתוּלֹתַי וּבַחוּרַי הָלְכוּ בַשֶּׁבִי (א׳, י״ח)	בָּנִים וּבָנוֹת תּוֹלִיד וְלֹא יִהְיוּ לָךְ כִּי יֵלְכוּ בַּשֶּׁבִי (כ״ח, מ״א)
Gates (*shaar*) and walls (*ḥoma*) will no longer function protectively.	חָשַׁב ה׳ לְהַשְׁחִית חוֹמַת בַּת צִיּוֹן נָטָה קָו לֹא הֵשִׁיב יָדוֹ מִבַּלֵּעַ וַיַּאֲבֶל חֵל וְחוֹמָה יַחְדָּו אֻמְלָלוּ (ב׳, ח׳) טָבְעוּ בָאָרֶץ שְׁעָרֶיהָ (ב׳, ט׳)	וְהֵצַר לְךָ בְּכָל שְׁעָרֶיךָ עַד רֶדֶת חֹמֹתֶיךָ הַגְּבֹהֹת וְהַבְּצֻרוֹת (כ״ח, נ״ב)

which enumerates the punishments that God will bring upon the nation if it sins. The term *Tokheḥa* does not properly account for the first part of the chapter (Deut. 28:1–14), which lists the blessings that God will bestow upon the nation if it obeys Him. Perhaps a more accurate title for the chapter is "*Berit*," or covenant, where both parties enter a relationship with full cognizance of their respective obligations. The same pattern appears in the other chapter known by the term *Tokheḥa* (Lev. 26).

The Punishment	Eikha	Deuteronomy 28
Israel will spiral downward (*tered*).[13]	וַתֵּרֶד פְּלָאִים (א', ט')	וְאַתָּה תֵרֵד מַטָּה מָטָּה (כ"ח, מ"ג)
Israel's king (*melekh*) will be exiled into the nations (*goy*).	מַלְכָּהּ וְשָׂרֶיהָ בַגּוֹיִם (ב', ט')	יוֹלֵךְ ה' אֹתְךָ וְאֶת מַלְכְּךָ אֲשֶׁר תָּקִים עָלֶיךָ אֶל גּוֹי אֲשֶׁר לֹא יָדַעְתָּ (כ"ח, ל"ו)
Israel will be mocked and disparaged among the nations (*haamim*).	סְחִי וּמָאוֹס תְּשִׂימֵנוּ בְּקֶרֶב הָעַמִּים (ג', מ"ה)	וְהָיִיתָ לְשַׁמָּה לְמָשָׁל וְלִשְׁנִינָה בְּכֹל הָעַמִּים אֲשֶׁר יְנַהֶגְךָ ה' שָׁמָּה (כ"ח ל"ז)
Parents will consume (*akhal*) their children, the fruit of their womb (*peri*) from hunger.	אִם תֹּאכַלְנָה נָשִׁים פִּרְיָם עֹלֲלֵי טִפֻּחִים (ב', כ') יְדֵי נָשִׁים רַחֲמָנִיּוֹת בִּשְּׁלוּ יַלְדֵיהֶן הָיוּ לְבָרוֹת לָמוֹ (ד', י')	וְאָכַלְתָּ פְרִי בִטְנְךָ בְּשַׂר בָּנֶיךָ וּבְנֹתֶיךָ (כ"ח, נ"ג)
The enemy will not honor (*lo yisa*) elders (*zaken*) or priests and will not act graciously (*lo yaḥon*) to elders and youth (*naar*).	פְּנֵי כֹהֲנִים לֹא נָשָׂאוּ וּזְקֵנִים לֹא חָנָנוּ · (ד', ט"ז)	גּוֹי עַז פָּנִים אֲשֶׁר לֹא יִשָּׂא פָנִים לְזָקֵן וְנַעַר לֹא יָחֹן (כ"ח, נ)
The enemy will come, as swiftly as an eagle (*nesher*).	קַלִּים הָיוּ רֹדְפֵינוּ מִנִּשְׁרֵי שָׁמָיִם (ד', י"ט)	יִשָּׂא ה' עָלֶיךָ גּוֹי מֵרָחֹק מִקְצֵה הָאָרֶץ כַּאֲשֶׁר יִדְאֶה הַנָּשֶׁר (כ"ח, מ"ט)
The phrase *al tzavar* (by our necks) describes Israel's burdens and exhaustion.	עַל צַוָּארֵנוּ נִרְדָּפְנוּ יָגַעְנוּ לֹא וְלֹא הוּנַח לָנוּ (ה', ה')	וְנָתַן עֹל בַּרְזֶל עַל צַוָּארֶךָ עַד הִשְׁמִידוֹ אֹתָךְ (כ"ח, מ"ח)

The rarity of some of the shared words and phrases strengthens the connection between these texts. The word *mano'aḥ* (Eikha 1:3 and Deut. 28:65), for example, appears outside of these passages only five times in the Bible.

---

13. See Ibn Caspi, Eikha 1:9, who observes this comparison.

God and His people base their relationship on a covenant, a contractual agreement with mutual terms and obligations. Clearly outlined alongside the consequences are distinct guidelines for maintaining the nation's well-being. Although this does not erase the trauma, the warning mitigates the sense that the punishment is unexpected, disproportionate, and unfair. The following verse may refer to the biblical covenant of Deuteronomy 28:[14]

> The Lord did that which He planned; He executed His word that He commanded from days of old. (Eikha 2:17)

As we will see, Eikha also references prophetic rebukes and warnings throughout the book. Prophetic exhortations include predictions of impending disaster and even explicit cautionary threats of the fall of Jerusalem, the destruction of the Temple, and the exile of Jerusalem's inhabitants. Had Israel only listened to the prophets, the nation might have avoided this situation.

The conclusion seems undeniable: Jerusalem has received her just desserts and she knew well in advance that this would be the consequence of her sins. Beyond the rebuke, the allusions to Deuteronomy 28 also contain an inspiring formula for rehabilitation. If the destruction of Jerusalem is a consequence of disobedience, then the situation is reversible, as stated in the *Tokheḥa* – embrace religious obligations and receive God's blessings. According to the Torah, God has forged an eternal, immutable covenant with Israel. Punishments, even those that appear catastrophic on a national level, do not abrogate that covenant – they affirm it.[15]

---

14. Interestingly, both Rashi and R. Yosef Kara refer to the covenant (*Tokheḥa*) of Leviticus 26 in their explanation of this verse. The *Targum* on this verse refers generally to God's words to Moses, without specifying a particular passage.

15. See Leviticus 26:42. The above approach is unlike the ancient Near Eastern lamentation over the destruction of the city of Ur, which adopts the fatalistic notion that a city's destruction permanently seals its fate: "Why do you concern yourself with crying? The judgment uttered by the assembly cannot be reversed... Ur was indeed given kingship, but it was not given an eternal reign. From time immemorial, since the Land was founded, until people multiplied, who has ever seen a reign of

R. Akiva notes this in the celebrated story of his reaction to the destruction of the second Temple:

> Rabban Gamliel, R. Elazar ben Azariah, R. Yehoshua, and R. Akiva...were coming up to Jerusalem. When they arrived at Mount Scopus, they tore their clothes. When they arrived at the Temple Mount, they saw a fox emerging from the Holy of Holies. They began to cry, but R. Akiva laughed [with joy]. They said to him, "Why do you laugh?" He said to them, "Why are you crying?" They said, "This is the place about which it was said, 'A foreigner who draws near shall die' (Num. 1:51). And now, foxes traverse it; shall we not cry?!" He said to them, "This is why I laugh... The verse made the prophecy of Zechariah contingent upon the prophecy of Uriah. Uriah said, 'Therefore, because of you Zion will be plowed up like a field' (Jer. 26:18). And Zechariah said, 'Old men and old women shall yet sit in the streets of Jerusalem' (Zech. 8:4). Until the [punitive] prophecy of Uriah was fulfilled, I was afraid that the [auspicious] prophecy of Zechariah would not be fulfilled. But now that the prophecy of Uriah was fulfilled, it is certain that the prophecy of Zechariah will be fulfilled!" They said to him, "Akiva, you have comforted us! Akiva, you have comforted us!" (Makkot 24b)

R. Akiva regards the destruction of the Temple as proof of God's ongoing involvement in His nation's fate. God did not abandon Israel; rather, He is carefully chastising His people, guiding them to behave properly. Ultimately, the fulfillment of a prophecy, even a punitive one, confirms the veracity of the prophetic tradition. Implicit in punishment is the truth of biblical theology and the faith in a restored glory, an idea that provides consolation and strengthens belief in a hopeful future.

---

kingship that would take precedence forever? The reign of its kingship had been long indeed but had to exhaust itself... Abandon your city... and accept the decree." (Translation taken from Black, J. A., Cunningham, G., Ebeling, J., Flückiger-Hawker, E., Robson, E., Taylor, J., and Zólyomi, G., *The Electronic Text Corpus of Sumerian Literature* [http://etcsl.orinst.ox.ac.uk/], Oxford 1998–2006.)

CONCLUSION

To summarize, we have seen three possible approaches to the theology of Eikha. First, perhaps we should not search for theology in the book, but rather examine it to uncover its rich portrayal of the nation's emotional response to God's role in the catastrophe. Second, the lack of a systematic theology may illustrate the complexity inherent in the bid to uncover God's elusive nature. Third, entwined into the weave of the book's construction are allusions to the *Tokheḥa* of Deuteronomy 28 (and other prophetic admonitions), indicating that these predicted events were avoidable had Israel behaved in accordance with their obligations.

Remarkably, despite the abiding theological questions, the heart of the book exhibits steadfast belief in God's goodness (Eikha 3:21–24). This testifies to the resilience of faith that lies at the core of human existence.

Biblical Poetry and the Book of Eikha

P oetry arouses passions, appealing as much to the imagination as to the intellect.[1] While prose aims primarily to inform, poetry seeks to impact.[2] It is natural, then, that a sustained expression of anguish such as Eikha adopts poetic form.

Although the distinction between poetry and prose (especially in biblical literature) remains murky,[3] the concentration of character-

---

1. For example, Leland Ryken, *Sweeter than Honey, Richer than Gold: A Guided Study of Biblical Poetry* (Bellingham, WA: Lexham Press, 2015), 27, explains: "Poetry is a more affective (emotional) type of discourse than ordinary expository discourse."
2. Both poetry and prose impact and inform. The mode of writing, however, illustrates its primary objective.
3. See A. Berlin, "Reading Biblical Poetry," in A. Berlin and M. Brettler, eds., *The Jewish Study Bible* (New York: Oxford University Press, 2004), 2097. J. L. Kugel, *The Idea of Biblical Poetry: Parallelism and Its History* (New Haven: Yale University Press, 1981), 63, observes that, "the same traits that seem to characterize Hebrew 'poetry' also crop up in what is clearly not poetry." Similarly, on p. 69, Kugel asserts that "to speak of poetry at all in the Bible will be in some measure to impose a concept foreign to the biblical world." Nevertheless, R. Alter, *The Art of Biblical Poetry* (New York: Basic Books, 1985), 5–6, disagrees with Kugel, maintaining that one can recognize poetic discourse. He further cautions that one should not overstate the difficulty of biblical poetry: "There remains much that can be understood about biblical verse ... it may exhibit perfectly perceptible formal patterns that tell us something about the operations of the underlying poetic system." In any case, scholars often bemoan the elusive nature of biblical poetry, defining it by the degree and concentration of poetic techniques, rather than by applying clear parameters.

istic poetic techniques used in the composition of Eikha marks it as poetry. Eikha employs elevated discourse, imagery, metaphors, parallelism, meter, rhythm, wordplay, repetition, sound patterns, multivocality, structure, and shifts in speakers to convey its grief-stricken tale. Due to the dense and terse nature of Eikha's poetry, to understand this delicately crafted poem – its themes, emotions, and theology – we must pay careful attention to the techniques used in its poetic composition.

Biblical books are not mere literature; they are religious texts, which present the human experience through the lens of the relationship between humans and God. In Eikha, mourning attains religious significance, as humans grapple with God amidst roiling emotions and tragic circumstances. In this chapter, I will examine the manner in which Eikha's poetic techniques shape the religious meaning of the text.

The following examination does not purport to be comprehensive, but rather representative. I will bring several examples from different categories of poetic techniques to illustrate the way they help convey the themes and theology of the book. As we progress through our study of Eikha, I will explore these poetic features as they arise.

IMAGERY AND METAPHOR

Although scholars do not concur on how to define poetry, most agree that a dominant feature is its attempt to spark the reader's imagination by using techniques such as imagery and metaphors.[4]

Poems often employ imagery intended to trigger the reader's senses, offering a visceral experience. Commonly, imagery appeals to the visual sense, evoking pictorial impressions that enable the reader to imagine the scene. Eikha vividly describes the terrible sights of Jerusalem's ruins: her desolate roads (1:4), foreigners entering her holy precinct (1:10), her sunken gates (2:9), elderly men in sackcloth, sinking to the ground in mourning (2:10), children languishing on the streets (2:11), people rendered wizened and unrecognizable by the ravages of starvation (4:8), foxes cavorting upon the ruins of the Temple (5:18), and more.

Eikha's imagery stimulates other senses as well. The reader hears Jerusalem weeping in the night (1:2), the sounds of the raucous rejoicing

---

4. Berlin, "Reading," 2101.

of the enemies (2:7), the children begging their mothers for a morsel of food (2:12; 4:4), and the jeers and whistles of gloating adversaries (2:16). The testimony of chapter 3's protagonist (known as the *gever*) evokes a brutal tactile sensation, as he describes his enemy cruelly breaking his bones (3:4) and viciously mangling him (3:11). Later, the nations express their revulsion toward Jerusalem's bloodied residents, withdrawing in disgust from any bodily contact: "Go away; do not touch!" (4:15). This scenario evokes a distinct mental image of a face filled with loathing and an involuntary recoil.

In recalling the past, the book evokes images of tasty delicacies (4:5), a contrast to the dry mouth and empty palate caused by the famine in Jerusalem (4:4). In a peculiar and savage anthropomorphic image, God also "consumes" in the book, swallowing Israel and her palaces (2:5). The most indelible (and gruesome) act of consumption in the book is women eating their children (2:20; 4:10), which elicits horror and revulsion.

The text does not specify the various odors that permeate the languishing city. The reader can only imagine the stench of death that pervades the houses (1:20) and emerges from the corpses that litter the streets (2:21). The text hints at an overpowering smell of the rotting garbage that clings to the residents of Jerusalem, who hug the refuse heaps to obtain warmth (4:5).

Poetry employs metaphors with a similar goal of engaging the reader. By referencing something unrelated, the metaphor allows for multifaceted meanings, involving readers in the act of interpretation and encouraging them to construct their own associations and insights.

Consider, for example, the initial metaphor of the book, which depicts the city as a widowed woman.[5] Jerusalem's suffering as a widow suggests her solitude, loss, vulnerability, despair, and precarious economic situation. After remembering her role as a wife, Jerusalem's betrayals rise to the fore, as the book recalls her former lovers: "She has no comforter from all her lovers" (1:2); "I called to my lovers; they

---

5. Biblical passages portray cities as women. Other examples include Isaiah 47:1–15 and Nahum 3:1–19. Note that the Hebrew word for city (*ir*) is feminine. We will discuss this at greater length in chapter 1.

deceived me!" (1:19).[6] It seems fitting that those who once respected Jerusalem now disparage her; having viewed her nakedness, they regard her as cheap (1:8).

Eikha also describes Jerusalem as a bereft mother whose children have been taken into captivity (1:5, 18), inclining the reader to empathize with Jerusalem's pain. Possibly, the maternal figure who consumes her children (2:20; 4:10) also alludes to Jerusalem.[7] In this representation, Jerusalem betrays her maternal nature, devouring her children instead of nurturing them.

Thus, the metaphor of Jerusalem personified as a female figure inspires multiple ideas: she is a vulnerable widow who has lost her present and a grieving mother who has lost her future. She is both perfidious and pathetic, sinner and victim. A resonant metaphor, the female Jerusalem simultaneously evokes sympathy and repugnance.

Another effective metaphor appears in Eikha 2:13. Describing Jerusalem's pain appears to be impossible; the verse begins by declaring that nothing can compare to Jerusalem's tragedy. Yet, as the verse winds to a close, the poet identifies something that reflects Jerusalem's agony, something utterly unexpected, underscoring the difficulty of finding an adequate comparison: "For as great as the sea is your brokenness; who can heal you?"

The sea emerges as a rich and diverse metaphor, conveying multiple ideas. First, the sea's vastness represents the endless breadth and depth of Jerusalem's pain. The water's salinity also recalls Jerusalem's copious tears (mentioned just two verses prior, in Eikha 2:11), plentiful enough to produce a veritable sea. Moreover, the sea is tempestuous, mirroring Jerusalem's state of unrest. In an evocative wordplay, the root used to describe Jerusalem's brokenness (*shivreikh*) functions as a homonym for waves that break upon the shore (*mishberei yam*), a

---

6. Note that the word "lovers" in Hosea 2:9, 12 references Israel's idolatry and betrayal of God. I will discuss other possible meanings of these verses when I examine chapter 1.

7. The starving and rapacious women in these verses seem to be residents of Jerusalem. Nevertheless, it is possible that this image evokes the figurative maternal figure of Jerusalem, suggesting that she too is complicit in the consumption of her populace.

phrase sometimes employed to describe one lost in a sea of despair (Jonah 2:4; Ps. 42:8).[8]

This is a fine example of the way in which metaphors can produce a rich multivocality. The sea evokes multiple associations that characterize Jerusalem's shattered emotional state.

As a final example, observe the metaphor provided by the *gever* in Eikha 3:10. As the description of his suffering at the hands of God gains traction, the *gever* appears to lose control, abandoning any semblance of theological restraint. In a frenzy of anguish, the *gever* asserts, "He [God!] is a bear lying in ambush for me, a lion in hidden places" (Eikha 3:10). This portrayal of God defies all accepted notions of God's ways. Rather than regarding God's actions as evenhanded and deliberate, the comparison suggests a bestial enemy, both predatory and arbitrary. This metaphor conveys the depths of the *gever*'s alienation from God, his utter incomprehension of his dismal circumstances. The wielding of this image cannot fail to capture the reader's attention, offering a striking glimpse into the *gever*'s religious state of mind.

PARALLELISM AND METER

Biblical poetry tends to employ binary sentences, divided into two parts by a slight conceptual pause. These sentences characteristically contain parallelism between the two parts.[9] Eikha's poetry, however, lacks frequent or strong parallelism. While some sentences still reflect some manner of parallelism and binary construct, many seem entirely devoid of it. Instead, the idea of the first line of the sentence frequently carries

---

8. Interestingly, the wordplay in Hebrew exists in English as well; the word *shever* means both broken and breakers of the sea.

9. Parallelism pairs the poetic lines of the binary sentence (either synonymously or antithetically), using lexical, grammatical, phonological, or semantic features. A rich and varied technique, parallelism does not fully duplicate (or contrast) two lines; the meanings of the lines always diverge slightly or greatly, thereby extending the meaning of the line in various ways. For more on this important topic, see J. L. Kugel, *The Idea of Biblical Poetry: Parallelism and its History* (New Haven: Yale University Press, 1981); R. Alter, *The Art of Biblical Poetry* (New York: Basic Books, 1985), 3–26; A. Berlin, *The Dynamics of Biblical Parallelism* (Bloomington: Indiana University Press, 1985).

over to the second line, furthering and developing the topic.[10] Consider the following three sentences in Eikha:

1. The roads to Zion mourn,
    for no one comes for the appointed day. (1:4)
2. Her king and officers are among the nations,
    there is no instruction. (2:9)
3. They cut off my life in a pit,
    and they cast a stone at me. (3:53)

These sentences do not contain lines that parallel one another; instead, the second line simply continues the idea presented in the first line. Though many of Eikha's binary sentences lack parallelism, it is present, especially toward the conclusion of the book.[11]

Corresponding to their parallelism, biblical binary sentences generally retain a balanced meter or rhythm in each part, supporting the thematic equilibrium.[12] However, although some passages in Eikha maintain the customary metrical symmetry, many of its sentences exhibit a distinctly different, imbalanced meter. In the early twentieth century, Karl Budde identified and proposed a term for Eikha's unusual meter,

---

10. Eikha's sentences tend to use a technique called enjambment, in which the syntax or meaning carries over to the next line without pause. See Dobbs-Allsopp, 19.

11. Although more than two-thirds of the book lacks parallelism, chapter 5 displays a predominantly parallelistic sentence structure. See Dobbs-Allsopp, 19, who claims that enjambment gives the book "a palpable sense of forward movement." According to this view, as the book draws to a close, its forward movement slows, as seen in the decline in enjambment. It seems to me that the return to parallel sentences represents a return to normalcy, to the convention of biblical poetry, and a discernable movement toward a harmonious, balanced world.

12. The idea that biblical poetry retains a metrical system remains a subject of controversy among scholars. Kugel, *Idea*, 292–99, objects to the possibility of finding a metrical arrangement in biblical poetry. Indeed, finding a clear metrical system in biblical poetry has proved elusive, despite the many attempts to do so. Certainly, no system has achieved any kind of scholarly consensus. Berlin ("Reading," 2099; *Lamentations*, 2) claims that binary lines tend to maintain balanced length and rhythm, even without adhering to a strict metrical system that can be measured in a precise and consistent manner.

dubbing it *"kina* (lamentations) meter."[13] *Kina* meter is uneven in a consistent fashion; the second part of the sentence tends to contain fewer accentuated units (stressed syllables) than the first part.[14]

I will illustrate Budde's theory by examining the meter of Eikha 4:7 (chapter 4 contains two binary sentences per verse). I have bolded the stressed syllable:

$$\begin{array}{ccccc} 1 & 1 & 1 & 1 & 1 & = 3 + 2 \\ \end{array}$$
Sentence 1: *Zaku nezireha misheleg*   *Tzaḥu meiḥalav*

$$\begin{array}{ccccc} 1 & 1 & 1 & 1 & 1 & = 3 + 2 \\ \end{array}$$
Sentence 2: *Ademu etzem mipeninim*   *Sapir gizratam*

The first part of each sentence contains three stressed syllables. In symmetrical biblical poetry, the second half should also have three stressed syllables, resulting in balanced meter. However, the second half of each of these sentences has two stressed syllables, creating an imbalance in the rhythm of the binary sentence.

Budde asserted that this metrical asymmetry is an apt characteristic of lamentation poetry.[15] The effect is a peculiar imbalanced rhythm, in which the second part of the sentence fades away. This conveys the book's inability to finish its sentences, a condition produced by exhaustion and despair. Cut off midway, the speaker chokes back the final word in his litany of suffering, tapering off into a disconcerting silence. Moreover, the uneven cadence produces an effect like Eikha's sparse parallelism; it mirrors an imbalanced world where harmony no longer prevails.

---

13. K. Budde, "Das hebraisches Klagelied," *ZAW* 2 (1882), 1–52.

14. The indicators of stressed syllables are part of the massoretic tradition that includes the vowels and cantillation points. First transmitted in written form in the seventh to tenth centuries CE, these massoretic points emerge as a late written addition to the biblical text.

15. W. H. Shea, "The Qinah Structure of the Book of Lamentations," *Biblica* 60 (1979), 103–6, broadens Budde's theory, suggesting that the overall structure of the book reflects a 3 + 2 pattern. Indeed, Eikha opens with three long chapters and decrescendos with the final two shorter chapters. Shea further perceives a 2 + 1 arrangement in the group of the first three chapters, followed by a 2 + 1 pattern in the final chapters (note that chapter 4 is twice as long as chapter 5).

The biblical listener, who hears not just the words but also the rhythm of the poetry, feels unsettled by its metrical lopsidedness, straining to hear the last beat of the sentence. Its absence jars the reader, who senses that the final word remains unspoken.

While the existence of this phenomenon remains debated, and it likely cannot be applied as widely as Budde proposed, some meaningful examples seem to support Budde's hypothesis that Eikha employs prosody with conscious artistry and design.[16] Consider Eikha 1:5, a verse that contains three binary sentences. The first and third sentences retain Budde's "*kina* meter," in which the second part of the sentence contains fewer stressed syllables than the first:

1   1   1   1   1   = 3 + 2

Sentence 1: *hayu tzareha lerosh   oyveha shalu*

1   1   1   1   = 3 + 1

Sentence 3: *oleleha halekhu shevi lifnei-tzar*

Unexpectedly, however, the middle sentence contains parallel meter, a balanced number of stressed syllables:

1   1   1   1   = 2 + 2

Sentence 2: *Ki-YHVH hoga   al-rov pesha'eha*

How can we understand the erratic metrical arrangement of this verse?[17] In this case, the verse's prosody clearly reflects its content. Sentences

---

16. Scholars have criticized this theory on various grounds. Some note that this metrical pattern also appears in poetry that is not elegiac. See G. B. Gray, *Forms of Hebrew Poetry* (New York: Ktav, 1972), 116. Others note that biblical laments do not always maintain *kina* meter. See Shea, "Qinah," 103, who makes both of the above points. Still others object to the assertion that the biblical metrical system rests on its stressed syllables. Nevertheless, Grossberg, *Centripetal*, 86, asserts that even if this meter does not characterize all biblical elegies, it can be established that this meter exists in Eikha.

17. The disparity between the metrical arrangements of the sentences in this verse is hardly unusual. Many verses in Eikha flit from even to uneven meter, some of which can be explained and some not. This, of course, contributes to many scholars' skepticism that one can identify a deliberate metrical arrangement in the book.

one and three describe an inharmonious world filled with injustice. The first sentence reflects upon the tranquility and success of Israel's enemies, known for their unremitting cruelty: "Her adversaries were at the head, her enemies were tranquil." The third sentence portrays the suffering of innocents, namely, the children: "Her young children went into captivity, before the adversary." These topics represent the crux of the theological question of evil. Why do wicked people prosper (*rasha vetov lo*)? Why do bad things happen to the righteous (*tzaddik vera lo*)? The metrical imbalance that bookends this verse reflects the discordant message of those sentences. Yet, at the heart of the verse there is a balanced sentence, one that restores the equilibrium of the verse – and of the world. "For the Lord made her grieve, because of the greatness of her transgressions." In His first appearance in the book, God enters as a stabilizing force, restoring faith that the world functions justly, even if we do not perceive it on the surface. The steady sentence at the heart of the verse expresses faith in divine justice, despite the storm of injustices that swirl around it.

Scholars continue to debate whether biblical poetry contains any metrical system. This brief examination does not intend to offer a sweeping conclusion to this long-running debate. Perhaps we can simply conclude that the search for a relationship between the metrical arrangement and the meaning of the text can sometimes yield elegant and meaningful results.[18]

THE ARTISTRY OF WORDS: SYNONYMS, SOUND PATTERNS, WORDPLAY, AND AMBIGUITY

Biblical poetry is terse, deploying its words laconically but with careful artistry. Eikha deliberately selects its vocabulary, sometimes offering a broad array of synonyms, repeating a word or sound, or employing words that contain dual or ambiguous meaning.

Eikha 2:1–10 employs a multitude of synonyms to describe the destruction of Jerusalem. The use of numerous verbs evokes a sense of

---

18. Kugel, *Idea*, 301, concedes that meter (in his view, "a loose and approximate regularity") is at times "clearly cultivated."

the scope and comprehensiveness of the destruction, and of misfortune besetting the city from every direction.

Eikha 3:47 is an example of a verse dense with assonance and alliteration, and with the recurrence of several consonants and vowels: *paḥad vaphaḥat haya lanu, hasheit vehashaver.* This striking repetition seems designed to hammer at the reader's senses, suggesting the unrelenting blows that the nation suffers.

Wordplay is an evocative verbal resource, drawing the reader into the act of interpretation. The reader simultaneously registers both the primary and secondary significance of the word, thereby constructing another layer of meaning for the poem. An apt example is the word *mo'ed,* which appears with different connotations throughout the book of Eikha. Its basic meaning is an appointed time or place, often one that is sanctified.[19] Eikha 2:6 refers to the "*mo'ed veshabbat,*" a conjunction that leaves little doubt that the reference is to hallowed time. In the same verse, the reference to *mo'ed* parallels God's sukka, indicating a consecrated place.

Eikha 1:4 observes the desolation of the once-bustling roads to Jerusalem, "for there is none that comes to the *mo'ed.*" The word *mo'ed* here is ambiguous and multivalent, referring both to sacred time (namely, the pilgrimage holidays) and to sacred place (namely, the Temple).

In an ironic twist, Eikha also uses the word *mo'ed* to refer to a divinely appointed time to destroy Jerusalem and her residents (1:15). The use of the word *mo'ed* to describe Jerusalem's destruction in place of her former celebrations evokes an agonizing contrast between the once hallowed city and its current devastation. Moreover, it indicates that God has turned against His holy city, transforming the appointed day of celebration into an appointed day of destruction. In an explicit acknowledgment of this reversal, Eikha 2:7 describes the enemies' raucous destruction of the Temple as sounding like the "*yom mo'ed.*" The cacophony of the demolition ironically and painfully recalls the joyous sounds of the festive celebrations.

---

19. For an example of an appointed time that does not appear to be sacred, see Genesis 18:4 or I Samuel 20:35. For an example of an appointed place that is not sacred, see Isaiah 14:31.

EIKHA'S SPEAKERS

Eikha lacks actual characters. Emerging simply as speaking voices, the multiple narrators of Eikha have elusive identities. These voices shift, changing from one verse to the next, and at times even in the middle of a verse. This literary device gives the reader insight into different perspectives throughout the book. In chapter 1, Jerusalem's evocative first-person account (1:11c–22, except 17) supplants the objective third person (1:1–11b, except 9c) description of Jerusalem. The first-person plural that appears for the first time in Eikha 3:40–48 offers a distinctly different point of view than the first-person singular. We can also distinguish between different first-person singular speakers: the first-person singular account of the individual *gever* (in chapter 3) is not necessarily identical to that of the first-person account of Jerusalem, which seems to represent the collective voice of her ill-fated residents.

The myriad voices in Eikha call attention to the complete absence of God's voice. Divine silence allows this book to focus exclusively on its portrayal of the human tragedy, and on the way people grapple with suffering. At the same time, God's reticence appears deliberate, indicating His ire. The absence of communication suggests that God punitively "hides His face," choosing to retreat from contact with His nation and withdraw into stony silence.

Let us examine one example in which the book's conscious switch of speaker aptly conveys Jerusalem's emotional state. The first time that we hear Jerusalem's voice, it breaks through unexpectedly, in the middle of a sentence in which the narrator is drily sketching Jerusalem's impurities, her downward spiral, and the absence of a comforter (Eikha 1:9). Following Jerusalem's impertinent interruption, in which she begs God to see her anguish ("Look, Lord, at my affliction, for the enemy is exalted!"), she immediately falls silent, reverting back to her composed posture. Two verses later, Jerusalem again interrupts the narrator's impassive account of her suffering, desperately beseeching God to take note of her:

> Her entire nation groans, they seek bread; they exchanged their precious delights for food, to restore their lives.
> "Look, Lord, and see! For I have become a glutton." (Eikha 1:11)

By allowing Jerusalem to interrupt the narrator mid-verse, the book implies that her despair erupts unbidden. Jerusalem has reached her breaking point; she cannot continue to maintain her silence as the narrator soberly recounts her misfortune.

We will examine the medium of Eikha's different voices throughout this study. The various shifts between speakers will sharpen our understanding of the tone and content of the book.

STRUCTURE: ALPHABETIC ACROSTIC AND CHIASTIC STRUCTURE

Poetry often conveys ideas through its configuration or structure. Lacking a plot, the poetic structure depends upon verbal artistry, which shapes the composition in a manner that is subtle but conscious. Structure in biblical poetry is both aesthetic and meaningful; buried within its design lie ideas of profound value. I will discuss two types of structural arrangements woven into Eikha's design: alphabetic acrostic and chiastic.

The conscious artistry of the book is perhaps most evident in the alphabetic acrostics of its first four chapters.[20] These acrostics show careful and deliberate assembly. Each verse opens with a subsequent letter of the alphabet.[21] Why adhere to such a formalistic construction? Presumably, this design cramps the free style of the poet. Why then are alphabetic acrostics common features of biblical poetry?[22]

This structure may simply be a memory aid, an especially useful device for remembering liturgical compositions in an era in which not everyone owned a prayer book.[23] This approach regards the structure as a technical and non-meaningful device.

---

20. Although chapter 5 does not conform to the acrostic structure, it does have twenty-two verses, which appears to be a deliberate allusion to an acrostic structure. Alternatively, it may simply represent a desire to maintain a consistent structural design.

21. Biblical acrostic structures frequently contain anomalies. In Eikha, chapters 2, 3, and 4 reverse the order of the *ayin* and the *peh*. I will discuss this later.

22. Psalms 9–10, 25, 34, 37, 111, 112, 119, 145; Proverbs 31; Nahum 1.

23. This seems to be the intention of the midrash (*Lekaḥ Tov Eikha* 1:1): "Why are the laments said in an alphabetic [structure]? So that they should be easily chanted by the mourners."

Alphabetic acrostics have a literary function as well. Suitable for maintaining order and compactness, this structure ensures that the poet's grief does not spill over and become unwieldy. By using an acrostic structure, the poet maintains control, despite the flood of emotions that accompanies his account.[24] As a literary device, the alphabetic design can also bind together the various ideas of the chapter. It provides a structural frame for the emotional account, which by its nature is scattered and frenzied. Some scholars suggest that the acrostic structure conveys the idea that in spite of the emotional tone and subject, Eikha is a rational, meticulous reflection on the terrible events.[25]

In Eikha, the alphabetic structure appears in four consecutive chapters, forming a pattern that involves recurring opening and closure. These alphabetic chapters move toward their inexorable alphabetic end; the tale of the downfall will reach its fateful conclusion when we reach the conclusion of the alphabet. However, there may be a positive message concealed in this repetitive alphabetic structure; after all, renewal follows every ending, emerging in spite of the destruction. Having concluded one melancholic description that leaves the reader with a sense of hopeless doom, the book appears to reawaken and acquire new energy, launching another alphabetical sequence, a new lease on life.

Acrostics most of all suggest totality, everything from A to Z.[26] Though Jerusalem's all-encompassing suffering is impossible to convey in words, by deploying all twenty-two alphabetic letters, the alphabetic chapters indicate their intention to employ the full range of linguistic possibilities. The following midrashim note that Eikha's alphabetic structure expresses totality (although they focus on the totality of Israel's sins, rather than on its grief):

---

24. N. K. Gottwald, *Studies in the Book of Lamentations* (London: SCM Press, 1954), 31, calls this the "judicious economy" of the book.

25. E. Assis, "The Alphabetic Acrostic in the Book of Lamentations," *CBQ* 69, 4 (2007), 717–18; W. F. Adeney, *Songs of Solomon and the Lamentations of Jeremiah* (London: Hodder & Stoughton, 1895), 66–67; Driver, *Introduction*, 459; Gottwald, 24.

26. One can discern this purpose in many compositions that employ alphabetic acrostics. For example, Psalms 145 expresses the comprehensive praise of God, while the alphabetic *vidui* (confession) of Yom Kippur expresses the totality of sinfulness.

> Why was [the book of Eikha] written in alphabetics? [R. Eliezer said:] Because Israel transgressed all the Torah completely. (Eikha Zuta 1:1)

> Why are the laments said in alphabetics?... Why was Israel penalized with an alphabetic? They sinned from *alef* to *tav* [i.e., A to Z], so they were punished from *alef* to *tav*. (*Pesikta Zutrata* [*Lekaḥ Tov*], Eikha 1:1)

Alphabetic chapters muster in a constricted space all the pain that the alphabet can encompass.

Deviations from the alphabetic acrostic draw the reader's attention, generating their own interpretive discussion. Why does the third chapter contain a triple alphabetic acrostic? Why does chapter 5 lack any alphabetic structure, but retain the twenty-two verse schema? Why is the customary order of the letters *peh* and *ayin* switched in chapters 2, 3, and 4, but retained in the first chapter?[27] For the moment, I will leave these questions aside, addressing them as they arise during the course of this study.

A chiastic structure is a literary device that involves a crosswise arrangement of concepts or words, which are repeated in reverse order, creating a ring structure (A B B' A').[28] This form of writing was common throughout the literature of the ancient Near East.[29] The Bible utilizes chiastic structures (in both prose and poetry) for a variety of purposes. They can be used, for example, to accentuate the concept of reward and punishment,[30] or simply to draw attention to parallels in the

---

27. Intriguingly, in the Qumran manuscript that contains the first chapter of Lamentations (4QLam), the *peh* precedes the *ayin*, conforming to the three other alphabetic chapters.

28. Many articles have been written about this structure. See, for example, Shimon Bar-Efrat, "Some Observations on the Analysis of Structure in Biblical Narrative," *Vetus Testamentum* 30 (1980), 154–73; Yehuda Raday, "Al HaKiasm BeSippur HaMikra'i," *Beit Mikra* (1964), 48–72 [Hebrew]. I discuss the chiastic structure of the book of Ruth in Y. Ziegler, *Ruth: From Alienation to Monarchy* (Jerusalem: Maggid, 2015), 461–65.

29. See John W. Welch, ed., *Chiasmus in Antiquity: Structures, Analyses, Exegesis* (Hildesheim: Gerstenberg Verlag, 1981).

30. See Genesis 9:6, whose tightly arranged language makes it an exemplar of chiastic structures, often used to illustrate the incontrovertible existence of chiasms in the Bible. See my discussion below of this verse, "Chapter One, Appendix 1: A Chiastic Structure."

composition. Sometimes the structure is concentric, in which the parallel sections revolve around a central axis that has no corresponding passage (A B C B' A'). This design highlights the central axis, which contains the vital idea of the composition.[31]

It may be possible to discern an internal chiastic structure in chapters 1 and 2 of Eikha, in which the first letter (*alef*) matches the last letter (*tav*) (*a"t*) and the second letter (*bet*) corresponds to the second to last letter (*shin*) (*b"sh*) and so on, creating an *a"t–b"sh* pattern.[32] In this scheme, the chapter appears as concentric circles that become increasingly narrower until the central meeting point of the chapter (verses 11 and 12), which contains its key idea. This structure provides a sense of cyclical rotation, representing an interminable calamity, a tale of destruction that has no exit. Jerusalem is as inconsolable at the end of chapter 1 as she is at the beginning,[33] and as troubled.[34]

Chapter 1's chiastic structure focuses attention on its inner core, the *kaf* and *lamed* verses (11 and 12), which contains an inner chiastic linguistic pattern:

ראה...והביטה

הביטו וראו

Look … see

See and look

Chapter 1 casts a spotlight upon its central idea: Jerusalem's loneliness. Having opened with Jerusalem's lonesome state in verse 1, at the

---

31. Several scholars maintain that this is the sole purpose of the structure. See, for example, Raday, *HaKiasm*, 51; D. N. Freedman, "Preface," in J. W. Welch, ed., *Chiasmus in Antiquity: Structures, Analyses, Exegesis* (Hildesheim: Gerstenberg Verlag, 1981), 7. I believe that one should also seek significance in the parallel passages that form the concentric circles around the center.

32. If chapters 3, 4, and 5 in fact lack a chiastic structure, this too requires an explanation. I will address this as part of our analysis of those chapters.

33. Note the phrase *ein la menahem* ("she has no comforter"), which appears in verse 2 (the *bet* letter), and the similar phrase, *ein menahem li*, in the corresponding *shin* letter (verse 21).

34. Note the corresponding root *tzar* in verses 3 and 20 (the letters *gimel* and *kaf*).

chapter's heart Jerusalem desperately yearns for someone, *anyone*, to look her way. Initially, she turns to God ("Look, Lord, and see!" – 1:11), beseeching Him to look her way and alleviate her isolation. However, God remains remote and inaccessible. Receiving no response, Jerusalem turns to the detached passersby. Desperately addressing these pedestrians, Jerusalem's pleas for attention ("See and look!" – 1:12) ring with plaintive and pitiful tones.

The overall structure of Eikha also appears to be chiastic. In this schema, chapters 1 and 5 correspond linguistically and thematically. Chapters 2 and 4 likewise contain numerous linguistic parallels and ideas unique to these two chapters. These similarities point to a crucial theological correspondence between the chapters, one that underscores the essential goal of the book. Moreover, this broad chiastic pattern highlights chapter 3, which stands at the pivotal center, directing our attention to the theology and faith at the book's nucleus. There, Eikha grapples with God's role in human suffering, providing a remarkable depiction of the deep core of human resilience, faith, and fidelity to God.

For the moment, I will refrain from developing this topic further, but we will continue to examine it as we progress through the book. At the conclusion, I will collate the ideas presented throughout, devoting the final chapter to understanding the manner in which Eikha's chiastic structure conveys its most fundamental theological ideas.

CHALLENGES OF POETRY

Writing about biblical poetry entails a unique set of challenges, especially when addressing an English-speaking audience. Interpreting any text in translation cannot do justice to the original. The nuances and associations of the Hebrew language tend to be obscured when writing in English. Moreover, biblical poetry is elliptical and multivalent. Its sentences bear multiple interpretations, its grammatical tenses alternate fluidly, and its language inclines toward denseness and terseness, lacking prepositions and explanatory phrases.[35] Engaging in linguistic discussions

---

35. As Berlin, "Reading," 2098, points out, biblical poetry typically and frequently omits the definite article, the accusative marker *et*, and the relative pronoun *asher*. Moreover, the style of biblical poetry is paratactic, in which connectives between

can become unwieldy, and can thus hamper the loftier goals of the book. In this commentary, I will not present all possible interpretations for each sentence. Unless there is a pressing reason to introduce the various options, or unless I feel that the text is purposely ambiguous, I will choose the reading I feel is best, based on interpretive and philological considerations. I have relegated some linguistic clarifications to footnotes, for those who feel inclined to pursue them. My goal is to introduce the reader to the themes and ideas of the book, as well as to the way that Eikha deploys literary artistry to evoke theological meaning. It is my hope that my selective interpretive methodology will succeed in presenting this book in its profundity and magnificence.

---

lines are absent or contain a conjunction (i.e., a *vav*) that can have several contradictory meanings (such as "and," "or," "but"). These omissions render biblical poetry particularly opaque and subject to multiple interpretations.

Eikha: Chapter One

A Desolate City

INTRODUCTION

The opening of the book of Eikha reveals a melancholic and lonely scene. Jerusalem sobs in anguish amidst the sights and sounds of the aftermath of destruction. Formerly a bustling metropolis, Jerusalem is now nearly desolate; the sounds of the priests mourning and the young women grieving echo in the abandoned city. Jerusalem's citizens abandon the city, plodding wearily toward an unknown fate. Jerusalem remains alone with her misery and memories of better times.

Is there a logical progression of ideas in this chapter? Perhaps not. It is possible that the absence of order best captures its timbre. The initial experience of grief is not cogent and analytic, but rather chaotic and turbulent. The chapter's attention flits from the desolate city to the hordes of itinerant exiles, the jeering enemy, the apathetic passersby, and back to a humiliated city. Portrayals of God vary widely, alternating between a God who actively punishes the city, an elusive God who refuses to take note of Jerusalem's pain, and a righteous God whose edicts are just. Erratic movement between one notion and its opposite illustrates the chapter's frenzied churn of emotions.

Nevertheless, Eikha's initial chapter strives to grasp the reason for this calamity, eventually attributing it to Jerusalem's sins. This effort involves a steady movement toward recognition of responsibility, a conclusion that allows Jerusalem to make sense of the madness. Two distinct routes lead to accountability, running parallel to the two separate speakers of the chapter: the third-person narrator (verses 1–11b) and Jerusalem's first-person account (verses 11c–22). The third-person narrator easily brandishes the notion that Jerusalem's sins led to this punishment (1:5), an assertion that tempers our compassion for the beleaguered city. The narrator's accusation gains traction in verse 8, with a stark proclamation of the city's guilt: "Jerusalem has surely sinned!" This denunciation shakes Jerusalem out of her silence, and she interjects in verse 9 with a howl of pain ("Look, Lord, at my affliction!").

When Jerusalem picks up the narrative in verse 12, she initially focuses more on her unbearable sorrow and on God's overbearing anger than on her culpability, to which she only alludes (1:14). Gradually, Jerusalem comes to recognize divine justice, acknowledging her own rebelliousness and boldly proclaiming God's righteousness (1:18). In the final verse of the chapter, Jerusalem explicitly references her sins, concluding her arduous journey toward an admission of guilt.

STRUCTURE

As noted, the shift in speaker divides chapter 1 into two basic units. Part 1 (verses 1–11b) is a third-person account of Jerusalem's desolation (aside from a brief interjection in verse 9). Part 2 (verses 11c–22) recounts Jerusalem's anguish in the first person (with one exception in verse 17).

Why does the chapter employ these different speakers? The third-person account describes Jerusalem from the outside, while the first-person account portrays Jerusalem's outlook. These perspectives offer different viewpoints on the catastrophe. It is much easier for the narrator to assign responsibility for the calamity to Jerusalem than for Jerusalem herself to confess. The narrator unflinchingly accuses Jerusalem of sinfulness, noting the wayward behavior that precipitated her punishment. This is not the case with Jerusalem's own account. She only gradually moves toward admission of sinfulness. Moreover, the city's self-portrait is far more poignant than the restrained account of the narrator. As an example, note the difference between the narrator's flat description of Jerusalem's weeping: "She surely cries in the night," and Jerusalem's evocative wail: "My eyes! My eyes! They flow with water." Jerusalem's anguished tale fosters identification and empathy.

If the more powerful speaker is Jerusalem, then why employ a third-person narration at all? Let us consider these two perspectives within the theological context of the book. While Eikha does not contain direct prophetic exhortation, it may be possible to discern a prophetic purpose in combining these viewpoints. Chapter 1 weaves together God's perspective (the third person) and the human perspective (the first person) into one complete cloth. This feat is the ultimate achievement of any prophet, who functions both as the representative of God to the people and of the people to God.

The bifurcated (some might say contradictory) job of the prophet is not simple, and some high-profile prophets fail to live up to this task. A midrash presents three types of prophets:

> One seeks the honor of the father [God] as well as the honor of the son [Israel]. One seeks the honor of the father, but not the honor of the son. And one seeks the honor of the son but not the honor of the father. Jeremiah seeks both the honor of the father and the honor of the son, as it says, "We have transgressed and rebelled, You did not forgive!" (Eikha 3:42) ... Elijah seeks the honor of the father, but not the honor of the son ... Jonah seeks the honor of the son but not the honor of the father. (*Mekhilta DeRabbi Yishmael, Bo, Parasha* 1)

This midrash views Jeremiah as the model prophet, the one who devotedly represents both God and humans. Interestingly, in its bid to portray Jeremiah as the prophet who strikes the ideal balance, the midrash draws from the book of Eikha rather than from the book of Jeremiah. In the latter, Jeremiah does not appear to be particularly sympathetic toward the errant nation.[1] His prophecies frequently express antipathy and anger, and Jeremiah seems more comfortable in his role as God's representative. Yet in the verse cited from Eikha (3:42), Jeremiah manages to strike a balance.

---

1. Jeremiah often becomes so angry at the people that he requests that God wreak vengeance upon them (Jer. 11:20, 12:3, 15:15, 17:18, 18:21–23, 20:12).

He condemns Israel for its sins while identifying himself as part of the nation by using the pronoun "we." That verse continues by championing Israel's position, accusing God of not exercising proper compassion.

It seems to me that Jeremiah exhibits similarly masterful prophetic skill in composing the first chapter of Eikha. The first part of the chapter proffers an objective, third-person viewpoint, which represents God's point of view. This allows room for scrutiny and censure of the errant city.[2] In the second part of the chapter, Jeremiah presents the situation from the viewpoint of the personified city, allowing the reader a glimpse into the mindset of the suffering nation.

PART 1 (EIKHA 1:1–11B): THE NARRATOR'S ACCOUNT

Eikha 1:1

אֵיכָה יָשְׁבָה בָדָד
הָעִיר רַבָּתִי עָם
הָיְתָה כְּאַלְמָנָה

רַבָּתִי בַגּוֹיִם
שָׂרָתִי בַּמְּדִינוֹת
הָיְתָה לָמַס

---

2. One midrash (Eikha Zuta [Buber] 1:1) assumes a different approach, maintaining that in Eikha, Jeremiah staunchly represents the people. Using the first part of chapter 1 as its example, this midrash presents the text as one half of a discussion between Jeremiah and God, in which Jeremiah's evocative descriptions of Jerusalem's pain in Eikha 1 are immediately countered by God's citation of verses that describe the sin that provoked these punishments:

> Jeremiah said before God, "Master of the Universe! Will the city that contains Your name and Your praise and most of her nation during the three festivals sit lonely ['How (Eikha) has the city sat alone!' (Eikha 1:1)]?" God said to Jeremiah, "Jeremiah, before you represent them, represent Me: 'How (Eikha) has [the city] become a harlot!' (Is. 1)." Jeremiah said, "She surely cries in the night!" (Eikha 1:2). And the Holy Spirit said to him, "And behold there the women are crying over the *Tammuz* [idolatry]!" (Ezek. 8:14). Jeremiah said, "Judah has been exiled (*galeta*) in misery and in terrible labor" (Eikha 1:3), and the Holy spirit said, "And she revealed (*vategal*) her nakedness!" (Ezek. 23:18).

How[3] has the city sat alone?
The city that was once so full of people
Has become like a widow

Great among nations
The princess of countries
Has become a tributary

The construction of this verse sets it apart, marking it as the opening of the chapter. While most verses in chapter 1 contain three binary (two-part) sentences, this verse contains two ternary (three-part) sentences. The final line of each stanza begins with the word *hayeta* ("has become"), signifying the change in fortune of the city. A city once teeming with people is now alone like a widow, and a city that was once regal is now subordinate to others.

Jerusalem's Isolation

The book of Eikha does not open with Jerusalem's destruction. Instead of describing the roar of the enemies or the crash of demolition, Eikha opens with the quiet sounds of devastation, the eerie echoes of an emptied city.

Loneliness dominates the opening chords of the book, illustrated poignantly by the metaphor of the widowed city, the *almana*, and acknowledged explicitly by the use of the word *badad* (lonely). Elsewhere in Tanakh, the word *badad* describes a destroyed city (Is. 27:10), a social outcast (Jer. 15:17), and a leper (Lev. 13:46). The image of Jerusalem sitting alone (*badad*) evokes these usages, focusing attention on the pain of her desolation, the abandonment of her loved ones, and her pariah status within the world. The phrase *yasheva badad* (used

---

3. The opening word, *Eikha*, is an elongated form of the word *eikh*, an interrogatory that asks: "How?" This word is a not so much a question as a rhetorical device, an expression of pain and confusion, the opening of a lament. The shortened word, *eikh*, opens Ezekiel's lamentation over the destruction of Tyre (Ezek. 26:17). Its lengthened version stretches out the word, ending in a vowel, which conveys the drawn-out sounds (of sobbing, shouting, or sighing) that accompany the rhetorical exclamation of despair. See below, Chapter One, Appendix 2: The Word "*Eikha*."

also about a leper in Leviticus 13:46) may allude to Jerusalem's culpability and sin, as noted by the *Targum*:

> The Attribute of Justice replied and said: "Because of the greatness of the rebellion and sin that was within her, she will dwell alone, as a person plagued with leprosy upon his skin, who sits alone." (*Targum Eikha* 1:1)

While the word *badad* primarily conveys the city's dreadful loneliness, a positive biblical usage of the word refers to Israel's singularity. Balaam prophetically proclaims that Israel is a "people that dwells alone (*am levadad yishkon*) and is not reckoned among the nations" (Num. 23:9), emphasizing Israel's uniqueness. Other verses using this term illustrate the way isolation can be positive, guaranteeing Israel's safety (Deut. 33:28; Ps. 4:9).[4]

This word may simultaneously point us to the cause of Israel's loneliness and to its solution. If only Israel had appreciated its singularity among the family of nations! Israel's desire to blend into the community of nations, her refusal to maintain her divinely mandated uniqueness, has turned a blessing of singularity (*am levadad yishkon*) into a curse of isolation (*yasheva badad*).[5] The experience of loneliness may be the very thing that can facilitate Israel's return to the ideal. Sitting alone can be a constructive experience for the battered city, reminding her that her isolated position is God's design and can facilitate Israel's destiny among the nations.

Metaphor: Widowed Jerusalem

A city's personification as a woman is a common biblical trope, one that emerges as a general theme of our chapter.[6] In Eikha, Jerusalem manifests her female persona both as a mother and as a wife, constructing a multifaceted portrait of the city's tragedy.[7] As a bereaved mother,

---

4. Jeremiah 49:31 uses a similar description regarding the security of Keidar.
5. This comes to expression in Israel's bid to forge political alliances (in contravention of prophetic guidance), a topic that will arise several times in Eikha.
6. See, for example, the description of Babylon in Isaiah 47 and Nineveh in Nahum 3.
7. Isaiah 47:8–9 also employs these metaphors when he describes Babylon's punishment. See the chart that compares Isaiah 47 and Eikha in the chapter, "Eikha and the Prophecies of Consolation in Isaiah."

Jerusalem's grief is incalculable. The loss of her inhabitants/children is the loss of Jerusalem's future, her hope, her destiny. It is also unnatural, a poignant portrayal of a topsy-turvy world in which a child predeceases a parent. The sorrow of a widow denotes a different kind of loss, one that exists more in the present than in the future, emphasizing her aloneness and vulnerability.[8]

The personification of Jerusalem, coupled with her human-like actions (such as sitting alone, crying and mourning), arouses empathy.[9] Her widowhood evokes physical and economic helplessness; the Bible often specifies the widow as one who deserves particular attention and care.[10] Strikingly, the city remains unnamed for the first three verses of the chapter.[11] Her anonymity mirrors her widowed state, suggesting that the loss of her husband signifies her loss of identity.[12]

---

8. Ibn Ezra, Eikha 1:1, understands the distinction quite differently. He claims that a mother's loss of children is endurable, because she still has a husband with whom she can bear more children. When a woman suffers the death of her husband, however, she has no hope of having more children, and she therefore loses her future.

9. The city and her structural components (walls, roads, gates, buildings) obtain human-like attributes throughout Eikha. The personification of the city as a single figure portrays her suffering as an individual. This overrides the impersonal nature of national calamity, with its mass number of sufferers, enabling the reader to focus upon the pain of one lonely figure. The city-as-widow also represents all her inhabitants, fused into a collective entity. Throughout the book, the city of Jerusalem can represent the physical city, the nation, or both.

10. For examples, see Exodus 22:20–23; Deuteronomy 10:18.

11. In verse 4, the book names Zion, while in verse 7, the name Jerusalem first surfaces. Eikha refers more frequently to Zion (thirteen times) than to Jerusalem (seven times). While many commentators assume that Zion and Jerusalem are synonymous, Ibn Ezra maintains that Jerusalem is the name of the city, while Zion is the area designated for the king (Ibn Ezra, Eikha 1:17). For more approaches to Zion's distinctive meaning, see J. Renkema, *Lamentations* (Historical Commentary on the Old Testament. Leuven: Peeters, 1998), 112; Dobbs-Allsopp, 52–53; P. R. House, *Lamentations* (Word Biblical Commentary 23B. Nashville: Thomas Nelson Publishers, 2004), 349.

12. See also Isaiah 4:1, which supports this notion. The semantic connection between the word *almana* (widow) and the appellation *Peloni Almoni* (meaning, "No-name") sustains the association between widowhood and namelessness (see Rashi, Ruth 4:1).

While her departed children are easily identifiable as Jerusalem's inhabitants, the identity of her deceased husband is less clear. Perhaps Jerusalem's husband, too, refers to her inhabitants, whose departure to exile has left her like a widow. Alternatively, God can be identified as the "deceased" husband of Jerusalem (in this case, representing the nation). After all, Israel's relationship with God is often described within a matrimonial context.[13] More significantly, following the exile and as part of the redemption, Isaiah 54:4–5 promises that the city shall not know the shame of widowhood any longer, for God will espouse her. The metaphor of Jerusalem widowed from her marriage to God raises some difficult questions. First, this metaphor seems odd. Would it not make more sense to describe Jerusalem as a divorcee, a city whose God has rejected her? Moreover, from a theological angle, how can one suggest that God is deceased?

The widow metaphor may be more useful than the divorcee metaphor because it evokes the city's sorrow, loneliness, and vulnerability, without placing blame.[14] Our initial encounter with the grieving city does not involve judgment or allude to her culpability, but relates only to her pain.[15] Slowly, as the chapter unfolds, we will have recourse to assign blame for the events, but for the moment, we simply note the city's loss.

To answer the theological question posed above, we rely upon the *kaf hadimayon*, the preposition that precedes the word widow, indicating that Jerusalem is "*like* a widow." This simile establishes a measure of equivalence between Jerusalem and a widow, but that does not mean that she is a widow in all aspects.

---

13. See, for example, Ezekiel 15; Hosea 2; Song of Songs. I will discuss this point again later in the chapter.

14. As Eikha Rabba 1:1 observes, this verse does contain a linguistic allusion to Jerusalem's betrayal. Its opening phrase describing Jerusalem's loneliness (*Eikha yashva badad*) evokes the scathing censure of the city's promiscuity (Is. 1:21): "*Eikha hayeta lezona*," "How has this city become a harlot!" This suggests that Jerusalem's widowed state stems from her infidelities.

15. Meshekh Ḥokhma (Eikha 1:1) notes that had the text wished to indicate that Jerusalem's loneliness stems from a deficiency in her relationship, it would have used the metaphor of a divorcee. In his view, the deceased husband is the nation, rather than God.

Nevertheless, the meaning underlying the image of Jerusalem's widowhood remains problematic. Is it possible that Jerusalem's metaphoric husband (whether God or nation) is like a deceased husband, never to return? Is Jerusalem's devastation hopelessly unalterable? The simile may reflect Jerusalem's state of mind in this chapter, her despair and her bleak outlook on the future. This is like other laments in this chapter: "The Lord has placed me in the hands [of those before whom] I cannot rise" (Eikha 1:14).

Even if the simile of the widow accurately reflects Jerusalem's despondency, is this a theologically tenable description? Jeremiah rejects this idea in a verse that seems to contravene Eikha 1:1:

> For Israel is not a widow, [nor is] Judah from his God, from the Lord of hosts. (Jer. 51:5)

Radak's explanation of the verse in Jeremiah is unambiguous:

> "For Israel is not a widow" – [S]he is not like a widow whose husband died and she is abandoned by him forever. Not so Israel! For her husband lives and exists, and if He left her in exile, He shall yet remember her and return to her and punish the enemies. (Radak, Jer. 51:5)

Rashi similarly refuses to accept that Eikha 1:1 actually likens Jerusalem to a widow. He stresses the significance of the *kaf hadimayon*, rejecting any substantive similarity. Instead, Rashi compares Jerusalem's lonely widow-like state to a different situation altogether:

> Not an actual widow, but like a woman whose husband went to a faraway land and his intention is to return to her. (Rashi, Eikha 1:1)

This creative reading is typical of Rashi's commentary, designed not necessarily to explicate the text (in this case, he seems to reject the simple meaning of widowhood) but, more importantly, to offer comfort and hope.[16] Rashi's viewpoint does, however, accurately reflect other biblical statements, in which God never completely abandons Israel.[17]

The lack of clarity regarding the identity of the dead husband remains salient. The reader experiences the loss, the widowed city's loneliness and anguish, without full knowledge of the precise nature of the tragedy. Instead, Eikha focuses on Jerusalem's overpowering grief, while the identity of her husband is of secondary concern. In refusing to name the deceased, Eikha allows room to hope that neither God nor Israel has forever forsaken Jerusalem. Present destruction leaves Jerusalem widow-*like* in her grief, but, lacking a corpse, no husband has permanently vanished.

Recalling Jerusalem's Past

Eikha's opening verse recalls Jerusalem's past glory; she was a city teeming with people, great among nations, the princess of countries. This focuses our attention on Jerusalem's astonishing fall. From her glorious heights of distinction, Jerusalem has fallen into the depths of wretchedness. While this is not the primary source of her pain, the change in her fortune undoubtedly bears upon Jerusalem's present state of shock and humiliation. Shattered expectations give rise to disorientation; Jerusalem's collapse leaves her bewildered.

Still, this opening line recalls past glory and dignity. This was no ordinary city. Jerusalem was a remarkable city, a thriving metropolis! Although Eikha lacks consolation, in recalling the greatness of this city, Eikha's initial verse makes the present situation slightly more bearable. It allows the inhabitants to remember the city's value and may even provide a flash of optimism, however miniscule. In the chapter "Eikha Rabba: Filling Eikha's Void," we will see how rabbinic interpreters employ this recollection of the past to coax consolation out of Eikha.

---

16. Rashi bases his approach on earlier rabbinic interpretation (Sanhedrin 104a and Eikha Rabba 1:3). It is typical of Rashi to choose, from among many rabbinic interpretations, an idea that consoles and uplifts.

17. See Leviticus 26:44; I Samuel 12:22; Isaiah 49:14–16.

Recollection of the past reminds us that Judaism does not focus exclusively on the present. Past events infuse the present with meaning. Similarly, present experiences incorporate awareness of the future – our aspirations, hopes, and expectations.[18] The timelessness of the Jewish historical experience has often enabled the nation to bear a miserable present.

Eikha 1:2

בָּכוֹ תִבְכֶּה בַּלַּיְלָה
וְדִמְעָתָהּ עַל לֶחֱיָהּ

אֵין־לָהּ מְנַחֵם
מִכָּל־אֹהֲבֶיהָ

כָּל־רֵעֶיהָ בָּגְדוּ בָהּ
הָיוּ לָהּ לְאֹיְבִים

She surely cries in the night
and her tears are upon her cheeks

She has no comforter
from all her lovers

All her friends betrayed her
Became her enemies

Picking up the theme of loneliness from the previous verse, this verse highlights the haunting absence of people supporting the sobbing city.

---

18. To describe the experience in which past is integrated into present and present antici-pates future, R. Joseph B. Soloveitchik coins the phrase, "unitive time-consciousness." See *Out of the Whirlwind: Essays on Mourning, Suffering, and the Human Condition*, eds. David Shatz, Joel B. Wolowelsky, and Reuven Ziegler (Jersey City: Ktav, 2003), 14–17. See also *Halakhic Man*, trans. Lawrence Kaplan (Philadelphia: JPS, 1983), 113–23, and "Sacred and Profane," reprinted in *Shiurei HaRav*, ed. Joseph Epstein (Hoboken: Ktav, 1994), 4–32.

Tears remain undried on Jerusalem's face; loved ones have abandoned her and friends have betrayed her.[19]

Quiet weeping reverberates through the night, aptly conveying the city's gloom.[20] The night scene highlights Jerusalem's loneliness, but it also points to her state of mind. Biblical usage suggests that night heightens Jerusalem's feeling of doom (Amos 5:18–20) and danger (Ob. 5; Jer. 6:4–5), her lack of clarity (Song. 3:1), confusion (Is. 59:9–10), terror (Ps. 91:5), and turmoil (Job 34:20).

Night is also a metaphor for God's elusiveness (Mic. 3:6). God is a source of light, illuminating Israel's path and clarifying the nation's purpose (Ps. 27:1; Mic. 7:8). When Israel walks in God's light, the nation's tread is confident, her path brightly lit (Is. 9:1; 60:1–3). Night conveys the opposite – confusion born of darkened paths, disorientation caused by abundant shadows, and God's inaccessibility. Jerusalem's future remains shrouded in darkness, obscured, uncertain, and terrifying.

Jerusalem's Lovers (*Ohaveha*) and Friends (*Re'eha*)

Jewish rituals of mourning revolve around human contact – seven days of social support, during which the community envelops the mourners in solace and sympathy. Following Job's tragedy, his three friends arrive to console him (Job 2:11). Without residents, how can Jerusalem be comforted? Who will alleviate her pain and offer her empathy? The absence of community means the absence of consolation, an important theme of this chapter.

Who are the loved ones who deny Jerusalem comfort? Who are the friends who betray her? Why do these associates of Jerusalem fail her in her time of need?

It is possible that the loved ones are the Judean residents of Jerusalem. Their love for the city is undeniable, and it will become clear in the next verse why they are unable to offer consolation. Forcibly taken into exile, Jerusalem's lovers cannot relieve her pain or wipe away her tears.

---

19. Rashi (1:2) explains differently: Her tears remain on her cheeks because she cries ceaselessly.
20. The dark night is particularly suited for weeping (e.g., Ps. 6:7; 42:9; 77:3; 88:2; Job 7:3.)

Alternatively, Jerusalem here represents not just the city but the entire nation of Israel, and the word *ohaveha* evokes the nation's illicit lovers, her unfaithfulness to God. Israel's betrayal of her monogamous relationship with God refers both to the worship of other gods (e.g., Hos. 2:7–15)[21] and to the political alliances forged with other nations (e.g., Jer. 22:20–22).[22] In this reading, the reference to Jerusalem's absent lovers evokes her culpability. Predictably, Israel's betrayals lead to disaster, leaving Jerusalem bereft of the lovers she has cultivated. This recalls the punishment prophesied by Hosea, who rebukes Israel for its betrayal of God:

> And she will pursue her lovers (*me'ahaveha*), but she will not catch up with them; she will search for them and not find them … And I will expose her disgrace in front of her lovers (*me'ahaveha*), and no person will save her from My hand. (Hos. 2:9, 12)

A midrash (Eikha Zuta [Buber] 1:6) suggests that these lovers are the false prophets. This intriguing proposal hints at the possible sincerity of the false prophets, since they are deemed *ohaveha* (those who love her). Jeremiah often describes these prophets foretelling peace and good tidings for the nation (e.g., Jer. 6:14; 14:13). While God pronounces these prophecies false, the prophets' intentions often remain obscure. Perhaps the midrash intends to suggest that these prophecies emerge from a genuine love for Jerusalem and the hope that their optimistic forecasts will prove true. Yet, in their failure to rebuke the nation properly, the false prophets ultimately cause her downfall. This midrash directs attention to the topic of the false prophets, which I will examine at greater length in chapter 2.

Re'eha (friends) may not be distinct from *ohaveha* (lovers).[23] Perhaps these two sentences are parallel, with an incremental intensification of

---

21. See *Targum* on Eikha 1:2: "And not one spoke consolation to her heart, from all of the gods that she loved to follow."
22. I will examine this idea at greater length in the discussion of Eikha 1:8.
23. See Rashi and R. Yosef Kara on Eikha 1:2. R. Yosef Kara avers that both terms refer to other nations.

meaning; while the first sentence describes the lovers who are not there to comfort, the second portrays this behavior as a betrayal.[24] Silence is a betrayal; their absence during Jerusalem's time of need transforms friends into enemies.[25]

Psalms 38:12 and 88:19 both juxtapose loved ones and friends. Like Eikha 1:2, in these psalms the loved ones and the friends of an anguished sufferer maintain their reserve:

My lovers and friends stand opposite my afflictions, and my intimates stand at a distance. (Ps. 38:12)

You distanced lovers and friends from me; my acquaintances are in darkness.[26] (Ps. 88:19)

The lovers and friends may not actively seek harm in any of these cases. However, their aloofness compounds the suffering and constitutes a betrayal of friendship.

An alternate reading sharply distinguishes between *re'eha* and *ohaveha*.[27] While the *ohaveha* are absent (possibly due to the exile), only the friends (*re'eha*) actually betray Jerusalem, recasting themselves as adversaries. These "friends" may refer to Israel's political allies, especially Egypt.[28] They never loved Jerusalem; their relationship was pragmatic, based on interests.[29] Prophets repeatedly caution against forging political alliances that offer Israel a false

---

24. According to this reading, it is unlikely that these terms refer to Jerusalem's exiled residents, who can hardly be blamed for their absence!

25. See Job 6:15–21, where Job refers to his brethren's absence as a betrayal.

26. In other words, I cannot see them; it is as though they are in darkness (Ibn Ezra, Metzudat David).

27. See Proverbs 18:24, which clearly distinguishes between the *ohev* and the *re'a.*

28. R. Yosef Kara (1:2) suggests that this may also refer to Babylonia and the Chaldeans (e.g., Ezek. 23:14–18) or Tyre. Other problematic political allies include Assyria and perhaps the neighbors of Israel and Judah (e.g., Moab and Ammon), with whom they forge shifting economic and political alliances. In II Kings 24:2, these neighbors are actively involved in Judah's destruction.

29. This recalls Henry Kissinger's famous remark: "America has no permanent friends or enemies, only interests."

sense of security and lead the nation to renounce their dependence upon God.[30] Indeed, when the Babylonians destroy Jerusalem, the Egyptians fail to save them.[31]

Possibly, the *re'eha* who betray Jerusalem refer to her populace, hinting at the nation's accountability. The nation betrayed Jerusalem by engaging in sinful behavior that spawns Jerusalem's calamity. This interpretation finds support in Jeremiah's oracle against Israel, which employs language that recalls our verse:

> Just as a woman betrays (*bageda*) her friend (*mere'ah*), so you have betrayed Me, house of Israel, says the Lord. (Jer. 3:20)

Language: The Totality of the Word *Kol*

The word *kol* appears twice in Eikha 1:2 to convey the comprehensiveness of Jerusalem's isolation. *All* her lovers and *all* her friends fail her. The frequent appearances of the word in this chapter – sixteen times in its twenty-two verses – convey the totality of the disaster. Jerusalem is not caught by *some* of her pursuers, but by *all* of them (1:3). Similarly, *all* her enemies rejoice in her downfall (1:21). *All* her gates mourn (1:4), and *all* her nation groans (1:11), miserable *all* day (1:13). *All* her glory has departed (1:6), and *all* her precious delights have been seized by the greedy grasping hands of the enemy (1:10). *All* those who once honored her now regard her cheaply (1:8), and God tramples *all* her strong men. This portrait of catastrophe illustrates the sweeping inclusiveness of Jerusalem's downfall: her total isolation, misery, defeat, suffering, betrayal, loss, and humiliation.

The closing *kol* in the chapter may be its most significant one.[32] In the final verse, Jerusalem assumes responsibility for God's punitive acts against her, declaring that God carries out His punishments, *al kol pesha'ai,*

---

30. Isaiah 20:3–6; 30:2–5; 31:1–3; Jeremiah 2:18, 25; Ezekiel 16:25–29; Hosea 5:13; 7:11; 8:9.

31. See II Kings 24:7; Jeremiah 37:5–8; Ezekiel 29:6–7. Ironically, this confirms Sennacherib's assessment of Egypt in II Kings 18:21.

32. Other usages of the word *kol* in this chapter involve Jerusalem's attempt to interact with others: She entreats *all* passersby to look at her (1:12), calls on *all* nations to listen to her and see her (1:18), and begs God to consider *all* of the wickedness of her enemies (1:22).

"because of *all* my sins." The chapter concludes with Jerusalem's categorical admission of her total sinfulness, which explains her total suffering. This brief examination of a key word in the chapter nicely captures its essence and the manner in which chapter 1 advances toward recognition of culpability.

Eikha 1:3

גָּלְתָה יְהוּדָה מֵעֹנִי
וּמֵרֹב עֲבֹדָה

הִיא יָשְׁבָה בַגּוֹיִם
לֹא מָצְאָה מָנוֹחַ

כָּל־רֹדְפֶיהָ הִשִּׂיגוּהָ
בֵּין הַמְּצָרִים

Judah has been exiled in suffering
And in terrible labor[33]

She sat among the nations[34]
And did not find respite[35]

---

33. The letter *mem* placed before the words suffering (*me'oni*) and terrible labor (*me'rov*) generally denotes a causative preposition. In other words, Judah is exiled *because* of the suffering (as Rashi suggests). It is not clear exactly what this means. In what way does the suffering cause the exile? The *Targum* on Eikha 1:3 explains that this refers to the oppression that Israel wrought upon the orphans and the widows, whom they enslaved and mistreated. According to this interpretation, the verse blames Israel for having engaged in immoral behavior, thereby bringing about her own punishment. Alternatively, R. Saadia Gaon explains the prepositions as a temporal description, "*after* much suffering and hard labor." Perhaps this simply describes the order in which the situation deteriorates: first suffering and slave labor, followed by exile. Possibly, this describes a state of mind: Judah's exile takes place as she suffers and labors.

34. Ibn Ezra notes that the Bible refers to Judah (like Israel and Egypt) variously as both feminine (e.g., Ps. 114:2) and masculine (e.g., Jer. 52:24; Zech. 2:16). In this study, I take my cues from Eikha, which treats the word Judah in this verse as a feminine construct.

35. Israel's restless state, *lo matze'a mano'aḥ* ("she did not find respite"), recalls a similar phrase in the covenant treaty (*Tokheḥa*) in Deuteronomy 28:65. As I noted in the earlier chapter, "Theology and Suffering," Eikha subtly weaves phrases from that

All her pursuers caught up with her
Between the narrow straits

Verse 3 shifts our attention from deserted, stagnant Jerusalem to the dynamism of exile. Exile is frenetic, in ceaseless flux. Israel's attempt to settle among the nations is futile and there is little choice except to continue moving. Those who pursue the itinerant deportees easily overtake them "between the narrow straits."

Though not explicit, the theme of solitude continues to surface, accompanying the nation into exile. The phrase *lo matza mano'aḥ* ("she did not find respite") recalls a similar phrase in Ruth 1:9. There, Naomi sends her daughters-in-law back to Moab with a blessing that they should find respite (*umetza'ena menuḥa*), each woman in the house of her husband. Judah's failure to find respite (*mano'aḥ*) in exile recalls Jerusalem's widowhood of verse 1, her absent husband, and her insecurity and loneliness.

The word *yasheva* offers a second hint to Judah's loneliness in exile. The second occurrence of the word in just three verses draws our attention back to its first appearance, "How has the city sat (*yasheva*) alone!" Though Judah sits "among" the nations in exile, the word *yasheva* evokes her loneliness. Sitting among strangers in a foreign land cultivates the existential loneliness of exile. This contrasts with the feeling of belonging that defines a nation in its own land.

Several words in verse 3 (*yasheva, vagoyim, mano'ah, matze'a*) ironically echo Israel's ideal state of settling in the land, the antithesis of exile. The word *yasheva*, here denoting the nation's unsuccessful bid to settle down in exile, is used elsewhere to promise Israel secure residence in its land (e.g., *lashevet*, Num. 33:53; or *viyshavtem*, Lev. 26:5). Just two verses ago, we glimpsed Jerusalem's former princely status among the nations (*rabbati vagoyim*, Eikha 1:1); in exile, Judah cannot even find respite among the nations (*vagoyim*). Dwelling in Israel is meant

---

covenant into the book. This catastrophe is not the product of random brutality; linguistic allusions indicate that Israel's violation of the terms of the covenant produces her calamity.

to be restful (*behaniaḥ*),[36] but there is no restfulness (*mano'aḥ*) in exile. Banishment is characterized by Judah's inability to find (*lo matze'a*), while the redemption from exile begins with the ability to find: "And you will seek from the [exile] the Lord your God and you will find [Him] (*umatzata*) when you seek Him with all your hearts and all your souls" (Deut. 4:29; Jer. 29:13).

The Egyptian Exile

Israel's experience of exile in Egypt echoes in the background of this verse. The word-pair *oni* and *avoda*, meaning suffering and labor, alludes to the Egyptian exile (Gen. 15:13; Ex. 1:11; Deut. 26:6). While the word *metzarim* seems to mean distress or narrow straits, it is orthographically identical to the word for Egypt, *Mitzrayim*. This wordplay evokes that original exile, the prototype of Israel's suffering and deliverance.

Other allusions to the narrative of Israel's servitude in Egypt are scattered throughout the chapter. The word *anaḥ*, describing the nation's groans, appears five times (Eikha 1:4; 8; 11; 21; 22), recalling the groans of the Israelites during their slavery in Egypt (Ex. 2:23). The word *mas*, tribute (Eikha 1:1), evokes the officers (*sarei misim*) in Egypt appointed to oversee their miserable labor (Ex. 1:11). Jerusalem's bitterness (Eikha 1:4) parallels Israel's bitterness in Egypt (Ex. 1:14); the pain that emerges three times in Eikha 1 (*makhov*)[37] is featured in Egypt as well (Ex. 3:7). The evils (*raatam*) of the enemy (Eikha 1:22) recall the evils committed by Egypt (*vayarei'u*, Deut. 26:6).

Despite these linguistic parallels, the Babylonian exile will not be like the exile in Egypt. It will be both shorter and less brutal, characterized by economic success and a thriving community, rather than enslavement and persecution.[38] Why, then, does this verse refer to the Egyptian exile when it describes the beginnings of the Babylonian exile? Perhaps at this preliminary stage, the assumption is that this exile will indeed

---

36. For additional examples, see Deuteronomy 3:20; Joshua 1:13; 23:1.

37. The word appears twice in verse 12 and once in verse 18.

38. The Al-Yahudu tablets constitute the earliest evidence of the Judean community exiled to Babylonia. Approximately 200 clay tablets dating from 572–477 BCE reveal an independent community, some of whose members are prosperous landowners involved in trade and business.

follow a pattern like the Egyptian one. Possibly, the text alludes to the Egyptian exile because it functions as the paradigm of exile in Tanakh.[39] In any case, recalling Egypt reflects the hopelessness of the chapter, as the community marches toward what will surely be a cruel fate.

There is a more uplifting aspect to these references to the Egyptian exile. The Bible presents the narrative of the enslavement in Egypt primarily as a story of God's salvation and Israel's redemption.[40] Jerusalem first addresses God in this chapter with a request: "Look (*re'eh*), Lord, at my afflictions (*oneyi*)!" (Eikha 1:9). This entreaty recalls God's promise to Moses that He intends to save His people from Egypt:[41]

> And the Lord said, "I have surely seen the affliction (*ra'o ra'iti et oni*) of My people in Egypt, and I have heard their cries because of his oppressors, and I know his pain. I will go down to save him from the hand of Egypt and bring him up from that land to a good and broad land, to a land flowing with milk and honey…" (Ex. 3:7–8)

In requesting that God see her afflictions, Jerusalem endeavors to enlist the compassionate God who redeemed the nation from Egypt and returned them to the land of their forefathers. The echoes of Egypt may sound ominous, but they also allude to God's eternal promise, His assurance of divine commitment. Evoking the Egyptian exile at this early stage of the Babylonian exile hints at the possibility of redemption and offers a subtle message of hope.

Eikha 1:4

דַּרְכֵי צִיּוֹן אֲבֵלוֹת
מִבְּלִי בָּאֵי מוֹעֵד

---

39. See, for example, Deuteronomy 28:68; Hosea 8:13; 9:3.
40. Allusions to the story of exile and redemption from Egypt also appear quite frequently in Isaiah's portrayal of exile and redemption from Babylonia. For some examples, see Isaiah 48:20–21; 52:7–12.
41. It also recalls God's promise to Abraham that He will deliver Israel from a foreign land, where they will suffer labor and affliction (Gen. 15:13).

כָּל־שְׁעָרֶיהָ שׁוֹמֵמִין
כֹּהֲנֶיהָ נֶאֱנָחִים

בְּתוּלֹתֶיהָ נּוּגוֹת
וְהִיא מַר־לָהּ

The roads to Zion mourn
for there is no one who comes on the festival

All her gates are desolate
Her priests groan

Her maidens grieve
And she is very bitter

After a brief glance at the exiles in verse 3, we will return our attention to Jerusalem, but not immediately. First, in verse 4, we experience the eerie solitude of the journey back to Jerusalem. We seem to have abandoned the wandering exiles of verse 3, relinquishing them to their exhausted misery. Progressing toward the city, we scan the dusty roads for pilgrims, but in vain; instead, we bear witness to their unnerving emptiness.[42] Arriving at the once-bustling entrance to the city, previously teeming with wayfarers and travelers, especially on the festivals, we bleakly observe the gates' desolation.[43] Priests, whose festival duties had once preoccupied them, now keen listlessly, emitting low and anguished groans. And the maidens! Their joy and vibrancy have dulled, their circle dances have ceased (Jer. 31:12). Wearily, they too issue sounds of grief, incomprehensible expressions of despair. Jerusalem herself is bitter, a despondent witness to her own collapse.

---

42. For a similar description of the desolation of roads (presumably of Jerusalem, although this is not explicit), see Isaiah 33:8.

43. In its portrayal of the ideal state of Jerusalem, Isaiah 60:11 describes her gates as always open day and night, ready to admit wealth and kings, and unafraid of invaders. Similarly, Psalms 122:2 describes people standing at the gates of Jerusalem, pausing for contemplation before proceeding toward the Temple.

The solemn priests and the joyous maidens would seem to be an incompatible pair.[44] Catastrophe unifies disparate factions in shared grief, erasing distinctions of age and social standing. All mourn equally. Perhaps this juxtaposition highlights the special role that both priests and maidens once played in the festival. As a complement to the dignified rituals of the priests, maidens cast off some of the solemnity, allowing the assembled masses to witness the exuberant celebration of the youth (see Judges 21:19, 21). Priests and maidens mourn the destruction with common cause, as each group has forfeited its unique role.[45]

Although the chapter mentions several groups (priests, maidens, children, officers), it does not single out any one group, focusing instead on the suffering of the general populace. The entire city joins in collective mourning. Even the anthropomorphized roads mourn, further emphasizing the entwined relationship between the city and her inhabitants.[46] Highways and gates, priests and maidens: all bemoan their meaningless existence and the cessation of their primary functions. A midrash explains the peculiar image of the grieving roads:

> *The roads to Zion mourn.* R. Huna said: All seek [to fulfill] their function. (Eikha Rabba 1:30)

The continuation of this midrash suggests that the roads mourn the loss specifically of their religious, rather than pedestrian, role:

> R. Avdimi from Haifa said: Even the roads seek [to fulfill] their function, as it says, "The roads to Zion mourn, for there is no

---

44. Commonly, maidens are mentioned alongside young men in biblical passages (see Deut. 32:25; Is. 62:5; Jer. 51:22; Ezek. 9:6; Amos 8:13; Zech. 9:17). This is true in Eikha as well (1:18 and 2:21).

45. See also Joel 1:8–9, where the verses describe the mourning of maidens and priests in successive verses.

46. R. Yosef Kara, Eikha 1:4, explains differently; it is not that the roads mourn, but rather that the people mourn the roads. In any case, the personification of objects animated by grief is a common biblical trope. See, for example, the mourning of the land in Hosea 4:3, the gates' misery in Jeremiah 14:2, and the mourning of the rampart and the wall in Eikha 2:8.

one who comes on the festival." It does not say, "For there are no station-houses for travelers…" rather, "For there is no one who comes on the festival." (Eikha Rabba 1:30)

Jerusalem is not just any city. All associated with Jerusalem – both people and objects – band together to facilitate worship of God in His sacred city. Correspondingly, when the city is destroyed, all join in mourning the loss of the city's sacred character and function.

Ambiguous Language: *Mo'ed* – Designated Time or Place?

Ambiguity attends the word *mo'ed* in Eikha.[47] *Mo'ed* derives from the word *yaad*, meaning appointed or designated. It can refer to a time or a place. In Eikha, this word refers variously to an appointed day[48] or to an appointed place, usually the Temple.[49] While the context often sheds clarity on its usage, in our verse, its meaning remains ambiguous. Ibn Ezra cites both possibilities:

> *Ba'ei mo'ed* – They would come on the festivals. But it is preferable in my eyes to interpret that this refers to the Temple, and it is called *mo'ed* because all Israel assemble by appointment there. Similarly, "in the midst of your appointed place (*mo'adekha*)" (Ps. 74:4), "they burned all the appointed places (*mo'adei*) of God…" (ibid. 74:8). (Ibn Ezra, Eikha 1:4)

Ibn Ezra concludes that the word *mo'ed* refers to the Temple, which used to attract throngs of pilgrims, who no longer visit.[50] Ibn Ezra brings as proof two texts from a psalm that describes the destruction of the Temple. His approach focuses our attention on the meaninglessness of

---

47. We noted this example in the introductory chapter, "Biblical Poetry and the Book of Eikha."
48. This day can be holy, namely a festival (Eikha 2:6), or a day appointed by God for destruction (Eikha 1:15).
49. See Eikha 2:6. The precursor to the Temple, the Tabernacle (*Mishkan*), is also referred to as the *ohel mo'ed*, commonly translated as "tent of meeting."
50. Similarly, Psalms 42:5 longingly recollects the hordes of celebrating pilgrims coming to the House of God.

the city without its sacred center.[51] Rashi offers the alternate interpretation, explaining that the word *mo'ed* refers to the festivals when pilgrims would visit Jerusalem.[52]

While translators must decide one way or another, it seems best to retain a dual meaning for the word *mo'ed* here. Everything in Jerusalem has ceased to function according to its purpose. This is especially noticeable in the emptiness of the sacred place (the Temple) during the sacred time (the festivals).

Embittered Jerusalem

Bitterness attends several notable biblical women: Hannah (I Sam. 1:10), the Shunemite woman (II Kings 4:27), Rachel (Jer. 31:14), and Naomi (Ruth 1:20). Common to all these women is the absence or loss of their children. Jerusalem's role as a mother figure in the book of Eikha is first hinted at here.[53]

Although this is an undeniably negative portrayal, midrashim characteristically find a ray of hope in associating Jerusalem with the bitter childless women. After all, none of these women remains miserable forever; each eventually obtains children, dispels bitterness, and replaces it with joy. In this vein, one midrash posits a stunning reversal of the loneliness that prevails in this chapter:

> "She has no (*ein lah*) comforter" (Eikha 1:2) – So says R. Levi: Every place in which it says, "she has none (*ein*)," she will have [what she lacks]. "And Sarai was barren; she had no child" (Gen. 11), and then she had one, as it says, "The Lord remembered Sarah" (Gen. 21). Similarly, "And Hannah had no children," and then she did, as it says, "For the Lord remembered Hannah." Similarly, "She is Zion, there is none that seeks her" (Jer. 30),

---

51. See also Rashbam, Eikha 1:4.

52. It appears that most translators and interpreters choose this reading, as I did in my translation above. See, for example, NJPS; Ibn Caspi, Eikha 1:4; Berlin, 41, 45.

53. Dobbs-Allsopp, 59, also sees a maternal allusion in the use of the root *tzar*, meaning distress, in verse 3 (*metzarim*), which evokes the pain of childbirth (Jer. 4:31; 49:24).

and she will have, as it says, "And a redeemer shall come to Zion" (Is. 59). Here too, you say that "she has no comforter." She will have, as it says, "I [God] am your comforter" (Is. 51). (Eikha Rabba 1:26)

Eikha 1:5

הָיוּ צָרֶיהָ לְרֹאשׁ
אֹיְבֶיהָ שָׁלוּ

כִּי־ה' הוֹגָהּ
עַל רֹב־פְּשָׁעֶיהָ

עוֹלָלֶיהָ הָלְכוּ שְׁבִי
לִפְנֵי־צָר

Her adversaries were at the head
Her enemies were tranquil

For the Lord made her grieve
Because of the greatness of her transgressions

Her young children went into captivity
Before the adversary

God enters the book for the first time alongside a blunt presentation of Israel's transgressions, the first explicit indication of Israel's accountability. While the verse does not elaborate the nature of Israel's sins, their central position in this verse highlights their pivotal role. Bookended by the bewildering success of the enemies and the terrible suffering of the children, Israel's unnamed sins lose some of their impact. How are these two topics – inexplicable injustice and human culpability – balanced in this verse? Are they mutually exclusive or complementary? To answer this, I will examine the substance, structure, and meter of this verse.

Poetic Composition and Theology

The first and third sentences of the verse focus on an unjust world. These sentences succinctly describe the problem of theodicy, which seeks to reconcile a good God with the existence of seemingly undeserved suffering. The paramount human quandary finds expression in two separate, but related questions:

1. Why do evildoers prosper? (*rasha vetov lo*)
2. Why do innocents suffer? (*tzaddik vera lo*)

The first sentence ("Her adversaries were at the head, her enemies were tranquil") describes the triumphant evildoers (presumably, the Babylonians). The word *shalu*, meaning tranquility, recalls Jeremiah's similar query, in which he describes his confusion regarding scoundrels who flourish:

> You are righteous, Lord. Shall I contend with you? I will still speak justice with you. Why do the ways of evildoers prosper? [Why do] all those who are traitorous [obtain] tranquility (*shalu*)? (Jer. 12:1)

In a psalm that celebrates Jerusalem, tranquility appears as a reward for those who love her:

> Ask after the peace of Jerusalem. Let those who love her obtain tranquility (*yishlayu*). (Ps. 122:6)

The enemies who obtain tranquility do not love Jerusalem; on the contrary, they cruelly assault her.

Captured children feature in the third sentence ("Her young children went into captivity before the adversary"), the archetype of suffering innocents. No transgression can ever account for the death of children. Thus, the children's torment creates a theological conundrum, characterized by feelings of outrage and incomprehension.

These sentences revolve around the verse's pivotal center. The core of the verse introduces simultaneously both God and the notion of Israel's culpability. God enters the book in a punitive role, balanced by Israel's sins ("For the Lord made her grieve because of the greatness of her transgressions").[54] God is responsible for Israel's misery, justly dispensing punishment.

We can gain some theological insight into this difficult verse by turning our attention to the covenant of Deuteronomy 28, which, among other things, lists the punishments to which Israel will be subject if they violate the covenant. Sentence 3 of our verse echoes the warning of Deuteronomy 28:41:

> You will give birth to sons and daughters and they will not remain for you, for they will go into captivity.

Deuteronomy 28:44 warns Israel of the consequences that come to fruition in sentence 1 of our verse:

> He will be the head and you will be the tail.

Thus, both sentences 1 and 3 in our verse – "Her adversaries were at the head" and "Her young children went into captivity" – echo the admonitions of Deuteronomy 28. By drawing on these forewarned punishments, Eikha indicates that the current situation is the predictable consequence of Israel's betrayal of the covenant.

It will always be difficult for humans to make sense of our world, which so often exhibits injustice. Evil people prosper, and innocents sometimes suffer. Nevertheless, this verse proposes that the world contains a deep core of justice. God's appearance at the center of this dilemma suggests divine justice, just as the subtle reference to Deuteronomy 28 hints at reasonable consequences. Even if humans cannot always understand, God's righteousness prevails

---

54. The word employed to convey Israel's sinfulness is *pesha*. Often used to describe a political infraction or rebellion (e.g., II Kings 1:1; 3:5), the term implies a willful act of rebellion.

at the heart of this verse, a resonant message as we contend with Jerusalem's calamity.

A strong correspondence emerges between meter and meaning in this verse.[55] As is typical in this chapter, verse 5 consists of three binary sentences. The first and third sentences retain characteristic "*kina* meter" (as discussed in the introductory chapter on biblical poetry), in which the second part of the sentence has fewer stressed syllables than the first, producing a limping and uneven rhythm.

1	1	1		1	1	= 3 + 2
Hayu	*tzareha*	*lerosh*		*oyveha*	*shalu*	

1	1	1		1		= 3 + 1
Olleleha	*halekhu*	*shevi*		*lifnei-tzar*		

Unexpectedly, the middle sentence maintains symmetrical meter, the customary meter of biblical poetry.

1	1		1	1	= 2 + 2
Ki-YHVH	*hoga*		*al-rov*	*pesha'eha*	

The sentences that describe rampant injustice maintain uneven and discordant meter, an apt reflection of the tension and dissonance that characterize the human condition.

The middle sentence is different; balanced meter manifests a harmonious worldview. This stark presentation belies the complexity of the human condition; it manages to restore equilibrium, conveyed both by its meter and by its content. Amid the turbulence of theological confusion, and surrounded by what appears to be an unfair world, one idea rings clear: Eikha maintains a deep-seated belief in God's justice. This conviction steadies and braces humans, who are beset by bewilderment in an inequitable world.

---

55. While I used this as an example in the study of meter in the chapter above, "Biblical Poetry and the Book of Eikha," I discuss it here in a slightly expanded fashion.

Eikha 1:6

וַיֵּצֵא מִבַּת־צִיּוֹן
כָּל־הֲדָרָהּ

הָיוּ שָׂרֶיהָ כְּאַיָּלִים
לֹא־מָצְאוּ מִרְעֶה

וַיֵּלְכוּ בְלֹא־כֹחַ
לִפְנֵי רוֹדֵף

Departed from the daughter of Zion[56]
Is all her glory

Her officers were like stags
They did not find pasture

And they walked without strength
Before the pursuer

For the second time (see also verse 3), Eikha turns its attention to
the sights outside of Jerusalem, to the far-flung places where her
inhabitants have gone. The verse bemoans the city's bygone glory,
without specifying what it has lost. The word *hadar* evokes an association with God's majesty (Ps. 96:6; 145:5), perhaps indicating that
God has left the city, taking His splendor with Him. However, the
continuation of the verse suggests that the departed glory is that of

---

56. A phrase that refers to the city as a daughter ("daughter of Zion/Jerusalem/Judah")
occurs thirteen times in Eikha. A similar phrase, "daughter of my nation," appears
five times in Eikha. These are common designations, used frequently by prophets.
These appellations appear to connote affection, protectiveness, or empathy for the
city. However, the term is not consistently employed toward Israel in a tender or
positive context (e.g., Micah 1:13; Eikha 4:6) and may be used ironically, preceding
the name of an enemy city (e.g., Jer. 46:11; Eikha 4:21–22). Berlin, 10–12, devotes a
short excursus to this expression.

the exiled officers.[57] Possibly, however, the departed glory refers to the final subject of the previous verse – namely, the young children gone into captivity. [58] Taken together, these interpretations merge, as the reader witnesses the depletion of Jerusalem's grandeur, dignity, and esteemed populace. As our eyes strain to follow these children into exile, we also glimpse the fleeing officers who fail to find respite. Turning back to the city, the reader observes a void in place of her previous majesty, which vanishes in the wake of her inhabitants' expulsion.

Three motifs recall the previous snapshot of exile in verse 3: the dogged motion of a weary people in flux, the relentless pursuer, and the way the exiles "do not find" respite or pasture. These repeated themes, appearing twice at the outset of the book (verses 3 and 6), crystallize a particular notion of exile. Exile is movement, unremitting persecution and pursuit, and an abiding inability to find repose.

These disturbing images portray exile as a hostile and challenging experience. Nevertheless, according to a midrash, the inability to find respite contains a hidden blessing:

> "And he sent the dove … and the dove did not find repose…" (Gen. 8:8–9). R. Judah bar Naḥman said in the name of R. Shimon, who said: Had she found respite, she would not have returned. Similarly, (Eikha 1:3), "She sat among the nations, and did not find repose." Had she found repose, they [sic] would not have returned. (Genesis Rabba 33:6)[59]

Since the nation does not find rest in exile, it does not have the opportunity to assimilate and disappear. As we will see in Eikha 4:15, the host countries repeatedly reject the Jewish refugees and do not allow them

---

57. Ibn Ezra, Eikha 1:6, suggests that this refers to the exiled monarchy; indeed the word *hadarah* often relates to the glory associated with royalty.
58. See Eikha Rabba 1:33.
59. See also Eikha Rabba 1:29. Rabbinic commentators sometimes put a positive spin on the hardships of exile, asserting that these difficulties prevent Israel from getting too comfortable and assimilating into its surroundings. For another example, see Eikha Rabba 1:28.

to integrate, thereby compounding their misery. The midrash suggests that this misfortune ensures that Israel maintains its distinctive national identity and its longing to return home.

Metaphor: Officers as Stags

Metaphors offer rich opportunities for interpretation. The word *ayyal* means a stag,[60] but a similar consonantal word can mean a ram (*ayil*).[61] In other biblical contexts, this consonantal combination connotes strength of leadership[62] and swift movement.[63] The verse portrays the previously powerful leadership as drained of energy, unable to find pasture or the basic means for survival. If they cannot find pasture for themselves, they certainly cannot help their people, whose sufferings are compounded by their leaders' impotence.

Rashi connects this inability to find food to the next part of the verse: starvation saps them of strength, which accounts for the stags' inability to flee from their pursuers. One privation leads to the next, creating a downward spiral of hardships.

The absence of pasture highlights God's absence. Biblical passages often depict God as a shepherd who nurtures and pastures His nation (Ps. 23; Jer. 23; Ezek. 34). Procuring pasture should be God's job; if the stags cannot find pasture, it is because God chooses not to help them. The leaders' failure in finding pasture also recalls their own deficiencies as shepherds of their people. No longer able to care for their

---

60. The word that means stag has a diacritical mark (the *dagesh ḥazak*) in the *yod*, as does the word in our verse. Therefore, I have translated stag. See Francis Brown, Samuel Rolles Driver, and Charles Augustus Briggs (hereafter BDB), *A Hebrew and English Lexicon of the Old Testament* (Oxford: Clarendon Press, 1951), 19.

61. This word does not have the *dagesh* in the *yod*, as does the word in our verse, though this reading is adopted by some of the early translations of Eikha 1:6 (e.g., Septuagint and Vulgate). These animals were used for both food (e.g., Gen. 31:38) and sacrifice (e.g., Ex. 29:31–32; 46:4–7). In this reading, the rams' inability to find pasture, along with their exhausted flight from the pursuers, implies Jerusalem's loss of food and sacrifices.

62. Some biblical passages refer to leadership with the word *eilei* (e.g., Ex. 15:15; Ezek. 17:13). BDB, *Lexicon*, 18, suggests that this may derive from the way the ram acts as the leader of the flock.

63. See Genesis 49:21; II Samuel 22:34; Isaiah 35:6.

own needs, much less the needs of others, the metaphor underscores the collapse of leadership.

Eikha 1:7

זָכְרָה יְרוּשָׁלַ͏ִם
יְמֵי עָנְיָהּ וּמְרוּדֶיהָ

כֹּל מַחֲמֻדֶיהָ
אֲשֶׁר הָיוּ מִימֵי קֶדֶם

בִּנְפֹל עַמָּהּ בְּיַד־צָר
וְאֵין עוֹזֵר לָהּ

רָאוּהָ צָרִים
שָׂחֲקוּ עַל מִשְׁבַּתֶּהָ

Jerusalem remembered
[During] the days of her affliction and wandering
All her precious delights
That were in the days of old

When her nation fell in the hand of the adversary
And there was none to help her
Her adversaries saw her
They laughed at her cessations [of activity]

This summary of Jerusalem's anguish concludes the description of Jerusalem's ruin (1–7). In the second part of this summary verse, we return to many themes already familiar to us (Jerusalem's fallen nation, her absence of support, her adversaries, and her paralysis). This verse also introduces a new torment for Jerusalem: the mockery of her enemies. Their jeers rudely intrude upon the muted sounds of Jerusalem's wretchedness: her cries in the night, the sobs and groans of priests and maidens. No longer alone, she is finally noticed. However, the observer is not an empathetic observer or a beloved companion, but rather a hate-filled foe, one who delights in her downfall. Loneliness is surely preferable to scorn.[64] Disparaged Jerusalem continues to suffer the enemy's mockery throughout the book.[65]

This verse centers on two of the characters in the story of Jerusalem's downfall: her nation and her enemies. God remains notably absent, despite His punitive (and justified) role in verse 5. Perhaps this indicates that Jerusalem has not fully accepted God's role in these events, nor has she come to terms with her own transgressions. This will change in the following verses (8–9), as the narrator denounces Jerusalem's sinfulness. At that point, Jerusalem turns directly to God, acknowledging His ongoing involvement in her tragedy.

While the second part of the verse employs many familiar themes, its first part introduces a new idea into the book – namely, memory. Recollections of the past can help Jerusalem contend with an unendurable present.

Before discussing the role of memory in Eikha, I would like to focus our attention on the structure and meter of this verse. We could divide this verse into either four standard-length sentences (instead of the usual three) or into two very long sentences (as I have done above). In either case, the structure of the verse distinguishes it from the surrounding ones.[66] Deviating from the accepted structure draws attention to this verse. Just as the opening verse (Eikha 1:1) highlights its distinctive

---

64. The contempt of the enemy is a particularly devastating experience (see Ps. 44:14–17; 79:4; 80:7; Jer. 48:26, 39; Zeph. 2:8, 10).

65. Eikha 1:21; 2:16; 3:46, 61–62. See also 3:14, where the mockery of one's own people is likewise intolerable.

66. Unsurprisingly, such a striking divergence leads some scholars to recommend an emendation, removing one of the lines to conform to the standard three-line verse (see, e.g., Hillers, 8–9, 68; Westermann, 112). I have many objections to the "emendation" approach. It is too facile, allowing any biblical scholar simply to excise what seems difficult, without properly contending with the possibility that it is deliberate. The subjective nature of this enterprise is also troubling. How should we emend the problematic verse? In the case cited above, which sentence should we remove? Is there any sentence that does not appear to be an organic part of the verse? It is difficult to make a compelling case, based on objective criteria, for any reconstruction of the verse. It is also worth noting that the verse as it stands appears in the ancient translations (Greek and Syriac).

placement by employing a unique structure (see the discussion there), so too does this verse, which serves as a summary and conclusion to the section describing Jerusalem's suffering.

In dividing this verse into two lengthy sentences, an intriguing metrical irregularity emerges in the first sentence. (The second sentence, with its focus on Jerusalem's anguish, has typically uneven *kina* meter [6 + 4], despite its uncommon length.) The meter of the first sentence is weighted in its second half (I have bolded the stressed syllable):

| | 1 | | 1 | | 1 | 1 | | 1 | = 5 stressed syllables |

Zakhera Yerushalayim yemei oniya umerudeha

| | 1 | | 1 | 1 | 1 | 1 | 1 | = 6 stressed syllables |

kol maḥamudeha asher hayu memei kedem

While in *kina* meter the first half of the sentence customarily retains more metrical beats than the second (6 + 4), the second half of this sentence is metrically longer than the first (5 + 6). The second half stretches and extends, signaling that the speaker cannot bear for this sentence to end. It appears that Jerusalem is thinking of the past, longingly conjuring up her former precious delights. Like someone experiencing a wonderful dream, Jerusalem prefers not to awaken to the reality of the painful present.

Zakhar: The Role of Memory

Appearing seven times in the book of Eikha, the word *zakhar* functions as a *leitwort*.[67] Memory plays a key role in Israel's national experience. In this verse, memory acts as a solace, a palliative to Israel's

---

67. M. Buber, *Darko shel Mikra* (Jerusalem: Bialik, 1964), 284, defined the *leitwort* (or leading word) as follows: "A word or linguistic root, which recurs within a text, a series of texts, or a set of texts in an extremely meaningful manner, so that when one investigates these repetitions, the meaning of the texts is explained or becomes clear to the reader, or at least it is revealed to a much higher degree." Umberto Cassuto stresses the significance of a sevenfold appearance of a root in identifying a *leitwort* of a narrative. See, for example, *A Commentary on the Book of Exodus* (Jerusalem: Magnes Press, 1967), 75, 91 ff.

pain. Recalling past glory allows Jerusalem to retain a semblance of her former majesty.[68]

Often in the Bible, the word *zakhar* obligates Israel. Recalling historical acts of divine salvation compels Israel to maintain its commitment to God.[69] Israel's remembrances are often onerous, but they can also be transformative. As we will see, Eikha 3:18–19 repeats the word *zakhar* three times in two pivotal verses. In these verses, the long-suffering *gever* of chapter 3 feels humbled by his memories, presumably because he recalls his violations of his commitments to God.[70] This begins his transformation from a self-absorbed victim (in 3:1–17) to a contemplative *homo religiosus* (in 3:21–39), illustrating how dramatic changes can occur in the wake of powerful recollections.

Memory plays an additional role in the covenantal relationship between God and nation. Not only must the nation remember God, but God commits Himself to remembering His covenant with His nation (e.g., Lev. 26:42; Ezek. 16:60; Ps. 111:5). Dashed expectations underlie the bitterness of the declaration in Eikha 2:1: "And He did not remember His footstool [the Temple] on the day of His anger." God's decision not to remember brings calamity in its wake. As time passes, however, God's pledge to remember Israel becomes a vital avenue for hope. The word *zakhor*, directed toward God, opens the final chapter of the book, as Israel collectively turns to God with a plea (Eikha 5:1): "*Remember, Lord, what befell us; look and see our disgrace!*" This request indicates Israel's trust in a relationship based on mutual remembrance, a conviction that sustains Israel during this crisis.

This verse caps Eikha's initial section (1:1–7) by touching on Jerusalem's recollections of her "precious delights" in "days of old."[71]

---

68. In Psalms 42:5, 7, however, memories of past time seem to increase the misery of the present.

69. For example, Exodus 13:3; 20:8–11; Deuteronomy 5:15; 24:9 25:17–19.

70. Though the verse does not explain why the *gever* feels chastened by his memories, it appears that he recalls his own responsibilities toward God, which he has not fulfilled properly. I will explore this at length in chapter 3.

71. This interpretation, which I adopt in my translation of the verse, coheres with the explanation of both Ibn Ezra and R. Yosef Kara. Rashi, however, explains that Jerusalem in exile remembered the catastrophe that brought on misery and suffering,

What are these precious delights and for which days of old does Jerusalem yearn?

Usage of the word *maḥamudeha* elsewhere in Tanakh helps sharpen our understanding of Jerusalem's treasured memories. Some passages use this word to refer to the Temple (Is. 64:10; Ezek. 24:21)[72] or its precious vessels (Joel 4:5; II Chr. 36:10, 19).[73] Others suggest that these precious delights are the inhabitants of the city:[74] one's children (Ezek. 24:25), spouses (Ezek. 24:16), or simply the general population. The precise nature of the recollection does not alter the meaning of our verse in any significant fashion. However, in later usages of this word, these distinctions will profoundly affect the meaning.

When were the "days of old" that Jerusalem recalls? Biblical passages do not employ this phrase in a consistent manner. The "days of old" can recall primordial time (II Kings 19:25; Is. 37:26),[75] or denote the days of the Patriarchs (Mic. 7:20). It can also refer to the monumental events of Israel's history, such as the splitting of the sea (Is. 51:9),[76] the period in the desert,[77] or the conquest of the land (Ps. 44:2–4).

The context of our verse suggests that Jerusalem is avidly remembering an ideal earlier period, one that she craves (see also Eikha 5:21).[78] Devoid of a specific reference, this verse allows readers to reflect upon the undisclosed period. Perhaps Jerusalem recalls the glorious era of the monarchy, and specifically its pinnacle under Solomon, when the

---

as well as the precious delights of former times. In Rashi's view, Jerusalem's recollections are both bad and good. In Ibn Ezra's reading, her present experience is miserable, but her recollections are positive.

72. See R. Yosef Kara on Eikha 1:11.

73. Eikha 1:10 supports this usage.

74. Eikha 2:4 supports this usage.

75. See Rashi on both verses cited. Rashi sometimes uses this phrase to mean primordial times (e.g., Rashi, Ex. 17:5).

76. See, for example, *Yalkut Shimoni, Beshalaḥ* 233; Radak ad loc.

77. See *Targum* and Radak on Jeremiah 2:2.

78. The ideal nature of this period may be suggested by the fact that the word "*kedem*" evokes the narrative of the creation of humans, prior to their sin (Gen. 2:8). For a similar unspecific use of the phrase to denote an ideal era, see Jeremiah 46:26. In contrast, Eikha 2:17 uses this phrase to reference God's early warning of retribution for sin, rather than an ideal time.

Temple brought glory and splendor to the city.[79] Solomon forged a vast kingdom, one that was prosperous, secure, and spiritually vitalized by the construction of the Temple. One can certainly imagine why Jerusalem would dwell on that era and regard it as an ideal.[80]

Mishbateha: A Wordplay

The root *shavat*, meaning to cease or desist, is at the core of the word *mishbateha*.[81] In its *hifil* verbal form, it can mean to exterminate or destroy (e.g., II Kings 23:5, 11; Jer. 36:29). In Eikha 1:7, the nominal form suggests the city's ruin.[82] It is not clear why this noun appears in the plural form;[83] perhaps it emphasizes the cessation of all forms of activity in the city.

Significantly, the word *mishbateha* alludes to Shabbat.[84] This wordplay evokes the terrible transformation wrought by destruction. Although on Shabbat work ceased, Jerusalem used to teem with activity, especially in the Temple (Is. 66:23; Ezek. 46:1–3). Linguistically invoking the once-bustling Shabbat brings Jerusalem's desolation sharply into focus.

Shabbat is the embodiment of God's covenant with His nation (Ex. 31:13), an emblem of Israel's dignity and nobility. Now, however, catastrophe elicits mockery. In lieu of admiration for her sanctified status, outsiders disdain Jerusalem for the enforced cessation of activity, for her *mishbateha*.

---

79. See Rashi, Psalms 77:7, where he explicitly uses this phrase to describe the experience in the Temple.

80. Leviticus Rabba 7:4 suggests that the similar phrase used to depict an ideal period in Malachi 3:4 (*keshanim kadmaniyot*) is a reference to the days of Solomon. See H. Angel, *Haggai, Zechariah, and Malachi* (Jerusalem: Maggid, 2016), 139, fn. 21.

81. A Qumran text reads *mishbareha*, her brokenness. That variance does not add anything in terms of meaning and lacks the marvelous wordplay with the word Shabbat that I will shortly discuss.

82. BDB, *Lexicon*, 992.

83. This plural form gave rise to midrashim that sought to explain the multiple cessations that occurred as a result of the destruction of Jerusalem. See, for example, Eikha Rabba 1:34.

84. Hosea 2:13 creates a wordplay between the verb *vehishbati*, meaning to destroy, and the word Shabbat. Rashi implicitly notes this wordplay by citing this verse in his commentary on Eikha 1:7.

Eikha 1:8–9

חָטְא חָטְאָה יְרוּשָׁלִַם
עַל־כֵּן לְנִידָה הָיָתָה

כָּל־מְכַבְּדֶיהָ הִזִּילוּהָ
כִּי־רָאוּ עֶרְוָתָהּ

גַּם־הִיא נֶאֶנְחָה
וַתָּשָׁב אָחוֹר

טֻמְאָתָהּ בְּשׁוּלֶיהָ
לֹא זָכְרָה אַחֲרִיתָהּ

וַתֵּרֶד פְּלָאִים
אֵין מְנַחֵם לָהּ

רְאֵה ה' אֶת־עָנְיִי
כִּי הִגְדִּיל אוֹיֵב

Jerusalem has surely sinned
Therefore, she has become an [object of] head-wagging[85]

All those who honored her belittle her
For they have seen her nakedness

She too groans
And she recoils backward

Her impurities are on her hems
She did not consider[86] her end

---

85. I will explain below why I have adopted the Ibn Ezra's translation of the word *nida*.

86. This translation follows Rashi's reading of the word *zakhera*. See below for an explanation of Rashi's interpretation.

> She spirals downward wondrously
> There is none to comfort her
>
> "Look, Lord, at my affliction
> For the enemy is exalted!"

The portrait of suffering abruptly gives way to harsh accusation: "Jerusalem has surely sinned!" Until now, Jerusalem's misery inclines the reader to empathize with her suffering. The tone shifts sharply here as the narrator points an accusatory finger at Jerusalem. A categorical statement correlates her sins with her wretchedness.

This verse moves rapidly from Jerusalem's culpability to the derisive reaction of others ("Therefore, she has become an [object of] head-wagging," and "All those who honored her belittle her"). Scorn is interspersed with descriptions of Jerusalem's exposure ("For they have seen her nakedness") and public humiliation in the form of defiled garments ("Her impurities are on her hems"). The outsiders are by no means the only ones who regard Jerusalem with disgust. Jerusalem displays self-loathing and shame, shrinking back from herself: "And she recoils backward."[87]

These verses contains a powerful metaphor of the city as a sullied figure whose moral impurities are visible to all. A distasteful image, it simultaneously establishes the city's humiliation and her patent culpability. Further compounding her guilt, this verse accuses Jerusalem of willful ignorance; she did not consider the consequences of her actions, thereby sending her spiraling uncontrollably toward her terrible fate. Condemned, disparaged, and culpable, no one wishes to console the dishonored city.

Metaphor: *Nida* and Nakedness

The metaphor of Jerusalem's feminine persona resonates throughout this chapter: her lonely widowhood, her absent lovers, and her captured children. Now, however, sympathy yields to disgust as the images of her

---

87. See Ibn Ezra, Eikha 1:8. R. Yosef Kara, ad loc., explains that Jerusalem wishes that she could move backward and retract her sinfulness.

nakedness and the stains on her hems come into focus. These images of an impure and exposed city follow the initial accusation of sinfulness.

At first glance, the word *nida* in verse 8 (which sounds like the word for a menstruant) appears to dovetail well with this image. Nevertheless, in contrast to its appearance in Eikha 1:17, the *dalet* in the word *nida* lacks a *dagesh*, the diacritical mark that indicates the doubling of the letter.[88] Accordingly, the root is not *n.d.d.*, but rather *n.o.d.*, meaning to wander. Based on this, Rashi explains that Jerusalem's sins transform her into an aimless wanderer (cf. Gen. 4:14).[89] In Rashi's view, Jerusalem's punishment is exile, which results in the disdain of those who previously respected her.[90] This same root (*n.o.d.*) can mean to move a body part, such as one's head – presumably as a gesture of either mourning or contempt.[91] Ibn Ezra adduces the latter meaning here, maintaining that this word describes the head-wagging of those who scorn Jerusalem.[92] I have adopted this reading in the above translation for the following reasons. Contextually, it flows naturally from verse 7, which concluded with the mockery of the enemies. The continuation of verse 8, moreover, expands on the theme – all those who once respected her now despise her. This reading is also consistent with Jeremiah 18:13–16, which warns "maiden Israel" that her sins will spawn desolation, followed by a description of passersby who will "wag their heads."[93]

---

88. The form of the word *nida* in verse 8 is a *hapax legomenon* (a word that appears only once in the Bible).

89. See also *Targum Eikha* 1:8; Eikha Rabba 1:35; Rasag, Eikha 1:8. The Greek translates *nida* with the word σάλον, which means turmoil: "Therefore, she is in turmoil." Possibly, this is an attempt to render the word *n.o.d.* in its Aramaic usage (fluttering or turmoil; see BDB, *Lexicon*, 626). Perhaps a similar meaning is indicated in Psalms 11:1.

90. See Hosea 9:17, where he describes exile with the word *nadad*.

91. This usage of the root *n.o.d.* juxtaposed with head (*rosh*) appears in Jeremiah 18:16 and Psalms 44:15 to describe the reaction of other nations to Israel's calamity. Based on the context, it appears to connote derision. In Job 2:11, the verb (lacking the word *rosh*) clearly indicates empathy.

92. Ibn Ezra cites Psalms 44:15 and (less clearly) Job 16:5. See also Hillers, 70.

93. It is not certain whether the wagging of the head in Jeremiah is a gesture of contempt (as in Ps. 44:15) or empathy (as in Nahum 3:7 or Ps. 69:21).

Despite the absence of the *dagesh* in the *dalet*, one can hardly avoid the obvious association with the menstruant *nidda*.[94] This use of the word *nidda* appears later in the chapter, linked there as well with the verb *hayeta*, meaning "to be" (1:17).[95] Moreover, this meaning coheres with the opening of following verse, in which Jerusalem's impurity upon her hems (presumably a reference to her menstrual blood)[96] becomes a metaphor for her moral and religious impurity, which is obvious to all who see her.

Perhaps in this context we can better understand the idea that "they have seen her nakedness (*erva*)."[97] What does it mean to see a city's nakedness? On one level, this refers to the manner in which the enemy destroys the physical city: stripping it of protective battlements and walls, baring its palaces and private inner chambers, and confiscating its treasures.[98] This pillage is not just physically devastating, but also shameful; the humiliation of ruin and vulnerability plays a central role in the city's misery, as her exposed defenselessness causes others to belittle her.[99] Moreover, the world sees through Jerusalem's facade of

---

94. Several biblical translations (Aquila, Symmachus, Syriac) render the word in this way. Rabbinic interpreters similarly note this association (e.g., Taanit 20a). See also Gottwald, 8; Albrektson, 63–64; Provan, 44; and House, 335. For more on the imagery of Jerusalem as a menstruant, see our discussion in Eikha 1:17.

95. The word *d.v.h.* also appears twice in this chapter (verses 13 and 22). While the primary meaning of *davah* is unwell or faint, the word also refers to a menstruant woman (Lev. 15:33; 20:18). Isaiah 30:22 employs the word *davah* as a metaphor for the impurities of idolatry.

96. Rasag and Rashi, Eikha 1:9, explain the verse in this sense. Alternatively, the impurities upon her hems could refer to the blood from the corpses littering the streets, which stains their garments (see also Eikha 4:13–15 and Psalms 106:38–39).

97. Prophets use similar metaphors to prophesy punishments against foreign cities, such as Nineveh (Nahum 3:5) and Babylon (Is. 47:3).

98. Seeing the nakedness of a city can also mean spying on it, noting its vulnerabilities (Gen. 42:9, 12). This meaning does not seem applicable to our verse.

99. The word *hiziluha* is derived from either the word *zol* or *zalal*. Both words have similar meanings – namely, to cheapen or to regard something as having little worth or value. In biblical Hebrew, some roots are classified as "weak roots," such as those with a *vav* in the middle or with a *heh* at the end, or those in which the second and third letters are identical. Conjugations of weak roots are often based on only two of the root letters (the "strong letters"). In many cases, we find a semantic fluidity between weak roots bearing the same two "strong" letters. In this case, the two

sanctity; her "nakedness" refers to the exposure of her previously hidden moral corruptions.

In adherence to the broader theme, exposure of Jerusalem's nakedness seems to be a fitting punishment for a city that betrayed her promise of fidelity to God; having willingly exposed herself to her illicit "lovers," Jerusalem is now punished by forced exposure.[100] As we will see, this scenario is described at length by various prophets, who regard Israel's betrayal of God as that of a wife who betrayed her husband. To properly understand the subtext of Eikha 1, let us examine the common metaphor of the spousal relationship between Israel and God, a relationship that Israel violated.

God and Israel: A Marital Covenant

The metaphor of the spousal relationship between God and His nation is a pervasive biblical theme, as noted by Ibn Ezra in his introduction to the Songs of Songs:

> Do not be surprised that [Solomon] compared *Kenesset Yisrael* to a bride and God to her beloved, for that is the way of the prophets. Isaiah said, "The song of my Beloved to His vineyard" (5:1), and also, "As the Bridegroom is joyous over the bride" (62:5). Ezekiel said, "Your breasts became ready and your hair was grown and you were naked and bare" (16:7), and also, "I covered your nakedness" (16:8), and, "I decked you out in jewelry" (16:11), and all that chapter [uses this metaphor]. Hosea said, "And I will betroth you

---

roots *z.o.l.* and *z.l.l.* share the same pair of strong letters (*z.l.*), and hence it is not surprising to find an overlap in their meaning. (I am grateful to Dr. Avi Shmidman for the above explanation.) Ibn Ezra first suggests that the word *hiziluha* means to belittle, functioning as an antonym of the word *kavod* (honor), and illustrating the radical change in Jerusalem's reputation ("All those who honored her belittle her"). Generally, *zol* (cheap) seems to function as the antonym of *yakar* (worthy), as in Jeremiah 15:19 (as cited by Ibn Ezra). Ultimately, Ibn Ezra seems to reject these readings, concluding that the root *zol* is different than the root *zalal*. He suggests (rather hesitantly) that the word here relates to the word *nazal,* meaning flow (as in Deut. 32:2). In this reading, the enemies cause Jerusalem to flow with tears.

100. While I present this viewing of Jerusalem's nakedness as part of her punishment, Ibn Caspi (on 1:8) seems to regard this as a description of her sin.

to Me forever" (2:21), "Go and love a woman" (3:1). And in the book of Psalms, "A Maskil. A song of love" (45:1), and, "Listen young woman and see, incline your ear" (45:11).

Biblical passages employ the spousal metaphor in various contexts. In its ideal state, this relationship evokes love, passion, monogamy, devotion, and abiding commitment between God and His nation. However, a committed relationship also entails obligations, incurring the risks for human infidelity, treachery, and immoral behavior.

Prophets frequently portray Israel's idolatry as harlotry.[101] Instead of maintaining her pledge of exclusivity, Israel betrays God, turning her attentions instead to foreign gods, often referred to as Israel's lovers. Less frequently, Jerusalem's harlotry refers to a general betrayal of God, not specifically having to do with idolatry (Is. 1:21; Hos. 5:4). Spousal infidelity may also refer to Israel's decision to forge political alliances instead of relying on God.[102] Malbim interprets several prophetic passages in this way:[103]

> "And you played the whore [with your neighbors, the Egyptians["
> (Ezek. 16:26)…this is the story when they turned to Egypt for
> assistance, and all this occurred during the days of Ahaz. (Malbim,
> Ezek. 16:26)

Israel's betrayal of God is destined for disaster. Unsurprisingly, Israel's infidelity to God causes a deep rift in their marital relationship. God implicitly threatens Judah with divorce (exile), a fate like that of her northern brethren:

---

101. See Radak's discussion in Jeremiah 3:1. This idea is already found in the Torah, where idolatry is referred to as harlotry (Ex. 34:15–16). The ceremony enacted by Moses when he finds the people worshipping the golden calf is intriguingly reminiscent of the *sota* ceremony, performed when a married woman is suspected of infidelity. See also Deuteronomy 31:16; Judges 2:17, 8:27, 33. We will examine several examples from prophetic passages, where this idea is common.

102. As noted in our examination of 1:2, prophets often rail against Israel's reliance upon political alliances.

103. See also Malbim on Ezekiel 16:28 and Jeremiah 13:25. However, most biblical interpreters assume that these passages refer to Israel's idolatrous practices.

Because of errant Israel's harlotries, I cast her off and I gave her a bill of divorce. And rebellious Judah did not fear, and she went and whored as well. (Jer. 3:8)

Moreover, having willingly revealed her nakedness to others, prophets warn that God will strip Jerusalem (and the nation) of her clothes and her dignity, displaying her humiliation to her former lovers.[104]

These prophetic passages shed light on Jerusalem's shameful state in Eikha 1:8–9. Having betrayed God by exposing herself to her "lovers," Jerusalem is now punished by forced exposure. Jerusalem receives due recompense for her misdeeds, forecast by prophets who castigated and cautioned her.

Yet, this metaphor contains within it potential for reconciliation. Despite His ire, God maintains His love for His cherished nation; prophets intersperse rebuke with expressions of eternal love. While denouncing Israel for betraying God (and threatening impending divorce), Hosea proposes a renewal of the relationship, unique in its emotional depth and intensity:

And I will strike a new covenant with [Israel] on that day… And I will betroth you to Me forever, and I will betroth you to Me in righteousness and justice and loyalty and compassion. And I will betroth you to Me in faith and you will know the Lord. (Hos. 2:20–22)

One cannot ignore the pathos that lies at the heart of this extraordinary proposition. Laced with passion and destined for sublimity, Israel's intimate relationship with God retains abiding promise.

---

104. See, for example, Hosea 2:11–12, Jeremiah 13:22–27, Ezekiel 16:35–39. In support of the approach that regards Israel's lovers as political allies, one scenario comes to mind. To bolster relations, King Hezekiah tries to impress the king of Babylonia by showing him the contents of his treasury (II Kings 20:13). Isaiah berates Hezekiah, prophesying that the king of Babylonia will eventually empty the coffers that Hezekiah so willingly exposed. This narrative nicely fits the metaphor in which Israel reveals her nakedness willingly, followed by her forcible exposure and ruin, when Babylonia conquers her.

Isaiah similarly offers Jerusalem God's pledge of renewal, following a period of punitive destruction, exile, and estrangement:[105]

> You will no longer be called Forsaken, and your land will no lon-
> ger be called Desolate. Instead, you will be called Desired, and
> your land, Wedded. For the Lord desires you, and your land will
> be wedded. As a young man weds a maiden, your inhabitants
> shall wed you, and as a bridegroom rejoices over his bride, so
> your God will rejoice over you. (Isaiah 62:4–5)

By recalling the metaphoric marriage between God and His nation,
Eikha evinces the once-passionate relationship:

> He compared Israel to a woman and said about her in feminine
> person, "[How has] she sat [lonely!]" (Eikha 1:1). God said: I said
> (Hos. 2:21), "And I will betroth you to Me with faith," "Come with
> Me from Lebanon, bride" (Song. 4:8), and now, you sit lonely.
> (*Pesikta Zutrata Eikha* 1:1)

When viewed within its broader biblical context, the spousal metaphor
extends beyond the terrible consequences of this chapter. It evokes a
relationship originally distinguished by mutual love and followed by
dramatic betrayal and painful separation. The prospect of joyous reunion
hovers on the horizon, a prophetic promise to which Israel clings during her period of estrangement from God.

"And She Recoils Backward"

Jerusalem's backward movement suggests regression, and anticipates
the downward spiral that occurs in verse 9. A midrash describes the
relentless worsening of Jerusalem's situation, as she spins inexorably
out of control:

---

105. In this section of Isaiah, the prophecies focus upon the period of return from the
Babylonian exile. For more on this topic, see the chapter entitled, "Eikha and the
Prophecies of Consolation in Isaiah."

And she recoils backward. There was no day that was not worse than the one before. This is as it says, "They have gone backward, not forward" (Jer. 7:24). (Eikha Rabba 1:3)

Another midrashic reading focused on Jerusalem's backward movement explains that the city withdraws from her noble roles:

And she recoils backward: backward from the priesthood, backward from kingship. (Eikha Rabba 1:3)

Biblical passages associate these offices with forward movements. Priestly sacrifices are said to be "brought close,"[106] while David thanks God for having brought him forward to kingship (II Sam. 7:18).[107] These dynasties represent advancement toward the ultimate aspirations of Israelite society: serving God and disseminating His name in the world. The destruction of Jerusalem and the Temple, along with the dissolution of the monarchy and priesthood, involve a backward movement away from Jerusalem's destiny.

Lo Zakhera

The word *zakhera* means to "remember." Nevertheless, the juxtaposition of *zakhera*, which usually refers to a past event, with "her end" (*aharita*), which seems to refer to a future one, results in an awkward formulation ("she did not remember her end").[108]

Several biblical interpreters resolve this problem by defining the word *zakhar* in an unconventional way. For example, Rashi proposes that *zakhar* means to "consider" or to think deeply about something.[109]

---

106. See, for example, Leviticus 1:2 and throughout the book of Leviticus.
107. Similarly, a midrash (Exodus Rabba 2:7) explains that God's words to Moses, "Do not draw near" (Ex. 3:5), inform Moses that he will produce neither kingship nor priesthood. See also the explanation of Ruth 2:14 in Shabbat 113b.
108. The identical phrase appears in Isaiah's description of Babylon's refusal to understand that her success is due to God's anger at His nation (Is. 47:7): "But you did not put these things on your heart; you did not remember your end." In the chapter "Eikha and the Prophecies of Consolation in Isaiah," I chart the extensive linguistic similarities between Eikha's description of Israel's sufferings at the hands of the Babylonians and the downfall of Babylon in Isaiah 47.
109. As noted, I translate the verse above in accordance with Rashi's interpretation.

According to Rashi, when Jerusalem sinned, she simply did not consider the ramifications of her transgressions. This approach does not diminish Jerusalem's complicity; instead, it suggests that the dynamic of sinning is so absorbing that the sinner is prone to disregard the consequences.

A midrash (*Pesikta Zutrata, Eikha* 1:9) raises the possibility that the word *zakhar* here means *yada*, to "know." This seems to exonerate Jerusalem somewhat, for she did not know that this would be her fate. But how is this possible? God clearly informed the nation that the punishment for sins is expulsion from the land. In fact, this same midrash earlier cites from a passage in Deuteronomy 18:10, whose context strongly indicates that Israel's sinfulness will lead to exile (see Deut. 18:9–12). It appears that Jerusalem's lack of knowledge is no excuse; her moral failure is that she chose not to remember God's admonition.[110]

In any case, the word *zakhar* clashes with its previous appearance in Eikha 1:7. There, Jerusalem painfully remembers the precious delights of her glory days, before her enemies plunged her into an abyss of grief. Our verse employs the same word, *zakhar*, to rebuke Jerusalem for not using her memory properly during her heyday.

Poetic Composition and Metrical Rhythm

Strikingly, the third sentence of verse 9 features Jerusalem's first-person appeal to God. The first two sentences conclude the narrator's description of the sullied, heedless, and lonely city, spiraling toward her own demise. In both of these initial sentences, the second half contains more metrical beats than the first: two stressed syllables in the first half of the sentence and three in its second half.[111]

1	1		1	1	1	$= 2 + 3$
Tumata beshuleha			*lo zakhera aḥarita*			

1	1		1	1	1	$= 2 + 3$
Vatered pela'im			*ein menaḥem la*			

---

110. See similarly R. Yosef Kara, Eikha 1:9.
111. To understand this better, see the chapter above, "Biblical Poetry and the Book of Eikha," where I discuss the metrical arrangement in biblical poetry.

The palpably weighted sentences seems to accord with their plunging movement. The first sentence ("her impurities are on her hems) sends the reader's eyes skittering rapidly down to the hems of Jerusalem's skirts, noticeably stained by her impurities. The second sentence opens by observing Jerusalem's downward spiral, its unnatural swiftness indicated by the brevity of the phrase. The metrical weightiness of the second half of each sentence suggests that Jerusalem remains slumped, finding it difficult to rise. Later in the chapter, Jerusalem will testify that this is indeed her present state: "The Lord has placed me in the hands [of those before whom] I cannot rise" (Eikha 1:14). Once again, we see how aptly Eikha's poetic techniques contribute to the meaning of the text.

Jerusalem's Interjection: "Look, Lord!"

Verses 8 and 9 harshly assign blame to Jerusalem for her own misery, accusing her of wanton sinning. Jerusalem's initial response seems muted; following the public exposure of her nakedness, she groans and recoils in shame (verse 8). Isolation follows collapse: "She spirals downward wondrously; there is none to comfort her." Her solitude seems to bring Jerusalem to her emotional breaking point; Jerusalem's voice intrudes mid-verse, appearing to interrupt the narrator's speech. After her brief, evocative plea ("Look, Lord, at my affliction!"), the third-person narration resumes (in verse 10), indicating that Jerusalem's interjection is unplanned, a function of her inability to restrain herself.

What precipitates Jerusalem's impertinent interruption of the narrator? The syntax suggests that Jerusalem's isolation, the absence of a consoler, forces her to turn directly to Him. She is desperate to find any means to alleviate her loneliness.

Possibly, it is her dawning recognition of God's role in these events that motivates Jerusalem to turn directly to God. As noted, in Eikha 1:7, Jerusalem ignores the idea stated in verse 5, which links God's punitive acts with her sins ("For the Lord made her grieve because of the greatness of her transgressions"). Now that her sins have been exposed in greater detail (1:8–9), she turns to God with a newfound understanding of His involvement. It is a gradual awakening; in our verse, she has not yet acknowledged her own guilt. At this stage, she still regards the evil of the enemy as the center of the calamity wrought by God, "Look, Lord, at my affliction, for the enemy is exalted!" We will see that in her next direct plea to God (1:11), Jerusalem will turn inward, another step in the slow, inexorable movement toward admission of her culpability.

God's Hidden Face

Jerusalem appeals to God to look at her and her misery, and to note the success of her adversaries. Until now, the word *raah* described the enemies' mocking and invasive gaze (verses 7 and 8). Conversely, now Jerusalem endeavors to draw God's empathetic attention to her sorry state.

Jerusalem's entreaty implies that God is not presently looking at Jerusalem. God's purposeful disregard of His nation is presented in Deuteronomy as the foreseen penalty for their idolatrous practices:[112]

> And the Lord said to Moses, "You are going to lie with your forefathers and this nation will rise up and whore after the gods of foreign lands...and he will forsake Me and violate My covenant that I have made with him. My anger will be kindled against him on that day, and I will abandon them, and **I will hide my face** from them. He will be as prey and many troubles and travails will find him. He will say on that day, 'Is it not because my God is not in my midst that these troubles have found me?' Yet **I will surely hide My face** on that day because of all the evil that he has done, for he turned to other gods." (Deut. 31:16–18)

The ominous day has arrived.[113] God has turned His face away from Israel, rendering Him both inaccessible and seemingly unconcerned

---

112. See also Deuteronomy 32:20.
113. Jeremiah also warns of this consequence, informing the people that God will scatter them among the enemies and show them His nape rather than His "face" (Jer. 18:17). Isaiah notes that this dire consequence came to fruition; God indeed hid His face from the people during the Babylonian exile (Is. 54:8; 64:6). See also Ezekiel 39:23.

with Israel's fate. This triggers Jerusalem's desperate plea: "Look, Lord, at my affliction!"

The minimal request, that God should "look and see" His nation, becomes a leitmotif of the book.[114] With the exception of chapter 4, every chapter contains this entreaty to God.[115] Before the nation can beg God to restore its fortunes, it must reestablish the foundations of communication with Him. The success of all further appeals rests upon whether God chooses to reinstate a relationship with Israel.

There may be a hidden benefit to God hiding His face from His nation. While the "face to face" relationship represents the ultimate aspiration of a religious person,[116] not everyone should aspire to this sort of intimacy. Living under God's scrutiny obliges humans to exercise utmost vigilance. When God gazes upon errant behavior, He responds with swift punishment, as noted by biblical verses that attribute punishment to God's direct gaze: "And I will set **My face** against that person."[117] Within this context, God's decision to turn His face away can be an act of charity, especially for a nation still steeped in sin.

Eikha 1:10–11

יָדוֹ פָּרַשׂ צָר
עַל כָּל־מַחֲמַדֶּיהָ

כִּי־רָאֲתָה גוֹיִם
בָּאוּ מִקְדָּשָׁהּ

אֲשֶׁר צִוִּיתָה
לֹא־יָבֹאוּ בַקָּהָל לָךְ

---

114. While 1:9 only asks God to "look" (*re'eh*), the complete phrase (*re'eh vehabita*) appears in 1:11.

115. In chapter 4, I will offer an explanation for this notable omission.

116. Moses realizes this sublime goal (Ex. 33:11; Deut. 34:10). It should be noted that God speaks to the entire nation at Sinai "face to face" (Deut. 5:4), thereby indicating that all Israel can attain this relationship.

117. Leviticus 20:3, 5; Ezekiel 14:8.

כָּל־עַמָּהּ נֶאֱנָחִים
מְבַקְשִׁים לֶחֶם

נָתְנוּ מַחֲמַדֵּיהֶם בְּאֹכֶל
לְהָשִׁיב נָפֶשׁ

רְאֵה ה' וְהַבִּיטָה
כִּי הָיִיתִי זוֹלֵלָה:

The adversary spread out his hand
Over all her precious delights

And she saw nations
Enter her Temple

About which You commanded
[Members] of Your congregation shall not enter[118]

Her entire nation groans
They seek bread

They exchanged their precious delights for food
To restore life

"Look, Lord, and see!
For I have become a glutton"

Jerusalem's breakthrough voice ceases just as suddenly as it emerged, and the narrator resumes his tale. Jerusalem's evocative plea seems to have affected the narrator. Instead of continuing his accusatory tone against the hapless city, he returns his attention to Jerusalem's suffering and to her enemy's brazenness.

---

118. I will discuss this translation below.

Ambiguous Language: *Yado Paras Tzar*

Verse 10 opens with the enemy's hand closing in on Jerusalem's precious delights. Recalling a similar phrase in verse 7, this appears to describe the greedy hand of a human enemy (Babylonia or her minions)[119] brandished against the city, seizing her precious objects (*mahamadeha*).

The enemy is not named, however, leaving open the possibility that this verse refers to the divine hand, commonly used to describe God's punishments and power.[120] The word *tzar* may not refer to the enemy at all, but can function as an adverb describing the manner in which a hand closes in "narrowly" (*tzar*) upon the treasures of Jerusalem. Perhaps the verse obscures the identity of the hand's owner in order to blur the distinction between God's hand and that of the enemy. Even if God does not actually wield the rod of punishment, He certainly guides the enemy's hand to punish His nation.[121]

At the conclusion of verse 10, the narrator directly addresses God ("You commanded"), in a bewildered bid to comprehend God's role in these events.[122] This direct address implicitly questions God's omnipotence: How is it possible that God did not prevent enemies from flouting His command and entering His hallowed precinct? Intimations of God's accountability likewise flutter and stir: How could God stand aside as evildoers defy His law?

---

119. Yevamot 16b (see also Rashi and Ibn Ezra on Eikha 1:10) asserts that this refers to the hands of Ammon and Moab. According to II Kings 24:2, Ammon and Moab were among the nations that invaded Judah alongside Babylonia. It is likely that Babylonia sent these surrounding nations to launch the assault, as they began their long march from Babylonia to Jerusalem. I will examine this approach below.

120. The Bible commonly refers anthropomorphically to God's "hand" to describe His power and actions (e.g., Ex. 9:3; Num. 11:23; Josh. 4:24).

121. See Isaiah 47:6. This does not absolve the conquerors of responsibility; God's accomplices undertake their role with enthusiasm, under the impression that their actions are of their own volition. See Isaiah 47:7, which describes the excessive cruelty of the Babylonian enemy, and their unwillingness to recognize that God commissions them to punish His nation. Isaiah contends with a similar situation in addressing the complicity of the divinely appointed Assyrian enemy; see Isaiah 10:5–19.

122. In this reading, the beginning of the verse describes God's hand in the third person, while at its conclusion the narrator turns to address God in the second person.

This shift into second person suggests prayer, as the speaker turns directly to God in his desperation. Jerusalem will again address God in second person briefly in verse 11 and will conclude the chapter with three verses directed toward God. This progression marks a growing boldness in addressing God, perhaps one that is born from an increased sense of isolation. It also marks a progression from an excessive focus on external enemies to a mounting recognition of God's role in these events.

Ambiguous Language: God's Command

> About which You commanded
> They shall not enter your congregation
> (*lo yavo'u vakahal lakh*)[123]

The translation above obscures the abstruseness of the sentence. What, in fact, did God command? Who is the subject of the words *lo yavo'u* ("they shall not enter")?

Some biblical interpreters understand this verse as a reference to Deuteronomy 23:4:[124]

> An Ammonite and a Moabite shall not enter (*lo yavo*) the congregation (*bikehal*) of the Lord. Even in the tenth generation, they shall not enter (*lo yavo*) the congregation of the Lord for eternity.

The phrase *lo yavo*, alongside the word *kahal*, congregation, forges a strong parallel between the verses. Observing the similarity between them, rabbinic interpreters explain that the verse in Eikha focuses on the Ammonites and Moabites, who have entered the Temple alongside the Babylonians:

> In the hour that enemies entered Jerusalem, Ammonites and Moabites entered with them, as it says (Eikha 1:10), "The adversary spread out his hand over all her precious delights, and she saw

---

123. I altered the translation from the one that I offered above in order to reflect the rabbinic interpretation examined below.
124. See Rashi and *Targum*, Eikha 1:10.

nations enter her Temple about whom You commanded, 'They shall not enter your congregation.'"[125] (Eikha Rabba Petiḥta 9)

A gemara offers a further elaboration of Ammon and Moab's heinous acts:

> R. Shemuel bar Naḥmani said in the name of R. Yonatan: About whom does it say, "The adversary spread out his hand over all her precious delights?" This is Ammon and Moab. When the idolaters entered the Sanctuary, everyone turned to the silver and gold, while [Ammon and Moab] turned to the Torah scrolls. They said, "[The scroll] in which it is written, 'An Ammonite and a Moabite shall not enter the congregation of the Lord,' must be burned in the fire." (Yevamot 16b)

In this rabbinic commentary, while the Babylonians concentrated on looting the Temple, the Ammonites and Moabites desecrated the holy Torah scrolls (the "precious delights" mentioned in the verse). According to some sources, this is the event that precipitates the final decree of destruction upon the Ammonites and Moabites (Zeph. 2:8).[126] This interpretation also explains the zeal of Israel's neighbors in joining the Babylonian enemy (II Kings 24:2). It shifts attention away from the contemporary enemy onto a more historic one, tapping into a rich and complex history of relations between Israel and her neighbors. The betrayal of Abraham's descendants by Lot's descendants is far greater and more painful than the impersonal conquest wrought by the voracious Babylonians.[127]

---

125. In this midrash, I translated Eikha 1:10 in accordance with the midrash's interpretation (but in contrast to my translation above).

126. Eikha Rabba Petiḥta 9, citing Ezekiel 25:8–11, adds a scenario in which Ammon and Moab see the cherubs in the Holy of Holies and mockingly accuse Israel of idolatry, thereby igniting God's wrath.

127. We will see something similar in Eikha 4:21–22, which reserves special anger for Edom, who also has a long-standing relationship with Israel (see also Ob. 1:10, 12). There will be no need for speculative interpretation there, as the verse explicitly names Edom as Israel's primary foe.

I have chosen a different direction for interpreting this verse. Despite the linguistic suggestiveness, there is no mention of the Ammonites or Moabites here or anywhere else in the book. While the rabbinic interpretation focuses on the identity of the nations who entered the Sanctuary, the translation that I propose above ("And she saw nations enter her Temple, about which You commanded [members] of Your congregation shall not enter") focuses on the *very act* of entering the Sanctuary. The holiness of the Temple disqualifies even members of God's holy congregation from entering. The wanton incursion of foreigners into this sacred site is another reminder of the desecration of the holy city, explaining the perplexity and outrage of those who witness it.

Jerusalem's Famine: Seeking Bread

Focusing for the first time on the misery of starvation, this depiction of hunger will reappear quite frequently in the book. The inclusive phrase *kol ammah*, "her entire nation," highlights the shared communal desperation that accompanies starvation. Absent sustenance, no one is more affluent than his neighbor; societal distinctions are leveled, everyone is hungry. Moreover, the value of material objects vanishes when there is no food for purchase;[128] everyone is eager to exchange valuable items for bread.

Ambiguous Language: Precious Delights (*Maḥamadeha*)

They exchanged their precious delights for food
To restore their lives

Verses 10 and 11 twice refer to Jerusalem's precious delights (*maḥamadim*). Previously (see the discussion of verse 7), I discussed several possibilities for identifying these *maḥamadim*. Based on biblical usage, this word could refer to the Temple, its valuable vessels, or human beings. To this varied list, rabbinic interpreters add the Torah scroll, as we have seen above.

---

128. See Ezekiel 7:19 and the less specific reference in Zephaniah 1:18. I will examine this further in Eikha 4:1.

The identity of the precious delights in verse 11 attains greater significance. Which *mahamadim* does Jerusalem offer in exchange for food? The words "to restore life" convey a desperate state. Jerusalem's inhabitants must undertake drastic measures to cope with the urgent situation. Did they sell the Temple vessels? Perhaps they peddled the sacred Torah scrolls in order to obtain sustenance?

Conceivably, this verse could allude to a more dreadful crime. If these precious delights refer to human beings, and presumably children, this may refer to the sale of the children on the slave market. Even more horrible is the possibility that this alludes to the cannibalism that we will witness in the continuation of the book. In this reading, Jerusalem's inhabitants *consume* their precious children "to restore life" (*lehashiv nafesh*). Ironically, Ruth 4:15 employs this very phrase (*meishiv nefesh*) to mean continuity through children. In our verse, the phrase may "justify" the consumption of children for short-term survival, while ignoring the way it precludes survival in the long term.

Jerusalem's Second Interjection: "Look, Lord, and See!"

The description of the nation using her precious delights for food precipitates Jerusalem's second brash intrusion into the narrator's monologue. This time, however, Jerusalem does not permit the narrator to resume his narrative. Instead, Jerusalem continues speaking (aside from one interruption) until the conclusion of the chapter.

Jerusalem's initial words depict her horror at herself, and at what she has become: "Look, Lord, and see, I have become *zolela*!" While the word *zolela*, similar to the word *zol*, may represent Jerusalem's cheapened value,[129] it can also refer to her gluttony (*zalal*).[130] In her heart-wrenching cry to God, Jerusalem recoils with self-recrimination over the manner in which starvation has transformed her. In what may

---

129. See Rasag and R. Yosef Kara, Eikha 1:11. See also Ibn Janach, *Sefer HaShorashim*, on the root *z.l.l*.

130. See Deuteronomy 21:20 and Ibn Ezra, Eikha 1:11. It is possible that the words *zol* and *zalal* are derivatives of the same strong two letter root (*z-l*), meaning worthless (as noted above in 1:8). According to BDB, *Lexicon*, 272–73, gluttony is the cheapening of the value of food, to the point that one squanders it.

be another allusion to cannibalism, Jerusalem has become a gluttonous consumer of her own children, a city that squanders her future.[131]

Jerusalem's second interjection is markedly different from her first. In verse 9, Jerusalem's entreaty to God ("Look, Lord, at my affliction, for the enemy is exalted!") is not self-reflective. There, Jerusalem remains focused on the enemy. Now she turns inward, focusing upon herself. While her first response fosters and reflects self-pity and turmoil, her subsequent, self-reflective address to God ("Look, Lord, and see, I have become *zolela!*") will eventually lead her to an entirely different conclusion. In this chapter's third and final direct appeal to God to look at her, Jerusalem will acknowledge that her misery is a consequence of her own rebellious behavior: "Look, Lord, for I am anguished; My insides churn, my heart turns over within me, for I have surely rebelled" (verse 20). By noting the progression of Jerusalem's direct appeals to God, we observe her slow and steady movement from self-centered suffering toward introspection, reconciliation with God, and assumption of responsibility.

PART 2 (EIKHA 1:11C–22): JERUSALEM'S ACCOUNT

Jerusalem's self-reflective words launch the second part of the chapter, in which she recounts her own tale in the first person. Using the word *hayiti*, she comments negatively on an essential aspect of her post-destruction self ("I have become a glutton"). Verse 1 opened the third-person account in a similar manner: twice using the word *hayeta* ("she has become"), verse 1 describes what Jerusalem has become following the calamity (a widow and a tributary). Here, Jerusalem asserts control over her narrative, offering us her own perspective on the events that have transformed her.

Eikha 1:12

לוֹא אֲלֵיכֶם כָּל־עֹבְרֵי דֶרֶךְ
הַבִּיטוּ וּרְאוּ

---

131. The spies of Numbers 13:32 describe Israel as a land that consumes its inhabitants, a negative depiction that requires interpretation (see also Lev. 26:38). Perhaps Jerusalem's gluttonous acts realize the negative vision of the spies.

אִם־יֵשׁ מַכְאוֹב כְּמַכְאֹבִי
אֲשֶׁר עוֹלַל לִי

אֲשֶׁר הוֹגָה ה'
בְּיוֹם חֲרוֹן אַפּוֹ

Not upon you, all you passersby[132]
Look and see!

Is there any pain like my pain
That has been committed against me?

When the Lord made me grieve
On the day of His burning anger

The second part of this chapter (verses 11c–22) features Jerusalem, who recounts her anguish in the first person (except for verse 17).

In the first part of the chapter, we observed Jerusalem from the outside, judging and censuring her. When she begins to speak, she springs to life, sharing the depths of her pain. We no longer regard her with disapproval; instead, we are party to her agony, experiencing it alongside her. In Jerusalem's direct plea to the passersby, "Look and see! Is there any pain like my pain?" she elicits the reader's attention, giving us pause to consider her suffering.

The introduction of Jerusalem's personal perspective shifts the narrative in other ways as well. In verse 5, the narrator balances his description of God's destructive role (*ki Hashem hoga*) with an explanatory statement that focuses on Israel's transgressions (*al rov pesha'eha*). Jerusalem uses a nearly identical phrase in verse 12 to describe God's harmful acts (*asher hoga Hashem*). However, Jerusalem follows this

---

132. Biblical interpreters generally understand this obscure phrase as an utterance of recoil tinged by horror, with the meaning, "That which was done to me should never happen to you!" See, for example, Eikha Rabba 1:40; Rashi and Ibn Ezra on Eikha 1:12. Sanhedrin 104b regards this phrase as a colloquial formula used to ward off danger from one's fellow.

description with the explanatory *beyom ḥaron apo*, "on the day of His great anger." Israel's sins do not play a role in Jerusalem's initial account. Instead, she claims that God's ire triggers His acts. Perhaps Jerusalem's misery obscures her ability to recognize the justness of God's action. Possibly she remains unconvinced that her sins warrant this terrible retribution, illustrating how difficult it is for Jerusalem to assume responsibility.

Jerusalem maintains that God singled her out for punishment. The word "me" (*li*) appears as a direct object of God's acts (*olal li*), hinting at this disquieting notion. A midrash regards Jerusalem's words as a complaint:

> "Look and see! Is there any pain like my pain?" He did not bring upon any nation what He brought upon me. He was not exacting from any nation in the way He was exacting with me! (Eikha Rabba [Buber] 1:3)[133]

The prophet Amos unabashedly asserts that God behaves in a more exacting fashion with His chosen nation:

> Listen to the word that the Lord spoke against you, children of Israel, upon the entire family that I brought up from Egypt, saying: Only *you* have I known from all the families upon the earth. Therefore, I will remember *you* for all your sins. (Amos 3:1–2)

God selected the children of Israel in order to cultivate a unique relationship with them. Chosenness entails both advantages and obligations. Closeness to God requires more vigilance; God expects more from those whom He nurtures and loves.[134]

The next few verses of Eikha contain an unflinching description of God's punishments. These expressions, while characteristic of Eikha

---

133. The citations of Eikha Rabba are generally taken from the Vilna edition of Eikha Rabba that appears in the Bar Ilan Responsa Project. On occasion, when the Vilna edition omits or abbreviates a central idea, I cite from Buber's edition of the Midrash.

134. See Ibn Ezra, Radak, and Malbim on Amos 3:2.

(and often found elsewhere in Tanakh), offer a harsh portrait of God. Taking a cue from the text, I will interpret these verses without sparing the reader, while attempting to grapple with some of the delicate issues that they raise.

Poetic Composition:
The Chiasm at the Center of the Chapter

Jerusalem addresses the passersby using the identical verbs that she used to address God in verse 11 ("look" [re'eh] and "see" [habita], in reverse order).

| Verse 11 | re'eh | vehabita |
| Verse 12 | habitu | ure'u |

This linguistic chiasm (AB BA), appearing in the center of chapter 1, draws the reader's attention to its central idea – Jerusalem's agonizing solitude.

Jerusalem's urgent plea to both God and passersby to relieve her loneliness highlights her desperate yearning for someone, *anyone*, to look her way. The chiasm also draws our attention to the absence of God's response. Jerusalem's first instinct is to turn to God, imploring Him to look her way and offer her respite from her wretched isolation (verse 11). God, however, does not appear to heed her cries. Therein lies the meaning of her address to the disinterested passersby in verse 12.[135] The significance of their identity lies in their very insignificance; these passersby are no one in particular. In her misery, Jerusalem grabs hold of the nearest person, begging for some sympathy, for a supportive glance, for some assurance that she is not utterly alone. Yet, from them as well, no response is forthcoming. Jerusalem remains miserably alone.

Eikha 1:13–15

מִמָּרוֹם שָׁלַח־אֵשׁ בְּעַצְמֹתַי
וַיִּרְדֶּנָּה

---

135. For another example of the usage of the passersby in this way, see Job 21:29.

פָּרַשׂ רֶשֶׁת לְרַגְלַי
הֱשִׁיבַנִי אָחוֹר

נְתָנַנִי שֹׁמֵמָה
כָּל־הַיּוֹם דָּוָה

נִשְׂקַד עַל פְּשָׁעַי בְּיָדוֹ
יִשְׂתָּרְגוּ

עָלוּ עַל־צַוָּארִי
הִכְשִׁיל כֹּחִי

נְתָנַנִי אֲדֹנָי
בִּידֵי לֹא־אוּכַל קוּם

סִלָּה כָל־אַבִּירַי
אֲדֹנָי בְּקִרְבִּי

קָרָא עָלַי מוֹעֵד
לִשְׁבֹּר בַּחוּרָי

גַּת דָּרַךְ אֲדֹנָי
לִבְתוּלַת בַּת־יְהוּדָה

From up high He sent fire in my bones
And it overpowered her[136]

---

136. The verb *vayirdena* contains multiple difficulties, rendering it impossible to translate with certainty. Its subject is unclear, with some (e.g., Ibn Ezra) suggesting it is the fire (referred to here in the masculine, as in Job 20:26), while others assume that it is God (see the Greek and Syriac *Targumim* and R. Yosef Kara). It is also difficult to identify the object that is overpowered. Although it could be Jerusalem, it seems unlikely that amidst a first-person description, Jerusalem suddenly refers to herself in the third person. Following Rashi and R. Yosef Kara, Y. Moshkovitz, "*Eikha*," in *Daat Mikra: Five Megillot* (Jerusalem: Mossad Harav Kook, 1990), 6 [Hebrew], suggests that the object is the bones referred to at the beginning of the sentence. The root of the verb is likewise uncertain. Interpreters (e.g., Rashi, Ibn Ezra, R. Yosef Kara) generally accept that the root of the word *vayirdena* is r.d.h., meaning to rule or

He spread a net for my feet
Sent me reeling backwards

He placed me in desolation
The entire day [I am] faint

My transgressions were twisted into a yoke in His hands
They became entangled[137]

They were lifted upon my neck
Made my strength fail

The Lord has placed me
In the hands [of those before whom] I cannot rise.

[God] trampled all my warriors [138]
In my midst

---

subjugate (see BDB, *Lexicon*, 921). Rashi also suggests the homonym *r.d.h.* (to scrape out; Judges 14:9), meaning to eviscerate. Possibly, this verb relates to the word *r.d.d.*, meaning to beat down or crush. It is uncommon to use any of these verbs to describe the effects of fire. Despite the linguistic distinction, the word *vayirdena* maintains a wordplay with the root *y.r.d.*, which signifies a downward movement (see the translation of NJPS and R. Alter, *The Hebrew Bible: A Translation with Commentary – The Writings* [New York: W. W. Norton, 2019], 650). This coheres well with the general downward movement depicted throughout the chapter.

137. Most interpreters assume that the word *yistargu* is related to the word *sarig*, meaning a vine. The verbal form of the word denotes the way the vines grow intertwined.

138. *Silla* is an active verb describing what God did to the warriors of Jerusalem. Rashi and Ibn Ezra explain the word to mean trample (from the root *s.l.l.*). A cognate word would be *mesila*, denoting a road that people traverse (e.g., Is. 11:16; 62:10). This explanation coheres well with the end of the verse, in which God treads on Judah as if she is in a winepress, although it renders the verse somewhat repetitive. Possibly, the verb *silla* relates to the word *solela*, meaning a piled-up mound (e.g., Jer. 50:26) or siege ramp (*solelot* in Jer. 32:24). In this reading, God piles up the bodies of Jerusalem's warriors, allowing the enemy entrance into the walled city. In Jeremiah 50:26, a similar verb evokes harvest (Hillers, 74, and Renkema, 168), mirroring the winepress image at the end of the verse. In this context, the verse recalls plentiful food, even as it depicts scenes from a besieged city.

> **He called against me an appointed time**
> **To break my young men**
>
> **The Lord stamped like a winepress**
> **On maiden daughter of Judah**

Turning her attention to God, Jerusalem describes the day of God's anger. Richly drawn metaphors impart the variety and force of these torments. First, God sends a fire from His heavenly abode, which penetrates Jerusalem's bones and overpowers the city. God spreads a metaphoric net for Jerusalem's feet, causing her to retreat.[139] He twists Jerusalem's transgressions into a thick rope,[140] and places it around her neck like a yoke, draining the city of its potency. Like a winepress, God tramples upon Jerusalem, squeezing out its vigor, as wine bleeds

---

139. God often spreads a net to punish sinners (Jer. 50:24; Ezek. 12:13; 17:20; 19:8; 32:3; Hos. 7:12; Ps. 94:13). On the flip side, God props up the feet of those who are loyal to Him (I Sam. 2:9; Ps. 18:34).

140. The difficulty of properly translating the *hapax legomenon* (singular word) *niskad* (which I have translated as "twisted," based on the context) constitutes one of the primary challenges in understanding this difficult verse. In his commentary on this verse, Ibn Caspi despairingly asks: "And how can we prophesy when we find a root and word once in all of the holy books?" He offers a possible suggestion for the word *niskad* ("to cleave"), but quickly retreats from this interpretation, admitting that it is not necessarily a correct reading.

Some interpreters offer a slightly different orthography of the word, writing it with a *shin* instead of a *sin*. (See Eikha Rabba 1:42, which may regard this as a wordplay, rather than an orthographic emendation.) The word *nishkad* with a *shin* means to pay attention, generally with the intent of punishment (see, e.g., Jer. 1:12). In other words, "God took notice of my weighty sins in His hand," a reading in which God's actions are preceded by His measured observations and premeditated decision to punish. The Greek translation has this reading, also rereading the word *ol* (yoke) as *al*, a preposition indicating that God pays attention to the sins. Rashi appears to remove the letter *sin* from the root, suggesting that the root is *n.k.d.*, meaning marked. He posits that God marks Jerusalem's sins, remembering them and administering retribution. The Aramaic *Targum* translates the word as "heavy," which seems to both switch the order of the letters and change its consonants: *niksha*, rather than *nishkad*. The breadth and variety of explanations make it nearly impossible to offer a definitive translation.

out of grapes. Depleted of her strength, Jerusalem collapses, without energy to rise.[141]

In the span of just three verses, God employs a wide range of punitive actions – scorching, trapping, choking, and crushing the people. The afflicted city retreats, languishes, and falls, battered mercilessly from all directions.

God's acts seem premeditated; nets suggest foresight and planning. Moreover, verse 15 depicts God planning the events in advance, by designating an appointed time (*mo'ed*)[142] to break Jerusalem's young strong men.

God's Responsibility for Jerusalem's Destruction

The description of Jerusalem's afflictions evokes the typical way enemies conquer and destroy a city. They set fire to the buildings, capture the inhabitants, place a yoke on their necks, kill the young strong men, and trample on the ruins of the razed city. In Jerusalem's account, the human intermediary vanishes; Jerusalem identifies God as the sole agent of her destruction.

Events that the narrator had previously attributed to human agency reappear in Jerusalem's description, in which she shifts the responsibility to God. In contrast to the narrator's account, Jerusalem maintains that *God* causes Jerusalem's desolation,[143] her failing strength,[144] her downward fall,[145] and the abuse of her young people.[146] Even Jerusalem's recoiling backwards, previously (in verse 8) ascribed to her own self-loathing, is here recast as God's doing (verse 13). The word *paras*, earlier used to describe the enemy's hand closing in on Jerusalem

---

141. The meter of the final sentence of 1:14 (2 + 3) recalls the meter that I discussed in 1:7 and 9, in which the second half of the sentence is metrically longer than the first. This uncommon meter weighs down the sentence, metrically conveying the heaviness that prevents Jerusalem from rising.

142. There is a bitter irony in using the word *mo'ed*, which evokes the appointed time to serve God (Eikha 1:4). This emphasizes the dramatic reversal that has taken place. We will encounter this again in Eikha 2:7.

143. Compare the word *shomema* in verses 4 and 13.

144. Compare the word *ko'aḥ* in verses 6 and 14.

145. Compare verses 7, 9, and 14.

146. Compare verses 5 and 15.

(verse 10), now refers to God carefully spreading the net that ensnares Jerusalem's feet (verse 13).

God's torment of Jerusalem linguistically (and ironically) recalls the ideal biblical relationship, in which God protects Israel from these selfsame travails and uses them instead to punish her enemies. Rather than spreading a net to trip Jerusalem, in Psalms 25:15 and 31:5 God delivers individuals from the nets that entrap them. In Isaiah 9:3 and Jeremiah 2:20, God breaks the yoke that has been placed on Israel, instead of twisting a yoke around her neck. Similarly, elsewhere God uses fire to destroy Israel's adversaries (e.g., Amos 1:3–2:5; Ezek. 39:6), sends Israel's enemies reeling backward (Ps. 9:4; 56:10), and crushes Israel's foes by stomping on them like a winepress (Is. 63:3; Joel 4:13). The day of God's anger is often depicted as one of punishment for Israel's enemies (e.g., Is. 13:13; Ps. 110:5).[147] The protective relationship between God and His nation breaks down as God wields His standard punishments against His own nation.

It is particularly noteworthy (and unsettling) that Jerusalem does not address God directly in this passage; she does not implore Him to rectify the situation. Instead, Jerusalem speaks about God in the third person, underscoring the alienation that prevails between them.

Despite Jerusalem's tone of outrage (and her difficulty in assuming responsibility, as noted previously),[148] there is one glimmer of self-accountability. God weakens Jerusalem by winding a twisted rope around her neck. This cord is constructed of Jerusalem's transgressions (*pesha'ai*); had she been blameless, God would not have had the means to manufacture the instrument of torture. In fact, *pesha* is the very word omitted by Jerusalem in verse 12. Although Jerusalem does not prop-

---

147. Prophets often warned that God's day of anger will negatively affect a sinful Israel as well. See, for example, Zephaniah 2:2–3. In a particularly poignant moment, Amos 5:18 lambasts those who yearn for the day of God, erroneously assuming that they will not be caught up in the punishment. For more on the topic of the day of God's anger, see our discussion of Eikha 2:1.

148. By calling the city in 1:15 "*betulat bat Yehuda*" (literally, "virgin daughter Judah"), Jerusalem implicitly rejects the accusation of the city's promiscuous behavior, perhaps even tendering a subtle protestation of innocence.

erly confess, her description of this cord of twisted sins gives us pause to consider its implications. The ruined city may well suffer beyond reason, but she cannot pretend to be entirely innocent of sin. Jerusalem moves steadily toward the goal of this chapter: admission of sinfulness.

Grapes of Wrath

The metaphor of God trampling on Judah like grapes in a winepress is vivid and violent, evoking in addition spilled blood. It also recalls similar metaphoric language used to describe the punishment of Israel's enemies. Isaiah 63:1–6 employs this image to depict God crushing Edom like one tramples on grapes in a winepress; Edom's red blood splatters, soiling the environs.[149] Similarly, Joel 4:13 describes a winepress overflowing with the blood of unnamed nations, the enemies of Israel. Now, Israel experiences a stunning blow, as God directs against her the punishments He had previously aimed at her enemies.

The wine image, however, also recalls more promising biblical metaphors. Biblical passages often liken Israel to a grapevine, a vineyard, or grapes; the following passage uses this metaphor to describe the manner in which Israel strikes roots in her land:[150]

> You transmitted a vine from Egypt, You expelled nations and You planted her.[151] You cleared her way, and You gave her roots, and she filled the land. Her shade covered the mountains and her branches, [were like] the cedars of God. You conducted her fruits until the sea, and her produce until the river. (Ps. 80:9–12)

Israel's comparison to a vine contains several layers of meaning. The vineyard produces wine, a highly desirable product. It has a regal association and may suggest Israel's princely status among nations. It is also associated specifically with Judah (Gen. 49:11), the kingship tribe whose

---

149. Isaiah 63 employs wordplay with the word Edom and the orthographically identical word for the color red (*adom*). See also Gen. 25:25, 30.

150. This is one of the dominant images of the Song of Songs, where the bucolic vineyards and the resulting wine surface repeatedly. See also Hosea 9:10. Leviticus Rabba 36:2 develops at great length the metaphor of the nation of Israel as a vineyard.

151. The word for vine (*gefen*) is feminine in Hebrew.

ancestral land produces grapes. Although the image of grapes crushed in the winepress is undoubtedly punitive, it implicitly recalls hopeful times, a noble nation.

Wine intoxicates, and while it can bring joy (Ps. 104:15) and foster a higher plane of consciousness, it often reduces humans to a state of crudeness and impropriety.[152] In fact, the vineyard contains the potential to produce greatness or baseness, nobility or vulgarity. Thus, the idyllic vineyard image easily becomes negative, and prophets bemoan the way the metaphoric vineyard betrays its owner. Despite favorable conditions and God's tireless labor on behalf of His vineyard (Israel), the vines sometimes produce inferior fruit:[153]

> My Beloved had a vineyard in Keren Ben Shemen. And He plowed it and He removed the stones from it, and He planted a choice vine in it. And He built a tower inside of it and He hewed out a vat in it. He had hoped to produce grapes, but it produced sour grapes... What shall I do more for My vineyard that I did not do for it? Why did I hope to produce grapes and it produced sour grapes? (Is. 5:1–4)

> And I planted a choice vine, an altogether faithful seed. How did you turn before Me into a corrupted foreign vine? (Jer. 2:21)

To punish the faithless vineyard, God dismantles its protective barriers, allowing the enemies to trample the vine and consume her fruits (Is. 5:5; Ps. 80:13–14). In Eikha 1:15, God Himself tramples Judah in a winepress.

Nevertheless, the trampling of grapes may also be interpreted positively. In a winepress, the process of making wine involves stepping carefully on the ripened grapes, thereby releasing the red liquid without crushing the seeds. Rather than wanton, unmediated violence, this image may suggest a careful balance of delicacy and power. God tramples Judah, administering a severe punishment

---

152. See, for example, Hosea 4:11; Isaiah 28:7–8. The negative results of the vineyard that Noah plants hints at its dangers (see Gen. 9:20–24).

153. See also Hosea 10:1; Ezekiel 19:10–14.

on the day of His anger. Nevertheless, it may be a measured act, designed not to crush the people entirely. Isaiah's prophecy hints at a similar idea:

> So says the Lord: Just as you find wine in every grape cluster, and you say, "Do not destroy it, for there is a blessing in it!" so I will do for my servants, [and I will] not destroy everything! (Is. 65:8)

When viewed within its broader biblical context, the metaphor in which God crushes Israel like grapes recalls the vineyard that God planted in the land, the hopes that it will produce fine grapes, and the bid to construct a regal society. One may also recall the poignant plea of Psalms 80, expressing the hope that God will return to favor His beloved vine:

> God of hosts! Return please, and look from the heavens and see, and remember this vine! (Ps. 80:15)

Eikha 1:16

עַל־אֵלֶּה אֲנִי בוֹכִיָּה
עֵינִי עֵינִי יֹרְדָה מַּיִם

כִּי־רָחַק מִמֶּנִּי מְנַחֵם
מֵשִׁיב נַפְשִׁי

הָיוּ בָנַי שׁוֹמֵמִים
כִּי גָבַר אוֹיֵב:

**Over these I weep
My eyes, my eyes, they flow with water**

**For a comforter is far from me
A restorer of my soul**

My sons became desolate
For the enemy has overcome

This verse concludes the first stage of Jerusalem's first-person account (1:11c–16). Wrapping up her tale, Jerusalem describes her weeping eyes, recalling the nocturnal tears of verse 2. The twice-repeated word *eini* (my eye) has several possible functions; each word may refer to one of her eyes (*Targum*),[154] or the repetition may seek to convey the torrential, ceaseless flow of tears (Rashi).

Following the tears, the chapter describes Jerusalem's loneliness, linking it to her weeping.[155] In the absence of a consoler, Jerusalem cannot quiet her sobs; she has no one who can relieve her pain or restore her morale. The absence of social support increases her misery, preventing her from moving toward recovery.

Al Eileh (Over These)

Over what does Jerusalem weep? She is surely referring to the previous verses, in which she describes the nation's suffering in torturous detail. Possibly, the word "these" also refer to the continuation of the verse, in which Jerusalem describes her desolate sons and the triumphant enemy.

A midrash focuses on the word *eileh*, suggesting that it refers to activities associated with the robust functioning of the religious and political institutions in Jerusalem:

> *Over these, I weep* ... R. Neḥemia said: Over the abolishment of the priesthood and the monarchy. This is as it says, "These (*eileh*) are the two sons [anointed by] oil who serve the master of all the land" (Zech. 4:14). They are Aaron and David. R. Yehoshua ben Levi says: Over the abolishment of Torah, as it says, "These

---

154. Because the word appears twice in succession, seemingly referring to both eyes, I have taken the liberty of translating both words in plural (my eyes), despite the singular form of the word (*eini*).

155. See verse 2, where her tears remain undried on her cheeks because she lacks a comforter (*menaḥem*). The theme of the elusive comforter (*menaḥem*) appears in our verse as well, alongside the description of her copious tears.

(*eileh*) are the statues and laws" (Deut. 12:1)... Zavdi ben Levi said: Over the abolishment of sacrifices, as it says, "These (*eileh*) shall you do for the Lord on your festivals" (Num. 29:39). The Sages said: Over the abolishment of the [priestly] shifts. (Eikha Rabba 1:51)

An alternate interpretation suggests that Jerusalem weeps not over her loss, but over the sins that led to her misfortune:

Over these I weep... R. Samuel bar Naḥmani said: Over idolatry, as it says, "These (*eileh*) are your gods Israel" (Ex. 32:4). (Eikha Rabba 1:51)

In this midrash, Jerusalem's words hint at the stirring of confession, in which the city assumes responsibility for her suffering. Though she tacitly acknowledges her sins in describing the rope woven with her transgressions (Eikha 1:14), Jerusalem mostly shirks responsibility in her initial first-person tale of woe (Eikha 1:11–16). This midrash anticipates the next part of the chapter (1:18–22), in which Jerusalem will admit her transgressions, expressing shame at her betrayal of God.

Eikha 1:17

פֵּרְשָׂה צִיּוֹן בְּיָדֶיהָ
אֵין מְנַחֵם לָהּ

צִוָּה ה׳ לְיַעֲקֹב
סְבִיבָיו צָרָיו

הָיְתָה יְרוּשָׁלִַם
לְנִדָּה בֵּינֵיהֶם

Zion spreads out with her hands
There is no comforter for her

> The Lord commanded against Jacob
> That around him shall be adversaries
>
> Jerusalem has become
> Like a menstruant among them

Jerusalem's first-person account in verses 11c–16 concluded with a tone of resigned hopelessness. Her cascading tears are no balm for her boundless grief, and a comforter remains elusive. Jerusalem's initial perception of the enemy's victory ("for the enemy is exalted," Eikha 1:9) intensifies with the description of the enemy's decisive triumph in verse 16 ("for the enemy has overcome"). Unable to continue, Jerusalem falls silent; her despair overtakes the narrative.

The narrator enters to fill Jerusalem's silence. Third person replaces first person for the duration of this one verse. Having drawn a tormented conclusion ("for the enemy has overcome!"), Jerusalem seems to have nothing left to say. Yet the narrator's speech induces Jerusalem to shake off her impotence and recognize her guilt. The narrator's words in verse 17 lead to the following verse, in which a chastened Jerusalem confesses her sins: "The Lord is righteous, for I have rebelled against His word!" (Eikha 1:18).

How do the narrator's words move Jerusalem to recognize God's righteousness and her own culpability?

To understand this, we will begin by examining Zion's obscure gesture, in which she "spreads out with her hands" (*peresa Zion beyadeha*).[156] To whom is this gesture directed and what does it mean?[157] Commentators submit a broad range of interpretations: Zion may be

---

156. The phrase *"paras yad"* appears in Eikha 1:10 to describe the enemy's hand looting the precious delights of Jerusalem. Westermann, 113, observes that Eikha 1:10 is an anomaly; nowhere else does the image of the spreading hand convey a hostile act. In an ironic twist, Jerusalem's desperate act in verse 17 mirrors the rampant violations of the enemy in verse 10.

157. One of the basic limitations of interpreting ancient texts lies in comprehending their cultural references. When it comes to the meaning of physical gestures, biblical interpreters engage in a good deal of speculation, most of which remains unsubstantiated.

expressing anguish,[158] attempting to call for help,[159] surrendering to God's punishment,[160] or illustrating her loneliness.[161]

The word *paras* alongside the word *yad* (hand) may indicate prayer. Isaiah 1:15 uses the phrase *paras kapayim* (spread hands) to describe a gesture of prayer. If that is the intended meaning, then Zion's prayer is futile; the verse continues by declaring that there is no one to console her. God certainly does not respond positively to Zion's gesture. Instead, He commands Jacob's enemies to surround Jerusalem, an overtly hostile response to Jerusalem's supplication.

Possibly, this phrase evokes prayer in an ironic fashion. Zion may stretch out her hands in a familiar gesture of prayer, but she does not turn to God. Instead, in a betrayal of God, Zion directs her desperate plea toward other nations, issuing a desperate but futile call for assistance.[162] This explains the continuation of the verse, which illustrates God's punitive response to Zion's misdirected pleas – God commands surrounding nations to respond with hostility to Jacob, and this confers pariah status upon Jerusalem. Subtly, this verse explains the justness of the situation: If only Jerusalem had properly turned to God in prayer, the events could have unfolded differently!

Poetic Composition: Jerusalem's Isolation

To highlight the city's isolation, this verse contrasts Jerusalem with those outside of her. The first half of each of the three sentences focuses on Israel (Zion, Jacob, or Jerusalem), while the second half turns its attention to outsiders, who could potentially lend support, sympathy, or aid to the troubled city.

---

158. Rashi tenders two interpretations, both of which construe this gesture as an expression of anguish. Based on Isaiah 25:11, he explains that the phrase *paras yad* depicts the grief-stricken way a sufferer waves his arms. Alternatively, Rashi suggests that this describes someone who squeezes his hands together so tightly that they nearly break.

159. Eikha Rabba 1:17.

160. Ibid. 1:52.

161. *Pesikta Zutrata*, Eikha 1:17, focuses on the word *beyadeha*, with her hands, explaining that Zion has to construct her own mourning carpets with her hands, because of the absence of comforters.

162. Moshkovitz, 8, explains the verse this way.

Zion speads out with her hands
    There is **no comforter** for her
The Lord commanded against **Jacob**
    That around him shall be **adversaries**
Jerusalem has become
    Like a menstruant among **them**

The response of outsiders ranges from inattention to antagonism to disgust; no foreign nation offers the much-needed empathy or assistance. Orchestrated by God, there seems to be little recourse for Judah's loneliness.

Nevertheless, God's command suggests His continued involvement in Jerusalem's fate. Although God deliberately surrounds Israel with threatening enemies, in terms of the sentence structure, God remains on Israel's side. The only appearance of God's name in the verse appears in the first half of the second sentence, as God punishes Jacob, indicating His ongoing personal association with His city.

Midrashim often emphasize the above idea, insisting that God's punishment does not spell rejection, and that God continues to dwell amidst Israel even when the nation is rife with impurities:

> A heretic said to R. Ḥanina: Now you are an impure people, for it is written, "Her impurities were on her hems" (Eikha 1:9). He responded to him: Go and see what it says there [about God]: "Who dwells with them in the midst of their impurities" (Lev. 16:16). Even at a time when they are impure, the divine presence dwells among them. (Yoma 56b–57a)

According to several rabbinic sources, God even accompanies His nation into exile, a sure indication of His enduring commitment to Israel.[163]

---

163. This idea is found in many midrashim. Note, for example, the poignant conversation between Jeremiah and God in Eikha Rabba *Petiḥta* 34, in which they discuss which one of them will be more effective in accompanying the nation into exile. See also Megilla 29a.

Perhaps it is the subtle presence of God alongside Israel that allows Jerusalem to resume her first-person account, reconcile with God, and declare His righteousness.

God's Commands

This verse contains God's second command (*tziva*) in this chapter. In verse 10, Jerusalem recalls God's former ban on the nations entering the Temple (*tzivita*). This indicated better times, when God's directives preserved the sanctity of the Temple, especially against foreign nations. In contrast, our verse portrays God commanding the nations to cultivate enmity against Israel.

By alluding to God's edict, verse 17 refocuses Jerusalem's attention on God. The vision of the triumphant enemies silenced her in the previous verse, and the narrator now steers her back to the pertinent topic: her relationship with God. This verse compels Jerusalem to rethink the question: Why did God orchestrate Jerusalem's downfall?

From this point until the end of the chapter (1:18–22), Jerusalem will focus the greater part of her attention on God. While she does refer both to the nations (1:19) and to her enemies (1:21–22), Jerusalem's human relationships are no longer her primary concern. She reopens her speech by mentioning God's righteousness (1:18) and closes it with three verses that directly address God (1:20–22).

Jerusalem the *Nidda* (Menstruant)

Maintaining that Jerusalem has become like a *nidda* (a menstruant) among the nations, this verse returns to the familiar metaphor of Jerusalem as a woman (widow, bereaved mother, or exposed woman). What is the meaning of the specific imagery of Jerusalem as a menstruant?

Menstruation represents a period of ritual impurity (*tuma*). Prophets sometimes employ this image as a metaphor for moral and religious defilement, especially in the land of Israel.[164] Ezra describes a land filled with idolatry, prior to Israel's conquest:

---

164. The prophets do not mean that menstruating women are religiously or morally corrupt; this is rather a metaphor used to describe impurity.

> The land ... is a ritually impure [literally, menstruant] land (*eretz nidda*), due to the impurities (*nidat*) of the nations of the lands, and their abominations with which they, in their impurities, filled it from one end to the other. (Ezra 9:11)

Ezekiel offers a similar description:

> The house of Israel sits on its land and they defile it with their ways and their deeds; their ways were like the impurities of the menstruant before Me. (Ezek. 36:17)

Our verse, however, employs the metaphor not to describe Jerusalem's sins, but rather her punishment of isolation. We find a similar usage in Ezekiel:

> And they put on their beautiful adornments in arrogance, and they made their abominable images and repulsive [idolatry]; therefore, I have made them like a menstruant. (Ezek. 7:20)

By weaving together Israel's abominable (impure) acts and God's decision to render her in a state of *nidda*, Ezekiel suggests that God repays her measure for measure. Impure activities beget treatment as one who is impure.

The ritual state of menstruation evokes isolation, since during that period married couples separate and refrain from physical contact (Lev. 18:19).[165] In our verse, the word *nidda* indicates Jerusalem's isolation; nations refrain from any contact with her. This image coheres well with the overarching theme of the chapter, which emphasizes Jerusalem's loneliness.

---

165. The separation of married couples during the woman's menstruation is not a punishment. Berlin, 58, notes that the menstruant is not a social outcast: "The Bible does not separate a menstruant from her family or from society." A menstruant woman may be an apt metaphor for isolation, but in a metaphor, not every aspect of the compared situations is necessarily parallel.

Even though the primary meaning of Jerusalem's *nidda* status in our verse relates to her isolation from other nations, the menstruant language recalls this chapter's theme of God's spousal relationship with Israel, now characterized by alienation. In his commentary on Ezekiel 36:17, Radak maintains that the *nidda* imagery points to a situation in which God distances Himself from Israel, precluding intimacy:

> *Like the impurity of the menstruant.* Because by way of a parable, the community of Israel is called God's wife, and He is her husband. During the period of sinfulness, [Israel] is likened to a menstruant, in which the husband is distant all the days of her menstruation and draws her near again after she becomes ritually pure. Likewise did God distance Israel and exile them to the lands of the nations because of their sins. In the future, He will return them, after they return to Him and purify themselves from their sins. (Radak, Ezek. 36:17)

Implicit within this idea is a measure of optimism, since the ritually impure period of menstruation is temporary.

> R. Yehuda said in the name of Rav: "[Therefore] she has become a *nida*."[166] This is a blessing. Just as the menstruant will become permissible [to her husband], so Jerusalem will again become permissible. (Taanit 20a)

God has sent Israel into exile, far from His dwelling place, because of her moral and religious impurities. A great blow to the relationship between God and His nation, this punishment precludes continued intimacy. Nevertheless, this is not a permanent state. Israel can renew the relationship by casting away its impurities. Reconciliation is not

---

166. This gemara interprets the word *nida* in Eikha 1:8 as referring to a menstruant. As noted previously, the word *nida* there does not have a diacritical mark in the *dalet* and therefore the simple meaning of the word appears more likely related to the root *n.o.d.*, meaning to wander.

elusive; the disruption of relations is provisional, wholly dependent upon Israel's behavior.

Eikha 1:18–19

צַדִּיק הוּא ה׳
כִּי פִיהוּ מָרִיתִי

שִׁמְעוּ־נָא כָל הָעַמִּים
וּרְאוּ מַכְאֹבִי

בְּתוּלֹתַי וּבַחוּרַי
הָלְכוּ בַשֶּׁבִי

קָרָאתִי לַמְאַהֲבַי
הֵמָּה רִמּוּנִי

כֹּהֲנַי וּזְקֵנַי
בָּעִיר גָּוָעוּ

כִּי־בִקְשׁוּ אֹכֶל לָמוֹ
וְיָשִׁיבוּ אֶת־ נַפְשָׁם

The Lord is righteous
For I have rebelled against His word

Listen, please, all nations!
And see my pain

My maidens and youth
Have gone into captivity

I called to my lovers
They deceived me

My priests and elders
Expired in the city

For they sought food for themselves
To restore their lives

Jerusalem resumes her account following the narrator's interjection, which appears to have triggered a remarkable transformation. Proclaiming that God is righteous, Jerusalem assumes responsibility for the situation, admitting that she has rebelled against God's word.

Following this admission, Jerusalem turns to address the nations, entreating them to hear her words and see her sons and daughters who have gone into captivity. Why is she so determined that the nations become participants in her tragedy?

Perhaps, once again, Jerusalem looks for someone, *any*one, to relieve her loneliness. As she notes, her children have gone into captivity and she is desolate and aggrieved. Even an outsider's attention can help relieve Jerusalem's unbearable isolation.

Possibly, Jerusalem turns to the nations in order to educate them. She calls on all the nations (*kol haamim*)[167] to witness God's righteousness and internalize the consequences of rebellion against God.[168] Addressed in this neutral way, these nations do not appear to be Jerusalem's enemies, but rather the potential recipients of the universal message of the Bible. In this schema, even during her great disaster, Jerusalem remains mindful of her role toward the nations.[169]

---

167. See similarly Micah 1:2. While some biblical interpreters (e.g., Radak, Malbim) understand Micah's address to the "nations, all of them," as a reference to the different tribes of Israel, the simple meaning is that Micah's prophecy contains a universal message, addressed to all of the nations of the world. See also Psalms 49:2, in which the similar opening of the psalm ("Listen to this, all of the nations!") prepares the reader for its universal message.

168. See Ibn Ezra on Eikha 1:18.

169. Isaiah, for example, describes Israel as "a light unto the nations"; see Isaiah 42:6, 49:6.

However, it is also possible that Jerusalem turns to the nations in reproach, to denounce them for their role in the disaster. At the beginning of the verse, Jerusalem admirably shifts the fault from God onto herself. She may not intend, however, to shoulder all the responsibility; her speech to the nations may indicate that Jerusalem lays partial blame for the situation upon them. Babylonia, of course, is directly accountable for Jerusalem's destruction. But there were also nations who allied themselves with the Babylonians, and others who were Jerusalem's erstwhile allies yet failed to come to her aid. In demanding that all the nations observe her pain and behold her children forcibly marching into exile, Jerusalem compels them to recognize their role in her calamity.

The following verse (1:19) opens with the description of unnamed loved ones (*me'ahavai*) who deceive Jerusalem. Are these loved ones the same anonymous nations from the previous verse? Perhaps Jerusalem now describes former political allies who have betrayed her, abandoning Jerusalem's notables to a miserable death from starvation.[170] The nature of the deception also remains unspecific. Have these loved ones actively betrayed Jerusalem, allying themselves with her enemies and revealing her confidences? Or have they simply left her plea unanswered, a passive betrayal of unfulfilled promises?[171]

Despite the possibility cited above, the word *me'ahavai* ("loved ones") appears to allude to an emotional connection between Jerusalem and her addressee. The intimacy of the reference suggests that Jerusalem has called to her citizens, who have deceived her.[172] The nature of this betrayal is less clear. Perhaps it refers to the intransigent sinfulness of the populace – an indirect betrayal to be sure, but one that is no less responsible for the ultimate collapse of the city.

---

170. Ibn Ezra understands the syntax of the verse differently. Reversing the order of the verse, he explains that because Jerusalem's usual advisors (priests and elders) died from starvation, she turned to outsiders, who then betrayed her.

171. See R. Yosef Kara, Eikha 1:19.

172. See, similarly, the above discussion on the word *ohaveha* in Eikha 1:2. Several midrashim (e.g., Eikha Rabba 1:54) suggest that the word *me'ahavai* refers to the prophets, false or otherwise. This also recalls one of the possible interpretations of Eikha 1:2.

These two verses retain several themes that echo previous verses. These include Jerusalem's request that outsiders see her pain (1:12), the exile of her children (1:5), the betrayal of her loved ones (1:2), and her desperate quest for food to survive ("to restore life," 1:11). Taken together, these repeated themes convey Jerusalem's loneliness and the certainty of her utter demise. Without food, she has no present; without children, she has no future.

Eikha 1:20–22

רְאֵה ה' כִּי־צַר־לִי
מֵעַי חֳמַרְמָרוּ

נֶהְפַּךְ לִבִּי בְּקִרְבִּי
כִּי מָרוֹ מָרִיתִי

מִחוּץ שִׁכְּלָה־חֶרֶב
בַּבַּיִת כַּמָּוֶת

שָׁמְעוּ כִּי נֶאֱנָחָה אָנִי
אֵין מְנַחֵם לִי

כָּל־אֹיְבַי שָׁמְעוּ רָעָתִי שָׂשׂוּ
כִּי אַתָּה עָשִׂיתָ

הֵבֵאתָ יוֹם־קָרָאתָ
וְיִהְיוּ כָמוֹנִי

תָּבֹא כָל־רָעָתָם לְפָנֶיךָ
וְעוֹלֵל לָמוֹ

כַּאֲשֶׁר עוֹלַלְתָּ לִי
עַל כָּל־פְּשָׁעָי

כִּי־רַבּוֹת אַנְחֹתַי
וְלִבִּי דַוָּי

Look, Lord, for I am anguished
My insides churn

My heart turns over within me
For I have surely rebelled

Outside the sword kills
Inside the house is death

They have heard that I groan
There is no comforter for me

All my enemies heard of my troubles and rejoiced
For You have done it

Bring the day you called for
And let them be like me

Let all their evil come before You
And do to them

As You have done to me
Because of all my transgressions

For my groans are many
And my heart is miserable

As the chapter nears its conclusion, Jerusalem issues an emotional second-person appeal to God, referring to herself with the personal pronoun *ani*, and to God with the personal pronoun *ata*. The bid to reconnect on a personal level illustrates Jerusalem's hope that she can reignite her relationship with God.

Jerusalem begins with a request: "*Look*, Lord, for I am anguished!" This is the third time in this chapter that lonely Jerusalem begs God to observe her (*re'eh*) in her wretchedness. Recalling verses 9 and 11, this stark request vividly illustrates Israel's feelings of abandonment.

God no longer looks at the nation; He has disengaged from their lives. Nevertheless, this may be more than a mere request for attention. Jerusalem seeks to end the period of God's punitive alienation, in which He "hides His face" from Israel. This would pave the way for repairing the frayed relationship. Moreover, God is merciful and kind; if He would only look at Jerusalem, He would surely take action to rehabilitate her and restore justice to the world.

Jerusalem's request contains a refreshing perspective. She does not ask God to look (*re'eh*) at her physical suffering, but rather to bear witness to her internal suffering, her shame, the pain that she has caused to herself by her behavior. Self-realization entails a newfound maturity, and Jerusalem develops into a more mature persona at the conclusion of the chapter.

Siege and Starvation

In verse 20, Jerusalem is metaphorically described as a physical body, whose innards churn and heart turns over in response to the crisis. These movements suggest heightened emotions, but they also convey the physical upheaval in Jerusalem. Her churning innards and overturned heart allude to the city's crumbling and collapse.[173]

A stark phrase (just five words in the Hebrew), "Outside the sword kills; inside the house is death," underscores the sense of looming and inescapable death.[174] Exiting their houses, Jerusalem's inhabitants encounter death by the enemy's sword. An unspecified death, presumably starvation[175] or plague,[176] vanquishes those who remain in their houses.

---

173. Rasag, Eikha 1:20, suggests that the churning of the innards describes the agonies of starvation.

174. This phrase echoes both the song of *Haazinu* (Deut. 32:25) and several prophetic forewarnings (Jer. 14:18; Ezek. 7:15). A similar phrase appears in the Sumerian *Lamentation over the Destruction of Sumer and Ur* (ANET, 618, lines 403–404): "Ur – inside it is death, outside it is death. Inside it, we die of famine, outside of it we are killed by the weapons of the Elamites."

175. See Jeremiah 14:18 and Ezekiel 7:15. See also Ibn Ezra, Eikha 1:21.

176. See, again, Ezekiel 7:15.

The house may refer more generally to the besieged city. In this schema, the death inside the house refers to the starvation that afflicts the besieged residents, while the outside implies surrender to the enemy that has surrounded it.[177] This coheres well with the description of the city in the previous verse, where residents die as they scrounge for food (1:19). Practically, however, there is little difference between the readings. In either case, Jerusalem turns to God in desperation and misery, anticipating imminent, ineluctable death.

Call for Vengeance

Eikha does not often look toward the future, concentrating instead on the trials of the present.[178] This may be one reason that Israel rarely beseeches God to change its fortune in Eikha. The penultimate verse of the book petitions God quite generally to "renew our days like [days] of old!" However, throughout the book, there is no request to return the captives from exile, to rebuild Jerusalem or the Temple, or to restore Israel's autonomy or monarchy. The nation seems reluctant to ask for anything beyond the first step of restoring communication with God, beseeching Him to pay attention, and to look and see His suffering nation.

One request for action weaves throughout the book, appearing as the resounding conclusion of this chapter. That is the call for God to take vengeance upon Israel's enemies.[179] This entreaty entails a quest for justice. It indicates an abiding confidence in God's omnipotence, alongside the belief that God desires the restoration of justice in the world. Less optimistically, this paltry request suggests Jerusalem's inability to ask God to remedy her own fate. In focusing outward, Jerusalem deflects attention away from her sinfulness, appealing to God to turn His eye instead to the evils of the enemies.

---

177. Berlin, 60, citing Ezekiel 7:15 (and Jeremiah 14:18) as proof texts. Nevertheless, the similar phrase in Deuteronomy 32:25 seems to imply that it refers to the actual house.
178. Rashbam, Eikha 1:1, notes this.
179. In his commentary on Eikha 3:66, R. Yosef Kara states that every chapter concludes with a call for vengeance against the enemies. See also Cohn, *Textual Tapestries*, 209–210. Strikingly, chapter 5 has no concluding plea for revenge, which apparently is due to the unique nature of that concluding chapter.

The mocking jeers of the enemies surfaced in verse 7, and their inexplicable success was the subject of verse 10. The problem of the wicked who prosper confounds and torments the suffering nation,[180] who again encounter the enemies' gloating at Israel's downfall in verse 21. This propels the nation to appeal to God for retribution.[181]

Interestingly, according to verse 21, the source of the enemies' schadenfreude is their understanding that *God* has brought punishment upon Jerusalem.[182] God, who had invariably protected Jerusalem, now crushes her, a fact that produces inordinate satisfaction for Israel's enemies.[183] By recalling that God wrought these events, Jerusalem somewhat ironically shifts the blame from the enemy back to God. Despite this, Jerusalem entreats God to bring vengeance upon these enemies, thereby proclaiming her abiding confidence in God's justice and commitment to punishing Israel's evil adversaries.[184]

The Final Sigh

Despite the positive developments examined above, chapter 1 concludes with a deep sigh of pain: "For my groans are many and my heart is miserable." Nothing in this chapter alleviates Jerusalem's pain. Admission of guilt only increases her shame, and the protracted plea for vengeance (spread out over two verses) compounds the sense that the quest for justice remains elusive.

---

180. See Ibn Ezra, Eikha 1:22.

181. The call for vengeance against evildoers, even those whom God commissions to punish Israel (e.g., Is. 10:5–12; 47:7), is a familiar element in biblical texts. See, for example, Psalms 22:4; 74:18–23; 79:6, 12; 83:14–18.

182. Based on Eikha Rabba 1:56, Rashi reads the words "for You have done it" as an accusation against God for originally separating Israel from the nations, thereby sowing the seeds of their enmity.

183. From the perspective of the enemies, Israel's situation may imply God's rejection of His nation. This idea is revived in Christianity's theological doctrine of supersessionism, in which the destruction of the Second Temple proves that God rejected the Jewish people, choosing the Christian community instead.

184. The word *raah* (evil) appears twice in these verses. Once it describes the evil wrought against Israel – namely, her sufferings and tribulations. The second usage depicts the evils of the enemies – namely, their brutality and cruelties. This parallel deployment of the word *raah* implies that the evils of the enemy are the cause of Israel's troubles, and must be dealt with as the priority.

As our chapter concludes, the word *rabbot* (indicating Jerusalem's abundant groans) recalls the intricate movements of the chapter. Its dual appearance in the opening verse conveys both the former multitudes of Jerusalem's inhabitants (*rabbati am*) and its previous princely status among the nations (*rabbati vagoyyim*). In a devastating twist of fortune, the same word in verse 3 describes the heavy labor (*rov avoda*) that Judah currently suffers in exile. Later in the chapter (1:5), this word conveys Jerusalem's copious sins (*rov pesha'eha*), which prompt God's punishment. The chapter closes with Jerusalem's profuse groans (*rabbot anhotai*), an audible response to the progression from prominence to pain, from sinfulness to destruction.

The Frame of Jerusalem's Account (1:11c–22)

The close of Jerusalem's narration (verses 18–22) parallels the launch of her speech (verses 11c–12) in a manner that highlights her stunning transformation.

Jerusalem opens her first-person account by addressing both God and the nations in a bid to alleviate her terrible isolation. She first petitions God in verse 11 to look and see her (*re'eh vehabita*). Immediately following this appeal, in verse 12, Jerusalem hails the passersby requesting that they look and see (*vehabitu ure'u*) her terrible pain (*makhov kemakhovi*). Addressing the passersby, Jerusalem identifies God as the perpetrator who has caused her pain on the day of His great anger. The passersby appear to be the only hope for alleviating Jerusalem's anguished loneliness.

When Jerusalem recovers her speech (following the narrator's interjection in verse 17), she again addresses both the nations and God (but in the opposite order). She appeals first (in verse 18) to the nations to listen to her and look at her pain (*re'u makhovi*). In contrast to her earlier address to the nations, here Jerusalem speaks of God's righteousness and her own rebelliousness (*mariti*). Jerusalem then turns to God (in verse 20), asking Him to look (*re'eh*) at her misery. This time, however, her misery is a product of her own rebelliousness (*ki maro mariti*), rather than God's erratic anger.

The frame of Jerusalem's first-person account (1:11c–22) forms a chiastic structure:

A: Verse 11– Look and see, **God!**

B: Verse 12 – See and look, **passersby**, at my pain!

B': Verses 18–19 – Listen and look, **nations**, at my pain!

A': Verses 20–22 – Look and see, **God!**

The contrast between Jerusalem at the beginning and the end of her speech is striking. Jerusalem has gradually reconciled to her own accountability, shifting blame from God onto herself. Moreover, the switch of the order in which Jerusalem addresses the nations and God illustrates Jerusalem's change in mindset. If at the outset of the chapter, the random passersby function as Jerusalem's final resort, at the chapter's conclusion, God is the final hope, the ultimate address for human supplication.

Several linguistic reversals between the opening of Jerusalem's first-person speech and its end further illustrate this contrast. At the outset, Jerusalem attributed God's punitive actions to indiscriminate divine wrath (1:12): "Is there any pain like my pain, that has been committed against me (*asher olal li*), when God made me grieve on the day of His burning anger?" By the end of the chapter, Jerusalem refers to God's punitive actions differently, acknowledging her own transgressions (1:22): "Do to them as You have done to me (*kaasher olalta li*) because of all my transgressions!"

Eikha 1:12 does not explain why God made Israel grieve (*asher hoga Hashem*), noting simply that this occurred on the day of God's anger. This verse disregards Eikha 1:5, which explains that God made Israel grieve (*ki Hashem hoga*) due to her great transgressions (*al rov pesha'eha*). By omitting any reason for God's fierce anger, Eikha 1:12 conveys a sense of injustice, reflecting her incomprehension of God's rage. In the concluding verse, Jerusalem evokes the transgressions noted in Eikha 1:5 but omitted from Eikha 1:12: "Do to them as You have done to me because of all my transgressions (*al kol pesha'ai*)!" At the end of the chapter, Jerusalem readily assumes responsibility, concluding with a clear pronouncement of God's justice.

CHAPTER ONE: IN SUMMATION

Although its alphabetic structure suggests order, the first chapter of Eikha is thematically haphazard. The chapter explores a range of topics, including Jerusalem's tears, the exile of her population, the groans and sorrow of the sufferers, the success and mockery of the enemies, the desecration of the Temple, the starvation of the population, and the inescapable, ever-looming certainty of death. The dizzying shifts between past and present, inside the city and outside, the Judean population and her friends, her lovers, and her enemies, is overwhelming and slightly bewildering. More disquieting are the different portraits of God in this chapter, compounded by the changing perspectives regarding Israel's culpability. The chapter features Israel's transgressions, pivots to focus on God's rage, then returns to Israel's sinfulness. Pronouncements of Israel's sins are juxtaposed alongside God's angry acts of violence, hurled mercilessly against the city. The chapter's turbulence and inconsistencies seem to epitomize Jerusalem's crisis; a formerly ordered world flounders as the nation hovers on the brink of cataclysm.

Nonetheless, a semblance of order emerges from the interchange of speakers in the chapter, creating a dialogue between the objective narrator in the first half of the chapter and Jerusalem in the second half. In reading the narrator's account, we remain distant from Jerusalem; although we empathize with her grief, we share the narrator's impartial judgments as he denounces her sins. In the second half of the chapter Jerusalem's voice breaks through, jarring the reader with her torrential tears, her raw pain, and her outrage at God's intemperance. These two separate movements lend the chapter thematic continuity and progression.

Each of these sections progresses ineluctably toward admission of sinfulness, a central motif of the chapter. The objective narrator arrives at sinfulness more easily, progressing briskly to this conclusion (verses 5, 8–9). Unsurprisingly, Jerusalem requires more time to internalize her sin. At first, she surmises that the enemy is the putative source of her misery (verse 9). Soon after, Jerusalem turns her attention to God, bemoaning His active role in her calamity (verse 12). Describing her suffering as the product of God's anger (verses 12–16), she dodges the guilty verdict hurled against her in verses 8–9. It requires the prompting of the narrator in verse 17 to propel Jerusalem to a final admission of guilt (verses 18–22).

One theme in particular holds this chapter together. Maintaining a consistently forlorn tone, chapter 1 features the loneliness of Jerusalem as she laments her departed populace. Ceaseless groans (verses 4, 8, 11, 21, 22) convey her grief, alongside five variations of the phrase "she has no comforter/helper" (verses 2, 7, 16, 17, 21). The word *shomem*, meaning desolate, appears twice (verses 4, 16),[185] while the word *maḥamadim* (precious delights) appears three times (verses 7, 10, 11) in the context of loss, underscoring Jerusalem's emptiness. Words that designate the negative, *ein* (verses 2, 7, 9, 17, 21) and *lo* (verses 3, 9, 10, 14, and twice in verse 6), reverberate throughout the chapter, focusing on what is absent from the city.

Ideas and themes repeatedly highlight Jerusalem's desolation. The city sits alone, and tears remain on her cheeks as she sobs in the night (verse 2). Zion's roads remain deserted, and they mourn the absence of pilgrims (verse 4). Jerusalem has fallen to the enemies, who have removed the city's splendor and inhabitants (verses 3, 6). Jerusalem's friends prove to be unreliable (verse 2), and her neighbors hostile (verse 17); even her loved ones do not answer her desperate call (verses 2, 19). Those who once respected Jerusalem now scorn her (verse 8), and the ritual impurity of the *nidda* surfaces as an apt metaphor for the city's solitary state.

Jerusalem's isolation finds singular expression at the center of the chapter (verses 11–12), where we encounter a linguistic chiasm (AB-BA). Jerusalem's desperate and futile entreaty to God that He observe her (*re'eh* [A] *vehabita* [B]), meets with silence and triggers her frenzied search for someone to notice her pain. Alighting upon some random passersby, she frantically seizes them, begging them to see her plight (*habitu* [B] *ure'u* [A]).

While highlighting Jerusalem's eerie emptiness – the absence of people, of loud sounds, of the city's characteristic hustle and bustle – the chapter largely disregards the destruction itself. It eschews any description of the demolition of the city and Temple,[186] the siege of the inhabitants,

---

185. The *Targum* on 1:21 adds the word "desolate" to verse 21: "May you summon against them that they may be made desolate like me."
186. Verse 10 briefly recounts the enemy entering the Temple and perhaps plundering it as well.

and the sounds and sights of Jerusalem's conquest.[187] This quiet chapter instead focuses primarily on the immediate aftermath of that conquest, registering the plaintive tones of horror as the city raises its head from the ashes to inspect the ruins. Anger is mostly absent;[188] shock and dismay prevail. Moans and quiet sobs thrum in the background, a symphony of desolation, a loud crash of silence.

---

187. One possible exception may be verses 13–15, which use metaphoric language to describe God tormenting Jerusalem with fire and nets, weakening the city and crushing her young men. Moreover, the laconic phrase in verse 20 seems to allude to the siege. However, the portrayal of the destruction remains muted, especially when compared to chapter 2.

188. As part of the exception noted in the previous footnote, verse 12 alludes to God's anger, a heated emotion that precedes the portrayal of God tormenting the city in verses 13–15.

Chapter One, Appendix 1

A Chiastic Structure

Although the structure of chapter 1 is not obvious, it appears to exhibit a chiastic pattern, buried within its carefully placed language. Revealing this pattern will yield some deeper meanings of the chapter.

As noted in the chapter on biblical poetry, a chiasm is a literary device that involves a crosswise composition of concepts or words, repeated in reverse order (A-B-C-C'-B'-A'). Genesis 9:6 offers a compelling example of a tightly arranged chiastic structure:

A	B	C	C'	B'	A'

Shofekh dam haadam   baadam damo yishafekh

He who **spills** the **blood** of a **human**,   by a **human** his **blood** will be **spilled**

Chiastic patterns do not always appear in such proximity. They are sometimes spread out over the course of a chapter or a narrative unit.[1]

---

1. Of course, as the spread of these structures gets wider, scholars regard their existence with increasing skepticism. See J. Berman, "Criteria for Establishing Chiastic Structure: Lamentations 1 and 2 as Test Case," *Maarav* 21:1–2 (2014), 57–58. See

To what end does the Tanakh construct its narrative and poetry in a chiastic structure? Chiasms appear in various ways and with various objectives. As we see in the example above, a literary unit may utilize a cyclical design to accentuate the concept of reward and punishment. Chiasms also draw attention to the parallels in a composition, prodding the reader to seek the meaning of the corresponding parts. At times, the chiastic structure forms a concentric design, in which the parts revolve around a central axis (A-B-C-B'-A'), highlighting its epicenter.[2] Chiasms create a cyclical structure, rather than a linear one. This type of composition can suggest that there is no exit from the situation at hand, no way forward.

The alphabetic design of Eikha chapter 1 reveals a consciously constructed unit.[3] By comparing the language of the verses in reverse order (first verse to last verse, second verse to penultimate verse, etc.), the chapter progresses incrementally toward its pivotal center.[4] Scholars have posited several variations of a chiastic structure for chapter 1, based on words and phrases that appear in each parallel set of verses.[5]

---

also J. W. Welch, "Criteria for Identifying and Evaluating the Presence of Chiasmus," *Journal of Book of Mormon Studies* 4:2 (1995), 1–14.

2. As noted in the chapter above, "Biblical Poetry and the Book of Eikha" (and I will further develop this idea in the final chapter of this book), the overall structure of Eikha is shaped in a concentric chiasm, designed to direct the reader's attention to its middle chapter.

3. See A. Condamin, "Symmetrical Repetitions in Lamentations, Chapters I and II," *JTS* (1905), 137–40; J. Renkema, "The Literary Structure of Lamentations [I]," in *The Structural Analysis of Biblical and Canaanite Poetry*, W. van de Meer and J. C. de Moor, eds. (Sheffield: Sheffield Academic Press, 1988), 295–97; House, 340–42.

4. I have noted the significance of the internal chiasm that lies at the center of chapter 1 (in verses 11–12). See also Renkema, "Literary Structure," 297.

5. I have not adopted the chiastic structure proposed by any one scholar, choosing instead to represent the correspondences that appear to me most persuasive. Scholars who present a chiastic design of chapter 1 include Cohn, *Literary Character*, 165 [Hebrew]; Moshkovitz, *Eikha*, 7–8; Berman, "Criteria," 64.

1 – *rabbati*
   2 – *ein la menaḥem*
     3 – *bein hameitzarim*
       4 – *kohaneha*
         5 – *halekhu shevi*
           6 – *Zion*
             7 – *tzar*
               8 – *kol*
                 9 – *God*
                   10 – **paras** *tzar*
                     11 – *re'eh vehabita*
                     12 – *habitu ure'u*
                   13 – **paras** *reshet*
                 14 – *God*
               15 – *kol*
             16 – *oyev*
            17 – *Zion*
         18 – *halekhu vashevi*
       19 – *kohanai*
     20 – *ki* **tzar** *li*
   21 – *ein menaḥem li*
22 – *rabbot*

This structure comprises some weaker associations and some more persuasive ones.[6] Some of the linked words and phrases seem common[7] or

---

6. Note that verses 7 and 16 contain a word-pair rather than the identical word (*tzar* and *oyev*, both words that mean "enemy"). See Renkema, "Literary Structure," 296, who suggests this parallel. Alternatively, A. Demsky, *Literacy in Ancient Israel* (Jerusalem: Magnes, 2012), 272–75 [Hebrew], suggests that the phrase *oniya umerudeha* (verse 7) corresponds to the phrase *eini yoreda* (verse 16) in terms of its alliteration.

7. As noted by Berman ("Criteria," 64), verses 8 and 15 contain the parallel word *kol*, although this word appears with high frequency in the chapter (sixteen times!). Moshkovitz (8) suggests a thematic parallel between verses 8 and 15, observing that they both contain a patent reference to Jerusalem's femininity. Verses 9 and

appear elsewhere in the chapter,[8] rendering the correspondence between the two parts not unique. Nevertheless, the broader framework unveils a remarkable design, one that seems deliberately woven into the artistic format of the chapter.[9]

This structure highlights two critical ideas. First, its cyclical design allows us to grasp the endlessness of Jerusalem's suffering. There is no way out of this relentless rotation of anguish. The chapter opens and closes with similar misery, with the absence of a consoler, and with a particular focus on the suffering of the priests. At its beginning, the chapter portrays the children going into captivity, and the very same dreadful image appears at its end. The chiastic structure casts a spotlight on the interminable pain of the fallen city, navigating the reader around a cyclical course that never moves forward and never arrives at any destination.

The concentric structure also draws attention to the chapter's center, the inner chiasm that lies at its focal point. We have already examined this inner chiasm, which features Jerusalem's repeated evocative outcry, "Look (*re'eh*) and see (*habita*)!" directed both to God and to the unlucky passersby. At the heart of this chapter, we encounter Jerusalem's desperate isolation, centrally located to highlight its pivotal role.

---

14 share a reference to God, albeit using different names (see Renkema, "Literary Structure," 294), but Berman ("Criteria," 67) notes that in the variant found in Qumran (4QLam), the identical name of God appears in these verses. All of the less persuasive examples (from a lexical viewpoint) appear in the correspondence between verses 7–9 and 14–16. For this reason, Condamin (*Lamentations*, 137–40) omitted these verses in his original presentation of this chapter's symmetrical structure.

8. The phrase "*ein menaḥem*," for example, appears in five variations in the chapter (see also verses 9, 16, 17), and not exclusively in the linked verses 2 and 21.

9. In his treatment of chapter 2, Berman ("Criteria," 61–63) persuasively argues that the concentrated presence of lexical correspondence in the chapter is unusual, and therefore significant. In contrast, when you search for a similar correspondence in chapters 3–4 of the book, you find only two possible pairs of congruent lexical elements in each chapter, even if you consider the most common words, such as *al* or *lo*.

Chapter One, Appendix 2

The Word *"Eikha"*

T he plaintive cry *"Eikha!"* – an elongated form of the interrogatory *eikh* ("How?") – opens chapters 1, 2, and 4. This word marks the chapters as lamentations, which open with a rhetorical question expressing incredulity, pain, and outrage.[1]

Isaiah employs the word *eikha* in his censure of Jerusalem, linking these biblical passages:[2]

---

1. Other laments use the shortened version of the interrogatory *eikh* to ask their rhetorical questions. David laments the deaths of Saul and Jonathan in II Samuel 1 by repeating three times, "How (*eikh*) have the mighty fallen!"

    The word *eikh* also appears in laments over cities. For example, Ezekiel 26:17 cites the eulogy that will be uttered after the destruction of Tyre: "How (*eikh*) you have been destroyed... this oft-praised city?" Zephaniah 2:15 cries over an unspecified city, "How (*eikh*) has [the city] become desolate?" Jeremiah 48:17 cites the lament of Moab's associates over her destruction: "How (*eikha*) has the strong staff been broken, the glorious rod?"

2. The association between these passages finds expression in liturgical practices. For example, the *haftara* read in most communities on the Shabbat preceding the fast of Tisha Be'Av (when Eikha is read) includes Isaiah 1:21. Megilla 31b suggests that the *haftara* read on Tisha Be'Av itself should open with Isaiah 1:21 (although most communities follow the second suggestion of the gemara, reading a passage that opens with Jeremiah 8:13).

> How (*eikha*) has she become a harlot, this faithful city? I filled
> her with justice, and righteousness dwelled there, and now [there
> dwell] murderers! (Is. 1:21)

Functioning as rebuke as well as lament, the word *eikha* may always
contain elements of both. Isaiah laments Jerusalem's fallen state, even
as he castigates her betrayal of God. Eikha's lament over Jerusalem
contains a strain of rebuke, suggesting that Jerusalem maintains some
responsibility for her calamity. The following midrash, commenting on
Eikha 1:1, notes this:

> R. Yehuda said: "*Eikha*" is a phrase of reproach, as it says, "How
> (*eikha*) has she become a harlot!" (Is. 1:21). (Eikha Zuta [Buber] 1:1)

Another midrash cites R. Yehuda's position as part of a debate regarding
the nature of the word *eikha* in Tanakh:

> R. Yehuda said: "*Eikha*" is a phrase of reproach, as it says, "How
> (*eikha*) can you say, 'We are wise and the Lord's instructions
> are with us?'" (Jer. 8:8). R. Nechemia said: "*Eikha*" is a phrase
> of lament, as it says, "And the Lord God called to Adam and he
> said to him, 'Where are you (*ayeka*)?'" (Gen. 3:9), [meaning,]
> "Woe to you (*oy lekha*)!" (Eikha Rabba 1:1)

Although R. Yehuda offers a different proof text in this midrash, he
again observes that the word *eikha* recalls prophetic rebukes. Perhaps
R. Yehuda means to suggest that God punishes in order to reproach,
offering an educational response to wayward behavior.

R. Nechemia disagrees with R. Yehuda, maintaining that the word
eikha signifies lament. Oddly, however, R. Nechemia chooses a proof
text from God's probing question to Adam following his sin. In fact,
God's reproachful query to Adam seems to constitute better evidence
for R. Yehuda's position. This verse is moreover an odd choice, given
that God's question to Adam is not *eikha* (how?), but *ayeka* (where are
you?). Orthographically, the consonants are identical, but the vowels
render these words significantly different. R. Nechemia's attempt to parse

the word *ayeka* into two words that express grief (*"oy lekha!"*, "woe to you!") is creative, but far from the simple meaning of the word. These implausible proofs indicate that R. Nechemia is willing to sacrifice the simple meaning in order to communicate a crucial idea. His reading suggests that even when God reprimands, He is actually expressing a lament. God's love for His people (and for Adam) is so pervasive that all His rebukes are laced with sorrow.

R. Nechemia's reference to Adam's sin also hints to a broader parallel between the story of Adam in the Garden of Eden (closeness to God, followed by sin and expulsion) and the story of the nation of Israel in its land (closeness to God, followed by sin and expulsion). I will explore this idea in Eikha 2:6.

Eikha: Chapter Two

Destruction and Anger

INTRODUCTION

Chapter 2 opens by offering the reader a vivid account of the obliteration of the city. Raucous forces hammer Jerusalem, methodically demolishing her magnificent buildings and fortified infrastructure. Despite its violence, the first part of the chapter maintains order; this is not a chaotic account but a systematic one. The alphabetic arrangement parallels the carefully designed execution of God's wrath.

Synonyms play a critical role in sketching the portrait of God's demolition. Verbs pour forth, creating a rhythmic tale of unrelenting destruction. Each sentence presents God administering a different sort of blow: God hurls and swallows, destroys and violates, chops and consumes, aims His bow and kills, wrecks and spurns. God strikes at each of Jerusalem's structures: her fortresses, buildings, palaces, and protective barriers. Divine wrath does not spare even His own house. The significance of the demolition of the Temple is indicated by the various appellations accorded it in this chapter, conveying its many facets and functions: "glory of Israel," "His footstool," "His hut (*sukko*)," "His appointed place," "His altar," "His Temple," "House of the Lord."

Chapter 2 returns repeatedly to Israel's plunging descent to the ground. The word *aretz* (earth) functions as a key word of the chapter, appearing eight times.[1] Fortresses collapse upon *the earth* (2:2) and *the earth* swallows Jerusalem's gates (2:9). Elders sit *on the earth* in mourning alongside young maidens who lower their heads *to the earth* in grief (2:10). Jerusalem spills her innards *on the earth* (2:11) while young and old lie dead *on the earth* in the streets of Jerusalem (2:21). Structures and inhabitants share the same fate. Sinking down to the ground in hapless mourning, they spill out their vitality, readying themselves for death and interment. Jerusalem's spiraling descent humbles her; towering structures and people crash to the earth, lying crumpled, degraded, and depleted of their former heights.[2]

The chapter unambiguously identifies God as the perpetrator of the destruction. Synonyms describe God's anger: He unleashes divine fury, wrath, rage, and ire (*apo, ḥori af, ḥamato, zaam*) upon His sacred city. God's wrath frames the chapter,[3] a consuming fire that incinerates its environs. Yet the chapter does not describe capricious divine action. God lays careful plans to destroy Zion's walls; spreading out a measuring line (verse 8), God proceeds to obliterate the city.

The chapter's presentation of God as the "enemy" is both unusual and deeply unsettling.[4] Initially, the narrator seems reluctant to present God as an enemy. Instead, the chapter depicts God withdrawing His right arm and allowing the enemy unfettered access to destroy Jerusalem (verse 3). Though its implications are terrifying enough, this description does not adequately convey the full force of His involvement. In the next

---

1. Seven of these depict the collapse and destruction of the city and her inhabitants. Once (2:15), the word *eretz* accompanies a remembrance of Jerusalem's former status, in which she was "a joy for all the land (*haaretz*)."
2. Prophets often describe high towers, buildings, or lofty trees as a metaphor for human arrogance. Hubris invariably leads to downfall, as both punishment and theological instruction. See Isaiah 2:9–22; Amos 2:9; Obadiah 1:3–4. See also II Chronicles 26:9–10, 15–16, where Uzziah's impressive building projects lead to his arrogance (termed a "high" heart).
3. See the reference to the day of God's anger in 2:1 and again in 2:21–22.
4. The portrayal of God as enemy is exceedingly uncommon in the Bible, appearing only in Isaiah 63:10, and perhaps also in Job 16:9, where Job appears to refer to God as "my adversary." I will discuss these passages when we examine Eikha 2:4. In several passages (e.g., Job 13:24; 19:11; 33:10), Job reverses this idea, asking why God considers *him* an enemy.

verse (verse 4), God transforms into the veritable enemy, positioning His potent right arm to strike. Eikha offers the reader an unexpected thunderbolt, an insight into the trauma and horror of humans who confront divine ferocity.

In chapter 2, destruction often focuses on the leadership, rather than on the general populace. Having failed in their task to guide the nation, kings, officers, prophets, and priests seem to bear the brunt of God's anger (verses 2, 6, 9).[5] The resultant dearth of religious and political leadership produces confusion. Order disappears along with a sense of security; God's instructions dwindle away, and guidance remains elusive (verse 9).

The focus on the leaders somewhat exonerates the general populace. Without effective supervision, how can anyone expect satisfactory religious performance from the laypeople? This chapter considers the possibility that Judah suffers an undeserved fate, an implication that emerges from other themes in the chapter as well. The dominant image of chapter 2 is the suffering and death of Jerusalem's young children, an unfathomable tragedy that precludes any suggestion of culpability. The tidy reconciliation of chapter 1, which concludes with Jerusalem's confident proclamation of God's righteousness (1:18), breaks down when we encounter the misery of the guiltless children.

The narrator's depiction of God's fury seems to reflect the latent human anger that simmers unabated throughout the presentation of the city's destruction. Jerusalem's outrage finally explodes at the conclusion of the chapter, where she turns against God in direct accusation (verses 20–22).

In this chapter, God's wrath is not balanced by an enumeration of Israel's sins, which appears nowhere in the first part of the chapter (and is significantly muted in the second half). Jerusalem herself never admits sinfulness. Lacking explanation or context for God's anger, the chapter maintains a tone of incomprehension. Nothing could properly explain

---

5. God measures the leaders by a different standard, having tasked them with the burden of guiding the nation toward proper religious observance. The failure of the leaders stands apart from that of the nation, and prophets often treat it separately from the deficiencies of the general society. See, for example, Jeremiah 22–23; Ezekiel 34.

the intensity and brutality that characterizes the assault on Jerusalem. The shame of chapter 1 has faded; this chapter considers only the trauma of the assault. In chapter 2, Jerusalem never reaches out to reconcile with God, remaining instead in her posture of outraged bewilderment, unabashed in her defiance and anger.

STRUCTURE

Chapter 2 is structurally like the previous one. Both chapters employ the identical opening word, *eikha*, signifying a lamentation, a rhetorical question that expresses incomprehension and pain. Both chapters consist of verses that contain three sentences.[6] Like chapter 1, chapter 2 is written in an acrostic; each subsequent verse begins with the successive letter of the alphabet.[7]

At first glance, the overall structure of the chapter likewise appears similar. The first half of chapter 2 (verses 1–10) relates its account of Jerusalem in an objective, third-person narration. Verse 11 shifts into the first person, offering a subjective report of Jerusalem's suffering, accompanied by a meaningful change in the tenor of the account.[8] However, unlike chapter 1 (verses 9, 11), no interruption occurs during the course of the narrator's report; Jerusalem does not offer her version until the narrator has finished. This suggests a neater tale, in which the chapter allots ample and equal time to each side to offer an account of the catastrophe.

Nevertheless, it is not quite so simple. Jerusalem falls silent after just two brief, but evocative verses (11–12). These verses offer a panoply of horror-filled images; helpless children, faint from starvation, lurch and weave, beg for a final morsel, lie faint, and finally (mercifully?) expire in their mother's bosoms. Following this agonizing description, Jerusalem concludes her grim report. What more can one say?

---

6. The three-sentence verse is unique to chapters 1 and 2.
7. In chapter 2, however, the order of the *ayin* and the *peh* is reversed. I will examine this in an appendix to this chapter.
8. Scholars differ widely in their understanding of the identity of the different speakers in the chapter. Some regard all of 2:1–19 as a monologue by the narrator, who speaks in both third and first person (e.g., Hillers, 40–48; Dobbs-Allsopp, 78–79; Berlin, 67). For a range of possible ways to divide the chapter and identify its various speakers, see House, 372–73.

Without recourse to Jerusalem's voice, verses 13–19 return to the third-person speaker. The narrator employs different strategies to persuade Jerusalem to resume her speech. Initially offering empathy, the narrator presumes to share the burden of the city's grief (verse 13). Following that, the speaker endeavors to ease Jerusalem's guilt (verse 14). Finally, the narrator adopts a more direct tactic, describing the external reactions to her tragedy (both empathetic and hostile), thereby prodding Jerusalem to endeavor to change her fortune (verses 15 and 16). The narrator's persistent efforts are to no avail; the city remains stubbornly silent. Perhaps Jerusalem's sobs choke her, precluding speech. Jerusalem may have given in to despair. Possibly, she defiantly refuses to plead her case before God. Regardless, Jerusalem remains mute and inaccessible.

The narrator, however, refuses to yield. In a final bid to rouse Jerusalem to speak, he recalls the starving children expiring on the city's streets (verse 19). This, the very same image that caused Jerusalem's silence, proves effective; Jerusalem finally explodes, issuing a shocking accusation in a second-person invective against God: "Look Lord, and see! To whom have You done this? When women consume their fruits, their well-nurtured children! When murdered in the Lord's sanctuary are the priest and prophet!... You murdered on the day of Your anger! You slaughtered, You did not pity!" (Eikha 2:20–21).

While theologically disturbing, accusation against God does not necessarily constitute heresy in the Bible. It can affirm human belief in a just and compassionate God with its insistence that God adhere to His righteousness. Abraham's words to God are instructive, as he searches for a way to persuade God not to destroy the cities of Sodom and Gomorrah: "Will the Judge of all the earth not do justice?" (Gen. 18:25). This audacious question illustrates the Bible's willingness to allow humans to interact boldly with God, especially when human impudence is predicated on deep-rooted belief in God's goodness. Jerusalem's relationship with God empowers her; when she emerges from the numb speechlessness that overwhelmed her in verses 13–19, Jerusalem remonstrates with God, reminding the reader of the meaningful relationship between them. Jerusalem's indictment of God's actions illustrates how deeply she entwines her fate with God's attentions. In the final analysis, the city's outrage stems from an underlying belief in a moral God.

PART 1 (EIKHA 2:1–10): THE NARRATOR'S ACCOUNT

To describe the assault on the city, the narrator harnesses several tools of verbal artistry. Most prominently, as noted, synonyms shape the narrative. God's purposeful destruction is the subject of nearly every sentence in the first eight verses of the chapter. These sentences generally contain a unique verb denoting destruction, followed by the direct object of destruction – namely, a part of the city or Temple. Approximately twenty sentences (within ten verses) conform to this general pattern. By varying words, syntax, and images and by subtly introducing nuances by means of linguistic allusions, the account conveys totality of destruction without becoming cumbersome.

Eikha 2:1

אֵיכָה יָעִיב בְּאַפּוֹ
אֲדֹנָי אֶת־בַּת־צִיּוֹן

הִשְׁלִיךְ מִשָּׁמַיִם אֶרֶץ
תִּפְאֶרֶת יִשְׂרָאֵל

וְלֹא־זָכַר הֲדֹם־רַגְלָיו
בְּיוֹם אַפּוֹ

How beclouds in His anger
Lord, the daughter of Zion

He threw from heavens to earth
The glory of Israel

And He did not remember His footstool
On the day of His anger

The three sentences of the opening verse contain three different verbs (becloud, throw, [did not] remember) alongside three appellations for Jerusalem (daughter of Zion, glory of Israel, [God's] footstool). While each term maintains an independent meaning or nuance, one goal is to heap on synonyms. These synonyms illustrate the variety of ways in which God wreaks destruction upon the city. They also allude to Jerusalem's multiple functions, all of which fail to elicit God's clemency. God disciplines the city that both reflects Israel's glory and functions as God's own footstool.

God is the subject of nearly all the verbs in this part of the chapter. Nevertheless, the opening sentence contains unusual syntax that seems designed to deflect attention away from God. Instead of placing the subject (God) prior to the verb (as is customary in Hebrew syntax), the verse begins with the verb (beclouds) and the cause (anger), both of which appear before the subject (God). This hints at a certain hesitation in identifying God as the destroyer. Ironically, the verse's unusual arrangement may wind up highlighting God, as the reader strains to identify the agent of destruction.

This first sentence contains another noteworthy feature. To connect God's angry actions to their object, the daughter of Zion, the sentence employs a connecting word that identifies definite direct objects (*et*). Often omitted from biblical poetry, the use of this word emphasizes the manner in which God deliberately targets the daughter of Zion, leaving no room to doubt that God's intended target is His city.[9] This word will appear again in the opening sentence of the following verse, ostensibly with a similar objective.

The initial verse of the chapter both opens with God's anger (*be'apo*) and closes with it (*beyom apo*).[10] Enveloped by God's fury, this verse displays the consequence of divine wrath, supporting the oft-cited rabbinic idea that divine anger always leads to punitive action:

> R. Yehoshua ben Karha said: Every fierce anger in the Bible is followed by a consequence. (Zevaḥim 102a)

Nouns: *Bat Zion, Tiferet Yisrael, Hadom Raglav*

The verse mentions three objects of God's punitive anger. The first sentence references *Bat Zion*, a common name in Eikha for Jerusalem.

---

9. See Dobbs-Allsopp, 79.
10. As noted, chapter 2 is similarly enveloped by the day of God's anger (appearing in verses 1 and 22). Structurally, verse 1 encapsulates the tenor of the chapter.

This term was associated with the city's regal elegance in 1:6. In our verse, God's anger casts a shadow over Jerusalem, obscuring her former loveliness.

Tiferet Yisrael seems not to be an appellation for something else, but rather literally to mean "Israel's glory." God not only wreaks physical destruction on Israel but also destroys her splendor. However, it is also possible to understand that Israel's glory is the Temple:[11]

> The Holy Temple and our glory (*tifartenu*), where our fathers praised You, has become a burning fire, and all our precious delights have been destroyed. (Is. 64:10)

The phrase *hadom raglav* (footstool) contains an anthropomorphism that alludes to the notion that God rests His "feet" on earth.[12] This metaphor sometimes refers to the Temple (Ps. 132:7),[13] while at times it refers specifically to the *aron* (ark), the sole furniture in the Holy of Holies (I Chr. 28:2). A passage in Isaiah 66:1 offers a broader perspective, suggesting that all the earth functions as God's footstool.[14] In our verse, this metaphor could refer to the Temple, the *aron*, or perhaps Jerusalem. God's neglect of His footstool indicates that He has deliberately ruptured the bond previously linking heaven and earth, discontinuing His relationship with His holy city.

Verbs: *Ya'iv, Hishlikh, Lo Zakhar*

The obscurity of the initial verb in this chapter, *ya'iv* ("becloud"), derives from its unusual verbal form. Some suggest that it is related to the word *taav*, abomination, which in its verbal form would mean to

---

11. Isaiah 13:19 refers to Babylon (presumably, the city) as the glory (*tiferet*) of the Chaldeans, raising the possibility that the glory of Israel refers to its capital city, Jerusalem.
12. See also Psalms 99:5.
13. See Eikha Rabba 2:3 and the *Targum* and Rashi on our verse. Using a similar metaphor, Ezekiel 43:7 refers to the Temple as "the place of the soles of My feet." See also Isaiah 60:13.
14. See R. Yosef Kara on Eikha 2:1.

render something abhorrent (Ezek. 16:52).[15] This would suggest that God piled filth and contamination upon Bat Zion – a fitting punishment for those who brought abominations into the Temple (Ezek. 5:11). While this meaning certainly fits with the context, it seems unlikely that the verbal form of the word *taav* would appear without the letter *tav*.

More likely (as I have translated above), the word *ya'iv* is the verbal form of the word *av*, which generally means thick clouds or a mass that obscures the light (e.g., II Sam. 22:12; Is. 25:5). In its verbal form, this word would mean that God plunged Jerusalem into darkness.[16] Darkness suggests impending doom; its ominous presence supplants the light, warmth, and guidance that was formerly present in God's holy city.[17] Jerusalem's light emanates from God's presence in the city.[18] It follows that when God abandons the city, Jerusalem's light vanishes. Our verse, however, implies a more direct cause for the darkness. The verb *ya'iv* portrays God deliberately placing a thick barrier between heaven and earth, blocking human access to light, the heavens, and God Himself.[19]

---

15. See T. F. McDaniel, "Philological Studies in Lamentations II," *Biblica* 49 (1968), 34–35. Berlin, 61, 66, adopts this translation, citing Psalms 106:40, which employs this verb to describe God's disgust at his nation due to their impure actions (see Ps. 106:39). The Aramaic translation of this verse appears to allude to this meaning by using the verbal form of the word *kotz*, meaning to despise.

16. See Rashi, Eikha 2:1. Ibn Ezra appears to agree that the verb *ya'iv* is related to the word *av* (cloud). However, he explains that this sentence prepares us for the next: God first lifted Zion up to the clouds so that He could throw her from heaven to earth.

17. See Isaiah 60:1–3, which describes Jerusalem as the bearer of God's light. Midrashim (e.g., Genesis Rabba 59:24) note Jerusalem's luminescence, as do the liturgical poets (e.g., the blessings linked to the *Shema* prayer in the morning service concludes, "Let a new light shine over Jerusalem so that we all merit quickly its light"). In a contemporary context, Naomi Shemer has popularized the notion of Jerusalem's radiance in her acclaimed song "Jerusalem of Gold" (and of copper and of light). Similarly, Eikha 4:1 opens by lamenting the tarnished gold, symbolizing Jerusalem's eclipsed shine.

18. Biblical passages often describe God as a source of light (e.g., Ps. 27:1; Mic. 7:9; Is. 60:19).

19. We will encounter a similar idea in Eikha 3:44, where God wraps Himself in a cloud to prevent Israel's prayers from reaching their destination.

Often, biblical passages employ the word *av* in a positive context. The *av* has cleansing power associated with repentance (Is. 44:22) and carries moisture that facilitates growth (Ps. 147:8). The *av he'anan* encases God when He speaks to the nation at Sinai (Ex. 19:9). This implies a protective role for the thick clouds, especially in the context of the human relationship with the divine.[20] In contrast to these positive usages, in our verse these masses of clouds have no positive function. God plunges the city into dense, impenetrable gloom.

God flings (*hishlikh*) the glory of Israel away from Him;[21] thrown from the heights of heavens, Jerusalem and her Temple crash heavily upon the earth.[22] A powerful metaphor of destruction, this image also conveys God's fierce rejection. God can no longer abide *tiferet Yisrael's* company in His heavenly domain, and He forcefully expels them. It seems that the glory of Israel formerly had an honored place in the heavens, serving as a direct conduit to God's throne. This recalls better times, but also renders the fall of Israel's glory that much more shocking; the colossal distance between the nation's previous elevated status and the present degradation is appalling. The well-known rabbinic dictum, "From a high roof to the deepest pit," signifying an acute and terrible change in fortune, has its source here.[23]

VeLo zakhar: Unlike the first two verbs, which depict God actively assailing His city, the verb *zakhar* is framed in the negative (*lo zakhar*), "He did not remember." At first glance, this verb suggests a retreat from God's furious assault. God simply does not remember His footstool; He is not aggressively acting against it.

Nevertheless, the negative formulation implies that God was supposed to remember; in choosing not to remember, God violates

---

20. The Zohar avers that Moshe could approach the divine presence manifested in a fire at the top of Mount Sinai only because he was encased in a protective cloud. See Zohar Shemot, *Vayakhel* 197a; *Pekudei* 229a.
21. The *hifil* form of this verb with God as its subject is frequently destructive. See Joshua 10:11; II Kings 13:23; 17:20; Jeremiah 52:3.
22. Rabbinic sources (e.g., Song of Songs Rabba 4:6; *Tanhuma, Vayakhel* 7) often maintain that the Temple's earthly manifestation has a counterpart in heaven.
23. See Ḥagiga 5b.

Israel's expectations. Moshe successfully pleads with God to remember His covenant with the forefathers and forgive Israel (Ex. 32:13; Deut. 9:27), and biblical verses often praise God for remembering His eternal covenant (Ps. 105:8; 136:23) and His loyalty to His nation (Ps. 98:3). This depiction of God may be less aggressive, but it kindles despair. God's decision not to remember implies intentionality, indicating the breakdown of a relationship founded upon an immutable belief in God's fidelity.

Judgment Day

Jerusalem was not destroyed in a day; to confine God's wrath to one day misrepresents the prolonged rampage against Jerusalem. Thus, the phrase "on the day of God's anger" is not necessarily literal. Rather, it employs a common biblical trope that alludes to a time in which God unleashes His judgments upon the world.[24] Biblical prophets often evoke this eschatological day, alternately referred to as "the day of the Lord," "the day of God's anger," or simply "that day" (*bayom/hayom hahu*).[25] This day involves divine scrutiny of human actions, which results in the punishment of evildoers and the restoration of justice to the world. Punishment can come in the form of a natural disaster or a war involving cosmic shifts. Biblical theology assigns to God full responsibility for these cataclysmic changes, relegating the human agents of war and destruction to a secondary or proxy role.

Naturally, divine judgment may be good or bad for Israel, depending upon their behavior. God's judgments upon Israel's enemies may be followed by a shift in the world order, paving the way for Israel to experience a national revival (Joel 4:14–21; Ezek. 38–39; Zech. 14). However, prophets also issue dire admonitions to Israel regarding that apocalyptic day (Zeph. 1:10–11; Ezek. 7; Joel 1:14). On that day, God may wield His judgments against Israel, who should not assume that they stand to gain

---

24. Biblical scholars discuss this topic extensively. For a review of some of the scholarship surrounding this subject, see Gottwald, 83 fn. 1.
25. For example, Isaiah 2:11–17; Joel 1:15, 2:1, 4:14; Zephaniah 1–2; Zechariah 14.

from God's concentrated attention.[26] That day, according to Eikha 2:1, has come and gone, leaving Jerusalem shattered in its wake.[27]

The day of God is not the apocalyptic end of the world. Biblical history, after all, does not end with the catastrophic events of 586 BCE.[28] Perhaps, then, the day of God may instead refer to recurring events throughout human history in which God's attention seems to focus upon the world, releasing divine judgment in a manner that disturbs the world order.[29] This could account for the ceaseless rise and fall of empires and the ever-changing shifts of power. Moreover, one could regard various historical events (including natural disasters and man-made catastrophes) as "the day of God." While humans or nature act as the ostensible cause of these events, biblical theology regards God as directing these affairs, notably those that effect dramatic changes in the world.

To have hope in the future after the destruction of Jerusalem, Israel must maintain a broad view of history. If Israel refrains from sinning and returns to God, surely the day will come when God turns His scrutiny upon the world and finds His nation meritorious. On that day, God will restore Israel's autonomy and punish their sinful enemies, allowing His nation to resume a leading role among the nations of the world.

---

26. Amos 5:18 admonishes stridently (and somewhat cynically) against those who long for "the day of the Lord." The verse in Amos suggests that one should be cautious about what one wishes for; only those deserving of God's favor will benefit from the day of divine scrutiny.

27. See also Eikha 1:12; 2:21, 22.

28. The significance of this point cannot be overstated. Although biblical history appears to conclude with the destruction of Jerusalem in II Kings 25, the historical biblical narrative resumes its account with Cyrus's decree and the return to Zion in the books of Ezra-Nehemiah, Haggai, Zechariah, and Malachi. This unexpected postscript is especially evident at the conclusion of the book of Chronicles, which closes with God spurring Cyrus to issue a declaration that Israel may return to Jerusalem and rebuild the Temple (II Chr. 35:22–23). Israel's history has resumed, and with it the hope for renewed opportunities to shape a better world.

29. In *The Guide of the Perplexed* II, 29, Maimonides adopts this approach, maintaining that "every day in which a great victory or a great disaster comes to pass is called 'the great and terrible day of the Lord'" (Maimonides, *The Guide of the Perplexed*, trans. S. Pines [Chicago: University of Chicago Press, 1963], 344).

Eikha 2:2

בִּלַּע אֲדֹנָי [לֹא] וְלֹא חָמַל
אֵת כָּל־נְאוֹת יַעֲקֹב

הָרַס בְּעֶבְרָתוֹ
מִבְצְרֵי בַת־יְהוּדָה

הִגִּיעַ לָאָרֶץ
חִלֵּל מַמְלָכָה וְשָׂרֶיהָ

The Lord swallowed; He did not pity
All the habitations of Jacob

He demolished in His rage
The fortresses of the daughter of Judah

He thrust down to the earth
Profaned the kingdom and her officers

While the previous verse has a vertical movement that directs the reader's gaze up (clouds, heaven, God) and down (Zion, earth, God's footstool), this verse offers us a horizontal landscape of destruction. God swallowed, demolished, and profaned a broad swathe of Judah: houses and fortresses, kingdom, and officers. The verse moves from the common habitations (possibly in the countryside)[30] to those protected by fortresses. This chapter gives special attention to the destruction of the royal elite of the city, first alluded to here: "[God] profaned the kingdom and her officers."

---

30. The term *na'ot* (from the root *n.v.h.*) can mean either habitations (see the parallelism with the word *bayit* in Proverbs 3:33) or pastures (see *Targum Eikha* 2:2; Ps. 23:2; Jer. 9:9). Some translations follow the former meaning (e.g., NJPS), while others follow the latter (e.g., Westermann, 141).

Verbs: *Bila, Lo Ḥamal, Haras, Higi'a, Ḥillel*

Five verbs portray the active destruction in this verse. God is the subject of each of the verbs: He swallowed, did not pity, demolished, thrust to the earth, and profaned His city.

Frequently employed as a verb of destruction, *bila* literally means "swallow." A verb that can describe the behavior of mindless animals (Jonah 2:1) and wicked people (Hab. 1:13), "swallowing" is an all-consuming act, one that engulfs and overpowers, leaving behind no remnant. It is often used to characterize the hostile act of an enemy (Hos. 8:7–8). This is how God describes the intentions of the *Satan* (Adversary) who induces Him to torment Job for no good reason (Job 2:3). Jeremiah depicts the Babylonian king Nebuchadnezzar swallowing Jerusalem in a serpent-like act of rapacious hunger (Jer. 51:34). In our verse, the Babylonian enemy recedes into the background; instead, it is God who swallows the city. This verb will appear twice more in verse 5 as part of a terrifying portrait of God's enmity. In its final appearance in Eikha (in 2:16), this verb is used by Israel's enemies, who gleefully proclaim, "We have swallowed!" The dual usage of this verb to portray both God and enemies illustrates how the chapter pairs them as collaborators in devouring Jerusalem.

For the second verse in a row, a verbal clause begins with the negative *lo*, highlighting what God does not do. In this case, God does not exhibit compassion (*lo ḥamal*), a phrase that will recur twice in this chapter (verses 17 and 21). The word *lo* suggests purposeful withholding, rather than passivity. God's compassion for His nation is commonplace (Is. 63:9; Joel 2:18; Mal. 3:17); one has the impression that God is suppressing His natural instinct.

Often used within a ritual sacred context, the word *ḥillel* means to profane something, or remove its sacredness. This verb can denote either sinfulness (Jer. 16:18) or punishment for sins (Is. 47:6), as in our verse. The desecration of the kingdom and her officers hints at their former consecrated status.[31] Finally, the orthography of the verb *ḥillel* parallels the nominal *ḥallal*, designating the corpses that languish on Jerusalem's

---

31. For a similar description of the manner in which God punishes the Davidic dynasty by desecrating their royal symbols, see Psalms 89:39.

streets in Eikha 2:12. This apt wordplay illustrates the defilement of the formerly pure city, now sullied by the corpses strewn in its midst.

Echoes of Prophecies

Language conveys meaning in many ways. Within the biblical canon, words tend to echo each other in a significant manner. When a word or phrase evokes another biblical passage, it hints at an inter-textual relationship that can offer a richer understanding of both passages.

Actualizing Prophecies of Admonition
The language of destruction in Eikha frequently evokes prophetic admonitions, indicating that they are now being fulfilled. The words *lo ḥamal* in our verse recall both Jeremiah and Ezekiel, who inform Judah of the possibility that God will withhold compassion from His people:[32]

> And I will also act in anger: My eye will not have compassion and I will not pity (*velo eḥmol*), and they will call out in my ears with a great shout, but I will not listen to them. (Ezek. 8:18)

The destructive verb *haras* likewise evokes Jeremiah's prophecy:

> So shall you say to him, "So says the Lord: Behold that which I built, I will destroy (*hores*) and that which I planted, I will uproot, along with all this land" (Jer. 45:4).[33]

The unusual phrase *higi'a laaretz* appears in Ezekiel 13:14 alongside another linguistic association with Eikha 2:2 (*haras*):

> And I will demolish (*harasti*) the wall that you covered with plaster, and I will make it reach the ground (*vehigaatihu el haaretz*); its foundations will be exposed and it will fall, and you will perish within it and you will know that I am the Lord. (Ezek. 13:14)

---

32. See also Jeremiah 13:14; Ezekiel 5:11; 7:4, 9; 9:10.
33. Jeremiah's opening prophecy also employs the word *haras* to caution of impending catastrophe; see Jeremiah 1:10.

By employing words that recall prophetic admonitions, Eikha indicates that this catastrophe was avoidable had the nation heeded the prophets' warnings. While this may be small comfort to those suffering in Jerusalem, it places these events within the broader biblical theology of destruction. This calamity is part of a larger historical plan, caused by Israel's sins, conceived by God, and foretold by prophets.

Reversing Prophecies of Doom

Prophetic texts of consolation likewise engage in dialogue with Eikha. Several passages transform Eikha's language of destruction into language of redemption, in a linguistic flourish designed to offer solace. In particular, Isaiah's "prophecies of consolation" (chapters 40–66) converse with Eikha, providing messages of hope while employing Eikha's language of destruction.[34] Isaiah 49:19, for example, alludes to the destruction described in Eikha 2:2, using its harsh words (*haras* and *bila*) to describe Israel's restoration:

> For your ruins and your desolate places and your destroyed land (*eretz harisuteikh*) will now be bursting with inhabitants, and those who consumed you (*mivale'ayikh*) will be distanced. (Is. 49:19)

Isaiah sketches a perfect reconstruction, using the very same language that conveyed the portrait of devastation. Throughout this study, we will encounter Isaiah's transposition of Eikha's gloom. I will explore the relationship between Eikha and Isaiah's prophecies of consolation more fully in a separate chapter, "Eikha and the Prophecies of Consolation in Isaiah."

The intersection between Eikha and the prophecies of redemption indicates that Jerusalem's destruction is not the end of her story.

---

34. Chapters 40–66 in the book of Isaiah concern themselves with a different period than that of Isaiah son of Amotz, who prophesied in the eighth century BCE. These chapters contain prophecies of consolation that appertain to the period following the calamity of 586 BCE. Explicitly referring to the community in the Babylonian exile, these prophecies tender promises of redemption and urge the Judeans to return to Jerusalem. (See, e.g., Is. 48:20; 52:9–10. Note also the explicit reference to Cyrus in Is. 44:28–45:1.) These chapters often linguistically reverse the book of Eikha, as noted by Eikha Rabba 1:23.

When the circumstances allow, God will reverse Jerusalem's calamity, returning her to her former status and glory. Embedded within destruction is the language of her restoration; as surely as Jerusalem is punished for her sins, God promises that her calamity will be reversed.[35]

Eikha 2:3

גָּדַע בָּחֳרִי־אַף
כֹּל קֶרֶן יִשְׂרָאֵל

הֵשִׁיב אָחוֹר יְמִינוֹ
מִפְּנֵי אוֹיֵב

וַיִּבְעַר בְּיַעֲקֹב כְּאֵשׁ לֶהָבָה
אָכְלָה סָבִיב

He hewed down in his smoking anger
All the horns of Israel

He withdrew His right hand backward
From before the enemy

And He burned in Jacob as a flaming fire
That consumes its surroundings

God's anger continues to smolder in this verse, bursting into lethal flames that consume everything in its environs. In the next verse, that same anger will surface (for the fifth time in the chapter) as a fire that spills over from God, surging forward to obliterate the tent of the daughter of Zion.

The first and third sentences in this verse conform to the general pattern. They each contain a verb denoting destruction (*gada, vayivar*)

---

35. This is the message of R. Akiva (Makkot 24b), who expresses joy in the fulfillment of the prophets' threat of destruction, inasmuch as it confirms the veracity of the prophets' messages of rejuvenation. I examined that anecdote in the chapter, "Theology and Suffering."

as well as mentioning the object that is destroyed (the horn of Israel, Jacob).[36] Unlike the surrounding sentences, the middle sentence of this verse does not have a direct object, nor does it contain an active verb of destruction; God merely withdraws His right hand, allowing the enemy unfettered entrance. Instead of featuring Jerusalem or some part of it, this middle sentence highlights the enemy, who, aided by God, seem destined to succeed.

Verbs: *Gada, Heshiv Aḥor Yemino, VaYivar*

The word *gada* means to hew down an object, often severing it from a biological connection. *Gada* can refer to the hewing down of trees which, once separated from their roots, fall and crash (Is. 9:9). By extension, this verb sometimes describes the felling of humans (Is. 10:33), whose height, grandeur, and immutability are likened to majestic trees.[37]

In this verse, the word *gada* modifies the "horn of Israel." This phrase recalls the magnificent horns of an animal, which serve as a symbol of their strength and glory. Hewing off Israel's horn may metaphorically connote the removal of Israel's might and splendor, leaving it defenseless and deformed.[38] The *keren* is also the accepted mode for anointing kings whose dynasty endures.[39] *Keren Yisrael* can therefore refer metonymically to the king, alluding to the termination of the Davidic dynasty (similar to the previous verse).[40]

---

36. The object that is burned in the third sentence is framed as part of a prepositional phrase, "and he burned in Jacob." Nevertheless, it appears that Jacob is the object destroyed by the fire. Alternatively, the object destroyed by the fire is the unspecific environs (*saviv*).

37. See Deuteronomy 20:19; Amos 2:9.

38. See Rasag on Eikha 2:3.

39. Y. Shekalim 6:1; I Samuel 16:2; I Kings 1:39. See also I Samuel 2:10: "And He shall give strength to his king and raise the horn (*keren*) of His anointed." See also Radak on II Samuel 22:3 and Psalms 132:17; Malbim on Psalms 89:25. Ibn Ezra (Eikha 2:3) suggests that this verse refers to both kingdoms (the Northern Kingdom of Israel destroyed by Assyria and the current destruction of the Southern Kingdom of Judah).

40. A midrash (*Yalkut Shimoni*, I Sam., 81) describes Israel as possessing ten horns. These ten horns include righteous people (Abraham, Isaac, Joseph, Moses, Messiah) and religious institutions (priests, Levites, Temple, prophecy, Torah), who function as Israel's splendor and strength, beautifying it and protecting it from harm. When

This phrase (*gada ... keren*) may hint to the sins that provoke this punishment. Biblical texts employ the word *gada* to instruct Israelites to hew down idolatry (Deut. 7:5; 12:3), and sometimes specifically the corners (literally, the horns) of the idolatrous altars (*karnei hamizbe'aḥ*) (Amos 3:14). The failure to obliterate idolatry entangles Israel in a condition of sinfulness that concludes with destruction.

God's second act in this verse is to withdraw His right hand (*heshiv aḥor yemino*). God's right hand is "glorious in power" and "shatters the enemies" to protect Israel at the Sea (Ex. 15:6).[41] Throughout biblical history, Israel continues to benefit from God's might, frequently depicted simply as God's right hand (e.g., Ps. 21:9; 44:4; 60:7). The removal of God's hand thus leaves Jerusalem defenseless, enabling the enemy to enter.[42] The enemy does not, however, assume the pivotal role in Jerusalem's destruction at this point; the human foe emerges briefly, only to fade quickly into the background, making way for God to resume His assault on Jerusalem.

Our verse continues its litany of destruction by describing a terrible conflagration that envelops Jerusalem. The perpetrator who lights the consuming fire is either God (who is the subject of every other sentence in this verse) or God's anger (God spills his rage out like fire in the next verse). Fire is a common symbol both of divine revelation (Ex. 24:17; Ps. 18:13–14) and of God's anger (Is. 66:15; Jer. 4:4) and punishment (Deut. 32:22). Shapeless and intangible, fire offers an apt metaphor for God's wrath, which incinerates offenders (Lev. 10:2; Num. 16:35; II Kings 1:9–14).

Fire also has beneficial qualities, offering warmth and light. Metaphorically, this conveys the favorable aspects of divine revelation – its clarity, protection, and mysterious splendor. Humans

---

Israel sins, these horns are removed and given to the idolatrous nations (see Dan. 7:7, 24). Despite the harshness of transferring Israel's horns to its enemies, this notion allows for the preservation of the glorious horns, which will be returned to Israel when Israel repents (in accordance with Psalms 75:11).

41. See R. Yosef Kara on Eikha 2:3.

42. The *Targum* on this verse adds that God withdraws His right hand so as not to give aid to His nation: "He drew back His right hand and did not help His nation from the enemy."

seeking spirituality and divine radiance sometimes encounter this fire. Thus, Moses veers from his path to contemplate the burning bush (Ex. 3:2–3), Elijah is spirited heavenward amidst flaming chariots and horses (II Kings 2:11), and Elisha perceives similar fiery cavalry surrounding and protecting him (II Kings 6:17). A fire that signifies God's glory burns at the top of Sinai (e.g., Ex. 24:17) and on the *Mishkan* (Tabernacle) at night (Ex. 40:38). In Zechariah's vision of the ideal state of Jerusalem, he describes God as a ring of fire around Israel, providing glory and protection:

> Jerusalem will be an unwalled city, [continually growing] from the multitude of people and animals in its midst. And I will be for her, says the Lord, a wall of surrounding fire; I will be a glory in her midst. (Zech. 2:8–9)

Despite its devastating primary message, the language used to depict Judah's destruction in this verse allows a glimpse of redemption. The hewing down of the horns of Israel evokes biblical passages that promise the cleaving of the enemy's horn (Jer. 48:25; Ps. 75:11). The horn also foretells the raising of Israel's horn, implying the restoration of her fortunes (Ps. 112:9). God's right hand appears elsewhere in biblical passages to strengthen and support Israel and deliver it from its enemies (Is. 41:10–11). The fire of destruction can easily transform into a protective fire, reflecting God's resplendence and His defense of Israel. Eikha weaves language of redemption into her language of destruction; echoes of salvation thrum quietly beneath the portrait of gloom.

Eikha 2:4

דָּרַךְ קַשְׁתּוֹ כְּאוֹיֵב
נִצָּב יְמִינוֹ כְּצָר

וַיַּהֲרֹג כֹּל מַחֲמַדֵּי־עָיִן

בְּאֹהֶל בַּת־צִיּוֹן
שָׁפַךְ כָּאֵשׁ חֲמָתוֹ

He bent His bow like an enemy
Steadied His right hand like an adversary

And He killed all those precious to the eye

In the tent of the daughter of Zion
He spilled out His anger like fire

God's agents vanish completely in this verse. Instead God comes into focus, bow in right hand, poised to smite Israel. An invincible foe (God is twice designated "enemy" in this verse and once more in the following verse), God plots and unleashes devastation. His right hand, held in abeyance in verse 3, now swings into action, smiting Jerusalem's precious inhabitants.

While the first and third sentences conform to the customary binary sentence structure, the verse's middle sentence is made up of a single line. This construction draws attention to the central sentence, whose stark disclosure jars the reader: God killed all those precious to the eye. This account requires no elaboration; the potency of the announcement lies in its austerity.

Who are those "precious to the eye"? In the previous chapter, the word *mahamadim* appeared several times (1:7, 10, 11). We considered the possibility that this refers either to objects or to humans. The context of our verse, however, clearly signifies humans. The phrase *hamad ayin* generally connotes members of one's immediate family, either spouse or children.[43] Here, the phrase most likely means children, preparing us for the central image of this chapter – the incomprehensible death of the children in verses 11–12.[44] The suffering of children reverberates

---

43. In I Kings 20:6 the phrase may connote either spouse or children – or more likely, both (see I Kings 20:5). Ezekiel 24:16–18 clearly refers to a wife, while Ezekiel 24:21, 25 seems to refer to children.

44. Eikha Rabba 2:8 likewise suggests that this phrase refers to the children. We should bear in mind that because Eikha appears to refer to all of Jerusalem's residents as the city's children (see 1:5), references to children could include her entire population. The midrash raises another possibility: that this phrase refers to the Sanhedrin, the legislative body, whose "eyes" (namely their understanding) are an important part

with injustice, drawing attention to the tense theological question that pervades this chapter.

God's Enmity

Does the *kaf hadimayon* (a comparative preposition) in *ke'oyev,* "like an enemy," mitigate the impact of describing God as an enemy?[45] Whether God is an actual enemy or simply behaves *like* an enemy seems to matter little so long as He is described in a hostile role. While exceedingly uncommon, this alarming portrait of God also appears in Isaiah.[46] Isaiah 63:10 depicts God functioning as Israel's enemy as a response to her betrayal:

> In His love, and in His compassion, He redeemed them, and He took them and bore them all the days. And they rebelled and grieved His holy spirit, *and He turned into their enemy and He battled them.* (Is. 63:9–10)

This portrayal of divine hostility has terrifying implications.[47] God's omnipotence renders him a formidable enemy indeed.

But despite the horror that attends the notion of God's enmity, there is no suggestion that the relationship between God and His nation has ended. When viewed within the context of Isaiah's historical overview, it becomes clear that the sole cause of God's hostility is Israel's egregious betrayal. Moreover, Isaiah follows the description of God's enmity with Israel's direct plea to God (Is. 63:16) and with Israel's trust in God's

---

of their job. This idea correlates well with the destruction of leadership, likewise a central feature of this chapter (Eikha 2:2, 6, 9).

45. Both the *Targum* (on this verse and especially on the next, where the *Targum* adds the word *damay,* meaning "similar to" an enemy, but not actually one) and the nineteenth century commentary *Palgei Mayyim* (on Eikha 2:5) emphasize the significance of this *kaf hadimayon,* insisting that God cannot be an actual enemy.

46. The adversary that Job refers to in 16:9 may be God, although Rashi maintains that it is the *Satan,* while others (e.g., Ibn Ezra, Metzudat David, Malbim) aver that God's anger empowers the human enemy to act.

47. *Sefer HaḤinukh* 87 discusses the philosophic implications of this anthropomorphic description of God.

parental love and commitment (Is. 63:16; 64:7). Reflecting upon the destruction of Jerusalem, the nation beseeches God to cease His anger:

> Do not be greatly wrathful with us, Lord,[48] and do not recall our sin for eternity! Look, please, at your nation, at all of us! Your holy cities have become a desert, Zion is like a desert, Jerusalem a desolation. Our holy Temple and our glory, where our fathers praised You, was consumed by fire and all our precious things were ruined. Will You restrain Yourself over these, Lord? Will You be silent and afflict us greatly? (Isaiah 64:8–11)

God does not answer immediately, but when He finally does His response is conciliatory and affectionate:

> For I will construct a new heaven and a new earth … and I will create Jerusalem as a joy and her nation as a delight. And I will rejoice in Jerusalem and I will delight in My people, and there shall not be heard in [the city] any more sounds of sobs or sounds of wails … And they shall build houses and dwell [in them], and plant vineyards and eat their fruit … They will not toil in vain and they will not birth [children destined] for horrors, for they are children of those blessed of the Lord, they and their descendants. And before they call, I will answer; they are yet speaking and I will hear. (Is. 65:17–24)

Despite its alarming implications, God's hostile response to Israel's transgressions will not endure endlessly, according to Isaiah. Israel's prayer generates forgiveness and a renewal of commitment, trust, and love between God and His beloved nation.

Eikha 2:5

הָיָה אֲ-דֹנָי כְּאוֹיֵב
בִּלַּע יִשְׂרָאֵל

---

48. We will discuss the way in which this phrase intersects with Eikha 5:22 in the chapter "Eikha and the Prophecies of Consolation in Isaiah."

בִּלַּע כָּל־אַרְמְנוֹתֶיהָ
שִׁחֵת מִבְצָרָיו

וַיֶּרֶב בְּבַת־יְהוּדָה
תַּאֲנִיָּה וַאֲנִיָּה

The Lord was like an enemy
He swallowed Israel

He swallowed all her palaces
He destroyed its fortresses

And He increased in the daughter of Judah
Mourning and moaning

God's enmity continues unabated, swallowing Israel and her palaces, steadily disposing of them until there are no more. The verb *bila* – appearing twice in rapid succession – depicts the total elimination of Jerusalem's buildings; wholly consumed, they leave no trace of having ever existed.

Many of the words in this verse featured previously in the first four verses of the chapter: God's enmity, the word *bila* (swallow), the fortresses, and the appellation *Bat Yehuda* make another appearance in our verse. The repeated words suggest that this verse is a recap, perhaps offering a conclusion to the relentless tale of Jerusalem's ruin.

The summary feel of the verse is further indicated by its final words. For the first time in this chapter we hear Judah's reaction. Wails of mourning indicate that destruction has ceased, allowing the city's inhabitants the respite needed to lament.

Nevertheless, the narrative pause turns out to be just that – a lull in the rampage, not its conclusion. In the next verses God will turn His attention to His own Temple, the sacred center of Jerusalem and the focus of its catastrophe.

A Verb of Destruction: *VaYerev*

In this verse, the verb *vayerev* portrays the escalation of mourning in Jerusalem. However, this is not the usual usage of this verb, which comes from the root *r.b.h.*, meaning to increase in numbers or greatness. God's original pledge to humankind includes the promise of fertility, using a form of this verb (Gen. 1:28; 9:1). Later, this blessing is bestowed specifically on Abraham's family (Gen. 22:17; 35:11), and then on the nation of Israel (Deut. 6:3; 8:1; 30:16). In sharp contrast to a word that tends to bestow divine blessing, God here increases Israel's mourning and moaning.

Rashi (Eikha 2:5) draws our attention to Exodus 1:20, which contains a verb with identical orthography: "And the nation increased (*vayirev*) and they became exceedingly powerful."[49] This linguistic reference to the promising beginnings of Israel's nationhood evinces terrible disappointment. Abundant blessings are gone, replaced by abundant calamities. However, this linguistic turnaround also reminds us that God bestowed those blessings upon the nation on a provisional basis, predicated upon Israel's obedience:

> For I am commanding you today to love the Lord your God, to follow His ways and observe His commandments, statutes, and laws – and you will live and *you will increase* and the Lord your God will bless you in the land that you are about to enter and possess. (Deut. 30:16)[50]

Possession of the land of Israel in particular, comes with stipulations – namely, the responsibility to maintain sanctity and follow God's laws. When the nation of Israel fails to live up to the stated prerequisites, God reverses and withdraws those divine favors.

Echoes of Prophecies

The phrase *taaniya vaaniya* is sometimes translated "mourning and moaning," a translator's flourish that preserves the poetic alliteration of the Hebrew.[51] Isaiah 29:2 deploys the same phrase to portray an upcoming

---

49. Rashi notes that the grammatical form of this verb is different in each of these verses.
50. See also, for example, Deuteronomy 6:3; 8:1.
51. See, for example, NJPS, New American Standard Bible. In his new translation, Robert Alter offers his own linguistic flourish to preserve these alliterative words,

calamity for Jerusalem.[52] Surprisingly, Isaiah's scenario does not end in disaster. Despite the mourning and moaning that anticipates the catastrophe, God miraculously saves His beloved city:

> And I shall cause distress to Ariel,[53] and there will be mourning and moaning... And it will come about with great suddenness. She shall be remembered by the Lord of hosts, with thunder and quaking and a great voice; storm and tempest and a conflagration of consuming flames. And it will be like a dream, a night vision, all the multitude of nations who are encamped against Ariel and all those who wage war against her and besiege her and trouble her. Like the hungry person dreams that he is eating and awakens, and his throat is empty, and like the thirsty person dreams that he is drinking and awakens, and he is faint [with thirst] and his throat is parched – this shall be [the experience] of the multitude of nations waging war against Mount Zion. (Is. 29:2, 5–8)

By referencing the miraculous salvation of Jerusalem in Isaiah, Eikha alludes to the contrast between the two scenarios. Mourning and moaning has once again beset the besieged city, but this time with no reprieve from God. If in previous circumstances Jerusalem's anxiety ended in divine salvation, in 586 BCE her privileged status appears to come to a sorry end. By utilizing a phrase previously associated with God's miraculous salvation of the city, our verse evokes the nation's bewilderment alongside its pain. Why does God fail this time to come to the aid of His beleaguered city? This question accords with the tenor of the chapter, which resonates with Israel's baffled perception of divine injustice.

---

translating them, "wailing and woe." See R. Alter, *The Hebrew Bible, III. A Translation with Commentary* (New York: W. W. Norton & Company, 2019), 653.

52. Isaiah appears to describe the averted disaster during Sennacherib's siege of Jerusalem in 701 BCE, an event that I discussed in the chapter "Historical Background."

53. Ariel is another name for Jerusalem; see A. Hakham, *Daat Mikra: Isaiah* (Jerusalem: Mossad Harav Kook, 1984), 288. In Ezekiel 43:15, the name Ariel refers specifically to the altar.

Despite the contrast between this scenario and the previous one, the linguistic allusion directs the reader to recall a wondrous event of biblical history. The phrase in Isaiah leads to God's brilliant might and vigorous defense of His nation, which results in a dramatic salvation. A subtle (nearly indiscernible) reference, these reminders allow the reader to grasp at a modicum of hope, buried amidst despair.

Eikha 2:6

וַיַּחְמֹס כַּגַּן שֻׂכּוֹ
שִׁחֵת מוֹעֲדוֹ

שִׁכַּח ה' בְּצִיּוֹן
מוֹעֵד וְשַׁבָּת

וַיִּנְאַץ בְּזַעַם־אַפּוֹ
מֶלֶךְ וְכֹהֵן

And He stripped His hut (*sukko*) like a garden
Destroyed His appointed place

The Lord made Zion forget
Holidays and Shabbat

And He spurned in His fiery anger
King and priest

God's furious onslaught turns abruptly from the city to its religious institutions.[54] He dismantles the city's failed religious infrastructure, destroying it alongside its inhabitants. God seems to act against His own interests as He directs His assault against all three dimensions of holy

---

54. If we interpret either the phrase *tiferet Yisrael*, "the glory of Israel" (see our discussion above), or *ohel bat Zion*, "the tent of the daughter of Zion" (see *Yalkut Shimoni*, II Sam., 145), as a reference to the Temple, then Eikha 2 has already alluded to God's destruction of the Temple.

experience: sacred space (*kedushat hamakom*), sacred time (*kedushat hazeman*), and sacred people (*kedushat haadam*). God crushes each one in turn, efficiently and methodically.

Even here, Eikha provides little by way of explanation; God does not elucidate or justify this assault on His sacred institutions. However, prophetic censures often revolve around Israel's errant religious lifestyle and its misuse of sacred space, time, and people.

Jeremiah, for example, describes the heinous acts performed by Jerusalemites in the holy Temple, where they seek impunity from God despite their corruptions:

> Will you steal and murder and fornicate and swear falsely and bring incense to the Baal, and chase after other gods that you do not know? And then, you come, and you stand before Me in this house, which has My name called upon it, and you say, "We have been saved," so that you can [continue to] do these abominations! Has this house that bears My name become a den of thieves? (Jer. 7:9–11)

Jeremiah's prophecy suggests that the Temple's destruction is no more than the nation deserves; their hypocritical behavior in the Temple impels God to terminate its functioning. The heinous crimes committed there undermine the very purity of the institution.[55]

Isaiah 1:12–13 records God's impatience with the abuse of sacred time (and sacred space) – namely, the false offerings that Israel brings to the Temple on both regular days and holy days, such as Rosh Ḥodesh and Shabbat. The fraudulent people are engaged in empty rituals, Isaiah claims; they are devoid of depth and sincerity, causing God to loathe the sacred days: "My soul abhors your new moons and appointed days. They have been a burden upon Me, which I cannot endure" (Is. 1:14). Isaiah's

---

55. Similarly, the corrupt actions of the high priest's sons, as they feigned service to God in the *Mishkan*, led to the dismantling of the *Mishkan* in Shiloh (II Sam. 2:12–17, 22). During the continuation of Jeremiah's prophetic rebuke (Jer. 7:14), he evokes Shiloh's destruction to illustrate the ruinous consequences of defiling the sacred space.

censure anticipates the eventual outcome. Destruction of Jerusalem will terminate those insufferable sacred days, days of pretense and treachery, lacking any correlation with the goals of sacred time.

Later, the prophet Jeremiah denounces Jerusalem for a more direct desecration of sacred time – namely, violation of Shabbat:

> So says the Lord: "Guard your souls and do not carry burdens on the Sabbath day or bring them in the gates of Jerusalem. And do not carry a burden out of your houses on the Sabbath day and do no work. Sanctify the Sabbath day as I have commanded your fathers." And they did not listen or incline their ears, and they hardened their necks so as not to listen or accept rebuke …
> "And if you do not listen to Me to sanctify the Sabbath day and to refrain from carrying burdens and entering [with them] into the gates of Jerusalem on the Sabbath day, I will set fire to her gates and it will consume the palaces of Jerusalem and not be extinguished." (Jer. 17:21–23, 27)

According to Jeremiah, God cautioned the people that He would destroy Jerusalem if they do not observe Shabbat properly. Following the implementation of this punishment, God obliterates the memory of holidays and Shabbat from Zion. This is a deserved punishment for an errant population, who have willfully disregarded observance of the sacred days.

Finally, our verse recounts God's rejection of His own anointed leaders, those imbued with extra sanctity and charged with the task of guiding the nation in worship of God.[56] Prophets regularly condemn the kings and priests who fail to observe God's law and properly care for His Temple:

> Like the shame of the thief who has been caught, so is the house of Israel shamed, they, their *kings*, their officers, their *priests*, and their prophets. (Jer. 2:26)

---

56. See Ibn Ezra's commentary on Eikha 2:6, where he explains that ideally, "the priest teaches the commandments and the king guards the Torah with his strength, and to these two were given the Torah."

In that time, says the Lord, the bones of the *kings* of Judah … and the bones of the *priests* … will be removed from their graves. And they will be exposed to the sun and to the moon and to all the hosts of heaven, whom they loved and worshipped and followed and sought and bowed to … (Jer. 8:1–2)

Characterized by backsliding and blunders, Judah's leadership has led the nation further into religious disarray. God scorns and punishes these leaders, whose lack of religious integrity and guidance leaves the nation in shambles.

This verse eliminates the holy city's frameworks for maintaining sanctity. God's rejection goes beyond punishing the sinful people and the corrupt city; He repudiates its celebrated role as the bearer of the nation's holy institutions.[57]

Metaphor: Stripping the Sukka like a Garden

Deriving from the word *sekhakh*, meaning thickets or boughs (often woven together to cover or protect), a sukka is a hut or a booth that functions as a temporary shelter.[58] This shelter may be for cattle (Gen. 33:17), warriors (II Sam. 11:11), field hands (Is. 1:8), or travelers (Lev. 23:43; Jonah 4:5). Popularly, the sukka is best known as the temporary lodging (with a woven protective covering of boughs, known as *sekhakh*) that God commands Israel to live in during the festival of Sukkot (Lev. 23:42).

In our verse, the word *sukko* contains a possessive pronoun, meaning God's sukka. It likely refers to the Temple, a place that offers shelter both to individuals seeking refuge under God's auspices (Ps. 27:5) and to the inhabitants of Jerusalem, who are shielded by God's Presence (Ps. 76:3).[59] In referring to the ravaged Temple as God's sukka (*sukko*), a word that connotes God's protective role, Eikha 2:6 resonates with tragic irony. No longer can God's Temple function as a shelter, as it

---

57. In his prophecies of return, Isaiah restores Jerusalem's status, calling her "the city of holiness" (Is. 48:2, 52:1). See also Nehemiah 11:1, 11.

58. BDB, *Lexicon*, 696–97.

59. Rashi and Ibn Ezra on Eikha 2:6 explain that *sukko* refers to the Temple. This seems to be the simplest meaning of the word in this verse.

falls victim to the tragedy that God has brought upon Judah. The word sukka also evokes an association with the festival. God demolishes His Temple just as He quashes celebration of the festivals, which brought throngs of pilgrims to the Temple. This sabotages Jerusalem's joyful and hallowed character.

The rarer verbal form of the word *ḥamas* ("violence"; see Gen. 6:11; 49:5) means to act violently.[60] This is sole biblical verse in which this powerful verb modifies God's actions. Perhaps this verse should be translated, "And He did violence to His sukka, like a garden."[61] However, in this reading, the meaning of the garden is quite obscure: Why would a garden be an object slated for destruction? In Jeremiah 13:22, the verbal form (*neḥmesu*) appears parallel to the word *gala*, meaning to reveal or expose. Accordingly, I (like many translators) have translated it here as "And He stripped."[62]

What does it mean to strip the Temple as one strips a garden? Rashi explains that just as one plucks the vegetables from a garden, so God ransacks His Temple.[63] Using the enemies as His agents, God pillages the Temple, emptying it of all items, large and small. The garden metaphor, with its absconded produce, alludes to the plundering of Jerusalem's food as the catastrophe unfolds. The result is hunger in Jerusalem, a prominent theme in the latter half of this chapter.

The garden metaphor also evokes the Temple's life-giving functions, the way its religious rituals provide food for the soul. Just as the

---

60. See, for example, Jeremiah 22:3; BDB, *Lexicon*, 329.
61. Moshkovitz, 12.
62. See Ibn Ezra's commentary on Eikha 2:6 and R. Yosef Ibn Janach in his *Sefer Shorashim* on the word *ḥamas*.
63. See Job 15:33, as cited by Rashi and others. While this particular metaphor does not appear anywhere else in the Bible, the Bible often compares Israel's destruction to the devastation of a place that grows produce. Consider Isaiah's parable of Israel as a vineyard, meant to yield grapes and fine wine (Is. 5:1–7). Once the vineyard betrays its owner, the owner removes its protective gates, exposing it to elements that destroy the vineyard and its produce. Likewise, Micah threatens that Zion will be like a plowed-up field (Mic. 3:12), and Jeremiah (12:10) bemoans that shepherds have destroyed God's vineyard (again, a metaphor for His nation) and trampled His field, rendering it a desolate wilderness.

garden without its fruits is no longer beneficial, so too the ransacked and ruined Temple has lost its vital purpose.

In the previous reading, the garden simply refers to a place that grows produce. Invariably, however, a biblical reference to a garden, especially in an obscure passage such as this, suggests an association with *the* garden, namely, the Garden of Eden:[64]

> And he stripped his sukka like a garden... R. Shimon bar Naḥmani said: Like the first man (Adam), as it says, "And He expelled the man..." (Gen. 3:24). (Eikha Rabba [Vilna] 2:10)

The Temple mirrors the Garden of Eden, a sacred locus that contains God's immanent presence.[65] Proximity to God (whether in the Garden of Eden or in the Temple) is both a privilege and a responsibility, requiring humans to exercise vigilance and careful obedience. Disobedience to God precipitates expulsion from God's proximity. A midrash parallels Adam's expulsion from the garden with Israel's expulsion from the Temple and the land:

> Everything that happened to Adam happened also to Israel. God brought Adam into the Garden of Eden and commanded him. [Adam] transgressed, and [God] sentenced him to ejection and expulsion, lamenting over him "Eikha!" "And He said to him, 'Where are you (*ayeka*)?'" (Gen. 3:9).[66] From where do we know

---

64. Similarly, rabbinic commentary often interprets the references to the unidentified gardens in Song of Songs as allusions to the Garden of Eden. See, for example, *Pirkei DeRabbi Eliezer* 14; Song of Songs Rabba 5:1; Numbers Rabba 13:2.

65. Psalms 36:8–9 suggests this connection by paralleling the word *eden* (which literally means "refreshing") with a reference to God's house. See also Ezekiel 28:13–20. Perhaps the most obvious connection is the cherubs, which in the Bible are associated exclusively with the Garden of Eden and the Temple. For further development of this topic, see my article in Hebrew, "The Return to Gan Eden in *Shir HaShirim*," in *BeHag HaMatzot*, ed. A. Bazak (Alon Shevut: Tevunot, 2015), 336–38. For more on this topic in English, see Ellen Frances Davis, "Reading the Song Iconographically," in *Scrolls of Love* (New York: Fordham University, 2006), 172–84.

66. This midrash is based on the orthographic equivalence between the word *eikha* and the word *ayeka*. In the above discussion of Eikha 1:1, we saw a different midrash

that He sentenced him to expulsion (*geirushin*)? As it is written, "And he expelled (*vayigaresh*) the man (Adam)" (Gen. 3:24). From where do we know that He judges him with ejection (*shiluḥin*)? As it is written, "And the Lord ejected him (*vayishalḥeihu*)" (Gen. 3:23). Likewise, God did to Israel. He brought them into the land of Israel...and He commanded them and said to them, "This is what you shall do, so that you will live, and this is what you shall not do."[67] And they transgressed His commands and He sentenced them to ejection and expulsion, as it says, "From My house I will expel them (*agaresheim*)" (Hos. 9:15). And He sentenced them to ejection (*shiluḥin*), as it says, "Eject (*shalaḥ*) from in front of Me and they will exit" (Jer. 15:1), and He lamented over them, "Eikha!" "How does the city sit lonely" (Eikha 1:1). (Eikha Zuta [Buber] 1:39)

In its use of the word garden in this obscure metaphor, Eikha 2:6 subtly alludes to the disastrous end of the original biblical story, one that anticipates and foreshadows the destruction of the Temple. The loss of the Temple harks back to the loss of the Garden of Eden, the earliest tragedy caused by humanity's insubordination. Israel now must contend with God's inaccessibility in a harsh world, brought about by her own rebellious waywardness.

Eikha 2:7

זָנַח אֲדֹנָי מִזְבְּחוֹ
נִאֵר מִקְדָּשׁוֹ

הִסְגִּיר בְּיַד־אוֹיֵב
חוֹמֹת אַרְמְנוֹתֶיהָ

(Eikha Rabba [Vilna] 1:1) that was likewise based on the orthographic correspondence between these words. See also Eikha Rabba *Petiḥta* 4.

67. This is not a direct citation of a biblical passage, although it echoes Numbers 4:19. (See also Gen. 42:18, where a similar phrase appears, but God is not the speaker and Israel is not the addressee!) The passage in Ezekiel 18:9–32 reflects this general notion, although not the words.

קוֹל נָתְנוּ בְּבֵית־ה'
כְּיוֹם מוֹעֵד

The Lord rejected His altar
He spurned His Temple

He delivered into the hands of the enemy
The walls of her palaces

They made sounds in the House of the Lord
Like the day of a festival

Despite the possessive form (*His* Temple, *His* altar), which emphasizes God's particular investment in these places, God persists in facilitating their collapse. This is unsurprising; God professed His willingness to destroy His own house at its very inception, explicitly informing Solomon of the Temple's conditional status:

> If you and your sons turn from Me and do not observe My commandments and the statutes that I have placed before you … then I will fling away from before Me the house that I have consecrated to My name… Everyone who passes this [house] will be astonished and whistle, and they will say, "For what did the Lord do this to this land and to this house?" (I Kings 9:6–8)

God disavows the place consecrated to His service. He actively enables the enemies to seize its palaces. Though the enemies have destroyed God's Temple, this verse makes it clear that they have not undermined God's omnipotence. Indeed, it is God who summons the enemies to punish His nation.[68] The notion of absolute divine power remains unmarred, despite the demolition of God's house.

The appalling reality is that Israel's enemies have prevailed; their whoops and cheers fill the House of God, replacing the sounds of festive

---

68. See for example, Isaiah 42:24–25; 47:7. Compare, similarly, Isaiah's explanation for Assyria's power and triumph over Israel (Is. 7:13, 18–19; 10:5–6).

worship. An ironic reminder (and a parody) of the joyful noise of festive celebration, the enemies' elated cries echo mockingly throughout the Temple precincts. The raucous din of devastation contrasts with the nation's silence. Bereft of their Temple and festive days, the nation remains in a mute daze, wordlessly moaning and mourning (Eikha 2:5) as their enemies raze the Temple.

Absent of the meeting place with God, the nation has no means for reconciliation with God; there are no sin-offerings and no Day of Atonement ceremony. The Aramaic *Targum* explicitly adds this point in its textual embellishment of Eikha 2:6:

> And He uprooted His Temple like a garden. *He destroyed the place established to atone for His people.* (*Targum Eikha* 2:6)

Ni'er (Spurned) and Psalms 89

The exact meaning of the word *ni'er*, signifying God's action or attitude toward His Temple, remains unclear.[69] In accordance with the first part of the binary sentence ("The Lord rejected [*zanaḥ*] His altar"), interpreters often suggest a parallel meaning for *ni'er* – "spurn" or "abhor."[70]

This verb appears only once more in the Bible, in Psalms 89:40, describing God's rejection of His covenant with the Davidic kings. Based on its usage in Psalms, Rashi explains that the word denotes abrogation, meaning that God causes the Temple to cease its function. Radak suggests that the word means to destroy, portraying God (once again) actively ruining His Temple.[71] Radak probably extrapolates this meaning from the parallel word in Psalms 89:40, *ḥillel*, used to describe God profaning the Davidic crown by flinging it upon the ground. Eikha 2:2 also describes God profaning (*ḥillel*) the kingdom, using the same word as Psalms 89:40.

Eikha's linguistic allusions to Psalms 89 draw attention to the similarity of substance and tone between that chapter and our own. Initially, Psalms 89 appears to sketch a portrait of divine munificence.

---

69. See BDB, *Lexicon*, 611.
70. Ibn Ezra translates hate or forsake. See also Moshkovitz, 13.
71. See Radak in his *Sefer Shorashim* on the root of the word *ni'er*.

Its first thirty-eight verses are a grateful recollection of God's promise to David of eternal dynasty (II Sam. 7).[72] Pivoting sharply, verses 39–52 veer from this idyllic portrait, expressing instead outrage and dismay over God's unfathomable abrogation of His promise. These latter verses in Psalms 89 describe the implication of the catastrophe of 586 BCE for the Davidic monarchy – the rejection of the Davidic king (verses 39–40), the razing of his fortresses (verse 41), the humiliation of his defeat (verses 42, 46) the victory of his enemies (verses 43–44), and the discontinuation of the dynasty (verses 45–46). The chapter culminates in an accusatory tone, employing a rhetorical question that illustrates the speaker's bewilderment:

> Where are Your steadfast loyalties of yesteryear, Lord, which You promised to David in your faithfulness? (Ps. 89:50)

Famously, Ibn Ezra (Ps. 89:2) cites a well-known "wise and pious" Spanish rabbi who refused to read this harsh chapter due to its insolent accusations against God.[73] This jarring psalm accords with Eikha chapter 2, which adopts a similar tone toward God, culminating in a direct accusation against Him (2:20).

Mo'ed: A Wordplay

The word *mo'ed* has appeared three times within the span of two verses (Eikha 2:6–7). Its first usage suggests an appointed place (the Temple), while its second appearance refers to an appointed time (namely, a festival).[74] Our verse (2:7) describes a sound that recalls the *yom mo'ed*,

---

72. Linguistic similarities that connect the first part of this chapter to II Samuel 7 abound, evoking the chapter that contains God's covenantal promises to David. See, for example, Psalms 89:27–28, 33 and II Samuel 7:14; Psalms 89:34 and II Samuel 7:15–16; Psalms 89:4, 21 and II Samuel 7:5, 8, 26.

73. In the chapter above, "Theology and Suffering," I discussed this bold approach, raising the possibility that Ibn Ezra's unnamed scholar is R. Yehuda Halevi, author of the *Kuzari*.

74. In Eikha 1:4, I discussed that the word *mo'ed* may be referring to either place or time (or perhaps both).

meaning the appointed day (or festival), but its location in the House of God alludes to the spatial *mo'ed* as well.

God has upended those spheres previously consecrated by Him. Instead of a time designated by God to be a hallowed celebration, God now selects a day for punishment (Eikha 1:5; 2:22). And in place of the sacred space where humans encounter the divine, God allows that place to be filled with the triumphant shouts of those who desecrate it.

Eikha 2:8

חָשַׁב ה' לְהַשְׁחִית
חוֹמַת בַּת־צִיּוֹן

נָטָה קָו
לֹא־הֵשִׁיב יָדוֹ מִבַּלֵּעַ

וַיַּאֲבֶל־חֵל וְחוֹמָה
יַחְדָּו אֻמְלָלוּ

The Lord determined to destroy
The wall of the daughter of Zion

He spread out a line
And did not withdraw His hand from swallowing

And He made the rampart and the wall mourn
Together they were miserable[75]

---

75. The word *umlal* often appears in conjunction with the word mourn, suggesting a similar or parallel meaning (see Is. 33:9; Jer. 14:2; Hos. 4:3). BDB, *Lexicon*, 51, translates it as to languish or be feeble. In biblical passages, the word variously describes the mourning/languishing of the produce, the land, the gates of the city, or humans. The context often involves food and children (see Is. 19:8; Jer. 15:9; Joel 1:10). The usage commonly evokes dashed hopes or expectations. For example, Jeremiah 14:2 describes the mourning (*umlalu*) of Judah's gates, once the center of its bustling trade and economic activity. Likewise, in our verse, Jerusalem's physical edifices mourn, in contrast to their previous strength and perceived immutability.

Instead of dwelling on the jubilant shouts of the enemies, this verse returns our attention to God, who is the actual perpetrator of the catastrophe. God's assault on Jerusalem is not a spontaneous outburst of divine wrath. Rather, God planned this catastrophe with forethought and careful preparation. Rashi notes that the word *ḥashav* is in the past tense, indicating that God contemplated destroying Jerusalem long before the actual *ḥurban*: [76]

> It has been many days since it occurred to God to do this [destroy the city]. As it says, "Because this city has aroused My anger and My wrath [from the day that they built it until today] and it must be removed from before Me" (Jer. 32:31). (Rashi, Eikha 2:8)

The line that God spreads appears to be a reference to the measuring line used by builders (see Jer. 31:38; Ezek. 47:3; Zech. 1:16), or perhaps to that used for assuming ownership of land (Is. 34:17). In an ironic parody of construction and possession, God carefully stretches out a line to measure Jerusalem for destruction and loss of ownership.[77] Instead of imposing order, this line inflicts disorder. Ibn Ezra likens this destructive line to the *kav tohu* (line of chaos) Isaiah (34:11) describes God using to wreak destruction upon Edom.[78]

Metaphor: The Personification of Jerusalem

To conclude the verse, God imposes mourning upon the ramparts and the walls of the city. These fortifications symbolize the city's defensive strength; the mourning of the walls and ramparts indicates their failure to function properly, leaving Jerusalem vulnerable to invaders.[79]

---

76. Jeremiah also uses the verb *ḥashav* to portray God's premediated decision to destroy Judah and Jerusalem (Jer. 18:11, 26:3, 36:3). In a positive reversal, Jeremiah (29:11) uses the word *ḥashav* to describe God contemplating and planning Judah's redemption.
77. For a similar usage, see II Kings 21:13; Isaiah 28:17. See also Amos 7:7–9.
78. The phrase *tohu vavohu* recalls the primordial chaos prior to God's creative structuring of the world (sometimes described with the same verb used here, *nata* – to stretch out). See Isaiah 40:22; 44:24; Jeremiah 10:12; 51:15. God, who created the world, maintains the right to destroy it when it is no longer fulfilling its purpose.
79. The city's ramparts and walls often emerge as a symbol of the city's strength, deriving from God's presence (see Is. 26:1; Ps. 48:14).

This verse's final sentence alludes to another loss that accompanies Jerusalem's destruction. The word "together" (*yaḥdav*), ironically recalls Jerusalem's unifying power: "Built-up Jerusalem: A city that knits people together (*yaḥdav*)" (Ps. 122:3).[80] The loss of the city spells the loss of national unity; instead of drawing the people together to worship God, Jerusalem's walls and ramparts unite in shared misery.

The city's external barriers assume personality and pathos in this verse.[81] The grief of the ramparts and walls mirrors that of Jerusalem's inhabitants, whose mourning and moaning (verse 5) resonate hauntingly. In our next two verses we will see the gates of the city sinking to the ground (verse 9), closely followed by the elders' similar action (verse 10). The city and her inhabitants mingle and merge in their collapse, a crumpled heap of once-vibrant buildings and humans.

Nevertheless, Jerusalem's destruction does not result in her demise, nor does it return her to her natural state as an inanimate city of stones. By preserving Jerusalem's human persona, by describing her mourning even as she succumbs, we can perceive Jerusalem's faint breaths. Dulled but not destroyed, under the layers of rubble Jerusalem remains alive. Thus, Israel can retain an emotional attachment to its vibrant city, despite the fact that it lies in ruins. If Jerusalem still lives, Israel will seek to return to her. Moreover, if the city still breathes, then so does Israel, whose immutability links to that of her city. The nation's hopes and aspirations rest on Jerusalem's continued existence.

Eikha 2:9

טָבְעוּ בָאָרֶץ שְׁעָרֶיהָ
אִבַּד וְשִׁבַּר בְּרִיחֶיהָ

---

80. Although there are different ways to interpret this verse, the above translation is based on the explanation of both Ibn Ezra and Radak on Psalms 122:3.

81. This personification of the city is common, as we have already seen in chapter 1. Jeremiah 14:2 (and Is. 3:26) also employs the image of Jerusalem's gates mourning. Rasag does not accept this anthropomorphic description of the city, explaining that this verse refers to the mourning of the *people* on the rampart and wall.

מַלְכָּהּ וְשָׂרֶיהָ בַגּוֹיִם
אֵין תּוֹרָה

גַּם־נְבִיאֶיהָ
לֹא־מָצְאוּ חָזוֹן מֵה׳

**Her gates sunk into the ground
He [God] shattered and destroyed her locks**[82]

**Her king and officers are among the nations
There is no instruction**

**Even her prophets
Did not find a vision from the Lord**

After eight active verses of destruction, God begins to recede into the
background. The physical city has been obliterated, Jerusalem's gates
sunk deeply into the ground, her defensive fortifications annihilated.
Having completed His task, God issues one final blow, shattering the
locks of the city, rendering her exposed and defenseless. God exits
the scene, abandoning Jerusalem to her fate, with no further instruction. The verse closes by focusing our attention upon the nation's
loss of guidance. Bereft of political leadership, religious instruction,
or prophetic visions, Jerusalem's inhabitants are left rudderless.

This verse describes the termination of divine communication.[83]
This absence of divine direction likely comes as a startling blow to the
nation, which had confidently proclaimed that it could plot against the
prophet Jeremiah without concern that it would thereby lose divine guidance: "For instruction will not desist from the priest, nor counsel from the
wise, nor a word from the prophet" (Jer. 18:18). They should have known
better; after all, God had cut off communication with His nation in the
past (Judges 10:14; I Sam. 3:1). Moreover, God's dire threat that He will
discontinue contact with the errant nation rings ominously throughout

---

82. See Ibn Ezra, who notes that God is the subject of this sentence.
83. For a similar description, see Psalms 74:9.

the prophets (Amos 8:11–12; Mic. 3:6), and particularly during the period prior to the *ḥurban* (Jer. 7:16; 11:14; 14:11;[84] Ezek. 7:26[85]). The terrible calamity of this verse is far from unexpected.

In a different interpretation of the verse, the *Targum* suggests that the phrase *"ein Torah,"* which I translated as "there is no instruction," constitutes an explanation for the catastrophic situation:

> Her king and officers were exiled among the nation *because they did not guard the words of the Torah.* (*Targum Eikha* 2:9)

Prompted by the word *torah*, which literally means "instruction" but often refers to the Pentateuch, the *Targum* assigns blame to the leaders for their own exile.[86] Biblical passages often describe the misdemeanors of Judah's kings and officers, whose errant behavior leads to their downfall.[87] Directing our attention to the behavior of the leadership also deflects attention from the nation, who flounder helplessly in the wake of their leaders' failings.

Eikha 2:10

יָשְׁבוּ לָאָרֶץ
יִדְּמוּ זִקְנֵי בַת־צִיּוֹן

הֶעֱלוּ עָפָר עַל־רֹאשָׁם
חָגְרוּ שַׂקִּים

---

84. While these three verses in Jeremiah specifically describe God refusing to listen to Jeremiah's prayer, this appears to be a step toward cutting off communication. See also Jeremiah 42:7, where God's response to Jeremiah's petition takes ten full days.

85. See Radak on Ezekiel 7:26, in which he compares the verse in Ezekiel to Eikha 2:9.

86. Rashi adopts this reading. Ibn Ezra explains that the phrase *"ein Torah"* is a consequence of the calamity (as I have suggested above). However, Ibn Ezra maintains that the Torah is not general instruction, but the actual Torah scroll that the king wrote and carried with him at all times. According to this reading, when the king went into exile, he did so without the royal Torah scroll, a tragic and symbolic punishment.

87. While examples abound, especially in the narratives of the book of Kings, the prophet Jeremiah is particularly concerned with the behavior of sinful kings and officers (see, e.g., Jer. 1:18–19; 2:26; 37:16).

יוֹרִידוּ לָאָרֶץ רֹאשָׁן
בְּתוּלֹת יְרוּשָׁלָםִ

They sit on the ground
The elders of the daughter of Zion fall still

They raise dust upon their heads
Put on sackcloth

They bow their heads to the ground
The maidens of Jerusalem

Chaotic destruction ends. The swirl of violent verbs ceases, and the tempo slows. As the loud clatter of destruction settles, silence envelops the desolate city. In what appears to be sluggish motion (especially in contrast to the dynamism of the previous verses), the elders mutely place dust on their heads and clothe themselves in sackcloth. Formerly vibrant young women incline feebly to the earth, dirtying their heads in dull imitation of their grief-stricken elders.[88] The elders' gravity is sobering. But the maidens' dispiritedness drains the scene of the potential vitality of youth, of optimism and hope.

These figures, collapsed upon the ground, mimic the collapse of the city. Their prostrate position indicates exhaustion, bereavement, and degradation.[89] Elders and maidens alike lack the drive to energize their surroundings, replicating the lifelessness of their disgraced city.

---

88. Isaiah 47:1, 5 employs remarkable linguistic similarities in its portrait of Babylon following her defeat. The prophet addresses the city with harsh instructions, indicating her impending destruction: "Go down and sit in the dust (*afar*), maiden daughter of Babylon (*betulat bat Bavel*) sit on the ground (*laaretz*)... Sit in silence (*dumam*)." The similarities between these passages call attention to the fact that Babylon will suffer an identical fate to the one that she wrought upon Jerusalem. In the chapter "Eikha and the Prophecies of Consolation in Isaiah," I compiled a chart illustrating the extensive similarities between Eikha and Isaiah 47.

89. See also Job 2:12; II Samuel 13:31; Joshua 7:6; Ezekiel 26:16.

Contact with the earth soils the respectable elders, who add to their filth by rubbing dust upon their heads.[90] The earth, and especially the dust (*afar*), recall both the creation of humans and humankind's inescapable mortality. God informed Adam, "For you are dust (*afar*) and to dust (*afar*) you shall return" (Gen. 3:19). Following the previous verse's description of the burial of the gates, which sink deep in the earth, Jerusalem's mourners likewise descend downward, surrendering to nature's inevitable pull. Strikingly, redemption involves the opposite movements: "Shake yourself, arise from the dust (*afar*), captives[91] of Jerusalem!" (Is. 52:2), and "Therefore he lifts up his head!" (Ps. 110:7).

Yidemu

The word *yidemu* (which I translated as "to fall still") connotes paralysis, a person stunned. This word can refer specifically to the cessation of speech (Ps. 4:5; 30:13) or movement (Josh. 10:12–13; Job 31:34).[92] In our verse, the word *yidemu* suggests the mourning and helplessness of the elders. What, in fact, can they say or do? Consolation is elusive, and wisdom is not forthcoming. The speechless elders compound the absence of instruction described in the previous verse.

Some scholars understand the word *yidemu* in an opposite sense, meaning to howl and wail in lament.[93] In this reading, verse 11 (which refers to Jerusalem's tears) follows directly from our verse, which records the wails of the elders. Their keening is accompanied by other formal gestures of mourning, such as sitting on the ground, placing dust on one's head, and donning sackcloth.

---

90. For other scenarios in which mourners place dust on their head, see Joshua 7:6; I Samuel 4:12; II Samuel 1:2; 15:32; Ezekiel 27:30; Job 2:12.

91. In translating the word *shevi* as captives, I have followed Radak's explanation, which I believe fits best in the context of the verse. *Targum*, Rashi, and Ibn Ezra translate this word with the meaning "to sit," which correlates the verse in Isaiah even more closely with our verse.

92. See BDB, *Lexicon*, 198–99.

93. Like the Akkadian word *damamu* (BDB, *Lexicon*, 199). See also Isaiah 23:1–2, 6, and Berlin, 71–72.

In either case, the elders and maidens perform acts associated with mourning.[94] Now that God has halted His assault on the city, its inhabitants begin contemplating their loss, and attending to their bereavement. Yet, Eikha will not dwell on mourning for long. It will soon turn its attention to the terrible sights in the city and the clamorous theological questions that accompany them.

Part 1 (Eikha 2:1–10): A Synopsis

God enters the first half of this chapter as a dynamic force, fiercely and systematically destroying Jerusalem. The third-person narrative adopts a seemingly detached tone, introducing a frightening depiction of God. God is the enemy in this section, purposefully demolishing His once beloved city. Fueled by anger (described six times in Eikha 2:1–5), God's resolve to punish His city does not abate. One can only surmise that Israel's sins cause God's wrath, though there is no mention of these sins. The destruction of Jerusalem is no human affair; Jerusalem is not the victim of political forces, but a target of God's judgment.

Synonyms abound; verbs vie with one another to describe God's assault. God throws, swallows, destroys, kills, strips, spurns, plans, and shatters. Blows come from every direction, mercilessly battering the city. Jerusalem cowers, crumbles, and collapses. The final blow comes when the gates sink underground, leaving no outward indication that they ever existed. All of Jerusalem's edifices lie prostrate, no longer majestic or dignified.

This section focuses more on Jerusalem's physical structures than on human casualties. Nothing is spared, not habitations, fortifications, palaces, rampart, or walls. The chapter pays special attention to the Temple, dwelling on the destruction of its different parts (altar, sanctuary). Various terms portray different aspects of the Temple; it is

---

94. While many of the characteristic behaviors associated with mourning do appear, others do not. Shoes are not removed, clothes are not torn, and no one fasts. (Of course, it makes little sense to fast when the city is beset by famine.) In fact, ceremonial mourning does not occupy a central role in this book.

God's footstool, Israel's glory, God's sukka, His meeting place, and the House of God.[95]

Destruction seems to go in the wrong direction. The Babylonian attack surely began at the perimeter of the city, breaking the locks, shattering the gate, and breaching the wall. It then likely proceeded into the city, reaching the Temple at its core only after destroying much else. Our chapter proceeds in a non-chronological manner. The opening verse directs our attention to God's footstool (the Temple). Demolition of the city continues outward (but repeatedly returning to the terrible sights of the destroyed Temple) until it reaches the external walls, gate and lock. Rejecting a chronological approach to destruction, the chapter chooses instead to focus attention on the heart of the crisis, its most critical event. The Temple, the sacred center of the relationship between God and His people, lies in ruins, leaving the people dismayed and shocked. Jerusalem's destruction reflects the disruption of this relationship, and the section ends with the severance of all communication.

Loss of relationship with God is compounded by the shattering of Israel's leadership. This section repeatedly focuses on the leaders. King (verses 2, 3, 6, 9), officers (verses 2, 9), priests (verses 3, 6), and prophets (verse 9) suffer. Yet they are not innocent victims, for they shoulder responsibility for the nation. Prophets often rebuke Judah's leaders for their spiritual deficiencies as well as their ineffective leadership and failure to guide Jerusalem. The exile of its leaders in verse 9 leaves Judah flailing, with no one to direct the people, alleviate their pain, or help them rehabilitate.

By focusing on the leaders (and omitting any explicit delineation of sins), this chapter sidelines the responsibility of the general populace. Although the chapter does not yet suggest that the nation has suffered unjustly, this focus on the leaders leaves room for that claim in the second half of the chapter. If the leaders bear responsibility for the calamity, why should the nation suffer their punishment?

---

95. Not all these terms necessarily refer to the Temple. However, each one does refer to the Temple in at least one other biblical passage. The Temple is termed Israel's glory (*tifartenu*) in Isaiah 64:10, God's sukka in Psalms 76:3, and God's footstool in Psalms 132:7.

PART 2 (EIKHA 2:11–22): JERUSALEM'S ACCOUNT

Eikha 2:11–12

כָּלוּ בַדְּמָעוֹת עֵינַי
חֳמַרְמְרוּ מֵעַי

נִשְׁפַּךְ לָאָרֶץ כְּבֵדִי
עַל־שֶׁבֶר בַּת־עַמִּי

בְּעָטֵף עוֹלֵל וְיוֹנֵק
בִּרְחֹבוֹת קִרְיָה

לְאִמֹּתָם יֹאמְרוּ
אַיֵּה דָּגָן וָיָיִן

בְּהִתְעַטְּפָם כֶּחָלָל
בִּרְחֹבוֹת עִיר

בְּהִשְׁתַּפֵּךְ נַפְשָׁם
אֶל־חֵיק אִמֹּתָם

My eyes are drained[96] of tears
My innards churn

My liver spills to the ground
Because of the brokenness of the daughter of my Nation

As the child and suckling faint
In the streets of the metropolis

To their mothers they say,
"Where is grain and wine?"

As they faint like the slain
In the streets of the city

As their soul spills out
To the bosom of their mothers

---

96. We will soon examine the different possible meaning for the word *kalu*.

> As they faint like corpses
> In the streets of the city
>
> As they spill out their souls
> In their mothers' bosoms

The second part of this chapter shifts noticeably from an objective, detached, third-person account of a ravaged city to a first-person description of human casualties.[97] Jerusalem now tells the story not of destroyed buildings but of human victims, of the brokenness of her nation.[98] She spotlights the poignant image of the children collapsed in the street, seeking food, and finally expiring in their mothers' arms. This is not an emotionally neutral image; passion replaces dispassion as children, rather than edifices, emerge as the focus. The enormous human tragedy comes sharply into focus.

The personified Jerusalem alludes to her physical ailments, describing her eyes, her internal organs, and her liver, which is spilled gruesomely on the ground.[99] This self-depiction connotes Jerusalem's ebbing energy and her impending demise. It also constitutes a vivid portrayal of the exile of her residents; Jerusalem has been eviscerated. Just as a person cannot exist without internal organs, Jerusalem cannot survive without her inhabitants.

---

97. The chapter does not specifically identify the first-person speaker as Jerusalem. Some scholars suggest that the narrator is speaking, shifting into first-person after concluding his third-person narration of Jerusalem's destruction (e.g., Berlin, 67, 72; Moshkovitz, 14). Others maintain that the speaker is God or the prophet, who identifies strongly with Israel's pain (see, e.g., Erhard S. Gerstenberger, *Psalms Part 2 and Lamentations*, FOTL XV [Grand Rapids: Eerdmans, 2001], 487–89; O. Kaiser, 143; House, 385). I find this latter approach unlikely, considering God's hostile role in the chapter and the first-person speaker's angry address to an adversarial God in 2:20–22. While the anonymous voice here may be the prophet Jeremiah, Jeremiah's role in the book is strikingly absent. It is more likely that, similar to the last chapter, Eikha offers Jerusalem the opportunity to speak in the second half of the chapter, so that she may represent the emotional perspective of the nation.
98. Jeremiah uses an identical phrase (*shever bat ammi*) in several contexts in his prophecies (see, e.g., Jer. 8:11, 21). The strong linguistic parallels between these verses and Jeremiah 14:17 (which also employs this phrase) suggests an intertextual relationship between these passages; Eikha shows that Jeremiah's warnings have been fulfilled.
99. For a similar description, see Job 16:13.

The verb *shafakh* (to spill out) appears twice in these two verses, drawing a parallel between the disemboweled city and her slaughtered inhabitants. The first time it describes Jerusalem's innards spilling on the ground (*nishpakh*). The same verb again appears (*behishtapeikh*) to describe the death of the children, who expire ("spill out their souls") as they lie cradled in their mothers' bosoms.[100] Their destinies inextricably linked, Jerusalem's fortune corresponds with that of her nation. Ultimately, Israel's prayers for the restoration of Jerusalem constitute prayers for her own restored fortunes.

Eyes and Tears (*Kalu VaDema'ot Einai*): Weeping or Paralysis?

Eikha 2:11 opens with Jerusalem's tears (*demaot*). This is not the first time that we witness the city's tears; Eikha 1:2 depicted Jerusalem crying in the night, her unwiped tears on her cheeks. Similarly, 1:16 depicted Jerusalem's eyes flowing with tears. The copious tears that have flowed since the opening of the book seem to have damaged Jerusalem's eyes, as indicated by one possible meaning of the verb *kalu* (ruin): "My eyes have been ruined by my tears."[101] This image of Jerusalem's ruined eyes dovetails with the portrayal of her churning innards and spilled liver; one by one, Jerusalem's organs fail her as her vitality ebbs away.

The verse acquires a different meaning if the verb *kalu* means completion.[102] In this reading, Jerusalem describes the cessation of her tears: "My eyes have ceased [shedding] tears," or, as I have translated above, "My eyes are drained of tears." Jerusalem has no more tears, no

---

100. In several biblical passages, this phrase (*shefokh nefesh*) means to pour out one's profound distress (I Sam. 1:15; Ps. 42:5). The context of our verse suggests that this is a physical image of children's lives draining from them as they take their final breaths.

101. Many scholars read the verse in this way (as in, e.g., Is. 10:23; Nahum 1:8). See Gordis, 136; Hillers, 32; Berlin, 63; House, 368; O'Connor, 36; Westermann, 142.

102. For example, Genesis 2:1; Exodus 39:32. Gottwald, 10, translates: "My eyes are spent with tears." For the reasons that I will explain, I have adopted a similar meaning in my translation, in spite of the awkwardness presented by the prepositional letter attached to the word tears (*vadema'ot*).

more strength for crying.[103] This represents a new stage in the city's grief. Paralyzed by the sights, Jerusalem becomes numb, unable to respond emotionally. Events later in the chapter bear out this reading. In verses 18–19, the narrator turns directly to Jerusalem,[104] pleading with her to cry, to sob, to spill out her tears before God. These verses imply that Jerusalem has discontinued her crying, as indicated by our verse.[105] Abrupt cessation of tears implies Jerusalem's newfound numbness, her inexorable slide into a dull, impassive stupor, caused by a deliberate suspension of emotion.

Jerusalem's eyes cease to function as a result of the awful sights of the children expiring on her streets. In a bid to rouse Jerusalem to prepare for her redemption, Isaiah offers her the opposite image, instructing her to raise her eyes and witness the return of her children:[106]

> Lift up your eyes to your surroundings and see everyone gathered and coming toward you! Your sons come from afar and your daughters carried tenderly on the hip. (Is. 60:4)

---

103. Psalms 69:4 contains an identical phrase (*kalu einai*). Exhausted by a sense of imminent annihilation, the psalmist describes his weariness, the failure of his voice, and the cessation of his eyes (*kalu einai*) while he waits for an answer from God. It is unclear there whether the eyes are ruined by copious tears or whether they cease to produce them, preventing us from drawing any direct conclusion from this verse.

104. Literally, "the wall of the daughter of Zion." I will discuss this unusual appellation in Eikha 2:18.

105. Significantly, the verse that begins with the letter *ayin* in our chapter (2:17) contains no reference to eyes. This seemingly insignificant omission becomes glaringly important when viewed in comparison with the other chapters of the book. The *ayin* verses of both chapters 1 and 4 (1:17, 4:17) contain an explicit reference to eyes. Two out of the three *ayin* verses in the triple acrostic of chapter 3 open with the word *eini* (my eye), and the middle verses refers to God's sight. Even in chapter 5, which lacks an acrostic but still retains the twenty-two verse structure, what would have been the *ayin* verse (5:17) contains the word *eineinu* (our eyes). Perhaps the omission of the eyes from the *ayin* verse in our chapter suggests that they have ceased to function.

106. See also Isaiah 49:18, 52:8.

The Death of the Children

Jerusalem's initial speech directs attention to the wretched children, presenting a dramatic close-up of their slow and excruciating death. They collapse and languish, plead (to no avail), feebly flail, and finally expire, taking their final breaths in their mothers' arms. These intense images elicit an emotional response from the reader, who cannot remain detached as a child utters his last desperate words.

The scene of the mothers and children functions both as a metaphor and as a literal image. On the metaphoric level, Eikha has already cast Jerusalem in the role of mother, with Judah's population assuming the role of her children (1:5, 18). In this context, Jerusalem is the one who experiences the excruciating pain of the mother, as she impotently bears witness to the suffering and death of her beloved children, her populace.

Nonetheless, this scene appears to be genuine and literal, a concrete description of interactions between mothers and children. Why does Jerusalem fixate upon the children, while ignoring the starvation of the rest of the population? Perhaps Jerusalem notices the children because they are the first to die of malnourishment. For now, they may be the only ones dying on Jerusalem's streets. It is more likely, however, that Jerusalem's attention rests on the children because their suffering exacts an immense emotional toll. The agonizing picture of children expiring in their mother's arms as they beg for a morsel of food is appalling and unnatural. Children should outlive their parents. Their demise spells the loss of the future, the loss of continuity.

Jerusalem also focuses on the suffering children in order to draw attention to the theological core of this chapter – namely, the sense of profound confusion. Children, especially infants, cannot incur blame. By painting a portrait of innocent victims, of the righteous who suffer inexplicably (*tzaddik vera lo*), this chapter presents the atrocities as incomprehensible.

This theological problem surfaces repeatedly in chapter 2, constituting its primary thesis. Unlike the previous chapter, this chapter catalogs the ways in which humans suffer for inexplicable reasons; regular folk are punished for their leaders' sins, and children die without having lived long enough to be culpable for their actions.

Jerusalem uses a strong phrase to describe her turmoil: *ḥomarmaru mei'ai*, "my innards churn." In the previous chapter, Jerusalem employed an identical phrase to describe her grief (Eikha 1:20: *mei'ai ḥomarmaru*). Appearing in two consecutive chapters, this rare phrase draws attention to the different theological positions of each of these chapters. In chapter 1, Jerusalem's anguish derives from her rebellion against God (Eikha 1:20): "Look, Lord, for I am anguished, my insides churn, my heart turns over within me, *for I have surely rebelled!*" This attitude characterizes chapter 1, which moves steadily toward accountability. In chapter 2, Jerusalem does not direct her address to God and does not assume responsibility for the catastrophe. Instead, she describes her physical and emotional turbulence, caused by the terrible sights of her shattered people and the suffering children.[107]

Mothers and Infants

These verses do not focus solely on the children. Verse 12 begins and ends with the mothers; the lexical placement of the word *imotam* illustrates the way the mothers enfold their dying children. Mothers are expected to shield their children, to protect them from all harm, including (perhaps especially) starvation. Infants cannot obtain food on their own; they rely on others. Under normal circumstances, mothers take responsibility for their children's welfare. Maternal instinct lies at the core of human compassion.[108] The mothers' failure suggests the severity of the situation. If the mothers cannot save their children from starvation, the storehouses must surely be depleted.[109]

---

107. Prophets did repeatedly admonish the people that their fate would devolve upon their children if they refused to cease their sinning. See, for example, Jeremiah 6:11, 9:20; both passages share several notable features with the descriptions in Eikha.

108. This is indicated by the etymological connection between the word *reḥem* (womb) and the word *raḥamim* (compassion). I will explore this idea at greater length in Eikha 4:10.

109. Berlin, 72, notes that the common (propitious) phrase "*dagan vetirosh*" is replaced here by the children's unique phrase requesting "*dagan vayayin*." Berlin suggests that this pair refers to food that can be stored. The mothers' silence in the aftermath of their children's pleas indicates that nothing remains in the storehouses.

However, we will see that this chapter later depicts mothers violating these norms, behaving without compassion. Mothers consume their children, rather than protecting and nurturing them (2:20). Perhaps the mothers in our verse are not as innocent as they seem. Possibly, it is not that the mothers *cannot* provide food, but rather that they actually *deny* their final stores to their children. The death of the children in their mothers' bosoms hints at the possibility that their mothers do not nurse them.[110] This reading is supported by the word *yonek* (suckling), used to describe the child. While it is possible that their milk has dried up for lack of nourishment, it is also possible that the mothers simply refuse to nourish their children, as this would deplete them of their own vital resources. This foreshadows the mothers' cannibalistic behavior described at the conclusion of the chapter (2:20). These verses also prepare us for the encounter with the cruel Judean mothers in Eikha 4:3–4, who refuse to suckle their infants. These images depict the dissolution of compassion, the failure of maternal instinct to nurture, which results in the death of the helpless children.

Poetic Composition:
The Chiasm at the Center of the Chapter

Verses 11–12 form the epicenter of chapter 2. Just as we saw in the previous chapter, these two middle verses contain a linguistic chiasm. Verse 11 describes Jerusalem's innards spilling (*nishpakh*) to the ground as she observes the children languishing (*be'atef*) on the streets (*birhovot*) of the metropolis. Verse 12 resumes Jerusalem's contemplation of the miserable children in reverse linguistic order, languishing (*behitatefam*) like corpses in the streets (*birhovot*) of the city, as they spill out (*behishtapekh*) their souls in the bosom of their mother:

נִשְׁפַּךְ לָאָרֶץ כְּבֵדִי...
בֵּעָטֵף עוֹלֵל וְיוֹנֵק בִּרְחֹבוֹת קִרְיָה

...בְּהִתְעַטְּפָם כֶּחָלָל בִּרְחֹבוֹת עִיר
בְּהִשְׁתַּפֵּךְ נַפְשָׁם אֶל־חֵיק אִמֹּתָם

---

110. See Ibn Ezra on Eikha 2:12, who notes the significance of the mother's role as the one who *nurses* the child.

The chiasm draws attention to the chapter's central idea, the death of the children in the public streets of the city.[111] No one comes to the children's aid; the adults lack either the resources or the desire to keep them alive. This bleak scenario calls for rectification. Will Jerusalem's streets ever again swell with young people, with sounds of joy, with a promising optimism? The prophet Zechariah offers a vision of Jerusalem's streets that consciously contrasts with the dismal images of Eikha:[112]

> So says the Lord of hosts: Once again, elderly men and women will sit in the streets (*birhovot*) of Jerusalem, and each person will have a staff in his hand because of his advanced years. And the streets (*urhovot*) of the city will fill with boys and girls playing in the streets (*birhovoteha*). (Zech. 8:4–5)[113]

When read within the broader canon, it becomes clear that the calamity of Eikha will be rectified; Judah will return from exile and rebuild her city. Israel's history continues, illustrating the nation's remarkable fortitude and reaffirming God's ongoing covenantal commitment to His nation.

Eikha 2:13

מָה־אֲעִידֵךְ

מָה אֲדַמֶּה־לָּךְ הַבַּת יְרוּשָׁלַ͏ִם

מָה אַשְׁוֶה־לָּךְ

וַאֲנַחֲמֵךְ בְּתוּלַת בַּת־צִיּוֹן

---

111. A similar scenario takes place on the streets of the city of blood, Nineveh, in Nahum 3:10. The parallel constructed between the punishment of the evil Nineveh and that of Jerusalem does not speak well of Jerusalem's sins.

112. See also the ideal image of tranquil streets filled with abundant prosperity in Psalms 144:13–14.

113. This poignant biblical passage was frequently cited by R. Yehuda Amital *z"l, Rosh Yeshiva* of Yeshivat Har Etzion. Having personally witnessed the Holocaust of the Jews of Eastern Europe (including one million children), R. Amital often marveled at the "miracle" of Jewish children thriving and frolicking in the streets of Jerusalem, as prophesied by Zechariah.

כִּי־ גָדוֹל כַּיָּם שִׁבְרֵךְ
מִי יִרְפָּא־לָךְ

How can I bear witness to you?
To what can I compare you, daughter of Jerusalem?

To what can I equate you, so that I can comfort you?
Maiden of the daughter of Zion

For as great as the sea is your brokenness!
Who can heal you?[114]

As the snapshot of the dying children fades, Jerusalem's speech abruptly
ends. Words cannot adequately represent the horror. Jerusalem has no
more tears, no more strength, no more words. Numbed by the horror,
Jerusalem becomes frozen and mute, unable to continue her narration
of the events.[115]

The narrator steps in to fill the chasm left by Jerusalem's silence.
Speaking directly to Jerusalem, the narrator presents a series of opaque
rhetorical questions. Can one bear witness to Jerusalem? Can anything
be compared to Jerusalem's situation? Is there anything that can console
the ruined city? The answer implied by these rhetorical questions is a
resounding no. The narrator presents these events as unprecedented
and incomparable. This produces a profound sense of helplessness, an
inability to provide consolation or a path to recovery.

Rhetorical Questions

"How can I bear witness to you?"[116]

---

114. Jeremiah 19:11 uses a similar phrase to prepare the inhabitants of Jerusalem for a
calamity that has no remedy. See also the language of Deuteronomy 28:35, which
delineates the punishments that the nation will receive if they disobey God.

115. Psalms 77 describes a similar situation, in which the psalmist cannot speak (77:5b),
and perhaps also cannot cry (77:5a), as a result of his theological reflections
(77:8–10). Lexical similarities connect this psalm to Eikha in other ways as well.

116. On translating the word as witness, see *Targum* and Ibn Ezra. Another biblical
usage suggests a warning or a solemn admonishment (deriving from the word

Scholars struggle to explain this peculiar rhetorical question: Why is it necessary for the narrator to bear witness to Jerusalem?[117] Bearing witness means that he observes her and validates her continued existence. It means that she is not insignificant, that her story continues to endure and interest others. However, this query suggests the opposite: The narrator wishes to say that he *cannot* bear witness for Jerusalem. Jerusalem's future remains uncertain, and she remains isolated in the enormity of her pain.[118]

"To what can I compare you?... To what can I equate you so that I can comfort you?"

The narrator's questions imply that no city has suffered like Jerusalem. Is this an accurate representation of the facts? Ancient cities frequently fell to their enemies, who murdered scores of innocent victims, including children. Additionally, why does the narrator assume that equating Jerusalem's pain with the pain of another would provide some sort of solace?[119]

"testify" and likely relating to the attempt to uphold divine testimonies, or laws). This word appears frequently to describe prophetic activity (e.g., II Kings 17:13; Jer. 11:7). In our verse, this meaning would suggest the narrator's despair ("how can I admonish you?"); there is no longer a point to prophetic rebuke when Jerusalem's brokenness is beyond repair. While this meaning segues nicely into the next verse, which accuses the prophets of failure, I think the context of our verse renders this meaning unlikely and therefore I have relegated it to a footnote.

117. As is common in biblical scholarship, numerous scholars prefer to resolve difficulties such as these by emending the text. Some (e.g., D. Hillers, 33, 39) follow the Latin Vulgate, changing the *dalet* to a *resh*, with the meaning *e'erokh*, "To what can I compare you." (The Vulgate likely was translating from a text that had the word with a *resh*, which is easily confused with a *dalet*. See, e.g., Radak, I Chr. 1:7; R. Yosef Kara, Josh. 9:4.) The Vulgate's emendation yields a series of three nearly identical rhetorical questions in a row, while the massoretic text produces a richer verse, containing a more diverse set of questions.

    Another solution is to regard the *dalet* in this word as doubled. The word would then mean "to strengthen" or "to encourage" (Ps. 20:9, 146:9): "How can I strengthen you?" See Gordis, 164. While this query makes sense in context, it is not plainly indicated by the form of the word, which lacks a *dagesh* (diacritical mark) in the *dalet*.

118. Dobbs-Allsopp, 96, observes that the book of Eikha itself bears witness to Jerusalem's pain, thereby memorializing her and testifying to her continued significance.

119. Rashi (Eikha 2:13) assumes that this is simply a psychological truth: when a suffering person hears of another person who suffers similarly, it provides solace. See also Rasag.

While the exact sense of this verse remains obscure, the narrator's queries seem designed to focus our attention on Jerusalem's loneliness. The narrator searches in vain for anyone who has experienced Jerusalem's pain, who can identify and empathize with her, offering her some measure of support and consolation. This recalls the loneliness theme of the previous chapter, often highlighted using the word *naham* (comfort). Employed five times in the negative in chapter 1 ("there is no comforter"), the sixth and final appearance of the word is in our verse in the guise of a rhetorical question. These questions suggest that nothing and no one can console Jerusalem. No one bears witness for her, and no one empathizes with her. Jerusalem's alienation is complete, her recovery elusive. Who, indeed, can heal her?

As I noted in chapter 1, the positive spin on Jerusalem's loneliness is her singularity. Jerusalem's glory is unlike that of any other city, deriving from God's presence (e.g.. Ps. 9:12; 48:2–4; 125:1). When God chooses Jerusalem, He imbues it with His own uniqueness and unparalleled status. Indeed, Jerusalem's situation is unlike that of any other city. Can a city that bore God's presence collapse?

Intriguingly, Isaiah's prophecies of consolation employ two verbs of this verse (compare and equate) to describe God's incomparability:

"And to whom will you compare Me, and I will be equated?" says the Holy One. (Is. 40:25)

"To whom will you compare Me and make Me equal? Liken Me so that I will be compared?" (Is. 46:5)

This may not resolve the verse's lack of clarity, but it does offer a solution to its quandary. While Eikha 2:13 longs for some company for Jerusalem, for someone with whom she can compare herself, this sort of comparison cannot hold up; ultimately, it is undesirable. Jerusalem's singularity links to God's singularity, and her destined reconstruction links to God's eternity.[120]

---

120. In Isaiah's prophecies of consolation, God designates Israel to bear witness to God's omnipotence, immutability, and singularity (Is. 43:10, 12; 44:8). This may function

Simile: The Vast Sea

The immense sea – roaring, terrifying, relentlessly wild – functions as an apt simile for Jerusalem's present condition. Like the sea, Jerusalem's pain crashes violently around her; there is no bottom, no anchor, and no way to cross it.[121] Jerusalem's brokenness overwhelms her, as the sea seethes with waves that crash into the shore, threatening to overrun its borders.[122] Elsewhere in Tanakh (e.g., Jonah 2:4; Ps. 42:8), these powerful waves are called breakers (*mashber*), a word that mirrors the brokenness (*shever*) of the city. The salty waters evoke tears, alluding perhaps to the cessation of Jerusalem's tears in verse 11. Possibly, the narrator uses this image to prod a paralyzed Jerusalem to grieve, to produce tears like the swelling sea.

Echoes of Prophecies: Isaiah's Restoration

The narrator fails to offer comfort in the wake of Jerusalem's pain. Just as the sea is seemingly infinite, so too is Jerusalem's suffering.

Isaiah's prophecies of consolation refer to these verses in Eikha, offering comfort where our narrator cannot. Initially, Isaiah calls to God to control the irrepressible sea and thereby to restore order to a chaotic world:

> Awaken, awaken, garb yourself with strength, arm of the Lord,
> Awaken like days of old, like ancient generations...
> Are You not the One who dried up *yam* (the sea), the great depths
> of the waters? (Is. 51:9–10)

Isaiah then cites God, who promises that He will personally offer Israel solace, and that He controls the wild sea:

---

as a cure for the helplessness expressed in our verse. Although there is presently no one who can bear witness for Jerusalem, when Israel assumes the responsibility of bearing witness to God, this will serve as testimony for God's city, where He will rest His glorious presence for eternity.

121. Psalms 104:25 and Job 11:9 allude to the vastness of the sea.

122. This image also suggests the return to a state of primordial chaos, before God established boundaries for the sea (Gen. 1:9–10). Jerusalem's destruction recalls a situation prior to Creation, when the world made no sense and had no order or structure, before God's word began to regulate the earth. Prophets frequently hint that God's punishments will undo creation and throw the world into chaos (see, e.g., Jer. 4:22–26; Ezek. 38:19–20; Zeph. 1:2–3).

> I, I, am He who comforts you (*menaḥemkhem*)... And I am the
> Lord your God, [Who] calms the sea and churns up its waves.[123]
> (Is. 51:12, 15)

Following this, Isaiah addresses Jerusalem directly, recognizing her brokenness and her misery, due especially to the misfortunes of her wretched
children, who faint and lie prone in Jerusalem's streets (recalling 2:11–12):

> Awaken, awaken! Arise Jerusalem, for you have drunk from the
> hands of the Lord the cup of His wrath... There was none to
> guide her from all the children that she birthed, and there is none
> to support her hand from all the children that she raised. Two
> [calamities] have befallen you. Who will show sympathy to you?
> Plundering and brokenness (*shever*), starvation and sword: Who
> can comfort you? Your children fainting, lying prone on every
> street corner...who are filled with the wrath of the Lord, with
> the rebuke of your God. (Is. 51:17–20)

Finally, Isaiah promises the reversal of Jerusalem's misfortunes, the
recovery of her dignity and future:

> Awaken, awaken! Garb [yourself] in strength, Zion!
> Garb yourself in clothes of majesty, Jerusalem, Holy City!
> For no longer will the uncircumcised and impure come
> against you.
> Shake yourself off, arise from the dust, captive Jerusalem.
> Unfasten the chains on your neck, captive daughter of Zion!
> (Is. 52:1–2)

Isaiah's prophecy reverses the image of the elders in 2:10, who place dust
on their heads and clothe themselves in sackcloth. Isaiah urges Jerusalem
to shake off the dust, to clothe herself in majesty, to prepare herself for

---

123. Jeremiah 31:34 uses an identical phrase to describe God. My translation of Isaiah
    follows Ibn Ezra's explanation of Isaiah 51:15. See also Jeremiah 6:16, cited by Ibn
    Ezra to explain the word *roga*.

the joy and dignity of liberation. Isaiah's prophecies of consolation rectify Jerusalem's dismal state, constituting a guarantee that the biblical story will move past catastrophe.[124]

Eikha 2:14

נְבִיאַיִךְ חָזוּ לָךְ
שָׁוְא וְתָפֵל

וְלֹא־גִלּוּ עַל־עֲוֹנֵךְ
לְהָשִׁיב שְׁבוּתֵךְ

וַיֶּחֱזוּ לָךְ
מַשְׂאוֹת שָׁוְא וּמַדּוּחִים

Your prophets prophesied for you
falsehood and triviality

And they did not reveal[125] your transgressions
To return you to your former state[126]

---

124. For a further elaboration of this theme, see the chapter, "Eikha and the Prophecies of Consolation in Isaiah."

125. The word *gilu*, meaning to reveal, evokes the word *gala*, meaning exile. This wordplay links the prophet's failure to reveal sin with the decree of exile.

126. The exact translation of this phrase, "*lehashiv shevuteikh*," remains unclear. Does the second word mean *shevi* (captivity) or *shuv* (return)? Sometimes the above phrase refers to returning captives (Deut. 30:3), while on other occasions the context suggests the restoration of one's fortune (Job 42:10), as I have translated above. In our context, it seems unlikely that accusation against the false prophets revolves around their inability to return the captives, given that the Judean exile and captivity occurs only now. A wordplay of these two roots is common (see, e.g., Ezek. 16:53; Hos. 6:11; Amos 9:14) and our verse likely alludes to the responsibility that the prophets bear for the upcoming exile and captivity of the Judean population. Moshkovitz, 15, maintains that this phrase hints to the word *teshuva*, meaning repentance. In this schema, the failure of the prophets includes their incompetence in persuading the people to repent and return to God.

And they prophesied for you
False and misleading oracles

The previous verse concluded with a question directed toward the broken Jerusalem: "Who can heal you?"[127] This verse directs our attention to the prophets, who could have provided the elusive cure. Turning to the prophets proves to be futile. They cannot offer a remedy, for they have failed Jerusalem and led her astray with their false prophecies. In a verse redolent with linguistic allusions to our verse, Jeremiah censures the false prophets for their ill-conceived and futile words:

> And they healed (*vayerapu*) the brokenness of the daughter of my people (*shever bat ammi*) fallaciously, saying, "Peace, peace!" But there is no peace. (Jer. 8:11)[128]

It seems more likely that the query that concludes the previous verse ("Who can heal you?") is rhetorical, expressing Jerusalem's terminal malaise. If that is the case, our verse functions differently: instead of a quest to find a healer, our verse searches for the cause of Jerusalem's condition. Settling on the prophets, the verse blames them for Jerusalem's catastrophe. To a degree, this functions as an exoneration of the populace. If the leaders bear primary responsibility, then the punishment of the common folk seems unnecessary or, at the very least, excessive. Once again, we see that this chapter shies away from condemnation of the people.

False Prophets
The Torah warns against false prophets (Deut. 13:2–6; 18:20), acknowledging their immense power to sway the public. The first challenge with

---

127. Several biblical passages (e.g., Is. 30:26; Ps. 147:3) present God as Israel's healer, rendering God as the obvious answer to the query. Jeremiah 30:12–17 depicts a scenario linguistically similar to Eikha, in which the nation's sins lead to terrible injuries. No one comes to her aid (the addressee is feminine in the passage) except God, who cures the nation from her wounds. The lexical similarity between our verse and Hosea 6:11–7:1 suggests that Jerusalem's remedy lies in revealing her sins and returning to God.
128. See similarly Jeremiah 6:14.

respect to these charlatans lies simply in identifying them.[129] Biblical narratives often present prophets without explicitly calling them false, even when the context clarifies that they are imposters.[130] This allows the reader to experience the complexity from the narrative point of view of the nation, who encounters the prophet without knowing whether he is authentic. False prophets begin to emerge at the beginning of the period of the divided monarchy, gaining significance as the monarchic period progresses toward rupture.[131] The pervasiveness and undue influence of the false prophets impinge upon God's genuine prophets, and both Jeremiah and Ezekiel devote a great deal of attention to the subject.[132]

Who are these false prophets? What is their aim? False prophets assume different guises, ranging from ingenuous to malevolent. Some false prophets appear to be political hacks, hired by the court to support the king's policies.[133] At times, a prophet seems to function as a political analyst, issuing messages that adhere to his geopolitical projection or that of the king whom he serves.[134] He may simply be an optimist, offering the people a hopeful view of a promising future. Other false prophets appear to be charlatans, deliberately inventing false visions that contradict God's message.[135]

---

129. Deuteronomy 18:21–22 acknowledges that recognizing a false prophet represents a difficult challenge. This complicated matter arises in several biblical stories (see I Kings 22; Jer. 28).

130. For example, the elderly prophet from Beit El is never called a false prophet, even though the text informs us that he lied (I Kings 13:19). Nor does the text refer to Hananiah ben Azur as a false prophet. He is simply called "*hanavi*" (Jer. 28:5), which is the same title appended to Jeremiah in the chapter.

131. The first story that revolves around a false prophet is that of the elderly prophet from Beit El in I Kings 13:11–32. Most biblical interpreters assume that he is a false prophet (e.g., *Targum Jonathan*, Rashi, Ralbag, Radak), even though he receives a true prophecy in I Kings 13:20 (therefore some biblical interpreters, such as the Abravanel, think otherwise). For more on this incident, see A. Israel, *I Kings: Torn in Two* (Maggid, 2013), 171–80.

132. See, for example, Jeremiah 27–29; Ezekiel 34. The description of the false and misleading prophecies in Eikha 2:14 shares linguistic similarities with several passages. See, for example, Jeremiah 23:12–13 and Ezekiel 13:6–16.

133. I Kings 22:5–14; Amos 7:12–15.

134. For example, some of the false prophecies issued with respect to Babylonia (Jer. 27:14, 16; 37:19) likely rely on the prophet's assessment of current events and his analysis of Babylonia's strength and power.

135. For example, Jeremiah 23:14, 26–27, 32.

Still others seem ideological, motivated by idolatrous beliefs.[136] Finally, it is possible that the false prophet is himself misled, wrongly believing that he has received visions or messages. The false prophet may be motivated by all or some of the above. One thing is clear: The false prophet operates independent of God; his messages are not the product of divine revelation:

> And the Lord said to me: "Falsehood these prophets are prophesying in My name. I did not send them, nor did I command them, nor did I speak to them!" (Jer. 14:14)

Immediately prior to the *ḥurban*, false prophets wreak havoc in several related but distinct ways. Pretenders offer insipid visions of peace and good fortune. They proclaim, "Peace, peace!" with no peace in sight (Jer. 6:14; 8:11; 23:17; Ezek. 13:10, 16), specifically promising that there will be security in Jerusalem (Jer. 14:13). False prophets tend to prefer a vapid message, whose murky objective is self-promotion rather than representing God. Even if these men mean well, by failing to warn of the possibility of disaster (Jer. 28:8; Ezek. 13:6; 22:28–30) they doom the nation to apathy, preventing repentance and hastening the disaster (Jer. 23:22).

False prophets may openly contradict Jeremiah's unpopular forecasts. When Jeremiah warns of catastrophe, they declare, "No evil will come upon you" (Jer. 23:17), and when Jeremiah informs them of the famine and death, they assure the populace that they will see neither sword nor famine (Jer. 14:12–13). False prophets' interpretations of specific political events clash with those of the true prophet and offer a more desirable prognostication. Inevitably, their popularity far outweighs that of the genuine prophet, who cannot manipulate or mitigate the severe divine message that he has received.

When Jeremiah tells the Judeans that God has decreed that they should accept Babylonia's rule (Jer. 27:11–13), false prophets contradict him, offering a message of resistance (Jer. 27:9, 14). Hananiah ben Azur deflects Jeremiah's prophetic advice to suffer the yoke of Babylonia with his dramatic pronouncement that the yoke of Babylonia will imminently be broken (Jer. 28:2–4). When Jeremiah says that Babylonia will attack

---

136. Ibid. 23:13.

Jerusalem, the false prophets refute his prophecy (Jer. 37:19). Jeremiah's warning that God will surely destroy the Temple is met with outrage, indignation, and a death sentence (Jer. 26:8–9, 11), which stem from a pervasive belief that God would not destroy His own house (Jer. 7:4).[137] When Jeremiah prophesies that Babylonia will ransack the remaining vessels of the Temple at God's behest (Jer. 27:21–22), charlatans promise the return of those vessels already plundered (Jer. 27:16). Jeremiah foresees a lengthy stay in Babylonia, while false prophets vehemently disagree, clamoring for Jeremiah's imprisonment and punishment (Jer. 29:21–32).

These prophets make Jeremiah's personal life difficult, often persecuting him physically to punish him and prevent him from prophesying. More importantly, they make his prophetic task impossible to fulfill, undermining his every attempt to present God's word to the people. Jeremiah cannot effectively have an impact upon the populace because no one listens to him; the nation prefers the soothing and vacuous words of the false prophets. Thus, these imposters do not foresee the upcoming disaster, nor do they inspire change for the better. Their influence is unquestionable, the damage they wreak is immeasurable, and the spiritual repercussions abound. Indeed, the false prophets bear a large share of the responsibility for Jerusalem's disaster.

Eikha 2:15–16

סָפְקוּ עָלַיִךְ כַּפַּיִם
כָּל־עֹבְרֵי דֶרֶךְ

שָׁרְקוּ וַיַּנְעוּ רֹאשָׁם
עַל־בַּת יְרוּשָׁלָ͏ִם

הֲזֹאת הָעִיר שֶׁיֹּאמְרוּ
כְּלִילַת יֹפִי מָשׂוֹשׂ לְכָל־הָאָרֶץ

---

137. It is unclear whether the false (*sheker*) words of Jeremiah 7:4 are spoken by the false prophets. Words of *sheker* are often associated with false prophets (Jer. 5:31; 14:14). See also the role of the "prophets" in the continuation of the story of Jeremiah 7, which takes place in Jeremiah 26.

פָּצוּ עָלַיִךְ פִּיהֶם
כָּל־אוֹיְבַיִךְ

שָׁרְקוּ וַיַּחַרְקוּ־שֵׁן
אָמְרוּ בִּלָּעְנוּ

אַךְ זֶה הַיּוֹם שֶׁקִּוִּינֻהוּ
מָצָאנוּ רָאִינוּ

They clapped their hands at you
All the passersby

They whistled and they wagged their heads
Over the daughter of Jerusalem

"Is this the city about which it was said,
'[She is] perfect in beauty, a joy for all the land'"?

They opened their mouths against you
All your enemies

They whistled and they gnashed their teeth
They said, "We have swallowed!

Yes, this is the day for which we waited!
We found it! We saw it!"

As Jerusalem persists in her muteness, the narrator fills the silence by peering outward, perusing reactions to the city's downfall. Some scholars read these verses as the narrator's continued (futile) search for someone who can heal Jerusalem.[138] More likely, the narrator looks

---

138. See Dobbs-Allsopp, 97; House, 389; Gottwald, 65. This reading is especially difficult given that Eikha 2:16 features the enemies. Why would the narrator turn to Jerusalem's enemies in search of a healer?

outward because he cannot bear to look inward at the frightful sights that pervade the city.

These two remarkably parallel verses direct our gaze away from Jerusalem's populace to observe how outsiders respond to her wretched state. Each of these verses names a different group (passersby and enemies), noting their non-verbal gestures (clapping, whistling, head-wagging, teeth-gnashing), followed by direct citation of their speech. I will begin by examining the unmistakable hostility of the enemies and will then turn to the opaque attitude of the neutrally dubbed "passersby."

The Malicious Enemies (Verse 16)

Verse 16 recounts the unambiguous gloating of Jerusalem's enemies. The adversaries do not attempt to conceal their hatred for Israel and their pleasure in Jerusalem's downfall and humiliation. While the passersby in verse 15 gesticulate with their hands, mouth, and head, all the gestures of the enemy involve their mouths. Like savage animals, Israel's foes open their mouths, threatening to consume their prey.[139] They whistle and gnash their teeth viciously, delighting in Jerusalem's pain.[140] While these movements do not actually harm Jerusalem physically, they portray her antagonists as beastly and inhuman, avidly devouring the news of her calamity. The focus on the violent movements of their mouths also prepares the reader for the vitriol that issues forth once the enemies begin to speak.

Unsurprisingly, the first word that the enemy pronounces also invokes animal-like oral imagery: "We have swallowed!"[141] Taking credit for God's punishment of His nation, the enemies crow triumphantly that they have swallowed, recalling the very word that described God's actions at the beginning of the chapter (Eikha 2:2, 5).

"Yes, this is the day for which we waited! We found it! We saw it!" Framed in the first-person plural, the enemy's gleeful words illustrate the personal nature of their hostility. In an unnerving display of *rasha vetov lo* (evildoers who prosper), Israel's foes attain their loathsome goals.

---

139. See Psalms 22:14 for a similar context.
140. See Psalms 35:16 and Job 16:9–10.
141. The one Hebrew word (*bilanu*) translates into three words in English.

Only the enemies find gratification in Eikha. The word *matza* (to find) has appeared in the book three times in the negative, illustrating the hardships that Israel has endured during the catastrophe: Judah cannot find rest (1:3), the officers cannot find pasture (1:6), and the prophets cannot find visions from God (2:9). In its fourth and final appearance, the enemies find that which they desired: Israel's misfortune.

Ambiguous Language: The Passersby (Verse 15)

The meaning of gestures and non-verbal communication varies from one culture to another. Nevertheless, since the hostility of the enemies is not in doubt, their whistles and teeth-gnashing are clearly expressions of malice. Yet, the reaction of the passersby in verse 15 is harder to interpret.

Modern scholars often blend the reactions in these two verses, assuming that the gestures of the passersby likewise reflect antagonism toward Jerusalem and that their words manifest derision.[142] This view is supported by the fact that the passersby and the enemies perform an identical action (*sharku*), implying shared sentiments. In this vein, several scholars interpret the word *sharak* to mean a hiss, which is surely a malevolent sound.[143] If this is the case, verses 15 and 16 are redundant; the passersby in verse 15 are just as much the enemy as those in verse 16.[144]

Perhaps this is the point. All outsiders disparage Jerusalem. Even those who seemed neutral prove to be otherwise in the aftermath of Jerusalem's disgrace. This fulfills Ezekiel's prophecy that Jerusalem would become friendless, that neighboring nations and passersby would observe her with disdain:

> And I will place you as a ruin and a shame among the nations who surround you, *in the eyes of every passerby*. (Ezek. 5:14)

---

142. For example, Hillers, 46, interprets the passersby's gestures as an expression of contempt; Gottwald, 40, 57, 93, avers that they mock and despise Jerusalem; O'Connor, 40, describes the passersby mocking and gloating, while Dobbs-Allsopp, 97, maintains that the passersby act no better than the enemies. House, 389, terms this group of passersby "the mockers," while Gerstenberger, 489, notes their disdain.

143. Gordis, 137; O'Connor, 40; House, 389; Gottwald, 79.

144. Dobbs-Allsopp, 97, explicitly makes this point, claiming that the passersby "act no better than the enemies."

However, the reaction of the passersby can be understood differently. Why assume that their attitude is gloating and scornful? Interpreters commit a grave injustice to the passersby by not considering that they may genuinely empathize with Jerusalem and grieve over her destruction.[145] Indeed, Jeremiah depicts a scenario in which nations will pass by Jerusalem's ruins and express astonishment, and possibly genuine regret:

> And many nations will pass by this city and they will say, each person to his friend, "Why did the Lord do this to this great city?" And they will say, "It is because they forsook the covenant of the Lord their God, and they bowed to other gods and they served them." (Jer. 22:8–9)

If we examine the nature of the three physical gestures that characterize the reaction of our passersby, an ambiguous picture emerges. They clap their hands, whistle, and wag their heads. Elsewhere in Tanakh, these gesticulations can express a range of emotions.

Balak claps his hands to express rage at Balaam's failure to curse Israel (Num. 24:10). A similar phrase in Job 27:23[146] (along with whistling) seems to communicate mockery, or possibly astonishment.[147] The word *sapak* appears in Ezekiel 21:17 as an expression of grief. Jeremiah 31:18 uses this gesture as a parallel to the word *niḥamti*, conveying remorse. The nature of hand clapping remains ambiguous; those who pass Jerusalem may clap their hands in shock, horror, disdain, grief, and even anger.

Despite the tendency of some scholars to translate the word *sharak* as a hiss, translating it as a whistle allows for a more neutral

---

145. Berlin, 74, recognizes the ambiguity of their reactions, allowing for the possibility that the passersby express genuine amazement, rather than hostility. Moshkovitz, 15–16, likewise regards the passersby as empathetic and pained by Jerusalem's state. See also Renkema, 288–91.

146. This verse substitutes a *sin* for the usual *samekh* in the word *sapak*.

147. Varying exegetical interpretations of Job 27:23 illustrate the ambiguity of its precise meaning. Malbim, for example, regards these as derisive gestures, while Metzudat David implies that it conveys astonishment.

interpretation.[148] The verb *sharak* appears quite frequently to describe a physical reaction to devastation (e.g., Zeph. 2:15). Sometimes the word appears alongside the word humiliation, in a negative context (Jer. 29:18), but often it is in conjunction with the word *yishom* (I Kings 9:8; Jer. 19:8; 49:17; 50:13), an expression of horror and disbelief.

The final gesture associated with the passersby involves a movement of the head, although the nature of that movement is unclear. While I have translated this as a wag, it could be a nod, a shake or a quivering, or perhaps something else. This phrase (*vayaniu rosham*) implies mockery in other biblical contexts (II Kings 19:21; Ps. 22:8; 109:25).[149] However, a similar phrase involving a movement of the head (*nod rosh*) and describing a response to Jerusalem's destruction (along with whistling), could likewise convey an array of emotions, ranging from grief to mockery (Jer. 18:16).

By accompanying (and reinforcing) their non-verbal gestures with speech, the verse offers a better way to clarify the meaning of the passersby's gesticulations. Their query is clearly articulated: "Is this the city about which it was said, '[She is] perfect in beauty, a joy for all the land'?" Because we do not actually hear the spoken words, it is difficult to discern their tone. Do the passersby recall Jerusalem's former glory with kindness, sorrow, pity, contempt, or glee?

To understand their words, we note the similar description of Jerusalem in Psalms 48:3: "Beautiful in elevation, joy of all the land." Further cementing the parallel, that psalm describes kings assembling to pass through the city (*avru*, recalling the passersby, the *ovrei derekh*) to witness the presence of God in its midst.[150] These regal visitors react intensely to the sight of Jerusalem: They are amazed, terrified, and panicked. Seized by trembling, the kings eagerly proclaim their newfound

---

148. Berlin, 74, cites a verbal communication with Moshe Greenberg in which he opined that the correct translation is whistle, not hiss.

149. Ibn Ezra suggests that the passersby do not issue a unified response. Some of them moan sadly over Jerusalem's state, while others wag their heads in mockery. Ibn Ezra seems to think that while some of these gestures likely express sympathy, the wagging of the head generally conveys scorn in Tanakh.

150. Elsewhere in Tanakh, the perfect beauty of the holy city indicates God's immanent presence (Ps. 50:2).

belief in God and His city: "Just as we heard, so we have seen, in the city of the Lord of hosts, in the city of *our* God! God shall establish this city for eternity!" (Ps. 48:9).

The precise background of this scenario remains elusive. It is possible that Psalms 48 describes the aftermath of Sennacherib's failed attempt to conquer Jerusalem in 701 BCE.[151] Local kings arrive in Jerusalem to confirm the rumors of the city's miraculous salvation. It turns out that Jerusalem indeed remains unscathed, her beauty and structural integrity intact. The royal observers respond with astonishment, recognizing that only God's direct intervention could have brought about Jerusalem's deliverance.

Although the historical context of Psalms 48 remains uncertain, its tone most certainly does not. Awed and overcome by evidence of God's presence in His city, these kings accept upon themselves God's rule, proclaiming their faith that He will protect Jerusalem eternally. In that psalm, God's presence rests in Jerusalem's palaces, which attain a reputation as a haven.[152] Eikha 2:15 records the reversal of Psalms 48. God unleashed His fury and allowed the enemies to destroy Jerusalem's palaces (2:5, 7). The passersby who now observe the fallen city must attempt to reconcile the dreadful sight with their long-held notions about Jerusalem. Those who believed in Jerusalem's invincibility as the special protectorate of God surely experience a great blow when they observe her in her present state. By evoking Psalms 48 in their query, the passersby seem to express their great disillusionment and incredulity.[153]

There are several advantages to portraying the relationship of the passersby to Jerusalem more positively. First, it mitigates the exaggerated isolationist approach offered by many biblical scholars. Instead of

---

151. Ibn Ezra (Ps. 46:1) cites an opinion that a nearby psalm (46) was written on the occasion of the miraculous salvation of Jerusalem from Sennacherib. To examine this idea further, see the chapter above, "Historical Background."

152. In verse 11, the psalm reflects on the righteousness that fills God's right hand (*yeminecha*). This word contrasts sharply with its appearance in Eikha 2:3–4, where God's right hand (*yemino*) acts in a hostile manner against Jerusalem's residents.

153. R. Yosef Kara (Eikha 2:15) describes the genuine sorrow of the nations over the loss of the Temple.

Jerusalem standing alone, surrounded by hostility, these verses offer a more realistic and even-handed picture, in which Jerusalem's downfall produces two different reactions – celebration of her misfortune, and genuine regret.

This balanced portrait also contains an important moral message. The Bible does not construct a one-dimensional account of Israel's relations with the nations. Although in Eikha Israel often harbors justified resentment toward her enemies, her betrayers, and those who rejoice in her downfall, the book carefully distinguishes between different factions of outsiders. There are the actual enemies who revel in Jerusalem's misery, but there are also those who empathize. Some of these outsiders appear to be righteous, preserving a vision of a holy city that contains God's presence. It is a moral imperative to distinguish between good and bad, to ensure that we judge people by their actions and not by their status as outsiders.

A similar message arises in other biblical narratives. The book of Exodus, for example, juxtaposes the story of Israel's archetypal foe, Amalek (Ex. 17), with the narrative of Jethro, the righteous Midianite who sets up Israel's judicial system (Ex. 18).[154] Saul later distinguishes between them, carefully instructing Jethro's descendants to separate from Amalek before he fulfills God's instructions to destroy them (I Sam. 15:6–7). Similarly, in Ezra (chapter 4), Israel's foes successfully petition the Persian king to thwart their attempt to rebuild the Temple. The following two chapters (Ezra 5–6) offer a description of two very different Persian kings (Darius and Cyrus), illustrating how each facilitates the Temple's rebuilding. The juxtaposition of these chapters highlights the distinction between good foreigners and bad, cautioning Israel implicitly not to treat all outsiders as antagonists.

In Eikha, this message is especially critical. Facing an existential crisis, Israel could easily hunker down in an isolationist

---

154. Ibn Ezra (Ex. 18:1) maintains that this is an artificial juxtaposition, taken out of its chronological order in order to link these narratives. As evidence, Ibn Ezra points to the linguistic parallels that draw attention to the similarities (and consequently the differences) between these narratives. Cassuto, *Commentary on Exodus* (Jerusalem: Magnes, 1967), 211–12, sketches a lengthier set of linguistic parallels between the narratives.

posture, regarding all outsiders with suspicion and hostility. The ability to rise above that defensive position and recognize that some outsiders remain allies necessitates a high degree of restraint and self-possession.

Finally, if the words of the passersby evoke Psalms 48, the narrator has contrived a way to offer Jerusalem a brief respite from her misery. Through echoes of Jerusalem's glorious past, the narrator reminds the reader of a time when the city's special status fostered hope and faith throughout the land.

Eikha 2:17

עָשָׂה ה' אֲשֶׁר זָמָם
בִּצַּע אֶמְרָתוֹ אֲשֶׁר צִוָּה מִימֵי־קֶדֶם

הָרַס וְלֹא חָמָל

וַיְשַׂמַּח עָלַיִךְ אוֹיֵב
הֵרִים קֶרֶן צָרָיִךְ

The Lord did that which He planned
He executed His word that He commanded from days of old

He destroyed and did not pity

And your enemy rejoiced over you
Your adversaries raised a horn!

Having completed his panoramic exploration of those who stand outside of Jerusalem, the narrator's attention returns to God, maintaining that He planned the disaster. This assertion quashes the exultant cries of Jerusalem's foes (verse 16), who eagerly sought credit for the city's disaster. God choreographed these events, not the enemies. Despite their confident proclamation, this is not their day, but rather the day of God (Eikha 2:1, 21, 22). It is not they who swallowed, but God (Eikha

2:2, 5). The enemies' arrogant assertions are patently false; they should not receive attribution for God's punitive actions.[155]

Planned and executed by God, the catastrophe is not an impulsive act of divine wrath. God warned Israel that this would be the result of their disobedience. When did God issue this warning? A midrash (*Pesikta Zutrata* [*Lekaḥ Tov*] Eikha 2:17) cites the following verse in Leviticus, which is part of the terms of the covenant between God and Israel:

> I will place your cities in ruins, and I will make your sanctuaries desolate and I will not savor your pleasing odors. And I will make the land desolate and your enemies who dwell there will be horrified over her. (Lev. 26:31–32)

Israel has long known the price of disobedience. In fact, God's patience with His nation has been remarkable; after years of sustained sinning and repeated prophetic admonitions, God finally implements the terms of the covenant. Upon return from exile, the nation acknowledges that the catastrophic destruction was fair and anticipated:

> And [the people] returned and said, "Just as the Lord of hosts planned (*zamam*) to do to us because of our ways and our deeds, so He has done with us." (Zech. 1:6)

Zechariah's word *zamam* recalls our verse, in which the narrator explains the theology of Jerusalem's destruction. By placing these events within the broader context of biblical history, the Jewish nation can accept their justice.

---

155. The alphabetic reversal of the letters *ayin* (which opens verse 17) and *peh* (which opens verse 16) in this chapter has generated different explanations, both homiletic (see Eikha Rabba 2:20) and historical (see, e.g., A. Demsky, "A Proto-Canaanite Abecedary Dating from the Period of the Judges and its Implications for the History of the Alphabet," *Tel Aviv* 4 [1977], 14–27). O'Connor, 40–41, suggests that this reversal of letters is a deliberate literary device alluding to the reversal of God's affections. Perhaps it draws our attention to the attempt of Israel's adversaries to assume credit for the devastation. In a deft literary flourish, the *peh* verse jumps in before its turn, illustrating the enemy's bid to usurp God's role. I will examine the historical explanation relating to the order of the alphabet in Appendix 2 following this chapter.

The implied acknowledgment of God's fairness lasts briefly, for just one short sentence, before returning to the bewilderment that prevails in this chapter. Similar to the structural anomaly in Eikha 2:4 (see the explanation there), the first and third sentences of our verse conform to the customary binary sentence structure, whereas the middle verse consists of a single, stark line:

He destroyed and did not pity.

This middle sentence stands alone, drawing attention to its dreadful content. This blunt statement shocks the reader, shifting abruptly from God's logical, well-planned execution of the covenant to His merciless destruction. In accordance with the general tenor of the chapter, this verse veers away from theodicy and back to its characteristic outrage and discomfiture, drawing on the language of the first part of the chapter. Once again, God does not pity (*lo ḥamal*, 2:2). Once again, the verb *haras* describes God's assault (2:2).

Following the description of the absence of divine mercy, the verse turns its attention to the triumph of the enemies, whom God aids and abets. They benefit from His determination to fulfill His word, and they raise their horns in exultant triumph. The enemy's celebratory horns recall the absence of Israel's horn, hewn down by God in His wrath (2:3). In this chapter, God functions both as Israel's enemy (2:4–5) and as an adjunct to Israel's foes. The theological conclusions are the same; in both representations, God emerges as Israel's primary adversary.

To compound the confounding portrait of God's enmity in this chapter, we observe the way its language contrasts with Psalms 37. A psalm of theological harmony, Psalms 37 depicts an ideal world in which all people receive just recompense. God thwarts and punishes evildoers and rewards those who trust in Him. In that psalm, the wicked plot (*zomem*) against the righteous, gnashing their teeth, poising their bows, and preparing to massacre (*litvoaḥ*) the virtuous (Ps. 37:12, 14). God intervenes, foiling their plot and ensuring that the upright prevail. Our chapter, however, perceives a very different world, in which God Himself plots against His people (*zamam*, 2:17), poising His bow (2:4) and massacring without pity (*tavaḥta*, 2:21).

Even if Jerusalem's current sinful residents are not like the righteous described in Psalms 37, the sharply contrasting portrait of God in Eikha 2 emerges as a vexing theological quandary, one that reverberates shockingly throughout the chapter. How could God destroy without mercy? Why would God bolster the hands of Israel's gleeful foes? How could God Himself behave as an enemy toward His nation?[156]

Eikha 2:18–19

צָעַק לִבָּם אֶל־אֲדֹנָי
חוֹמַת בַּת־צִיּוֹן

הוֹרִידִי כַנַּחַל דִּמְעָה
יוֹמָם וָלַיְלָה

אַל־תִּתְּנִי פוּגַת לָךְ
אַל־תִּדֹּם בַּת־עֵינֵךְ

קוּמִי רֹנִּי בַלַּיְלָה
לְרֹאשׁ אַשְׁמֻרוֹת

שִׁפְכִי כַמַּיִם לִבֵּךְ
נֹכַח פְּנֵי אֲדֹנָי

שְׂאִי אֵלָיו כַּפַּיִךְ
עַל־נֶפֶשׁ עוֹלָלַיִךְ

הָעֲטוּפִים בְּרָעָב
בְּרֹאשׁ כָּל־חוּצוֹת

Their hearts cried out to the Lord
Wall of the daughter of Zion[157]

---

156. I will explore the way Eikha continues to intersect with Psalms 37 in chapter 3; see Appendix 1 of that chapter.
157. I will attempt to explain this difficult phrase below.

> Let your tears flow like a stream
> Day and night!
>
> Do not let yourself cease
> Do not stop up your eyes!
>
> Get up! Cry out in the night
> At the top of each watch
>
> Pour out your heart like water
> Before the face of the Lord!
>
> Lift up your hands to Him
> Because of the lives of your children
>
> Who are fainting from hunger
> On every street corner

Identified in the previous verse as the primary perpetrator, God is also Israel's only address – and therefore her sole hope. This galvanizes the narrator, and he passionately addresses Jerusalem, whose tears (and words) ceased in verse 11. In a series of five imperative sentences, the narrator urges Jerusalem to direct a torrent of tears to God.

In this energetic and poetic passage, the narrator employs several literary tools to beseech Jerusalem to weep. First, the narrator exhorts Jerusalem's eyes to flow like a stream, day and night.[158] Time is of the essence; she cannot afford to sleep. The narrator further presses Jerusalem to rise at the beginning of every night watch to cry out her pain.[159] In this way, Jerusalem will assume the role of the custodian of her people. She must act as a sentry who defends and shields her people without slumber.

In accordance with Jerusalem's own perspective (e.g., 1:20; 2:11), the narrator portrays her as a corporeal being; he appeals to her eyes,

---

158. For a similar image, see Jeremiah 8:23.
159. For this translation, see Gordis, 168.

heart, hands, and, implicitly, her mouth, to advocate on behalf of her children. The assumption that Jerusalem can continue to function belies her self-perception, as she described her physical body breaking down, churning and emptying her innards onto the ground (2:11). Nevertheless, the narrator encourages Jerusalem to assume control over her own destiny, instead of allowing outsiders to use their bodies (hands, mouth, head, teeth) to define her condition (2:15–16).

The narrator proposes that Jerusalem pour out her heart like water before God. While this is a unique phrase,[160] both the words "pour" and "heart" appear as key words in the book of Eikha (seven and ten times, respectively). In chapter 1, Jerusalem describes her physical response to her misery (1:20): "My insides churn, my *heart* turns over within me." Two verses later, the chapter concludes with the words (1:22), "For my groans are many, and my *heart* is miserable." In our verse, the narrator presses Jerusalem to revive her feckless heart and direct it toward God. The word *shafakh*, to pour or spill over, appears four times in this chapter in a variety of contexts. In verse 4, God pours out His wrath. In verse 11, Jerusalem spills out her innards onto the ground. In the central image of the chapter, the children spill out their souls into their mothers' bosoms (verse 12). With these frightful images in stark relief, Jerusalem must end her stubborn silence; considering the dire situation, she must allow her heart to spill over as she addresses God. Because God has poured out His wrath like fire (verse 4), it is especially important for Jerusalem to spill out her heart like water, which can extinguish God's fiery rage.

What is the goal of all these tears – supplication or lamentation? If Jerusalem's tears could actually save the children's lives and restore some dignity to the city, we could well understand the urgency of the narrator's tone; much would be at stake in this appeal and there would be no time to lose. However, Jerusalem already lies in ruins, depleted of her vibrancy. Perhaps the goal is to help Jerusalem weep therapeutic tears, to urge her to abandon her mute numbness. Though Jerusalem (mirroring her populace in 2:10) lies prostrate on the ground following the catastrophe (2:11), the narrator calls on her to arise (*kumi!*), to cry

---

160. The metaphoric description of the heart spilling over appears only here and in Psalms 62:9. Hannah similarly describes her prayer as pouring out her soul (I Sam. 1:15).

out in the dark night, thereby setting in motion the process of rehabilitation.[161] In this way, the narrator prods Jerusalem back to life, offering her meaningful actions and a path to recovery.

The narrator's directive is also designed to reinstate communication between Jerusalem and God. God's destructive mission concludes with a calamitous crash of silence; even prophets receive no vision from God (2:9). As noted in the previous chapter, the state in which God withdraws from His people, "hiding His face" (*hester panim*), is an anticipated penalty for Israel's sins. By requisitioning Jerusalem to advocate for her populace before "the face (*penei*) of the Lord," the narrator prods the city to lay the groundwork for reconciliation with God.

As the narrator's speech begins to reach its climax, a structural anomaly draws our attention to his final words. Instead of three sentences, verse 19 has four sentences.[162] The elongated verse illustrates the extra effort the narrator invests in inducing Jerusalem's cries. It also draws our attention to the final sentence in the verse, the "surplus" sentence. Instead of giving up on Jerusalem, the narrator makes one final bold attempt to provoke her tears by recalling the image of the children collapsing from hunger on the street. By reviving the appalling scenario lying at the core of this chapter, the narrator harks back to the very reason Jerusalem chose to become mute, the image that precipitated her stony, numb silence. After seven long verses of Jerusalem's paralysis, the narrator's speech draws to a resounding conclusion, as he finishes making a case for Jerusalem to resume speaking. His final argument rests in the crucial last sentence: For the sake of the children, Jerusalem must resume her cries!

---

161. In a similar vein, Isaiah urges Israel several times to arise (*kumi*) and rejuvenate following her suffering and destruction (Is. 51:17; 52:2; 60:1).

162. I discussed a similar variance in Eikha 1:7. As is customary, some scholars recommend removing a line in a bid to conform to the general structure of the poem. See, for example, Hillers, 40, who recommends removing the fourth line because it is not an imperative beseeching the city to cry. As I have already noted, I eschew emendations of this sort, preferring to seek out a meaningful idea that underlies the textual irregularities. In my opinion, by removing this line, Hillers removes the linchpin sentence of this passage, as explained above.

An Obscure Phrase: Their Hearts Cried Out to the Lord, Wall of the Daughter of Zion

The opening statement of these impassioned verses contains many difficulties, confounding commentators. The subject, those whose hearts cried out to God, remains uncertain,[163] as does the identity of the "wall of the daughter of Zion."[164] The fact that this sentence is not formulated as an imperative also sets it apart from the rest of the verse, leaving its role open to interpretation.

In keeping with the rest of the verse, this sentence seems to issue an implicit call to Jerusalem's walls to cry out to God. The "wall" likely represent the whole city.[165] This expression hints at the city's protective barricade, one that no longer functions to protect or defend it (see 2:8).[166] The reference to the wall may also prepare us for the narrator's call to Jerusalem to cry out at the beginning of the night watches.[167] Sentinels stand on the wall; this phrase implores Jerusalem's wall to resume her role as guardian of her people, to protect them and advocate on their behalf.

Yet, the phrase lacks an imperative. "Their hearts cried out to the Lord, wall of the daughter of Zion" may simply describe the frozen silence that prevails following the catastrophe. The narrator

---

163. Ibn Ezra assumes that the subject is the enemies, who are mentioned at the close of the previous verse. In this reading, the shouts are not in supplication, but in triumph against God. This reading is difficult within the context of this verse. Moreover, Ibn Ezra (like the Aramaic *Targum*) separates the first half of the sentence, describing the enemies' cries, from the second half, which addresses the wall of the daughter of Zion. He connects the second half of the verse to that which follows it, assuming that the narrator beseeches the wall of the daughter of Zion to let her eyes flow like a stream day and night.

164. Because *tzaak* (cry) is masculine singular and *ḥoma* (wall) is feminine singular, it seems unlikely that the narrator is describing the wall crying out here. Moreover, the hearts are plural, deepening the confusion that prevails in this sentence.

165. This figure of speech, known as a synecdoche, refers to a thing by the name of one of its parts – for example, using the word "suits" to refer to businessmen or "wheels" to refer to a car. In this case, the wall becomes a synecdoche for the city. Some scholars conclude that God is the wall or defensive shield of Zion, based on Zechariah 2:9 (see, e.g., Gottwald, 12; Renkema, 311).

166. During the period of the return to Zion, Jerusalem's broken wall is a source of great concern to Nehemiah (see Neh. 2:13–17), who undertakes to rebuild it (Neh. 3–6).

167. Berlin, 75, makes this observation.

bemoans the situation, in which the hearts of the people certainly cry out to God, but their lips remain sealed, their voices stifled (as symbolized by the wall that closes around their cries). The opening of the verse describes the paradox of Jerusalem's deep desire to reconnect with God alongside her paralysis. In this context, the wall represents Jerusalem's emotional barrier, the impermeable shell that she has built around herself. In the continuation of this passage (verse 19), the narrator pleads with Jerusalem to pour out her heart like water before God.

In his prophecies of Israel's renewal, Isaiah presents the opposite scenario:

> For the sake of Zion, I will *not* hush, and for Jerusalem's sake I will *not* be silent... Upon your walls Jerusalem, I have appointed guards all day and all night, they will never be hushed. Those who mention the Lord, do not become silent! And do not let Him become silent,[168] until He establishes and places Jerusalem as a glory in the earth! (Is. 62:1, 6–7)

As we have seen, Isaiah's prophecies of consolation (chapters 40–66) address the exiled Judean community, encouraging their return from Babylonia. As part of his redemptive message, Isaiah often reverses Eikha's calamity, promising the restoration of Jerusalem, her voice, and her vigilant sentries on the wall.

Eikha 2:20–21

רְאֵה ה' וְהַבִּיטָה
לְמִי עוֹלַלְתָּ כֹּה

אִם־תֹּאכַלְנָה נָשִׁים פִּרְיָם
עֹלֲלֵי טִפֻּחִים

---

168. This reading is like that of Metzudat David and the NJPS translation of the verse. The Malbim suggests that the verse refers to the righteous in the generation who cannot remain silent until Jerusalem's fortunes are restored.

אִם־יֵהָרֵג בְּמִקְדַּשׁ אֲדֹנָי
כֹּהֵן וְנָבִיא

שָׁכְבוּ לָאָרֶץ חוּצוֹת
נַעַר וְזָקֵן

בְּתוּלֹתַי וּבַחוּרַי
נָפְלוּ בֶחָרֶב

הָרַגְתָּ בְּיוֹם אַפֶּךָ
טָבַחְתָּ לֹא חָמָלְתָּ

Look Lord and see!
To whom have You done this?

When women consume their fruits[169]
Their well-nurtured children!

When murdered in the Lord's sanctuary
Are the priest and prophet!

They lie on the ground in the streets
Young men and old

My maidens and youths
Fallen by the sword

You murdered on the day of Your anger
You slaughtered, You did not pity

The narrator has achieved his aim, and Jerusalem at last resumes her speech. Tears are absent and the tone of her response is more outrage

---

169. The term for offspring in Tanakh is often "fruit" (e.g., Gen. 30:2; Deut. 7:13). In our context, the use of the word fruit to mean children horrifically contrasts with its usual usage, illustrating the grim situation in which children substitute for food.

than supplication, but Jerusalem finally summons up her energy to address God: "Look Lord and see![170] To whom have You done this?" Hostile words, unyielding in their steely fury, they are not designed to elicit divine sympathy but to express Jerusalem's anger at the atrocities. Jerusalem's pent-up pain surges and overflows, bursting forth with a harsh indictment generated by unadulterated horror. She demands that God witness the ghastly sights and remonstrates with Him over the death of children and religious leaders. Yet, Jerusalem's aim is not merely for God to witness the grim reality. Instead, she hurls these sights at Him accusingly ("To whom have You done this?"), implicitly challenging the way that He runs His world.

Once again, it is the sight of the innocent children that particularly galls Jerusalem. God's purposeful actions (*olalta*) and the death of the children (*olelei*) are inextricably linked using striking wordplay.[171]

Jerusalem accosts God with a world that has come unhinged, where the inconceivable has occurred. Is it possible that mothers, whose natural instinct is to protect and nurture, could be driven mad by starvation and consume their own children?[172] This query draws attention to the moral unravelling of the populace. Moreover, the sanctuary that once offered purity and asylum, now harbors the murderers of its custodians.[173] Can it be that God allows the desecration of His holy sanctuary by the slaying of its priests and prophets?[174] These rhetorical

---

170. In chapter 1, I noted the pervasiveness of the request that God "look and see" (*re'eh vehabita*) throughout the book.

171. The horror of these sights is not mitigated by the fact that this scenario is foretold as a consequence of Israel's disobedience (Lev. 26:29; Deut. 28:57; Jer. 19:9; Ezek. 5:10).

172. Metaphorically, Jerusalem may subtly refer to her own guilt in cannibalizing her "children" (namely, her residents), who are expiring in her streets.

173. Although neither Jerusalem nor the Temple functioned as an official city or place of refuge, the stories of both Adoniyahu (I Kings 1:50–53) and Yoav (I Kings 2:28–34) grabbing hold of the altar suggest that the altar was popularly treated as a place of asylum. While bloodshed is avoided in the Temple (II Kings 11:15), sometimes circumstances allow for it (as in the case of Yoav above).

174. Midrashim (*Sifra, Behukotai* 2:6; Eikha Rabba 1:51) view this as an allusion to the stoning death of Zechariah ben Yehoyada, a priest and a prophet who was killed in the Temple by the orders of the Judean king Yoash (II Chr. 24:20–21).

questions hang in the air. Jerusalem has not finished sketching her litany of horror. Vigorous maidens and lads, filled with youthful vibrancy, are cut down cruelly by the sword. Sprawled on every street lie the young and the old, fallen side by side: the past and the future intertwined in a macabre death posture.

Jerusalem concludes her survey of the absurd by pointing a finger at God and issuing a blazing accusation featuring four second-person words: "*You* murdered on the day of *Your* anger, *You* slaughtered (*tavaḥta*), *You* did not pity!" An especially violent word for God's massacre, the verb *tavaḥ* often describes the slaughter of animals for food.[175] The noun *tabaḥ* can mean a cook, further cementing the sense that this word describes preparation for eating.[176] The accusation that God "slaughtered" the populace of Jerusalem fuses with the image of mothers consuming their children, implicitly saddling God with responsibility for that atrocity.

The verb *tavaḥ* also refers to the slaughter of people, although generally in the context of God's punishment of Israel's enemies (Is. 14:21; 34:2, 6; Jer. 48:15) or the behavior of especially wicked people (Ps. 37:14). Using this word implies that God slaughtered His people like the enemy – or worse, like animals, without regard for the sanctity of human life.[177]

In this section, Jerusalem tests the limits of human discourse with the divine, as she hurls her fierce indictment against God. As we have noted, accusation of God is not heresy; Jerusalem's anger does not deny God, but rather affirms the relationship, illustrating Jerusalem's foundational belief in divine responsibility, authority, and involvement in her fate.

---

175. Genesis 43:16; Exodus 21:37; Deuteronomy 28:31; I Samuel 25:11.

176. See, for example, I Samuel 8:13; 9:23. Pharaoh's *sar hatabaḥim* (Gen. 37:36) functioned either as the royal chef (see Rashi, Gen. 37:36) or the royal executioner (*Targum*, Nahmanides, and Ḥizkuni on Gen. 37:36). The latter possibility finds support in the fact that the Babylonian military general, Nevuzaradan, is called the *rav tabaḥim* (II Kings 25:8). See also Daniel 2:14.

177. Biblical passages that employ the word to describe the projected punishment of the wicked in Israel, similar to our context, include Isaiah 63:12; Jeremiah 12:3; Ezekiel 21:15.

In the aftermath of the Holocaust, Elie Wiesel expresses a similarly intense, fury-filled accusation, fueled by an enduring faith in divine accountability and power:[178]

Blessed be God's name? Why, but why would I bless Him? Every fiber in me rebelled. Because He caused thousands of children to burn in His mass graves? Because He kept six crematoria working day and night, including Sabbath and the Holy Days? Because in His great might, He had created Auschwitz, Birkenau, Buna, and so many other factories of death? How could I say to Him: Blessed be Thou, Almighty, Master of the Universe, who chose us among all nations to be tortured day and night, to watch as our fathers, our mothers, our brothers, end up in the furnaces? Praised be Thy Holy Name, for having chosen us to be slaughtered on Thine altar?[179]

The passage in Eikha 2:20–21 portrays humans adopting an audacious stance. Jerusalem rages at a world lacking in compassion, a world directed and managed by God. The book of Eikha permits Jerusalem to rage – an impudent posture, to be sure, but one that is tempered by Jerusalem's commitment to maintaining a meaningful relationship with God.

Eikha 2:22

תִּקְרָא כְיוֹם מוֹעֵד
מְגוּרַי מִסָּבִיב

וְלֹא הָיָה בְּיוֹם אַף־ה'
פָּלִיט וְשָׂרִיד

---

178. Eliezer Berkovits, *Faith after the Holocaust* (Jerusalem: Maggid Books, 2019), 68, avers that asking where God is during calamity is the correct question for those who retain faith in God: "Not to ask it would have been blasphemy... Faith, because it is trust in God, demands justice of God."

179. Elie Wiesel, *Night*, trans. M. Wiesel (London: Penguin, 2006), 67.

אֲשֶׁר־טִפַּחְתִּי וְרִבִּיתִי
אֹיְבִי כִלָּם

Call for an appointed day (*mo'ed*)
Against my terrors all around[180]

And there was not, on the day of the Lord's anger
A refugee or survivor

Those whom I nurtured[181] and raised
My enemy obliterated

The final verse of chapter 2 is ungainly and difficult to translate. In the awkward translation above, I have preserved the textual clumsiness for the purposes of understanding the upcoming discussion.

The most pressing problem of the verse lies in its inconsistent tenses. The verse opens with a future tense, *tikra*, "call," in which Jerusalem petitions God to consecrate an appointed day.[182] This day is

---

180. The identity of the *megurai misaviv* is difficult to determine. (Similar confusion surrounds this same phrase in other passages where it appears: Jer. 6:25; 20:10; 46:5; 49:29; Ps. 31:14. All appearances of this phrase seem to indicate a hostile context.) The root *gur* can mean to reside, to stir up strife, or to fear (BDB, *Lexicon*, 157–59). In accordance with this variety of meanings, the phrase *megurai misaviv* can indicate the encircling terrors (Ibn Ezra, Eikha 2:22), the enemies who battle Jerusalem (Hillers, 34; Berlin, 65), or the neighbors who dwell around Jerusalem (Rashi, Eikha 2:22; Gottwald, 12). Gordis, 138, conflates these meanings somewhat, suggesting the translation "my hostile neighbors roundabout." Note his explanation on p. 169. Moreover, because the phrase *megurai misaviv* lacks a preposition preceding it, it is unclear whether God is calling an appointed day against the *megurai misaviv* or recruiting them to join Him in executing punishment on the appointed day.

181. See Ibn Ezra, Eikha 2:22, and Ibn Janach, *Sefer HaShorashim*, on the word *tipuḥim*.

182. The word used here is *mo'ed*, which literally means an appointed day, but is generally used in Tanakh to refer to a festive day. On the ironic use of that word in this chapter, see our discussions in the chapter above, "Biblical Poetry and the Book of Eikha," Eikha 1:4 and 2:7. For biblical passages in which God's destruction is likewise described as a celebration or festive sacrifice, see Isaiah 34:1–7; Zephaniah, 1:7–8; Jeremiah 46:10; Ezekiel 39:17.

the day of God's judgment, involving punishment and destruction. The verse continues by describing in past tense (*velo haya*) the absence of a survivor on the day of God's anger. If this day has not yet occurred, then why does the verse shift to the past tense, describing the results of this day?

Possibly, the shift to the past tense expresses confidence in God's inevitable punishment of the enemies; although it has not yet taken place, Jerusalem describes it as though it has. However, this reading does not cohere with the general tone of the verse, whose intent is not to proclaim confidence in God.

Most commentators find it necessary to reinterpret one of the verbs. Some change the future tense (*tikra*) to a past tense (e.g., Rashi), while others read the past tense (*haya*) as a future tense (e.g., R. Yosef Kara). The verse may therefore describe what God has already done (called a festival to massacre Judah) or what Jerusalem calls on God to do (call a festival to massacre Judah's enemies). Thus, biblical interpreters produce two radically different readings.

If the verse is in the past tense, then Jerusalem continues the demoralizing description of what God has done to her populace.[183] God called an appointed day of His anger (similar to 2:1, 7), a day in which He enacted His judgment against Judah and Jerusalem. The *megurai misaviv* are the human agents designated by God to carry out His task. Thus, the verse reads: "*You called* for an appointed day to those fearsome ones who surround me. And there was not, on the day of the Lord's anger, a refugee or survivor. Those whom I nurtured and raised, my enemy obliterated!" Following the numb silence that prevailed in Eikha 2:13–17, Jerusalem once again speaks. However, she does not suddenly acquire hope and beseech God to change her fortune. Instead, Jerusalem maintains her pessimistic outlook, describing her horrified outrage at the dismal sights surrounding her. At no point in this chapter do the events trigger effective action or the optimism necessary to precipitate a bold request from God.

---

183. For this reading, see Rashi, Eikha 2:22; Moshkovitz, 18; Gordis, 138; House, 370; Hillers, 34.

Alternatively, some interpreters read the entire final verse in future tense.[184] In this schema, our chapter concludes as do the other chapters in the book, with a plea that God take vengeance against Israel's enemies: "Call as a festive day against my enemies that surround me. And *do not let there be* on the day of God's anger a refugee or a survivor. Those whom I nurtured and raised, my enemy obliterated!" Although God is the primary cause of the destruction, His human agents offer their services eagerly. Therefore, these enemies deserve punishment; their enthusiasm and cruelty are unmitigated by the fact that they unknowingly execute God's will.[185] This petition expresses a request for justice. In order to begin rebuilding, God must first punish the evil enemies and restore a sense of fairness to the world.[186]

It is impossible to select the best reading of this verse. Each translation is equally plausible, and each contributes significantly to our understanding of the conclusion of chapter 2. I propose, therefore, that this verse contains a deliberate ambiguity, constructed with the express purpose of maintaining both meanings. On the one hand, the final verse retains the despondent tone of the chapter, in which Jerusalem helplessly describes the terrible events and God's role in them. On the other hand, this verse also describes Jerusalem's petition to God to take vengeance upon her enemies. Though the request is a minimal one, each chapter concludes with it, paving the way toward a new world order in which Jerusalem can rebuild on the foundations of restored justice.

The Identity of the Enemy

The chapter concludes with two stark words: *oyevi khilam* ("My enemy obliterated"). Who is the enemy who has destroyed those whom Jerusalem nurtured and raised? While it could be the human enemy, we

---

184. See, for example, R. Yosef Kara.
185. See Isaiah 47:6. For a discussion on the theology of God punishing those whom He appointed to commit evil, see Maimonides, *Hilkhot Teshuva* 6:5, and Raavad there.
186. See T. Granot, "That This Song May Answer Before Them Forever," in The Israel Koschitzky Virtual Beit Midrash (http://etzion.org.il/en/song-may-answer-them-forever): "Revenge on the wicked, even if the time is not yet ripe for a repealing of the decree, is God's signal that He is acting in history on our behalf, and that everything that happens to the world is just."

cannot forget that the chapter refers to God as an enemy three times. Written in singular form,[187] the foe at the conclusion of this chapter may indeed be God. The act of obliteration certainly harks back to God who, at the very least, has empowered the enemy. The chapter concludes with Jerusalem's final statement of horror and helplessness at the pernicious acts that have obliterated her future.

The Final Words: The Death of the Children

Unsurprisingly, the chapter concludes with its most haunting image, the death of the children. Even if the verse contains a call for vengeance in its first part, its final five words suggest a moan of pain rather than the intense fury felt in previous verses. Jerusalem seems to have deflated; the chapter ends with a terrible absence of hope, a declaration of the enemy's triumph.

Jerusalem speaks in the first person, emphasizing the personal nature of the tragedy: "[Those whom] *I* nurtured and [whom] *I* raised, *my* enemy destroyed."[188] Despite the emotionally charged subject, Jerusalem does not address the enemy directly in this final sentence. If God is the enemy of this sentence, the disappearance of the direct address mutes the intensity of Jerusalem's words. Previously, Jerusalem had unflinchingly pointed her finger directly at God in fierce accusation (2:20–21). Now, however, we hear Jerusalem's subdued whimpers, almost as though she is mumbling to herself in dismay, "Those whom I nurtured and raised, my enemy obliterated."

God's persistent silence is deafening, leaving Jerusalem's final words to reverberate in the void. Israel may speak, but unlike her words at the end of chapter 1, she resists any admission of sinfulness. Instead, chapter 2 concludes with a defiant timbre: Why indeed does the world function in this incomprehensible way? The problem hangs in the air, defying an answer.

---

187. Many translations (e.g., Greek, Aramaic, Latin) render the word "enemy" here in the plural form.

188. By employing the word *tipaḥti* (nurtured), Jerusalem harks back to the mothers of verse 20 who consume the children they have lovingly reared (*olelei tipuḥim*). This suggests again that Jerusalem herself is the mother who consumes her "children" in this chapter.

CHAPTER TWO: IN SUMMATION

Thematic, linguistic, and technical-structural similarities suggest a strong connection between chapters 1 and 2 of Eikha. Shared themes include: Jerusalem's vanished glory (1:6; 2:15), the tears in Jerusalem's eyes (1:16; 2:11), a terrible dearth of food in the city (1:19; 2:12), violation of the Temple (1:10; 2:7), the destruction of the *mo'ed* (an appointed place or time; 1:4; 2:6), a consuming fire (1:13; 2:3), Jerusalem as a physical body with a heart (1:20, 22; 2:19), the desolate or sunken gates of the city (1:4; 2:9), the mocking enemies (1:7, 2:16) and their schadenfreude (1:21; 2:16, 17), the exile among the nations (1:3; 2:9), and the appearance of priests (1:4, 19; 2:2, 6, 20), officers (1:6; 2:9), elders (1:19; 2:21), maidens (1:4; 2:10), passersby (1:12; 2:15), and *olalim*, young children (1:6; 2:11).

Specific linguistic parallels also link these chapters. Unusual phrases appear in both chapters, such as *mei'ai homarmaru*, portraying the city's churning innards (1:20; 2:11), God's deliberate destruction using the verb *olal* (1:12, 22; 2:20), the appellation *betulat bat Yehuda/ Zion* (1:15; 2:13), the days of old, *yemei kedem* (1:7; 2:17), the call to God to look and see, *re'eh vehabita* (1:11; 2:20), the lexical combination of the word call (*kara*) alongside the word *mo'ed* (1:15; 2:22), and the phrase "maidens and young men," *betulotai uvahurai* (1:18; 2:21).

Technical and structural similarities include the lament-like word *eikha*, which launches both elegiac chapters, the alphabetic structure that gives it order, and the shift from the third-person speaker to Jerusalem herself at the chapter's center. These, along with Jerusalem's role as the chapters' pivotal emotive force, as well as the focus on the physical city and her personified grief, bind the two chapters together in structural, substantive, and linguistic ways.

However, while at first the structural division of the chapters appears broadly similar, a closer examination indicates otherwise. Jerusalem recounts her share of the story at length in the second part of chapter 1, but speaks only briefly after her initial appearance in the second part of chapter 2. Following her succinct portrayal of the dying children (2:11–12), Jerusalem refuses to continue her account, defying the reader's expectation and ignoring the attempts of the narrator to elicit her speech. Jerusalem resumes speaking in verses 20–22 only after the narrator pointedly uses the image of the dying children to persuade her to communicate. When Jerusalem's speech recommences, it does not emerge gently; she does not turn to God in shame-filled admission of culpability, as she did at the conclusion of chapter 1. Instead, accusations against God burst forth in an explosion of anger; confusion and fury intermingle to produce a vehement tirade.

Each of these chapters likewise maintains a distinct tone. The first chapter focuses on the eerie void that hovers over Jerusalem following the destruction, while the second chapter details the actively destructive forces assailing Jerusalem. The dismantling of Jerusalem is methodical; the enemy devastates her buildings, palaces, fortresses, walls, and Temple. Synonyms abound, as various verbs of destruction lend the account depth and intensity. The chapter pays special attention to the destruction of the political, religious, and military leadership; kings, priests, and officers are profaned, spurned, and exiled, leaving Jerusalem's populace rudderless, lacking guidance or instruction.

The chapter presents God engaging in an unremitting assault on His city, pummeling it from every angle. Opening with an act of furious divine violence, God hurls the glory of Israel from the heavens to the earth. This launches the chapter's recurring theme of a downward plummet, represented by the eightfold appearance of the word *aretz* (ground). The entire city seems to come crashing to the ground as Jerusalem's structures totter and collapse (2:2) and her gates sink into the earth (2:9). Mirroring the fall of the city's structures, its inhabitants likewise drop to the ground. Elders sit on the bare earth, dazed by mourning (2:10), maidens' heads sag to the ground (2:10), Jerusalem's innards spill out onto the earth (2:11), and elders and youth lie dead on the blood-soaked earth of Jerusalem (2:21). This theme reveals not simply the city's physical collapse, but her spiritual downfall as well.

At their theological core, these chapters are more different than they are similar. Chapter 1 moves toward admission of sin and reconciliation with God, while chapter 2 does nothing of the sort. Chapter 1 concludes with Jerusalem's shame and guilt, alongside her declaration of God's righteousness, while chapter 2 concludes with Jerusalem's outrage and defiance, alongside her declaration of God's culpability.

God's antagonistic posture predominates throughout the chapter. Sometimes, the text resists calling God an enemy, preferring instead to depict Him allowing Jerusalem's enemy access to His city (verses 3, 7). However, the chapter does not always deal gently with the reader's sensibilities; verses 4 and 5 refer to God as an enemy three times in rapid succession. The final reference to the anonymous enemy (2:22) may point to God, even if He employs human agents to execute His destructive designs.

God's anger burns fiercely and actively throughout chapter 2. The day of God's anger envelops the chapter, appearing in its first, penultimate, and final verse (2:1, 21, 22). The chapter employs various synonyms and expressions – anger (*hori af*, 2:3), wrath (*heima*, 2:4), and fury (*zaam apo*, 2:6) – to construct a sweeping portrait of divine ire. In contrast, God's anger appears only once in chapter 1, alongside His punitive actions (verse 12); in chapter 1 Jerusalem endeavors to elicit God's attention (verses 9, 11, 20), turning to God in her grief. To compound its frightening portrait of God's fury, chapter 2 repeatedly describes God's pitiless stance (*lo hamal*, verses 1, 17, 21) as well as His inaccessibility. God withdraws from the city, withholding guidance (2:9), vision (2:9), and speech. God is merciless and wrathful in our chapter.

Divine anger mirrors and provokes the human anger that intensifies at the chapter's conclusion. Jerusalem's initial speech (2:11–12) expresses pain and horror. When Jerusalem resumes her speech at the end of the chapter, she challenges God and flings her words defiantly at Him, shifting sharply from her role as numb victim to that of enraged critic. Jerusalem's angry speech empowers her, allowing her to revive following emotional paralysis. This produces defiance; the savagery of the divine assault on the city and the death of the innocent children leave no room for submission, no possibility of quietly accepting the divine decree.

Jerusalem does not find theological tranquility in chapter 2, which recounts a tale of righteous people who suffer without cause (*tzaddik vera lo*). The people suffer unjustly from the leaders' blunders, especially those of the false prophets (2:14).[189] The chapter reserves its most lurid

---

189. The only mention of sin in the chapter is in the context of the failure of the prophets to reveal the sins to the people. This chapter does not assign responsibility for the catastrophe to the general populace. If anyone is to blame, it is the failed leadership.

details to describe at its core the unfathomable death of innocent children. Scandalized by these events, Jerusalem does not primarily blame her enemies; she lodges her most strident complaint against God, who bears ultimate responsibility. Lacking a solution for the theological quandary, the chapter ends without repairing the relationship between God and His nation. Its final words can be spun into a question, laced with disbelief: "Is it possible that those whom I nurtured and raised have been obliterated by my enemy?"

Chapter Two, Appendix 1

A Chiastic Structure

Like chapter 1, this chapter displays a chiastic pattern:

1 – *beyom apo, velo*
  2 – *lo ḥamal, laaretz*
    3 – *ke'esh… **akhela** saviv*
      4 – ***shafakh** ke'esh ḥamato*
        5 – *A-donai, bevat*
          6 – Tetragrammaton
            7 – *oyeiv, keyom*
              8 – *Bat Zion*
                9 – *nevi'eha, ḥazon*
                  10 – *Bat Zion, betulot Yerushalayim*
                    11 – *nishpakh, be'atef, birḥovot*
                    12 – *behitatfam, birḥovot, behishtapeikh*
                  13 – *Bat Yerushalayim, Betulat Bat Zion*
                14 – *nevi'ayikh, ḥazu*
              15 – *Bat Yerushalayim*
            16 – *oyvayikh, hayom*
          17 – Tetragrammaton
        18 – *A-donai, bat*
      19 – ***shifkhi** kamayim libeikh*
    20 – *im **tokhalna** nashim piryam*
  21 – *lo ḥamalta, laaretz*
22 – *beyom af Hashem, velo*

Some of these linked pairs have strong and unique linguistic associations, while others are less persuasive.[1] Nevertheless, the overall structure maintains a robust chiastic design, which does not appear to be random.[2]

What is the meaning of this structure? Its cyclical design indicates that the chapter does not progress in a linear fashion. It opens and closes with the day of God's anger (*yom apo*) and His pitiless stance (*lo ḥamal*). God's judgments encircle the chapter and there is no respite or escape from that fury; it swirls tempestuously, imprisoning Jerusalem in its furious power.

Despite the cyclical, unending situation, one parallel seems designed to hint at a solution. Eikha 2:4 describes God pouring out His anger like fire, which incinerates the city. Its parallel verse in 2:19 features the narrator pleading with Jerusalem to cry out to God, to pour out her heart like water. Water extinguishes fire, suggesting that prayer and petition can function as the solution for divine wrath.

The concentric structure draws the reader's attention toward its pivotal center.[3] As in the previous chapter, an inner chiasm lies at its midpoint, focusing our attention upon its most important idea.[4] This chapter revolves around the innocent children who languish on the city streets. The theological centerpiece of the chapter unveils Jerusalem's perplexity and pain as she witnesses calamity that defies human understanding.

---

1. For example, the Tetragrammaton in verses 6 and 17 is not a unique word, nor is it unique in the chapter, appearing in five additional verses (verses 7, 8, 9, 20, 22), for a total of seven appearances. The word *bat* (appearing in two separate pairs of verses: 8 and 15 and 10 and 13) also appears seven times in the chapter.

2. As noted in Chapter One, Appendix 1, Berman ("Criteria," 61–63) persuasively argues that the concentrated presence of lexical correspondence in the chapter is statistically rare and therefore compelling.

3. As the chapter moves toward its center, the word pairs become increasingly persuasive, creating verse pairs that contain intertwined language and perhaps also parallel themes. See the word pairs of verses 9 and 14 (which focus on the failure of the prophets' visions) and 10 and 13 (which focus on Jerusalem and her different appellations).

4. In Eikha 2:11–12, I noted the linguistic chiasm at the center of this chapter: *nishpakh* ... [*be'atef* ... *birḥovot*] + [*behitatefam* ... *birḥovot*] ... *behishtapekh*.

Chapter Two, Appendix 2

The Reversed Order of the *Ayin* and the *Peh*

T he first four chapters of the book of Eikha are composed as alphabetic acrostics, in which each verse opens with a subsequent letter of the alphabet. While chapter 1 maintains the familiar order of the alphabet, chapters 2, 3, and 4 reverse the positions of the *ayin* and the *peh*. Thus, in our chapter, verse 16 opens with the letter *peh*, while verse 17 opens with the letter *ayin*.

Eikha Rabba offers a homiletic explanation for this conspicuous reversal, playing on the meaning of the words *peh* (mouth) and *ayin* (eye):

> Why did the *peh* precede the *ayin*? Because they said with their mouths what their eyes had not seen. (Eikha Rabba 2:20)[1]

---

1. Sanhedrin 104b attributes this behavior to the errant spies, who prevented the Israelites from entering the land for forty years (Num. 13–14). This in accordance with the tradition that the spies (whose punishment was decreed on the same day that the Temple was destroyed) retain some responsibility for the *ḥurban*.

The midrash suggests that one of the sins of the people is that they spoke rashly, without understanding or basis.

The midrash draws its greatest support for this idea from chapter 3. The initial *peh* verse (3:46)[2] opens with a reference to the mouths of the enemies,[3] followed by three successive references to "my eye" in verses 48, 49, 51 (the first reference actually appears in the third *peh* verse [48], anticipating the manner in which the first and third *ayin* verses [49 and 51] open with the word *eini*, my eye). In chapter 3, the mouth quite literally precedes the eyes, in a manner that suggests the triumph of the cruel mouths, which produce fear and horror (3:47). Unlike the midrashic homily, in this case the mouth belongs to the enemy (not to Israel), while the eyes are the sufferer's tool for eliciting God's compassion.

The above midrash also draws our attention to the significance of mouths and eyes in Eikha. Appearing five times, the word "mouth" twice describes God (1:18; 3:38) and twice describes the enemies (2:16; 3:46). On the one occasion where the mouth is that of a member of Israel, the sufferer (*gever*) of chapter 3 ruminates that humans should not speak, but rather put their mouths in the dust (3:29). Eyes appear even more frequently – ten times – but they always fail to see; generally they serve to produce tears. On the one occasion they are used for sight, they fail to see that which they seek (4:17).

The midrashic approach notwithstanding, archaeological finds shed a different light on this irregular alphabetical arrangement.[4] Early Semitic abecedaries (writings that record the alphabet in order, probably used for educational purposes) from the pre-exilic era of Israel, consistently place the *peh* before the *ayin*.[5] To date, no abecedary from

---

2. Chapter 3 contains a triple acrostic, which means that there are three *peh* verses followed by three *ayin* verses.
3. The first word in the initial *peh* verse is *patzu* (they opened), while the third word is *pihem* (their mouths).
4. See, for example, Demsky, "Proto-Canaanite," 14–27.
5. Abecedaries that have this reversed order include one from approximately 1200 BCE found at Izbet Sarta, three abecedaries on one jar from Kuntillet Arjud dated to approximately 800 BCE, and probably also the abecedary found at Tel Zayit from the tenth century BCE. An unprovenanced ostracon with three abecedaries from the sixth century BCE also places the *peh* before the *ayin*. Interestingly, the earliest manuscripts (fourth and fifth centuries CE) of the Septuagint translation of the

that era has been found that has the *ayin* preceding the *peh*. It seems likely, therefore, that early Hebrew (Proto-Canaanite) originally developed with the *peh-ayin* arrangement, and only later adopted the *ayin-peh* arrangement found in other Western Semitic languages.[6]

In spite of the compelling nature of the historical explanation, the fact that biblical alphabetical compositions generally adhere to the *ayin-peh* order (including the first chapter of Eikha)[7] suggests that the switch in Eikha's middle chapters is a deliberate technique used to convey an idea. O'Connor, for example, maintains that this reversal of letters is a conscious literary device designed to allude to the reversal of God's affections.[8]

In our chapter, the *ayin* verse describes God's role in the destruction, while the *peh* verse depicts the gloating enemies. Perhaps the reversal draws our attention literarily to the way God withdrew in order to allow the enemy to enter (as stated explicitly in 2:3). Alternatively, the reversal may draw our attention to the attempt of Israel's adversaries

---

alphabetic poem of Proverbs 31 (*eshet ḥayil*) have the *peh* preceding the *ayin*. See E. Tov, "Recensional Differences Between the Masoretic Text and the Septuagint of Proverbs," in H. W. Attridge, et al., *Of Scribes and Scrolls: Studies on the Hebrew Bible, Intertestamental Judaism, and Christian Origins Presented to John Strugnell* (1990), 53.

6. The order in Hebrew may have changed due to the influence of Western Semitic languages such as Ugaritic and Aramaic, which used the *ayin-peh* order. M. First suggests that this occurred during the Babylonian exile, where the Aramaic alphabet predominated. See "The *Pe/Ayin* Order in Ancient Israel and Its Implications for the Book of Psalms," in *Esther Unmasked* (New York: Kodesh Press, 2015), 229.

7. Most biblical alphabetic compositions (Prov. 31; Ps. 9–10, 25, 34, 37, 111; 112; 119, 145) use the *ayin-peh* order, in contrast to the three middle chapters of Eikha. Some scholars believe that other alphabetic compositions may originally have had a *peh-ayin* order, which was not preserved due to its anomalous appearance. Amos Hakham brings a rabbinic source to support his assertion that Psalms 34:16–17 was originally constructed in a *peh-ayin* order (which makes better sense in the context of the chapter). See Amos Hakham, *Daat Mikra: Psalms* (Jerusalem: Mossad Harav Kook, 1990), vol. 1, 189–90, fn. 9. See also First, "*Pe-Ayin* Order," 207-29. I am grateful to Mitchell First for his helpful comments, including the reference to Amos Hakham's footnote. Intriguingly, the Qumran scroll of Eikha (4QLam) reverses the order of the *peh* and the *ayin* in chapter 1, rendering its order consistent with the remaining alphabetical arrangements of the book.

8. *Lamentations*, 40–41. The broader phenomenon hints at the centrality of the theme of reversal in the book, as developed extensively in Gottwald, 53–62.

to assume credit for the devastation. In a deft literary flourish, the *peh* verse jumps in before its turn, illustrating the enemy's bid to usurp God's role. Thus, this striking structural element can reflect and enhance the themes of the chapter.

Eikha: Chapter Three

The Suffering of the Individual

INTRODUCTION

The uniqueness of chapter 3, the structural center of the book, is immediately discernable: its unusual triple acrostic sets it apart from the other chapters.[1] It therefore has sixty-six verses, as opposed to the twenty-two verses of the other four chapters.[2] While this technical difference draws our attention, other distinctive elements of the chapter are substantive. The absence of the word "*Eikha*" at its opening suggests that this chapter is not composed as a lament. More significantly, a unique first-person voice launches the chapter; the speaker introduces himself as a *gever*, a lone individual.[3]

---

1. The only other biblical composition that has a multiple alphabetic design is Psalms 119, which has an eightfold acrostic.
2. Substantively, this chapter is no longer than the previous chapters. Each verse of chapter 3 contains only one sentence, while verses in both chapters 1 and 2 usually contain three. In terms of word count, chapter 3 is nearly identical in length to chapters 1 and 2 (all three of these chapters have between 330 and 350 words).
3. While both chapters 1 and 2 contain first-person accounts, the individual speaker seems to represent a collective "I" of Jerusalem, rather than a lone individual. Similarly, some scholars regard the *gever* of chapter 3 as a collective "I" (see the review

The connection between this chapter and the rest of the book initially seems tenuous. In a book concerned with national calamity, the central chapter focuses upon the misfortunes of an individual, offering a portrait of how one suffering person contends with God and copes with travail. I will attempt to establish that this chapter fits into the book's broader framework, both linguistically and thematically.

The anonymous *gever*'s personal account enables the reader to focus on the experience of an individual who suffers physically, emotionally, and religiously.[4] The sufferer navigates through the morass of his misery, experiencing religious growth along the way. Every person who experiences adversity can regard this *gever*'s journey as his own.

The *gever*'s experience can rightly be termed a journey, inasmuch as he progresses in a linear fashion (albeit with some twists) during the course of the chapter. The linear progression marks this chapter's distinctness as surely as the technical differences noted above. Constructed in a chiastic fashion, the previous two chapters maintain a cyclical form that conveys the hopelessness of ceaseless suffering. This chapter, in contrast, moves from despair to contemplation to hope, in a steady motion forward. The *gever* at the beginning of the chapter is not the same as the *gever* at its conclusion, though his external circumstances appear unchanged.

Chapter 3 omits the major motifs of the previous chapters, including the fall of Jerusalem and the Temple, and the suffering, starvation, and exile of the Judean inhabitants. There are no priests, kings, or leaders, no maidens or young men, no vulnerable, dying children, and no hint of a national tragedy. Even the suffering of the individual is not directly connected to the events of 586 BCE.[5] Instead, this chapter is uniquely concerned with

---

of scholarship that holds this position in Hillers, 62), but in my view, this reading is less plausible in this chapter. Support for regarding the *gever* as an individual speaker can be found in Ibn Ezra, Eikha 3:1, and Hillers, 64 (Hillers also refers to other scholars who maintain this position).

4. As we will see, the individual first-person account gives way to the plural first-person later in the chapter. Nevertheless, the dominant figure remains the individual, whose voice will reassert itself as the chapter moves toward its conclusion.

5. Perhaps the chapter was not originally written about the ḥurban. It matters little, as this chapter's linguistic and thematic connections to other chapters indicate that it is an integral part of the book, a chapter that guides the individual to cope with tragedy.

theological reflection, considering the nature of God and His interactions with humans. The suffering individual of this chapter seeks and finds hope in God – the only lengthy message of hope in the book. The chapter also discusses the lessons that one may draw from suffering, and several erroneous conclusions that one should scrupulously avoid. Prayer, repentance, and communal responsibility follow these reflections, stemming from a distinctive optimistic timbre that lies at the heart of chapter 3.

STRUCTURE

While scholars suggest different ways to divide chapter 3, I propose a broad threefold division that reflects its general progression: [6]

> Part 1 – Verses 1–18: A First-Person Account of Suffering
> Verses 19–20: Transition Verses
> Part 2 – Verses 21–39: Theological Reflections
> Part 3 – Verses 40–66: A First-Person Account of Suffering

These general sections subdivide further, as we will see when we examine them in greater depth. Part 3, for example, opens with a first-person plural voice that calls on the community to repent, confess, and pray (verses 40–42), followed by a detailed description of collective communal suffering (verses 43–47). Only afterward does the individual voice reemerge to conclude the chapter (verses 48–66). This shift in speaker indicates that the third section is not monochromatic; the section unfolds in a manner that necessitates further subdivision.

The above threefold division draws attention to several significant ideas. First, the central axis around which this chapter (and therefore the entire book) revolves is its theological reflections. Parts 1 and 3 frame the contemplative center with the suffering of an individual. Moreover, a close examination will reveal that parts 1 and 3 distinctly differ from one another due to the theological reflections in part 2. Following profound contemplation of God's ways and having internalized the lessons that he draws from his examination, the sufferer becomes a member of the

---

6. Unlike previous chapters, the change in speaker does not define the structure of chapter 3.

community. He then uses his personal experience to benefit that community. He has acquired hope and faith, and he petitions God directly – no longer viewing God as an opponent, but rather as a support upon whom he can depend.

I do not mean to claim that this chapter moves the book away from the grief-stricken tone of Eikha by transforming despair into hope. In fact, chapter 4 once again plunges the reader deep into the despondency of the current situation. Eikha does not mask its grisly reality with a veneer of false optimism. Nevertheless, it is significant to note that at the core of this book, hope prevails, alongside theological reflections that transform human suffering into a meaningful experience.

Uniquely positioned as a chapter that has no counterpart, this chapter's placement as Eikha's central axis underscores its significance. Chapter 3 is the linchpin of the book, its theological centerpiece. All events revolve around the contemplative center, mirroring the contemplative center that lies at the core of every human being and represents the secret of human resilience. At the heart of human experience lie conviction, confidence, and courage. Eikha is not merely a book of human suffering, but rather one that allows people to find a deep strain of tranquility within the maelstrom of existence, enabling them to find faith in a turbulent world.

Technical Note to the Commentary on Chapter 3

For the first part of the chapter (verses 1–18), I have divided my commentary into units based on the alphabetic division. I have done so primarily for technical reasons, so that I can discuss this lengthy section in manageable parts. I do not mean to suggest that these three-verse alphabetic segments are independent units.[7] As we examine the themes in the chapter, I will frequently note the way ideas flow as a continuum from one alphabetic unit to the next. For the remainder of the chapter (verses 19–66), I will divide the section thematically, rather than alphabetically.

---

7. D. Grossberg, *Centripetal and Centrifugal Structures in Biblical Poetry* (Atlanta: Scholars Press, 1989), 88, maintains that the book weaves a verbal root within the three lines of each alphabetic segment, unifying it into a stanza.

PART 1 (EIKHA 3:1–20):
AN ACCOUNT OF PERSONAL SUFFERING

Eikha 3:1–3

אֲנִי הַגֶּבֶר רָאָה עֳנִי
בְּשֵׁבֶט עֶבְרָתוֹ

אוֹתִי נָהַג וַיֹּלַךְ
חֹשֶׁךְ וְלֹא־אוֹר

אַךְ בִּי יָשֻׁב
יַהֲפֹךְ יָדוֹ כָּל־הַיּוֹם

I am the man who has seen affliction
by the rod of His anger

Me, He led, and He walked me
In darkness and not light

Only against me He returns
His hand turns[8] all day

The *gever* opens his tale of woe by focusing upon himself, using the word *ani*, I.[9] Completely absorbed by his own misery, the *gever* repeatedly employs self-referential words at the beginning of the chapter, such as *oti* (which opens verse 2) and *bi* (the second word of verse 3). Rashi observes the *gever's* self-absorption, suggesting that he regards himself as the singular recipient of God's attention:

---

8. The phrase, *yahafokh yado*, seems to imply a repeated beating (see, e.g., *Targum*, Ibn Ezra). The word *yahafokh* (to turn) also recalls the destruction of Sodom and Gomorrah, the Bible's paradigmatic sinful cities, overturned (*vayahafokh*) and annihilated by God (Gen. 19:25).

9. This opening word is particularly distinctive, given that chapters 1 and 2 open with the word *Eikha*, and chapter 4 will again revert to that inaugural word.

Only against me He returns. I alone am struck continuously, for all
the cycles of His blows are upon me. (Rashi, Eikha 3:3)

It seems unduly self-centered to focus on one's own suffering in a book
that dwells at length on the nation's collective suffering. Perhaps for this
reason R. Yosef Kara reads the *gever's* complaint as a communal one,
relating to the fate of the nation:

> *Only against me He returns, His hand turns all day.* All the nations
> sin, but there is no nation in the world that God punishes for sin,
> except Israel. (R. Yosef Kara, Eikha 3:3)

While R. Kara's interpretation alleviates the narcissistic quality of the
gever's statement, it does not cohere well with the context of the chapter.
The *gever* tells a story of personal (not national) adversity; in his tale, he
remains fixated upon himself.

The Identity of the *Gever*

Who is this *gever*, who recounts his travails with such pathos? Biblical
interpreters have suggested several possibilities. Some simply regard the
gever as an Everyman who seeks to instruct others in the lessons acquired
from his personal experience.[10] Others suggest that the *gever* represents
the nation, the collective "I" (perhaps even the voice of Jerusalem, as
we encountered in chapters 1 and 2).[11] Many point to a specific historical figure, generally identified as Jeremiah.[12]

---

10. See, for example, Hillers, 122; Renkema, 348–52; Dobbs-Allsopp, 106–9.
11. See, for example, O. Eissfeldt, *The Old Testament: An Introduction,* P. Ackroyd, trans.
    (New York: Harper and Row, 1965), 502–3; Albrektson, *Studies in Text and Theology
    in the Book of Lamentations* (Lund: Gleerup, 1963), 127–29; Gottwald, 37–42. Gordis,
    171, critiques this approach, noting that it is difficult to reconcile with the references to
    an individual, particularly in the middle section of this chapter (verses 27–29, 35–36).
    In any case, it would be highly irregular to have a male *gever* represent Jerusalem.
12. For a list of the many scholars who conclude that Jeremiah is the speaker (along
    with a summary of the different positions that scholars hold on this subject), see
    House, 405–6. A midrash suggests that this *gever* is Job (Eikha Rabba 3:1), while an
    outlying opinion suggests that the figure is Jehoakhin, although the evidence for this
    remains flimsy (see Norman Porteous, "Jerusalem: Zion, The Growth of a Symbol,"

Rashi identifies the *gever* as Jeremiah, who uses the chapter to recollect the difficulties and challenges of his prophetic career:

> *I am the man who has seen affliction.* Jeremiah was bemoaning and saying: I am the man who has seen affliction, who has seen more misfortune than any of the other prophets who prophesied about the destruction of the Temple. For in their days the Temple was not destroyed; in my days, it was. (Rashi, Eikha 3:1)

Linguistic and thematic parallels between the *gever's* account and Jeremiah's personal story support Rashi's contention. Note, for example, the *gever's* description of his alienation from his people:

> I was a laughingstock for all my nation, their plaything all day. (Eikha 3:14)

In one of Jeremiah's most evocative laments over his role as prophet, he similarly bemoans his isolation and the misery of his prophetic mantle:

> I was a laughingstock all day; everyone mocks me. (Jer. 20:7)

We likewise hear echoes of Jeremiah's misfortunes in the *gever's* account of his imprisonment in a pit (3:52, 55; see Jer. 38:6), as well as the beatings he suffered (3:30; see Jer. 20:2; 37:15).

In identifying the *gever* as Jeremiah, Rashi builds upon the tradition of Jeremiah's authorship of Eikha. It seems logical to assume that the personal account in a book belongs to its author, who introduces his own life experiences as they become relevant.

Nevertheless, the chapter does not indicate anywhere that the *gever* is Jeremiah. It is also not clear why Jeremiah's individual story

---

in *Verbannung und Geimkehr, Rudolph Festschrift*, W. Randolph, ed. [Tubingen: Mohr, 1961], 244–45). Saebø, "Who is 'the Man' in Lamentations 3? A Fresh Approach to the Interpretation of the Book of Lamentations," in *Understanding Poets and Prophets*, A. G. Auld, ed. (Sheffield: Sheffield Academic Press, 1993), 302–4, suggests that the man is Zedekiah.

should be relevant to the book of Eikha. The prophet stands above the people, outside of them, judging and chastising them; his personal experience seems to bear little resemblance to the ordeals of the common person. Moreover, Jeremiah's suffering takes place at the hands of his Israelite compatriots and not the Babylonian enemy. Are the Israelites the *gever's* cruel antagonists? And if so, the lessons he draws from his troubles have little resonance for those who have caused them. Why should Jeremiah's personal hardships appear in a book about national calamity?

After raising the possibility that Jeremiah composed this chapter about his life, Ibn Ezra suggests that the chapter is written from the perspective of "every person from Israel," namely, Everyman.[13] Instead of focusing on a specific individual, the chapter spotlights a figure whose experience of suffering is archetypal. The chapter employs figurative language of suffering (as found also in Job and Psalms) to describe a universal experience, designed to apply to all sufferers. Everyman is also No-one, inasmuch as the details of the account may not apply in a precise sense to any individual. This chapter concerns human suffering in general, rather than a specific person or specific events.

Featuring an individual, rather than a community, has several advantages. First, it is easier to cultivate empathy for one person than for large numbers of sufferers.[14] Moreover, if one individual represents every person, then it underscores what is common to all, allowing individuals to discover a shared experience. This fosters a sense of community among the sufferers.[15] The *gever* arrives at this realization, as is evident by his shift to a collective plural voice when he addresses his

---

13. Even if Jeremiah wrote this chapter about no one in particular, it is understandable that he would draw upon his personal experience when composing it, without intending to suggest that it is his story. That could account for the correlations between Jeremiah's life and the suffering *gever*.

14. Similarly, in commemorating the Holocaust, museums and memorial ceremonies often focus on the stories of individuals and families, rather than on the collective. This allows for empathy and identification, more so than the account of the collective, which can feel too vast and overwhelming to comprehend.

15. Eikha 3:14 alludes to the isolation that initially accompanies the sufferer in his grief. Once the sufferer joins a community (3:40–47), his loneliness dissipates, relieving one aspect of his pain.

fellow sufferers in verses 40–47. In these verses, the individual briefly merges with the community of sufferers. Sharing one's pain does not simply alleviate the isolation of grief, it can also provide meaning to the ordeal, becoming useful and beneficial to others.

If all suffering follows a common trajectory, this chapter takes on a didactic quality. The *gever's* journey from lonely agony to theological reflection to renewed hope functions as a blueprint for the suffering individual. This chapter guides people on their challenging journeys, so that they do not flounder and stall, or become paralyzed by despair. This chapter both integrates into Eikha and rises above it, functioning independently to offer solace and guidance for all those who suffer, regardless of the context or circumstances of their woe.

The word *gever* may offer a clue to the identity of the man in the chapter. *Gever* is certainly not the most common word used to refer to an adult male in the Bible. Synonyms for man include *ish* (the most common referent), *enosh*, and *adam*. While often interchangeable within a sentence, synonymous words tend to retain subtle distinctive meanings, thereby enriching a language.

Etymologically, the word *gever* relates to *gevura*, strength, and may refer to a man who wields physical or military strength.[16] Perhaps the *gever* uses this self-description ironically or bitterly, underscoring his abuse and defeat in spite of his physical might.[17] The *gever* may also refer to someone who has spiritual strength,[18] or inner strength, the heroic ability to overcome suffering:[19]

Happy is the *gever* whom You make suffer, God, and You teach him from Your instructions. (Ps. 94:12)

---

16. See, for example, Judges 5:30; Joel 2:8. One interpretation of the phrase *keli gever* (vessels of a *gever* in Deut. 22:5) is weapons (Nazir 59a). The physical strength of the *gever* may also relate to his fertility (Ps. 127:3–5).

17. In Eikha 1:16, the word is used as a verb, describing the enemy overpowering Jerusalem (*gavar oyev*).

18. See, for example, Jeremiah 17:5–7; Psalms 40:5.

19. This is corroborated by Akkadian wisdom literature, where the anonymous sufferer is called a *gever*.

Unsurprisingly, Job refers to himself as a *gever* at the opening of his discourse (Job 3:3). The word *gever* appears with unusual frequency in Job, the book that contends most directly with human suffering. We will examine the *gever's* tale as the story of Everyman – the archetypical sufferer who serves as a model for how to cope with suffering.

Who Is the Perpetrator of the *Gever's* Suffering?

Sixteen excruciating verses recount the brutality that the *gever* endures. He is struck with a rod and led in darkness, swallowed and smashed, poisoned, burdened by iron fetters, ambushed and mangled, set up as a target and riddled with arrows. The perpetrator remains anonymous; the *gever* employs a hidden third person to veil his identity.

According to Rashi, God is the disciplinarian in these verses:[20]

> *By the rod of His anger.* Of the one who dominates and strikes –
> He is God. (Rashi, Eikha 3:1)

The divine anger that burned so fiercely in the previous chapter continues unabated in chapter 3 (both 2:2 and 3:1 employ the word *evrato*).

Several words highlight the absence of divine benevolence, indicating that God exchanges His previous acts of liberation for punitive ones. For example, the divine hand that once delivered His people (Ex. 14:31; Ps. 74:11) now strikes the *gever* mercilessly (verse 3).[21] Consider

---

20. Many translators and interpreters agree with Rashi's approach. Some translators actually insert the word God or a capitalized "He" into the translation (e.g., NRSV, NJPS). I have committed a similar heavy-handed act of interpretation by capitalizing the He in my translation, thereby implicating God. Scholars who assume that God is the hidden enemy of this chapter include Westermann, 170–72, and Dobbs-Allsopp, 109–11. Some commentators do not regard God as the implied perpetrator. Ibn Ezra, for example, acknowledges but rejects this reading, preferring to identify the perpetrator as the human adversary. See also O'Connor, 47. As noted, I have adopted Rashi's approach in my translation and commentary.

21. This is not to say that God employs His "hand" only to deliver His people. Many biblical passages describe God punishing His nation with His "hand" (e.g., Is. 5:25; Jer. 21:5; Ps. 39:11). Nevertheless, the ideal usage of God's "hand" appears in the story of the liberation from Egypt, in which Israel witnesses God's "great hand" liberating

also the *gever*'s opening statement that he has seen his own affliction (3:1). God frequently "sees the afflictions" of His people (Ex. 3:7; Ps. 31:8). The *gever*'s description in 3:1 implicitly points to the absence of God's customary regard for sufferers. Withdrawn kindnesses coupled with God's wrathful acts produce a frightening depiction of divine antagonism.

God hovers ominously, if obliquely, in the background of this verse. By excluding any direct mention of God, the *gever* consciously diverts attention to himself, focusing the narrative on his suffering. The *gever*'s unwillingness to name God may also indicate the extent of the alienation between them.

Psalms 23

The rod of God's anger (*shevet*) that conducts the *gever* through darkness recalls God's comforting rod (*shivtekha*) in Psalms 23:4. In that idyllic chapter, God shepherds the vulnerable individual as He would a sheep, ushering him to rest in green pastures and guiding him to walk along a tranquil watercourse (23:2). God safeguards his circuitous route, steering him on his way (23:3). "Even when" (*gam ki*) he finds himself in a valley of deep darkness, this person does not fear, for he knows that God is with him (23:4).

The sufferer in Eikha 3 reverses the idyllic portrait of Psalms 23.[22] God again accompanies him on a difficult journey, but this time He drives him into darkness, leading him toward danger and persecution. Afflicting him with the rod (*shevet*) that once comforted (3:1), God deliberately thwarts and impedes the *gever*'s journey, building a stone wall to block him (3:9), twisting his pathway (3:9), and diverting his route (3:11). No one offers food, water, or restful pastures to the *gever* on his perilous perambulations, and God offers only obstructions. "Even when" (*gam ki*) he calls out in his desperation, his prayer is blocked; no one answers or heeds his cries (3:8).

The *gever*'s dark and obstructed journey illuminates his befuddled state of mind. His convoluted movement toward an uncertain destination reflects the *gever*'s disorientation, as he makes his way through this

---

them from slavery (e.g., Ex. 14:31). Any use of God's "hand" against Israel seems to be a terrible reversal of the desired state.

22. See Hillers, 65–66.

crisis. Danger swirls around; will he survive this calamity? Will he find a path and a safe terminus? Darkness suggests God's absence, even as God is the one who leads him into this circuitous and perilous route. This sketch reflects the *gever's* inability to find a foothold or a steady course in a world shaken by calamity.

The arduous journey also draws attention to the actual journey toward exile, a grueling trek fraught with dangers and lacking a clear destination.[23]

Isaiah's prophecies of consolation often describe a journey that starkly contrasts with the hopeless one in Eikha. Rallying the nation to return to their land, Isaiah describes the journey homeward in language that simultaneously recalls Psalms 23 and overturns Eikha 3:[24]

> I will lead the blind on a road that they did not know; on pathways they did not know, I will guide them.[25] I will turn darkness before them into light and the twisted paths to a straight plain. These things I have done; I will not abandon them. (Is. 42:16)

> Saying to the prisoners, "Exit!" To those who are in darkness, "Reveal yourselves!" They will pasture on the roads, and on every high place will be their pastures. They will not be hungry and they will not be thirsty, and the heat and sun will not strike them, for the One who has compassion on them will lead them, and He will guide them along springs of water.[26] (Is. 49:9–10)

---

23. The word *nahag*, describing God leading the *gever* into darkness (3:2), is used similarly to describe the Assyrians leadings captives into exile in Isaiah 20:4.

24. Intriguingly, the Aramaic *Targum* reads Psalms 23 as a description of Israel's return from the exile in Egypt, recording the journey from exile to redemption. See also Exodus Rabba 25:7. Radak, Psalms 23:1, suggests that this psalm may have been written for the people to sing as they returned from exile.

25. The words *derekh* (roads) and *netivot* (pathways) recall (and reverse) Eikha 3:9. Isaiah 35 depicts a similar description of a secure and comfortable journey (verses 6–8), in which there will be no lion or vicious beast who can attack them (verse 9). This reverses the image of the lion and bear in Eikha 3:10, whose threatening appearance occurs between two descriptions of a dangerous journey.

26. The word *yenahagem* (lead them) recalls Eikha 3:2, while the word *yenahalem* (guide them) evokes Psalms 23:2.

Biblical narratives present a continuum of events. Just as surely as exile can follow redemption, redemption can follow exile. After Israel's period of exile, Isaiah promises that a new redemption awaits, offering a promise of renewal.

Eikha 3:4–6

בִּלָּה בְשָׂרִי וְעוֹרִי
שִׁבַּר עַצְמוֹתָי

בָּנָה עָלַי וַיַּקַּף
רֹאשׁ וּתְלָאָה

בְּמַחֲשַׁכִּים הוֹשִׁיבַנִי
כְּמֵתֵי עוֹלָם

He wore away my flesh and my skin
He broke my bones

He built against me and encircled [me]
[With] poison and hardship

He made me dwell in darkness
Like the eternal dead

Daily beatings take their toll upon the *gever*, wearing away his flesh and skin and shattering his bones.[27] Unable to move and surrounded by perils on all sides, the *gever* feels trapped and immobile; darkness closes in on him as though he is entombed.

The *gever* flails in different directions, employing metaphors that convey the range and intensity of his afflictions. The expression, "He built against me and encircled [me]," evokes a siege (II Kings 25:1;

---

27. This interpretation (adopted from Ibn Ezra, Eikha 3:4) reads verse 4 as a direct continuation of verse 3 (in spite of the alphabetic division). As I previously observed, the alphabetic division does not necessarily divide the chapter into separate units.

Deut. 20:20),[28] such that the *gever's* physical afflictions align with the trials of a city. The physical deterioration of his body mirrors the breakdown of a city whose internal infrastructure is crushed (like his pulverized bones), and whose external barricades (like his flesh and skin) are peeled away.

The phrase *shibar atzmotai*, "he broke my bones," indicates that the tormentor inflicts excessive violence upon him. Yet it also may convey a slow demise by debilitating disease as in the case of Hezekiah, who utilizes this phrase to describe the agonies of his illness (Is. 38:13).

The *gever's* torments do not merely threaten him with imminent death, but actually simulate its horror. Darkness is a death-like experience,[29] and the peeling away of the *gever's* flesh suggests the post mortem rotting of his body (Job 13:28).

The *Targum* (Eikha 3:6) observes that darkness signifies imprisonment as well as death: "He placed me in a dark prison, like the dead that go to another world." Darkness can also signify imprisonment (e.g., Ps. 107:14).

The *gever* conveys his experience by employing language depicting various types of hardships (siege, sickness, imprisonment, death). Rich use of figurative language allows the *gever's* personal situation to apply to a broad spectrum of sufferers, each of whom can find an aspect of his own experience in the *gever's* tale.

Suffering without Accountability

At this point in the chapter, the *gever* assumes no responsibility for his misfortunes. He portrays himself as a victim of God's actions, without considering his own role. This absence is especially glaring when compared to other passages in Tanakh that employ similar phrases.

The *gever's* description of the torment of his flesh and bones (*besari veatzmotai*) recalls a similar word pair in Psalms 38:4:

---

28. See the *Targum* on Eikha 3:5: "He built a siege against me and surrounded the city, and he uprooted the leaders and drained them."

29. Psalms 88 describes death similarly, using images of darkness, powerlessness, and imprisonment. In contrast to Eikha 3, the individual of Psalms 88 beseeches God to save him from this near-death experience. For similar imagery used to describe death, see also Psalms 49:20; Eccl. 6:3–4; Job 10:19–22.

There is no perfection in my flesh (*bivesari*), because of Your anger; there is no wholeness in my bones (*baatzamai*), *because of my sin.*

Unlike the *gever* of our chapter, the individual of Psalms 38 explicitly recognizes that his physical afflictions stem from his sin.

Psalms 32:3 portrays a sinner whose silence in lieu of confession caused him such pain that his "bones wore away" (*balu atzamai*). Psalms 32:5–6 strongly recommends confessing and admitting transgressions. Only then can a sinner begin his road to reconciliation with God and recovery from his pain. The *gever* describes his own pain using similar language (*bila besari...shibar atzmotai*). However, he does not acknowledge his sins nor does he turn to God in supplication. By comparing these expressions, we may conclude that the true source of the *gever's* pain is not his tormentor, but rather his own silence and resistance to acknowledging his sin.

We find another stark contrast to the *gever's* attitude in Psalms 143:3, where the psalmist describes himself entombed in darkness: "The enemy...made me dwell in darkness like the eternal dead." The supplicant directs his pleas to God, the obvious address for his troubles. Once again, in comparison with other biblical passages, the *gever's* alienation from God and denial of responsibility is evident. The *gever* does not explicitly assume responsibility until verse 39. As I noted in chapter 1, the movement toward recognition of sin is notoriously difficult and takes time, effort, and religious maturity.

Eikha 3:7–9

גָּדַר בַּעֲדִי וְלֹא אֵצֵא
הִכְבִּיד נְחָשְׁתִּי

גַּם כִּי אֶזְעַק וַאֲשַׁוֵּעַ
שָׂתַם תְּפִלָּתִי

גָּדַר דְּרָכַי בְּגָזִית
נְתִיבֹתַי עִוָּה

He built a wall around me and I cannot exit
He weighed down my chains

Even when I cry and plead
He shuts out my prayer

He built a wall on my roads, of hewn stones[30]
He twisted my pathways

The *gever* uses images of entrapment to describe his helplessness. God constructs roadblocks that encircle the *gever*,[31] impeding and perhaps immobilizing him.[32] Perhaps this obstructed road is the one that leads the chained *gever* into exile,[33] or perhaps it depicts the streets of destroyed Judean cities, clogged by heaps of rubble.

In any case, the blocked roads are also figurative, meant to convey the *gever*'s state of mind, his confusion and existential insecurity. The *gever* plods along on a road that does not take him anywhere. His path is twisted and blocked; he does not know how to arrive at his destination. Moreover, chains weigh down his feet; his heavy footsteps further impede him.

Structurally, this alphabetic unit (the *gimel* verses) has an interesting feature. The first and third *gimel* verses open with the verb *gadar*, "to construct a wall." They surround the middle verse of the alphabetic unit, which features the *gever*'s first attempt to pray. The endeavor is futile; just as the wall surrounds the middle sentence, the *gever*'s prayer is stonewalled, and cannot penetrate to God.

---

30. The hewn stones (*gazit*) that obstruct the *gever*'s road recall linguistically (and ironically) the hewn stones used to construct the Temple (I Kings 5:31; 6:36).

31. Dobbs-Allsopp, 112, notes the irony of using imagery of construction within a book that commemorates destruction.

32. Rashi on Eikha 3:7 explains the word *gadar* as follows: "He made a wall opposite me to imprison me."

33. Rashi (ibid.) explains that the wall that surrounds the chained *gever*, from which he cannot escape, consists of troops ready to ambush. Rashi's precise intention is unclear. He may be describing the siege around the city, or perhaps the troops that accompany the captives into exile, guarding them so that they do not flee.

A: *Gadar*: A wall built around the *gever* (verse 7)
  B: *Gam ki ezak*: The obstruction of the *gever's* prayer (verse 8)
A': *Gadar*: A wall built on the *gever's* road (verse 9)

Job, the quintessential sufferer, employs similar imagery and vocabulary to describe his plight. Lamenting his unanswered prayers, Job describes the wall that surrounds him as he walks on a path that has been plunged into darkness.

> Know that God has wronged me; He surrounded me with His fortress. Indeed, I cry violence and I am not answered; I plead and there is no justice. He built a wall (*gadar*) around my route and I cannot pass, and He places darkness upon my pathways. (Job 19:6–8)

Where is God? Why does God rebuff the *gever's* prayer in 3:8? Is this just another example of God's wrathful intransigence? Intriguingly, the *gever's* entreaties omit an address. The entire verse lacks the second person; the *gever* may cry and plead, but he does not direct his petition to anyone, and he does not mention to whom he prays. Instead, the first person appears three times in this verse: "*my* cries," "*my* pleas," "*my* prayer." Submersed in his suffering, this *gever* cannot see outside himself. Just as the *gever* does not mention God by name, deepening the alienation between himself and God, he cannot find God in prayer because he sees only his own misery. God does not respond to the *gever's* supplication because the *gever* neglects to address Him, preferring to wallow in the echoes of his own wails.

Encircled by figurative barriers that he has constructed around himself, the *gever's* self-absorbed speech bounces off the walls and boomerangs back to him. Retreating into his misfortune, the *gever* directs his speech to no one, deepening his solitude. Poignant cries echo futilely within the sealed chamber of the *gever's* misery.

Eikha 3:10–12

דֹּב אֹרֵב הוּא לִי
אֲרִי בְּמִסְתָּרִים

דְּרָכַי סוֹרֵר וַיְפַשְּׁחֵנִי
שָׂמַנִי שֹׁמֵם

דָּרַךְ קַשְׁתּוֹ וַיַּצִּיבֵנִי
כַּמַּטָּרָא לַחֵץ

He is a bear lying in ambush for me
A lion in hidden places

He diverted[34] my roads and mangled me
He made me desolate

He bent His bow and stood me up
As a target for His arrow

New and disturbing animal imagery emerges, of wild and irrational
tormentors. The *gever's* bestial oppressor lies hidden, waiting to tear
him apart. As disconcerting as it may seem, Rashi explicitly states that
this figurative portrayal refers to God: "God turned into a bear lying in
ambush for me."[35] We encountered a hint in this direction earlier, when
God voraciously swallows Israel (2:2, 5). A discomfiting image, the portrayal of God as a ravenous animal challenges the notion that God torments the *gever* for his sins. Animals do not act with logic; they simply
pounce on whatever prey crosses their path.

Once again, the *gever* finds himself on a perilous, twisted road.
This time, the dangers materialize; his tormentor attacks him with

---

34. Some commentators on this verse (Rashi, R. Yosef Kara) explain that the word *sorer*
derives from the word *sir*, meaning thorns. Like in Hosea 2:8, God paves the *gever's*
roads with thorns that render his journey painful. This interpretation also alludes to
the desolation along the roads that have become overgrown and thorny from lack
of maintenance and travelers (see Is. 34:13).

35. Hosea 13:7–8 portrays God in a similar manner. Eikha Rabba 3:4 maintains that
these savage animals refer to Israel's brutish enemies – namely, the Babylonian
general Nebuchadnezzar (who destroyed the First Temple) and the Roman general
Vespasian (who destroyed the Second Temple).

animal-like savagery.[36] The *gever's* desolation is complete.[37] No one comes to save him; the roads contain only hostile elements.[38]

The word that depicts God positioning the *gever* as a target is *darakh* (verse 12). A wordplay with the word *derekh*, meaning road (verses 9 and 11), this word links the *gever's* journey (where he is a target of wild beasts) to God targeting him with His bow.

This targeting marks a significant pivot in the *gever's* narrative.[39] No longer an arbitrary act of abuse, the tormentor singles out the *gever* in a deliberate and focused decision. Emotionally, this must be a terrible setback for the *gever*. He begins to understand that he is not the victim of capricious happenstance or indiscriminate cruelty; rather, God chooses to afflict him. From a theological viewpoint, however, this is a step forward. It is but a small step from this realization to the inescapable conclusion that God is meting out punishments for his sins. The *gever's* newfound comprehension represents both an emotional shock and a theological development.

Eikha 3:13–15

הֵבִיא בְּכִלְיוֹתָי
בְּנֵי אַשְׁפָּתוֹ

הָיִיתִי שְׂחֹק לְכָל־עַמִּי
נְגִינָתָם כָּל־הַיּוֹם

---

36. The *Targum* translates the hapax legomenon *pashaḥ* as meaning *shasa*, which can describe the way in which an animal is ripped apart (Lev. 1:17; Judges 14:6).

37. In using the word *shomem*, which previously described the desolation of Jerusalem, her gates, and her children (Eikha 1:4; 13, 16), the *gever* creates another parallel between his experience and that of the city.

38. While the verse does not specifically mention the absence of fellow travelers (as opposed to the explicit description in Eikha 1:4), the *gever's* desolation and vulnerability suggest his isolation. The *gever* seems entirely unaware of any human being other than himself. His misfortunes loom large; he is completely absorbed in his own experience.

39. Biblical interpreters disagree as to whether God sets up the *gever* as a target in order to shoot at him (Rashi), or if his tormentor places him in a vulnerable position, so that anyone who wishes to shoot at him may do so easily (R. Yosef Kara). Similar language in Eikha 2:4 suggests that God fires the arrows at him here as well. See also the next verse (3:13). For further support for Rashi's reading, see Job 16:12.

הִשְׂבִּיעַנִי בַמְּרוֹרִים
הִרְוַנִי לַעֲנָה

He brought into my innards
The sons of His quiver

I was a laughingstock for all my nation
Their plaything all day

He satiated me with bitterness
Saturated me with wormwood

Having situated the *gever* as a target, the tormentor releases the bow-string and arrows penetrate the *gever*'s innards.[40] The arrows are poetically termed the sons of His quiver, ironically recalling biblical passages that refer to Israel as God's sons (Deut. 14:1; 32:19–20).[41]

To compound his isolation, the *gever* endures the mockery of his own people, who ceaselessly taunt him for sport.[42] Atypical within the book, the cruelty of the *gever*'s own nation sets his suffering apart from theirs. Not only do his fellow countrymen fail to commiserate with him, they deliberately demean and demoralize him. Why is this tormented *gever* a laughingstock? Possibly, the scorn of the people derives from his suffering; when his fellows see that God singles him out for punishment, they regard him as deserving of his tribulations. If his penalty is divinely ordained, he rightly earns their scorn; his misfortune must be a just consequence of his own heinous crimes.

Verse 15 describes a new torment for the *gever*. He is coerced into imbibing bitterness and wormwood, which penetrate his innards just as the arrows did in verse 13. This time, toxic fare enters his body by way

---

40. Once again, an idea continues across the boundaries of the alphabetic unit. The tormentor aims the arrows at the end of the *dalet* unit (verses 10–12), but only looses them at the beginning of the *heh* unit (13–15).

41. In an idyllic psalm, Psalms 127:5 offers a reversal of this image by describing a contented *gever*, who "fills his quiver" with his sons instead of arrows.

42. Some biblical commentators read *ammim* or *am* instead of *ammi* (Rasag; Ibn Ezra; R. Yosef Kara). In this reading, other nations jeer at the *gever*, not his own comrades.

of the mouth, corroding his intestines.[43] Possibly, this alludes to the starvation caused by the siege; in his desperate hunger, the *gever* must satiate himself with bitter and unpalatable victuals.[44] The language may be figurative, an apt way of describing the bitterness that he endures and internalizes.[45] The bitter *merorim* recall the ritual food eaten to commemorate the Exodus from Egypt (Ex. 12:8). Compelled to swallow bitterness without hope for God's liberation, this is an ironic linguistic allusion to the narrative of God's salvation.

Eikha 3:16

וַיַּגְרֵס בֶּחָצָץ שִׁנָּי
הִכְפִּישַׁנִי בָּאֵפֶר

He broke my teeth with gravel
He made me cower in ashes

God breaks the *gever's* teeth with gravel, silencing him at least temporarily. Perhaps this alludes to the consequences of starvation; compelled to eat whatever he can find on the ground, the *gever* consumes food mixed with pebbles that grind down his teeth and splinter them.[46] Cowering[47] in ashes (see also Job 2:8) is associated with mourning,[48] humiliation,[49] human insignificance, and mortality.[50]

---

43. For a similar description, see Jeremiah 9:14.
44. For a similar idea, see the *Targum* on Eikha 4:9.
45. See Jeremiah 9:18; Proverbs 5:4.
46. Rashi cites a midrash (Eikha Rabba 1:22) that offers a similar understanding of this verse.
47. For this translation of this hapax legomenon (*hikhpishani*), see R. Yosef Kara. Rashi offers a different translation, in which God muzzles the *gever* with ashes, presumably by stuffing them into his mouth (see also Ibn Ezra). This is an apt continuation of the first part of the verse, where God neutralizes his mouth, rendering it ineffective.
48. Isaiah 61:3; Jeremiah 6:26.
49. Ezekiel 28:18; Psalms 102:9–11.
50. Genesis 18:27; Job 30:19. Both verses use the phrase "*afar va'efer*," which connotes human mortality as well as insignificance.

Portrait of the Suffering *Gever* (Eikha 3:1–16): A Synopsis

Verse 16 concludes the lengthy description of the *gever's* suffering (1–16). Utilizing multiple metaphors, the *gever* paints an agonizing and diverse portrait of human misery. Beaten, poisoned, mangled, devoured, broken, entombed, imprisoned, chained, pierced, and scorned, the *gever* endures an assortment of horrors. One torment follows another in rapid succession, bringing to mind the prophecy of Amos:

> When a person flees from the lion, and the bear confronts him, and he enters the house and rests his hand on the wall, and the snake bites him. (Amos 5:19)

Even if he manages to emerge alive from one torment, another affliction awaits; there is no escape from misfortune.

As we have noted, this account does not necessarily portray the specific story of one person's suffering. Figurative language and a broad variety of experiences sketch a universal experience of woe. The *gever* represents the prototypical sufferer.

Several images recur in this section and deserve special attention. God leads the *gever* into darkness (verses 2, 6), a frightening and ominous blackness reminiscent of death (Ps. 88:11–13; Job 10:21–22; Eccl. 6:4). Darkness evokes other biblical associations as well: severe distress (Is. 8:22), imprisonment (Ps. 107:10), and divine punishment (Ex. 10; Ezek. 32:7–8). The day of God's judgment, in which He sentences humankind, often invokes darkness (see Joel 2:1–2; 4:14, Amos 5:18; Zeph. 1:15). Darkness also represents the absence of divine light (Ps. 27:1), which indicates the absence of righteousness (Is. 59:9) and of God's beneficent presence (Is. 60:1–3; Mic. 7:8). Partially for this reason, darkness obscures understanding (Ps. 82:5; Eccl. 2:14), blinding people to justice.

Images of darkness coalesce with the theme of the *gever's* contorted and dangerous road (verses 9, 11). Darkness confuses him and diverts him from his intended path. These depictions merge and intertwine; the *gever* describes a difficult journey, characterized by befuddlement and fear. These portrayals are both literal and metaphoric. Without God as a guide and a support, the *gever* walks in figurative darkness, along twists and turns that take him toward no real destination. This describes the *gever's* general instability, but also perhaps, an actual journey into exile, a convoluted path that reverses the theological and national trajectory of every member of the nation.

Encirclement emerges as a predominant image of this section. God's hand circles the hapless *gever*, returning repeatedly to strike him (verse 3). God surrounds him with poison and hardship (verse 5) and builds a wall around him; there is no exit (verse 7). Literal experience once again merges with the figurative, alluding to the frame of mind of the victim, who feels trapped, caged, surrounded on all sides.[51] There is no escape, not even through prayer (verse 8).

This encirclement is reminiscent of the prowling movement of an animal stalking its prey, advancing in rings until he pounces and tears it apart. Animal imagery abounds in this section. Portrayed as a wild animal who lies in ambush (verse 10), God assaults the *gever* with ferocity. Scraping at his flesh and skin and breaking his bones, God mangles him (verses 4, 11). It is an unnerving depiction, in which the *gever* portrays God as brutal and inconceivably arbitrary. In this schema, God operates without a plan, tackling his prey for no apparent reason and with no obvious goal. However, as the description progresses, the *gever* gropes his way toward a different perception of God's role in his misfortune. Once God positions him as a target, singling him out for deliberate abuse, the divine image shifts and comes into focus. Indeed, God has attacked him, but this was no arbitrary occurrence. It becomes clear that God has selected the *gever* for punishment. This new realization will accompany the *gever* on his ruminations in the next section, which will end with a pronouncement of human accountability.

---

51. The circular movement with no escape reminds us of the structure of chapters 1 and 2, which is circular and chiastic. Nevertheless, as we will see, this chapter will turn out to be linear in structure, allowing the *gever* to emerge from his cyclical misery.

Job and the *Gever*

Unsurprisingly, our *gever* emerges as a Job-like figure, whose trials evoke those of that classic sufferer of biblical literature.[52] As noted, Job refers to himself as a *gever* (Job 3:3). Although Job's personal narrative is considerably longer than our *gever's* account, which is concentrated into sixteen verses, the *gever's* language often evokes Job's. According to Job, God encircles him (19:6), builds a wall on his path, and submerges his pathways in darkness (19:8). God steeps Job in bitterness (9:18) and positions him as a target (16:12). Job feels God's rod (9:34), suffers animal-like attacks (10:16), and describes the shriveling of his "skin and flesh" (19:20). Job wallows in ashes (2:8) and pleads and cries with no divine response (20:7). He also feels alienated from God and his fellows, who mock both Job and the *gever* in strikingly similar ways (compare Job 30:9 to Eikha 3:14). The suffering of the religious person obtains a universal character; these similarities can help us isolate aspects of suffering that are common to all people, particularly within a religious framework.

Eikha 3:17–18

וַתִּזְנַח מִשָּׁלוֹם נַפְשִׁי
נָשִׁיתִי טוֹבָה

וָאֹמַר אָבַד נִצְחִי
וְתוֹחַלְתִּי מֵה׳

**And my soul rejected peace
I forgot goodness**

**And I said, "My endurance is lost
And my hope in the Lord"**

A cry of helpless despair follows on the heels of the *gever's* horror-filled account. The *gever* declares that he (or his "soul") has abandoned any hope for peace (*shalom*). The quest for "*shalom*" represents the

---

52. See Berlin, 85.

focal point of biblical aspirations, both for individuals[53] and for the nation.[54] It connotes more than just physical peace; the word *shalom* also alludes to inner tranquility, a sense of wholeness. All this eludes the persecuted *gever*, who cannot conceive of obtaining *shalom* ever again. Indeed, this word appears only once in Eikha, in this negative context.

The *gever* also proclaims that he has forgotten goodness. He has lost a basic sense of well-being, of a satisfactory existence.[55] No longer does the *gever* entertain even this minimal aspiration; goodness is not even a possibility for him. A conclusive utterance of despair follows this proclamation (3:18): "And I said, 'My endurance is lost, and my hope in the Lord!'" Depleted of energy and lacking hope, this testimonial seems on the verge of bringing this chapter and the *gever*'s life to a miserable close.[56] There is nothing more to say, no more strength, and no more

---

53. For example, at the conclusion of Song of Songs (8:10), the *Re'aya* (the female figure) finally "finds *shalom*," a climactic moment that represents the apex of the book. The word *shalom* also represents the ultimate objective of several idyllic psalms (Ps. 29:11; 125:5; 128:6), and appears as the conclusion of the blessing of the *kohanim* (Num. 7:26), the concluding blessing of the *Amidah*, the conclusion of the Grace after Meals, and the message of the final mishna in *Shas*.

54. Note, for example, the description of Solomon's ideal reign in I Kings 5:4. In Song of Songs, Solomon (Shelomo) has a relationship with the Shulamit (Song 7:1), and they are situated in Yerushalayim. All these key words (Shelomo, Shulamit, and Yerushalayim) relate to the word *shalom*, indicating its supreme importance for constructing an ideal nation. See also Psalms 122:4, 6.

55. The word *tov* in Genesis 1 appears a key seven times, suggesting that this is a primary goal of creation. In the book of Eikha, the word *tov* also appears seven times, indicating its central importance for the book. Five of these appearances are in chapter 3, as I will shortly discuss.

56. R. Yosef Kara (Eikha 3:18–19) explains the loss of hope in an evocative passage: "My hope in the Lord is lost. What hope can a person have if he is imprisoned in a dark place? And if the prison is constructed by hewn stones that are walled around him? And if he is incarcerated in heavy chains and the prison is closed around him from all directions so that his voice cannot be heard from outside when he shouts? And outside of the prison, his pathways are twisted so that even if he breaks through a wall of the prison, he cannot return to the road that he walked on. And not only that, but 'He is a bear lying in ambush for me' and therefore, my hope to escape has been lost."

faith in a positive outcome. The word *avad*, used here to express the loss of strength and hope, contains intimations of death.[57]

In one of Jeremiah's uncommon hope-filled prophecies, he uses the words *tova* and *shalom* to illustrate the reversal of this despair:

> And I will return the captives of Judah and the captives of Israel and I will build them as of old … And they will be for Me a name, joy, glory, and splendor more than all the nations of the earth, who will hear of all the *good* that I will do for them and will be fearful and agitated because of all the *goodness* and all the *peace* that I will bring for her. (Jer. 33:7, 9)

Verse 18 of Eikha precipitates a turning point, which occurs quite dramatically in the upcoming verses.[58] What causes the *gever's* unexpected pivot? In verse 18 the *gever* names God for the first time. Previously, God has been an omnipresent but nameless and hidden third person, whose absence resonates loudly. Against the backdrop of his despair, the *gever* finally calls God by name, grimly dismissing the possibility of retaining any hope in Him.

Yet, in expressing his loss of hope in God, the *gever* utters God's name. This triggers a stunning transformation.[59] The self-absorbed *gever* begins to emerge from his shell, seeing outside of himself for the first time. With the name of God upon his lips, the *gever* launches an interior monologue, in which he ponders God's ways and explores the relationship between God and humankind.

---

57. Numbers 17:27; Jonah 1:6; Esther 4:14, 16.

58. Hillers, 69, maintains that when a person introduces his lament with self-reflective words, "I said," it signifies a turning point. See also Psalms 31:23; 94:18; 139:11; Isaiah 6:5; 38:11; 49:4.

59. In one of his essays ("Thou Shouldst Enter the Covenant of the Lord," in *On Repentance*, ed. P. Peli [Jerusalem: Maggid, 2017], 113–45), Rav Soloveitchik discusses two different processes that lead people to repentance. Sometimes repentance begins as a rational process, whereby people gradually arrive at the logical conclusion that life without God is not worthwhile. Often, however, repentance begins as an emotional process, in which people are struck by a sudden, desperate need to reconcile with God. Our chapter appears to depict the latter process. Having uttered the name of God, the *gever* abruptly desires a relationship with Him, setting into motion a series of ruminations that lead to a total transformation.

Eikha 3:19–20

זְכָר־עָנְיִי וּמְרוּדִי
לַעֲנָה וָרֹאשׁ

זָכוֹר תִּזְכּוֹר
וְתָשׁוֹחַ עָלַי נַפְשִׁי:

When I remember my affliction and wandering[60]
[It is like] wormwood and poison

When I truly remember
My soul sinks down upon me

Two obscure verses transition the *gever* from despondency (verse 18) to renewed hope in God (verse 21).[61] The transformation itself is remarkable. The same soul (*nefesh*) that rejected any possibility of peace in verse 17 begins to change in verse 20 as he describes his soul (*nefesh*) sinking within him.[62] Yet the precise meaning of these transition verses remains murky, and biblical interpreters have translated them in radically different ways. The reading I adopted above has the *gever* speaking to himself,

---

60. The phrase "affliction and wandering" appears in one other place in Eikha (1:7), where Jerusalem speaks of her miseries. The experience of the *gever* again merges with the city's hardships.

61. The obscurity of these verses is compounded by the fact that some interpreters identify verse 20 as containing a *tikkun soferim*, an alteration of the original text designed to preserve God's honor. Not all sources identify a *tikkun soferim* here, and no source that does records the original reading or identifies the words that contain the problem. This makes it incredibly difficult even to speculate about restoring the original verse. For more on the *tikkun soferim* in this verse, see C. D. Ginsburg, *Introduction to the Masoretico-Critical Edition of the Hebrew Bible* (London, 1897), 361. For more on *tikkunei soferim* in general, see Saul Lieberman, *Hellenism in Jewish Palestine* (New York, 1950), 28–37.

62. As I will note, this sinking (*shaḥaḥ*) of his soul may also be understood in radically different ways. I prefer to see this as the beginning of the humbling of the narcissistic *gever* (see a similar usage of the verb *shaḥaḥ* in Isaiah 2:9, 11, 17). His self-absorbed misery precludes his ability to see a broader picture, which he only starts to see when he mentions God and begins to ponder His ways.

reflecting pensively on his afflictions.[63] Another common interpretation portrays the *gever* directing these words toward God.[64] I will explore each of these possibilities, considering how each one contributes to the *gever's* forward movement at this critical turning point of the chapter.

In the above translation, the *gever* is self-consciously ruminative, sharing his remembrances with the reader. The opening word, *"zekhor,"* conjures up his memories of bitterness and pain. The *gever* does not confine himself to these unpleasant feelings for long. He quickly becomes contemplative, arriving at a truly spectacular conclusion: suffering begets humility.[65] Why do his reflections humble him? The *gever* does not clarify this point. Possibly, the experience of suffering reminds him of humanity's essential weakness, mortality, and vulnerability. More compellingly, the *gever* is beginning to acknowledge that which he will specify only at the conclusion of his ruminations: suffering that is linked to sin engenders humility, inducing every individual to recognize his own accountability for his plight (3:39).

An alternative reading has the *gever* turning to God and demanding that God remember the *gever's* pain.[66] Here, the *gever* undergoes a

---

63. Rashi (Eikha 3:20) views this as the *peshat*, the simple reading of the verse. See also Rasag on verse 20 and the Greek translation of the verse. Scholars who adopt this general approach include Hillers, 50, 69–70; O'Connor, 47; Dobbs-Allsopp, 117.

64. For example, R. Yosef Kara. Further complicating matters, some interpreters separate these transition verses, explaining that the *gever* addresses God in verse 19 and himself in verse 20 (e.g., Gordis, 141, and see R. Yosef Kara on *Eikha* 3:19–20). Others maintain the opposite: the *gever* addresses himself in verse 19 and God in verse 20 (Westermann, 161, 172). Multiple readings of these transition verses make it impossible to conclude with any certainty the simple meaning of these verses.

65. One interpretation of the soul sinking down within him is that this is a description of humility. Some scholars suggest that this describes the crushing weight of the *gever's* troubles that press down on him (O'Connor, 48), or a depiction of the *gever's* inner despondency (Dobbs-Allsopp, 117; Berlin, 82–83). Note that Psalms 42:5–6 describes a person's memories that lead to his soul sinking down – namely, his misery. These readings, however, simply circle back to the description of the *gever's* suffering. Considering the transitional role played by these verses, I prefer the reading above, in which recollections of his misery lead him forward toward newfound humility.

66. See R. Yosef Kara on Eikha 3:20, who understands verse 20 not as an imperative, but as a statement of fact: "You will surely remember [my sufferings], but until that time comes, my soul sinks down upon me." See also Eikha Rabba 3:7 and Rashi's citation of it as the aggadic explanation of verse 20.

more abrupt transformation, refusing to relinquish hope in God, despite his words in verse 18. Instead, he musters up his last bit of strength and beseeches God, "Remember my affliction and wandering, like wormwood and poison! You must surely remember that my soul sinks down upon me!" In this scenario, suffering begets petition. This is the final recourse; if the *gever* does not turn to God, he has no option other than to abandon hope completely.[67] By enlisting God to remember him and his misery, the *gever* begins his turnaround.

Instead of choosing between these readings, I prefer to assume that Eikha intentionally weaves multiple meaningful interpretations into these verses.[68] Each reading offers an important understanding of how one can transition from hopelessness to renewal, from alienation to reconciliation with God.

No matter how we understand these verses, we must observe the pivotal role played by the word *zakhar* ("remember") in this book.[69] Featured a key seven times throughout the book, the word appears three times in these two transitional sentences. The *gever's* recollections (or his request that God recollect) launch the turning point of the chapter, spinning the *gever's* thoughts in a new direction. This swivel indicates the important role that memory plays in one's relationship with God. Even when a person feels most alienated, asserting that he has utterly abandoned hope in God, he can turn to his memories to remind himself

---

67. R. Yosef Kara explains Eikha 3:19 as follows: "Even though I could have said, 'I have lost my strength and hope in the Lord'... I will not be silent from crying out and beseeching Him and petitioning Him, saying: 'Remember my affliction and wandering that were like wormwood and poison.'"

68. Rashi, too, cites an explanation that he calls the simple meaning, followed by the homiletic explanation, which he also deems legitimate. Similarly, Ibn Ezra (in his *dikduk hamilot*) brings both possible readings of the word *zekhor* in verse 19 (either a description of his own recollections or an imperative addressed to God). However, in his explanation of the verse, he prefers the reading in which the *gever* describes his own recollections, as I have translated above. Similarly, in his explanation to verse 20, although he alludes to two interpretations, Ibn Ezra prefers the interpretation in which the *gever* is remembering pensively.

69. I discussed this word at greater length in its first appearance in the book (Eikha 1:7).

of God's eternal covenant and obligations to Israel.[70] On the flip side, remembering also reminds him of his promises to God, which he has violated. This sobering thought humbles him and compels the *gever* to begin an exploration of his obligations toward God.

PART 2 (EIKHA 3:21–29): THEOLOGICAL REFLECTIONS

This unit, positioned at the core of the book of Eikha, is its structural and theological center. It explores God's nature and the way in which humans grapple with suffering. This brief section is not a well-developed discourse on theology. For that, one would do better to turn to the book of Job, which is the classic and most elaborate biblical discussion of theodicy. In Eikha, the *gever* offers a condensed treatise of just nineteen sentences, laconically illustrating how humans struggle with their understanding of God and their own role in a world filled with anguish.

This middle section of Eikha refuses to lament the miserable fate of humanity, embarking instead on a series of reflections on the nature of both God and humans. The section progresses steadily, illustrating how human beings can regain equilibrium, and even advance, in spite of their grim situation. These ruminations are not comprehensive, nor are they prescriptive; they offer a fleeting but arresting glimpse of human resilience and faith.

Not all scholars regard these verses as an independent unit.[71] Although opinions vary widely, Rashi makes a rare structural comment on 3:21: "This I shall place upon my heart, therefore, I will hope":

---

70. Note the threefold appearance of the word *zakhar* in Leviticus 26:42, in which God's assurance that He will remember His nation echoes promisingly after a terrible litany of divine punishment. Similarly, see Leviticus 26:45; Jeremiah 31:19; Ezekiel 16:60; Psalms 106:46. In Exodus 2:24, God "remembers" His covenant and saves Israel from their oppression in Egypt. This idea is so important that it plays a central role in the Mussaf service of Rosh Hashana, where we ask God to "remember us with a favorable memory, and recall us with a remembrance of salvation and compassion."

71. The vast array of opinions with regard to the division of chapter 3 is overwhelming. For example, House, 430, continues the first section until verse 24 and regards verses 25–39 as a unit, while Westermann, 189, continues the opening unit until verse 25. Hillers, 65, prefers to continue the first section of the book until verse 39. Dobbs-Allsopp, 116–19, views verses 19–24 as an independent unit. O'Connor identifies a unit in 3:22–42, which she terms "Divine Mercies," while Berlin's division (verses 22–39) is close to the one that I have adopted (Berlin, 92).

And what is the "this" that "I shall place on my heart" [verse 21]? "The kindnesses of the Lord shall not cease" [verse 22] until, "Of what shall a living person complain?" [verse 39]. (Rashi, Eikha 3:21–22)

According to Rashi, the *gever* expands upon his confident statement in verse 21 in the eighteen verses that follow (22–39).[72] I will adopt this approach and examine the section in accordance with Rashi's understanding.

To begin this analysis of this middle section of the chapter, we need to understand how these verses flow from one to the other. I divide this section into three subunits (each of which I will examine independently):[73]

A. Verses 21–26: **God's Compassionate Ways (*Ḥesed* and *Raḥamim*): Reacquiring Hope**

B. Verses 27–30: **The Role of the Suffering Individual**

A'. Verses 31–39: **God's Compassionate Ways (*Ḥesed* and *Raḥamim*)**

The subunits (A and A') that surround the pivotal center of the book (B) contain similar subject matter, describing God's positive attributes with identical words (*ḥesed and raḥamim*). Faith in God's goodness envelops the nucleus of Eikha.

At the book's core, the central section of the central chapter, lies a section that I have termed "The Role of the Suffering Individual." Its structural centrality indicates its pivotal role in the book. Deep in the recesses of the book lies human tenacity, an abiding faith in the human ability to survive.

---

72. Dobbs-Allsopp, 117, posits that the "this" that gives the *gever* hope refers back to his suffering, rather than forward to his reflections on God. I have adopted Rashi's reading, which I think is more logical; why, after all, should his suffering cause him to hope? Moreover, Rashi's reading is more meaningful; hope is born of faith, not pain.

73. Many biblical scholars do not accept this division. As noted, the division of the chapter engendered a vast array of different opinions. The division of this section is no less controversial (and, of course, many scholars do not regard this as a "unit" at all).

Eikha 3:21–26

זֹאת אָשִׁיב אֶל־לִבִּי
עַל־כֵּן אוֹחִיל

חַסְדֵי ה׳ כִּי לֹא־תָמְנוּ
כִּי לֹא־כָלוּ רַחֲמָיו

חֲדָשִׁים לַבְּקָרִים
רַבָּה אֱמוּנָתֶךָ

חֶלְקִי ה׳ אָמְרָה נַפְשִׁי
עַל־כֵּן אוֹחִיל לוֹ

טוֹב ה׳ לְקֹוָו
לְנֶפֶשׁ תִּדְרְשֶׁנּוּ

טוֹב וְיָחִיל וְדוּמָם
לִתְשׁוּעַת ה׳

This I shall place upon my heart
Therefore, I will hope

For the kindnesses of the Lord do not cease
For His compassion does not end

They renew themselves every morning
Great is Your trustworthiness!

"My portion is in the Lord," my soul says
Therefore, I will hope in Him

The Lord is good to those who wait for Him
To the soul who seeks Him

> **It is good to hope and be silent**
> **For the salvation of the Lord!**

God's Compassionate Ways (*Ḥesed* and *Raḥamim*): Reacquiring Hope

The *gever's* remarkable transformation produces an emotional turn-around, in which he hauls himself out of the depths of despair and recovers his optimism. Transposing the linguistic expressions of hope-lessness uttered in verses 17–18, the *gever* reanimates and reclaims his relationship with God.

The thread that draws this subunit together and defines it as a section is the word *yaḥal*, meaning to hope. The final words of the *gever* in verse 18 flatly assert that he has lost hope (*toḥalti*) in God. Truly a wretched state, loss of hope in God dooms the individual to despon-dency, marking the final, inexorable slide toward a meaningless existence.

The first step toward recovery, then, is to restore hope in God. As the *gever* progresses through his reflections, his confidence and faith escalate. Buoyed by the idea that his ponderings can facilitate hope (*al kein oḥil*, verse 21), his words contradict his avowed loss of hope just three sentences prior! After two sentences in which he briefly rumi-nates on God's compassion and faithfulness, the *gever's* optimism again mounts. This time, his proclamation of hope contains a direct object: "Therefore I will hope *in Him*!" (*al kein oḥil lo*, verse 24). The *gever's* newfound confidence further reinforces his hope in God. Using a differ-ent word to describe his hope (*kava*), the *gever* grasps an encouraging truth: "The Lord is good to those who wait for Him!" (verse 25).[74] He, of course, stands to gain from this realization, as he now identifies as one who hopes in God. In a spectacular conclusion to this recovery of hope,

---

74. I have translated the word *kava* as wait, to distinguish between the two words with similar meanings. Isaiah uses the word *kava* in a similar context, noting that God supports those who hope in Him / wait for Him (Is. 40:31), and they will not be shamed (Is. 49:23).

the *gever* describes a particularly stalwart type of hope (*yaḥil vedumam*, verse 26): silent, unwavering, and utterly confident in God's salvation.[75]

In just five sentences, the *gever* has embarked upon an extraordinary internal journey. The same soul (*nafshi*) that rejected peace and forgot goodness in verse 17, sinking low in verse 20, has emerged with renewed vigor. In verse 24, the *gever's* soul (*nafshi*) proclaims with deep conviction, "My portion is in the Lord ... Therefore, I will hope in Him!"[76] In the following verse (25), the soul (*nefesh*) actively seeks God, anticipating His goodness. This entire process occurs internally; the *gever's* soul transforms despite the unchanged external situation.

While the first seventeen verses of the chapter refuse to name God (referring to Him in the hidden third person), the *gever* names God as his final word in verse 18, in an expression of terrible bereavement: "My endurance is lost, and my hope in the Lord!" In our section, the *gever's* connection to God grows steadily, as indicated by the fourfold mention of God's name in verses 21–26, which also concludes with the name of God: "It is good to hope and be silent for the salvation of the Lord!" The significance of this cannot be overstated. Having experienced terrible atrocities that he attributes to God, it is astonishing that the *gever* desires to reconcile with God and succeeds in doing so.

The *gever* begins to perceive God differently in this section. Instead of wrath, he perceives benevolence, as God renews kindness/loyalty (*ḥesed*)[77] and compassion (*raḥamim*) each day. A powerfully simple notion – God's unceasing magnanimity and fidelity – reassures

---

75. This is not the defeated silence of the conquered elders of Jerusalem that we encountered in Eikha 2:10 (*yidemu*). Instead, the *gever* has managed to produce a noble, dignified silence (*vedumam*), whose stated goal is to wait patiently, with perfect faith in God's deliverance. These similar-sounding words seem to derive from different roots (*d.m.m.* and *d.o.m.*). Nevertheless, their meanings are similar, as is often the case of the weak root, as I noted in Eikha 1:8–9.

76. See, similarly, Psalms 16:5; 73:26.

77. The word *ḥesed* connotes an array of similar (but not identical) meanings: loyalty, compassion, generosity, goodness, kindness, and steadfast love. Due to its importance and the ambiguity of its precise meaning, several monographs have been written about this word in Tanakh. See, for example, Nelson Glueck, *Hesed in the Bible* (Cincinnati: Hebrew Union College Press, 1967); Katherine Doob Sakenfeld, *The Meaning of Hesed in the Hebrew Bible: A New Inquiry* (Missoula: Scholars Press

the *gever* that he may continue to rely on God's goodness, no matter the present situation. Indeed, God's kindnesses toward His followers are ever refreshed, so that even the most downtrodden and despondent can retain hope for rapid recovery.

These divine attributes (*ḥesed* and *raḥamim*) appear frequently in biblical passages describing God[78] and evoke the formulaic portrayal of God's compassion and kindness in Exodus 34:6–7.[79] This description of God's munificence follows the incident of the golden calf. It becomes a fundamental principle of God's relationship with His nation that sin and punishment will be followed by divine compassion and forgiveness.[80] There is good reason, then, for the *gever* to acquire hope when he recalls God's attributes; no calamity can signify the termination of God's loyalty and mercy.

Divine goodness emerges alongside God's benevolent attributes. In contrast to the *gever's* previous utterance that rejected the possibility of goodness (verse 17), in verse 25 the *gever* uses the word *tov* (good) to modify God ("The Lord is good"), qualifying it somewhat by adding "to those who seek Him." Surprisingly, the *gever* does not constrain God's benevolence to the pious or righteous, but rather to those who sincerely yearn for Him, a broader and more easily accessible goal.[81] Because the *gever* has recently become that individual who seeks God, this realization allows him to anticipate receiving God's goodness.

The *gever's* newfound understanding of God ameliorates his previous alienation, characterized by the hidden third-person references to God in the beginning of the chapter. In our section, the *gever* turns to God in a direct address: "Great is *Your* trustworthiness!" This easy familiarity speaks both of God's faithfulness and of human trust in God.

---

for the Harvard Semitic Museum, 1978); Gordon R. Clark, *The Word Hesed in the Hebrew Bible* (Sheffield: JSOT Press, 1993).

78. See, for example, Joel 2:13; Jonah 4:2; Psalms 86:15; 103:8; 145:8.

79. There is some exegetical debate as to who actually formulates this classic notion of God's attributes. The subject of the word "*vayikra*" (Ex. 34:6) may be either God (as explained by most medieval interpreters, including, e.g., Rasag, Ibn Ezra, Sforno) or Moses (see, e.g., *Targum Yerushalmi* on this verse).

80. See also the use of this formula after the incident of the spies in Numbers 14:18–20.

81. Compare to Psalms 145:18.

Strikingly, the *gever* now seems certain that God is accessible, if only he can muster up the faith to turn to Him.

Eikha 3:27–30

טוֹב לַגֶּבֶר
כִּי־יִשָּׂא עֹל בִּנְעוּרָיו

יֵשֵׁב בָּדָד וְיִדֹּם
כִּי נָטַל עָלָיו

יִתֵּן בֶּעָפָר פִּיהוּ
אוּלַי יֵשׁ תִּקְוָה

יִתֵּן לְמַכֵּהוּ לֶחִי
יִשְׂבַּע בְּחֶרְפָּה

It is good for a *gever*
To bear a burden in his youth

He should sit in solitude and be silent
When it is placed upon him

He should place his mouth in the dust
Perhaps there will be hope

He should give his cheek to the one who strikes him
He should suffer it in shame

The Epicenter of the Book:
The Role of the Suffering Individual

This is the central passage of the book, indicating its importance.[82] According to the division that I have delineated, this middle section

---

82. Unlike the previous chapters, this chapter does not maintain a chiastic structure or operate in a circular manner, progressing instead in a linear fashion. In the

of the *gever's* ruminations is the middle unit of the middle chapter of Eikha. Its subject differs from that of the surrounding subunits, which reflect on God's compassionate ways. The *gever* appears at the center of his own musings; God does not feature at all at the apex of the book. In his reflections, the *gever* considers the lessons that he may draw from his suffering and that which he may gain from his experiences.

This focus on the individual is crucial, but God's absence in this section raises questions. Who imposes the "burden" on the sufferer? To which abuser should the sufferer submit his cheek? Rashi (3:28) assumes that God is the hidden subject responsible for the *gever's* afflictions. Indeed, the continuation of these theological reflections suggests as much.[83] Yet, by not naming God, these verses highlight the *gever* and his reflections. At its core, this book seeks the inner resources that enable humans to survive in a world filled with suffering.

"It is good (*tov*) for a *gever* to bear a burden in his youth" (3:27). The word *tov* opens this middle section, as it opens the previous two verses of the alphabetic *tet* unit of chapter 3.[84] The word marks a smooth continuity from one subunit to the next, as well as a striking progression in the *gever's* thoughts. As the *gever* ruminates on what is good, he transitions from his contemplation about God (who is *good* to those who seek Him, verse 25), to a meditation on how it is *good* for a person

---

previous circular chapters (1 and 2), the quantifiable midpoint is the *kaf* and *lamed* verses (verses 11 and 12), which appear as the hinge around which the concentric chapters revolve. In this noncircular chapter, I have taken the liberty of defining its midpoint elsewhere (in the *tet* and *yod* verses) based on the substance and themes of the chapter. Moreover, I have assigned the first two *tet* verses to the previous sub-section (based on the word *yaḥal*, as noted above). All structural divisions of this chapter remain uncertain; the one that I have presented seems to me to have the most substantive significance, as I will try to illustrate.

83. See also R. Yosef Kara, Eikha 3:28. These exegetes do not comment on the identity of the one who strikes the *gever* in 3:30, although their comment on 3:28 seems to suggest that God perpetrates all the *gever's* woes in this section.

84. This is not typical of the alphabetic units in this chapter, which generally vary their opening words. The only other example is the *kaf* unit, in which all three verses open with the word *ki*. The eightfold *tet* unit in Psalms 119 employs the word *tov* as its opening word in five out of the eight verses, suggesting that this is a commonplace word in alphabetic compositions (see also Ps. 37:16; 112:6; 145:9; Eikha 4:9), although there remain other possible options (Ps. 34:9; 111:5; Prov. 31:18; Eikha 1:9; 2:9).

to behave (hoping in silence for God's salvation, verse 26). The final conclusion is that it is *good* for an individual to bear a burden in his formative years (verse 27). Suffering begets good; one's ordeal has value. The *gever* proceeds from an outward glance (toward God) to an inward one (his own behavior), settling finally on a general description of what is "good" for all human beings.

The central section is didactic in nature, its opening reminiscent of instructive statements found in the book of Proverbs.[85] The *gever* offers advice meant to be universally applicable, opening with the expansive (but not personal) statement that bearing a burden in one's youth is beneficial.

Why is it good to bear a burden in one's youth? Perhaps the idea that it is good to suffer *only* in one's youth, when one has the stamina and resilience to tolerate hardship. Yet, it seems that the statement maintains a positive outlook toward youthful suffering. Some commentators suggest that the yoke refers not to abstract suffering, but to punishment for sins.[86] Possibly this is because those who are punished for their sins in their youth will be spared later in life. Others regard this suffering in youth as a formative experience, one that is instrumental in constructing the human persona. In this schema, it may be good for people to experience adversity early on in order to prepare them to face life's inevitable suffering later, when their strength has waned.[87] More positively, individuals who encounter difficulties in their youth acquire courage and build a robust character. They can learn to rely on God and on their own inner resources, gaining strength to endure whatever hardships may come their way.

---

85. Many statements in Proverbs begin with the word *tov*, in a bid to counsel a general audience as to what is "good." See Proverbs 8:19; 12:2; 13:22; 16:8. Moreover, the youth (*naar*) is a prominent figure in Proverbs, a book whose hortatory content includes specific advice about how to educate the young to the proper path. For examples, see Proverbs 22:15; 23:13–14.

86. See, for example, R. Yosef Kara. A *Targum* of Eikha 3:28 suggests that one who suffers punishment for his sins in this world will arrive in a perfect state in the next world.

87. See House, 416, extrapolating from C. F. Keil, *Jeremiah, Lamentations*, J. Martin, trans. (Grand Rapids: Zondervan, 1872, reprinted, 1980), 415.

The burden (*ol*) may refer not to suffering or even punishment for sin, but rather to the encumbrance of sin itself (see the use of the word *ol* in Eikha 1:14), which stymies the *gever* in his ongoing quest for a relationship with God.[88] Bearing this burden teaches the *gever* the terrible consequences of sin and the agony of living without God.[89] From this experience, the *gever* acquires the desire to work hard to maintain an ongoing relationship with God.

The Significance of Words

Several words that appear at the core of the book echo earlier words or anticipate subsequent usage, offering clues as to the critical idea that lies at the book's center. The word *gever* appears at the opening of the chapter (*ani hagever*, 3:1), drawing attention to the fact that the *gever* who discovers good in his suffering (*tov lagever*, 3:27) is the same figure who launched the chapter with the account of his misfortunes. If we identify that *gever* as Everyman, then this central section strives to instruct every suffering individual to find goodness in his travails.

Words that appear only twice in the entire book (once at the epicenter) may be especially valuable for understanding its essence.[90] The word *ol*, yoke or burden, appears only one other time in the book. In 1:14, the word refers to Jerusalem's transgressions, woven together by God to form a suffocating yoke around her neck. There, the word *ol* appears as part of Jerusalem's complaint, her protracted description of God's wrathful actions. In the center of the book, however, the word *ol* is linked with the *gever's tov*, suggesting that sins, or any heavy yoke,

---

88. Alternatively, the yoke can be a metaphor for God's commandments, which every individual must eventually shoulder and which one should begin experiencing in one's youth. See the *Targum's* translation of Eikha 3:27. Berlin, 94, cites this approach, recalling Jewish tradition that regards the commandments as a yoke (see, e.g., Mishna Berakhot 2:2; *Sifra, Shemini* 10:12). While this is a valuable idea, I find this approach less textually compelling, as it disregards the suffering of the *gever*, focusing instead on the positive onus of God's commands.

89. R. Soloveitchik develops this idea; see his *On Repentance*, 117–29.

90. Similar observations enhance one's understanding of the book of Ruth. See Ziegler, *Ruth*, 476.

can be beneficial, not suffocating, and can lead to good (as noted in the discussion above). In chapter 3, the *gever* expresses gratitude for the yoke, recognizing that he must bear it with purpose. The book uses this word to engage in an internal dialogue, shifting from one approach to a markedly different one.

The word *badad* also appears only twice in the book: once at its opening (1:1) to describe Jerusalem's unbearable loneliness, and once here (3:28) to encourage the experience of solitude. The central section of Eikha again transforms misery into a constructive experience, in which loneliness allows one to acquire confidence, patience, and stalwart faith.[91] The *gever*'s solitude is an opportunity for introspection and a reminder that he can truly rely only on God.

Also appearing twice in the book is the word *leḥi* (check). The cheeks (*leḥeya*) wet with undried tears in Eikha 1:2 reappear here as part of the sufferer's courageous embrace of his own suffering: "He should give his cheek to the one who strikes him."

The word *afar* (dust) also appears only twice in the book. It first describes the mourning rituals of the elders, who, having witnessed the devastation of Jerusalem, despondently rub dust on their heads (2:10). This act evokes the lowly origins and tragic fate of humans, who emerged from dust and will inevitably return to dust (Gen. 3:19). Here, however, the sufferer embraces his mortality and his humble pedigree. The suffering individual welcomes God's designs with serenity, patience, and submission: "He should place his mouth in the dust (*afar*); perhaps there will be hope."[92]

---

91. The Mishna in Avot 3:2 sees this verse as a description of the individual who learns Torah in solitude.

92. While some regard the word *ulai*, "*maybe* there is hope," in a negative way, as though the *gever*'s hope falters and fades (e.g., O'Connor, 51), I regard it as a reflection of humility before God. Biblical passages often moderate their descriptions of God's acts with the word *ulai*, "maybe" (see, e.g., Josh. 14:12; I Sam. 14:6; II Kings 19:4). This word indicates that God's ways are not predictable, and humans cannot command God to act at their behest. Humans should approach God with uncertainty, hoping that He will see fit to do that which we require.

Other words in this central section appear in the book more than twice, but in a significantly changed manner. Unlike the wretched elders who dejectedly sit on the ground, mourning silently (*yidemu*) in agonized helplessness (2:10), the word *yidom* appears in 3:28 as a positive act (he *should* sit in solitude and be silent, *veyidom*). In the critical center of the book, the *gever's* silence is constructive, suggesting faith in God and surrender to His plans.[93]

The word "mouth" also obtains significance in relation to its usage elsewhere in the book. In 3:29, placing one's mouth (*pihu*) in the dust seems to be an expression of subservience and obedience, in which the *gever* deliberately silences himself, allowing no words to issue from his lips.[94] While the word "mouth" appears several times in Eikha, this exact form of the word – *pihu* – also appears only in 1:18 at a revelatory moment in the chapter.[95] There, Jerusalem concedes that she has rebelled against God's mouth (*pihu*), thereby bringing upon herself all of God's just punishments. The two appearances of the word *pihu* clash and then merge; that which issues from God's mouth is quite different from whatever may emerge from the human mouth. God's authoritative instructions ring truthfully and righteously, while the suffering individual should place his mouth in the dust, not daring to utter words of complaint or protest. To do so would fail to recognize the supremacy of God's *pihu*, of His just design.

The final word of this section, *herpa*, means shame, and it offers a curious endorsement of the experience of degradation: "he should suffer it in shame." There are several reasons why the *gever* might conclude that humans should embrace their own dishonor.

---

93. Rashi (Eikha 3:28) explains that he should fall silent because of his understanding that God has decreed this against him. Rashi reads the word *ki* as "because," rather than "when," unlike the manner in which I have translated it above. Note also that Rashi explains the word *yidom* here as waiting, not as silence, disagreeing with the *Targum* on this verse.

94. Ibn Ezra suggests that it denotes prostration, in which the individual bows low to the earth in recognition of God's decree, until dust enters his mouth. See also *Targum* on 3:29.

95. The word *peh* appears three other times in the book: twice, the enemies' mouth spews vitriol against the suffering Jerusalem (2:16; 3:46), and once the word *peh* describes God's just instructions (3:38).

First, it can be a character-building experience. Second, it puts human beings in their proper place, reminding them that they must combat their natural inclination toward hubris. Human conceit inevitably produces sin, and the experience of disgrace may be a much-needed reminder of the danger and fallacy of human vanity. Humiliation (*ḥerpa*) is twice thrust before God in Eikha (3:61; 5:1), with the assumption that it will prod God to act on His people's behalf. This may be because God pities those who have been shamed, or perhaps because God's honor (and dishonor) is woven deeply into that of His nation.[96] In any case, *ḥerpa* can, it seems, have a positive effect.

This central section of the book advocates the proper conduct for a suffering individual, having accepted the axiom that bearing a burden is good. Strikingly, the book does not explain how it arrives at these startling conclusions. The *gever* merely states, rather unequivocally, that it is good for humans to bear a yoke, to sit in silence and solitude, to place their mouths deferentially in the dust and wait for the possibility of hope, and to accept beatings and dishonor. Why is any of this good? The book leaves it to each individual to determine how suffering can be constructive, and the manner in which it can build one's character and relationship with God. In any case, people should accept hardship with equanimity and humility, and regard suffering as ennobling or at least formative.

In the sections that surround the core of the book, the *gever* expresses faith in God and His merciful ways. At its center, in the deepest recesses of the book, the *gever* express faith in humankind and faith in himself. Even as the *gever* grapples with an external struggle, he embraces the internal tranquility that allows for a faith-filled existence. The book's nucleus mirrors that of the human individual, who can regard his life's trials as an opportunity to search deep within and find the faith that lies at his innermost core. As it turns out, calamity need not destroy one's

---

96. The word *ḥerpa* is often used in conjunction with Israel's enemy, whose bid to shame Israel is also an attempt to dishonor God (e.g., I Sam. 17:10, 26, 45; II Kings 19:4). See also Psalms 74:10. I discuss this topic at greater length in Eikha 5:1.

convictions, serving instead as a conduit to discovering them; adversity can foster faith in a turbulent world.

Introduction to Verses 31–39:
God's Compassionate Ways (*Ḥesed* and *Raḥamim*)

This dense section (Eikha 3:31–39) defies easy translation or explanation. Statements may be read as questions, and the questions may be actual or rhetorical, depending on the interpreter's inclination.[97] The array of possible interpretations stymies any clear translation of this passage, making it nearly impossible to offer a conclusive reading. I have translated the section to the best of my understanding, while referring to alternate readings in the footnotes. To compound the difficulty of this section, its thematic coherence remains obscure. How does this section proceed from one idea to the next? What is its overriding message?

Perhaps this section consciously endeavors to maintain a measure of obscurity. Indeed, any discussion of theodicy (namely, the bid to defend God's goodness and omnipotence while evil exists in the world) seems to necessitate a deliberate vagueness, reflecting the uncertainty that accompanies any grappling with this topic.

Eikha 3:31–33

כִּי לֹא יִזְנַח לְעוֹלָם
אֲדֹנָי

כִּי אִם־הוֹגָה
וְרִחַם כְּרֹב חֲסָדָיו

כִּי לֹא עִנָּה מִלִּבּוֹ
וַיַּגֶּה בְּנֵי־אִישׁ

---

97. The only verses that should certainly be read as a question are those that open with an interrogative (verses 37 and 39). Other attempts to place a question mark at the conclusion of a sentence involve creative liberties taken by the interpreter. Placing a question mark at the end of a statement completely reverses its meaning, resulting in a radically changed verse.

For He shall not reject forever
Lord

For even when He causes grief
He will then have compassion, out of His great kindness

For He does not torment from His heart [deliberately]
To cause people grief

The previous section (verses 27–30) struck a confident tone, advising the sufferer to bear his misfortune in solitude, silence, and submission. Why should the sufferer yield to this advice? The three initial verses of this subunit (verses 31–33) are the *kaf* verses, each of which begins with the explanatory *ki*. These sequential verses return our focus to God, declaring three separate contentions regarding God's attributes. These statements support the idea of compliance, affirming that God is responsible for the suffering individual, who should therefore calmly accept his burdens.[98]

Three brief axiomatic statements about God's punitive decrees appear in the *kaf* verses: these punishments are temporary, ultimately compassionate, and meaningful (that is, not random). Presented as manifest truth, there is no attempt to explain or substantiate these ideas. This is not an expansive treatise on theology, but an attempt to offer basic guidelines for the religious sufferer.

Statement one:
For He shall not reject forever,
Lord.

---

98. Rashi (Eikha 3:31) reads the section in this manner, explaining that the fact that God does not reject humans forever is a good reason to submit silently to God's decree. R. Yosef Kara (3:31) makes a similar point: "And now he gives a reason for all that was said above. Why is it 'good for the *gever* that he should bear a burden in his youth' and there is no greater good for a person than that 'he should sit in solitude and silence,' throughout everything that God places upon him? 'He should put his mouth in the dust...he should give the one who strikes him his cheek' – 'For the Lord will not reject forever!'"

A blunt proclamation, this sentence does not easily divide into two parts. The most likely division (as I have noted in my translation above) places undue weight on the sentence's first section, "For He shall not reject forever." Its second part consists of one stark word. No longer fixated upon the human sufferer, the chapter again turns its attention to God. While the book previously admits that suffering derives from divine rejection (see the word *zanaḥ* in 2:7), Eikha here asserts that God's rejection is not without end. Moreover, by employing the same word (*zanaḥ*) that the *gever* used to express his soul's rejection of peace in 3:17, this verse clarifies why there is still no cause for despair. God will not abandon a sufferer forever; there is no reason to lose hope.[99]

Statement two:
For even when He causes grief,
He will then have compassion, out of His great kindness.

God's kindness and compassion remain axiomatic; this is a basic principle of the Bible. Nevertheless, human suffering calls into question the notion of God's boundless goodness.

While Eikha does not offer a programmatic discourse on this topic, it does adopt certain assumptions. First, it does not absolve God of responsibility for human suffering. Explicitly acknowledging that God causes grief (without yet explaining why),[100] this verse likewise continues by promising that God's compassion will soon alleviate that grief. Recalling the opening section of the ruminations (3:22–23), this verse maintains that God's kindnesses will always rekindle, even when they seem to have been suspended or terminated. Finally, this verse assumes that God's afflictions are not the norm; they are always a temporary

---

99. This idea appears often in Tanakh. See, for example, Psalms 77:8; 103:8–9.

100. Rashi (Eikha 3:32) prefers not to ignore this omission in the verse, which leaves a troubling theological void. He therefore adds an explanation for God's afflictions – namely, that God brings grief because of man's sins, an idea that will appear only in Eikha 3:39, at the conclusion of this section.

interval, soon to be replaced by God's natural state, His abiding compassion and kindness.

Statement three:
For He does not torment from His heart [deliberately]
To cause people grief.

Finally, the verse asserts that God does not desire to cause people grief. He is not capricious or cruel. But this reassuring thought fails to address the critical question: Why, then, *does* God afflict people? No answer is forthcoming.[101] The individual has yet to state the obvious; for the moment, the word sin remains noticeably absent from the discussion.

Eikha 3:34–36

לְדַכֵּא תַּחַת רַגְלָיו
כֹּל אֲסִירֵי אָרֶץ

לְהַטּוֹת מִשְׁפַּט־גֶּבֶר
נֶגֶד פְּנֵי עֶלְיוֹן

לְעַוֵּת אָדָם בְּרִיבוֹ
אֲדֹנָי לֹא רָאָה

By crushing under his feet
All the prisoners of the earth

By distorting the laws of a *gever*
Before the presence of the Most High

By corrupting a human in his dispute
[All of the above] the Lord does not see

---

101. Once again, Rashi (Eikha 3:33) fills the void by explaining that God only afflicts people when they have sinned.

An alphabetic unit, verses 34–36 each begin with a *lamed* introducing an infinitive clause describing an injustice: trampling hapless prisoners, distorting laws, corrupting disputes.[102] This section evokes the unfairness that prevails among humans.[103] People can be cruel and arbitrary, sadistically relishing the torment of others.

According to these verses, God does not behave in a perverse manner, as do humans.[104] God does *not* sanction or condone these injustices. Rashi (3:34–36) explains that the negative *ki lo* at the beginning of verse 33 applies to all the portrayed injustices. Each represents something God does not desire and would never inflict.[105] Rashi also understands the definitive statement at the conclusion of the final *lamed* verse ("The Lord does not see")[106] as referring to *all* the previously delineated corrupt behaviors.[107] God does not see or identify with any

---

102. The language of these verses evokes biblical laws that demand uprightness, particularly in treatment of the unfortunate and helpless (e.g., Ex. 23:6; Deut. 24:17; 27:19). Perhaps for this reason, the *Targum* adds the adjective *misken* (meaning "poor") to describe the sufferer in verses 35–36.

103. Westermann, 178, discerns in the background of these verses the voice of someone who has suffered unjustly. I see no reason to assume that these verses refer to someone's specific experience. All the ruminations in this section seem to be of a general nature, designed to relate to anyone and everyone who has suffered.

104. See also Job 8:3.

105. It seems apparent throughout that the intention here is *not* to thrust these injustices as accusations at God, but rather to maintain the opposite. In order to maintain that reading, we must either apply the final clause of the *lamed* verses ("The Lord does not see") to all the earlier statements in verses 34–36 or apply the first two words of verse 33 (*ki lo*) to all the following verses, which are then read in the negative (Rashi offers both of these readings). In this elliptical state, these statements preserve the uncertainty of the claimants, indicating that human beings do not easily exonerate God, especially in the wake of terrible misfortune.

106. Interpreters explain the phrase, "The Lord does not see," in vastly different ways, emerging with quite different readings of this section. Westermann (*Lamentations*, 162, 166, 178; and Berlin, 81, 83) read this as a rhetorical question: "Does not the Lord see it?" This reading indicates that sufferers should take comfort in the fact that God sees all human injustice. O'Connor (*Lamentations*, 52) offers a completely different reading, claiming that Eikha portrays God choosing not to see or respond to human suffering (as indicated in Eikha 1:9, 11, 20; 2:20). This reading suggests that these ponderings include an accusation, or at the very least an uncomfortable theological confusion.

107. This is as I have offered in my translation above. See also Gordis, 181.

of the immoral deeds cited in the *lamed* verses; He cannot bear or tolerate injustice. God does not crush prisoners under His feet[108] or behave
with corruption in His judgment of humans. God remains above the
immoral machinations of humans.[109] Thus, there must be an explanation for God's decision to inflict grief.

Eikha 3:37–39

מִי זֶה אָמַר וַתֶּהִי
אֲדֹנָי לֹא צִוָּה

מִפִּי עֶלְיוֹן לֹא תֵצֵא
הָרָעוֹת וְהַטּוֹב

מַה־יִּתְאוֹנֵן אָדָם חָי
גֶּבֶר עַל־חֲטָאָיו

Who was it that spoke, and it came to be?
Was it not the Lord who commanded?

Does not the mouth of the Most High issue
Bad and good?

Of what can a living person complain?
Each *gever* of his own sin!

---

108. Ibn Ezra's explanation of the verse is that it raises the possibility that God sits in
the heavens, while unfortunate human beings remain prisoners of the earth, locked
together in a world that operates in accordance with God's whim. This (rejected)
idea represents a theology of horror, in which God deliberately traps humans in
order to crush them.

109. While this point seems self-evident, scholars note that the Bible's portrayal of
God's morality constitutes one of its great contributions to the world. According
to N. Sarna, *Understanding Genesis* (New York: Schocken Books, 1970), 16–18, the
fundamental difference between polytheism and monotheism is that a system
of many gods "inevitably engendered a multiplicity of ethical values and moral
standards." By introducing one supreme God whose essential nature is ethical, the
Bible establishes a universal moral order.

At this point, a conclusion seems within reach; it is perhaps even inescapable. Yet, it remains elusive for just a little longer. For another two
verses, the ruminations continue, exploring a final theological question:
God's omnipotence. While this section has invested plenty of effort in
establishing God's axiomatic goodness and justice, and confirming that
God is *willing* to prevent evil, the question of God's omnipotence remains
critical. As Epicurus reportedly asked: "Is God willing to prevent evil,
but not able? Then He is not omnipotent."[110]

A contradiction arises between God's inability to tolerate injustice and the injustice that continues to prevail. Perhaps, then, God's
omnipotence is not certain; perhaps there are forces that overwhelm
God's desire for justice and goodness.

Two brief verses put these uncertainties to rest:

> Who was it that spoke, and it came to be?
> Was it not the Lord who commanded? [111]
>
> Does not the mouth of the Most High issue
> Bad and good?[112]

These rhetorical questions establish God's control over the world,
including the bad things that occur. By broaching God's omnipotence

---

110. The following formulation, attributed to Epicurus but not found in his extant
    writings, is often regarded as the basic formulation of the problem of theodicy:
    "Is God willing to prevent evil, but not able? Then He is not omnipotent. Is He
    able, but not willing? Then he is malevolent. Is He both able and willing? Then
    whence cometh evil? Is He neither able nor willing? Then why call him God?"
111. This verse has generated a wide variety of interpretations. R. Saadia Gaon, for
    example, explains it as follows: "Who has ever said that something will be and it
    was, if God did not command that it should be?" R. Yosef Kara maintains that it
    follows from the previous verse: "If someone tells you that this is so, namely that
    God enjoys corrupting humans in their disputes and crushing under His feet all
    the prisoners of the earth, do not believe them, because God did not command
    this thing." See also the *Targum*, which offers an entirely different interpretation.
112. This verse also has widely disparate interpretations, which produce opposite mean-
    ings. Gordis (*Lamentations*, 143, 175, 182–183), for example, does not regard this as a
    rhetorical question, but rather as a statement, firmly declaring that God is *not* the
    source of evil in the world. This view is like Elifaz's in Job 5:6–7.

via rhetorical questions, the verses draw the readers in, expecting them to acquiesce vigorously to these patent truths. Indeed, God created the world with the spoken word. Simply by uttering, "Let there be," the world emerged into existence (Gen. 1:3, 6, 14). If God created the world, He has power over it.[113] Moreover, God assumes responsibility for everything – bad as well as good.[114] Everything comes from God, and everything is part of the just, divine plan.[115]

If we accept that God is responsible for all evil and that He does not conjure it on a whim or for His own delight, these contemplations can finally draw to their resounding, dramatic conclusion: Of what then can a living person complain? Each *gever* of his own sin!

As the word "sin" surfaces for the first time in the chapter, its absence from the first thirty-eight verses becomes glaringly apparent. Nevertheless, it is not entirely clear what this finale means to convey. Is it a confession of sin, the *gever's* blunt recognition that he must have transgressed? Or is it an avowal of human limitations in trying to comprehend God?

Rashi regards this as a recognition of his sinfulness, the logical conclusion of this contemplative passage:

> And if I come and say, "This evil did not come from His hand, but was a coincidence that it happened to me," this is not so, for whether bad or good events, who was it that spoke, and it came to be? Was it not God who commanded, and from His mouth did not both good and bad emerge? And so, of what can a living person complain?... Each individual can complain about his sins, *for they bring misfortune upon him.*[116] (Rashi, Eikha 3:38)

---

113. Many biblical passages assume this. See, for example, Isaiah 40:22–23; 42:5; Psalms 33:6–11.

114. This reading broadly follows Rashi's first interpretation of verse 38. However, Rashi's second interpretation (along with the interpretations of R. Saadia Gaon, Ibn Ezra, and R. Yosef Kara) does not regard this as a rhetorical question, but rather as a definitive statement: It is *not* from God's mouth that human evil and good emerge! Read in this way, it means quite the opposite. God does not cause evil; humans alone are responsible for evil in the world.

115. For a similar idea, see Amos 3:6, Isaiah 45:7, Job 2:10.

116. See also Eikha Rabba 3:40 and R. Yosef Kara's commentary on Eikha 3:39.

According to this approach, no misfortune exists in a vacuum. If someone suffers, he must recognize his own culpability.[117] He certainly should not complain in a manner that suggests rebellion or renunciation of responsibility.[118] The obvious next step is self-introspection, which occurs in the verse that follows this revelation: "Let us search our ways and examine them and we will return to the Lord" (Eikha 3:40).[119]

The age-old problem of evil people who prosper and good people who suffer arises in the wake of this unequivocal conclusion. Rather than address this inscrutable question, I propose another way to understand the conclusive statement: "Of what can a living person complain? Each *gever* of his own sin!" Philosophical attempts to resolve the mystery of God's providence inevitably fail. Instead, the sufferer has only one recourse, and that is to turn inward and consider how these events can produce change. While humans can never comprehend God's designs, we can control our own responses. Therefore, the critical question is not a helpless, "Why did this happen?" but rather a practical, "What can each individual do in the wake of suffering?"[120] In this schema, the direct

---

117. A gemara (Berakhot 5a) offers a more complex approach, explaining that there are various reasons a person may suffer:

> Rava (some say R. Ḥisda) says: If a person sees that painful sufferings visit him, let him examine his conduct. For it is said: "Let us search our ways and examine them and we will return to the Lord" (Eikha 3:40). If he examines and finds nothing, he should attribute it to the neglect of the study of the Torah. For it is said: "Happy is the person whom You cause to suffer, God, and from Your Torah You teach" (Ps. 94:12). If he did attribute it to this and still did not find [this to be the cause], it is certain that these are sufferings of love. For it is said: "For whom the Lord loves He rebukes" (Prov. 3:12).

118. The only other use of the word *yitonen* appears in Numbers 11:1, where the word illustrates Israel's rebellious complaint against God in the desert.

119. R. Yosef Kara notes the connection between verses 39 and 40, maintaining that after the *gever* recognizes the connection between sins and suffering (verse 39), he searches his ways for the specific sins that he has committed (verse 40). Maimonides, *Hilkhot Aveilut* 13:12, advocates a constructive response to tragedy (one should examine his deeds), without necessarily accepting a causal relationship between sins and suffering.

120. This is Rav Soloveitchik's general approach to suffering in his essay *Kol Dodi Dofek*, D. Z. Gordon, trans. (New York: Yeshiva University, 2006), 1–11. For analysis of this view, see Reuven Ziegler, *Majesty and Humility: The Thought of Rabbi Joseph B. Soloveitchik* (Jerusalem: Urim, 2012), 249–71.

correlation between sins and misfortunes dissipates. Instead, humans choose a constructive response to their travails, one that involves introspection and self-improvement.

PART 3 (EIKHA 3:40–66):
A FIRST-PERSON ACCOUNT OF SUFFERING

Having paused to introspect and to consider God's ways, the proper response to suffering, and human accountability, the *gever* returns in the third section of this chapter to the account of misfortune.[121] A comparison between this account of suffering and the one at the beginning of the chapter illuminates the dramatic transformation that has taken place. Themes resurface from the first section of the chapter; prayer remains blocked and the sufferer is still entrapped, overwhelmed by misfortunes and tribulations. Yet, the *gever's* progression is remarkable. Utterly altered by his ruminations, he reconstructs his relationship with God and community, acquiring at the same time a new perception of himself.

In this section, the *gever* first speaks in first-person plural, unexpectedly appearing in the role of a leader among a community of sufferers. In verse 48, the *gever* returns to the first-person singular for the duration of the chapter. However, when the first-person speaker reemerges, he does not initially focus upon his own private tragedy, concentrating instead on the suffering of the nation. In verse 52, the *gever* resumes his personal account. However, as we will see, he is a changed man, even if his grim circumstances are essentially unchanged.

I am inclined to divide the final section of this chapter into three subsections, based on both speaker and substance:

A. Verses 40–47: The Communal Speaker – Repentance, Prayer, and Complaint

B. Verses 48–51: The Individual Speaker – An Advocate for the Community

---

121. Although he is never called the *gever* in this section, I will assume that the identity of the speaker remains unchanged and that chapter 3 tells a consistent tale of the *gever*.

C. Verses 52–66: The Individual Speaker – A First-Person Account of Suffering

Eikha 3:40–47

נַחְפְּשָׂה דְרָכֵינוּ וְנַחְקֹרָה
וְנָשׁוּבָה עַד־ה׳

נִשָּׂא לְבָבֵנוּ אֶל־כַּפָּיִם
אֶל־אֵל בַּשָּׁמָיִם

נַחְנוּ פָשַׁעְנוּ וּמָרִינוּ
אַתָּה לֹא סָלָחְתָּ

סַכֹּתָה בָאַף וַתִּרְדְּפֵנוּ
הָרַגְתָּ לֹא חָמָלְתָּ

סַכֹּותָה בֶעָנָן לָךְ
מֵעֲבוֹר תְּפִלָּה

סְחִי וּמָאוֹס תְּשִׂימֵנוּ
בְּקֶרֶב הָעַמִּים

פָּצוּ עָלֵינוּ פִּיהֶם
כָּל־אֹיְבֵינוּ

פַּחַד וָפַחַת הָיָה לָנוּ
הַשֵּׁאת וְהַשָּׁבֶר

Let us search our ways and examine them
And we will return to the Lord

Let us lift up our hearts in our hands
To God in the heavens

We have transgressed and rebelled
You did not forgive

You covered Yourself in anger and You pursued us
You killed and You did not pity

You covered Yourself with a cloud
To prevent prayer from passing through

You placed us in filth and refuse
In the midst of the nations

They opened their mouths at us
All our enemies

Fear and pitfall are our lot
Horror and brokenness

The Communal Speaker:
Repentance, Prayer, and Complaint

The word sin remains suspended in mid-air after verse 39, as we eagerly wait to see how the *gever* will proceed following his realization. Confession produces repentance, followed promptly by prayer and more confession. The *gever* appears to function in a new role, inspired by his experience and introspection.

The key to understanding the *gever*'s transformation begins by noting his unexpected (and unprecedented) shift from a first-person singular voice to a first-person plural one.[122] The *gever* now speaks as part of a community. He has abandoned the posture of a forlorn individual, whose isolation from his community is an additional source of woe. One cannot forget his plaintive description from verse 14: "I was a laughingstock for all my nation, their plaything all day." The *gever* never

---

122. The plural voice appears in Eikha here for the first time, reappearing in 4:17–20, and again throughout chapter 5.

explains the cause of this social alienation; it remains simply one of his many trials, another reason for self-pity and despair.

The *gever's* sense of isolation from his nation in verse 14 mirrors his sense of alienation from God (indicated primarily by the fact that he does not mention God by name for the first seventeen verses of the chapter). Perhaps it was his estrangement from God that spawned his alienation from the community, which is bound together by its members' shared relationship with God. It seems evident that the *gever's* misery produces a narcissistic obsession with his woes, the inability to see beyond his own grisly experiences. Seeing neither God nor his fellow humans, the *gever* finds himself in a state of utter aloneness.

How, then, has the *gever* recovered a relationship both with God and with his community? First, as the *gever* progresses on his journey, his self-absorption begins to diminish, other people come into focus, and he observes that they too suffer. Similarly, the dissipation of his self-centered misery allows him to see God.

Comparison of verses 8 and 44 – two substantively similar verses, in which the speaker bemoans the failure of his prayer to reach God – throws the *gever's* transformation into sharp relief. In verse 8, the *gever's* prayer was so self-centered that he did not even acknowledge the recipient of his pleas. Verse 8 lacks an addressee, a "thou," focusing exclusively on the *gever* as he bemoans the futility of his prayers: "Even when *I* cry out and when *I* plead, *my* prayer is shut out." In content, verse 44 is not substantially different from verse 8; the communal speaker again laments that prayer fails to reach its destination. Yet, there is no trace of the self-absorbed victim of the first section. Verse 44 obscures the "I" (or "we") who prays, referencing instead the divine addressee twice in the second person: "*You* covered *Yourself* with a cloud to prevent prayer from passing through." The contrast between these verses illustrates the shift that has taken place. No longer consumed by his own misery, the *gever* acquires the ability to see beyond his self-absorbed reality.

Once the *gever* reconciles with God, he can regain membership in his community. As noted, the community is linked by its shared relationship with God. When an individual member of the nation of Israel breaks off his relationship with God by sinning, this negatively affects his connection with the community as well. The converse is also true;

by repairing his relationship with God, the *gever* finds himself once again a part of the covenantal community of Israel.

Why, though, does the *gever* choose to speak in the plural form? Why abandon the intensely personal narrative to link up to the national tragedy? It is now that the *gever* transforms his personal misfortune into a constructive affair, making his own suffering useful. Inspired to share his revelations, the *gever* urges others to join him in introspection and repentance. Thus, the *gever* joins his community, not simply to alleviate his loneliness, but to motivate them to take part in his newfound transformative journey.

The word *derakhenu* also indicates the change in the *gever*. At the beginning of chapter 3, the *gever* described God blocking or twisting his route, deliberately leading him astray (3:9, 11). The word *derekh* (road) appears at the opening of this section in a very different manner (3:40), "Let us search our ways (*derakhenu*; literally, "our roads") and examine them, and we will return to the Lord." Amidst a call for communal repentance and prayer, the community internalizes its guilt, assuming responsibility for walking on the proper course; God is no longer held accountable for their wayward path.

Yet contrition is fleeting, and the *gever* sharply alters his conciliatory tone (verse 41): "We have transgressed and rebelled, *You* did not forgive!" Complaint supplants the remorseful call to repentance and prayer.[123] The second-person accusation ("*You* did not forgive!") replaces the first-person plural of confession ("*We* have transgressed and rebelled"), establishing an adversarial relationship between the community and God.[124] Each side has betrayed the other; both parties assume a measure of culpability.[125] Casting off sorrowful confession, the community indulges instead in delineating its grievances, which grow in intensity.

---

123. The *Targum* mitigates the indictment in this verse by adding a phrase to its translation: "We have transgressed and rebelled, *and because we did not return to You*, You did not forgive."

124. Dobbs-Allsopp, 123, points out that aside from the "I" in verses 1 and 63, this is the only place in the chapter in which independent pronouns are used.

125. The midrash cites this verse as evidence of Jeremiah's even-handedness as a prophet (*Mekhilta DeRabbi Yishmael, Bo, Parasha* 1). See our discussion in the introduction to Chapter One.

Flinging accusations at God in a series of rapid-fire second-person verbs, the community's anger at God is personal and direct (verses 42–45): "*You* did not forgive, *You* covered *Yourself* in anger, *You* pursued us, *You* killed, *You* did not pity, *You* covered *Yourself* with a cloud… *You* placed us in filth and refuse!"

In a jarring reversal, the *gever* who finally discovered sin and launched repentance now has the audacity to renew his complaints and reproach God, treating Him as an adversary. How has this occurred?[126]

When speaking to God, the community has different privileges than the individual. It has the right to speak directly to Him with the expectation that He will heed and forgive. After all, the covenant that God made with the forefathers obligates Him to maintain fidelity to the national entity,[127] though not necessarily to individuals. Rejoining his community empowers the *gever*; in the plural form, he can address God in a manner that an individual never could. In a similar vein, a gemara accords special powers to collective prayer, noting that God pays particular attention to the pleas of the community:

> What is the meaning of the verse: "And my prayer will be to You Lord at an acceptable time" (Ps. 69:14)? When is an acceptable time? At the time that the congregation is praying… R. Natan says: From where do we know that God does not reject the prayers of the many? As it says (Job 36:5), "Behold, God does not reject the mighty."[128] (Berakhot 8a)

---

126. Berlin, 96, opines that the *gever* concludes, disturbingly, that there is no actual relationship between repentance and divine forgiveness. But why should he expect there to be? Even if God allows for a causal connection between penitence and forgiveness, He does not promise it as an immediate, automatic response. The expression of disappointment in the absence of divine forgiveness seems to be beyond reasonable expectations. For this reason, I will suggest above that this new tone is rooted in the sense of entitlement felt by the communal entity.

127. See Exodus 32:13; Leviticus 26:42; II Kings 13:23.

128. This seems to be the intended translation of the verse according to the Gemara (see Rashi in his commentary to Berakhot 8a). This is not, however, the simple meaning of the verse in Job 36:5.

The communal voice also tempers the aggrieved words. Protests and grievances become supplication and prayer in the communal mouth. Defined by its shared commitment to serving God, the community's outrage is muted by the unbreakable bond between God and His nation.

The communal speech concludes by describing a miserable reality, familiar from other depictions in the book. Enemies prevail, opening their mouths in gloating mockery, just as they did in Eikha 2:16. The community's final words express horror and brokenness (see 2:11, 13). The highly alliterative word-pairs *"paḥad vaphaḥat"* (fear and pitfall) and *"ḥashet vehashever"* (horror and brokenness),[129] suggest that these words work in tandem, cooperating to entrap the victim, who cannot escape his terrible fate.[130] Dodging the fear (*paḥad*), he falls in the pitfall (*paḥat*); even if he can manage to extract himself from the horror (*shet*), he is certain to be overwhelmed by brokenness (*shever*).

Misery aside, this speech depicts a community empowered by its unified voice. The *gever*, moreover, has undergone a significant personal transformation, as indicated by the shift to a communal voice. Speaking as a communal "we," the *gever* rises above his lonely, self-absorbed victimhood. He has become an advocate and leader of his nation, employing his personal tragedy to rally others to return to God.

Eikha 3:48–51

פַּלְגֵי־מַיִם תֵּרַד עֵינִי
עַל־שֶׁבֶר בַּת־עַמִּי

---

129. I call these word-pairs "highly alliterative" because each pair shares two common consonants at the beginning of the word, deepening the feeling of reiteration. *Paḥad* and *paḥat* are distinguished only by a *dalet* and a *tav*, which are also similar sounds.

130. Note the use of these words in Isaiah 24:17–18: "Fear, pitfall, and a snare upon you, inhabitants of the land. And those who run from the sounds of fear will plunge into the pitfall, and he who goes up from the pitfall will be caught in the snare..." Based on the similar linguistic usage, Rashi interprets the words "fear and pitfall" in Eikha 3:47 as an indication of a hopeless attempt to escape misfortune: "When we fled the fear, we plunged into the pitfall." See also Jeremiah 48:43–44.

עֵינִי נִגְּרָה וְלֹא תִדְמֶה
מֵאֵין הֲפֻגוֹת

עַד־יַשְׁקִיף וְיֵרֶא
ה׳ מִשָּׁמָיִם

עֵינִי עוֹלְלָה לְנַפְשִׁי
מִכֹּל בְּנוֹת עִירִי

Streams of water flow from my eye[131]
Over the brokenness of the daughter of my nation

My eye flows and does not stop
Refusing to cease

Until He looks and sees,
Lord, from the heavens

My eye does harm[132] to my soul
Because of all the daughters of my city

The Individual Speaker:
Advocating for the Community

After the communal speaker's brief appearance, the voice of the individual reemerges. But now we encounter a completely changed man. The *gever* who recounted his narrative at the opening of the chapter was self-absorbed and alienated from his community; this transformed individual expresses his consuming grief for the suffering of his nation. He does not look inward, but outward; it is concern for others that produces his tears. Willingly assuming the role of representative of his

---

131. For a similar metaphor, see Psalms 119:136.
132. The word *alal* generally means a deed or an action. In this verse, translating the word as an action makes little sense. Because in the book of Eikha the word often has a negative connotation, indicating an action meant to do someone harm (see 1:12, 22; 2:20), I have offered the above translation (following some modern translations such as House, 402).

people, he turns his grief-stricken sobs into an instrument designed to force God's attentions.

Eyes and eyesight emerge as the dominant images of this passage (3:48–51).[133] Referring to his own eyes in three out of four of the verses, the individual describes the streams of tears that prevent him from accomplishing anything beyond his incessant weeping. Even should he seek a respite, his eyes seem to act independently of him, adamantly refusing to stop their tears. Two of the *ayin* verses (49 and 51) begin with the word *eini* (my eye), surrounding the middle *ayin* verse (50), which focuses on God's sight.[134] In a bid to enlist God to look at him, the *gever* encircles God with his tears.[135]

The attempt to coerce God to respond recalls the story of Ḥoni HaMe'agel:

> Once it happened that the month of Adar had nearly finished, and the rains had not fallen. They sent [a message] to Ḥoni HaMe'agel, "Pray, so that rain will fall!" He prayed and no rain fell. [Ḥoni] drew a circle and stood in it, the same way that Habakkuk the prophet did… [Ḥoni] said to Him, "Master of the Universe! Your children have placed their hopes in me that I am a [favored] member of Your household. I swear in Your great name that I will not move from here until You have mercy on Your children!" Rain began to trickle [in small amounts]. His students said to him, "We believe that the rains have come only to free you from your oath." [Ḥoni] said [to God], "This is not what I requested. Rather, [I requested] rain that fills the cisterns, ditches, and caves." The [rain then] fell with angry force… [Ḥoni] said to Him, "This is not what I requested. Rather, [I requested] desirable rain, of

---

133. Once again, the subdivisions do not seem to be dependent on the alphabetic sub-units (see my explanation of verses 27–30 above). While the first two *peh* verses were part of the community's speech, the third *peh* verse (48) shifts into the first-person speaker, containing the leading word of this subsection (48–51), *eini*, directly in the center of the verse.

134. In verse 50, the word *ayin* (eye) is noticeably absent; God's corporeality is omitted, even as the individual demands that God look and see.

135. R. Yosef Kara (3:50) explicitly links verse 49 and 50 in this way.

blessing and bounty." Rain [then fell] in a satisfactory way until all the nation went up [for shelter] to the Temple Mount because of the rain. (Taanit 23a)

Ḥoni boldly advocates for his nation, in imitation of the prophet Habakkuk. The *gever's* manner of representing his people recalls the actions of biblical and rabbinic leaders who are willing to act with impertinence before God on their nation's behalf.

The *gever* does not petition God to deliver his people from suffering or engage in any specific action to alleviate their situation. Instead, he returns to the recurring request in the book, a minimal one, to be sure; God (who seems to have turned away in anger, as warned in Deut. 31:17–18) should *look* at His nation.[136] If God looks down from heaven and witnesses the terrible suffering of His people, He will undoubtedly have compassion and deliver them from their misery. After all, God is merciful. This is precisely what occurred at the inception of God's relationship with the nation of Israel, when they were enslaved in Egypt (Ex. 2:25; 3:7–10). Forcing God's attention is the first step in effecting change.

Chapters 2 and 3: Eyes That Weep

To understand the significance of this copious weeping, we turn our attention back to chapter 2, viewing our chapter as its continuation.[137] There, Jerusalem bears witness to the starvation of the children who languish and die in the streets. She explains the cessation of her tears (2:11),[138] attributing it to the "brokenness of the daughter of my nation." Following her description, Jerusalem falls silent, lacking the energy or

---

136. See Eikha 1:9, 11; 2:20; 5:1. For similar biblical verses, see Isaiah 63:15; Psalms 33:13.
137. This idea rejects the position held by some scholars that the book of Eikha is a loosely connected collection of songs. See, for example, Westermann, 191, and the discussion about the unity of the book in the chapter above entitled, "Introduction to Eikha." In my opinion, the linguistic and thematic connection between these passages indicates deliberate arrangement, in which these verses in chapter 3 rectify chapter 2.
138. In Eikha 2:11, I offered different understandings of Jerusalem's words, "*kalu vadema'ot einay.*" There, I explained why I prefer the above interpretation, which coheres better with the flow of the chapter.

desire to speak. For several verses (2:13–17), the narrator fills Jerusalem's silence, until he finally addresses Jerusalem directly, pleading with her to resume her weeping and turn to God in prayer (2:18–19):

> Let your tears flow like a stream day and night!
> Do not let yourself cease; do not stop up your eyes!
> Get up! Cry out in the night, at the top of each watch!
> Pour out your heart like water before the face of the Lord!

The narrator achieves a modicum of success; in verse 20, Jerusalem does at last resume her speech. However, Jerusalem declines to weep, remaining in a state of partial, perhaps willful, paralysis. Chapter 2 concludes without resolving the problem of Jerusalem's discontinued tears. She has withdrawn, impeding her ability to heal, and perhaps, to reconcile with God.

As the *gever* develops in chapter 3, he reacquires the ability (or inclination) to cry. Our passage is filled with copious tears, using words that recall Jerusalem's previous refusal to cry. In 2:18, the narrator urged Jerusalem to let her tears flow down (*horidi*) like a stream (*naḥal*). In our passage, the individual proclaims that his eye will flow down (*teirad*) like streams of water (*palgei mayim*).[139] Pressing Jerusalem further, the narrator in chapter 2 insisted that she should not cease her weeping (*al titni fugat lakh*), that she should not allow her eyes (*bat einekh*) to stop (*al tidom*). The individual in our chapter declares that this is precisely his intention: "My eye flows and does not stop (*velo tidmeh*), refusing to cease (*me'ein hafugot*)."

Viewing the book as a continuous narrative, chapter 3 offers a slight but significant progression forward. Moving past the emotional paralysis of chapter 2, this chapter reopens the floodgates, allowing the sufferer to weep freely.

One final point cements these chapters together even more securely, illustrating the forward trajectory of the book. As noted, in 2:11, Jerusalem attributed her occluded tears to the "brokenness of the

---

139. In Job 20:17, the words *peleg* and *naḥal* appear in tandem, maintaining similar meanings.

daughter of my nation." Chapter 3 attributes the return of those tears
to the very same situation: "Streams of water flow from my eye over *the
brokenness of the daughter of my nation*."[140] That which caused Jerusalem's
absence of tears in chapter 2 has the opposite effect at the end of chapter
3, allowing the narrative of Eikha to progress, one paltry step at a time.

Eikha 3:52–66

צוֹד צָדוּנִי כַּצִּפּוֹר
אֹיְבַי חִנָּם

צָמְתוּ בַבּוֹר חַיָּי
וַיַּדּוּ־אֶבֶן בִּי

צָפוּ־מַיִם עַל־רֹאשִׁי
אָמַרְתִּי נִגְזָרְתִּי

קָרָאתִי שִׁמְךָ ה'
מִבּוֹר תַּחְתִּיּוֹת

קוֹלִי שָׁמָעְתָּ
אַל־תַּעְלֵם אָזְנְךָ לְרַוְחָתִי לְשַׁוְעָתִי

קָרַבְתָּ בְּיוֹם אֶקְרָאֶךָּ
אָמַרְתָּ אַל־תִּירָא

רַבְתָּ אֲדֹנָי רִיבֵי נַפְשִׁי
גָּאַלְתָּ חַיָּי

רָאִיתָה ה' עַוָּתָתִי
שָׁפְטָה מִשְׁפָּטִי

רָאִיתָה כָּל־נִקְמָתָם
כָּל־מַחְשְׁבֹתָם לִי

---

140. A verse containing a similar idea appears in Jeremiah 14:17.

שָׁמַעְתָּ חֶרְפָּתָם ה'
כָּל־מַחְשְׁבֹתָם עָלָי

שִׂפְתֵי קָמַי וְהֶגְיוֹנָם
עָלַי כָּל־הַיּוֹם

שִׁבְתָּם וְקִימָתָם הַבִּיטָה
אֲנִי מַנְגִּינָתָם

תָּשִׁיב לָהֶם גְּמוּל ה'
כְּמַעֲשֵׂה יְדֵיהֶם

תִּתֵּן לָהֶם מְגִנַּת־לֵב
תַּאֲלָתְךָ לָהֶם

תִּרְדֹּף בְּאַף וְתַשְׁמִידֵם
מִתַּחַת שְׁמֵי ה'

They surely entrapped me like a bird
My enemies, for no reason

They cut off my life in a pit
And they cast a stone at me

Water floated above my head
I said, "I have been decreed against!"

I have called out Your name, Lord
From the depths of the pit

You have heard my voice
Do not obstruct Your ear to my groans and my cries

You have been close on the day that I called You
You have said, "Do not fear"

You have fought, Lord, the battles of my soul
You have redeemed my life

You have seen, Lord, my perversions
Judge my judgments!

You have seen all their vengefulness
All their thoughts are upon me

You heard their taunts, Lord
All their thoughts are against me

The lips of my antagonists and their logic
Are against me all day

When they sit and when they stand, look!
I am their plaything!

Return to them what they deserve, Lord
Like the work of their hands

Give them anguish of heart
Let Your curse be upon them

Pursue them with anger and destroy them
From under the heavens of the Lord

The Individual Speaker:
A First-Person Account of Suffering

This section returns us to the personal tale of the suffering individual. The first three verses (3:52–54) recall the first section of the chapter (3:1–16). Images of encirclement predominate here as before, fostering the oppressive sensation that there is no escape. If previously the *gever* was encircled by poison (3:5) or stone walls (3:7), here he is enclosed by a pit (3:53). The pit begins to fill with water, which rapidly rises, threatening to engulf him; he is on the verge of drowning and there seems to be no way to escape the rising tide (3:54).[141] The *gever's* distress is compounded by the stone cast at him in the pit (3:53). While some commentators envision enemies pelting him with rocks,[142] others suggest that the enemies place one large stone upon the pit to block any possibility of escape.[143]

The animal imagery also recalls the earlier account. Previously, the adversary's animal-like qualities surface repeatedly; he maims and mauls (3:4, 11) like a bear or a lion (3:10). Similarly, the *gever* here compares himself to a hunted animal, an innocent and helpless bird (3:52).[144] Even if the sufferer no longer explicitly likens his enemy to an animal, he portrays him as a predator tormenting his prey. The sufferer maintains that his enemies plague him for no discernible reason (3:52), perhaps merely for recreation or applause.

The individual's unfortunate circumstances may be actual or metaphorical; physical hardship mirrors spiritual and emotional distress. Descent into the pit accompanied by the feeling of entrapment evokes the doomed descent into the netherworld, the ineluctable movement toward death.[145] The pit also functions as a prison, from which escape is impossible without assistance.[146] The waters that overwhelm him recall his copious tears of 3:47–48, which now threaten to drown him in endless sorrow. The sufferer's grim situation climaxes in a one-word exclamation of desperate surrender (3:54), *"Nigzarti!"* – "I have been decreed against!" Hope is lost, and the end rapidly approaches.

---

141. For a similar image, see Psalms 69:2–3, 15–16.

142. R. Yosef Kara, Eikha 3:54–55; Hillers, 74.

143. Rashi and Ibn Ezra, Eikha 3:53. See also Daniel 6:18. Note that the stone appears in a singular form in this verse.

144. For a similar image, see Jeremiah 16:16. The image of the trapped bird evokes Sennacherib's siege of Jerusalem, where he inscribes in his annals that he made Hezekiah "a prisoner in Jerusalem, his royal residence, like a bird in a cage." See the discussion of this incident in the chapter above, "Historical Background."

145. For a similar description of misfortune, see Psalms 7:16; 88:4–7. Being thrown into a pit invariably arouses associations with Joseph (Gen. 37:24; 41:14) and Jeremiah (Jer. 38:6), although I do not think that we should make too much of these similarities. In my opinion, the pit is used to elicit a feeling of hopeless entrapment, rather than an allusion to specific stories or characters.

146. Rashi, Eikha 3:53. See also Jeremiah 38:6–13.

However, in the next verse (3:55), this hopelessness abruptly disappears, replaced unexpectedly by a direct call to God: "*I have called out Your name, Lord, from the depths of the pit!*" Upon hitting rock bottom, "from the depths of the pit," the *gever* inexplicably fills with newfound optimism and exclaims God's name. This surprising turnaround occurs without so much as a warning, leaving the reader unprepared for it. The *gever's* very desperation appears to launch this transformation. As he lies at the very bottom of the pit, the sufferer reaches deep into himself and finds the ability to call on God.[147]

The sudden recovery mirrors the *gever's* turnaround at the beginning of this chapter. After the *gever* recounts the litany of his hardships (3:1–16), reality overwhelms him as he sinks into despondency (3:17–18): "My soul rejected peace, I forgot goodness. And I said, 'My endurance is lost and my hope in the Lord.'" Yet, in the next verse (3:19), the *gever* suddenly embarks upon the movement toward self-rehabilitation, probing his memory to find consolation and optimism. I suggested earlier that this remarkable shift occurs at the mere utterance of God's name, which precipitates the *gever's* transformation.

Possibly, the *gever's* proclamation ("I have called out Your name, Lord, from the depths of the pit") does not refer to his present circumstances, but rather to the beginning of this chapter, when he called on God's name while steeped in hopelessness. We can similarly explain the sufferer's statement about his soul: "You have fought, Lord, the battles of my soul (*nafshi*)" (3:58). The *gever's* spiritual recovery rapidly transmuted from a hopeless soul (3:17), to a humbled soul (3:20), to a soul that sought and found its portion in God (3:24–25). In this chapter, God redeems the *gever* not simply from physical peril, but from the danger of abandoning hope and faith in God.

After calling on God's name (3:55), the suffering individual continues speaking to God, addressing Him in second person nearly twenty

---

147. This spiritual resilience is certainly not unique to Eikha; in fact, it appears to be a fairly common occurrence. Many psalms describe one who has relinquished hope, only to be revived by a sudden, baffling recovery, in which he either directly addresses God or enlists God to rescue him. See, for example, Psalms 18:5–7; 22:13–14, 17–21.

times. He also specifies God's name four additional times before the conclusion of the chapter (3:59, 61, 64, 66). In fact, the Tetragrammaton appears seven times in the final section of chapter 3 (verses 40–66).[148] The centrality of God's name in this section contrasts starkly with the absence of God's name in the initial section.[149]

What precisely does the *gever* want from God in this final passage of the chapter? First, the *gever* calls on God (3:55), describing God listening to his prayer (3:56). This is a revision of his previous statements, in which he accuses God of shutting out his prayers and deliberately obstructing them (3:8, 44). He then describes God drawing near to him and offering explicit verbal assurance: "Do not fear!" (3:57). These are the only words that God actually utters in the book (though they are cited by the human speaker in God's name), and they draw our attention to the *gever*'s newfound perception of God's accessibility.

After recognizing God's willingness to listen and respond, the *gever* confidently asserts that God has intervened in his disputes (*"ravta… rivei nafshi"*), redeeming his life (3:58). This bold declaration confirms the *gever*'s proclamation in 3:35–36 that God abhors the perversion of disputes (*"le'avet adam berivo"*).

The *gever* moreover notes that God *sees* his perversions and the enemy's vengeful behavior (3:59–60).[150] This rectifies a previous predicament in the chapter, one that echoes throughout the book – namely, that God has turned His face away from His suffering nation. Just a few verses prior, the *gever* had boldly demanded that God look from

---

148. The remaining two appearances are in 3:40, 50. We have had several occasions to note the significance of a sevenfold appearance of a word in a biblical passage, which according to Cassuto renders it a key word. See Cassuto, *A Commentary on the Book of Exodus* (Jerusalem: Magnes Press, 1967), 75, 91 ff. I thank my student Margot Botwinick for pointing out this sevenfold appearance of God's name in the final section of chapter 3.

149. Names of God also appear seven times in the middle section of the chapter (3:21–39): the Tetragrammaton appears four times and *A-donai* three. In the final section, in addition to the sevenfold appearance of the Tetragrammaton, the name *A-donai* appears once. I have rendered both the Tetragrammaton and the name *A-donai* as "Lord," while *E-lokim* has been rendered simply as God, as is customary in Bible translations.

150. Much depends upon the tense of the verbs in this section, as I will discuss shortly.

the heavens, avowing that he will weep unceasingly until God grants his petition (3:49–50). Now the *gever* twice asserts his confident belief that God is looking (3:59, 60); nevertheless, in 3:63, the sufferer again entreats God to look at his antagonists, employing the imperative verb, "*Habita!*"[151] Once God looks out from heaven, He is bound to see not only the suffering of the wronged, but also the malevolence of the wicked.

In the climactic finale of the chapter, the *gever* seeks to kindle God's ire at the enemies who taunt, plot against, and torment the speaker.[152] He outlines a detailed plan for God's vengeance. God should give them anguish of the heart, His curse should be upon them, and He should pursue them with anger and destroy them. This is no more than they deserve; the *gever* is careful to specify that retribution should be in accordance with their own deeds.

The *gever*'s request that God "pursue [the enemies] with anger" (3:66) employs words previously used to describe God's punishment of His nation, "You covered Yourself in anger and You pursued us" (3:43). In this call for vengeance, the sufferer endeavors to shift God's attention from His nation to the enemies, who perpetuate injustice. The call for vengeance that closes each chapter of Eikha is not mere vindictiveness.[153] This plea looks toward the restoration of divine justice. The bid to restore the world to its proper moral order begins with the punishment of those who have caused harm to others.

By turning directly to God throughout this section, the sufferer illustrates that he no longer regards God as the enemy. Unlike the first section, in which the *gever* refers to his tormentor in the singular, in this section the enemy appears in plural form. Here, a malevolent group

---

151. As I have noted, the word-pair "*Re'eh vehabita*" ("Look and see!") appears in every chapter of the book except chapter 4 (1:11; 2:20, 5:1). Both words appear in the final section of chapter 3 (3:59, 60, 63), although not juxtaposed so closely as in the other chapters.

152. While here (verse 61) the context suggests that the taunts are directed against the *gever*, the word *ḥerpatam* often connotes blasphemy or mockery of God (see, e.g., I Sam. 17:26, 45; Ps. 74:10, 18, 22). The *gever* may use this word to suggest that the enemies' taunts are also an offense to God, in a bid to spur God to act against them. See my discussion of the word *herpa* in Eikha 5:1.

153. As I previously noted, R. Yosef Kara (3:65) observes that this idea closes each chapter.

(perhaps a foreign nation) seeks to harm the suffering individual. This constitutes one of the most significant transformations in the chapter. In contrast to the first section, where the *gever* assigns God responsibility for his woes, in this final section, the external enemies are guilty, and God is the *gever's* guardian. It is perhaps for this reason that the *gever* no longer employs the motif of darkness to describe his grim situation. In the first section, God leads him in darkness without light (3:2), and, surrounded by peril, darkness closes in on him as though he were already dead (3:6). Although the sufferer still experiences encirclement and imprisonment, he omits any mention of darkness. With God at his side, divine light accompanies the sufferer. Death, moreover, vanishes from his lexicon; instead, he focuses on his "life," first endangered (3:53) and then redeemed by God (3:58).[154]

The root *a.v.t.* offers an instructive model for understanding the trajectory of chapter 3. The word (*iva*) is used in the first section to describe God deliberately perverting the *gever's* pathways (3:9). In the contemplative middle section of the chapter (3:36), the *gever* asserts that God cannot abide perversions of justice (*le'avet adam berivo*). This reflection inspires the *gever* to reconsider his understanding of God as his enemy. In the final section of the chapter, the sufferer confidently notes that God has seen his perversions (*avatati*) (3:59) and can, consequently, be called upon to restore justice.[155] The *gever's* perceptions have completely changed; he no longer regards God as his adversary, but as his protector, one who sees and responds to the perversions of his actual enemies.

At the conclusion of the chapter, the *gever* stands firmly within his community. He had originally expressed his feeling of alienation from his nation by asserting plaintively, "I was a laughingstock for all my nation, their *plaything all day*" (3:14). This statement highlights the *gever's* isolation, and his perception that his countrymen take pleasure

---

154. The *gever's* description of his deathlike ordeal (3:6) overpowers the initial section of the book. The *gever* feels nearly dead: dulled, insensible, and lifeless. He seems to return to life only after he finishes ruminating about God, when he states vigorously, "Of what shall the living person complain, each *gever* over his own sins!"

155. Based on the context, most commentators identify these perversions as the injustices that his enemies have inflicted upon him. See *Targum*, Rashi, Ibn Ezra, and R. Yosef Kara on Eikha 3:59.

in his misery, perhaps even afflicting him for sport. The *gever* at the end of the chapter again describes the taunts of his adversaries, who maliciously regard him as a *"plaything"* (3:63), plotting against him *"all day"* (3:62). However, the agents of his misery are no longer his compatriots, but rather his enemies. By repeating words that appear in his initial statement of alienation from his community and transposing them onto the actual enemy, the chapter illustrates the *gever's* remarkable transformation. As the *gever* reacquires God and his community, his perspective and his narrative alter, and he rejuvenates.

Ambiguous Language:
The Verbs of Verses 56–61

Has God already intervened on the individual's behalf in this section or is the speaker petitioning God to do so? Much depends upon the nature of the verbs in verses 56–61, which has been the subject of scholarly debate. While some of the verbs are easily identifiable as imperatives ("Do not obstruct… Judge my judgments… Look"), others are ambiguous.

These ambiguous verbs at first seem to be in the past tense ("You heard… You were close… You said… You fought… You redeemed… You saw"), describing God's prior actions to aid the sufferer.[156] This gives the sufferer hope that God will deliver him from this situation as well. It appears, however, rather doubtful that chapter 3 would devote so much space and energy to describing God's salvation in an unrelated episode. The current situation seems sufficient to occupy the sufferer's thoughts and it is unlikely that he would remove his attention from it for such a prolonged time.

Some scholars suggest that these verbs are in the precative perfect tense, in which the sufferer beseeches God in the present, expressing a wish or request: "Hear my voice… Be close… Say to me, 'Do not be afraid'… Fight my fight… Redeem my life… See my injustice."[157] These

---

156. R. Yosef Kara (3:56–57) reads some of the verbs in this way, maintaining that some of the past-tense verbs refer to God's liberation of the enslaved Israelites from Egypt. See also Rashi, Eikha 3:57–58; Westermann, 164; House, 402, 426.

157. See Rasag on Eikha 3:58. Hillers, 52; Berlin, 81, 97; Dobbs-Allsopp, 126. The precative perfect is close to an imperative but has a less demanding quality.

verbs thereby link up with the imperative verbs to turn this section into a plea for help; the sufferer implores God to intervene in his ordeal. In this schema, the chapter ends without any concrete results; the best one can aim for is to appeal to God for assistance.

We can also understand the verbs in the present perfect tense (as I have translated above). This tense expresses actions that are complete, but also have consequences for the present.[158] These verbs construct statements steeped in faith and hope that God will immediately respond to the sufferer's predicament, if He has not done so already.[159] In this reading, the sufferer expresses bold confidence in God and His deliverance, giving the impression that it has already happened or is currently occurring. God has heard him, and has drawn close, having assured him that he should not fear. God has also fought on his behalf, redeemed him, and seen his predicament. Though I have adopted this approach, I am not at all certain that this is the only way to understand the verbs in this passage. It seems likely that the verb tense is deliberately ambiguous, mingling different aspects of the sufferer's perception of God's role in his salvation.

Why are the verbs in this section so ambiguous? In all these readings, God's role is to protect the sufferer. Lack of clarity as to whether He has already delivered this individual from peril, whether He is now in the process of delivering him, or whether the sufferer requires His assistance, may be the very point. This deliberate blurring of the verbs describing God's actions indicates the *gever's* unwavering confidence in God's deliverance. Has God already saved? Has He yet to do so? It does not seem to matter very much. Hope-filled memories of God's past deliverance become the basis for optimism that He will save in the future. This has bearing on the way in which people regard their present, and their ability to maintain faith in God even when circumstances seem hopeless. It is the *gever's* religious transformation that matters here, and these verbs illustrate the staunchness of his faith in God.

---

158. Perhaps this is Ibn Ezra's intention in his commentary on 3:56–57.
159. Gottwald, 61, notes that the perfect tense reflects the writer's firm conviction.

CHAPTER THREE: IN SUMMATION

Chapter 3 deviates from the circular course set by the previous two chapters. It charts instead a linear course, progressing from despair to contemplation and then to hope. Contemplation spawns comprehension of responsibility and consequently moves the *gever* toward reconciliation with God. To arrive at these conclusions, the *gever* draws from his deep resources of faith, depicted at the core of the chapter, which is also the pivotal center of the book.

Nevertheless, the ending of the chapter is far from triumphant. The suffering *gever* resurfaces in 3:52–66, his plight still miserable, his immediate prospects grim. The individual continues to feel entrapped and maligned, taunted and tormented.

Although the *gever's* external circumstances do not change over the course of the chapter, he undergoes an inner transformation. The third section of the chapter illustrates his astonishing development. Possibly the most significant transformation occurs as he abandons his self-centered victimhood and begins to perceive those around him. The *gever* no longer regards God as his adversary, nor does he feel alienated from his compatriots. Instead, he advocates on his people's behalf and enlists God as his protector. This process allows him to restore a relationship with both God and his community, alleviating his loneliness, restoring his meaningful existence, and facilitating his recovery.

Chapter 3 opens with the word *Ani*, "I," introducing a self-absorbed individual whose narcissistic obsession with his hardships alienates him from his surroundings. The chapter closes with the name of God, illustrating that the *gever* has learned to look beyond the narrow scope of his own grief. Though God never directly intervenes in the chapter (or in the book),[160] in this final section the sufferer hears God's words, senses His immanence, and anticipates the restoration of divine

---

160. This constitutes a remarkable omission within the context of a biblical book. God's absence from the book suggests that in this era of punishment and exile, people must cultivate the ability to find a relationship with God even if a divine response is not forthcoming or easily discerned. This is one of the primary challenges of Judaism following the destruction of the Temple and the subsequent waning of prophecy.

justice. By the end of his process of introspection, the *gever* has indeed found God, deep within the recesses of his own inner being.[161]

---

161. I complete the writing of this commentary on Eikha 3 – a striking chapter of human faith and determination – as I sit in my home in Alon Shevut on 11 Tevet, 5777, the day that my neighbor, Second Lieutenant Erez Orbach, was laid to rest. Erez was killed by a terrorist in Jerusalem on the fast day of 10 Tevet. Despite a medical condition that exempted him from army service, Erez insisted on serving, and volunteered for the Israeli army, eventually enrolling in an officers' course. He was an exemplar of idealism, fortitude, and dedication, a committed soldier, and a spiritual young man who had a great deal more to contribute to his family, community, and nation. I dedicate this chapter to his blessed memory. *Yehi zikhro barukh.*

Chapter Three, Appendix

Psalms 37 and Eikha 2 and 3

T his appendix will illustrate the way Eikha, chapters 2 and 3, dialogue with Psalms 37. I have appended a Hebrew chart with the linguistic parallels at the end of the appendix.

Psalms 37's alphabetic acrostic sketches an orderly world.[1] Sustaining an idyllic worldview, the psalm ingenuously expresses an unwavering belief in God's ultimate intention to destroy evildoers and reward those who trust in Him:[2]

---

1. Psalms 37 situates its alphabet acrostic at the beginning of every second verse. Acrostic compositions typically vary the way they construct their design.

2. The *mizmor* uses various terms to refer to wicked people. The word *rasha* or its plural, *resha'im*, appears thirteen times (although if we include the verbal *yarshienu* in verse 33, cognates of the word appear fourteen times), but a wide range of terms for evil appear throughout the *mizmor* (*mere'im* twice, *osei avla, posh'im, osei mezimot*). In total, this *mizmor* refers to the wicked and evildoers nineteen times, leading the Soncino edition of Psalms to subtitle Psalms 37, "The Problem of Evil" (A. Cohen, *The Psalms* [London: Soncino Press, 1945], 111). In my view, this psalm is not about the problem of evil, but rather the absence of the problem (even though evil exists). Reference to righteous people (*tzaddik*), appears nine times (with the substantive *tzedaka* in verse 6, it appears ten times), which is eleven times more than the word appears statistically in passages of similar length in the book of Psalms [I thank alhatorah.org for providing the resource that makes this statistic available].

331

Do not contend with evildoers, do not envy those who commit perversions. For, like the grass, they will rapidly fade, and like the verdant vegetables, they will wither. Trust in the Lord and do good, live in the land and guide with faith. Take pleasure in the Lord, and He will give you your heart's desires. (Ps. 37:1–4)

Psalms 37 never fluctuates from its serene worldview, in which sinners fade away, leaving a world filled with justice and peace:[3]

For evildoers shall be cut off and those who hope in the Lord, they will inherit the land. A bit longer and there will be no wicked, and you will look to his place and he will be gone. And the humble will inherit the land, and they will take pleasure in the abundant peacefulness. (Ps. 37:9–11)

At no point does the psalm wrestle theologically with God's ways or with the wicked who lurk in the backdrop. Despite the pervasive presence of evil, the chapter expresses staunch certainty that God supports the righteous and punishes the wicked:

For the Lord loves justice and will not forsake His faithful ones; they are guarded forever, and the seed of the wicked ones will be cut off... The wicked watches for the righteous and desires to kill him, but the Lord will not forsake him in his hand and will not let him be condemned when he is judged. Hope in the Lord and guard His way and He will lift you up to inherit the land; you will see the wicked ones cut off! (Ps. 37:28, 32–34)

Instead of dwelling on the evildoers' deeds, Psalms 37 focuses on their destruction. The only extensive description of their villainous activities appears in verses 12 and 14:[4]

---

3. Justice is referred to three times in the nominal form and once in its verbal form. The word *shalom* (peace) appears twice.

4. In later verses, Psalms 37 briefly alludes to the deeds of the wicked. Verse 21 notes that "the wicked one borrows and does not repay," while verse 32 depicts a more threatening situation: "The wicked watches for the righteous and desires to kill him."

The wicked one maliciously plots against the righteous one, and he gnashes his teeth at him ... Wicked ones draw their sword and bend their bow to cause the poor and impoverished to fall, to slaughter those whose road is straight. (Ps. 37:12, 14)

Intertwined within this portrayal of malevolent schemes, verses 13 and 15 remain calm, unruffled by the blustering brutishness of the wicked. Verse 13 features God scoffing at the evildoer who believes that his wickedness can prevail against God's justice:

The Lord will laugh at him, for He sees that his day has come. (Ps. 37:13)

Following the extensive description of the evildoers' bid to slaughter the innocent (verse 14), the psalm coolly proclaims the imminent downfall of the wicked, whose own weapons will turn against them:

Their swords will enter their own hearts and their bows will be broken. (Ps. 37:15)

This faith-filled psalm does not falter even for a moment. Its unwavering confidence in God's justice remains its most striking feature, presenting a theology of steadfast belief in a divinely ordered and just world.

EIKHA 2 AND PSALMS 37

Eikha 2 contends with a grim reality, one that clashes with the halcyon portrayal of divine justice of Psalms 37. A disquieting depiction of the seemingly indiscriminate torment of the populace of Judah, Eikha 2 features the suffering of children. These innocents do not receive God's benevolent protection; instead, the chapter depicts God as an adversary, the prime cause of suffering.

In its presentation of the situation, Eikha 2 consciously argues with Psalms 37, drawing from its language, and disagreeing with its conclusions. Points of disagreement between Eikha 2 and Psalms 37 include the following questions: Do righteous people suffer (from famine)? What happens to evildoers? What is God's role in suffering?

According to Psalms 37:18–19, innocents do not go hungry during times of famine (*re'avon*). Furthermore, Psalms 37:25 asserts: "I was a young man, and I have also grown old, and I have never seen a righteous person forsaken, nor his children seeking bread." This claim rings hollow in Eikha 2, as the innocent children clamor for food (verse 12) and languish from starvation (*raav*) in the streets (verse 19).[5] In another twist on its riposte to Psalms 37:25, Eikha 2:21 addresses the tranquil description of the young man (*naar*) who has turned old (*zakanti*), issuing sage observations on life as he accrues wisdom. In an ironic inversion of the psalm's peaceful portrait, Eikha employs the same two words (*naar* and *zaken*) to describe the corpses that litter Jerusalem's streets:

> They lie on the ground in the streets, young men (*naar*) and old (*zaken*). (Eikha 2:21)

In Eikha's view, young men do not always age, nor do the elders necessarily retire in peace. In Eikha's reality, people may be cut down indiscriminately, victims of a cruel and unjust world.

In the harmonious portrait of Psalms 37, the success of the evildoers is illusory and ephemeral (37:2). Shortly, the evildoers' day of reckoning (*yomo*) will arrive (37:13) and they will vanish (37:10, 13, 20, 28) and not be found (*velo nimtza*) (37:36). Therefore, righteous people should not envy the wicked, but should instead trust God, do good, and anticipate salvation (37:3–7). Hope (*kavei*) in God, urges the psalm, and you will witness the destruction of the evildoers (37:34). Eikha refutes these axioms by using similar language to present the triumphant crowing of Jerusalem's enemies: "Yes, this is the day (*hayom*) for which we waited (*kivinuhu*)! We found it (*matzanu*)! We saw it!" (Eikha 2:16). According to Eikha 2, the evildoers have not disappeared and those who hope in God have not triumphed.

Land is a key motif of Psalms 37; the word *eretz* appears six times in the chapter. Five of these appearances link to the verb *yarash* (inherit),

---

5. Eikha does not clarify whether the parents of the children are righteous, as required by Psalms 37:25. It matters little; all children qualify as the innocents of Psalms 37:18, who, according to verse 19, will remain satiated during times of starvation (*re'avon*).

offering a simple promise that the humble, the blessed, the righteous, and those who hope in God will surely inherit the land. Contrast this with the eightfold appearance of the word *eretz* in Eikha 2, which depict a downward movement in which Jerusalem – her buildings and her population – comes crashing down from the heights.[6] That chapter contains no theological explanation for the loss of the land; dispossession does not link to sin, leaving the reader flailing for an explanation of the destruction.[7]

The psalm depicts the confidence of the righteous person, who does not stumble even as evildoers plot to kill him. This is because the righteous person speaks wisdom and justice, preserving God's instructions (*torah*) in his heart (*libo*) (37:30–31). In contrast, Eikha 2:9 bitterly declares that there is no longer instruction (*torah*), that Jerusalem's prophets no longer receive any prophecies from God. This leaves the populace with no choice other than to shout and spill out their hearts (*libam*) before God (2:18–19).[8]

Psalms 37 urges trust in God, who supports the righteous and thwarts the enemy, deflecting his evil actions. The evildoers unsheathe their sword (*ḥerev*) and bend their bow in order to cause the poor people to fall (*lehapil*), but their designs will come to naught (verses 14–15). In fact, even if the righteous one falls (*yipol*), he will not be cast away, for God supports his hand (*yado*) (37:24). God will certainly never abandon the righteous in the hands of the enemy (verse 33)! In Eikha's view, all of this is nonsense. God readily relinquishes Jerusalem into the hands (*beyad*) of the enemy (2:7), and God is assigned blame for the fall (*naflu*) of the youth by the sword (*veḥarev*) (2:20–21).

In Eikha's most audacious inversion, chapter 2 portrays God in language used by Psalms 37 to describe evildoers. While Psalms 37 depicts the wicked people as "the Lord's enemies" (37:20), Eikha 2:4–5, portrays *God* acting as the "enemy," poised to strike Jerusalem. Like the

---

6. The only exception is the use of the word *eretz* in Eikha 2:15, which cites the way passersby formerly regarded Jerusalem as "a joy for all the land (*haaretz*)."

7. As I noted, the only reference to sin in chapter 2 is an indirect one, in which the narrator accuses the false prophets of failing to reveal Jerusalem's sins (2:13).

8. The hearts of the people appear twice in these verses in a posture of desperate entreaty.

evildoers in 37:13, in Eikha 2:4, God draws His bow (*darakh kashto*), killing all the precious ones.

Eikha 2:20–23 thrusts a direct indictment at God, accusing Him of causing the calamitous events in which so many youths have fallen by the sword (*naflu beḥarev*). The verses conclude with a scathing second-person denunciation of God, "You murdered on the day of Your anger, You slaughtered (*tavaḥta*), You did not pity!" These verses recall the language of the evildoers' deeds in Psalms 37:14: the sword, the fallen victims (*lehapil*), and the violent word *tavaḥ* (slaughter).

Eikha 2:16–17 cleverly manipulates Psalms 37:12, which describes the wicked one maliciously plotting (*zomem*) against the righteous and gnashing his teeth against him (*ḥorek...shinav*). Eikha 2:16 likewise describes the rapacious glee of Israel's enemies, who gnash their teeth (*veyeḥarku shen*) at the delightful news of Jerusalem's misfortune. However, the word *zomem* appears in 2:17 to describe God – rather than Israel's enemies – executing His premeditated designs (*asher zamam*) against the people.[9] Eikha 2 blurs the distinction between God and the evildoers, offering a harsh portrayal of divine hostility.

God's wrath (*af, ḥori, ḥamato, zaam*) abounds in Eikha 2, leaving terrible destruction in its wake. These words clash significantly with Psalms 37:8, which advises people to desist from anger (*af*) and abandon rage (*heima*), and not be wrathful (*titḥar*),[10] lest they come to evil.

Eikha 2 categorically rejects the worldview of Psalms 37, which presents God as the champion of justice. It presents instead an adversarial God, who wreaks havoc and causes human suffering, including the inexplicable death of innocent children.

---

9. The word *zomem* indicates a plot, conceived with virulence aforethought, to harm another. Biblical passages generally employ this word either to portray God's punishments (e.g., Jer. 51:12; Zech. 8:14–15) or the malevolent plots of the wicked (Deut. 19:19; Ps. 31:14).

10. The root (and meaning) of the word *titḥar* (the *hitpa'el* appears three times in Psalms 37) is a matter of some debate. Many interpreters assume that this is the verb often used in combination with *af*, and means to burn or be kindled with anger. See Ibn Ezra on Psalms 37:1, 7 (although he offers a different translation of the same word in 37:8).

EIKHA 3 AND PSALMS 37

In its opening verses, Eikha 3 resumes the tone of anger at God found in chapter 2. God's enmity emerges with battering force, as the *gever* describes his experience as God's victim. God once again (3:12) bends His bow against the hapless *gever*, like the evildoers of Psalms 37:14. In Eikha 3, God repeatedly diverts the *gever's* path (*derakhai*), surrounding it with a wall of stones (3:9) and perverting its course (3:11). This contrasts with God's support of the *gever's* feet in Psalms 37:23, enabling him to walk on his road (*darko*).[11] And in place of God's mockery of the wicked in Psalms 37:13 (*yishak*), the mockery (*sehok*) of the *gever's* detractors reverberates in Eikha 3:14, compounding his suffering.

Psalms 37 sees a world filled with peace (37:11, 37), goodness (37:3, 27), and hope (*hithollel*) in God (37:7).[12] The *gever's* experience causes him to flatly discard these perceptions (3:17–18): "My soul rejected peace, I forgot goodness. And I said, 'My endurance is lost and my hope (*tohalti*) in the Lord.'"

Up to here, Eikha has pointedly utilized phrases from Psalms 37 in order to dispute the naiveté of the idyllic *mizmor*. However, as the *gever* of Eikha 3 transforms, the chapter shifts from despair to hope, allowing the *gever* to reacquire his faith in God. Alongside this process, Eikha's attitude to Psalms 37 shifts, gradually incorporating its simple faith into its own outlook. To illustrate this, the book once again adopts the language of Psalms 37, but this time in an affirmative manner.

The *gever's* turnaround begins in Eikha 3:21. Pondering God's ways, he declares that he now has hope (*al ken ohil*). Abstract hope rapidly evolves and becomes hope *in God* (*al ken ohil lo*, 3:24). God is good (*tov*) to those who hope in Him (*kovav*, 3:25), leading the *gever* to his final movement toward faith that endures independent of circumstances (3:26): "It is good to hope and be silent (*yahil vedumam*), [waiting] for the salvation (*teshuat*) of the Lord." The *gever* seems to internalize this

---

11. The road (*derekh*) emerges as a key word in Psalms 37, appearing five times. The way suggests a pilgrimage, a unidirectional journey toward God. Verse 14 refers to the righteous innocents as "those whose road is straight."

12. Hope in God appears twice more in the psalm (37:9, 34), using a different word for hope (*kaveh*).

advice, falling silent two verses later (3:28): "He should sit in solitude and be silent (*veyidom*), when it [the burden] is placed upon him."

The *gever*'s newfound faith draws directly from the worldview of the psalm that Eikha had previously disputed and rebuffed. Psalms 37 perceives a world of *tov*, which appears three times as a stark contrast to the illusory power of the evildoers and their wicked ways.[13] Moreover, Psalms 37:7 advises its listeners to be silent (*dom*) as they wait for God and to have hope in Him (*hitholel lo*). Those who hope (*kovei*) in God will receive just reward from Him, as they will inherit the land (Ps. 37:9). Psalms 37:34 again counsels the righteous to hope (*kavei*) in God, concluding with a promise that the salvation (*teshuat*) of the righteous will come from God, who will actively save them (*yoshi'em*) from the evildoers (Ps. 37:39–40). Following its initial rejection, Eikha 3 reconciles with the simple worldview presented in Psalms 37. This reconciliation with God introduces serenity into the book.

Eikha initially rejects the simple faith of Psalms 37, arguing with it, transposing its language, and contradicting its themes. However, Eikha's view does not remain static. It transforms as the book progresses from chapter 2 to chapter 3, illustrating a struggle that unfolds within Eikha as it contends with the question of God's goodness. By noting the complex way in which Eikha weaves Psalms 37 into its chapters, we can better understand the book's struggles, and its unsteady movement toward the theological reconciliation that takes place at its pivotal center.

תהילים ל"ז	איכה
(יח) יוֹדֵעַ ה' יְמֵי תְמִימִם וְנַחֲלָתָם לְעוֹלָם תִּהְיֶה: (יט) לֹא־יֵבֹשׁוּ בְּעֵת רָעָה וּבִימֵי רְעָבוֹן יִשְׂבָּעוּ:	שְׂאִי אֵלָיו כַּפַּיִךְ עַל־נֶפֶשׁ עוֹלָלַיִךְ הָעֲטוּפִים בְּרָעָב בְּרֹאשׁ כָּל־חוּצוֹת: (ב', י"ט)

---

13. The word *tov* appears three times in the *mizmor* (Ps. 37:3, 16, 27) and three times in the middle of Eikha 3 (verses 24, 25, 26).

תהילים ל"ז	איכה
(כה) נַעַר הָיִיתִי גַּם־זָקַנְתִּי וְלֹא־רָאִיתִי צַדִּיק נֶעֱזָב וְזַרְעוֹ מְבַקֶּשׁ־לָחֶם:	שָׁכְבוּ לָאָרֶץ חוּצוֹת נַעַר וְזָקֵן בְּתוּלֹתַי וּבַחוּרַי נָפְלוּ בֶחָרֶב הָרַגְתָּ בְּיוֹם אַפֶּךָ טָבַחְתָּ לֹא חָמָלְתָּ: (ב', כ"א)
(יג) אֲדֹנָי יִשְׂחַק־לוֹ כִּי־רָאָה כִּי־יָבֹא יוֹמוֹ: (לו) וַיַּעֲבֹר וְהִנֵּה אֵינֶנּוּ וָאֲבַקְשֵׁהוּ וְלֹא נִמְצָא: (לד) קַוֵּה אֶל־ה' וּשְׁמֹר דַּרְכּוֹ וִירוֹמִמְךָ לָרֶשֶׁת אָרֶץ בְּהִכָּרֵת רְשָׁעִים תִּרְאֶה:	פָּצוּ עָלַיִךְ פִּיהֶם כָּל־אוֹיְבַיִךְ שָׁרְקוּ וַיַּחַרְקוּ־שֵׁן אָמְרוּ בִּלָּעְנוּ אַךְ זֶה הַיּוֹם שֶׁקִּוִּינֻהוּ מָצָאנוּ רָאִינוּ: (ב', ט"ז)
(לא) תּוֹרַת אֱלֹהָיו בְּלִבּוֹ לֹא תִמְעַד אֲשֻׁרָיו:	מַלְכָּהּ וְשָׂרֶיהָ בַגּוֹיִם אֵין תּוֹרָה גַּם־נְבִיאֶיהָ לֹא־מָצְאוּ חָזוֹן מֵה': (ב', ט') צָעַק לִבָּם אֶל־אֲדֹנָי (ב', י"ח) שִׁפְכִי כַמַּיִם לִבֵּךְ נֹכַח פְּנֵי אֲדֹנָי (ב', י"ט)
(יד) חֶרֶב פָּתְחוּ רְשָׁעִים וְדָרְכוּ קַשְׁתָּם־לְהַפִּיל עָנִי וְאֶבְיוֹן לִטְבוֹחַ יִשְׁרֵי־דָרֶךְ: (טו) חַרְבָּם תָּבוֹא בְלִבָּם וְקַשְּׁתוֹתָם תִּשָּׁבַרְנָה:	שָׁכְבוּ לָאָרֶץ חוּצוֹת נַעַר וְזָקֵן בְּתוּלֹתַי וּבַחוּרַי נָפְלוּ בֶחָרֶב הָרַגְתָּ בְּיוֹם אַפֶּךָ טָבַחְתָּ לֹא חָמָלְתָּ: (ב', כ"א)
(כד) כִּי־יִפֹּל לֹא־יוּטָל כִּי־ה' סוֹמֵךְ יָדוֹ:	הִסְגִּיר בְּיַד־אוֹיֵב חוֹמֹת אַרְמְנוֹתֶיהָ (ב', ז)
(כ) כִּי רְשָׁעִים יֹאבֵדוּ וְאֹיְבֵי ה' כִּיקַר כָּרִים כָּלוּ בֶעָשָׁן כָּלוּ:	הָיָה אֲדֹנָי כְּאוֹיֵב בִּלַּע יִשְׂרָאֵל בִּלַּע כָּל־אַרְמְנוֹתֶיהָ (ב', ה')
(יד) חֶרֶב פָּתְחוּ רְשָׁעִים וְדָרְכוּ קַשְׁתָּם לְהַפִּיל עָנִי וְאֶבְיוֹן לִטְבוֹחַ יִשְׁרֵי־דָרֶךְ:	דָּרַךְ קַשְׁתּוֹ כְּאוֹיֵב נִצָּב יְמִינוֹ כְּצָר וַיַּהֲרֹג כֹּל מַחֲמַדֵּי־עָיִן (ב', ד') דָּרַךְ קַשְׁתּוֹ וַיַּצִּיבֵנִי כַּמַּטָּרָא לַחֵץ: (ג', י"ב)
(יד) חֶרֶב פָּתְחוּ רְשָׁעִים וְדָרְכוּ קַשְׁתָּם לְהַפִּיל עָנִי וְאֶבְיוֹן לִטְבוֹחַ יִשְׁרֵי־דָרֶךְ:	שָׁכְבוּ לָאָרֶץ חוּצוֹת נַעַר וְזָקֵן בְּתוּלֹתַי וּבַחוּרַי נָפְלוּ בֶחָרֶב הָרַגְתָּ בְּיוֹם אַפֶּךָ טָבַחְתָּ לֹא חָמָלְתָּ: (ב', כ"א)
(ח) הֶרֶף מֵאַף וַעֲזֹב חֵמָה אַל־תִּתְחַר אַךְ־לְהָרֵעַ:	אֵיכָה יָעִיב בְּאַפּוֹ אֲדֹנָי אֶת־בַּת־צִיּוֹן (ב', א') שָׁפַךְ כָּאֵשׁ חֲמָתוֹ: (ב', ד') גָּדַע בָּחֳרִי־אַף כֹּל קֶרֶן יִשְׂרָאֵל (ב', ג')
(יב) זֹמֵם רָשָׁע לַצַּדִּיק וְחֹרֵק עָלָיו שִׁנָּיו:	עָשָׂה ה' אֲשֶׁר זָמָם בִּצַּע אֶמְרָתוֹ אֲשֶׁר צִוָּה מִימֵי־קֶדֶם הָרַס וְלֹא חָמָל (ב', י"ז)

תהילים ל״ז	איכה
(כג) מֵה' מִצְעֲדֵי־גֶבֶר כּוֹנָנוּ וְדַרְכּוֹ יֶחְפָּץ:	אֲנִי הַגֶּבֶר רָאָה עֳנִי בְּשֵׁבֶט עֶבְרָתוֹ: (ג', א') גָּדַר דְּרָכַי בְּגָזִית נְתִיבֹתַי עִוָּה: (ג', ט') דְּרָכַי סוֹרֵר וַיְפַשְּׁחֵנִי שָׂמַנִי שֹׁמֵם: (ג', י"א)
(יג) אֲדֹנָי יִשְׂחַק־לוֹ כִּי־רָאָה כִּי־יָבֹא יוֹמוֹ:	הָיִיתִי שְּׂחֹק לְכָל־עַמִּי נְגִינָתָם כָּל־הַיּוֹם: (ג', י"ד)
(יא) וַעֲנָוִים יִירְשׁוּ־אָרֶץ וְהִתְעַנְּגוּ עַל־רֹב שָׁלוֹם: (ג) בְּטַח בַּה' וַעֲשֵׂה־טוֹב שְׁכָן־אֶרֶץ וּרְעֵה אֱמוּנָה: (ז) דּוֹם לַה' וְהִתְחוֹלֵל לוֹ	וַתִּזְנַח מִשָּׁלוֹם נַפְשִׁי נָשִׁיתִי טוֹבָה: וָאֹמַר אָבַד נִצְחִי וְתוֹחַלְתִּי מֵה': (ג', י"ז-י"ח)
(ז) דּוֹם לַה' וְהִתְחוֹלֵל לוֹ (לד) קַוֵּה אֶל־ה' וּשְׁמֹר דַּרְכּוֹ וִירוֹמִמְךָ לָרֶשֶׁת אָרֶץ בְּהִכָּרֵת רְשָׁעִים תִּרְאֶה: (לט) וּתְשׁוּעַת צַדִּיקִים מֵה' מָעוּזָּם בְּעֵת צָרָה: (מ) וַיַּעְזְרֵם ה' וַיְפַלְּטֵם יְפַלְּטֵם מֵרְשָׁעִים וְיוֹשִׁיעֵם כִּי־חָסוּ בוֹ:	חֶלְקִי ה' אָמְרָה נַפְשִׁי עַל־כֵּן אוֹחִיל לוֹ: טוֹב ה' לְקֹוָו לְנֶפֶשׁ תִּדְרְשֶׁנּוּ: טוֹב וְיָחִיל וְדוּמָם לִתְשׁוּעַת ה': (ג', כ"ד-כ"ו)

340

A Chapter of Numb Pain

INTRODUCTION

Chapter 4 veers away from the story of the individual, returning the book to its account of national tragedy. Two-thirds the length of the previous two chapters, chapter 4 has the same twenty-two verses as chapters 1 and 2, but each verse contains just two sentences instead of three. Brevity indicates despair; there is not much left to report, speech seems increasingly pointless. Jerusalem can no longer sustain its starving populace; the city's fall and the exile of her inhabitants appear imminent.

Chapter 4 focuses attention on a wide swath of Jerusalem's populace – its children, mothers, Nazirites, prophets, and priests. By singling out particular groups, the chapter offers a glimpse of individual experiences, a panoply of human tragedy. Vivid metaphors merge with a graphic portrait of suffering, focusing particularly on the horrors of famine. In its wake, Jerusalem's inhabitants treat precious jewels and once-cherished children with similar indifference, mothers abandon their humanity, and corpses litter Jerusalem's streets. Details of the famine assault our senses; we visualize the infants' parched tongues and we hear the children's desperate pleas for bread.

Despair colors this chapter in dark hues; the lustrous gold, shining white, and rosy-cheeked vigor of Jerusalem's bright past fade, giving way to dark tones, the shadowy color of despondency. Blackened by hunger and desiccated by thirst, people no longer recognize their fellows. Lack of recognition metaphorically suggests antisocial behavior; society breaks down as hunger predominates, and every individual seeks his or her own survival at the expense of another.

Strikingly, this chapter lacks petition or prayer. Unlike the first three chapters, the first-person speaker does not address God, not even to issue the minimal request that God look at the nation or the characteristic final plea for vengeance. With little faith that God will intervene on His nation's behalf, this chapter tumbles toward a bleak conclusion, bereft of God or hope in His salvation.

Despite its gloomy outlook, this chapter does not end on a despondent note. Even if the chapter does not contain a petition to God, it expresses belief in ultimate justice. In a surprising reversal, the chapter concludes with a confident declaration of a just future. Edom will surely meet its deserved fate. Sins have caused this catastrophe; repudiation of sins will surely overturn it. The lessons learned from the previous chapter resonate clearly as the narrator utters his promising conclusion: "When your sins cease, daughter of Zion, He will not continue to exile you!"

STRUCTURE

The speakers in this chapter deviate from the pattern established in chapters 1 and 2. As in those chapters, the third-person narrator opens the chapter. In a matter-of-fact voice, the detached narrator indicates resignation. However, while those chapters shift from the objective speaker to a more emotional first-person account at the midpoint, in chapter 4, the first-person narrator seems to have vanished.[1] The third-person account continues long past the chapter's midpoint.

The speaker finally changes in verse 17, not to the first-person singular but to the first-person plural, which narrates the final dashed hopes of the nation. The communal voice musters its last reserve of strength in a desperate quest to find a last-minute reprieve. These verses move

---

1. A first-person singular reference to *"bat ammi"* appears in verses 3, 6, and 10. Lending the speaker some personality, it does not change his anonymity and the sense that he speaks not from the personal perspective of the city/people, but rather as an outside observer.

rapidly from brief hope to utter despair, culminating in the enemy's pursuit, ambush, and ultimate success. The account concludes as the leader falls into a snare, bringing all hopes of continued autonomy to a crashing halt.

In the wake of the community's failure, the third-person narrator reemerges with his sights gamely set upon the future, in which the enemy will receive his due and Israel will return from exile. The third-person account in verses 21–22 contains several second-person addresses. It intersperses harsh imprecations directed at the Edomite enemy ("daughter of Edom") with a message of consolation for the "daughter of Zion." These final verses offer a modicum of hope at the conclusion of a chapter shrouded in despondency.

Thematically (but not in terms of its speaker), this chapter divides into two parts, as do chapters 1 and 2. For the most part, it tells a chronological story, moving from siege and famine (verses 1–10), to conquest and exile (verses 11–20).

The account of famine proceeds as one would expect. The vulnerable children suffer first (verses 4–5), but as the famine progresses, the adult population experiences its effects as well (verses 7–9). The horrific climax of the famine appears in verse 10, which depicts the women cooking their children in a desperate bid to survive.

The second half of the chapter also plays out in a sequential fashion. One brief verse (11) depicts the actual conquest of Jerusalem. Following that, blood-stained blind people wander the streets (verse 14) – a metaphor for the obtuse sinners, but also an apt description of the impurity and filth that saturate Jerusalem. Siege and destruction give way to exile, releasing the people from the entrapment of the starving city, but launching a period of aimless wandering and harsh rejection by the diaspora nations (verses 15–16).

The chapter returns our view to a community still in Jerusalem (verses 17–20) even after we have seen the populace's movement toward exile (verse 15). This back-and-forth description may accurately describe the reality, in which exile occurs in stages, and we return to Jerusalem in order to witness the next wave of expulsion. More poignantly, this chapter illustrates the difficulty of abandoning Jerusalem. Although the reader follows the exiles on their journey outside of the city, our attention immediately returns to Jerusalem, as we relive her terrible last moments of impending doom.

Exile brings other nations to the foreground. Portrayed three times (verses 15, 17, and 20), these nations rebuff and betray the Judean community. Conditions for co-existence vanish; hope in a leader who can navigate Israel's relationship with the nations disappears when he is captured. Israel's relationships with other nations proves useless and often harmful, leaving her vulnerable and alone. Chapter 4 concludes with one final glance at the nations, contrasting the daughter of Zion with her nemesis, the daughter of Edom. Despite Israel's present isolation, the chapter ends by offering a glimpse of a better future, in which roles are reversed; Edom receives due punishment while Zion's exile ceases.

I have divided the chapter as follows, based on the chapter's themes:

Part 1 – Verses 1–10: The Famine
Part 2 – Verses 11–20: Destruction and Exile
Part 3 – Verses 21–22: An Epilogue – Hope and Justice

PART 1 (EIKHA 4:1–10): THE FAMINE

Eikha 4:1

אֵיכָה יוּעַם זָהָב
יִשְׁנֶא הַכֶּתֶם הַטּוֹב

תִּשְׁתַּפֵּכְנָה אַבְנֵי־קֹדֶשׁ
בְּרֹאשׁ כָּל־חוּצוֹת

How the gold is dimmed
The fine gold altered

The holy stones spilled
On every street corner

Opening with the familiar cry of "*Eikha*," chapter 4 returns to the tone of lament sounded in chapters 1 and 2. Bemoaning the fate of the city's precious objects, chapter 4 sets out on its anguished course, assessing the impact of the siege upon its victims.

The verse seems at first glance to be literal. Contrasting past glory to the present misery, it highlights Jerusalem's drastic fall from splendor to dullness, a painful contrast between the city as it was and as it is now.[2] Objects of value no longer shine; their value depreciated, they litter the streets. Why in fact do these precious gems spill onto the street? Is this caused by exhaustion, carelessness, or neglect?

As many scholars note, gold does not dim. Perhaps, then, it has become sullied, covered in dirt, having been tossed into the street along with the people's once-valued treasures. More likely, the verse suggests that the gold's *value* has dimmed; after all, of what value are precious jewels when one can no longer exchange them for food? During famine, once-precious gems litter the streets, ignored by all passersby, a stunning symbol of a city desperate for food.[3]

These expensive objects recall the past glory of Jerusalem, the royal city. Evoking the magnificent palaces of the Davidic kings (see I Kings 10:14–25), the discarded gold and precious stones illustrate the dissolution of the wealth and splendor of Jerusalem's past.

Jerusalem's Temple also comes to mind, a resplendent building glistening with gold (see: I Kings 6:20–22, 30; 7:48–50; Jer. 52:19), and representing God's majesty.[4] The "holy stones" that now lie in the street evoke Jerusalem's former sacred status, a city that bore the divine presence.

---

2. See Eikha 1:1, where I noted the phenomenon of comparing the past to the present in the book. I will examine this at greater length later in this chapter (4:5, 7).

3. R. Yosef Kara (4:1) notes how unlikely it is that one would dispose of precious jewels. However, Ezekiel 7:19 warns of just this situation, explaining that silver and gold cannot fill stomachs during a famine. See also Zephaniah 2:18.

4. The Aramaic *Targum* on this verse (4:1) refers explicitly to the gold and luster of the Temple.

What exactly are these holy stones that lie neglected in the street?[5] They may be the structural stones of the Temple (see I Kings 5:31, 7:9–12), scattered in the street following the Temple's destruction.[6] Possibly, the "holy stones" are the Temple treasures, the costly gemstones that lie in its coffers. More specifically, they may refer to the precious stones set on the ephod and breastplate of the high priest, each one etched with the name of one of the twelve tribes (Ex. 25:7; 28:15–21).[7] These stones once rested proudly on the high priest's chest as he brought the sacrificial service, confirming his role as the representative of all twelve tribes. Tossed unceremoniously into the streets, these stones emerge as a symbol of the nation. The failed high priest, the chief custodian of the Temple, has not managed to protect the sacred space, the city, or the people.

Read independently, the verse highlights the depreciation of Jerusalem's value. It does not shine or warrant respect; the city no longer maintains its royal and sacred status. However, the following verse (4:2) suggests that the primary sense of this verse is figurative, a metaphor for the treatment of Zion's children, who were once valued as gold. The "holy stones" that spill onto the streets represent people, an interpretation supported by the engraving of names onto the precious stones of the high priest's breastplate. In this reading, the children of Zion become mirrors of their holy Temple; the Temple's demolition parallels the destruction of Jerusalem's residents.

The phrase that describes the public place where the stones lie, namely, "on every street corner" further suggests that the stones represent the children. This exact phrase appears in Eikha 2:19 to describe the dying children of Jerusalem, who languish from famine "on every street corner." This unique phrase (appearing only in these two places in Eikha) links the two images, confirming that our verse refers to the

5. For a review of this topic, see J. A.Emerton, "The Meaning of ʾabnē qŏdeš in Lamentations 4:1," *ZAW* 79 (1967), 233–36.

6. See the Latin Vulgate, which translates: "The stones of the sanctuary are scattered at the top of every street." This reading suggests that Eikha 4:1 describes the aftermath of the destruction of the Temple. Generally, however, the first ten verses of the chapter focus on the famine, which is more likely a product of the ongoing siege prior to the Babylonian penetration of the city.

7. See R. Yosef Kara on 4:1.

children, who languish in the streets, depleted of their value.[8] The verb that describes them "spilling out" into the streets also evokes the starving children of 2:12, who "spill out" their lives in their mothers' bosoms. The neglect of the children at the opening of chapter 4 points to the breakdown of humanity, as well as the collapse of Jerusalem's future.

Isaiah's prophecies of return from Babylonia to Jerusalem reverse this image of the precious children. Their homecoming bedecks the city with glittering splendor:

> Hasten your children[9] [to return] ... Lift up your eyes and see all of them gathering and coming to you, I swear, says the Lord. For you shall wear them all like jewels and adorn yourself with them like a bride ... So says the Lord God: "I will raise My hand to the nations and lift up My banner to peoples, and they will bring your sons in their bosoms and carry your daughters on their shoulders. Kings shall tend to your children and their queens shall be your nursemaids..." (Is. 49:17–18, 22–23)

Isaiah's prophecy of return envisions venerated children worn proudly like jewels, carried tenderly and treated with respect.[10] Reversing the indifference displayed toward the children in Eikha, this passage restores hope in a glorious future.

Another passage in Isaiah visualizes the restoration of Jerusalem's splendor – a city rebuilt, resplendent, and bejeweled:

---

8. This exact phrase appears only twice more in Tanakh (Is. 51:20; Nahum 3:10). Intriguingly, this phrase always describes children who lie "on every street corner," a symbol of a society that has lost its future, along with its moral compass. Other biblical passages refer to scenes that take place in the streets (*ḥutzot*) but lack the complete phrase that we are discussing here. I will return to this topic in our discussion of Eikha 4:14–15.

9. Because God addresses Jerusalem in this section, the "children" probably refer to all Jerusalem's residents and not just youngsters. This may also be the identity of the "children of Zion" in Eikha 4:2.

10. Similarly, God promises Moses that the children of slavery will leave Egypt bedecked in jewels (Ex. 3:22), a symbol of restored dignity.

Behold I will pave your stones with colored mortar, and I will lay sapphires as your foundations.[11] I will place your battlements as pearls and your gates of polished jewels, and all your border [walls] of cherished stones.[12] And all your children shall be disciples of the Lord and great peace [upon] your children. (Is. 54:11–13)

Isaiah seamlessly shifts from the ornamented city to her populace, linking the reestablishment of the city with the reanimation of her inhabitants.[13] Similarly, throughout the book of Eikha the fate of the city and that of her inhabitants intertwine. Jerusalem's splendor depends upon the glorious return of her children bedecked in jewels, and the splendor of the nation relies upon the restoration of glory to Jerusalem.

Eikha 4:2

בְּנֵי צִיּוֹן הַיְקָרִים
הַמְסֻלָּאִים בַּפָּז

אֵיכָה נֶחְשְׁבוּ לְנִבְלֵי־חֶרֶשׂ
מַעֲשֵׂה יְדֵי יוֹצֵר

**Precious children of Zion
Who were valued as gold**

**How have they been considered as earthenware jars
The work of the hands of a craftsman?**

---

11. Aside from the reference to precious stones, several words link Isaiah 54:11 to Eikha chapter 4: the sapphires (see Eikha 4:7) and the city's foundations (destroyed in Eikha 4:11). Jerusalem's gates in the following verse (Is. 54:12) also connect to Eikha 4:12.

12. It is not possible to identify the stones (and other words) of this verse with certainty. I have tried to adhere to the *Targum* and Rashi's interpretations, although Rashi brings several possibilities to translate *shimshotayikh*.

13. The oft-cited rabbinic interpretation of Isaiah 54:13 likewise intertwines the centrality of the children in the city and its physical reconstruction (Berakhot 64a): "R. Eliezer said in the name of R. Ḥanina: Torah scholars increase peace in the world, as it says, 'And all your children shall be disciples of the Lord and great peace [upon] your children.' Do not read 'your children' (*banayikh*), but rather 'your builders' (*bonayikh*)."

A second cry of *"Eikha"* appears in this verse, the final one in the book. Intensifying the elegiac tone, the repetition prepares the reader for a particularly difficult chapter, a grim portrait of the city's collapse.

This verse elucidates the meaning of the previous verse, which described the valuable and holy jewels of Jerusalem, tossed aside like trash.[14] These turn out to be a metaphor for the once-precious and dazzling children of Zion,[15] who were valued like gold, and are now like earthenware pots, commonplace and disposable.[16] While initially the chapter appears concerned with objects, it actually focuses upon people, upon the human suffering in the city.

The worth of children does not exactly mirror that of gold. Gold's value vanishes when society lacks sufficient nourishment to survive, while human beings have inherent value.[17] To safeguard its future and maintain its morality, a society should especially care for its children, whose value cannot be measured in currency. The callous treatment of the priceless children suggests the collapse of basic societal responsibility.

Why have these children been demoted, deemed comparable to earthenware jars? Who is it that actually regards the children of Zion in this way? Possibly, it is the city herself who metaphorically devalues her inhabitants, withdrawing her protection and allowing the enemies to

---

14. See R. Yosef Kara on 4:1. Eikha constructs these verses so that the reader first encounters verse 1 on its own merit, and only afterward reads verse 2, which offers new meaning to the first verse. This indicates that verse 1 retains its literal meaning as well.

15. Rashi (and *Targum*) on 4:2 highlights the parallel between the physical appearance of the *benei Zion* and the appearance of the gold. Similarly, R. Yosef Kara (4:2) focuses on the way this metaphor describes the dulled appearance of the people, rather than their diminished value.

16. As noted, *"benei Zion"* may refer to the general population, and not only to the children (see, e.g., Berlin, 106). The next verses (3–4) refer to the actual children. This may indicate that verse 2 also refers to the youngsters (Dobbs-Allsopp, 131).

17. Unlike money, the value of gemstones may also lie in their beauty, rarity, and luminous appearance. Song of Songs 5:11–15 describes the magnificence of the *Dod* (the male figure in Song of Songs), whose physical body is overlaid with gold and studded with jewels. The *Dod's* head is described with two synonyms for gold (*ketem* and *paz*) found in our passage. This similarity suggests that precious jewels are a good metaphor for describing an ideal image of human singularity and radiance. For more on this topic, see our discussion of Eikha 4:7–8.

do as they please. Perhaps it is God. The chapter later describes mothers deserting their children during the famine (4:3–4, 10). Possibly, then, this verse refers to the parents, who disregard the value of their own children, allowing them to languish in the gutter, where they suffer from hunger (verse 4) and cold (verse 5). This portrait of parental neglect stems from the horrors of famine, which depletes people of their physical and moral vigor; indeed, their very humanity suffers in its wake. Hunger demoralizes and dehumanizes. As the food supply dwindles and Jerusalem's residents suffer the slow and agonizing effects of the famine, hope for the future fades, alongside the inclination or ability to sustain the children.[18]

Metaphor: The Work of the Hands of the Craftsman

The children are likened to earthenware jars, which are the work of the hands of a human craftsman. Biblical passages often hint at the breakability of manufactured vessels, considered to have meager value in biblical times (Is. 30:14, Ps. 2:9). Because people regarded earthenware vessels as disposable items, they treated them carelessly, like refuse, unceremoniously tossing them away when their usefulness ceased.[19] Jeremiah recoils from this attitude toward humans:

> Is this man, Kanyahu,[20] like a broken and despised pot? Is he a vessel that no one desires?[21] Why were he and his descendants picked up and thrown on a land that they knew not? (Jer. 22:28)

The reference to a human artisan (*yotzer*) suggests a comparison to God, who is often termed a *yotzer* (Is. 45:7; Jer. 10:16; Amos 4:13). Human

---

18. It may be supposed that not everyone behaved in an identical fashion. It is certainly probable that there were exceptions to this description (and the ones that will follow). In painting this harsh picture of society's moral collapse, this chapter portrays a general failing of Jerusalem's populace, a horrifying result of hunger and despair.

19. Ancient sites filled with shards constitute evidence that society treated these objects as being of little worth.

20. This is a reference to the penultimate king of Judea, Jehoakhin.

21. The phrase "a vessel that no one desired" is sometimes used to depict a particularly harsh treatment of humans in biblical prophecies (Jer. 48:38; Hos. 8:8).

hands construct inferior products, such as earthenware vessels, which do not require great skill.[22] In contrast, the Bible attributes God's creation of humans to His artisanship (Gen. 2:7–8; Is. 64:7; Zech. 12:1). It is therefore a surprising and terrible demotion for the children of Zion to be designated the work of a human. This reduces them in terms of both their worth and their divine origins.

Jeremiah uses a similar metaphor to warn Israel of the consequence of their sins:

> The word that came to Jeremiah from the Lord, saying, "Arise and go down to the house of the craftsman (*beit hayotzer*) and there I will let you hear My words." And I went down to the house of the craftsman and there he was doing work upon the stones.[23] And the vessel that he was making from clay was ruined in the hands of the craftsman, and he began again and made another vessel, one that was good in the eyes of the craftsman. And the Lord said to me, "Like this craftsman, can I not do this to you, house of Israel?" says the Lord. "Like clay in the hands of the craftsman, so you are in My hands, house of Israel." (Jer. 18:1–6)

As the divine manufacturer of the human being, God warns that He has free rein to do what He wishes with His creations. Like the potter, who can throw away an unsatisfactory vessel, God may choose to destroy the people who do not fulfill the purpose of their creation. Jeremiah's prophecy resonates frighteningly against the backdrop of this verse. God's warning has been implemented. The value of humans has been reduced to that of earthenware vessels – the work of the Divine Craftsman who is no longer satisfied with His creation.

---

22. Several prophets use this argument to denigrate idols, which are fashioned by human hands, the work of a mortal artisan (Is. 40:19, 44:9–12; Hab. 2:18).

23. The word for stones here is *ovnayim*, which appears in only one other place, describing a birthing stone for humans (Ex. 1:16). The strengthens the analogy between the human craftsman making and breaking his earthenware vessels and the Divine Craftsman who expresses willingness to destroy His human creations.

Eikha 4:3–4

גַּם־תַּנִּים חָלְצוּ שַׁד
הֵינִיקוּ גּוּרֵיהֶן

בַּת־עַמִּי לְאַכְזָר
כַּיְעֵנִים בַּמִּדְבָּר

דָּבַק לְשׁוֹן יוֹנֵק אֶל־חִכּוֹ
בַּצָּמָא

עוֹלָלִים שָׁאֲלוּ לֶחֶם
פֹּרֵשׂ אֵין לָהֶם

Even jackals[24] draw out a breast
And nurse their young

The daughter of my nation is cruel
Like the ostriches in the desert

The tongue of the suckling cleaves to his palate
In thirst

Children ask for bread
They have no provider

These verses indirectly accuse the mothers of cruelty, without identifying them or explicitly depicting their refusal to nurse their children. Instead

---

24. The word *tanim* is generally considered to be the plural form for the jackal (see BDB, *Lexicon*, 1072). Nevertheless, the *ketiv* reads *tanin*, which variously refers to a serpent (e.g., Ex. 7:9, 10, 12, 15) or a mythological sea-monster (e.g., Ps. 74:13). Thus, the Septuagint translates this word as serpent (see also Rasag), while the Vulgate translates it as sea-monsters. Because serpents do not nurse their young, the identification of this creature with the serpent is unlikely. The presumed cruelty of the venomous serpent (see Deut. 32:33, where the same word *akhzar* appears regarding the poisonous serpent) probably fuels this identification (see Eikha Rabba 4:6).

of naming the mothers, the verse accuses an elliptical *bat ammi*, "daughter of my nation," of cruelty. The phrase *bat ammi* refers generally to the nation, appearing five times in the book, and three times in the first section of chapter 4 (4:3, 6, 10). On three occasions, the reference appears in a longer sentence that describes the people's terrible brokenness, "*al shever bat ammi*," in the context of famine, anguish, and the disintegration of the moral fabric of the nation (2:12; 3:48; 4:10).

The possessive form and parental tone of *bat ammi* suggests affection and empathy. Indeed, in chapters 2 and 3, the appellation is linked to a first-person emotional response. Chapter 4 employs the term *bat ammi* three times in the first half of the chapter, climaxing in the full phrase, *al shever bat ammi*. Despite the emotional resonance of the appellation elsewhere, chapter 4 employs it in a dry, unemotional tone, devoid of tears. This surprising tone is compounded by the awful contexts in which the appellation appears. It first describes the cruel mothers who refuse to nurse their infants, then details a terrible punishment,[25] worse than that of Sodom. Finally, it appears during the most horrific act of all: the mothers consuming their children. The dissonance between the term and the absence of emotion epitomizes the detachment characteristic of chapter 4. This chapter offers a dry narration of the horrific events, a depiction of a traumatized nation numbed by suffering and resigned to despair.

The Maternal Instinct

Breastfeeding is a nutritional drain on the mothers, whose refusal to nurse their children indicates a decision to sustain themselves rather than their offspring.[26] As a result, the suckling babes remain parched,

---

25. When I examine Eikha 4:6, I will discuss whether the word *avon* refers to the nation's iniquity or punishment.

26. Though it is possible that their milk has dried up as a result of their own lack of nutrients (see, e.g., Moshkovitz, *Eikha*, 32), the verse suggests that this decision is a result of cruelty, a decision that negates the maternal instinct. Rashi (4:3) elucidates this choice: "They see their children crying out for bread but there is no one who will give to them, because their lives precede that of their children's lives due to the famine." The *Targum* on 4:3, presumably distressed by the scathing portrayal of the mothers, interprets the verse differently: "Even the indulged daughters of Israel

with no one to alleviate their terrible thirst.[27] The maternal instinct plays a foundational role in human compassion.[28] Childrearing cultivates a willingness to sacrifice one's own selfish needs and offer kindness to another person. The disappearance of parental compassion endangers empathetic human interactions.

The maternal instinct exists in the animal kingdom as well. Mammals reliably nurse their young, though it requires extra nutrition and renders the mothers vulnerable to predators. In Eikha, however, mothers refuse to suckle their young, allowing their maternal instinct to atrophy. The contrast between the loyalty of the animal mothers and the treachery of the Judean mothers stuns the reader.[29] Israel has lost not only its humanity, but also the primal generosity that humans share with the animal kingdom.

The final sentence of this description ("children ask for bread, they have no provider") indicates that the neglect of the children is not limited to mothers who refuse to nurse their infants. Adults have stopped caring for children, leaving them to fend for themselves. The children's plaintive request for food hangs heavily in the air, as no response is forthcoming. Perhaps there is no bread left in the city, leaving the adults helpless and mute.[30] Possibly, they simply refuse to share their meager rations. With parental morality undermined by starvation, the instinct to nurture their children recedes and dissipates.

---

drew out their breasts to children of the nations, who are similar to serpents, while the great members of my nation were given over to cruel ones, and their mothers mourn over them like ostriches in the desert." In this reading, the cruel ones are the enemies, whose children are breastfed by the Judean women. It is not clear whether the *Targum* intends to say that the enemy coerces the Judean women to breastfeed their children or if this is a description of the great compassion of the Judean women.

27. In Isaiah's prophecies of reversal and redemption, God promises that He will not forsake those parched by thirst and will provide them with abundant water (Is. 41:17–18).

28. Note the etymological connection between the Hebrew words *reḥem* (womb) and *raḥamim* (compassion). See BDB, *Lexicon*, 938.

29. Other biblical passages similarly criticize Israel by contrasting them unfavorably with animals. See, for example, Isaiah 1:3; Jeremiah 8:7.

30. During the Babylonian siege on Jerusalem, the city does in fact run out of bread. See II Kings 25:3.

Metaphor: Ostriches in the Desert

Not all animals behave as nobly as mammals, and this verse draws a sharp distinction between animals who suckle their young (jackals) and those who do not (ostriches). It does not, however, appear that the jackal is a paradigm of compassion. Rashi explains that despite its willingness to suckle its young, the jackal is a cruel animal. This is suggested by the word *gam* (*"even* jackals draw out a breast and nurse their young"), which indicates that this behavior is unexpected. Yet, even the unkind jackals show more compassion than the Judean mothers.

Following the scathing contrast between the human mothers and the jackals, the verse compares them to the ostriches (*ye'enim*) of the desert.[31] What do we know about these desert birds that can help us to understand this comparison? Malbim identifies the bird in Job 39 (*renanim*) as an ostrich (*bat yaana*).[32] Job describes a cruel and neglectful mother-bird, who abandons her offspring without compunction:

> The wing of the ostrich (*renanim*) is joyous… but she abandons her eggs on the ground and they are warmed in the dirt. And she forgot that a foot could crush them and a beast of the field could trample them. She is indifferent to her children as though they are not hers. (Job 39:13–16)

Even a hint of a comparison to this neglectful bird constitutes a scathing critique of the Judean mothers, whose indifference to their children puts them in the company of cold-hearted creatures.

---

31. For this identification, see BDB, *Lexicon*, 419, which conflates the *ye'enim* of our verse and the more frequently mentioned *bat hayaana* (e.g., Lev. 11:16; Deut. 14:15). Hullin 64b similarly discusses whether the *bat yaana* is identical to the *yaana*. I thank my father, Prof. Allen Zeiger, for this reference, which he came across in his devoted daily learning. Generally, I wish to thank him for his contribution and his frequent phone calls in which he shared relevant passages from that day's *daf* of Gemara. I wish my father many years of continued *talmud Torah*.
32. Malbim, Job 39:13. BDB, *Lexicon*, 943, notes that the words *ye'enim* and *renanim* sound similar. The word *renanim* may be related to the word *ranan*, which means to give a ringing cry; BDB explains that the ostrich is a "bird of piercing cries."

Though the verse contrasts the jackal and the ostrich, these animals frequently appear together in biblical passages, a gloomy pair whose natural setting is among the detritus of destruction.[33] Jackals and ostriches frequent ruins, preferring the overgrown nettles of deserted habitations (Is. 13:21–22; 34:13).[34] The sounds that they utter evoke mourning (Mic. 1:8), and (perhaps for that reason) they are natural company for those who are miserable (Job 30:27–30). Despite the contrast between them in Eikha 4:3, their coupled appearance conjures a backdrop of devastation; their presence hints at the impending destruction of the city.

Eikha 4:5

הָאֹכְלִים לְמַעֲדַנִּים
נָשַׁמּוּ בַּחוּצוֹת

הָאֱמֻנִים עֲלֵי תוֹלָע
חִבְּקוּ אַשְׁפַּתּוֹת

Those who ate delicacies
Are desolate in the streets

Those raised in crimson silk
Embrace refuse heaps

This verse directs the reader to look back and forth, contrasting the splendid past with the dismal present, offering a brief glimpse of Jerusalem's former glory, a pampered life of comfort and prosperity. Jerusalem's

---

33. Isaiah 43:20 describes this pair as animals that live in the desert, like the *ye'enim* of the desert in our verse. Life in the desert (like life during a siege) encourages selfish behavior because conditions for survival (especially obtaining food and water) are so harsh.

34. I have only referenced verses in which the jackal and the ostrich appear together. Many biblical verses confirm that jackals prefer to live among ruins (Jer. 9:1, 10:22, 49:33, 51:37; Mal. 1:3). Jeremiah 50:39 mentions that the ostrich frequents ruins.

inhabitants once ate delicacies fit for a king,[35] rare and tasty. Raised in bright crimson clothes, or perhaps clothes of silk,[36] Jerusalem's populace once enjoyed royal luxuries. Juxtaposing the portrait of Jerusalem's formerly regal existence with the current poverty of the besieged city heightens the calamity. Jerusalem has experienced a dramatic reversal of fortune.[37]

The situation is so dire that it resists parallelism; nothing in the present remotely resembles the past. Consider the first sentence:

> Those who ate delicacies
> Are desolate in the streets

True parallelism would require the second half of the sentence to focus on food; Instead of delicacies, one may expect the populace to eat plain food, such as bread. In our verse, however, in place of delicacies there is nothing, just desolation. It appears that there is no food at all in Jerusalem.[38]

The second sentence similarly deviates from direct parallelism:

> Those raised in crimson silk
> Embrace refuse heaps

Instead of crimson silk, one would expect the verse to describe Jerusalem's residents clothed in rags. Yet, it appears that no garments

---

35. Genesis 49:20 employs the word for delicacies found in our verse alongside the word "king," *maadanei melekh.*
36. The word *tola* means a worm (see Ex. 16:20). When applied to clothing, it is not clear whether it refers to a worm used as a dye to produce a scarlet color (BDB, *Lexicon,* 1068–69, suggests that the *tola* is the insect *Coccus ilicis*), as suggested by Isaiah 1:18 (and see Rashi on 4:5), or a silkworm (*Bombyx mori*). It is not possible to determine the correct reading, which in both cases points to regal, luxurious clothing. My translation ("crimson silk") preserves both possibilities.
37. Hannah's song in I Samuel 2 catalogs God's ability to reverse people's fortunes in an abrupt and dramatic fashion, both for better and for worse. In I Samuel 2:8, Hannah describes God extracting the impoverished from the refuse heap (*mei'ashpot yarim evyon*). This is the opposite image of the one in our chapter, in which the prosperous wind up hugging the refuse heap (*ḥibeku ashpatot*). See also Psalms 113:7.
38. For confirmation of the absence of bread in the city, see II Kings 25:3.

are available in the besieged city; residents of the city cling to the refuse piles for warmth.[39]

It is a public and undignified scenario – the weak and starving lying in the streets, lacking food and clothes. Family structures have disintegrated and no one has the ability or the interest to care for dying relatives. Lodging also appears scarce, leaving the populace huddled in the refuse heaps for warmth. Possibly, these unfortunates are not searching for heat, but scavenging for food. Ibn Ezra explains that this image refers to the treatment of the corpses: "They embrace the refuse heaps. For they are tossed out like dung, and no one buries [them]." Whatever the exact meaning of the phrase, one thing is certain: Jerusalem's aristocratic lifestyle is no longer; her surviving inhabitants cling to survival amidst dismal conditions.

Eikha 4:6

וַיִּגְדַּל עֲוֺן בַּת־עַמִּי
מֵחַטַּאת סְדֹם

הַהֲפוּכָה כְמוֹ־רָגַע
וְלֹא־חָלוּ בָהּ יָדָיִם

And the sin of the daughter of my nation was greater
Than the transgression of Sodom

Which was overturned in an instant
And no hands lay upon it

Turning abruptly from the images of horror, the narrator appears to veer toward acknowledgment of sin. In comparison to Sodom, it seems that Jerusalem is penalized excessively. It stands to reason, muses the narrator, that Jerusalem's sins must outweigh those of Sodom. A midrash derives this idea based on a literary parallel:

---

39. R. Yosef Kara on Eikha 4:5.

"And the sin of the daughter of my nation was greater" (Eikha 4:6) – R. Yehoshua ben Neḥemia said in the name of R. Aḥa: It says with regard to the tribes of Judah and Benjamin something that it does not say with regard to the Sodomites. With regard to the Sodomites it is written, "Their sin was *very* weighty" (Gen. 18:20), but with regard to the tribes of Judah and Benjamin it is written, "And He said to me: 'The iniquity of Israel is *very, very* great'" (Ezek. 9:9). (Eikha Rabba 4:9)

Ezekiel offers a similar idea, castigating Jerusalem for corruptions that exceed those of both Samaria (the capital of the exiled Northern Kingdom of Israel) and Sodom:

> Your elder sister was Samaria who, along with her daughters, settled to the left of you. Your younger sister, who is settled on your right, was Sodom, along with her daughters. You did not go in their ways and practice their abominations. Shortly after,[40] you *exceeded* their corruptions in all your ways! (Ezek. 16:46–47)

Our verse appears to offer a humble admission of the nation's sins, yet this submissive posture seems oddly incompatible with the rest of this chapter. A litany of horror saturated with outrage drives this chapter forward, without pause to consider the cause or assume responsibility for the calamity. Perhaps for this reason, some biblical interpreters understand the words *avon* and *ḥatat* as references to punishment rather than sin:

> There is a *ḥatat* and an *asham* sacrifice, whose explanation is that they *follow* the sin and transgression.[41] And [these words refer to] the unfortunate *consequence* [of sin] ... And the meaning is that the evil that came upon Israel was greater than the evil that came upon Sodom... (Ibn Ezra, Eikha 4:6)[42]

---

40. See Radak, Ezekiel 16:47 for this translation of the obscure phrase "*kimat kat.*"
41. Ibn Ezra brings several biblical passages to support his contention: Genesis 15:16, I Samuel 28:10, and Genesis 4:13.
42. See also Ibn Ezra on Isaiah 53:6. Gordis, 147, 189, explains similarly.

In this schema, this verse contains neither confession nor acknowledgment of culpability. It seeks solely to illustrate the severity of Jerusalem's punishment, which eclipses even that of Sodom, often referred to as the archetype of a punished society.[43] However, even without reinterpreting the words *avon* and *ḥatat*,[44] the tenor of the verse does not appear to be confessional. The tone suggests grievance, and the main point of the verse is certainly the harshness of Jerusalem's punishment.[45]

According to our verse, Jerusalem's punishment dwarfs Sodom's in two respects. First, Sodom's destruction is instantaneous; they do not have to suffer the prolonged agony of starvation. Second, God alone administers Sodom's punishment, which means that no human enemy raises its bloodstained hands against Sodom. Brutish human hands lay waste to Jerusalem, which suffers the dishonorable misfortune of destruction by a mortal enemy.

How indeed can Jerusalem's fate be worse than that of Sodom, arguably the Bible's most infamously immoral society? Perhaps we should question the premise of the verse. The assumption that Jerusalem's punishment is worse than Sodom's remains correct only if this catastrophe leads to Israel's annihilation. If so, then a quick death would be preferable to a slow one, and a God-inflicted disaster would be preferable to the disgrace of a military invasion. Chapter 4 assumes that the nation's end steadily approaches, and that the conclusion of this story will be like that of Sodom. It turns out, of course, that this assumption is incorrect. A remnant of Israel survives; there is yet a possibility for national revival. In retrospect, Israel will see that the contrast drawn between Sodom's instantaneous death and Jerusalem's slow demise illustrates God's mercy toward His nation, not His excessive severity.

Sodom and Jerusalem

The comparison to Sodom draws our attention to the heinousness of Jerusalem's crimes. Sodom emerges as the Bible's most compelling

---

43. See, for example, Isaiah 1:9; Jeremiah 49:18; Amos 4:11.

44. Rashi (Eikha 4:6), for example, interprets the words *avon* and *ḥatat* as sin.

45. Daniel 9:12 similarly claims that God punished Jerusalem more than any other nation (though he maintains that God's punishment is justified).

example of how not to construct a society. A city devoid of morality, Genesis 19:4–5 describes how the men of Sodom surround Lot's house, demanding to rape his guests. When Lot attempts to deflect them, their response indicates their disdain for justice (*mishpat*): "Has one come here to live and he dares to judge (*vayishpot shafot*)?" Later, the prophet Ezekiel recalls Sodom's societal iniquities:

> Behold, this was the sin of Sodom, your sister: She and her sisters had the arrogance of satiation of bread and untroubled tranquility. But she did not support the hand of the poor and needy. (Ezek. 16:49)

Sodom's prosperity and security do not foster generosity or consideration for the less fortunate. It turns out that fewer than ten righteous people dwell in Sodom; this paucity of virtuous residents seals its fate (Gen. 18:20–33). God eradicates Sodom and her surrounding communities, sprinkling the ruins with salt so that nothing can grow there ever again.[46] As far as the Bible is concerned, Sodom can produce nothing of value for the world.

The antithesis of Sodom, Jerusalem is a city with a purpose, positioned to disseminate God's teachings to the world (Is. 2:2–3). God Himself fills Jerusalem with justice and righteousness (Is. 1:21; 33:5). This becomes Jerusalem's defining feature; some suggest that for this reason, early kings of Jerusalem added the word *tzedek* (righteousness) to their royal names:[47]

> "And Malki-Tzedek, the king of Shalem" (Gen. 14:18). [Shalem] is Jerusalem, as it is written, "And His shelter was in Shalem" (Ps. 76:3). And all kings of Jerusalem are kings of *tzedek*, such as Adoni-Tzedek, as it is written in the book of Joshua: "Adoni-Tzedek, the

---

46. Deuteronomy 29:22; Zephaniah 2:9.
47. While this practice did not continue with the Judean kings of Jerusalem, some kings do maintain names that recall Jerusalem's higher purpose. Solomon (Shelomo) evokes peace (*shalom*), Jehoshaphat evokes justice (*mishpat*), and the final king of Judah is renamed Zedekiah by the Babylonians, recalling the earlier kings whose names contained the word *tzedek*.

king of Jerusalem" (10:1). Because Jerusalem is a place of righteousness and peace, and it cannot tolerate injustice and violence and abominable acts for a lengthy period; therefore, it spits out the transgressors who dwell there. (Radak, Gen. 14:18)[48]

In the passage cited above (Gen. 14:18), Malki-Tzedek, king of Shalem (identified as Jerusalem by many biblical commentators), greets Abram with food and blessings on his victorious return from war. Abram graciously accepts Malki-Tzedek's greetings. In the same passage, the king of Sodom also comes to greet Abram, who rebuffs him (Gen. 14:22–24). This chapter draws a sharp distinction between Abram's regard for the two cities. Abram favors the king of Shalem and disassociates himself from the king of Sodom.[49] This incident serves to set up the contrast between Sodom (the city of injustice, slated for annihilation) and Jerusalem (the city of justice, slated to disseminate God's laws).

Unfortunately, the city of Jerusalem does not live up to these lofty expectations. Prophets frequently compare Jerusalem's sins to those of Sodom, issuing dire warnings against its inhabitants' Sodom-like behavior.[50] These verses tend to highlight Israel's moral corruptions, in keeping with Sodom's social depravity.[51] By failing to maintain a just society and show the world God's righteousness, Jerusalem fails to fulfill her purpose, thereby condemning herself to the fate of Sodom.[52]

---

48. This Radak is based on Genesis Rabba 43:6.
49. For more on this encounter, see Y. Levy, "Jerusalem in the Torah (II): Avram's Encounter with the King of Sodom and with Malki-Tzedek," in The Israel Koschitzky Virtual Beit Midrash (https://etzion.org.il/en/jerusalem-torah-ii-avrams-encounter-king-sodom-and-malki-tzedek).
50. See Isaiah 1:10, 3:9; Jeremiah 23:14; Ezekiel 16:2, 46–47.
51. Even in its present situation, where Jerusalem's residents all suffer from hunger, Eikha 4 depicts a Sodom-like attitude that infiltrates Jerusalem's populace; they fail to respond to the young children who plead for bread.
52. As noted above, the fates of these cities eventually diverge: Sodom receives a fatal blow while Jerusalem revives. Written with a near-sighted view of Jerusalem's ongoing collapse, Eikha 4 intertwines Jerusalem's fate with the fate of Sodom.

Eikha 4:7–8

זַכּוּ נְזִירֶיהָ מִשֶּׁלֶג
צַחוּ מֵחָלָב

אָדְמוּ עֶצֶם מִפְּנִינִים
סַפִּיר גִּזְרָתָם

חָשַׁךְ מִשְּׁחוֹר תָּאֳרָם
לֹא נִכְּרוּ בַּחוּצוֹת

צָפַד עוֹרָם עַל־עַצְמָם
יָבֵשׁ הָיָה כָעֵץ

Her Nazirites were [once] brighter than snow
Shinier than milk

Their body [bone][53] was ruddier than pearls[54]
Their limbs,[55] sapphires

Their appearance [now] is darker than black
They are not recognized in the streets

Their skin has wrinkled on their bones
It was dry like wood

---

53. The word *etzem* literally means "bone" (see my translation of the same word in the next verse). Nevertheless, it seems evident that the general sense here is body, as in Proverbs 16:24 (see Metzudat Zion). I have included the word "bone" in brackets in order to draw attention to the contrast between its appearance here (where the *etzem* links to a healthy ruddy appearance) and in the following verse (where the same word indicates a wizened, shrunken appearance).

54. It is not possible to identify the precise stone denoted by *peninim* (Rasag explains rather vaguely that it is a precious stone). While modern Hebrew uses this word to mean pearls, many scholars suggest a stone with a redder hue, such as coral. See also Ibn Caspi on 4:7.

55. *Gizra* means something chiseled. I translated it as "limbs," as they form the distinctive outline of the human body.

A remarkably vivid portrait, these verses employ vibrant color and highly descriptive language to draw a contrast between the radiance of satiation and the ashen shades of hunger. Verse 7 draws a sparkling picture of the health and vigor of the "Nazirites" of Jerusalem. The following verse presents a portrait in shadowy tones; the scene is drained of its colorful vibrancy, portraying desiccated bodies wrung of sustenance.[56]

The starving Jerusalemites are "not recognized in the streets." Malnutrition has erased familiar features from the shrunken faces.[57] Acquaintances, colleagues, friends, family, and intimates vanish; with recognition gone, human fellowship dissipates. Anonymity prevails, fostering alienation and the unravelling of social ties. The populace of Jerusalem wastes away in a mass of visceral hunger.

Nazirites: Nobility or Religious Elite?

These verses focus upon the appearance of the Nazirites, whose downfall represents a particularly dramatic reversal of fortune. Who are these Nazirites, and why do they elicit so much attention?

Some interpreters maintain that the Nazirites of this verse are the nobility, who are adorned with a *nezer* (crown) upon their heads.[58] At first, we recall the nobles' glittering countenances, brimming with vitality. Crimson and shiny white tones swirl around them; they are robust due to their satiation and prosperity.[59] The collapse of these figures is abrupt. Lacking a transition to soften the blow, the next verse tenders

---

56. Berlin, 103–4, notes the effective use of color in these verses. The switch from the vivid colors of verse 7 to the dull, sepia tones of verse 8 can be compared to a color movie that suddenly fades into black and white.

57. Job's suffering also makes him unrecognizable to his friends (Job 2:12), hinting at their estranged relationship.

58. Rashi says that *nezireha* means *sareha*, her rulers, because the ruler wears a *nezer*. Alternatively, this could refer to the priests, especially the high priest, who has a *nezer* placed upon his head (see Ex. 29:6, 39:30; Lev. 8:9; 21:12). Berlin, 101, refers to Genesis 49:26 and Deuteronomy 33:16 to adduce evidence for this reading. Moshkovitz adds Nahum 3:17 as a proof text.

59. The word *ademu*, describing the ruddy hue of the former populace, recalls the ruddy and vigorous David (*admoni*), who is described in the same verse maintaining a "fine appearance" (I Sam. 16:12; 17:42).

a gruesome portrait of the demotion of the starving nobles – shriveled, unrecognizable shells of their former selves.

Possibly, the focus on the degradation of these noble figures suggests that they are especially deserving of severe treatment. Often, the higher classes do not distribute wealth in a charitable fashion, using their position to benefit only themselves and even to subvert justice at the expense of the poor.[60] A famine is a fitting end for a city steeped in social injustice; in the absence of food, the rich suffer alongside the poor, erasing the social inequity between them. Nevertheless, this verse is less an indictment than a litany of horror; it contains no accusation or hint of culpability. These aristocrats appear to function as a mirror for the city's lost splendor. The decay of the sparkling elite reflects the erosion of the city's magnificence.

Another approach identifies these Nazirites as the voluntary ascetics described in Numbers 6:1–21, who do not drink wine. Even the ascetic Nazirites maintained a healthy appearance in God's bounteous city; how much more so the general populace, who drink wine that enhances their radiance (Ps. 104:15).[61]

The Nazirites' vow to abstain from cutting their hair spotlights them as the conspicuous spiritual elite of the society. The initial word used to describe them is *zaku*, a word that sometimes connotes physical luminescence (Job 25:5), but more often refers to religious purity (Ps. 73:13; Job 11:4). In the current situation, all that has changed. Despite their snow-white purity, the righteous Nazirites have been degraded, their glow has dimmed. In the absence of any suggestion of wrongdoing, the Nazirites have suffered a miscarriage of justice; their fate remains an incomprehensible tragedy, a theological quandary.[62]

---

60. See, for example, Jeremiah 5:26–28. In 22:13–17, Jeremiah accuses the king, Jehoakim, of acting unjustly toward the common people.

61. Rashi asserts an opposite reading, claiming that the Nazirites' long hair augmented their beauty, constituting the reason they feature as the emblem of Jerusalem's former glory.

62. Amos 2:11–12 accuses the Nazirites of participating in Israel's iniquities along with the prophets. Nevertheless, there is little indication in Eikha 4:7–8 that the Nazirites acted wrongly; in fact, the description of their snow-white purity suggests otherwise.

Like the death of innocent children, the deterioration of these religious role models turns our attention to the central theological issue in this chapter.[63] Chapter 4 features people who suffer inexplicably: children, Nazirites, and perhaps also the unfortunate parents, who are driven to inhuman behavior due to the ravages of hunger. The image of the withered Nazirites leaves us bewildered, contributing to the overall tenor of the chapter.

However we understand the precise identity of the Nazirites, they appear to be leaders of the community. In contrast to the children, the leaders tend to be the last people affected by the ravages of famine. The Nazirites' starvation hints at impending doom. Jerusalem's demise looms.

Song of Songs

The health and beauty of the former residents of Jerusalem evoke a passage in Song of Songs in which the *Re'aya* describes the physique of her beloved *Dod* in splendid metaphoric detail:

> My Beloved is dazzling and ruddy (*tzaḥ ve'adom*)…his head is of fine gold (*ketem paz*)…his eyes are like doves on streams of water awash in milk (*beḥalav*)…his hands are rolls of gold (*zahav*)…his stomach is a tablet of ivory, inlaid with sapphires (*sapirim*). (Song. 5:10–14)

Remarkable linguistic overlap connects the idyllic image of the *Dod* with the noble former inhabitants of Jerusalem in Eikha 4. Both passages use three synonymous terms for gold (*zahav, ketem,* and *paz*), and both passages refer to precious stones, including sapphires. The radiance of these figures is indicated by the word *tzaḥ* (which I translate above as dazzling)[64] and identical words are deployed to indicate their red and

---

63. This is like the theological approach of chapter 2. Chapters 2 and 4 constitute parallel chapters, mirroring each other in tone, substance, and theological approach. I will develop this idea at the end of this chapter, and I will refer to it again when I discuss the overall structure of the book.

64. See BDB, *Lexicon*, 850.

shiny white hues (*adom* and *ḥalav*). The correlation indicates that these passages maintain similar perceptions of vigor and health, using familiar tropes to depict the ideal appearance.[65]

Rabbinic commentaries often interpret Song of Songs not as a human love story, but rather as one that develops between God and His nation. According to this reading, Song of Songs 5:10–16 describes God's radiance and glittering splendor.[66] Intriguingly, this schema suggests that the magnificent appearance of the Jerusalemites prior to the crisis mirrors God's splendor.[67] Jerusalem's noble residents once were the representatives of God's majesty.[68] This privileged position has its perils; when Jerusalem's residents cease to represent God properly, they are deemed unfit for this enviable role. At that point, the splendor of Jerusalem's citizens dissipates, their glory disappears, and their glimmering presence fades into shadows, replaced by a hollowed-out image of dulled, shriveled grandeur.

Eikha 4:9

טוֹבִים הָיוּ חַלְלֵי־חֶרֶב
מֵחַלְלֵי רָעָב

שֶׁהֵם יָזֻבוּ מְדֻקָּרִים
מִתְּנוּבֹת שָׂדָי

Better were the corpses [who died] from the sword
Than the corpses [who died] from famine

---

65. Similarly, Song of Songs 1:4–5 depicts unnaturally blackened skin in a negative manner, paralleling the attitude in Eikha 4:8.

66. Many of these descriptions of the *Dod* make their way into the medieval poem known as *Anim Zemirot* (*Shir HaKavod*), which is a sustained praise of God.

67. The word *sapir* (4:7) appears in several contexts that seem to describe God (Ex. 24:10; Ezek. 1:26). The metaphoric description of God in Daniel 7:9 also contains parallels to Eikha 4:7.

68. I Chronicles 29:23 presents King Solomon sitting on the throne of God. King Solomon becomes the manifestation of God's reign, and represents God's majesty. For similar ideas, see also I Chr. 17:14, 28:5; II Chr. 9:8.

For they flowed from punctures
From the produce in the field[69]

The word "better" (*tovim*; literally, "good") is an ironic opening for a verse where the "good" refers to those who died by the sword. In praising an instantaneous death, the verse reiterates the main point of verse 6. Any death is better than the prolonged suffering of starvation, even the violent annihilation of Sodom.[70]

Understanding the second half of the verse remains difficult. The context suggests that it portrays death by famine, although the description of the corpses "flowing from punctures" indicates a sword wound. The sentence appears to contain an ellipsis, an omitted word. Though typically one can discern the missing word from the context, in this sentence that presents a challenge. Thus, biblical commentaries offer different possible readings.

According to Rasag, the sentence focuses solely on the agonizing death by famine. He explains that the flow refers to a discharge produced by the body due to the absence of food. The puncture described in the verse functions as a simile, which Rasag would read: "They flow *as if* they had been pierced by the sword."[71] Similarly, Rashi explains that as the people starved, the smell of the enemies' roasting meat rose from the fields outside the besieged city. The smell would cause their bodies to respond (produce gastric juices), and their stomachs would distend and rupture.[72]

---

69. As we will see, this verse is extremely difficult to translate. The above translation reflects R. Yosef Kara's and R. Yeshayahu di Trani's approaches. While it offers a close translation of the words, it does not adequately convey the terrible starvation featured in this verse.

70. See Bava Batra 8b, which refers to this verse in explaining why death by famine is worse than death by sword.

71. In Rasag's reading, the missing word is *kemo*, expressing similarity. His reading does not reflect the traditional punctuation, which places a comma between the word "punctures" and "the produce of the field."

72. See Eikha Rabba 4:14. This approach does not require the addition of any word and does not adopt Rasag's explanation that the puncture is a simile. In this explanation, the word *medukarim* means the actual rupture of the stomach.

R. Yosef Kara also reads this as a description of the ghastly death of those who died by starvation. His explanation of the verse is that the starved populace ate copious amounts of inedible growth from the fields, causing their shrunken stomachs to burst. R. Yeshayahu di Trani likewise assumes that the inedible produce of the field led to their deaths. In his reading, their desperate need for food caused the starved population to eat roots and burrs that punctured their innards, causing internal bleeding.[73] In both of these readings, the verse is not elliptical, and reads: "Those who died by sword were better off than those who died by famine, for they flowed from punctures caused by the produce in the field."

Ibn Ezra reads the second part of the sentence as a description of death by the sword: "Those who died by sword were better off than those who died by famine, for [those who died by the sword] flowed from punctures, [but were satiated] by produce of the field." In this reading, those killed by the sword still went to their deaths with a full stomach, a fate far preferable to death by starvation.

Finally, we might divide the second sentence into two; the first part describes death by sword (parallel to the first part of sentence one) and the second describes death by famine (parallel to the second part of sentence one). This would produce the following translation: "Those who died by sword were better off than those who died by famine, for *they* flowed from punctures, while *they* died from lack of produce of the field."

Multiple readings offer various ways to explain the specifics of this verse. All agree, however, on its basic message: a quick death is preferable to death by starvation. To illustrate this point, the next verse will present the chapter's most appalling image, a scenario whose horror looms large in a book that overflows with dreadful images.

Eikha 4:10

יְדֵי נָשִׁים רַחֲמָנִיּוֹת
בִּשְּׁלוּ יַלְדֵיהֶן

---

73. See also *Targum* on this verse and the gloss in Rashi, presumably added by one of his students.

הָיוּ לְבָרוֹת לְמוֹ
בְּשֶׁבֶר בַּת־עַמִּי

The hands of compassionate women
Cooked their children

They were food for them
In the brokenness of the daughter of my people

A spare statement, the calm of this verse belies its madness, the emblem of an unbalanced world. Women consuming their children represent a cataclysm, the unraveling of society.[74] The verse dispassionately notes the collapse of the Judean populace, her utter brokenness (*shever bat ammi*).[75] Famine has drained Jerusalem of its moral fiber, and society moves inexorably toward its demise.[76]

Devoid of emotion, judgment, or pain, this verse creates striking dissonance between the subject matter and the detached description of it. This contrasts with Eikha 2:20, where Jerusalem howls in anguish,

---

74. Most midrashim (e.g., Eikha Rabba 2:23; Lekaḥ Tov Eikha 4:10) and biblical interpreters (e.g., Rashi, R. Yosef Kara, Ibn Ezra) assume that the cannibalism described in the book (here and in 2:20) is literal. However, Eikha Rabba 4:13 radically reinterprets this verse, such that the cannibalism did not take place. Hillers, 89, raises the possibility that the book presents cannibalism as a literary trope that describes the last dreadful state of the famine. Alternatively, he suggests that the book wants to illustrate the fulfillment of the curses of Deuteronomy 28.

75. The narrator employs the possessive form in referring to the nation (*bat ammi*, "daughter of my people"), which seems to suggest some type of emotional involvement. As we have noted, the narrator displays no emotion when he refers to Jerusalem as *bat ammi* in this chapter (4:3, 6, 10).

76. II Kings 6:24–30 recounts a similarly harrowing tale, in which women consume their children during a famine. Writers have often depicted how famine reduces people to a bestial existence. See, for example, Josephus's depiction of the famine when Jerusalem was besieged by the Romans during the Second Temple Era (*Wars of the Jews*: Book V, chapter 10, paragraph 3). Vasily Grossman offers one of the most evocative descriptions of the impact of famine that I have read, when he portrays the deliberate starvation that Stalin caused in the Ukraine in the 1930s. See Vasily Grossman, *Everything Flows*, trans. R Chandler, E. Chandler, and A. Aslanyan (New York: New York Review Books, 2009), 123–38.

furiously pointing an accusing finger at God: "Look Lord and see! To whom have You done this? When women consume their fruits, their well-nurtured children!" The narrator's detachment here conveys apathy; he appears unmoved by the terrible sights. How can the narrator present this horror in such an understated fashion?

Language is deemed inadequate to express the scope of the horror; the narrator may prefer to allow the reader to experience the scene without commentary. This dispiritedness may also be designed to mirror that of the hapless mothers who consume their children. Suffering spawns numbness, extinguishing the ability to muster up feeling. This links up with the other failings that we have encountered in this chapter due to the famine: callousness, alienation, and now apathy.

Womb (*Reḥem*) and Compassion (*Raḥamim*): A Wordplay

As noted earlier, the word *raḥamaniyot* (compassionate women) evokes the *reḥem* (womb), highlighting the inherent connection between motherhood and compassion.[77] A midrash notes this, basing itself on our verse:

> Why is the womb called a *reḥem*? Because it should produce compassion (*mitraḥem*). However, due to the terrible sins, that compassion transformed into cruelty, and she became cruel to her son, like a mongoose,[78] which bears and then eats her children... Therefore it says, "The hands of compassionate women cooked their children." (Midrash Aggada [Buber], Deuteronomy 1)

The womb lays the foundation for human compassion, as is evident from the etymology of the word *raḥamim*. In a stunning display of altruism, a mother shelters her child for nine months in her womb, nurturing, protecting, and sustaining her fetus with her body.[79]

---

77. See BDB, *Lexicon*, 938.
78. Although the mongoose has not cultivated a particular reputation for this behavior, feline carnivores (like the mongoose) have been seen killing and eating their young.
79. To the best of my knowledge, the only biblical narrative that describes a mother's compassion using the word *raḥamim* is I Kings 3:26.

Compassion, however, is not restricted to mothers. All people can cultivate compassion, whether or not they have a womb that has borne a child.[80] Once a child emerges from the womb, that child continues to require altruistic care and devotion, acts that cultivate compassion among anyone who participates – male and female. Fathers also appear as paradigms of compassion in Tanakh:

> As a father has compassion (*kiraḥem*) for his children, so does the Lord have compassion for those who fear Him. (Ps. 103:13)

Raising children teaches people to form relationships based on selflessness, commitment, and shared resources. The experience of childrearing fosters a unified society. It educates its members to overcome their innate self-centeredness and links them together in a shared quest to create an altruistic and robust community.[81]

The mothers' betrayal represents a flagrant inversion of normalcy, biological behavior gone awry. The dissolution of the maternal instinct indicates the implosion of human compassion.[82] As the basis for human relationships evaporates, society invariably collapses.

Where is God and where is His compassion in this chapter? In chapter 2, the image of women consuming their children causes Jerusalem to hurl an angry accusation at God (Eikha 2:20). Our verse lacks any such accusation. In fact, God has been noticeably absent from chapter 4, and will only surface to pour out His wrath upon the city in verse 11.

---

80. Biblical passages describe compassion between brothers (Gen. 43:30) and fellow humans (Zech. 7:9; Ps. 112:4), as well as among kings (Neh. 1:11), court officials (Dan. 1:9), and even formerly cruel captors (I Kings 8:50) or enemies (Jer. 42:12).

81. I am not claiming that only those who raise children attain these ideals, nor would I claim that everyone who raises children does so; rather, the basis of these ideals in a society stems from the extraordinary experience of bearing and nurturing life.

82. In a related (but not identical) manner, Sisera's mother twice employs the word *reḥem* as she gloats that her son surely rapes the women whom he captures (Judges 5:30). With this utterance, she seems to betray and violate her role as mother, abandoning any semblance of compassion.

The word *raḥamim* (ironically describing the women who cook their children) recalls the recent expressions of confidence in God's compassion from the previous chapter (Eikha 3:22, 32). Biblical passages generally associate *raḥamim* with God, whose compassion appears in Tanakh far more frequently than that of humans.[83] What has happened to divine compassion? In our verse, the mothers have discarded compassion; perhaps this indicates that God has as well.

> "The hands of compassionate women" – when Jeremiah saw this, he began to shout and cry before God. He said, "Master of the Universe, which nation has experienced troubles like these? Where is Your compassion? Where is Your kindness? Is it not written, 'For the Lord your God is a merciful God'? You turned compassion into cruelty; You stood up from the chair of compassion and sat [instead] on the chair of judgment."[84] (Midrash Aggada [Buber], Deuteronomy 1)

The dissipation of the mothers' compassion mirrors the dissipation of God's compassion. This idea gathers strength in the following verse. There, God pours out His fury against Jerusalem, igniting a fire that "consumes" the city's foundations. These verses juxtapose the scene in

---

83. God's compassion appears in dozens of contexts. The following is not a comprehensive list, but an attempt to show the breadth and scope of the idea. One of God's essential defining features is His compassion (Ex. 34:6; Deut. 4:31; II Sam. 24:14; Joel 2:13; Jonah 4:2; Ps. 86:15; 103:8; 111:4; 145:8–9), which He often extends to Israel (Deut. 30:3; II Kings 13:23; Is. 14:1; 49:10, 13; 54:7–10; Jer. 12:15; 30:18; 42:12; Ezek. 39:25; Hos. 2:21; Mic. 7:19; Zech. 10:6). Moreover, trust in God's compassion emerges as a foundational principle in prayer and petition (Ps. 40:12; 51:3; 69:17; 79:8; 103:5; 116:5; 119:156; Dan. 9:9, 18; Neh. 9:17, 19, 27–31). According to Kiddushin 30a, the central verse in the book of Psalms opens with the words, "And He is compassionate!" (Ps. 78:38), thereby underscoring the centrality of divine compassion in that book.

84. In the continuation of this midrash, God defends His actions, accusing Israel of sins that warrant this punishment: "The Holy Spirit responds to him and says to [Jeremiah]: Which nation…has acted as Israel has acted? 'When murdered in the Lord's sanctuary are the priest and prophet' (Eikha 2:20). By the measure of what people mete out, so it will be meted out to them."

which mothers cook their children with the depiction of God's fire that consumes Jerusalem. Compassion no longer arrives from its expected sources: neither from the mothers nor from God.

God's compassion for His nation has its limits. Prophets warned that God may withdraw His compassion from His nation, deliberately abandoning His natural inclination in order to punish them (e.g., Is. 9:16; Jer. 13:14; 16:15).[85] Divine punishment comes in the form of the cannibalism of the mothers, whose terrible plight has caused them to discard their innate compassion. This recalls Deuteronomy 28:53, where God warns Israel of the consequences of breaking the covenant:

> And you will eat the fruit of your womb, the flesh of your sons and daughters that the Lord your God has given you, in the siege and straits that your enemies have pressed against you. (Deut. 28:53)

The nation is now suffering the repercussions of abrogating their contract with God. While this does not mitigate the horror of the scene, it explains the absence of divine compassion, situating the events within a context of sin and punishment.[86]

Still, one searches for some remnant of divine compassion, a modicum of relief from this harsh predicament. Is it possible there is none to care for Israel, that Israel should no longer expect supererogatory love from God? Eikha 4 may not offer relief, but in his prophecies of consolation, Isaiah relates directly to this omission:

> And Zion said, "The Lord has forsaken me, and the Lord has forgotten me." Can a woman forget her child, [will she] have no compassion on the child of her womb? Even if *they* do forget, I

---

85. An essential component of God's compassion, stated at the outset (Ex. 33:19), is that God can bestow His compassion on whomever He chooses, without having to explain His decision.

86. Chapter 4 does not focus on the sinfulness or responsibility of the people. Nevertheless, the book maintains a consistent linguistic thread linking it to biblical passages indicating that these events are a consequence of ignored prophetic warnings and violations of the covenantal relationship with God.

will not forget you! I have engraved you on the palms [of My hands], your walls are always before Me. (Is. 49:14–15)

God's love is comparable to parental love in terms of its passion and commitment.[87] Yet, as we have seen, extenuating circumstances can cause human mothers to abandon their primal compassion. Nonetheless, the breakdown of human compassion does not spell the end of divine compassion. God may choose to withdraw His compassion in order to punish Israel. However, in this striking passage in Isaiah, God assures Zion that His compassion for His nation outweighs that of a biological mother; God's abiding commitment for His nation can never be abrogated.

Part 1 (Eikha 4:1–10): A Synopsis
The first half of chapter 4 (1–10) describes the heavy toll that famine exacts on society, both morally and physically. This section twice declares that other deaths (specifically that of Sodom and death by sword, but presumably meaning *any* death) are preferable to famine. The depictions of the starving city illustrate this point well, exhibiting the extensive damage that famine wreaks on society.

The effects of the famine are felt gradually as the chapter unfolds, mirroring the slow spread of starvation throughout Jerusalem. The suffering and demise of the vulnerable children occurs in the earliest stages (4:2–5). Unabated, the famine continues to plague the city, collecting victims until even the stronger members of society deteriorate and languish (4:7–8). The final verse (4:10) records the desperate straits of a city deep in the throes of utter starvation – only this can account for the incongruous act of women consuming their children.

Mothers and children frame the chapter's description of the famine, illustrating the unravelling of the city's compassion and moral fabric. At the opening of the chapter (4:1–5), Jerusalem's mothers neglect their

---

87. Jeremiah 31:19 compares God's compassion to the natural, instinctive one of a parent. Jeremiah does not clearly refer to a mother; some biblical commentaries (Radak, Metzudat David, Malbim) maintain that the verse refers to the connection between a father and a child.

once-valued children, refusing them even the most elemental care. At the conclusion of the section (4:10), the mothers pay attention to their children, but only as a means of sustenance.

Birth, motherhood, and nursing reverberate throughout this first section, underscoring their thematic centrality. Several scholars note the wordplay between *shever*, which means brokenness (4:10), and *mashber/mishbar* that alludes to birth, namely, the breach of the womb (e.g., II Kings 19:3; Hos. 13:13).[88] The difficult word "*ḥalu*" in verse 6 evokes the writhing pain and fear that accompanies birth (Is. 26:17–18; Mic. 4:9; Ps. 48:7).[89] Eikha 4:7 employs milk as a metaphor to evoke the healthy glow of the Nazirites. This links up to the image of the female jackal's breast, generously unsheathed to suckle her young, in contrast to the Judean mothers who cruelly resist nursing their parched children (4:3–4). Perhaps the word *saddai* (which I rendered "the field," but literally means "my fields") in 4:9 also evokes a wordplay with the *shad* (breast) of Eikha 4:3,[90] drawing a parallel between the field that sustains the population and the breast that sustains the infant. The betrayal of the mothers mirrors the betrayal of the land, whose produce no longer sustains her people. As hope for seed (food and children) rapidly fades, images of birth emerge, ironically recalling all that has been lost.

---

88. See BDB, *Lexicon*, 990–91; Berlin, 109. It is also noteworthy that the same word (*shever*) can allude to food, such as corn or grain, which must be broken (threshed) to eat (Gen. 42:1; 44:2; Amos 8:5; Neh. 10:32). Sometimes this word appears in a verbal form to mean the purchase of grain (Gen. 43:4; Deut. 2:6; Is. 55:1). The brokenness (*shever*) of the people in Eikha, therefore, also hints to the inability to obtain any food.

89. See the discussions on the various possible meanings of this word in Gordis, 189; Hillers, 80. See also Dobbs-Allsopp, 132, who notes the allusion to childbirth.

90. Some scholars believe that there could be an etymological connection between words written with the letter *shin* and those written with the *sin* (which use the same letter, even if they produce different sounds). Harris, *Canaanite Dialects*, 33–35, concludes that these two phonemes coincided in much of the Canaanite area, rendering an etymological connection such as this one possible. Another example is a proposed connection between the word *shevua* (oath) and the word *sava* (satiated). See Yael Ziegler, *Promises to Keep: The Oath in Biblical Narrative* (Leiden: Brill, 2008), 6.

A visceral section, Eikha 4:1–10 explicitly references many body parts in various states of health and corrosion. Hands, breast, tongue, palate, bone, limbs, skin – all draw our attention to the intense physicality of the chapter which, after all, conveys the physical effects of hunger. Famine dehumanizes, forcing people to focus on their bodily functions as they slowly deteriorate and fail.

Vivid imagery presents the famine in a series of snapshots, as one might paint an artistic piece, representing not every individual feature, but rather those that capture the moment, the emotion, and the horror. Images remain frozen in various contortions of agony: humans treated as earthenware pots, spilling onto the street and littering it with bodies; nursing mothers who indifferently turn their backs on their infants; children issuing anguished pleas for bread, to no avail; blackened faces and shrunken skin covering skeletal shadows of human forms; and near-corpses dying on the streets, joining those who have already expired from sword wounds and starvation.

The chapter partially alleviates the terrible scene by unexpectedly conjuring equally vibrant images from the past, of the world that the nation has lost. Viewed beyond the ghastly landscape of death, the past beckons, a bright memory that glitters and shines, providing a glimpse of a prosperous and pampered life, nearly forgotten in the current misery. From the heights of luxury, Jerusalem has collapsed into the pit of despair. Yet, by evoking the past, this terrible section offers a sliver of consolation to a nation steeped in degradation, briefly allowing the reader to recollect Jerusalem's former nobility.

PART 2 (EIKHA 4:11–20): DESTRUCTION AND EXILE

The second part of chapter 4 widens the lens, shifting from a close-up look at the famine and its human casualties to a general description of the city's destruction. It appears that the siege has ended, releasing the enemy into the city. Destruction follows rapidly; the city goes up in flames, which consume its foundations and force the survivors into exile. Jerusalem's refugees scatter and wander, continuously reliving the story of their chaotic final moments.

This second part of the chapter (verses 11–20) divides into two sections, based on the speaker. The first section (verses 11–16) continues the detached perspective of the narrator, whose calm demeanor clashes jarringly with the horror he describes. The narrator assigns responsibility for the carnage to God (verse 11) and to the nation's religious leaders (verse 13), without any accompanying outrage.

The second section of this part (verses 17–20) employs a first-person plural voice, summoning the community to describe the final, frantic moments of life in Judea, an account imparted with a rising pitch of anxiety and despair.

A. Verses 11–16: Third-person description
B. Verses 17–20: First-person plural description

Eikha 4:11–12

כִּלָּה ה׳ אֶת־חֲמָתוֹ
שָׁפַךְ חֲרוֹן אַפּוֹ

וַיַּצֶּת־אֵשׁ בְּצִיּוֹן
וַתֹּאכַל יְסוֹדֹתֶיהָ

לֹא הֶאֱמִינוּ מַלְכֵי־אֶרֶץ
כֹּל יֹשְׁבֵי תֵבֵל

כִּי יָבֹא צַר וְאוֹיֵב
בְּשַׁעֲרֵי יְרוּשָׁלָ͏ִם

The Lord completed His wrath
Spilled out the anger of His nostrils

He lit a fire in Zion
And it consumed her foundations

The kings of the land did not believe
[Nor did] all the inhabitants of the world

That an adversary and enemy would come
Into the gates of Jerusalem

Focusing primarily on human affairs, this entire chapter only twice refers to God.[91] These two references surround the account of the city's destruction (4:11–16), illustrating God's active role in the events. In His first appearance (4:11), God wrathfully demolishes the city, setting a fire to Zion. The narrator's tale of Jerusalem's destruction concludes as God scatters the nation before consciously averting His gaze (4:16).

The brief but intense report of Jerusalem's annihilation consists of just one verse (4:11), which appears to be an abridged version of the lengthy account in Eikha 2:1–10. Two expressions of anger attend God's actions, recalling God's intense fury of chapter 2. Both *hamato* (2:4) and *haron apo* (2:1, 3, 21, 22)[92] link to specific words in chapter 2; here, too, divine anger emerges as the primary cause of the catastrophic events. God's wrath spills over and erupts in a fiery conflagration, just as it did in 2:3–4, consuming (*vatokhal*) the physical infrastructure of the city (the word *akhela* describes the consuming fire in 2:3).

In an ironic reversal of chapter 3's declaration that God's compassions are never *completely* spent (*ki lo khalu*, 3:22), 4:11 depicts God *completely* pouring out His anger upon the city (*kila... et hamato*). Despite the optimistic tone that emerged in chapter 3, chapter 4 returns to describe the grim reality, one that bears little resemblance to the hope-filled center of the book.

God's explosive anger contrasts with the impassivity of both the narrator and Jerusalem's populace. The nation displays no discernible reaction to the violent destruction of her city. Those who survive wander blindly in the streets and out of the city, mutely enduring the taunts that follow their perambulations (verses 14–15).

Reactions from around the world fill the void created by the blank silence of Jerusalem's survivors. Kings of the land and citizens

---

91. A third mention of God in the chapter appears as part of the epithet for the leader (4:20): "anointed of the Lord."
92. Sometimes the word *af* appears without the full phrase, *haron af*.

of the world cannot believe that enemies have succeeded in penetrating Jerusalem's gates. Some scholars reject this description as historically improbable, suggesting that it is simply a literary trope employed to convey the scope of the shock and the presumed importance of the city.[93] Let me propose, however, that this reaction harks back to Sennacherib's failed attempt to conquer Jerusalem, an event that cast a mythological aura upon the sacred city. Sennacherib's military campaign was wildly successful and well publicized; yet, with all of his troops and military resources, he was unable to conquer Jerusalem.[94] Kings and civilians likely concluded that Jerusalem was inviolable, the special protectorate of God.[95] With Jerusalem's fall, it seemed that the inconceivable had occurred: Jerusalem's enemies had succeeded in penetrating the sacrosanct city, defying long-held beliefs, and leaving the world flabbergasted.

Eikha 4:13

מֵחַטֹּאת נְבִיאֶיהָ
עֲוֹנוֹת כֹּהֲנֶיהָ

הַשֹּׁפְכִים בְּקִרְבָּה
דַּם צַדִּיקִים

**On account of the sins of her prophets
The iniquities of her priests**

**Who spill out in her midst
The blood of the righteous**

An incomplete sentence, this verse opens with the causative *mem* ("*On account of* the sins of her prophets, the iniquities of her priests...")

---

93. See, for example, Berlin, 110; Provan, 116–17.

94. For more details on this event and its archaeological evidence, see the chapter above, "Historical Background."

95. See my explanation of Psalms 48:5–9 in the chapter "Historical Background."

linking it either backward to explain the destruction of the city (4:11),[96] or forward to explain why blind people wander in the streets, defiled by blood (4:14–15).[97]

Linguistically, both readings can be maintained. The word *shafakh* in our verse links the verse backward, to 4:11; God spilled out (*shafakh*) His anger on the city, *because* the priests and prophets spill out (*hashofekhim*) the blood of the righteous in her midst.[98] Blood (*dam*) links our verse to the one that follows it. The copious blood shed by the religious leaders (4:12) anticipates the scene in the following verse, in which blood contaminates the blind people who wander the street. Carefully placed between verses 11 and 13, our verse likely functions in a dual capacity; harking backward and forward to explain both the destruction of the city and the bloody desecration of its unseeing pedestrians.

This verse flatly blames the religious leaders, denouncing both priests and prophets.[99] By featuring the iniquities of the leadership, the chapter shifts our attention away from the general populace.[100] Like chapter 2, chapter 4 avoids highlighting the people's guilt, possibly alluding to it (tangentially) in verse 6,[101] and again at the chapter's conclusion,

---

96. See R. Yosef Kara, Eikha 2:13.

97. See Dobbs-Allsopp, 133.

98. The word *shafakh* also links to the description of the precious stones (a metaphor for the children) that spill (*tishtapekhna*) onto the streets of Jerusalem in 4:1. This linkage suggests that that horror also derives from the behavior of the religious leaders, who spill (*hashofekhim*) the blood of innocents. The word *shafakh* constitutes a *leitwort* in the book, appearing seven times in total, mostly in the context of death, fury, and carnage. This word only appears in chapters 2 and 4, creating a linguistic connection between those chapters.

99. This resembles Eikha 2:14. The similarities between chapters 2 and 4 continue to accumulate, coalescing to form a collaboration of thought, ideas, and language.

100. In contrast, House, 444, maintains that similar to chapters 1, 2, and 3, this passage lays the responsibility "at the feet of a sinning people." I propose that chapters 1 and 5, which hold the general populace accountable, differ from chapters 2 and 4, which lay the primary responsibility at the feet of the leaders. I will discuss this and other distinguishing features of these pairs of chapters in an upcoming chapter: "The Structure of Eikha: Faith in a Turbulent World."

101. As noted previously, some biblical interpreters understand the words *avon* and *ḥatat* in 4:6 as references not to sin, but rather to punishment. Even if one does interpret

which deviates from the general tone of the chapter. The absence of the populace's guilt links up with the righteous who suffer inexplicably in the chapter (children too young to have known sin, ascetic Nazirites pure as white snow, the righteous) to form the theological backdrop of this chapter. In contrast to the tension and outrage expressed in chapter 2, the atmosphere of chapter 4 remains oddly expressionless in reaction to the injustice. Paralysis sweeps through the dulled city, which lacks the energy to protest even the most profoundly disturbing events.

Murder or Metaphor?

Although priests and prophets do not work in tandem in a formal sense, they occasionally appear as a team due to their shared role as religious leaders, banding together to promote common goals.[102] More often, however, biblical passages link priests and prophets as the subjects of prophetic castigations[103] and shared punishment.[104] Positioned as the nation's religious leaders, they share responsibility when things go wrong. The power of their office can corrupt, allowing both prophets and priests the opportunity to engage in unscrupulous behavior.

Eikha 4:13 flings a scathing accusation at these religious leaders, censuring them for spilling the blood of righteous innocents. Do the priests and the prophets commit actual murder? Perhaps this accusation refers to a specific event. In Jeremiah 26, when the prophet speaks of the Temple's possible destruction, the priests and prophets seize Jeremiah, declaring that he deserves death (26:1–9). Some sort of trial ensues, in which these priests and prophets play the role of Jeremiah's prosecutors, insisting that he receive a death sentence (26:11). The officers and the people defend Jeremiah (24:16), who ultimately survives due to the actions of Aḥikam ben Shafan (26:24). The role of the priests and prophets in this incident, and their insistence that the

---

the words as referring to Israel's sins, the purpose of that verse is more to bemoan Israel's punishment than to condemn its sinfulness.

102. See I Kings 1:32, 45; II Kings 23:2; Zechariah 7:3.

103. See Isaiah 28:7; Jeremiah 2:26; 23:1; 32:32; Zephaniah 3:4.

104. See Jeremiah 4:9; 14:18.

innocent prophet be sentenced to death, may account for the accusation in our verse.[105]

More likely, our verse does not refer to a specific event. Even if they do not actually shed blood, the priests and prophets are held responsible for allowing violence to spread in Jerusalem. A hundred and fifty years earlier, Micah described the corruption in Jerusalem, castigating these leaders for unscrupulous leadership that led to bloodshed:

> Listen to this, leaders of the House of Jacob and officers of the House of Israel, who loathe justice and twist all that is straight. [You have] built Zion with *bloodshed* and Jerusalem with perversion. Her leaders judge for bribes, and her *priests* teach for pay, and her *prophets* prophesy for money and on the Lord they rely, saying, "Is not the Lord in our midst?[106] No harm shall come to us!" (Mic. 3:9–11)

When Jerusalem's leaders neglect their duties, society no longer functions in a viable manner, occasioning bloodshed.[107] Ezekiel describes Jerusalem as a city of blood, filled with abominations and depravity.[108] While he does not specifically blame the priests and the prophets for

---

105. It seems unlikely that this is an isolated incident. During the course of the chapter, we learn of a previous incident, in which the king Jehoakim kills Uriyahu the prophet for a similar offense (Jer. 26:20–23). While that incident does not explicitly mention the involvement of the priests and prophets, its appearance as part of the account of Jeremiah's trial hints at their culpability. It is unclear whether the priests and prophets acted out of a sincere belief that Jeremiah blasphemed God. Other passages indicate that corruption was rampant among this leadership elite, who acted with political expedience so as to maintain their popularity (see Jer. 6:13–15; 8:10–12).

106. This verse reflects a prevailing attitude among Jerusalem's inhabitants, who believe that because God dwells in Jerusalem's Temple no evil can affect Jerusalem. Jeremiah rails against this notion (see Jer. 7:1–15), which seems to gain traction following the miraculous salvation of Jerusalem from Sennacherib's siege.

107. See Jeremiah 2:34; 7:6; Ezekiel 22:1–16; 33:25–29.

108. Ezekiel 22:1–16; 23:31.

this, he does single out both prophet[109] and priest[110] for their involvement in defiling the land.

In several biblical passages, God decrees destruction upon Judah and Jerusalem in the wake of Manasseh's long, corrupt reign.[111] The Judean king's depravities include idolatry and mass murder. Manasseh spills so much innocent blood in Jerusalem that it fills the streets, a literal or metaphoric description of a polluted city. Two separate verses link God's decree of Jerusalem's destruction to the innocent blood (*dam naki*) that Manasseh spilled (*shafakh*) in Jerusalem (II Kings 21:16; 24:4). These acts echo linguistically in our verse (*shofekhim* and *dam tzaddikim*). Although the Tanakh does not blame the priests and prophets during Manasseh's reign, our verse may suggest that the religious leaders bear (perhaps indirect) responsibility for the king's actions.[112] Indeed, the job of the religious leadership (especially the prophets) is to censure when necessary.

Instead of guiding the people to repentance, the prophets and priests flatter the errant nation, offering them false messages of security and complacency:[113]

> From the youth until the adults, all greedily take profits, and from *prophet* to *priest*, all engage in falsehood. And they repair the brokenness of My people glibly, saying, "Peace! Peace!" And there is no peace. [They should] be ashamed! For they have committed abominations. But they are not ashamed, they do not know embarrassment. Therefore, they will fall among the fallen when I punish them; they will fail, says the Lord. (Jer. 6:13–15)[114]

---

109. Ibid. 22:24, 28.

110. Ibid. 22:25.

111. See II Kings 23:26; 24:3–4; Jeremiah 15:4.

112. Jehoakim also spills innocent blood, according to Jeremiah 22:17.

113. See Jeremiah 2:8; 5:31. Eikha 2:14 similarly assigns responsibility to the prophets for their failure to castigate the people for their sins and induce them to repent.

114. See, similarly, Jeremiah 23:11.

The religious leadership could have averted disaster. Instead, they assure their constituents that everything is fine, that "no harm shall come upon you" (Jer. 23:17), thus preventing the nation from repenting. In this way, prophets and priests bear responsibility for the massacre of innocents and the carnage wrought upon the city.

Eikha 4:14–15

נָעוּ עִוְרִים בַּחוּצוֹת
נְגֹאֲלוּ בַּדָּם

בְּלֹא יוּכְלוּ
יִגְּעוּ בִּלְבֻשֵׁיהֶם

סוּרוּ טָמֵא קָרְאוּ לָמוֹ
סוּרוּ סוּרוּ אַל־תִּגָּעוּ

כִּי נָצוּ גַם־נָעוּ
אָמְרוּ בַּגּוֹיִם לֹא יוֹסִפוּ לָגוּר

The blind wander in the streets
Polluted by blood

So that no one is able
To touch their clothing

"Turn aside, impure one!" they call to them
"Turn aside, turn aside, do not touch!"

As they flee and wander
The nations say, "Let them not continue to dwell [here]!"

A vivid portrait, the verse first focuses our attention on the blood that desecrates the blind people, staining them so thoroughly that no one can bear to touch their clothing. Jerusalem's bloodstained populace have fallen victims to a myriad of atrocities wrought by violent enemies, who maim and kill, saturating the city with blood.

The blood that pollutes the city is not simply a consequence of the enemies' butchery, but also alludes to the defilement caused by sin.[115] Continuing the trajectory of the previous verse, in which Jerusalem's religious leaders spill the blood of righteous innocents, verse 14 describes blood overflowing into the streets of the city. Read metaphorically, the polluting "blood" alludes to a noxious atmosphere in the sacred city. Steeped in iniquity, the streets of Jerusalem soil those who walk there.[116]

To describe the aftermath of the destruction, verse 14 focuses on the blind individuals who pick their way through the bloody streets of the city. Contaminated by blood, no one wants to touch their clothing or approach them. A hostile voice deflects the repulsive itinerants, repeating the alienating call "*Suru!*" ("Turn aside!") three times in rapid succession. Driven forward by the unidentified voice, the sightless ramblers wander, suddenly finding themselves among the nations. An apt description of the aimless movement toward exile, the evacuees flee, drift, and roam.[117] Arriving at an unnamed place, the exiles hear the dogged rejection of "the nations," who univocally proclaim that these contaminated refugees will not be permitted even a temporary residence.

The vague and surreal quality of the tale, which offers some gruesome details while remaining elliptical in so many others, tenders a remarkably lifelike portrayal of the muddled and dazed journey from a ruined city to an unwelcoming diaspora. The account leaves the reader with more questions than answers, as it withholds basic information that could clarify and sharpen the scene.

---

115. For a similar metaphoric meaning of impurity, see Isaiah 64:5. See also Numbers 35:33–34 and Ezekiel 22:1–31, where bloodshed and sins contaminate the land.

116. The context of Isaiah 59:3, which employs an identical phrase, *nego'alu vadam*, "polluted by blood," indicates that the primary meaning of the phrase is not literal but figurative, a reference to Israel's iniquities. We will soon examine this chapter at greater length.

117. In the above description, I have conflated two possible understandings of the word *natzu*, both related to the word "feather." As I will suggest below, it appears that the word depicts either a bird in flight or the drifting motion of the feather in the wind.

Who are the blind people wandering the streets, soiled by blood? Why does the scene immediately focus upon them in the aftermath of the destruction? Perhaps the verse features them because they are the most conspicuous of the wounded. Blinded by the enemy, who also blind the city's king, Zedekiah (II Kings 25:7), these hapless victims constitute visible evidence of the butchery that has taken place in the city. The enemy has not even bothered to exile them. Disregarded as potential threats because of their recently imposed handicap, they are left to forage the streets of the city, alone and bloodied, vulnerable and dazed.

Ibn Ezra suggests that this blindness is not literal, but rather a description of the manner in which residents wander dazed through the streets.[118] Blindness evokes tentative and fumbling movements, and can be a metaphor for confusion and lack of understanding.[119]

Blindness can also be employed as a metaphor for a corrupt nation, who do not see truth or justice.[120] Isaiah berates a corrupt nation, in a depiction that has some striking linguistic similarities to our passage in Eikha:

> Your transgressions have separated between you and your God, and your sins have made Him hide His face from listening. For your hands *are polluted with blood*, and your fingers with transgressions, your lips have spoken falsehood and your tongue utters perversions... They rush to *spill innocent blood*, their thoughts filled with wickedness, plundering and brokenness litter their routes. They know not peaceful ways and there is no justice in the circuits; they pervert their pathways; all who tread them know no peace. Therefore, justice is far from us and righteousness cannot reach us; we hope for light and there is darkness, for brightness,

---

118. See also Rasag, Eikha 2:14.

119. See, for example, Deuteronomy 28:29. Consider also the textual presentation of Isaac's blindness as an introduction to the narrative in which Isaac attempts to give the blessing to Esau (Gen. 27:1), or the way in which Eli's blindness conveys his obliviousness (I Sam. 3:2).

120. Exodus 23:8 notes metaphorically that bribes can "blind those who can see," and cause the perversion of justice. See also Rashi's explanation of Isaiah 35:5; 56:10.

but we walk in gloom. We grope the wall *like blind people,* and we fumble as though we have no eyes, we stumble in the afternoon, as if in darkness. (Is. 59:1–3, 7–10)

Prophets also employ blindness as a metaphor for the nation in exile, referring to the absence of God, and the consequent lack of clarity or guidance.[121] Those who blindly wander Jerusalem's streets have begun their inexorable movement toward exile, with its attendant darkness and disorientation.[122]

However we understand the blindness, it emerges as an appropriate punishment for a myopic nation who have heedlessly ignored God's instructions:

I will bring distress on the people and they will walk like blind people, for they have sinned to the Lord. (Zeph. 1:17)

Following the above analysis, we can offer several possibilities for the specific identity of the blind people. They may represent the general population of Jerusalem, the miserable survivors of the carnage.[123] They may be the errant leaders of the previous verse (prophets and priests), who are saturated with the blood of innocents.[124] These erstwhile religious guides now blindly wander the city, a fitting demotion for the sinful prophets or seers,[125] who failed to educate their constituents to see properly.[126] Contamination and impurity saturate their clothing, an apt end for the priests who failed to wear the priestly

---

121. See Isaiah 35:3–10; 42:7; 43:8; and Radak on Isaiah 35:5.
122. While the verse does not explicitly state that the streets in which the blind wander are Jerusalem's, it seems unlikely that these unidentified *ḥutzot* are anything else. Nevertheless, by the conclusion of 4:15, these blind people find themselves among the nations (presumably in exile), although it remains unclear how and when they got there.
123. See Hillers, 90; Dobbs-Allsopp, 133.
124. See Westermann, 202; Berlin, 111; House, 444–45.
125. Prophets are sometimes called *ha'roeh,* "the seer" (I Sam. 9:9).
126. In a similar context, Radak and Ibn Ezra explain Isaiah 56:10 as a description of the false prophets, who are meant to see but are actually blind.

vestments in holiness and failed to infuse the people with sanctity and purity.[127]

Recoil from the blood-drenched clothes of the blind gives way to an explicit cry, "Turn aside, impure one!" Who speaks these words: enemies or compatriots, accomplices or innocent observers? These disembodied words seem ambiguous in tone: Is this a jeer, a yelp, a shriek? Does it emerge from pity, disgust, fear, or shock? Initially it appears that solicitous passersby or compatriots speak these words, warning others to be alert to the impurities in the city;[128] yet the words grow more intense, sounding increasingly strident and antagonistic.[129] The speaker shrilly repeats the word *"suru"* twice more, followed by a panicked exclamation, "Do not touch!" Rapid movement follows; suddenly these polluted undesirables find themselves immersed within the nations who also speak, their words mingling with the rebuff of the unidentified speakers. The nations leave no doubt as to their hostile intentions; rejecting the wretched wanderers, they firmly announce, "Let them not continue to dwell [here]!"

The verse does not offer a clear picture, suggesting that the journey into exile does not develop in a sequential or methodical fashion. Two words describe movement: *natzu* (which appears to be related to the word feather, to a bird in flight or the drift of the feather)[130] and *na'u* (wander – a word that also appears in the

---

127. Ezekiel 22:26 castigates the priests sharply for shirking their duties: "Her priests did violence to My teachings, and they violated My holiness, they did not distinguish between sacred and profane and they did not teach [the distinction] between pure and impure, and they closed their eyes to My Sabbath, and I have been profaned amongst them."

128. This evokes the call of the leper in Leviticus 13:45, which seems to be good advice for those who surround him; he most certainly does not speak these words to abase himself. As noted in our comments on Eikha 1:1, Leviticus 13:46 contains a striking parallel to Eikha 1:1, drawing another connection between a nation tainted by impurities and the impurity of the leper. See also Eikha Rabba Petiḥta 21.

129. The *Targum's* translation of Eikha 4:15 suggests that the nations speak these words in a hostile tone.

130. Ibn Ezra and BDB, *Lexicon*, 663. An alternate understanding relates the word to the root *notz*, meaning ruin or destruction (e.g., Is. 37:26; Jer. 2:15). Based

previous verse).[131] The exiles appear to both flee and drift, reflecting a muddled state, a panicked and aimless journey, whose destination matters little.[132] One thing about the journey seems clear: the cacophony of background voices resonates with antipathy, relentlessly pursuing the exiled nation as they wander. Harsh words confront them whenever they approach, thrusting them toward their next unknown destination. The exiles are untouchable and unwelcome; defilement clings to them.

The refugees will eventually wash their bloodstained clothing, but the notoriety of their contamination accompanies them on their wanderings. Nations recoil from this community, beset by troubles, and stained by the ignominious repute of their sin-filled city. Tainted, moreover, by God's rejection, the exiled community bears its disgrace heavily, haunted by the revulsion that it encounters.

Israel's defiled state does not exempt the nations from responsibility for their despicable behavior. The rejection by the diaspora countries encapsulates the tragic essence of Israel's exile, one that continues to unfold over the course of Jewish history. The nation of Israel wanders and are often banished unceremoniously by the locals, in an echo of the sentence, "Let them not continue to dwell here!"

This is an alarmingly accurate verse; from our historical vantage point, we can identify the taunting nations with chilling certainty. Alexandria utters these words in 415. Mainz in 1012. France in 1182, 1254,

---

on his understanding of the *Targum* on Leviticus 1:16, Rashi maintains that this word signifies filth, parallel to the word *nego'alu* in 4:14. See Rashi there and on Zevaḥim 65a. Nahmanides on Leviticus 1:16 disagrees with Rashi's understanding, explaining our verse in a manner similar to that of Ibn Ezra. Eikha Rabba 4:18 (and R. Yosef Kara) relates this to the word *naatz*, meaning to anger, explaining that the verse provides a theological explanation for the exile as it occurs: "For they angered God."

131. As in the case of Cain, the punishment for bloodshed is wandering (*na*); this word appears twice in the story of Cain (Gen. 4:12 14) and twice in Eikha 4:14–15.

132. Isaiah offers a similar description in reverse, of two divergent versions of the exiles' journey home (Is. 60:8): "Who are these who fly like a cloud, like doves to their cotes?" The exiles will return both on a cloud, which randomly blows them toward their land, and like doves, whose instinctive desire to return to their homes drives them directly toward their targeted destination.

1322, 1359, and 1394. Naples in 1288. England in 1290. Bern in 1392. Upper Bavaria in 1276 and 1442. Warsaw, Lithuania, and Sicily in 1483. Spain in 1492. Portugal in 1496. Brandenburg in 1410. Nuremberg in 1499. Frankfurt in 1614. Prague in 1542 and 1561. Germany in 1935.[133]

The nations' rejection, while demoralizing, ultimately preserves Israel's distinctive character, preventing them from assimilating into their environment. Isaiah 59 linguistically evokes Eikha 4:14–15 in a bid to return Israel from its exile:

> Burst out and sing together, ruins of Jerusalem! For the Lord has consoled His nation, redeemer of Jerusalem. The Lord exposed His holy arm in the sight of all the nations, and all of the gathered of the earth will see the salvation of our God! "Turn aside, turn aside (*suru, suru*), go out of there, do not touch impurity (*tamei, al tiga'u*)! Go out of [the diaspora],[134] cleanse yourself, oh bearers of the vessels of the Lord!" (Is. 52:9–11)

According to the book of Isaiah, the Judean community is not permanently stained by impurity. If they wish to reacquire purity and become the bearers of God's vessels, Israel must leave the impure diaspora and return to their land, bearing the Temple's holy vessels. Thus, they can reassume their position as the nation consecrated to God, one that bears God's message of holiness to the world.

Jerusalem's Streets (*Ḥutzot*)

This chapter features snapshots of public ruin, emphasizing Jerusalem's streets: precious jewels strewn on every street corner, former nobility languishing and dying on the streets, shadows of human figures roaming the streets, unrecognizable in their withered starvation, and finally, blind people aimlessly wandering the streets, defiled and ashamed. The word *ḥutzot* appears four times in this chapter, a chapter that violates

---

133. This is an abridged list, intended to offer a general impression of the scope of the phenomenon.
134. See Rashi and Radak on Isaiah 52:11.

basic human privacy and turns people out of their houses to die publicly, disgracefully, and anonymously.[135]

The public scene obtains theological significance when we recall that Jeremiah decries the rampant idolatry,[136] injustice,[137] and evil[138] that pervade Jerusalem's streets (*ḥutzot*). For that reason, God pronounces a sentence of public death upon Jerusalem's residents:

> And the nation to whom the [false prophets] prophesy shall be flung into the streets (*ḥutzot*) of Jerusalem from starvation and the sword, and there will be no burial for these, for them or for their wives, or for their sons and daughters, and I will spill upon (*shafakhti*) them their evils. (Jer. 14:16)

It is fitting that a nation that sins publicly and without shame dies disgracefully on the streets. Employed both to describe their sins and their punishment, the word *ḥutzot* hints at the justice of the nation's end.

This understanding can inspire Israel's repentance (Jer. 33:8), followed by a vision of restored vivacity and joy in the streets (*ḥutzot*) of Jerusalem:

> So says the Lord, "There will yet be heard in this place about which you say 'It is destroyed; there are no humans and there are no beasts in the cities of Judah and in the streets (*ḥutzot*) of Jerusalem'... [You shall yet hear] sounds of festivity and sounds of joy, sounds of the groom and sounds of the bride, a voice saying, 'Praise the Lord of hosts, for the Lord is good, for His kindness is eternal!' as they bring thanksgiving sacrifices to the House of the Lord. For I shall restore the captives of the land as they once were," says the Lord. (Jer. 33:10–11)

---

135. Chapter 2 offers similar public scenes of people languishing and dying in the streets. In that chapter, two different words represent the streets: the word *ḥutzot* appears twice (2:19, 21) and the word *reḥovot* twice (2:11, 12).

136. Jeremiah 7:17; 44:17, 21.

137. Ibid. 5:1.

138. Ibid. 44:9.

Employed variously to describe Jerusalem's sins, punishment, and promises of restoration, the word *hutzot* offers a sweeping view of the city's turbulent but ultimately propitious history. Jeremiah's hopeful prophecy serves as the basis for the seventh blessing recited at a wedding, a prayer that today echoes through the wedding halls that cram Jerusalem's streets: "Soon, Lord our God, let there be heard in the cities of Judah and in the streets (*hutzot*) of Jerusalem, sounds of festivity and sounds of joy, sounds of the groom and sounds of the bride!"

Eikha 4:16

פְּנֵי ה' חִלְּקָם
לֹא יוֹסִיף לְהַבִּיטָם

פְּנֵי כֹהֲנִים לֹא נָשָׂאוּ
וּזְקֵנִים לֹא חָנָנוּ

The Lord's face scattered them
He did not continue to look at them

The faces of priests, they did not lift up
And to the elders, they did not show favor

God enters for the second time in this chapter, scattering Jerusalem's residents further into exile.[139] God's action (*lo yosif lehabitam*) recalls the words of the nations (*lo yosifu*), who rebuff the exiled community in the previous verse. In turning His face away from the Jerusalemites, God intensifies their experience of alienation; even their God refuses contact with them. Moreover, by withholding His guidance, their sightlessness worsens. The disgrace of the priests in this verse likewise hampers the nation's ability to obtain purity, submerging them more deeply in a state of contamination. This verse exacerbates the alienation, blindness, and impurity of the exiles found in previous verses.

---

139. For this meaning of the word *hillekam* ("scattered them"), see Genesis 49:7.

What does it mean that God's face scattered them? Several biblical passages feature God's face in a punitive context (Lev. 20:3, 6; 26:17; Ezek. 14:8). For this reason, some interpreters explain the phrase to mean His anger, an emotion evident on people's faces.[140] The phrase may simply refer to divine attention, which, when turned toward a sinner, results in punishment:

> The Lord's face is against those who do evil, to obliterate their memory from the earth. (Ps. 34:17)

During the siege of Jerusalem, Jeremiah warns Zedekiah:

> "For I have placed My face against this city, for evil and not for good," says the Lord. It shall be given into the hands of the king of Babylonia and it shall be burned by fire. (Jer. 21:10)

After the incident of the golden calf, God explains the danger of maintaining His presence among a sinful nation:

> And the Lord said to Moses, "Say to the children of Israel: You are a stiff-necked nation; [if for] one instant I will go up in your midst, I will destroy you." (Ex. 33:5)

This can help us better understand God's warning that, under extreme circumstances, He will hide His face from His nation, abandoning them to their fate (Deut. 31:16–18; 32:20). In the above examination of Eikha 1:9, I posited that this disciplinary action contains an underlying kindness. When God gazes directly at sinful humans, punishment follows, swift and sweeping. An intimate "face to face" relationship has its perils, necessitating extra vigilance. When people are behaving sinfully,

---

140. See Ibn Ezra on Eikha 4:16, who employs the elliptical reference to *paneha* (her face) in I Samuel 1:18 as a proof text that the word can mean anger. Although Hannah's anguish seems to predominate over her anger, the narrative refers to Penina's attempt to goad Hannah to anger in I Samuel 1:6–7, while Hannah refers to her own anger in I Samuel 1:16.

it is far preferable that God turn His face away, thereby preventing the inevitable disciplinary action.

Repeatedly in Eikha, God's elusiveness gives rise to the speaker's painful sense of abandonment, provoking his evocative cry: "Look Lord (*re'eh*) and see (*vehabita*)!" Variations of this plea surface in chapter 1 (verses 9 and 11), chapter 2 (verse 20), chapter 3 (verses 59, 60, 63), and chapter 5 (verse 1). Only chapter 4 deviates from this standard request, refraining from addressing God at all.

Eikha 4:16 can explain the reason for this omission. The consequences of God's attentions resonate with horrifying impact, as "God's face" flings away the wretched exiles, scattering them to far-flung places. Instead of requesting God's attentions, the verse offers a welcome respite from them, stating that, "He did not continue to look at them (*lehabitam*)." Chapter 4 avoids any attempt to reverse this situation, fearing that God's further attention could destroy the nation. Instead of repairing its relationship with God, in chapter 4 the nation prefers to focus inward. Alone and isolated from God, Israel tends to its wounds and maintains its tenuous survival among the nations until it is ready to reinstate intimacy with God without danger of destruction.

The Priestly Blessing

The priestly blessing simulates the experience of encountering God *panim el panim*.[141] As the priests face the nation, they utter the three sentences that God instructs them to say, invoking God to turn His face to the community in blessing (Num. 6:24–26):

> The Lord shall bless you and guard you.
> The Lord shall shine *His face* upon you and give you favor.
> The Lord shall lift up *His face* to you and bestow upon you peace.

This blessing conjures an ideal situation, in which God's "face" confers bounty and harmony upon His nation, whose faces are upturned to the priests to receive God's blessings.

---

141. See Sotah 38a and Maimonides, *Hilkhot Tefilla* 14:7, 11.

Yet, 4:13 depicts sinful priests, who fail to carry out their tasks faithfully. The priestly blessing subsequently vanishes, along with any semblance of purity, leadership, or religious integrity. The "face to face" blessing malfunctions in our verse, where the word "face" appears twice: God's face punishes the people and the priests' faces suffer a tragic fate.

Several intriguing references to the elusive priestly blessing crop up in our verse.[142] In a linguistic reversal of the final sentence of the priestly blessing ("The Lord shall lift up [*yisa*] His face"), the verse declares that no one "lifts up" (*nasa'u*) the priests' faces. Instead of God conferring favor upon His nation (*viḥuneka*), the verse maintains that no one shows favor (*ḥananu*) to the elders. Blending seamlessly into the grim portrait of divine abandonment, the priestly blessing flickers and disappears; as God withdraws His blessing, Israel sinks deeper into the morass of its defilement.

Ambiguous Language:
Who Dishonors the Priests and Elders?

The second half of the verse lacks a subject, leaving ambiguous the identity of those who disrespect the priests and the elderly. Possible culprits range from the nation to the enemy to God. The widely disparate options illustrate the richness of Eikha's poetry, which allows readers to encounter significantly different readings of the same verse.

Some interpreters understand the culprit to be Israel.[143] Why, in fact, does God scatter the people? According to this understanding, God's action is a response to the nation's flagrant insolence toward the consecrated priests and esteemed elders. Linguistically, this reading obtains support from the word *penei*, which appears twice in this verse. The first appearance describes God's face scattering the nation into exile, while its second appearance describes the dishonored faces of the priests, an egregious act committed by a nation that receives its punishment.

---

142. Scholars note that the priestly blessing crops up frequently in biblical passages, most notably in the book of Psalms. See for example, L. Liebreich, "The Songs of Ascent and the Priestly Blessing," *JBL* 74 (1955), 33–36; M. Fishbane, "Form and Reformulation of the Biblical Priestly Blessing," *JAOS* 103 (1983), 115–21. See also Angel, *Haggai, Zechariah, and Malachi*, 128–29.

143. See Rashi on Eikha 4:16.

Why does Israel no longer respect its priests and elders? This may be a result of the leaders' own behavior. Alternatively, it shows the breakdown of societal norms. Veneration of the religious leadership derives from their role in society. The priests deserve reverence due to their public tasks, performed on behalf of the nation in the Temple. When the nation no longer honors its priests, this signifies the nation's disregard for Temple worship and for service of God.

The stature of elders varies from one culture to another. Care for the elderly depends upon compassion, and respect depends upon appreciation of accumulated wisdom. A rabbinic homily suggests that the word *zaken* (elder) is an acronym for the phrase *"Zeh kana ḥokhma,"* "This one has acquired wisdom."[144] To ensure that society accords them proper respect, Leviticus 19:32 mandates veneration of the elderly: "You shall rise before the aged and you shall honor the face of the elderly." Our verse portrays the violation of this directive; no one shows favor to the elderly. In a society lacking compassion or respect for the other, the weaker members of society suffer from the neglect of those who should care for them. This chapter features society's failure to care properly for its vulnerable members, both young and old.

Some biblical interpreters maintain that this describes the havoc that the *enemies* wreak on society.[145] In this reading, the second half of the verse describes what occurs *after* God scatters the people, when the enemies do not behave with respect toward their victims. This reading finds support in Eikha 5:12, where the actions of the marauding enemies include a description of their mistreatment of the elderly: "The faces of the elderly, they did not honor." The similarity between these verses suggests that both refer to the same villain who disrespects the vulnerable aged – namely, the enemy.

This approach obtains further confirmation from Deuteronomy 28:49–50, where God ominously warns Israel of the consequences of violating the terms of their covenant with God:

---

144. See, for example, Kiddushin 32b; *Sifra, Kedoshim* 3:7; *Seder Olam Rabba* 30; Ruth Zuta [Buber] 4:2.
145. *Targum Eikha* 4:16; Moshkovitz, 35–36; House, 446; Gordis, 193.

The Lord shall bring against you a nation from afar... an audacious nation, *who will not lift up the face of the elderly* and will not
show favor to the young.

God cautions Israel that, if they sin, an enemy nation will arrive who will
not "lift up the faces" (*lo yisa fanim*) or "show favor" (*yaḥon*) to their
victims. Our verse fulfills that threat: the priests' faces are not lifted up
(*lo nasa'u*) and the elderly are not shown favor (*lo ḥananu*), presumably by the enemy.

Although plural verbs describe the perpetrators of this dis-
respectful behavior, God may be the subject of the entire verse.[146]
First, God scatters His nation, and then He disgraces her priests and
elders. This is an act of divine justice, wrought upon sinful leaders.
Indeed, the priests have brought this upon themselves, as is evident
from the blood that they shed in Eikha 4:13. While Eikha does not
feature the sins of the elders, Ezekiel often depicts them as evildoers
who flout their role as wise counselors and caretakers of tradition
(14:1–8; 20:2–4).[147]

In the final analysis, the identity of the one who brings this ruin
upon the priests and prophets matters less than the result. This chapter draws our attention to the unravelling of Jerusalem's leaders. In the
span of a few short verses, prophets and priests foster terrible violence,
and priests and elders forfeit their honor. Ezekiel 7:26 features prophets,
priests, and elders as the triumvirate who are the source of all wisdom.
Their current downfall represents the foundering of leadership. Lacking
guidance, hierarchy, or authority, the people stumble into exile, rudderless and bewildered.

Instead of choosing among these readings, I prefer to assume that
Eikha intentionally weaves multiple meaningful interpretations into this
verse. Each reading offers an important understanding of the identity

---

146. See Hillers, 84, 91.
147. Ezekiel concludes the prophetic castigation of the elders (Ezek. 14:1–8) with ominous words that evoke Eikha 4:16: "*And I shall place My face against* that person
and I will make him a sign and a byword, and I will cut him off from his people
and you will know that I am the Lord" (Ezek. 14:8). See also Ezekiel 8:11–12.

of those who disrespect Judah's men of stature, thus contributing new insight into the nation's culpability, the unscrupulous behavior of the enemies, and the way that divine justice is brought to bear against the sinful leaders.

Eikha 4:17–19

עוֹדֵינוּ תִּכְלֶינָה עֵינֵינוּ
אֶל־עֶזְרָתֵנוּ הָבֶל

בְּצִפִּיָּתֵנוּ צִפִּינוּ
אֶל־גּוֹי לֹא יוֹשִׁעַ

צָדוּ צְעָדֵינוּ
מִלֶּכֶת בִּרְחֹבֹתֵינוּ
קָרַב קִצֵּינוּ מָלְאוּ יָמֵינוּ
כִּי־בָא קִצֵּינוּ

קַלִּים הָיוּ רֹדְפֵינוּ
מִנִּשְׁרֵי שָׁמָיִם

עַל־הֶהָרִים דְּלָקֻנוּ
בַּמִּדְבָּר אָרְבוּ לָנוּ

Our eyes still strain [to see]
Our futile aid

In our anticipation, we anticipate
A nation that does not deliver

They entrapped our steps
[We could not] walk on our streets

Our end nears, our days completed
For our end arrives

399

> **Our pursuers were swifter**
> **Than the eagles of heaven**

> **They chased us on the mountains**
> **In the deserts, they ambushed us**

These verses utilize the first-person plural, describing Jerusalem's last days from an insider's perspective. The collective voice casts a spotlight upon one last group of nameless survivors who remain hiding in the shadows of the ruins. We are privy to a brief but intense glimpse of the final moments of the city's endurance, just before the total eradication of her inhabitants.

This section employs rich poetic technique to convey the unfolding tale of terror. Highly alliterative,[148] it obtains a staccato beat, a hammering effect that mimics the unremitting pursuit and the inexorable march toward a disastrous end. The threefold structure of the second half of verse 18 has a similar effect. Instead of the customary binary sentence, this verse offers three clipped phrases depicting the inescapable end: "Our end nears. Our days completed. For our end arrives."[149]

These sentences also feature several intriguing wordplays. Verse 17 weaves together the gerund and verbal form of the word *tzafa* (to anticipate), illustrating the intense anticipation of the elusive savior (*betzipiyatenu tzipinu*). Verse 18 combines the verb that modifies the enemies who entrap, *tzadu*, with the similarly sounding word *tze'adenu*, our footsteps. These alliterative words tangle the relentless hunt with the stumbling steps of the hunted, illustrating how the implacable enemy impedes movement.

The scene opens with the eyes of the survivors desperately scanning the horizon in hope of a last-minute reprieve. Eyes have two primary functions: they see and they produce tears. In its tenfold references to eyes,

---

148. The unusual alliteration includes three words in rapid succession that begin with *ayin*, followed by four *tzadi* words, and then four words that begin with *kof*.

149. In Hebrew, the effect is even more pronounced, as the first two sentences contain two words, while the third has two beats (although it has three words, there are only two stressed syllables).

Eikha mostly features eyes that weep (or refrain from tears), impeding their sight. Eikha 4:17 is the sole verse in the book in which eyes function to see, but in vain.[150] The communal gaze keenly anticipates but ultimately fails to see the hoped-for savior. This coheres well with the metaphor of the body's physical breakdown that runs throughout this chapter, illustrating the deterioration of the city and its populace. More significantly, it features the *absence* of sight, signifying the confusion of a battered population.

Amid a rising pitch of anxiety, the realization dawns that assistance will not arrive. Panic wells up as hope wanes, and Jerusalem's frightened residents hunker in their homes, increasingly aware that the end has arrived.[151] Unexpectedly, the fugitives emerge from hiding to flee from their pursuers; they burst into view, roaming the mountains and the desert. Their attempt to find refuge in formidable terrain fails; the enemies are everywhere, trapping, ambushing, and hunting the hapless group of survivors.

The enemies surface gradually in these verses. They are obscured in the initial verse, ostensibly because the remaining inhabitants scan the horizon for the anticipated savior. The enemies linger in the shadows in verse 18, an implicit threat to those who dare venture out into the public spaces. In verse 19, the enemies gain momentum, emerging in a rush of zeal. Soaring effortlessly over the mountains, they keep an "eagle eye" on their unfortunate prey, while doggedly pursuing them, even into the desert, where they ambush the Jerusalemites.

The verse does not identify the highly anticipated savior, leaving the impression that his identity is of little importance. The focus is on the flailing community, who fruitlessly search for a rescuer. It appears, though, that they seek a particular redeemer whose arrival is expected.

---

150. Eikha 2:11 employs the same verb (*k.l.h.*) to modify the word *ayin*. There, the word refers to tears (or the cessation of tears), while here it refers to the exhaustion of eyes that watch for a savior who does not come. See BDB, *Lexicon*, 477.

151. The word *ketz* appears twice in verse 18, recalling Ezekiel chapter 7, which features this word to describe Jerusalem's impending end (Ezek. 7:2–6). This terrible chapter in Ezekiel contains several intriguing parallels to Eikha, illustrating that its primary goal is to prepare Judah for the upcoming catastrophe that finds expression in Eikha. Compare, for example, Ezek. 7:15 to Eikha 1:20; Ezek. 7:19 to Eikha 4:1; Ezek. 7:20 to Eikha 1:8; Ezek. 7:26 to Eikha 4:13, 16.

Who is the community awaiting? In the first part of the verse, the identity of the "helper" (*ezratenu*) remains open-ended, allowing the reader to suppose that the community pins its final hope upon God. After all, God is frequently portrayed as the helper (*ezer*) of both individuals (Gen. 49:25; Ex. 18:4) and His nation (Deut. 33:26; Is. 41:13–14; 49:8; Ps. 33:20; 44:27). Israel often trains its eyes (*kalu einai*) upon God, in yearning and hopeful anticipation (Ps. 69:4; 119:82, 123). The prophets repeatedly assert that Israel can rely only on God to deliver them (Is. 20:3–6; 30:2–5; 31:1–3; Jer. 2:18; Hos. 5:13; 7:11; 8:9). At first it seems possible that this group of survivors has finally internalized this message.

The second half of the verse squelches the hope that Israel looks to God for its salvation. Informing us that the community's eyes are trained upon a *nation*, the verse continues by portraying this nation as one "that does not deliver." Evidence suggests that the potential liberator is Egypt, whose friendship proves tenuous in the moment of Jerusalem's great need.[152] Jeremiah 37:5 relates that the Egyptian ally sets out to aid Judah against Babylonia, an act that initially frightened the Babylonians, who withdrew temporarily from Jerusalem. The Egyptians soon changed their minds about helping (*le'ezra*) Jerusalem, reversing course and returning to Egypt (Jer. 37:7–8).[153]

Egypt's change of mind should not come as a surprise to the nation. Prophets often berate Israel for their undue reliance upon Egypt, which prevents Israel from properly depending upon God. God warns them that their alliance with Egypt will be futile for this very reason (Is. 20:6; 30:2–5; 31:1–3). Isaiah 30:7 employs language that strongly evokes our verse ("And Egypt's help [*yazoru*] is futile [*hevel*] and empty"), as noted by Rashi, who cites it here.[154] In fact, God already informed

---

152. See Rashi on Eikha 4:17. See also Ibn Ezra, who adds that they may have been relying on Assyria as well. Presumably, Ibn Ezra draws this idea from biblical passages that refer to Israel's misguided reliance on these two nations (Jer. 2:18; Hos. 6:11). See also Eikha 5:6.

153. See also II Kings 24:7 and Ezekiel 29:6–7.

154. Isaiah 31:1–3 uses the word *ezer* four times in describing Israel's reliance on Egypt's help and the futility of depending upon their assistance. See also Eikha 1:7, which states simply that no one helps (*ozer*) Jerusalem.

Jeremiah (37:6–10) that Jerusalem's desperate hope that Egypt will deliver her from calamity will prove futile.

The savior's failure to arrive illustrates the bankruptcy of the original alliance; Israel seals its own fate by pinning its hopes on a human ally instead of on God. In comparing the relentless enemies to the eagles in heaven, the verse evokes God's customary role as savior.[155] God redeems His people on the wings of eagles, conveying His swiftness and protectiveness over His nation (Ex. 19:4; Deut. 32:11). The enemies who pursue the last group of survivors seem to overtake even God, flying faster than God's salvation. This, of course, is not because they are swifter than God. God chooses to suspend the activities of His redemptive eagle in order to bring an eagle-like nation from afar, soaring and relentless, to punish the errant nation (Deut. 28:49; Jer. 4:13).

The enemy's actions linguistically recall God's actions against His nation in the previous chapter. God *pursued* His nation (Eikha 3:43) and lay in *ambush* for the *gever* (Eikha 3:11), allowing the enemy to *hunt* him like a bird (Eikha 3:52). By interweaving the enemies' hostile acts in this chapter with God's punishment of the previous chapter, Eikha reminds us that the enemies are the agents of God's punishment, acting in pursuance of divine will.

Eikha 4:20

רוּחַ אַפֵּינוּ מְשִׁיחַ ה'
נִלְכַּד בִּשְׁחִיתוֹתָם

אֲשֶׁר אָמַרְנוּ
בְּצִלּוֹ נִחְיֶה בַגּוֹיִם

**The breath of our nostrils, anointed of the Lord
Was captured in their traps**

---

155. The metaphor also conveys their speed (II Sam. 15:23) and their ability to follow the fugitives even to their secure refuge in the mountains and deserts.

About [whom] we said
"Under his shadow, we will live amongst the nations"

The first-person collective account comes to a stunning and tragic conclusion with the capture of the national leader: the breath of their nostrils, the anointed of God.[156] This unnamed figure had inspired confidence, and the community unanimously anticipated his success, asserting that this leader would surely cast his protective shadow over them.[157]

Yet, this leader also fails them. The unusual syntax of the verse draws our attention to the sharp contrast between hope and disappointment. Focusing first upon the leader's prestige and status, the verse then tersely describes his capture, which represents a climax of Jerusalem's fall. In a staggering reminder of more hopeful times, the verse returns to cite the earlier words of an optimistic populace. These words fall as a terrible blow, reverberating ironically and trailing off bleakly as the nation falls into silence, bereft of their leader, bereft of hope.

Chapter 4 (like chapter 2) often focuses our attention upon the loss of leadership (verses 7, 13, 16). This, however, remains the only verse in the book that actually refers to an individual with a specific, if unnamed, identity.[158] By remaining anonymous, the leader retreats further into the shadows, impotent and feeble, unable to deliver the city from its misfortune. Nevertheless, the question remains: who is the leader who revived his people, imbuing them with newfound confidence? I will examine the possibilities raised by biblical interpreters,

---

156. As the organ of breathing, the nostrils often describe anger (especially when coupled with the word *ḥaron*), in a vivid portrayal of the fierce quick breaths that accompany anger (see Eikha 1:12; 2:1, 3, 21, 22). The phrase "breath of the nostrils" sometimes describes God's powerful ability to whip up a strong wind (Ex. 15:8; II Sam. 22:16). In our context, it seems to indicate someone who can breathe new life into the nation (see Gen. 2:7 and 7:22, where the breath of the nostrils simply signifies life). Possibly, the similar phrase in Job 27:3 suggests that this leader will revive them religiously by restoring their "spirit of God."

157. The protective shadow of this leader, appointed by God, evokes the shadow that God casts over those under His protection (see also Ps. 17:8, 91:1).

158. In Eikha 2:6, 9, the king is mentioned in general terms, but he has neither character nor specific attributes. Eikha often mentions general groups (e.g., priests, prophets, officers, mothers, children, elders, youth) without identifying anyone by name.

but in the final analysis, the leader's identity remains unclear, as elusive as the nation's dashed hopes.

Many scholars assume that the verse alludes to King Zedekiah, who reigns in Jerusalem during its final days.[159] He is appointed by the Babylonians in 597 BCE after they exile King Jehoakhin along with Jerusalem's notables (II Kings 24:17). Zedekiah allows for the possibility that a remnant of the nation will remain in Jerusalem even as the Babylonians assert their hegemony over the region.

Jerusalem's residents may well speak optimistically about the newly appointed Zedekiah, who can help them survive Babylonia's aggressive stance toward Judah: "Under his shadow, we will live amongst the nations!"[160] This scion of the Davidic dynasty ("anointed of the Lord") revives the people's hopes ("breath of our nostrils"), offering them a reprieve from a rapidly deteriorating political disaster. Tragically, Zedekiah's reign is all too brief, ending in disaster as the king surreptitiously tries to escape the city, but to no avail. Apprehended by the Babylonian soldiers ("captured in their traps") and abandoned by his terrified infantry, Zedekiah's leadership draws to a close (II Kings 25:4–5). The Babylonian soldiers bring him to their king, who summarily executes judgment upon him, killing his sons, blinding him,[161] and exiling him in chains to Babylonia (II Kings 25:6–7).[162]

Zedekiah, however, appears to be an unlikely candidate for the superlatives ascribed to the leader in this verse. Although Zedekiah, a descendant of David, technically bears the title "anointed of the Lord," this king repeatedly scorns the word of God, according to Jeremiah 37:2.[163] Moreover, Zedekiah is a weak king, placed on the throne by

---

159. Ibn Ezra adopts this position and R. Yosef Kara cites it as the first possibility (and presumably the one he feels is most logical) of the three opinions he cites. See also Hillers, 92; House, 448.

160. Berlin, 113, raises the possibility that the citation refers to Zedekiah's rebellion against Babylonia. See II Kings 24:20, Jeremiah 52:3.

161. The reference to the blind people who wander the city in Eikha 4:14 may further cement a relationship between this chapter and King Zedekiah's misfortune.

162. These events appear also in Jeremiah 39:1–7; 52:1–11; Ezekiel 12:12–14.

163. See also Jeremiah 32:1–5, where Zedekiah imprisons Jeremiah because of his prophecy. Nevertheless, Zedekiah is not the most sinful king from the Davidic line – he seems to waver between listening to Jeremiah's prophecies and disobeying them.

the Babylonian enemy. It seems particularly inappropriate to refer to Zedekiah as "the breath of our nostrils," a unique phrase that bespeaks exaltation and the ability to reinvigorate the nation.[164] Perhaps the nation simply reveres and adores the Davidic line, indiscriminately pinning their hopes on any king belonging to God's chosen monarchic lineage.

Many of the traditional commentaries assert that this verse refers not to Zedekiah but to Josiah.[165] Exegetes who adopt this approach often assert that Jeremiah composed it originally as a lamentation over Josiah's death.[166] While this was a deeply troubling event, its occurrence twenty-three years before Jerusalem's fall should render it largely irrelevant in Eikha 4. Why hark back to such a distant tragedy while writing about the current disaster, whose catastrophic impact far outstrips that of Josiah's death?

Those who espouse this approach likely focus upon Josiah's exceptional virtue, and the manner in which he breathes new spiritual life into the faithless people.[167] Truly, this "breath of our nostrils, anointed of the Lord" embarks upon an extraordinary path, reforming the nation, destroying idolatry, and centralizing worship of God in the Temple (II Kings 23; II Chr. 34–35). Some biblical passages (Jer. 3:11–12; II Chr. 34:9) suggest that the exiles from the Northern Kingdom begin to trickle home.[168] Josiah's religious campaign coincides with the waning of Assyrian power, and the Davidic king asserts his hegemony over the Northern Kingdom, restoring the land of Israel to its

---

See Jeremiah 34:8–11, 17–22; 37:3–4. This finds expression in Zedekiah's personal relationship with Jeremiah, as may be evidenced especially in Jeremiah 37:17–38:28. From this story, Zedekiah appears to be a weak leader, caught between the foolhardy advice of his palace officials and Jeremiah's word of God.

164. While this phrase refers to God's actions several times (as noted above), this appears to be the only biblical passage in which it describes a human.

165. *Targum* and Rashi on Eikha 4:21; Taanit 22b; *Seder Olam Rabba* 24.

166. For more discussion of the impact of Josiah's death, see the chapter above, "Historical Background."

167. II Kings 23:25 asserts that there was no king before him or after him who returned to the Lord "with all his heart and all his soul and all his strength."

168. Megilla 14b asserts that Josiah seeks God's word from the prophetess Huldah and not from Jeremiah because the latter had gone north to bring back the ten tribes.

original undivided state.[169] All this offers hope that Josiah is the figure destined to fulfill the optimistic prophecy of Isaiah 11:1–12:6. Under Josiah's leadership, Israel retains the hope that it will thrive among the nations, rebuilding a powerful kingdom respected among nations ("Under his shadow, we will live amongst the nations"). Israel's hopes come to an abrupt end when Josiah dies in battle with the Egyptians. Our verse suggests that the killers of Josiah capture him in a trap, ostensibly alluding to the manner of his death, caught in the maw of the Egyptian war machine.

The death of the righteous king launches the theological struggles that characterize the period following Josiah's death up until the events of our chapter.[170] Events seem to spiral out of control, leaving a theologically distraught nation. In this schema, we can better understand Rashi's contention that Jeremiah wrote all of chapter 4 as a lamentation over Josiah's death.[171] At first glance, this appears implausible, given that chapter 4 describes the siege and starvation in Jerusalem, the destruction of the city, and the exile of her inhabitants – all of which occur long after Josiah's death. Yet, Josiah's death is the theological backdrop of Eikha 4, whose core idea remains the unexplainable nature of divine justice, the fact that righteous people suffer. The theological quandary that lies at the heart of the chapter takes root and grows following Josiah's death. Events merge, weaving a variegated tapestry of confusion and outrage. For this reason, many exegetes assume that our verse alludes to Josiah, whose death propels the nation toward an inexplicable calamity.

Rashbam identifies the leader in this verse as Gedalya ben Aḥikam, the final leader of the Judean community. Following the destruction of the city and the exile of the majority of her populace,

---

169. Josiah enacts his reform in the area of the Northern Kingdom, thereby indicating his hegemony there (see II Kings 23:15, 19; II Chron. 34:6–7). Josiah also goes to battle with Pharaoh Necho as he travels through Megiddo in the Jezreel Valley, indicating that Josiah regards himself as the ruler of that area, deep in what was formerly the area of the Northern Kingdom (see Radak, II Kings 23:29; Eikha Rabba 1:53).

170. For more on the way the theological impact of this event echoes throughout prophetic passages, see the chapter above, "Historical Background."

171. Rashi, Eikha 4:1. See also Eikha Rabba 4:1.

the Babylonians permit a small number of poor Jerusalemites to remain in Judah (Jer. 39:10), appointing Gedalya as their official leader (Jer. 40:5, 7). Gedalya urges the remaining Judeans to accept their situation and regroup under Babylonian auspices (Jer. 40:9–12). In an act of great treachery, Yishmael ben Netanya (at the behest of the king of Ammon) murders Gedalya and his cohorts (both Judean and Babylonian), perpetrating a bloodbath upon the remnant of the Judean community (Jer. 41:1–10). Fearing that the Babylonians will avenge the death of their soldiers and appointed leader, the remaining Judeans flee the country, headed for Egypt (Jer. 43:2–7). This flight is a final act of betrayal against God's word and is condemned by Jeremiah, who had advised them that God wants them to remain in Judah (Jer. 42:7–22).

Several factors likely compel Rashbam to identify the leader in this verse as Gedalya. First, Rashbam appears to read the chapter as a chronological continuum. The capture of the leader (verse 21) takes place in the chapter *after* the destruction (verses 11–14) and exile from the city (verses 15–16). If one assumes that the chapter records the events in order, this leader must be Gedalya, who oversees the small community that remains in Judah following the exile. Gedalya also appears to be a virtuous and responsible leader, who represents the last Judean hope, "the breath of our nostrils."[172] Moreover, Gedalya has gained the trust of the Babylonians, a leader about whom the people may say, "Under his shadow, we will live amongst the nations."

Nevertheless, it is inaccurate to refer to Gedalya as the anointed of God. He is not a descendant of the house of David, nor does God appoint him to his position. If this verse is not about the end of the Davidic dynasty, its impact resonates less significantly. After all, Gedalya is only a temporary leader, appointed by the enemy to shepherd the survivors of a beaten nation. Moreover, in this schema, the one who lays the trap is not the external enemy – Babylonia or Egypt – but rather the internal enemy, Gedalya's fellow Judeans. For these reasons, I am

---

172. The fast that commemorates Gedalya's murder, traditionally observed on 3 Tishrei, acknowledges the significance of his death, which represents the end of the paltry community remaining in Judah.

less inclined to accept Rashbam's opinion, which represents a minority position among biblical interpreters.

However we understand the specific identity of the unnamed leader who has been trapped and captured, the tone and message of the verse is a dejected one. As the chapter begins to wind down, Judah recalls its last hope, a leader who could have salvaged the community. The optimism that first surrounded the leader deflates and vanishes in a tragic finale.

PART 3 (EIKHA 4:21–22):
EPILOGUE – HOPE AND JUSTICE

The final verses (21–22) directly address both the Edomite enemy and the daughter of Zion. The conclusion of chapter 4 focuses mostly upon vengeance; the dust seems to have settled on the destruction, and the nation fixes its attention upon the impending misfortune of its enemies. It also appends a laconic strategy for its own return from exile, introducing a brief ray of light at the chapter's end.

Eikha 4:21–22

שִׂישִׂי וְשִׂמְחִי בַּת־אֱדוֹם
יוֹשֶׁבְתִּי בְּאֶרֶץ עוּץ

גַּם־עָלַיִךְ תַּעֲבָר־כּוֹס
תִּשְׁכְּרִי וְתִתְעָרִי

תַּם־עֲוֹנֵךְ בַּת־צִיּוֹן
לֹא יוֹסִיף לְהַגְלוֹתֵךְ

פָּקַד עֲוֹנֵךְ בַּת־אֱדוֹם
גִּלָּה עַל־חַטֹּאתָיִךְ

**Be joyous and happy, daughter of Edom
Who lives in the land of Utz[173]**

---

173. For the connection between Edom and Utz, see Genesis 36:28.

The cup will pass over you as well[174]
Get drunk and bare yourselves

[When] your transgressions cease, daughter of Zion
He will not continue to exile you

[When] your transgressions are remembered, daughter of Edom
He will reveal your sins

Following the capture of her leader, the community abruptly falls silent. The narrator picks up the narrative, turning directly to address Judah's enemy. Flinging bitter words at the Edomites who revel in Jerusalem's downfall, the narrator issues a curse/prediction that they will receive their just retribution. In the final verse of the chapter, the narrator addresses Zion and Edom in inverse relation to one another. Using the feminine *"bat"* as part of each nation's epithet, the narrator then depicts the state of her transgressions, sketching antithetical outcomes for each nation: Bat Zion will invariably cease her transgressions, while Bat Edom's transgressions will surface. By employing the word *"gala"* about each of these nations, the narrator further contrasts them; Zion will not remain in exile (*lehagloteikh*), and Edom's sins will be revealed (*gila*).

God remains oddly obscured in these final verses. While He will most likely be the one to punish Edom, discontinue Zion's exile,[175] and reveal Edom's sins, the narrator omits any direct reference to God. Having turned away from His nation in verse 16, God does not seem inclined to intervene on their behalf. Moreover, Israel may not actively wish to court God's involvement, given the disastrous consequences of His attentions. In either case, God's absence from the chapter's conclusion illustrates that this chapter does not reconcile with God or with His judgments.

---

174. We will presently discuss the meaning of this phrase. While most commentators assume that *kos* means cup, a possible secondary meaning is the bird *kos*, which tends to haunt ruins (see Ps. 102:7).

175. Ibn Ezra suggests that the subject of the phrase, "He will not continue to exile you," harks back to the mention of God in verse 20. Alternatively, he suggests that the subject may be Zion's sins, which until now have actively caused her exile.

Despite God's absence from the verse, the narrator expresses deep conviction that Zion's sinning will end, thereby reversing her fortunes. The linguistic link between God's decision not to continue to look at His nation (4:16: "*lo yosif lehabitam*") and the reversal of Judah's exile (4:22: "*lo yosif lehagloteikh*") indicates the narrator's confidence that God's disregard for His nation is an impermanent state. God may now hide His face from His nation, temporarily removing Himself from their misfortunes. However, God's covenant with Israel remains eternal and unbroken, even as Israel's adversaries sustain fleeting triumphs. Thus, even as Israel suffers her lowest moments in the book, the narrator adroitly anticipates a change of fortune, remaining stalwartly confident in redemption.

Chapter 4 closes on an unusually optimistic note. Its final verse recognizes that Israel's exile is not a permanent state. Termination of sinfulness will surely coincide with the termination of punishment. The narrator also expresses confidence in the impending punishment of Israel's enemy. Strikingly, instead of issuing a plea to God to destroy the enemies, as in previous chapters, the narrator describes reprisal against Edom as an inevitable occurrence.

The Edomite Enemy

Chapter 4 concludes with a call for vengeance against Israel's enemies. Oddly, the verse explicitly mentions Edom, rather than the Babylonians, the perpetrators of the destruction.[176] Possibly, the narrator singles out Edom because Israel expected allegiance from them, based upon their neighborly proximity,[177] or upon the family ties that bind the Edomites to

---

176. Edom's prominent role in the Tanakh has generated several monographs on the subject. See, for example, E. Assis, *Identity in Conflict: The Struggle between Esau and Jacob, Edom and Israel* (Winona Lake, IN: Eisenbrauns, 2016).

177. It should not surprise us that Israel expresses more bitterness against her neighbors than against the enemies who came to conquer her from afar. Although some biblical narratives portray enmity between Israel and Edom, II Kings 3 illustrates military cooperation between the neighboring countries, which likely shared some measure of economic relationship as well. These neighbors now eagerly rejoice and even participate in Israel's destruction. It is difficult to avoid the comparison to the complicit involvement of many of the Jews' neighbors in the Holocaust. For more on this topic, see Jan Tomasz Gross, *Neighbors: The Destruction of the Jewish Community in Jedwabne, Poland* (London: Penguin, 2000); Barbara Engleking, *Such a Beautiful*

Israel.[178] Edom violates the expectation of brotherly loyalty (see Amos 1:11; Ob. 12), a betrayal in some ways worse than the cruelty of the conquerors.[179]

Edom's precise role in Jerusalem's suffering remains unclear. In Eikha 4:21, the Edomites appear to be engaged in raucous celebration, ostensibly sparked by Judah's misfortune.[180] Edom's delight in Jerusalem's downfall finds expression in a psalm's description of Edom's cheers as Babylonia dismantles the city:

> Remember, Lord, against the sons of Edom, the day of Jerusalem, as they said, "Strip her! Strip her! (*Aru! Aru!*) Until [we see] her foundations!" (Ps. 137:7)

Invoking the glee expressed by the Edomites in the psalm, Eikha 4:21 scathingly advises Edom to strip herself (*titari*) in a final bawdy drinking spree before she suffers retribution.[181]

The prophet Obadiah similarly describes Edom's delight in Jerusalem's calamity:[182]

Sunny Day... – Jews Seeking Refuge in the Polish Countryside, 1942–1945 (Jerusalem: Yad Vashem Publications, 2016); and the movie *Shoah* by Claude Lanzmann.

178. Edom is identified with Esau, Jacob's brother, in Genesis 36:1, 8.

179. The assumption that Israel expects Edom's allegiance is based on the word "brother," which appears in both the prophecies of Obadiah and Amos referenced above. See also Deuteronomy 2:2–8 and 23:8, which offer Edom special familial treatment as befits a brother. Many biblical passages regard Edom as a long-standing enemy, from whom we have little if any expectations of allegiance and whose destruction we actively seek (Is. 34:8; 63:1–4; Jer. 49:7–22; Ezek. 25:12–14; 35: 1–15; Joel 4:19; Ps. 137:7; II Chr. 20:10–11; 28:17).

180. See Ibn Ezra, Eikha 4:21, who asserts that Edom's joy and cheers of approval at Jerusalem's downfall lead to this condemnation of Edom. In support of this, Ibn Ezra cites Psalms 137:7.

181. This translation of the word *titari* follows Ibn Ezra's understanding of the word (see also Radak in his *Sefer Shorashim* on the word *ara*). *Targum*, Rashi, and R. Yosef Kara understand it differently, to mean either to empty the cup or to empty the contents of one's stomach, namely, to vomit.

182. There is much discussion about the historical context of Obadiah's undated prophecy. Many scholars assume that these events relate to the Edomites' role during the Babylonian conquest, as reflected in Eikha 4:21–22. For a review of opinions on this matter, see Yehuda Kiehl in *Daat Mikra*, 4–5.

Because of the violence [done to] your brother Jacob, you will be covered with shame and cut off for eternity. On the day that you stood opposite them, on the day that foreigners absconded with his wealth, and strangers came into his gates, and a lot was cast against Jerusalem – you were like one of them! Do not gloat[183] on your brother's day, on the day of his calamity, and do not rejoice over the sons of Judah on the day of their destruction, and do not open your mouth wide on the day of distress. (Ob. 1:10–12)

Obadiah affixes another layer to Edom's offensive behavior:

Do not enter the gates of my nation on the day of their disaster, do not gloat you also, in his misfortune, on the day of his disaster, and do not loot his wealth on the day of his disaster. Do not stand on the crossroad to cut off his refugees, and do not capture his survivors on the day of his distress! (Ob. 1:13–14)

Edom does not merely celebrate Jerusalem's downfall or stand by as enemies destroy her. In Obadiah's description, Edom enters Jerusalem opportunistically, looting the wealth of those maimed, killed, or exiled, and rounding up those who manage to escape.[184] This evil behavior may underlie our verse's particular censure of Edom.

One final reason for this chapter's focus on punishing Edom relates to Edom's broader role in biblical ideology.[185] The fates of Israel and Edom appear to be linked in the Bible; Edom's good fortune is

---

183. While the word literally means simply to look, the context suggests that it means to look with satisfaction, or to gloat. See the translation of the NJPS and BDB, *Lexicon*, 908. For similar uses, see Micah 7:10; Ezekiel 28:17; Psalms 22:18.

184. See also the apocryphal book *I Esdras* (4:45), which maintains that the Edomites actively burned the Temple during the Babylonian conquest.

185. Rabbinic sources offer another explanation for Edom's biblical prominence. Midrashim (e.g., *Sifrei* Deuteronomy 343) and Rashi (Eikha 4:21) perceive Edom as a precursor to Rome, which destroys the Second Temple. See also the Aramaic *Targum* on Eikha 4:21 (Yemenite manuscript edition), which reads, "the city of Rome," for *"bat Edom."* The suggestion that this chapter anticipates Rome's destruction of Jerusalem, followed by the prolonged exile, reflects another attempt to account for the special attention accorded to Edom in chapter 4.

predicated on Israel's bad fortune and vice versa.[186] This idea harks back to the oracle that Rebecca receives while she is pregnant with Jacob and Esau, who wrestle in her womb:

> Two nations are in your womb and two peoples will separate from your innards; and one nation will be mightier than the other, and the elder shall the younger serve. (Gen. 25:23)

Isaac alludes to a similar idea when he blesses Esau:

> And you shall live by the sword and you shall serve your brother. But it will be when you shall rule,[187] you shall break his yoke from upon your neck. (Gen. 27:40)

This verse hints to an ongoing inverse relationship between the two nations.[188] Vengeance on Edom signifies Israel's redemption.[189] By exchanging Israel's misfortune with Edom's, our verse sets in motion the reversal of Israel's fortune. Indeed, this may be the best reason for singling out Edom at this point in the book. Expressing his hopes for a total reversal of the world order, the narrator anticipates Edom's downfall and Zion's simultaneous restoration.

---

186. See Rashi on Genesis 25:23. Many rabbinic sources posit an inverse relationship between Jacob's fortunes and those of Esau, in which one's rise is contingent upon the other's fall. See Genesis Rabba 6:5; Megilla 6a.

187. This translation follows Rasag, Radak, and Ibn Ezra. For similar usages of this meaning of the word *tarid*, see, for example, Genesis 1:28; I Kings 5:4. See also my examination of Eikha 1:13.

188. See Kli Yakar and Or HaHayim in their commentaries on Genesis 27:40. For other biblical verses that juxtapose their fortunes, see Joel 4:19–20; Amos 9:11–12; Obadiah 1:18, 21.

189. Isaiah 34 describes Edom's punishment immediately prior to his depiction of Israel's redemption (in chapter 35), thereby juxtaposing and linking the two events. This can also account for the unusual placement of the prophecy against Edom in Ezekiel 35, ensconced within the prophecies of Israel's redemption. Possibly, this can explain why Isaiah singles out Edom in 63:1.

Metaphor: The Cup of Punishment

The narrator acerbically encourages Edom's merriment, cheering on their decadent behavior, as a prelude to their ultimate punishment. In addition to Edom's gleeful celebration of Judah's downfall, we also observe their vulgar and hedonistic parties. The expression that the narrator uses to allude to Edom's punishment recalls these inebriated festivities: "The cup will pass over you." What is this cup that will pass over Edom? Both *Targum* and Rashi regard the cup that will pass over Edom as a metaphor for troubles.[190]

The unnamed executor of Edom's punishment is surely God, who frequently punishes (both Israel and the nations) by administering this metaphoric cup of punishment. What is the nature of the drink? Sometimes God administers a toxic brew. In a visceral image, Isaiah 51:17 describes it as a cup of God's wrath, which issues forth like a poisonous broth, killing those who imbibe it.[191] This cup sometimes simply contains wine, inducing a state resembling drunkenness,[192] in which the one punished exhibits uncontrollable and shameful behavior.[193]

Jeremiah 25:15–28 uses this cup as a metaphor for geopolitical upheavals, specifically for the Babylonian conquest of other nations, who stagger and fall, drunk, incoherent, and vomiting. This constitutes a sharp metaphor for the inner workings and vulnerabilities of powerful empires, who rise and fall in a seesaw of shifting power struggles. Felled

---

190. This reading, adopted by Rashi, appears in the Yemenite manuscript edition of the Aramaic *Targum* on the verse.

191. See also Psalms 60:5.

192. Y. Rozenson, "Divine Providence Over Israel and Over the Nations," *Megadim* 9 (1990), 57 [Hebrew], maintains that the primary idea of this metaphor is to illustrate that God's punishments deliberately cause confusion, which prevent the recipient from repenting. In his view, this metaphor hints to the finality and imminence of God's punitive action.

193. See Jeremiah 51:7; Ezekiel 23:32–34. This seems a fitting punishment for a nation steeped in hedonism. Habakkuk 2:15 rebukes a person who forces his friend to drink until intoxicated so that he can see his nakedness. The prophecy continues by warning this individual that the cup in God's right hand shall be used against him, to bring him disgrace in place of respect (Hab. 2:16). Some prophecies describe God simply punishing a nation with drunkenness, though they lack the image of a cup. See Jeremiah 13:13; 48:26; 51:39; Obadiah 16.

by their own gluttony, hedonistic parties suggest a voracious and insatiable desire for conquest.[194] Their appetite renders them helpless and muddled, pawns of their own quest for power. In Jeremiah's prophecy, nations do not control their own destinies; God will turn their rapacious thirst against them, and they will drink a cup of noxious/intoxicating brew.

By using the word "also" (*gam*), our verse implicitly links Edom's cup of punishment with Israel's punishment: "The cup will *also* (*gam*) pass over you."[195] In anticipation of Israel's redemption, Edom will switch places with Zion, receiving her punishment in due course, as in Isaiah's prophecy:

> So says the Lord, your Lord who fights for His nation: Behold, I have taken from your hands the cup of poison, the bowl, the cup of My wrath. You shall not continue to drink from it anymore. And I will place it in the hands of your tormentors, who said to you, "Lie down and let us pass over you." And you placed your back like the ground and like the street for those who passed. (Is. 51:22–23)

CHAPTER FOUR: IN SUMMATION

Chapter 4 maintains a factual tone, recounting shattering events in a terse, unemotional style. Like chapters 1 and 2, chapter 4 seems to divide substantively into two main parts; unlike in chapters 1 and 2, Jerusalem refrains from speech in this chapter. Jerusalem is exhausted, numbly witnessing the atrocities but lacking the energy to comment or cry out.

A sustained eyewitness account of the siege and famine in Jerusalem, the first part of the chapter (verses 1–10) initially focuses on the children, who emerge as its most poignant and memorable image. The calamity (and especially the food shortage) wreaks havoc upon the vulnerable and innocent victims, who previously were Jerusalem's glory,

---

194. Jeremiah 25:26 suggests that Babylonia will also eventually drink from that cup, after the others have done so. Evil empires inevitably fall, victims of their own appetite for conquest.

195. See Jeremiah 25:17–18, where Jerusalem and Judah drink from God's cup of wine, a metaphor for the Babylonian conquest. Both Utz and Edom also drink from this cup, according to Jeremiah 25:20–21.

her jewel and pride. Flitting back and forth between glittering images from a magnificent past and a survey of the bleak present, the shifting snapshots aptly convey the city's terrible downfall.

The second section of the chapter (11–20) follows what appears to be a chronological continuum, recording events that occur after the breach of the city. Instead of describing the enemies pouring into the battered city, the opening salvo depicts God flinging His wrath against the city, igniting it in a fiery display of divine anger. Disbelief follows, as foreign kings absorb Jerusalem's disaster. In Jerusalem, survivors blindly pick their way through city streets, unmindful of the blood that flows and contaminates, sullying the city, her survivors, and anyone associated with her. At this point, the chapter assumes a disoriented tone, painting an impressionistic portrait of shadowy figures moving aimlessly from the city to exile. Unidentified voices call out to these dazed figures, referring in disgust to the impurities that cling to the populace as they are driven from their city. God surfaces once again to scatter them further afield, wreaking yet more havoc on a shattered nation. Briefly, the communal voice breaks through, recounting the frantic last moments in the city, and concluding with the capture of their leader, God's anointed, who represents the final, futile hope for the nation's survival.

This chapter seems hopeless; it spins out of control, moving disjointedly but inexorably toward unmitigated disaster. Nevertheless, the structure of this chapter is *not* chiastic: it does not present a cyclical, unending catastrophe. In fact, as the narrative spirals toward a devastating conclusion, a modicum of hope surfaces, allowing the chapter to emerge from its dark despair. It concludes by offering the most hopeful moment in the book, asserting that Israel's sins will surely end, as will her exile.

Chapter 4 bears striking similarities to chapter 2 in terms of its content, structure, and language. These common features direct the reader to compare the two chapters, whose most significant shared theme is the way each grapples with God and His role in human suffering.[196]

---

196. In an upcoming chapter, I will discuss the overall structure of Eikha, collating (and abridging) the above comparisons between chapters 2 and 4. There, I will emphasize the theological similarities between these chapters (as well as those between chapters 1 and 5), and how they direct our attention to the theology of the book.

Pictorial and intense, chapters 2 and 4 depict the sights and atrocities in detail, vividly portraying the calamity that unfolds in the streets of Jerusalem. The unforgettable image of these chapters is that of the children, who languish on the streets, weak and expiring from starvation. Equally haunting, if only because of its unfathomable cruelty, these chapters feature mothers who eat their children, once-merciful women who are now both the victims and the perpetrators of unspeakable atrocities. These mothers are ill-fated and helpless, but also shockingly heinous.

God pours His wrath upon the city in these chapters, resulting in a fiery conflagration that destroys its very foundation. Both chapters focus upon the blow to the political leadership; kings, officers, and the anointed of God are violated, spurned, trapped, captured, and exiled. As explanation, these chapters point to the sins of the leaders, especially the religious leaders: prophets, priests, elders. Loss of leadership entails a dizzying lack of guidance; Jerusalem's residents seem disoriented and bewildered. Following God's active destruction, He recedes and disappears; the nation receives no direction from God as He turns away from His people, refusing to look their way. In both chapters, the people keep their tears and prayers in check; it is difficult to petition God once He has abandoned them.

Other nations play an important role in both chapters; outsiders have mixed reactions to Jerusalem's calamity. Some display shock and disbelief, while others respond with scorn, exultation, and celebration. Each of these chapters includes a citation of exultant enemies whose words communicate their enmity. Their joy rings derisively, and chapters 2 and 4 each close with the hope that God's vengeance will crush these contemptuous foes.

Structurally, the book aligns chapters 2 and 4 in chiastic relation to each other; they divide into two similar sections, but in opposite order. The first ten verses of chapter 2 describe the destruction of the city, corresponding to the second half of chapter 4 (verses 11–20). The second section of chapter 2 features the famine (11–21) and its terrible effect upon the children, in parallel with the first ten verses of chapter 4. Both chapters conclude, as noted, with vengeance upon the enemies.

Chapter 2	Chapter 4
The Destruction: Verses 1–10	The Famine: Verses 1–10
The Famine: Verses 11–21	The Destruction: Verses 11–20
Call for God's Vengeance: Verse 22	God's Vengeance: Verses 21–22

In addition to the thematic similarities, the language of the two chapters is remarkably parallel, highlighting the common features noted above: God's fiery anger, the terrible scenes on Jerusalem's streets, the hapless and starving children, the nation's (or Jerusalem's) straining eyes, the sneering joy of the enemies, the failure of the leaders (kings, prophets, and priests), the brokenness of the shattered nation, and the city's destruction by fire. Linguistic parallels appear in the following chart:[197]

Chapter 2	Chapter 4
He *spilled out* (*shafakh*) His *anger* like fire. (2:4)	[The Lord] *spilled out* (*shafakh*) the *anger* of His nostrils. (4:11)
On every street corner (*berosh kol ḥutzot*). (2:19)	On every street corner (*berosh kol ḥutzot*). (4:1)
As the child and suckling (*olel veyonek*) faint in the streets of the metropolis. To their mothers they say, "Where is grain and wine?" (2:11)	The tongue of the suckling (*yonek*) cleaves to his palate in thirst. Children (*olelim*) ask for bread, they have no provider. (4:4)
My eyes (*einai*) are drained (*kalu*) from tears. (2:11)	Our eyes (*eineinu*) still strain (*tikhlena*). (4:17)
And your enemy rejoiced (*vayesamaḥ*) over you. (2:17)	Be joyous and happy (*simḥi*), daughter of Edom. (4:21)
My liver spills (*nishpakh*) to the ground... as they spill out (*behishtapeikh*) their souls in their mothers' bosoms. (2:11–12)	The holy stones spilled (*tishtapekhna*) on every street corner. (4:1)
	The iniquities of her priests, who spill out (*hashofekhim*) in her midst the blood of the righteous. (4:13)

---

197. For those who prefer a Hebrew chart, it appears below in the chapter "The Structure of Eikha: Faith in a Turbulent World."

Chapter 2	Chapter 4
He profaned the kingdom (*mamlakha*) and her officers. (2:2) And He spurned in His fiery anger king (*melekh*) and priest. (2:6) Her king (*malkah*) and officers are amongst the nations, there is no instruction. (2:9)	The kings (*malkhei*) of the land did not believe. (4:12)
He destroyed (*shiḥet*) its fortresses. (2:5) He destroyed (*shiḥet*) His appointed place. (2:6) The Lord determined to destroy (*lehashḥit*) the wall of Bat Zion. (2:8)	The breath of our nostrils, anointed of the Lord, was captured in their traps (*bish'ḥitotam*). (4:20)
Because of the brokenness of the daughter of my nation (*al shever bat ammi*). (2:11)	In the brokenness of the daughter of my people (*beshever bat ammi*). (4:10)
How beclouds in His anger (*be'apo*), Lord? ... And He did not remember His footstool on the day of His anger (*beyom apo*). (2:1) He hewed down in his smoking anger (*baḥori af*). (2:3) And He spurned in His fiery anger (*bezaam apo*) king and priest. (2:6) You murdered on the day of Your anger (*beyom apekha*)! (2:21)	The Lord completed His wrath, spilled out the anger of His nostrils (*ḥaron apo*). (4:11)
And he burned in Jacob as a flaming fire (*esh*) that consumes (*okhela*) its surroundings. (2:3)	He lit a fire (*esh*) in Zion, and it consumed (*vatokhal*) her foundations. (4:11)
Even her prophets (*nevi'eha*) did not find a vision from the Lord. (2:9) Your prophets (*nevi'ayikh*) prophesied for you falsehood and triviality. (2:14) When murdered in the Lord's sanctuary are the priest and prophet (*venavi*)! (2:20)	On account of the sins of her prophets (*nevi'eha*), the iniquities of her priests. (4:13)

Chapter 2	Chapter 4
They wagged (*vayaniu*) their heads over the daughter of Jerusalem. (2:15)	The blind wander (*na'u*) in the streets … as they flee and wander (*na'u*). (4:14–15)
As the child and suckling faint in the streets (*birhovot*) of the metropolis. (2:11)	[We could not] walk on our streets (*birhovoteinu*). (4:18)
And they did not reveal (*gilu*) your transgressions. (2:14)	He will not continue to exile you (*lehagloteikh*).… [When] your transgressions are remembered, daughter of Edom, He will reveal (*gila*) your sins. (4:22)

Appearing a total of seven times in the book of Eikha (but only in chapters 2 and 4), the verb *shafakh* depicts death (children spill out their life), fury (God spills out His wrath), and carnage (priests and prophets spill the blood of innocents). In these painfully public chapters, the reader views the flagrant spectacle of suffering and death that occurs both in the city's streets (*hutzot*: 2:19, 21; 4:1, 4, 8, 14) and its open spaces (*rehovot*: 2:11, 12; 4:18).

In Eikha 2:11, Jerusalem describes her eyes, worn out from tears (*kalu … einai*). An identical expression appears in Eikha 4:17 to describe the eyes of the community, worn out from straining to see a savior who does not arrive. A striking linguistic similarity, this draws our attention to the absence of tears in these chapters. Nevertheless, chapter 2 has an evocative, passionate tone, while chapter 4 maintains an emotional numbness that clashes with the painful sights it describes.

Both chapters feature the incomprehensible horror of the death of innocents, primarily the children and sucklings, too young to have known sin. Similarly, both chapters feature the death of righteous figures: chapter 2 focuses on the death of priests and prophets in the Temple (presumably while attending to their religious duties), while chapter 4 spotlights the ascetic Nazirites and the *tzaddikim* (innocent righteous), slaughtered by the wicked leaders.[198] A profound sense of divine injustice forms the theological backdrop of these chapters, compounded by

---

198. Whereas chapter 2 suggests that the slaughtered priests are the innocent party, chapter 4 presents the priests as the killers of innocents. Perhaps the priests who faithfully serve in the Temple remain pious, while those who wander the streets get into trouble.

the absence of a description of the sinfulness of the general populace.[199] Instead, these chapters place the burden of the events upon the leaders, prophets, and priests, deflecting the people's guilt. These chapters recognize God's role in the nation's misfortune, which seems to them unwarranted and disproportionate.

Unrelieved by a clear sense of theological culpability and focused on the intensity of God's anger and its brutal outcome, chapters 2 and 4 display both confusion and defiance. Neither chapter properly reconciles with God. Instead, they retain a tenor of theological uncertainty, fraught with an abiding inability to comprehend the events that have occurred.

The End of the Chapter: The End of the Book?

Chapter 4 concludes in an unexpectedly hopeful manner. Its final two verses seem almost an addendum, a separate entity from the rest of the chapter. Offering hope (and perhaps even a glimpse of theological reconciliation), verses 21–22 assert that when sinning ends, so will punishment. These verses could perhaps have functioned as the conclusion of this calamitous book. Indeed, the first word of 4:22 is *tam*, which suggests completion and conclusion. Followed by the word "sins," the verse explains that the cessation of sinning will lead to return from the exile. Moreover, enemies will receive their due recompense, and justice will be restored to the world. This conclusion of chapter 4 looks in a new direction, envisioning an optimistic end to Zion's calamity.

However, Eikha does not end with these verses. The book cannot yet conclude because chapter 4 ends without a direct address to God. The community, exiled and detached from their land and their city, still feels alienated from God. Despite the optimism at the end of Eikha 4, the community lacks the courage and strength to call upon

---

199. As noted above, Eikha 4:6 alludes to the *"avon"* of the people. Some biblical interpreters understand it to mean punishment rather than sin. In any case, the purpose of the verse is not to condemn the nation's sinfulness, but to bemoan their annihilation. The conclusion of chapter 4 also contains a reference to the nation's sins. This reference, however, coheres with the anomalous nature of the conclusion of the chapter, which mentions sinfulness in order to offer guidance and hope for ending the exile.

God directly. The book cannot end with a community that lacks the inner resources to petition God.

The ability to see a broader picture along with the possibility of a just world, both of which emerge at the conclusion of chapter 4, re-imbue the community with confidence and vigor. This paves the path to the final chapter, which opens with the community's direct and evocative appeal to God.

Eikha: Chapter Five

A Communal Petition
and Lament

INTRODUCTION

The composition of chapter 5 sets it apart from the previous chapters. Especially noticeable is the absence of an alphabetic acrostic, even though this chapter contains twenty-two verses, as would a Hebrew alphabetic sequence.[1] The dissolution of the alphabetic structure may indicate the ebbing of the all-encompassing pain that characterized previous chapters, the community's fatigue, or the breakdown of any semblance of order.[2]

Each verse of this chapter contains one brief binary sentence. The list of woes emerges in a staccato beat, relentlessly battering the reader with dull but persistent force. The book has become increasingly

---

1. Some scholars have proposed various acrostics that replace the alphabetic. I will soon introduce one intriguing proposition.
2. J. F. Burg, "Biblical Acrostics and their Relation to Other Ancient Near Eastern Acrostics," in W. W. Hallo, B. W. Jones, and G. L. Mattingly (eds.), *The Bible in Light of Cuneiform Literature: Scripture in Context* (ANET Studies 8; Lewiston, NY: Edwin Mellon Press, 1990), 286, notes that the disappearance of the acrostics in chapter 5 indicates the poet's exhaustion.

shorter; its life force diminishes as the community loses the strength to articulate their grievances.[3]

Unlike previous chapters, chapter 5 opens with three imperative verbs asking God to intervene, instead of the elegiac opening, *"Eikha."* Omitting the word *"Eikha"* indicates that this chapter is not primarily a lament. *"Kina* meter" likewise dissipates, and sentences revert mostly to the balanced meter of biblical poetry.[4] Written almost entirely in the first-person plural, the communal nature of the chapter suggests organization; possibly, it was written after some time elapsed.

The chapter opens with a collective appeal to God, a communal prayer.[5] Chapter 4 concluded with the conviction that Israel's exile will end. Nevertheless, that optimistic projection remained obscured in an amorphous future, dependent upon factors that have yet to occur. Jerusalem's shame and suffering are still ongoing, God remains elusive and silent, and Israel cannot yet manage to turn to Him. In chapter 5, the community summons the remains of its energy and turns directly to God, presenting their tragedy for His examination.

Despite the distinctive compositional features of this chapter, which suggest the possibility of a renewed relationship with God, the chapter maintains its blunt assessment of the dismal reality. Recalling chapter 1, it circles back to the original account of Jerusalem's calamity. Jerusalem remains desolate, a widowed city, characterized by loss and

---

3. Chapter 4 maintains two sentences in each verse, and chapters 1 and 2 have three sentences per verse. Chapter 3 likewise has one sentence for each verse, but contains three times the number of verses. Thus, chapters 1, 2, and 3 have 66 sentences, chapter 4 has 44 sentences, and chapter 5 has 22 sentences. The book of Eikha weakens and dwindles, mirroring the community's ebbing vitality.

4. The first three sentences of the chapter function as notable exceptions to this, suggesting perhaps that as the chapter gains momentum, it achieves a more balanced (and less grief-stricken) tone. Another exception is verse 14, which is also composed in *kina* meter. The epilogue to the chapter, which in my view functions as the epilogue to the book, returns mostly to *kina* meter, circling back to the painful reality of mournful lamentation.

5. Several Greek manuscripts introduce this chapter with the words "A prayer," or "A prayer of Jeremiah." Scholars note that national laments often conclude with a prayer for God's intervention, as in Psalms 28:9; 44:27. See, for example, Grossberg, *Centripetal*, 102.

by the word *"ein"* ("there is none").[6] The community petitions God to remember, look, and see their humiliation, following this with a harrowing catalogue of their losses.

Communication with God has been limited in the book, and this bid to mend ties suggests renewed faith. As part of its movement toward reconciliation with God, the community twice interrupts the litany of suffering to contemplate why these events have occurred. Initially refusing to assume responsibility, the community assigns it instead to their predecessors (5:7). As the chapter progresses, it gropes its way toward admission of sinfulness, giving rise to a communal assumption of responsibility: "Woe to us for we have sinned!" (5:16). It remains unclear what precisely precipitates this conclusion, which emerges without warning, in a sudden flash of clarity.

The bulk of the chapter has the community focused inward in a first-person plural description of their distress (5:2–18). Toward the conclusion of the chapter, the community again turns directly to God, first in a description of His eternity (5:19) and then in a (perhaps rhetorical) question that contains a hint of a plea (5:20). In verse 21, the community's boldness reaches its zenith, as they petition God to intercede and restore His relationship with His nation. Nevertheless, the book concludes with God's silence; the community heaves a final sigh of despair, ending the chapter (and the book) with an expression of bewilderment and pain, flung directly at God: "For You have surely rejected us, You have been greatly wrathful against us" (5:22).

This is the only chapter that contains just one speaker.[7] The voice of the anguished individual has faded, yet the collective voice of the community somehow endures. Rising from the ashes of a shattered nation, it insists on its right to petition God. Although the book eschews

---

6. The word *ein* (none) appears five times in chapter 1 (primarily referring to the absence of a comforter) and three times in chapter 5. This underscores the similarity between these chapters, both of which describe a desolate city, emptied of her glory and bereft of her inhabitants. The word *ein* appears only twice more in the rest of the book (once in chapter 2 and once in chapter 4).

7. The chapter shifts into third person in verses 11–14, in order to describe the way in which specific groups (women, maidens, officers, elders, young men, youth) are affected by the calamity.

unrealistic positivity or fraudulent solutions, chapter 5 restores the community's prayerful mode. In this petitionary chapter, the community transforms its paralyzing grief into a communal mission to regain God's attention and reopen the channels of communication.

STRUCTURE

We cannot divide the structure of chapter 5 based on its speakers, as the communal first-person speaker dominates the chapter. Dividing the chapter on thematic grounds elicits problems as well. Most of the chapter recounts the losses suffered by the community. Starting with the loss of life's necessities (housing, drink, and food), and proceeding to a description of torment and humiliation, the list of grievances arrives at its climactic calamity – namely, the desolation of the Temple Mount. The chapter ends with several disjointed statements: a brief theological reflection, a hope that flares up and extinguishes, and a lament over God's wrathful rejection.

Based on this thematic progression, some scholars divide the chapter as follows:[8]

> Part 1 – Verse 1: Petition
> Part 2 – Verses 2–18: List of Grievances
> Part 3 – Verses 19–21: Praise of God
> Part 4 – Verse 22: Closing Lament

Alternatively, we can divide the chapter based on two reflective comments, constituting two pauses that interrupt its catalogue of misfortune. This division draws the reader's attention to the way that chapter 5 grapples with the theological implications of the calamity. The first seven verses cite the community's initial deflection of responsibility, "Our fathers sinned and they are no more, and we suffered for their iniquities!" (verse 7). The following nine verses climax with an opposite conclusion, linguistically evoking the earlier assertion, only to invert it: "Woe to us for we have sinned!" (verse 16). This division leaves the final six

---

8. Although they do not have identical divisions, scholars who adopt this basic outline include Westermann, 212–13; Hillers, 103; Dobbs-Allsopp, 142.

sentences of the chapter with no clear linguistic or thematic connection to the first sixteen verses; they function instead as an epilogue both to the chapter and to the book. This division yields the following structure:

Part 1 – Verses 1–7: Grievances Without Culpability
Part 2 – Verses 8–16: Grievances and Recognition of Sinfulness
Part 3 – Verses 17–22: Epilogue: Concluding Reflections

Both divisions offer different perspectives on the principal idea of the chapter. The first emphasizes its petitionary mode, albeit recognizing that the "prayer" consists of a list of complaints rather than direct communication with God or praise of Him. The second division highlights the theological grappling that takes place in this chapter, the community's valiant and successful bid to arrive at recognition of sinfulness. The second division regards the final verses as a separate entity, which may function as an epilogue not only for the chapter, but also for the entire book. I will adopt this second approach in my reading of this chapter.

Is Zechariah the Author of Chapter 5?

According to some scholars, chapter 5 opens with an acrostic that functions as a colophon.[9] Its initial two words, "*Zekhor YHVH*," form the name Zechariah. Following this opening, the first letter of each line of verses 1–3 (there are two lines in each verse) produce the word "*hanavi*," or "the prophet."[10] Perhaps this opening ascribes authorship of this chapter to Zechariah the son of Berechiah, who prophesied during the period of the return to Zion (520–518 BCE).[11]

---

9. A. Rosenfeld, "Acrostics in Eikha, Chapter 5," *Sinai* 110 (1992), 96 [Hebrew]. The acrostic is as follows:

(א) **זְכֹר יְ-ה-ו-ה** מֶה הָיָה לָנוּ הַבִּיטה וּרְאֵה אֶת חֶרְפָּתֵנוּ:
(ב) **נַחֲלָתֵנוּ** נֶהֶפְכָה לְזָרִים בָּתֵּינוּ לְנָכְרִים:
(ג) **יְתוֹמִים** הָיִינוּ וְאֵין אָב אִמֹּתֵינוּ כְּאַלְמָנוֹת:

10. This kind of acrostic, known as a mesostic, appears in some biblical alphabetic acrostics, such as Psalms 111–12.
11. There is another prophet named Zechariah, the son of Jehoyada, who was murdered in the Temple following his prophecy, at King Joash's command (II Chr. 24:20–22). While several midrashim (*Sifra, Behukotai* 2:6; *Eikha Rabba* 1:51) assert that Eikha

If Zechariah wrote this chapter at the end of the sixth century BCE, this would confirm that it was composed after the previous chapters (as suggested above). Several linguistic points support a connection between Zechariah and Eikha 5. Zechariah opens his prophecy by reminding the people of God's anger with their fathers (namely, the previous generation who suffered the *ḥurban*).[12] The word that launches Zechariah's prophecy (appearing twice in his opening sentence, 1:2) is *katzaf,* which appears in the final verse of Eikha (5:22): "You have been greatly wrathful (*katzafta*) against us." Zechariah's next sentence (1:3) advises the people to return to God so that He will reciprocate: "Thus says the Lord of hosts: Return to Me... and I will return to you." This verse linguistically evokes but also counters the penultimate verse of Eikha, which demands the opposite order of events: "Return us to You, Lord, and we will return."[13] These linguistic connections indicate that Zechariah's book consciously picks up where Eikha 5 trails off, in a conscious bid to reconcile the nation and God.[14]

What is the significance of this possible ascription? Why would Zechariah write Eikha 5? The prophecies of Haggai and Zechariah are designed to spearhead the rebuilding of the Temple (520–516 BCE), offering encouragement and inspiration to the small community that has returned from exile. The litany of loss in Eikha 5 climaxes with the loss of the Temple, whose desolation is identified as the primary source of despair. Indeed, the foxes that desecrate the hallowed ground likely still cavort there during the time of these post-exilic prophets, who endeavor to inspire the Judeans to launch the rebuilding of the Temple.

2:20 alludes to this incident, I see no reason to assign authorship to this earlier Zechariah.

12. Although the identity of the fathers who were the object of God's anger is unstated, the context suggests that this refers to the generation of the *ḥurban*. See Rashi on Zechariah 1:2.

13. A midrash (Eikha Rabba 5:21) notes the disagreement between these verses, thereby acknowledging their interconnectedness.

14. The fact that biblical books dialogue with each other does not necessarily mean that they have a common author. I have not, after all, suggested that Isaiah 40–66 and Eikha share the same author, despite their numerous cross-references. I only raise this possibility here because of the intriguing colophon at the opening of the chapter.

Possibly, chapter 5 lends further impetus to the community to undertake this project.

Zechariah (along with Haggai) achieves his prophetic objective (Ezra 5:1–2), successfully persuading the Judeans to rebuild the Temple and thereby reverse the Babylonian destruction of their sacred center. Possibly for this reason, R. Akiva joyously remembers Zechariah's prophecy when he witnesses the terrible sight of the foxes desecrating the site of the second *ḥurban*. Zechariah does not simply prophesy change, he believes in it, spearheads it, and shepherds it to fruition.

PART 1 (EIKHA 5:1–7):
GRIEVANCES WITHOUT CULPABILITY

Eikha 5:1

זְכֹר ה' מֶה־הָיָה לָנוּ
הַבִּיטָה וּרְאֵה אֶת־חֶרְפָּתֵנוּ

Remember, Lord, what befell us
Look and see our disgrace

The chapter opens with the community firing three imperative verbs at God, beseeching Him to remember (*zekhor*) what has happened to them, to look (*habita*), and to see (*ure'eh*) their humiliation.

Positioned as the key opening word in chapter 5, the word *zekhor* makes its seventh and final appearance in the book. Memory and forgetfulness frame the chapter, underlining its significance.[15] Elsewhere in Tanakh, memory plays an important role in bringing about a reversal of God's decree of destruction (Gen. 8:1). It also marks the mutual and immutable relationship between God and Israel: God often obliges Israel to remember pivotal events,[16] while promising that He will remember

---

15. In verse 20, the community posits a rhetorical question: "Why should You forget us forever?"

16. The obligatory nature of remembering specific events finds liturgical expression in the "six remembrances," instituted at the conclusion of the daily morning prayer service.

His nation, and not reject them or abandon them in exile (Lev. 26:42–45). Nevertheless, in Eikha's only previous usage of the verb *zakhar* that clearly relates to God,[17] the word appears in the negative: "And He did *not remember* (*velo zakhar*) His footstool on the day of His burning anger" (Eikha 2:1). God's decision *not* to remember sets in motion the destruction of Jerusalem in chapter 2. Aloof and distant, God refuses to recall His Temple, obliterating Jerusalem's only hope for a reprieve. Eikha's final chapter launches with an appeal to God to remember, setting in motion the opposite trajectory, in which God remembers His nation and rebuilds the city and Temple. In our examination of chapter 3, I noted that the word *zakhar* functions as a pivot for the *gever's* transformation, whether it involves his own remembrances or his appeal to God to remember. Employing the same word that propelled the turnaround of chapter 3, Eikha's final chapter endeavors to bring about a similar pivot toward restoration of the community's relationship with God.

The two remaining imperative verbs in the verse (*re'eh* and *habita*) echo previous petitions directed toward God. Chapters 1 and 2 contain direct appeals to God that He look (*re'eh*) and see (*habita*) His nation (1:11; 2:20). The speaker in chapter 1 entreats God twice more simply to look (*re'eh*) at him (1:9, 20), although he omits the second verb, *habita*, in these verses. Chapter 3 employs both verbs in succession (though not in conjunction) in relation to God (3:59, 60, 63), either as an appeal to God or as a description of God's actions. Chapter 4 appears to consciously refrain from issuing this appeal, asserting that "[God] did *not* continue to look at them (*lehabitam*)."[18] Chapter 5 revisits the customary petition in its initial verse, a heartfelt plea to restore communication. This functions to restore the failed communication of chapter 4, revealing the community's determination to renew its ties with God.

It is customary to declare Israel's obligation to remember the Exodus from Egypt, the experience at Sinai (also known as Ḥorev), the eternal war against Amalek, the nation's recalcitrant behavior during their wanderings in the desert, the punishment of Miriam when she spoke against Moses, and the sanctification of the Shabbat.

17. It is unclear whether the three appearances of the word *zakhar* in Eikha 3:19–20 describe God's memory or human remembrances.

18. For an explanation of this, see my discussion of Eikha 4:16.

Despite their frequent appearances, these three verbs appear in conjunction only in this verse. The word *zekhor* suggests that the community is alluding to events that occurred in the past, while the request to look and see them evokes their current state of distress. Ibn Ezra notes this, explaining the verse as follows:

> *Zekhor*: The [plea to] "remember" is in the heart and [the plea to] "look" is with the eye. Its explanation: [Remember] all the troubles that passed over us prior to the exile, and [look at] the disgrace that we are presently in. (Ibn Ezra, Eikha 5:1)

According to Ibn Ezra's reading, this chapter integrates Israel's past troubles with its present misery.[19] It is difficult to separate the past from the present in this chapter. Which of the inventory of calamities do they recall from the perspective of exile, and which represent an account of their present situation? It seems impossible to discern one from the other. Nevertheless, one thing seems clear: This chapter describes an unbroken continuum of loss that began while they were still living in Jerusalem and accompanies them following the city's destruction. The nation finds it difficult to heal; living with its losses, it unceasingly recalls its hardships, mixing past catastrophes and present ones.

Before embarking on a lengthy description of the dismal situation, the chapter summarizes it in one Hebrew word: *herpatenu*, "our disgrace."[20] Calling upon God to bear witness to its humiliation, the community expresses the emotional fallout from the terrible events, the helplessness and torment that expunge human dignity.

Biblical passages often link the reputations of God and Israel, such that shaming Israel demeans God as well. Goliath's pugnacious speech, designed to taunt and humiliate Israel (I Sam. 17:10, 25), also

---

19. Although Ibn Ezra does not specify, it seems probable that he refers to the events that occurred in Jerusalem up to and including its destruction by the Babylonians. Nevertheless, R. Yosef Kara (Eikha 5:2) asserts that the past events include those associated with the exile of the ten tribes by the Assyrians in the eighth century BCE. Although he does not adduce Eikha 5:6 to support this claim, R. Kara is likely influenced by the reference to Assyria and Egypt in that verse.

20. We encountered the word *herpa* twice in chapter 3 (verses 30 and 61).

aims to humiliate Israel's God (I Sam. 17:45).[21] When Israel experiences troubles, enemies of Israel question God's fidelity to His nation or His very omnipotence. Taunts such as, "Where is your God?" (Mic. 7:10; Ps. 42:11), reverberate hauntingly, compounding the people's suffering.

In the context of Eikha, God's ostensible abandonment of Israel to a terrible fate endures as a source of disgrace for His people and for God, leaving lingering questions about God's power, loyalty, and trustworthiness.[22] The prophet Ezekiel describes the Babylonian exile as a desecration of God's name:[23]

> And I poured my wrath upon them because of the blood that they spilled upon the land, and they sullied it with their idolatries. And I scattered them among the nations, and they spread out through the lands; according to their ways and their deeds I judged them. And they came to the nations that they arrived there, and *they desecrated My holy name* when the [nations] said about them, "These are the nation of the Lord and from His land they were exiled!" And I had compassion upon My holy name, which the house of Israel had profaned amongst the nations where they had arrived. (Ezek. 36:18–21)

The linkage between Israel and God in the eyes of the world adds dimension and depth to the appeal that God see Israel's humiliation. Perhaps by observing Israel's disgrace, God will witness the public desecration of His own name. This may induce Him to repair Israel's situation, restoring honor to the nation that reflects God's honor.

Indeed, in a stunning redemptive moment, Ezekiel describes God swooping in to redeem His people from the Babylonian exile and restore them to their land and good fortune. God does this not because

---

21. The same word that appears in our verse (*ḥerpa*) appears in each of these verses in I Samuel 17.
22. This and similar arguments are propounded by prominent biblical figures in their attempts to persuade God to have mercy on His nation (see Ex. 32:12; Num. 14:13–16; Joel 2:17; Ps. 79:10).
23. See also Isaiah 52:5; Psalms 74:7–10.

they deserve it, but in order to sanctify His name following its terrible
desecration:

> So says The Lord God: Not for you I act, house of Israel, but for
> My holy name, which you have desecrated among the nations...
> And I will sanctify My great name... and the nations will know
> that I am the Lord – says the Lord God – when I manifest My
> holiness through you before their eyes. And I will take you from
> among the nations and I will gather you from all the lands and I
> will bring you to your land. And I will sprinkle pure water upon
> you, and you will be purified... I will give you a new heart and
> I will place a new spirit in your midst... and you will live in the
> land that I gave to your fathers, and you will be for Me a nation
> and I will be for you a God. (Ezek. 36:22–28)

In petitioning God in Eikha 5:1 to witness their humiliation, the nation
appeals not just for sympathy, but for deliverance. God's desire to sanctify His name among the nations will surely stir Him to remove the
humiliation and restore Israel's dignity.

Eikha 5:2–5

נַחֲלָתֵנוּ נֶהֶפְכָה לְזָרִים
בָּתֵּינוּ לְנָכְרִים

יְתוֹמִים הָיִינוּ וְאֵין אָב
אִמֹּתֵינוּ כְּאַלְמָנוֹת

מֵימֵינוּ בְּכֶסֶף שָׁתִינוּ
עֵצֵינוּ בִּמְחִיר יָבֹאוּ

עַל צַוָּארֵנוּ נִרְדָּפְנוּ
יָגַעְנוּ וְלֹא הוּנַח־לָנוּ

Our estates are turned over to strangers
Our houses to foreigners

> We became orphans without a father
> Our mothers are like widows
>
> Our water we drank [in exchange] for money
> Our trees came for pay
>
> Pursued by our necks[24]
> We wearied and they gave us no respite

Following the brief petition of verse 1, the community offers a self-portrait of devastation that is both resolute and concise. Ordinary life unravels as the chapter steadily lists the loss of the basic exigencies of existence: land, homes, fathers, husbands, drinking water, and wood. Households and family structure collapse. Exhaustion sets in, driven by the pursuit of a relentless enemy.

Although the chapter does not open with the customary word that signifies lament (*"Eikha!"*), the first three verses employ the meter of lamentation that I identified in previous chapters (*"kina* meter").[25] Initially, the chapter presents itself as a lament; the community seems to sob and swallow its words, unable to complete its sentences as it recalls its misfortune. Beginning in verse 4, however, the account is tempered by balanced meter, reflecting an equilibrium heretofore unseen in the book. Perhaps (as I suggested above) time has passed since the catastrophe, allowing the community to regain its footing and reflect sorrowfully on events without choking back tears.[26]

---

24. The phrase *al tzavarenu*, which I have loosely translated as "by our necks," may be an idiom that points to an enemy in close pursuit. Perhaps it refers to a yoke borne on their necks as the enemy drives the Judean community into captivity. I will examine this shortly.

25. For an explanation of *kina* meter, see the introductory chapter "Biblical Poetry and the Book of Eikha."

26. Eikha Rabba 2:4 portrays R. Yoḥanan engaging in more extensive exegetical analysis of Eikha's text than Rebbe (R. Yehuda HaNasi). The midrash rejects the possibility that R. Yoḥanan is a more skilled exegete, concluding instead that Rebbe, who lived a generation before R. Yoḥanan, recalls the catastrophe with sobs, preventing him from a sober analysis. It is worth pointing out that Rebbe was born sixty-five years *after* the destruction of Jerusalem!

Verse 2 contains two parallel sentences, portraying foreigners and strangers ousting Judah's inhabitants from their estates and homes. The ancestral land (*naḥalatenu*) parallels the houses (*bateinu*), while the invasive foreigners (*zarim*) parallel the strangers (*nokhrim*), as they work in tandem to displace the Judeans. Homelessness is not the only problem; this description alludes to the psychological effect of witnessing others enjoying the fruits of your labors, taking for themselves what is rightfully yours.[27] The *Tokheḥa* in Deuteronomy warned of this scenario:[28]

> You will betroth a woman, and another will lie with her, you will build a house and you will not dwell in it, you will plant a vineyard but will not consecrate it. Your ox will be slaughtered in front of your eyes and you will not eat from it, your donkey will be stolen from in front of you and will not return to you, your sheep will be given to your enemies … a nation that you do not know will consume the fruits of your land and all of your labor. (Deut. 28:30–33)

The loss of the *naḥalot* (land estates) represents another disruption of the nation's religious commitments. A family's *naḥala* is an inalienable possession, bequeathed to it by God (Num. 36:2; Josh. 18:4–6, 10; 21:41), and returned to the family without fail every Jubilee year (Lev. 25:10, 13, 23). Biblical passages and later rabbinic sources discourage families from selling their houses and land,[29] while encouraging other members of the same family to buy the family estates if they do appear on the market (Lev. 25:25–34).[30] This attitude contains strong religious undertones, displayed clearly in the words of Navot, who refuses to sell

---

27. It is instructive to draw from the contemporary experience of those who survived the Holocaust. Returning shattered from the camps or their hiding places, they generally found their houses occupied and their furniture requisitioned. This experience compounded their sense of displacement and alienation.

28. See also Jeremiah 6:12, where the prophet warns the people that their houses will be given to others because of their sinfulness.

29. See *Tosefta Arakhin* 5:6 and Maimonides, *Hilkhot Shemitta VeYovel* 11:3, which discuss the religious strictures involved in selling ancestral property.

30. See Numbers 36:7, 9, which takes pains to ensure that the land inheritances remain within the tribe. See also Micah 2:2, where the prophet berates the people for the evil they have committed in taking the houses and family estates of others. While

his ancestral property to King Ahab (I Kings 21:3): "The Lord forbid me that I should give the inheritance of my forefathers to you!" God bequeathed upon the family their portion of land and it would be an act of ingratitude and impiety to relinquish it.

In addition, the word *naḥala* also often refers to the land as a whole, not simply to the individual family portions. God bestows the land upon Israel (Deut. 4:21, 38), who have the responsibility and privilege of maintaining it. The collapse of this system represents yet another loss of divine endowments, a bequest that vanishes along with all that God had previously given them.[31]

The verb that describes the upheaval in verse 2 is *nehefkha*, meaning to overturn. This word frames the description of Jerusalem's disarray, appearing again in verse 15 to portray the replacement of joyful dance with gyrations of agony. Employed in various contexts, the verb *hafakh* can signify the complete transformation of an object (Ex. 7:15, 17; Jer. 13:23; Joel 3:4), a person (I Sam. 10:6), a state of mind (Ex. 14:5), or a city (Jonah 3:4). It also alludes to a change of fortune, often effected by God (Deut. 23:6; Jer. 31:12). More specifically, this word frequently describes the overturning of Sodom and Gomorrah (Gen. 19:21; Is. 13:19; Jer. 49:18; Amos 4:11; Eikha 4:6), formerly thriving cities transformed into wasteland. The word suggests an upside-down state, a sweeping scope of destruction, and an unlikely, if not impossible, recovery.

Following the loss of property and houses, the community describes the dissolution of family and household. Fathers disappear, leaving behind orphaned children and widowed mothers.[32] Strikingly, the verse does not clarify what has happened to these men, remaining

---

this may refer specifically to the act of stealing, the reference to houses and *naḥalot* suggests the violation of the law of family property.

31. In our verses, Israel has lost the promise of both "*menuḥa and naḥala*" (Deut. 12:9). The loss of *menuḥa* (the resting place) is referenced linguistically in 5:5 (*velo hunaḥ lanu*). Strikingly, God bemoans the loss of His house (*beiti*) and estate (*naḥalati*) in Jeremiah 12:7. God's misfortunes are linked with Israel's, which may ultimately provide some consolation for Israel. See also Eikha Rabba *Petiḥta* 24.

32. The description of the widowed population recalls the city's widowed state at the beginning of the book (Eikha 1:1). The word *almana* links chapters 1 and 5 and illustrates the merging of the city's experience with that of the community.

focused on loss. The men's absence suggests either their death in battle or their capture by the enemies.[33]

Reduced to a populace of orphans and widows, the nation is especially vulnerable, lacking provisions and protection. This hints to the impending collapse of the social infrastructure.[34] If all members of society have become defenseless and needy, then no one can offer the widows and orphans assistance; everyone is equally disadvantaged.

The reference to the absent father also may allude to God,[35] who has deliberately withdrawn from His nation. In this scenario, the people's vulnerable state has no possible reprieve, as they cannot even invoke the special protection God generally to widows and orphans (Deut. 10:18).

Moving rapidly to the next atrocity, the community describes the loss of their resources. In a metrically balanced verse, which contains synonymous parallelism, verse 4 flatly presents the situation. Deprived of control over their land, the local population must pay for their water and trees, resources generally unrestricted and free of charge, certainly for locals.[36] In this description, the enemies who currently retain the rights to the water and trees remain in the background; the verse focuses on the survivors, forced to pay others for the right to live in their own land.[37]

Following these losses, the community depicts its exhaustion; with the enemy in pursuit, they cannot find respite.[38] In the context of the litany of loss, this verse seems out of place. Moreover, it remains unclear what the verse is describing. Is it the enemies propelling them toward exile, where they find no rest? Is it their capture and enslavement? Or perhaps it portrays the Judean community toiling upon their land to

---

33. R. Yosef Kara maintains that the fathers are not actually gone; rather, their inability to help their children and families denies the fathers their paternal role. Lacking their essential ability to nurture their families, their wives are *like* widows and their children *like* orphans.

34. See, for example, Exodus 22:21; Deuteronomy 24:17, 19–21; 26:12–13.

35. See, for example, Exodus 4:22; Jeremiah 31:8; Hosea 11:1.

36. See Ibn Ezra and R. Yosef Kara on Eikha 5:4.

37. Ibn Ezra asserts that this describes the siege prior to the actual destruction.

38. The phrase "*lo hunaḥ*" ("they gave us no respite") recalls the causative verb commonly used to describe God's intervention in helping the Israelites obtain secure settlement in the land (Deut. 12:10; Josh. 23:1). Used negatively in verse 5, the word highlights the withdrawal of God's support.

produce food they will never enjoy.[39] The last possibility seems most consistent with the rest of the chapter, which appears to represent the current situation of Jerusalem's populace (see verses 2, 11, 18).

The initial phrase of verse 5, "pursued by our necks," is unclear. Perhaps this is an idiom that represents the enemy "breathing down its neck," suggesting close pursuit that is both unremitting and threatening. Many biblical interpreters (both traditional and modern) assume that the phrase alludes to a yoke of enslavement, metaphoric or actual, placed upon their necks.[40] This leads to the exhaustion and inability to rest described in the next part of the verse.[41] In this reading, the verse in its entirety portrays the condition of forced labor imposed upon them by others.[42] Alternatively, the verse may simply evoke the community's state of mind; weary and drained, they feel relentlessly pursued.[43]

Eikha 5:6

מִצְרַיִם נָתַנּוּ יָד
אַשּׁוּר לִשְׂבֹּעַ לָחֶם

We gave a hand to Egypt[44]
[To] Assyria, for our fill of bread

---

39. R. Yosef Kara asserts that the correct translation of the word *hunaḥ* (which contains a massoretic dot in the letter *nun*) is that others did not leave us the fruits of our toil. He maintains that without the dot, the meaning would be that we could not find rest. Indeed, the verb seems to be in a causative form, suggesting that others cause our state. However, it could mean that others did not allow us to rest, rather than that they prevented us from enjoying the fruits of our labor.

40. See Rashi, R. Yosef Kara; Hillers, 95; Westermann, 208, 214. Ibn Ezra reads this verse as a continuation of the previous one: "If we bring the water or the trees upon our necks, the enemies pursue us and our toil is for naught, for they do not leave for us that which we have brought."

41. The pursuit, exhaustion, and inability to find rest all recall chapter 1 (see verses 3 and 6), which functions as a parallel to chapter 5.

42. Verse 13 contains a similar depiction of forced labor.

43. See Berlin, 119.

44. The phrase, "To give one's hand," often refers to the forging of an alliance (e.g., Ezek. 17:18; I Chron. 29:24). Rashi explains that we stretched out a hand in order to obtain assistance from these countries, while R. Yosef Kara asserts that this verse describes

To understand Assyria's role in this verse, we must address two issues: the period in which the community seeks an alliance with Assyria and the reason for the alliance. When did the nation seek an alliance with Assyria?[45] Does verse 6 (like verse 7) portray past events (as a prelude to describing the sins of the fathers) or is it a continuation of the description of the current situation?

Perhaps this verse describes ties forged during the Babylonian siege, in which Jerusalem's desperate and hungry populace scrambles for bread to survive. It is difficult, however, to understand the reference to Assyria.[46] In what way did Assyria assist Judah during the calamity brought about by the Babylonian empire? The Assyrian empire had collapsed long before, and it no longer played any major role in Judah's fate. Some scholars conclude that "Assyria and Egypt" is simply Ancient Near Eastern shorthand for the broad swath of land from the southwest (Egypt) to the northeast (Assyria).[47] Others suggest that "Assyria and Egypt" is a term used for improper alliances, even if the reference is not to these specific powers.[48]

Alternatively, this verse may not describe the present situation. Possibly, this looks backward at earlier events, trying to make sense of the current horrific circumstances and preparing us for the verse that follows. Israel's dependence upon alliances with foreign powers (including Assyria) are repeatedly condemned by prophets,[49] constituting one of the main sins that spawns this calamity.[50] This reflection leads to the

---

the creation of an unequal relationship, in which Judah must obey and accept the dominance of the nation to whom it extended its hand.

45. I previously discussed the role of Egypt during this crisis (see Eikha 4:17). The community that remains in Judah following the exile emigrates to Egypt soon after the murder of Gedalya ben Aḥikam (Jer. 43:7). The decision to go to Egypt, taken against Jeremiah's express counsel (Jer. 42:7–22), illustrates their continued reliance on Egypt for both political support and abundant food (see Jer. 42:14, cited by R. Yosef Kara in his commentary on Eikha 5:6).

46. One edition of the *Targum* removes Assyria from this verse.

47. Berlin, 119, suggests this and the following idea as well.

48. See, for example, Jeremiah 2:18, 26; Hosea 7:11; 12:2.

49. See, for example, Hosea 7:11; Isaiah 31:1–3; Jeremiah 2:18.

50. I have previously examined the problem of forging alliances with other nations, most notably in chapter 1, where this theme emerges prominently. See 1:2, 8, 17, 19.

following verse, in which the community holds the sins of the fathers responsible for the disaster.

The intent of the phrase "for our fill of bread" remains ambiguous. Does it seek to exonerate the desperate nation, offering an excuse for their behavior? In this reading, the tone of the verse is defensive; the starving community had little choice but to forge alliances if they wished to obtain food.[51] This phrase recalls God's role in providing sustenance for His nation (Ex. 16:12). It seems that Judah's dependence on other nations stems from God's abandonment; had God taken care of us and satiated us with bread, we would not have had to turn to outside sources. Read in this way, the community offers an excuse for their ill-advised alliances.

Possibly, however, the phrase "to satiate with bread" does not imply a desperate grasp for survival, but rather a greedy desire for a life of luxury. The phrase *sava leḥem* sometimes describes the lifestyle of the wealthy, one of corrupt extravagance and overindulgence.[52] Intriguingly, this phrase appears in a hostile exchange between the nation and Jeremiah, which takes place after the survivors of the catastrophe go to Egypt instead of obeying God and remaining in Israel. Jeremiah urges them to cease their idolatry, maintaining that their sins brought about the catastrophe in Jerusalem (Jer. 44:1–14). The surviving Judeans hold the opposite view, asserting that it was only when they worshipped idols that they prospered:

> This thing that you spoke to us in the name of the Lord, we shall not listen to you. For we will continue doing that which we said, to bring incense to the Queen of the Heavens and we will pour libations for her as we and our forefathers, our kings and

---

See also the discussion of 4:17. These alliances obviate the people's reliance on God, causing Israel to rely instead on untrustworthy (and essentially powerless) nations. To compound this problem, these alliances with other nations influence Israel to worship those nations' idols, either because the allies require it, or because the gods of the stronger nations appear more powerful.

51. While there is no evidence that Israel ever allied itself with Assyria to obtain food, Israel did often go down to Egypt to obtain food during a famine. House, 463, interprets this phrase as figurative, explaining that the quest for "bread" is in fact one for political assistance.

52. Ezekiel 16:49 employs the phrase to describe Sodom's corrupt prosperity. For another negative use of this phrase, see Proverbs 30:22.

officers did in the cities of Judah and in the streets of Jerusalem.
And we were satiated with bread and we lived well and saw no evil.
However, since we stopped bringing incense to the Queen of the
Heavens and pouring her libations, we lost everything, and we
perished by the sword and by hunger. (Jer. 44﹕﹡ ﹡﹡)

The nation's warped perspective causes them to seek prosperity by worshipping idols. It is possible that the use of this phrase in Eikha 5:6 intimates that the community forged improper alliances not in a desperate
quest for basic survival, but in order to perpetuate a distorted value system. In this reading, the community acknowledges that Judah formed
alliances out of a crass desire for sumptuous living.

Eikha 5:7

אֲבֹתֵינוּ חָטְאוּ וְאֵינָם
וַאֲנַחְנוּ עֲוֹנֹתֵיהֶם סָבָלְנוּ

Our fathers sinned and they are no more[53]
And we suffered for their iniquities[54]

This verse pauses to reflect, offering a brief theological statement that
focuses on the sins of "our fathers" (*avoteinu*) alongside the present
condition of "us" (*anaḥnu*), their descendants. It is not clear, however,
whether the statement aims to contrast or compare the behavior of the
fathers and their descendants. Does the community issue this utterance
in a tone of outrage or compliance? Is this a protest or a submissive
statement of confession?

Interpreting this verse largely depends upon our understanding of
the word *avonoteihem*. Do we bear the father's sins or their punishment?

---

53. Eikha 5:3 also employs the word *ein* ("there is none") to depict the fathers' absence,
    leaving vulnerable orphans and widows. In our verse, the fathers' absence leaves
    the community vulnerable, bearing the burden of the fathers' sins.
54. I can only choose one interpretation to translate the verse. This obscures the verse's
    complexity, and its multiple layers of interpretation. In the text that follows, I will
    elaborate on the possible translations and explain why I chose the above translation.

Moreover, what is the meaning of the word *savalnu*, which means to bear a heavy load (sometimes a figurative one, as in our verse)? Does it mean that the community suffers that load as a punishment, or carries it willingly to perpetuate the behavior of the fathers?

One reading assumes that the community admits that it continues to bear (namely, perpetuate) the sins of the fathers.[55] Both Ibn Ezra and R. Yosef Kara explain that the community draws an equivalence between their fathers' transgressions and their own, which together result in the current calamity.[56] Bearing the weight of accumulated sinfulness, the present generation suffers the punishment deserved by their ancestors along with that which they themselves have earned. This reading resolves the theological problem implied in this verse, namely, children suffering for the deeds of their parents.[57] Many rabbinic interpreters explain that children suffer for the sins of their parents only when they perpetuate their sinful behavior.[58]

Alternatively, the verse draws a contrast between the sins of the fathers and the (unfair) suffering of the children for their fathers' sins. In this reading, the community voices a theological protest, outraged that they suffer for the crimes of previous generations.[59]

Is this a realistic assessment? Biblical passages from the period of the *ḥurban* note that the Judean community believes that they suffer for the sins of others. To counter this, both Jeremiah and Ezekiel endeavor to convince the people of their own guilt and of God's justice:

> In those days they will no longer say, "Fathers eat sour grapes and the teeth of the children are blunted." Instead, each person dies

---

55. The above translation does not reflect this approach, which would instead translate: "Our fathers sinned, and they are no more, and we perpetuated their iniquities."

56. Daniel 9:16 contains a confession in plural form in which "our sins" link up with "the sins of the fathers" to cause the destruction of Jerusalem.

57. While Exodus 34:7 states that God visits the sins of the parents upon the following generations, several biblical passages assert the opposite – namely, that children do not die for the sins of their parents, nor do parents die for the sins of their children: Deuteronomy 24:16; II Kings 14:6; Ezekiel 18:1–20; II Chronicles 25:4.

58. See Sanhedrin 27b; *Targum Onkelos* and *Yonatan*, Rashi, Ibn Ezra on Exodus 34:7.

59. The mention of Assyria in the previous verse may support this reading; the community recalls alliances forged by past generations, as a prelude to foisting responsibility upon them.

for his own sin; every person who eats sour grapes shall have his teeth blunted. (Jer. 31:28–29)

What do you mean by citing this proverb upon the land of Israel, when you declare, "Fathers eat sour grapes and the teeth of the children are blunted"? I swear, says the Lord God, that you shall no longer speak this proverb in Israel. Behold, all lives belong to Me, the life of the father and the life of the child, [both] belong to Me and [only] the soul of the sinner shall perish! (Ezek. 18:2–4)

Despite the adamant position of the prophets, one can sense that this message does not easily convince the people, who prefer to deflect responsibility.[60]

Within this context, it seems likely that the verse reflects the popular notion that God treats their generation unfairly. The verse reads better as a grievance, as I have rendered it above: "Our fathers sinned and they are no more, and we suffered for their sins!" The tension between responsibility and suffering and the theological quandary that it creates climax in this simple utterance.

Josiah and the Suffering Servant

Isaiah 53 uses the word *saval* twice, describing a servant of God who suffers for the sins of others.[61] In the first instance, the word *saval* describes the pain that the sufferer bears for the sins of others:

---

60. Under the circumstances, their position is understandable. As we have seen, during the national calamity, children die alongside adults, and righteous people suffer alongside those who are sinful. This situation, typical of any national catastrophe, leaves acute theological questions that remain unanswered. It seems easiest to assert that God does not run His world in a just manner, as the Judean community seems to maintain in Eikha 5:7. Moreover, Exodus 34:7 plainly notes that God visits the sins of one generation upon the following generations (although sometimes exegetes interpret the verse differently). I will discuss below the reason that this generation in particular regards itself as righteous in contrast to their predecessors – a perception that is erroneous, yet emerges from a genuine assessment of their generation's deeds.
61. See Rashi (Is. 53:4, 11, 12), who reads Isaiah 53 in this way.

Indeed, he carried our sickness and he bore (*sevalam*) our pain. We thought that he was plagued, struck, and tormented by God. Yet, he was wounded for our transgressions, crushed by our iniquities... And the Lord struck him for the iniquity of us all. (Is. 53:4–6)

In the second appearance of the word *saval* (Is. 53:11), the sufferer bears the iniquities of others (*avonotam hu yisbol*), in a description linguistically linked to our verse (*avonoteihem savalnu*).

Who is the servant who suffers and how can he shed light on our verse? Rabbinic interpreters offer a range of possible identities.[62] I will focus on one suggestion that can help understand the attitude of outrage in Eikha 5:7. Abravanel suggests that one level of understanding is that the pious servant refers to the worthy Judean king Josiah, who dies in battle despite his righteousness.[63] In Abravanel's view, Isaiah 53 contains several harsh expressions of protest over Josiah's undeserved death. Josiah, after all, invested his energies and resources in ridding the country of idolatry and guiding the people to worship God properly.

The outrage of the Judean community in Eikha 5:7 may be better understood within the context of Josiah's death. Josiah transforms the community, enlisting them to join in his religious fervor. Many members of Jerusalem's current populace witnessed (and participated in) the reforms of King Josiah, ostensibly repenting their sinful idolatry. It is no wonder that the nation regards itself as undeserving of punishment. Why should they suffer for the idolatrous sins of previous generations?

---

62. Many exegetes maintains that the sufferer represents the collective Israel during the period of exile (e.g., Rashi, Is. 53:3, 8; Radak, Is. 52:13; R. Yosef Kara, Is. 53:13; Ibn Kaspi, Is. 53:13; Kuzari II:34; Metzudat David, Is. 52:13; Malbim, Is. 53:4). Ibn Ezra (Is. 53:2) raises the possibility that this section represents only the pious people in Israel, those who *behave* as servants of God. Others search for an individual sufferer: the Messiah (Ibn Ezra, Is. 52:13, brings this as one possibility; see also *Targum Yonatan*, Is. 52:13 and 53:10) or Jeremiah (Rasag, Is. 52:13). See Shadal's overview of interpretations in his commentary on Isaiah 52:13.

63. Abravanel interprets the entire passage twice, in extensive detail. First, he interprets it as if the suffering servant is Israel. The second time, the sufferer is Josiah.

Nevertheless, according to Jeremiah, Josiah's generation repented half-heartedly.[64] Rabbinic interpreters likewise note the people's insincerity, explaining that Judah's populace deceived their virtuous king, pretending to rid their houses of idolatry, while actually continuing these practices.[65] A well-known midrash vividly depicts the nation's duplicity:

> [Josiah] would send a pair of students to purge their homes of idolatry. When they would enter, they would not find anything. However, when they left, [the inhabitants] would say, "Close the doors." When they closed the doors, there was a graven image inscribed there [on the back of the door].[66] (Eikha Rabba 1:53)

If their repentance were fraudulent, why would they declare their innocence in Eikha 5:7? Perhaps this simply reflects human nature. People are notoriously self-deceptive when it comes to their own behavior. Indeed, it should not surprise us if the Judeans perceive themselves as innocent, even when they are not.

Alternatively, they may feel that no matter how much they sin, their righteousness far surpasses that of their predecessors. Unlike Judah's inhabitants during the reign of Manasseh, they at least engaged in a modicum of reform, even if it was lackluster. Moreover, several biblical passages assert that God's decree against Jerusalem and the Temple is a result of the sins of Manasseh, prior to Josiah's reform. Thus, the utterance of Eikha 5:7 rings with some measure of accuracy.

This protest does not represent the chapter's conclusive theological utterance. Even if initially the community expresses a grievance, it changes its mind in verse 16, when it finally assumes responsibility: "Woe

---

64. See Jeremiah 3:6–10. For further discussion of this topic, see the chapter above, "Historical Background."

65. In Abravanel's reading of Isaiah 53, he notes that although some may assume that the generation of Josiah was likewise righteous, Isaiah 53:6 supports the rabbinic notion that the people had not properly embraced Josiah's reforms.

66. This midrash appears to be based upon Isaiah 57:5–13, and especially verse 8.

to us for we have sinned!"[67] Chapter 5 (like chapters 1 and 3) gropes its way to recognition of sinfulness and confession. This process is exceedingly difficult, but it reflects the courage and maturity of the Judean community. In this way, they begin the healing process of repentance.[68]

PART 2 (EIKHA 5:8–16):
GRIEVANCES AND RECOGNITION OF SINFULNESS

Eikha 5:8–10

עֲבָדִים מָשְׁלוּ בָנוּ
פֹּרֵק אֵין מִיָּדָם

בְּנַפְשֵׁנוּ נָבִיא לַחְמֵנוּ
מִפְּנֵי חֶרֶב הַמִּדְבָּר

עוֹרֵנוּ כְּתַנּוּר נִכְמָרוּ
מִפְּנֵי זַלְעֲפוֹת רָעָב

**Servants ruled us
There was none to extricate us from their hand**

**We risk our lives to bring bread
Because of the sword in the desert**

**Our skin was darkened as though by an oven
Because of the fevers of starvation**

Moving briskly from one horror to the next, the chapter presents an array of images. The inventory of the people's devastation continues with the

---

67. Those who read the statement in verse 7 as a confession of sorts would say that verse 16 is simply restating verse 7. In my opinion, the contrast between the verses lends them drama and significance.

68. As Maimonides notes (*Hilkhot Teshuva* 1:1), repentance begins with confession of sins.

loss of their autonomy followed immediately by severe economic woes, compounded by the threat of death by sword. Their inability to obtain food in the perilous situation results in starvation, which discolors their skin. The distorted appearance of the malnourished community increases their degradation.

The Judeans surrender their sovereignty to others, to individuals dubbed "servants." Who are the servants who attain political power over the community? This may refer to the nations who cooperate with the Babylonian masters, functioning as their governors over conquered territory.[69] These nations are themselves conquered, servants of the Babylonians.[70]

Presumably, however, those who "ruled us" refers to the enemies who have conquered Judah – namely, the Babylonians. Why would Eikha label the Babylonians "servants"? The *Targum* suggests that this epithet relates to Genesis 10:10, which presents Babylon as a descendant of Ham, who was cursed by Noah to servitude.[71] Perhaps this verse simply reveals a disdainful attitude to the Babylonian conquerors,[72] whose power endures fleetingly, fizzling out not long after it reaches great heights.[73] This may be what Isaiah 23:13 means when it speaks of

---

69. Some scholars adduce II Kings 25:24 as evidence that the servants of the Babylonians governed Judah following the destruction of Jerusalem. Nevertheless, the parallel passage in Jeremiah 40:9 suggests a different reading of the verse in II Kings, according to which the Babylonians themselves rule over the remaining Judean community.

70. Ibn Ezra suggests that this refers to Edom, a country once ruled by Israel. If so, it recalls the passionate anger toward the Edomites expressed at the conclusion of chapter 4.

71. This, however, is not entirely accurate. In actuality, Canaan, son of Ham, is cursed with servitude (Gen. 9:25–27), and Babylon is a descendant of Kush, the son of Ham (Gen. 10:6–10).

72. The word "servants" could refer to the Babylonians, in keeping with Jeremiah's reference to Nebuchadnezzar as God's servant, "*avdi*" (Jer. 27:6). This reading would change the tone of the verse, offering a positive context in referring to the Babylonians as servants of God. I find this interpretation implausible.

73. Based on the brevity and fleeting intensity of Babylonian rule, *Ḥazal* explain that Babylonia's success was orchestrated by God for the sole purpose of destroying Jerusalem and the Temple (e.g., Ḥagiga 13:2; Eikha Rabba 1:31; Gittin 56b; R. Yosef Kara on Eikha 1:5).

Babylonia (Chaldea) dismissively: "Behold the land of Chaldea; this is the people that never existed."[74]

In any case, this depiction points to an upended social system, a complete reversal of fortune and roles. Chaos reigns as the uncouth and uneducated govern others.[75] When formerly suppressed people take charge, their unpreparedness and resentments can find expression in excessive cruelty toward those whom they now dominate.[76]

Bleakness overpowers verse 8, as the community states poignantly, "There was none to extricate us from their hands." This desperate utterance again evokes their futile reliance upon Egypt, which fails to rescue Judah from the Babylonian invasion.[77] The word *porek* also hints to God, who extricates (*vayifrekenu*) His nation from its enemies (Ps. 136:24). The community offers no reason for the absence of a savior. It is simply a fact that the Judean community acknowledges, and an apt illustration of their hopelessness and helplessness.

Nothing particularly new attends the depiction of starvation in verse 9. The Jerusalemites risk their lives for bread (as they did in Eikha 1:19), a commodity in short supply (see Eikha 2:12; 4:4). Venturing to far-flung places in a quest to survive, they risk a trek into the desert (see Eikha 4:19) to obtain bread (see also 5:6, where they make unwise alliances for bread).[78] Malnutrition alters their appearance, which becomes blackened and wrinkled,[79] as in Eikha 4:8. This concise summary of

---

74. An obscure verse, the NJPS translation renders it, "This is the people that has ceased to be."
75. Isaiah 3:4 warns of this sort of situation. See also Ecclesiastes 10:5–7.
76. See Proverbs 30:21–22, which does not elaborate, but certainly recognizes the danger of a servant turned ruler.
77. Note the previous discussion of this episode in Eikha 4:17.
78. It seems odd to go to the desert on a quest for bread. Perhaps this indicates their desperation. Possibly, the sword of the desert comes to *them*, as wild bands emerge from the nearby desert looking to procure food. In this reading, simply venturing out of the city (possibly to obtain hidden stores of food; see, e.g., Jer. 41:8) endangers them. The desert may even be a literary trope, portraying the city as a desert-like society, in which lawlessness reigns and the sword determines who obtains food.
79. See R. Yosef Kara's translation of *nikhmaru* in Eikha 5:10.

hunger illustrates its centrality in the book.[80] Famine remains the most pressing problem, depleting the community of its vigor, morality, dignity, and identity.[81]

Eikha 5:11–14

נָשִׁים בְּצִיּוֹן עִנּוּ
בְּתֻלֹת בְּעָרֵי יְהוּדָה

שָׂרִים בְּיָדָם נִתְלוּ
פְּנֵי זְקֵנִים לֹא נֶהְדָּרוּ

בַּחוּרִים טְחוֹן נָשָׂאוּ
וּנְעָרִים בָּעֵץ כָּשָׁלוּ

זְקֵנִים מִשַּׁעַר שָׁבָתוּ
בַּחוּרִים מִנְּגִינָתָם

Women were tortured in Zion
Maidens in the cities of Judah

Officers were hung by their hands
They did not honor the faces of the elders

Young men bore a grindstone
And youth stumbled with wood

Elders ceased from the gates
Young men from their songs

---

80. Jeremiah's prophecies ominously warn the people of "sword and starvation" (Jer. 16:4). The people and their false prophets dismiss these warnings (Jer. 5:12; 14:13, 15), which ultimately leads to the fulfillment of the prophecies, as we see in these verses.

81. As I have noted, it is difficult to date this chapter in a precise manner. Whether the events occur before, during, or after the destruction of Jerusalem, the ruinous situation remains generally the same.

The community pauses its collective tale to look around at the various groups affected by the calamity. The first-person plural description temporarily fades; the community cannot speak as a collective "we" about the women, the young maidens, the officers, the elders, the young men and the youth. Snapshots of humiliation emerge; each sentence tersely recounts the misery of a distinct sector of Judah's populace.

Opening with the women and the young maidens, the verb used to describe their debasement is *inu*. This word means to torment or afflict, and often connotes sexual assault.[82] Both torment and degradation, the rape of women in warfare hints at the powerlessness (or absence) of the male population, who cannot protect their wives and daughters. The fading authority of the former leadership in verse 12 illustrates this well. Officers are publicly hung by their (now ineffectual) arms,[83] and the elders receive no respect.[84] Who has committed these atrocities? This point remains suspended without clarification; it matters little who is responsible for the community's disgrace.[85]

The next snippet (verse 13) offers a snapshot of backbreaking labor, presumably compulsory. This explains what has happened to the strapping men who generally protect the women and ensure that the elderly are respected. The select young men bear a grindstone and the youth stumble under the weight of lumber. It is unclear whether there is any point to this labor; is it compulsory and pointless, or do they

---

82. See Genesis 34:2; Deuteronomy 21:14; Judges 9:24; II Samuel 13:12. See also Ibn Ezra on Eikha 5:11.

83. It is unclear whose arms Eikha 5:12 describes. It could be the arms of the enemy, who use their power (that is, their arms) to string up the officers. Alternatively, the officers may be hung by their arms in a grotesque posture that recalls crucifixion. This coheres well with the general debasement featured in this section. Moreover, the enemy's general absence from this section suggests that the verse refers to the arms of the Judean officers, rather than those of the enemy.

84. Regarding the identity of those who did not honor the elders, see the discussion of Eikha 4:16.

85. The fact that the enemy remains unnamed leaves open the possibility that the section describes general lawlessness that prevails in the city, perhaps following its conquest. The perpetrators may be the enemy or the enemy's lackeys (Edom or Moab), or even (horrifying as it sounds) wicked inhabitants of the city who take advantage of the chaos and disorder to commit atrocities of their own.

engage in it to obtain the scarce necessities of life?[86] Again, this seems less important than the humiliation attached to the grueling labor,[87] and the fact that it prevents the men from attending to the critical role of protecting their city.

Nothing in Judah functions properly. Elders no longer sit in the gates, where they once rendered judgment,[88] and lent an air of authority and wisdom to the bustling cities. Young men cease their music, busy with their burdens.

In this unembellished catalogue of degradation and abuse, no one has been spared. Old and young, male and female, officers and young men – all fall prey to the agony and shame of conquest. The people of Judah lack dignity and freedom. Normal human activity dwindles and fades as the tale of Jerusalem's catastrophe begins to wind to an end.

Eikha 5:15

שָׁבַת מְשׂוֹשׂ לִבֵּנוּ
נֶהְפַּךְ לְאֵבֶל מְחֹלֵנוּ

The joy of our hearts has ceased[89]
Our circle dances have turned to mourning

Returning to its collective self-portrayal, the community describes the cessation of its joy, the abrupt discontinuation of its merry dances. Movement does not cease; instead, exuberant dance shifts seamlessly into twisting agony. Joy vanishes from their hearts; life as they knew it ceases to exist.

---

86. Rashi (Eikha 5:13) regards this as the condition under which the Babylonians drive the young men into exile.

87. Some scholars suggest that bearing a grindstone is women's work (e.g., Is. 47:2) or that of prisoners (e.g., Judges 16:21), and is designed to humiliate the men (see, e.g., Hillers, 105). However, the verse describes them carrying the grindstone, not using it to grind flour.

88. *Targum* adds the word Sanhedrin to his translation, indicating that this verse illustrates that the Sanhedrin ceases its function.

89. The verb *shavat* (to cease) appeared in the previous verse as well, depicting the cessation of normal activity in the city.

The brief allusion to the past recalls the city's high-spirited energy before it was overturned (*nehepakh*). The word for joy, *masos*, recalls Jerusalem's effect on the world, as described in Eikha 2:15: "Is this the city about which it was said, '[She is] perfect in beauty, a joy (*masos*) for all the land?'" Jerusalem's existence inspired widespread joy, whether because of God's evident presence in her midst (Ps. 46:5–6; 48:2), God's morality that emanated from the city (Is. 2:3; Ps. 102:22), Jerusalem's splendor (Ps. 48:3), her festive gatherings (Hos. 2:13), or her role as a unifier of tribes and peoples (Ps. 122:3–4). Jerusalem's destruction has the opposite effect, terminating joy and leaving behind a cheerless existence.

This verse fulfills Amos's dire prophecy:

> And I will transform (*vehafakhti*) your celebrations to mourning (*le'evel*) and all your songs to lamentation. (Amos 8:10)

Joy does not simply disappear; in Amos's prophecy, God turns it into mourning. Yet this reversal is not unidirectional. Just as God can transform joy into grief, He can transform grief back into joy. Jeremiah promises a reversal of this catastrophe using language and ideas similar to those found in Amos and in our verse:[90]

> Then the maiden will rejoice in her circle dance (*bemaḥol*), with young men and elders together, and I will turn (*vehafakhti*) their mourning (*evlam*) into joy (*lesason*) and I will comfort them and make them happy from their anguish. (Jer. 31:12)

Eikha 5:16

נָפְלָה עֲטֶרֶת רֹאשֵׁנוּ
אוֹי־נָא לָנוּ כִּי חָטָאנוּ

---

90. A similar reversal appears in Psalms 30:12. Berakhot 55b recommends reciting verses of transformation – Psalms 30:12 and Jeremiah 31:12 (along with Deut. 23:6) – in order to reverse a bad dream. Each of these verses features the word *hafokh*.

The crown of our head has fallen
Woe to us for we have sinned!

In a poignant climax of despair, the community proclaims decisively, "The crown of our heads has fallen!" The fallen crown may refer to the collapse of the Davidic dynasty (Jer. 13:18), the loss of God's regal presence (Is. 28:5), or, more generally, the ruin of the noble city, her majestic Temple, and her aristocratic populace. The crown also functions as a figurative reference to the glory of the king (Song. 3:11) and of Israel (Ezek. 16:12). Its removal causes dishonor (Job 19:9). Isaiah's prophecy of renewal includes the restoration of Jerusalem as a glorious crown (Is. 62:3), along with the reinstatement of joy and protection for the city.

This concludes the chapter's litany of loss and suffering. In a flash of cognition, the community issues a final theological statement: "Woe to us, for we have sinned!" Lending coherence to the chapter, this realization reverses the previous theological musing that foisted responsibility onto previous generations (verse 7). Sixteen verses into this chapter, the community finally assumes responsibility for its fate. Gradually, perhaps inevitably, the nation recognizes its culpability. Jeremiah describes the Judean community engaged in a similarly poignant admission:

> We lie in our shame and our disgrace covers us, for we have sinned to the Lord our God, we and our fathers, from our youth until today, and we did not listen to the voice of the Lord our God. (Jer. 3:25)[91]

This admission parallels the conclusion of chapter 1 (see 1:18, 20, 22). The tentative but steady movement toward recognition of sinfulness envelops the book of Eikha, constituting the theological crux of both chapters 1 and 5. Recognition of human responsibility alongside trust in God's righteousness frames the book, enclosing the other three chapters, which often display outrage and bewilderment vis-à-vis God. Having attained this recognition, they can approach their theological quandaries in a new light. Within the context of faith in a righteous God, one

---

91. See also Jeremiah 14:20.

can press further and deeper, asking questions that have no attainable answer, secure in the knowledge that faith surrounds and buffers the bid to understand.

This concludes the main text of chapter 5. We can now turn our attention to the summary thoughts, which function as an epilogue both for the chapter and for the book.

PART 3 (EIKHA 5:17–22):
EPILOGUE – CONCLUDING REFLECTIONS

Eikha 5:17–18

עַל־זֶה הָיָה דָוֶה לִבֵּנוּ
עַל־אֵלֶּה חָשְׁכוּ עֵינֵינוּ

עַל הַר־צִיּוֹן שֶׁשָּׁמֵם
שׁוּעָלִים הִלְּכוּ־בוֹ

Over this our hearts were miserable
Over these our eyes darkened

Over the desolation of Mount Zion
Foxes prowl on it

The book winds down by focusing on the central element of the communal disaster. The destruction of the Temple emerges as the true cause of the nation's misery.[92] The sacred center of Israel's universe is gone, the symbolic meeting place between God and His nation. This calamity spawns confusion and hopelessness. How, after all, can Israel mend her ruptured relationship with God without the Temple, priests, sacrifices, and the Temple rituals associated with the Day of Atonement? How can Israel hope to reconstitute itself as a nation, lacking the nucleus around which everything revolves?

---

92. The threefold use of the word *al* (about) opening each sentence of verses 17 and 18 indicates that these three sentences are connected, and that the deepest cause for misery is the desolation of the Temple Mount (see also Rashi on Eikha 5:17).

The terrible loss elicits a physical response;[93] hearts fill with misery and eyes darken,[94] presumably flooded with tears.[95] Despite the references to hearts and eyes, the city lacks any physical presence. Even the Temple Mount, once the bustling heart of the sacred city, is lifeless and desolate. Only foxes, which haunt sites of destruction, frequent its ruins.[96] Impure animals roam through areas previously restricted to the impure, to non-priests, and to non-Israelites, even encroaching upon the Holy of Holies. Distinctions evaporate, sanctity is breached, and Jerusalem lies in ruins amidst its shattered convictions.

R. Akiva and the Foxes

These events, though grievous, do not come without warning. The covenant of Leviticus 26 explicitly lays out punishments should the people violate God's statutes:

> And I will place your cities in ruins, and I will render your Temples desolate,[97] and I will not savor your pleasing odors. (Lev. 26:31)

The destruction of Jerusalem and her Temple occurs for a reason, as part of an ongoing relationship with God. Had the community kept to its commitments, the calamity could have been avoided. This perspective allows for a solution; after ascertaining the behavior that led to the catastrophe, the nation can repair its conduct and begin the process of reconstruction.

---

93. Hearts and eyes frequently appear together in biblical passages, constituting a word pair that signifies an intellectual or emotional experience involving understanding (Proverbs 23:26) or yearning (Num. 15:39; Jer. 22:17). Sometimes, a third body part, ears for hearing, appears alongside these. See Ezekiel 40:4.
94. I have previously noted the significance of eyes and weeping in the book. Intriguingly, the reference to eyes in chapter 5 appears in verse 17, which, according to the sequence of the alphabet in chapters 2–4, should have been the *ayin* verse.
95. See Ibn Ezra on Eikha 5:17.
96. See Ezekiel 13:4, which links foxes to ruins. In Song of Songs 2:15, foxes are the figurative symbol of ruined relationships.
97. According to the *Sifra* on this verse, the plural "Temples" includes all places of worship (including synagogues and study halls).

An oft-cited incident involving R. Akiva applies our verse to the destruction of the Second Temple, arriving at a hopeful conclusion:[98]

> R. Gamliel, R. Elazar ben Azariah, R. Yehoshua, and R. Akiva…
> were coming up to Jerusalem. When they arrived at Mount
> Scopus, they tore their clothes. When they arrived at the Temple
> Mount, they saw a fox emerging from the Holy of Holies. They
> began to cry, but R. Akiva laughed [with joy]. They said to him,
> "Why do you laugh [with joy]?" He said to them, "Why are you
> crying?" They said, "This is the place about which it was said,
> 'A foreigner who draws near shall die' (Num. 1:51). And now,
> foxes traverse it; shall we not cry?!" He said to them, "This
> is why I laugh [with joy]… The verse made the prophecy of
> Zechariah contingent upon the prophecy of Uriah. And Uriah
> said, 'Therefore, because of you Zion will be ploughed up like a
> field' (Jer. 26:18). And Zechariah said, 'Old men and old women
> shall yet sit in the streets of Jerusalem' (Zech. 8:4). Until the
> [punitive] prophecy of Uriah was fulfilled, I was afraid that the
> [auspicious] prophecy of Zechariah would not be fulfilled. But
> now that the prophecy of Uriah was fulfilled, it is certain that
> the prophecy of Zechariah will be fulfilled!" They said to him,
> "Akiva, you have comforted us! Akiva, you have comforted us!"
> (Makkot 24b)

R. Akiva regards the destruction of the Temple as an event that is part of the ongoing relationship between God and His nation. The fulfillment of a prophecy, even a punitive one, confirms the veracity of the prophetic tradition. This in turn provides comfort and faith in a hopeful future. Standing amidst the ruins of Jerusalem, R. Akiva succeeds in renewing his colleagues' faith in prophecy.

---

98. Although I cited this source in full in the chapter above, "Theology and Suffering," I decided to bring it again in the context of the verse upon which the anecdote rests.

Eikha 5:19–20

אַתָּה ה' לְעוֹלָם תֵּשֵׁב
כִּסְאֲךָ לְדֹר וָדוֹר

לָמָּה לָנֶצַח תִּשְׁכָּחֵנוּ
תַּעַזְבֵנוּ לְאֹרֶךְ יָמִים

You Lord shall sit forever
Your throne is from generation to generation

Why should You forget us forever
Forsake us for the length of days?

Demonstrating once again the remarkable vitality of faith, the book
moves toward its conclusion with a brief philosophic musing, a declaration of God's eternity and His continued reign. This reflective statement
emerges without warning, a burst of clarity that follows the sorrow-filled
observation of Zion's desolation. Turning directly to address God, the
community employs the personal pronoun, *ata*, to assert the fact of
God's immutable existence.

Despite the ruins of the Temple Mount, God's sovereignty
endures. Phrased as an incontrovertible theological statement, the
community pronounces God's independence from any physical structure. As biblical prophets repeatedly assert, God's existence does not
depend upon the Temple, nor does a building function as a measure
of His omnipotence.[99] Biblical texts often describe God's throne in the
heavens, expressing God's transcendent reign.[100] The Aramaic *Targum*
on this verse explicitly makes this point: "You Lord are forever, *the
house of Your dwelling is in the heavens*, the throne of Your glory is for

---

99. In asserting God's willingness to destroy His own Temple, Jeremiah indicates that
God's power does not depend upon it. Many of the nation consider Jeremiah's
assertion blasphemous and do not accept this theological premise. See Jeremiah,
chapters 7 and 26.
100. See Isaiah 66:1; Psalms 11:4; 103:19.

generations." The destruction of God's Temple on earth does not spell the end of God's dominion over the world.

The description of God seated on a throne evokes divine judgment.[101] This image suggests that the desolation that envelops Jerusalem is punitive, a result of God's verdict. But it also leads into the next two verses, in which the community hurls questions at the seated judge (verse 20), followed by a request for reprieve and clemency (verse 21).

What is the nature of the parallel questions of verse 20: "Why should You forget us forever? [Why should You] forsake us for the length of days?" Do they express complaint, supplication, or resolute faith?

Possibly, the questions reflect the nation's irrepressible bitterness.[102] God's judgment against the long-suffering nation endures, with no end in sight and unrelieved by any divine indication of regret or compassion. In this reading, the questions constitute a bitter challenge to God's ongoing decree. The bold request that follows this verse (verse 21) is driven by desperation, a wild flailing that obtains no results (verse 22).

R. Saadia Gaon regards the questions in verse 20 as an entreaty. In his view, the community pleads with God: "Do not forget us forever, nor forsake us for the length of days!" Recalling the prayer that launched the chapter (verse 1), "Remember, Lord," the community concludes the chapter by entreating God not to forget them. The petitionary mode seems to gain momentum, and the verse that follows contains an even bolder appeal to God (verse 21): "Return us to You, Lord, and we will return; renew our days like [days] of old!" This reading highlights Israel's newfound activeness and faith in prayer.

This verse may pose rhetorical questions, whose implied answers reflect the community's persistent faith. Would You, God, actually forget us forever? Is it possible that You would forsake us for the length of

---

101. See Psalms 9:8–9; Rashi on Psalms 45:7; Proverbs 20:8. See also Malbim's explanation of I Kings 22:19; Psalms 29:10, and the interpretation in Exodus Rabba 4:3 of God sitting on a chair in Isaiah 6:1.

102. See, similarly, the question that follows the destruction of the Temple in Psalms 74:1: "*Why*, God, have You rejected for eternity?"

days? After all (as Rashi comments), God took an oath of fealty to His nation, an assurance that is rooted in His own eternity![103] Any proclamation that asserts God's eternity therefore functions as a recollection of God's enduring commitment to Israel. In this reading, these questions constitute a confident utterance, rhetorical questions that express resolute trust in God's loyalty to His nation.

In Rashi's view, God's eternity functions as a panacea for the nation's temporary troubles, reassuring Israel that God will certainly not reject Jerusalem or her people forever. Employing the same two verbs, Isaiah reassures Zion, who fears that God has abandoned the city:

> And Zion said, "The Lord has *forsaken* me, and the Lord has *forgotten* me." Can a woman forget her child, have no compassion on the child of her womb? Even if they do forget, I will not forget you! (Is. 49:14–15)

God, who convened an everlasting covenant with His people, has no intention of forsaking or forgetting His people. In contrast with the opening of the book, which focused on Jerusalem *sitting* lonely and abandoned in a posture of grief and isolation, the book closes with God, regally *seated* upon His everlasting throne. This image of God's eternal strength provides hope for Israel's eventual restoration.

These philosophic musings do not yield an unambiguously encouraging resolution, underscoring the complexity of the book's conclusion. Short on solace, grasping for confidence in a future, and still mired in its calamity, the book does not end with a decisive pivot toward recovery. Instead, the ambiguous philosophic musing seems designed to convey a motley mixture of the community's sentiments: bitterness, muted hope (expressed in prayer), and a deep chord of faith.

---

103. Rashi bases this on the interpretation in Berakhot 32a of Exodus 32:13. While Rashi does not clarify that he reads these questions as rhetorical, that seems to be the implication of his comment. See also Ibn Ezra and R. Yosef Kara on Eikha 5:20.

Psalms 102

As noted above, the mere remembrance of God's eternity can transform the community's state of mind. Consider, for example, Psalms 102, which depicts an abrupt and remarkable movement from despair to rejuvenation.

Characterized by anguish, loneliness, and despair, the first section of Psalms 102 (verses 1–12) depicts a state of physical and existential danger. Distanced from God, the poet hovers on the brink of an abyss, bereft of hope and support:

> Lord, listen to my prayer and allow my cries to come before You! Do not hide Your face from me on the day that I am anguished! Incline Your ear to me! On the day that I call, answer me quickly! For my days vanish in smoke and my bones char as on a pyre. Struck like grass, my heart withers, and I even forget to eat my bread. With the sound of my moans, my bones cleave to my flesh …. For I eat ashes like bread and my drink mixes with tears. Because of Your anger and wrath! For You carried me, and then You flung me aside. My days stretch like a shadow and I wither like grass. (Ps. 102: 2–6; 10–12)

From the bowels of profound despair, the chapter suddenly pivots, shifting its attention from its own misery to God. What effects this transformation? The following laconic sentence:

> And You, Lord, shall sit forever, and Your remembrance is from generation to generation. (Ps. 102:13)

Terse and undramatic, this utterance produces an astounding change in the tone and subject of the chapter. Suddenly, in the next verse, the poet reacquires an abundance of confidence, brimming over with optimism and excitement. The verses that follow portray God in His compassion, energetically reconnecting with His people, reconstructing their city, and restoring their national dignity:

> You will surely arise and have compassion on Zion, for it is time to be gracious to her, the appointed time has come!... For the Lord has built Zion and He may be seen in His glory. He has turned

to the prayer of the desolate and has not spurned their prayer…
For He looks from the height of His holiness, the Lord beholds
the earth from the heavens. To hear the groaning of the prisoner
and release those destined for death. In order that we recount
the name of the Lord in Zion and His glory in Jerusalem, when
the nations gather together with the kingdoms to serve the Lord.
(Ps. 102:14, 17–18, 20–23)

The brief mention of God's eternity functions as a bridge that propels the sufferer from utter despair to joy, hope, and confidence in his
renewed fortune.

The brief utterance at the end of Eikha (nearly identical to that
in Psalms 102:13) allows for the possibility of a similar transformation.
Although Eikha does not progress past the statement of God's eternity, by
inserting the transformative verse of Psalms 102 at its conclusion, Eikha
leaves tantalizing hope in its wake. This proposed reading can alleviate
the conclusion of Eikha, which seems to trail off into a desolate, hollow
future. By alluding to Psalms 102:13, Eikha suggests that the nation will
experience a similar turnaround, emerging from despair into a triumphant and glorious restorative period.

Events of the past century lend new resonance to our understanding of Psalms 102. Its first section uncannily evokes the Holocaust. Any
inmate of the Nazi concentration camps, whose days vanished like smoke
and stretched out like a dark and ominous shadow (102:4, 12), could easily have spoken the words of the psalm. Deprivation and hunger left their
bones cleaving to their flesh, while the subdued moans suggest the depletion of their energy (102:6). Their moans were drowned out by the mocking degradations of the enemy, who reviled and cursed the nation of Israel
(102:9). In their humiliation and privation, all food tasted like ashes and
all drink mixed with tears (102:11). Withered bodies mirrored the wither-
ing of souls. Most painfully, Psalms 102 records the desperate, unanswered
pleas that the sufferer flings at God, imploring Him to respond (102:2–3).
God's silence rings louder than the ebbing cries of the wretched poet.

Yet, in an instant, the portrait of a wretched nation shifts, transforms, and revitalizes. In an exhilarating and dramatic pivot, the Jewish
people rise from the ashes of destruction and energetically embark upon

the project of rebuilding their historic homeland. After two thousand years of wandering in an often-hostile diaspora, the State of Israel emerges – a mere three years after the Holocaust – offering a restored existence for the Jewish people. In an evocative fulfillment of the second section of Psalms 102, God appears to rise from His eternal throne (102:13–14), answering the prayers of His nation (102:18, 20–21), releasing them from imprisonment (102:22), and showering them with renewed compassion (102:14). An abrupt and stunning divine about-face begets the rebuilding of Jerusalem and the restoration of its splendor (102:17). A revitalized Jerusalem draws the attention of the world, which acquires new regard for God's omnipotence, His glory, and His name (102:16, 22–23).

The events of the past century affirm the unassailable fact of God's eternal reign. The enduring covenant with God allows a nation in the throes of misery to maintain hope for a promising future.

Eikha 5:21

הֲשִׁיבֵנוּ ה' אֵלֶיךָ וְנָשׁוּבָה
חַדֵּשׁ יָמֵינוּ כְּקֶדֶם

Return us to You, Lord, and we will return
Renew our days like [days] of old

Rhetorical questions ("Why should You forget us forever?") give rise to hope, which surges forward in this uniquely spirited request. Overcoming the book's largely defeatist attitude, the community finally asserts itself optimistically, petitioning God to take initiative and restore a hopeful future.

The anomalous nature of this bold request emerges with greater clarity when we consider the previous direct appeals to God. Over the course of the book's five chapters, Eikha submits either decidedly minimal requests or those that seek redress rather than reinstatement. On several occasions, the book issues a direct entreaty, imploring God merely to look at His nation or His city.[104] This minimal request offers more of an insight into the current broken state of the relationship (as God averts His eyes from

---

104. See Eikha 1:9, 11, 20; 2:20; 3:63; 5:1.

His nation) than hope for its imminent restoration. Bitter supplications for divine vengeance upon enemies also do not reflect forward-thinking plans for renewal.[105] Until this point in the book, Israel's requests remain steeped in a bitter present rather than focused on a quest for a brighter future.

The precise nature of the community's request in 5:21 remains subject to debate. The *Targum* understands the verse as a plea to God to help us repent, while Ibn Ezra regards the petition as a concrete bid to return the community to Jerusalem, thereby restoring the daily service of God. Whatever its precise meaning, this verse features striking mutuality between God and Israel.[106] Though the community petitions God to initiate reconciliation ("Return us to You"), it continues with a promise to mirror God's action ("and we will return"). Without God's initiative, reconciliation seems impossible,[107] but Israel assumes its share of responsibility for the reestablishment of the relationship.

The request simultaneously looks forward and backward, encapsulating a timeless Jewish perception of history. Steeped in an unbearable present, the beleaguered community yearns for a glorious past (*kedem*), anticipating the reinstatement of that glory in a revitalized future.

What are these days of old?[108] Can we identify the glorious past that the community desires? R. Yosef Kara offers a general timeframe:

> Like the days when Israel was immersed in [its] land and Jerusalem and her environs were settled in tranquility... Like the days when [God] chose Jerusalem to be a throne for [Him]. (R. Yosef Kara, Eikha 5:21)

According to R. Kara, Israel longs for a period of peaceful existence in the land, characterized (and facilitated) by harmonious co-existence with God.

---

105. See Eikha 1:22; 3:64–66 and our discussion on Eikha 2:22.

106. See, similarly, Jeremiah 31:17. Other biblical verses simply petition God to return us to Him, omitting the mutuality expressed in our verse. See Psalms 14:7; 85:5.

107. Interestingly, when God calls Israel to penitence in Zechariah 1:3, He reverses the order, commanding Israel to initiate the return to God: "Return to Me, says the Lord of hosts, and I will return to You!" See also Malachi 3:7.

108. In examining the phrase *yemei kedem* in Eikha 1:7, I noted that biblical passages do not employ this phrase consistently to refer to one specific event.

Although R. Kara does not identify a specific era, his description evokes the glorious period of Solomon, a time of tranquility and security in Jerusalem. Solomon's cardinal act is his construction of the Temple, which enshrines God's presence in the city and infuses the nation with new spiritual fervor and prospects. In fact, a midrash explains the similar phrase "years of old (*shanim kadmoniyot*)" (Mal. 3:4) in this way:

> "The offerings of Judah and Jerusalem will be pleasing to the Lord like the days of yore and the years of old" – "the days of yore" [refers to] the days of Moses, while "the years of old" [refers to] the years of Solomon. (Leviticus Rabba 7:4)

As the community experiences its devastating spiritual and physical collapse, it looks back at an ideal period in Israel's national history, issuing a courageous plea to God to return the community to that era.

This phrase also evokes the primordial ideal, the story of the Garden of Eden.[109] The sparse description of the garden includes the elliptical information that God plants the garden "*mikedem*" (Gen. 2:8). Translated in different ways, this word can indicate either a spatial (in the east) or a temporal (long ago) setting.[110] Whatever its precise meaning, the phrase *yemei kedem* linguistically evokes the Garden of Eden.[111] Thus, the final request in the book petitions God to restore the shattered community to the primeval period of humanity.

---

109. The different approaches delineated do not necessarily contradict one another. The era of Solomon (and especially his construction of the Temple) itself constitutes an ideal recreation of the Garden of Eden. See Yael Ziegler, "Paradise Regained: *Eretz Yisrael* and the Garden of Eden," in *The Koren Maḥzor for Yom HaAtzma'ut and Yom Yerushalayim* (Jerusalem: Koren, 2015), 101–8. The longing for Solomon's period and the longing for the Garden of Eden represent similar quests.

110. Biblical commentators argue over the correct interpretation of the word *kedem*. *Targum Onkelos*, Genesis Rabba 15:3, Ibn Ezra, and Nahmanides translate this word in a temporal context, explaining that God planted the Garden of Eden before the creation of humans. However, Rashi and Radak prefer a spatial explanation, maintaining that the word *kedem* indicates an eastern location for the Garden.

111. Eikha Rabba 5:21 notes this connection. See also Rashi's comment on the phrase *yemei kedem* in II Kings 19:25 and Isaiah 37:26, suggesting that it refers to the primordial era.

Israel longs to return to Eden both because humanity existed in pristine purity and actively engaged in an intimate relationship with an immanent God.[112] Moreover, the desire to return to the garden bespeaks of the yearning to return to the original purpose of humankind, before humans sin. In alluding to the Garden of Eden, the community displays its aspiration to return to a harmonious life, in which humans tend a fertile earth, animals do not threaten humans, man and woman live in partnership, and humans interact with God in obedience to His will.[113]

Eikha 5:22

כִּי אִם־מָאֹס מְאַסְתָּנוּ
קָצַפְתָּ עָלֵינוּ עַד־מְאֹד

For You have surely[114] rejected us
You have been greatly wrathful against us[115]

---

112. I am referring to the initial description of the lifestyle in the garden, presented laconically in the second chapter of Genesis. The third chapter depicts the unravelling of this harmonious lifestyle, caused by disobedience and betrayal. The narrative offers no information regarding the timeframe of these events. How long do Adam and Eve live in that ideal existence prior to their sin and expulsion? The timeless nature of the narrative leaves this question unanswered.

113. For a more detailed description of the harmonious and ideal lifestyle of the Garden of Eden and its theological aim, see Ziegler, "Paradise," 101–8.

114. The translation of the word *im* (in general and in this verse in particular) has long occupied exegetes and scholars (see, e.g., the review of the scholarship in House, 470–71). I have translated the word *im* as an asseverative rather than a conditional word. The *Targum* adopts this approach, translating the phrase "*ki im*" as *arum* ("because"), an asseverative statement. Ibn Ezra, however, translates the word *im* as conditional, rendering the following reading of Eikha's final verse: "For even if You have rejected us in our sins, You have already been excessively angry with us!" Ibn Ezra's following words anticipate imminent redemption: "And He in His mercy will have mercy upon us." This interpretation steers in an optimistic direction. While this hopeful reading alleviates the dismal tone of Eikha's conclusion, the verse's use of strongly negative vocabulary ("*ma'os me'astanu … katzafta*," indicating divine rejection and wrath) makes it difficult to maintain.

115. Interpreters and translators have explained this verse in a broad variety of ways, some of which render completely opposite meanings. I have chosen not to examine the range of possibilities, selecting instead the interpretation that I believe best

A glimmer of hope emerged briefly in verse 21, only to disappear in verse 22, eclipsed by the misery that overtakes the book. Appropriate to its context, the book ends on a sober note, as the community emits a concluding sigh of despair.

Two words dominate this final verse: *maas* (rejection) and *katzaf* (anger). Harsh expressions of divine abandonment and wrath, these words offer a bleak depiction of the community's perception of God at the conclusion of the book. The community appears to respond to its own query directed toward God in Jeremiah 14. As in our verse, the verse in Jeremiah employs the doubling of the word *maas* (rejection) in its address of God:

> Have You surely rejected (*ma'os maasta*) Judah? Has Your soul been repulsed by Zion? Why have You struck us, and we have no remedy? [We] hope for peace, but there is no good; for a time of healing, but behold there is terror. (Jer. 14:19)

The heartfelt question is followed by a sincere confession. Recognizing its sins, the community entreats God to maintain His relationship with Israel for the sake of His own honor (Jer. 14:20–21).[116]

The book of Eikha does not venture in the confessional direction found in Jeremiah 14. Submerged in a dismal reality, the community does not attempt to convince God to offer clemency. Israel desists from praying to God, from asking Him to extinguish His anger. Instead, Eikha remains engulfed in theological despair, anchored to a reality in which God remains distant and angry. Suffering overshadows any visions of a hopeful future as the community resignedly shoulders the burden of its present. In the closing moments of the book, the Judean community remains consumed by sorrow, heaving a final mournful exhalation.

---

reflects the spirit and tone of the words of the book's conclusion. For a review of the different possible readings of this verse, see Gordis, 197–98.

116. In an interesting twist, *Soferim* 18:4 states that Jeremiah 14:19–22 should be read on Tisha Be'Av.

As we have seen, the prophecies to the Babylonian exiles in Isaiah 40–66 often counter Eikha's hopelessness, offering a panacea to the events that mark Israel's catastrophe.[117] In its bid to prepare Israel to return from exile, the book of Isaiah counters the language found at the end of Eikha, assuring Israel unequivocally that God has certainly not rejected them, "*lo me'astikha*" (Is. 41:9), nor will He ever forsake them (Is. 41:17). More significantly, Isaiah 64:8 records a plea to reverse the final words of Eikha (*katzafta aleinu ad me'od*, "You have been greatly wrathful against us"):

> Lord, do not be excessively wrathful (*al tiktzof... ad me'od*), and do not forever recall sin, please look at Your nation, at all of us! (Is. 64:8)

When read in its broader canonical context, one finds relief for the despondency of Eikha's conclusion. Yet, Eikha refuses to conclude on a note of false optimism or facile recovery from disaster. The book's commitment to an honest representation of human suffering makes it truthful, accessible, and relevant.

A Community Custom: Repetition of the Penultimate Verse

Despite the book's unyielding honesty, an abiding danger lurks in its conclusion. Eikha's final note of despair leaves the community of Israel hovering over a perilous abyss, uncertain of its future. This ending is especially jarring during the annual public reading of the book on Tisha Be'Av.[118] Eikha's final verse leaves the listeners stunned, flailing in the misery of an excruciating present and an unknown future.

During its exilic history, Israel endures persecutions and difficulties, calling into question God's continued fidelity. Eikha's ending, which exudes despondency over God's abandonment, may weaken Israel's

---

117. For more on this topic, see the upcoming chapter, "Eikha and the Prophecies of Consolation in Isaiah."

118. Y. Shabbat 16:1 offers anecdotal evidence of the custom of reading Eikha on the fast of Tisha Be'Av. However, it appears as an official custom only in *Soferim* 14:3; 18:5.

already precarious faith. With this in mind, an empowering tradition developed in which the public reading of the book does not conclude with its final verse.[119] Instead, following the completion of the reading, the congregation chants the uplifting penultimate verse aloud, followed by the communal reader who echoes their reading. In this way, the community resists and even undermines the final despondent message of the book.[120] Refusing to accept despair, the community exercises its privilege to petition God, concluding our public reading of Eikha with a bold request: "Return us to You, Lord, and we will return, renew our days like [days] of old!"

Eikha Rabba: Finding Hope in Eikha

Rabbinic sources also brought their authoritative weight to bear on Eikha's dismal conclusion.[121] The authors of Eikha Rabba, who were forced to contend with their own communities' calamities following the destruction of the Second Temple, could not allow Eikha to foster despair. Instead, midrashim often reverse the simple meaning of the book, abandoning fidelity to the text in order to coax from it hope and optimism. To this end, Eikha Rabba becomes a study in creative exegesis. As an example, consider the way Eikha Rabba interprets the despondent final verse of the book:

---

119. This seems to be an early custom, mentioned in some Massoretic manuscripts (it does not, however, appear in the Leningrad Codex). A possible reference to this custom appears in Y. Berakhot 5:1 (see the explanation of the Maharsha, *Ḥiddushei Aggadot*, among others, although Rabbeinu Yonah explains the Yerushalmi differently). There is some evidence that this custom is found among early liturgical poets (*paytanim*), such as R. Eliezer Hakalir. Rashi cites this custom in his commentary on Eikha 5. See also Rama, *Oraḥ Ḥayyim* 559:1. This tradition is applied broadly, so that we avoid concluding any public reading on an inauspicious note. See Maimonides, *Hilkhot Tefilla* 13:5, 7. Thus, the custom of the community when attending a public reading that concludes the books of Isaiah, *Trei Asar* (namely, Malachi), and Ecclesiastes is to chant the uplifting penultimate verse following the conclusion of the reading, which ends on a negative note.

120. This coheres well with the special rights and power accorded to the community of Israel that I discussed in chapter 3.

121. In an upcoming chapter, I will explore the rabbinic interpretation of the book of Eikha in Eikha Rabba.

"For you have surely rejected us. You have been greatly wrathful against us." R. Shimon ben Lakish said, "If [God] rejects, there is no hope; but if [God] is wrathful, there is hope, because anyone who gets angry will eventually be appeased." (Eikha Rabba 5:22)

CHAPTER FIVE: IN SUMMATION

Chapter 5 is brief, lacking the pathos, elaboration, and many of the compositional features found in previous chapters. It has no alphabetic acrostic, no first-person singular speaker, and no elegiac opening word (*"Eikha"*). Instead, chapter 5 petitions God to look and see the community's devastation and shame. The bulk of the chapter consists of a first-person plural list of the community's losses, interrupted twice by theological statements that illustrate its movement toward accountability.

In its final reflections, the book flits rapidly from one topic to the next, allotting each a sentence or two in summary. The four topics of the book's epilogue trail off without closure, leaving the reader to carry on contemplating the book's final, raw ruminations. Eikha's summary first directs our attention to the nation's most painful loss, namely, the Temple, the sacred center of Israel's world. It then engages in a concise theological exploration, replete with a simple statement of God's eternal reign followed by several (perhaps rhetorical) questions regarding God's continued relationship with His nation. A fleeting optimistic request for restoration fades immediately, replaced by a sigh of despair, an abiding acknowledgment of God's continuing alienation and anger.

Chapter 5 bears striking similarities to chapter 1 in terms of its content and language. These common features direct the reader to compare the two chapters, whose most significant shared characteristic is their theology. The similar manner in which each of them reconciles with God's justice, eventually coming to grips with their own culpability, constitutes the essence of these chapters.[122]

Quiet and haunting, chapters 1 and 5 focus mainly on the nation's losses, rather than on the active destruction of the city. A key word is *ein* (none), indicating what has disappeared from the life of the nation.

---

122. For more on the importance of these chapters' shared theology, see my upcoming chapter, "The Structure of Eikha: Faith in a Turbulent World."

These chapters observe the cessation of activity in the once-vivacious city, whose gates are now desolate. Widows (*almana*) feature only in these two chapters, their loneliness and vulnerability an emblem of the city's pain. Eyes darken, while mourning and miserable hearts predominate.

Neither chapter 1 nor chapter 5 focuses upon the innocent children or the culpable leaders. Instead, they give equal weight to a broad swath of Judah's populace: priests, maidens, children, officers, young men, elders. All of Judah is responsible for the calamity and no one has been spared.

Both chapters grope their way toward admission of sinfulness. Each displays a degree of hesitancy – the initial attempt to deflect responsibility (1:12 and 5:7) – followed by a resounding statement of culpability (1:18 and 5:16).

In addition to the thematic similarities, the language of the two chapters is remarkably parallel, highlighting their common features: a city overturned, desolation in her gates, the cessation of all activity. Festivities have transformed into mourning, marked by miserable hearts, and darkened or flowing eyes. The neck appears only in these chapters, burdened and pursued. The community seems exhausted, lacking respite, engaged in a desperate, perilous quest for bread. Young men break and stumble, the officers have lost their splendor, and the specter of vulnerable, widowed loneliness hovers over the chapters. Death seems inescapable, the houses no longer protect their inhabitants, and the sword awaits. The longing for days of old breaks through as some measure of relief for the empty, desolate reality.

The linguistic parallels appear in the following chart:[123]

Chapter 1	Chapter 5
The city…has become *like a widow* (*ke'almana*) (1:1)	Our mothers are *like widows* (*ke'almanot*) (5:3)
Over these (*al eileh*) I weep, my *eyes*, my *eyes*, they flow with water (1:16)	*Over these* (*al eileh*) our *eyes* darkened (5:17)

---

123. For those who prefer to see the chart in Hebrew, I have supplied this same chart in Hebrew in the chapter below, "The Structure of Eikha: Faith in a Turbulent World."

Chapter 1	Chapter 5
The roads to Zion *mourn,* for there is no one who comes on the festival (1:4)	Our circle dances have turned to *mourning* (5:15)
My heart *turns over* (*nehpakh*) within me (1:20)	Our estates are *turned over* (*nehefkha*) to strangers (5:2)
	Our circle dances have *turned* (*nehpakh*) to mourning (5:15)
All her *pursuers* caught up with her (1:3) And they walked without strength before the *pursuer* (1:6)	*Pursued* by our necks, we wearied, and they gave us no respite (5:5)
For my groans are many and my *heart is miserable* (*libi davai*) (1:22)	Over this our *hearts were miserable* (*daveh libenu*) (5:17)
Jerusalem has surely *sinned* (1:8)	Our fathers *sinned* and they are no more (5:7) Woe to us for we have *sinned!* (5:16)
She sat amongst the nations and *did not find respite* (*mano'aḥ*) (1:3)	Pursued by our necks, we wearied, and *they gave us no respite* (*hunaḥ*) (5:5)
They became entangled; they were lifted upon my *neck* (*al tzavari*), made my strength fail (1:14)	Pursued by our *necks* (*al tzavarenu*), we wearied, and they gave us no respite (5:5)
[They] made my strength fail (*hikhshil*) ... He called against me an appointed time to break my *young men* (*baḥurai*) (1:14–15).	*Young men* (*baḥurim*) bore a grindstone and youth stumbled (*kashalu*) with wood (5:13)
Her entire nation groans, they seek *bread.* They exchanged their precious delights for food to restore *life* (*nafesh*) (1:11)	We risk our *lives* (*benafshenu*) to bring *bread,* because of the sword in the desert (5:9)
Outside the *sword* kills, inside the house is death (1:20)	We risk our lives to bring bread, because of the *sword* in the desert (5:9)
All her *gates* are desolate (1:4)	Elders ceased from the *gates* (5:14)
They laughed at her *cessations* [of activity] (*mishbateha*) (1:7)	Elders *ceased* (*shavatu*) from the gates (5:14)

Chapter 1	Chapter 5
Departed from the daughter of Zion is all her glory (*hadara*). Her *officers* were like stags (1:6)	*Officers* were hung by their hands; They did not honor (*nehdaru*) the faces of the elders (5:12)
All her gates are *desolate* (1:4) He placed me in *desolation* (1:13) My sons became *desolate* (1:16)	Over these our eyes darkened: over the *desolation* of Mount Zion, foxes prowl on it (5:18)
Jerusalem remembered [during] the days of her affliction and wandering, all her precious delights that were in the *days of old* (*miymei kedem*) (1:7)	Return us to You Lord and we will return, renew our *days* like [days] *of old* (*yamenu kekedem*) (5:21)
The Lord has placed me in the *hands* [of those before whom] I cannot rise. (Eikha 1:14).	Servants ruled us, there was none to extricate us from their *hand* (5:8)
Zion spreads out with her *hands*, there is no comforter for her (1:17)	We gave a *hand* to Egypt (5:6)
Outside the sword kills, inside the *house* is death (1:20)	Our estates are turned over to strangers, our *houses* to foreigners (5:2)
She has no (*ein*) comforter from all her lovers (1:2) And there was none (*ein*) to help her (1:7) She spirals downward wondrously, there is none (*ein*) to comfort her (1:9) Zion spreads out with her hands, there is no (*ein*) comforter for her (1:17) They have heard that I groan, there is no (*ein*) comforter for me (1:21)	We became orphans without (*ein*) a father, our mothers are like widows (5:3) Our fathers sinned and they are no more (*ve'einam*), and we suffered for their iniquities (5:7) Servants ruled us, there was none (*ein*) to extricate us from their hand (5:8)
When her nation *fell* in the hand of the adversary and there was none to help her (1:7)	The crown of our head has *fallen* (5:16)

I will return to examine these shared features and their contribution to the shape and purpose of the book of Eikha in the chapter below examining Eikha's structure.

Eikha and the Prophecies of Consolation in Isaiah

Eikha is a book of suffering, filled with enormous pain, bewilderment, despair and outrage. It offers no hope and no guidance for rehabilitation; the final verse trails off with a sigh of despair: "For You have surely rejected us, You have been greatly wrathful against us."

However, Eikha does not exist in a vacuum. Surprisingly, the biblical narrative, and the story of the nation of Israel, do not conclude with exile. Cyrus allows the Judeans to return to Jerusalem and rebuild their Temple and community. While some of the biblical books of this period (such as Ezra-Nehemiah, Haggai, and Zechariah) record both great excitement and great disappointment, these events imbue the nation with unanticipated potential for success. As the biblical story marches forward past exile, Israel's optimistic outlook takes shape: redemption can follow exile, dispersion and loss of autonomy do not spell the end of the nation.

The "prophecies of consolation" in the book of Isaiah (chapters 40–66) focus on the period of the return to Zion.[1] These prophecies

---

1. Not all these prophecies of consolation console; some of these chapters offer harsh rebuke, over both past and present misdemeanors. Nevertheless, overall, these chapters offer optimistic messages, designed to launch and maintain a hopeful period of the return to Zion.

present Cyrus as God's messenger (44:28–45:2) and urge the Judeans to leave Babylonia (48:20). Other prophecies address a personified Jerusalem, advising her that God is returning to the city along with her children (namely, her exiled populace), and promising Jerusalem a glorious future. These chapters pulse with jubilation and excitement; redemption is at hand, and Israel will return to a dazzling city. These prophecies maintain a special relationship with the book of Eikha, creating a dialogue between the book of destruction and the biblical passages that mark its reversal.

Ḥazal recognize the remarkable linguistic exchange between the books.[2] Noting that the prophet Isaiah lived long before the redemptive events, they explain that Isaiah preempts Jeremiah's harsh composition of rebuke by providing prophecies that offer a remedy in advance of the calamity:[3]

> R. Neḥemia said: Even though Jeremiah cursed them using an alphabetic structure [in] Eikha [chapter 1], Isaiah preempted and cured them for each verse until [the final one]. (Eikha Rabba *Petiḥta* 21)

The midrash cites an alphabetical catalogue of suffering in Eikha chapter 1 (attributing authorship to Jeremiah), following the opening of each

---

2. Biblical scholars also observe the various ways in which Lamentations correlates with the prophecies of consolation in Isaiah. See, for example, P. T. Willey, *Remember the Former Things: The Recollection of Previous Texts in Second Isaiah* (Scholars Press, 1997); B. Sommer, *A Prophet Reads Isaiah: Allusion in Isaiah 40–66* (Stanford: Stanford University Press, 1998); T. Linafelt, "Living Beyond Lamentations: The Rhetoric of Survival in Second Isaiah," in *Surviving Lamentations: Catastrophe, Lament and Protest in the Afterlife of a Biblical Book* (Chicago: The University of Chicago Press, 2000), 62–79.

3. This midrash indirectly relates to the question of when chapters 40–66 of Isaiah were composed. The first chapters in Isaiah (1–12) relate to events that took place during the mid-eighth century BCE, while the chapters at its end (40–66) relate to events that took place in the sixth century BCE. The midrash assumes that Isaiah wrote these chapters prophetically, in advance of the event. Ibn Ezra (Is. 40:1) seems to suggest (in a typically cryptic fashion) that these chapters were not written by Isaiah, but presumably by a later prophet. For further discussion of this topic, see Amnon Bazak, *To This Very Day: Fundamental Questions in Bible Study* (Jerusalem: Maggid, 2020), 149–59.

verse with a corresponding prophecy in which Isaiah rectifies the situation. These are some selected examples from the midrash:

> Jeremiah [in Eikha] said (1:2): "She surely cries in the night."
> Isaiah said (30:19):[4] "She shall surely *not* cry."

> Jeremiah [in Eikha] said (1:4), "The *roads* to Zion mourn."
> Isaiah said (40:3): "A voice calls: Clear the *road* for the Lord in the wilderness."

> Jeremiah [in Eikha] said (1:5), "Her adversaries were at the head."
> Isaiah said (60:4), "Those who tormented you will come to you bowed."

> Jeremiah [in Eikha] said (1:6), "Departed from the daughter of Zion is all her glory."
> Isaiah said (59:20), "And to Zion will come a redeemer."

> Jeremiah [in Eikha] said (1:8), "Jerusalem has surely sinned."
> Isaiah said (44:22), "I have erased her sins like a cloud."

> Jeremiah [in Eikha] said (1:10), "Her entire nation groans, they seek bread."
> Isaiah said (49:10), "They will not be hungry, and they will not be thirsty."

> Jeremiah [in Eikha] said (1:17), "Zion spreads out with her hands, there is no comforter for her."
> Isaiah said (51:12): "I, I am your comforter."
> (Eikha Rabba 1:23)

---

4. In its search for corrective verses, the midrash does not distinguish between the earlier and later prophecies of the book of Isaiah (although most of its examples are drawn from the "prophecies of consolation" at the end of Isaiah).

This literary midrash lays the groundwork for viewing Eikha alongside the book of Isaiah. It turns out that the destruction of Jerusalem does not spell the nation's end; Isaiah's prophecies direct the biblical reader to the next stage of biblical history, in which God reverses Eikha's dismal situation. Exile is followed by return, just as consolation follows grief.

The book of Isaiah's extensive and specific references to Eikha suggest a conscious effort to counter the latter's grim conclusions. Following the lead of the midrash, I will expand upon the way in which Eikha's language of despair links to Isaiah's language of hope. I have scattered references to Isaiah's reversals of Eikha throughout this book. This chapter expands on those brief references, collating them into a thematic whole. Nevertheless, this is hardly a comprehensive exploration of the topic, which requires book-length analysis.

Eikha's most alarming feature is its absence of consolation. The six-fold appearance of the word *naham* fails to provide the expected comfort. Employed five times in chapter 1 as part of a negative formulation (1:2, 9, 16, 17, 21: there is no comforter for you), and once as a rhetorical question in 2:13 ("To what can I equate you, so that I can comfort you?"), the dearth of consolation leaves Israel flailing without hope.

To counter this, God Himself consoles the inconsolable nation in the book of Isaiah. The prophecies of consolation open with God twice uttering the word *nahem* (Is. 40:1): "Comfort (*nahamu*), comfort (*nahamu*) My people!" God's consolation does not end there; the word *nahem* weaves throughout these lyrical chapters, providing solace and hope (e.g., Is. 49:13; 51:3, 12). Swaddling these chapters in divine consolation, the word *nahem* appears three times in rapid succession in the final chapter (Is. 66:13): "As a man whose mother comforts him, so I will comfort you, and in Jerusalem you shall find comfort!"

God does not merely offer words of comfort. The prophecies in Isaiah counter specific aspects of Israel's wretchedness. Consider for example, Eikha's initial chapter. Opening with a haunting image of a desolate city (the word *shomem* appears twice in chapter 1), Jerusalem's loneliness is metaphorically expressed by her widowed state. The city sits alone as her sobs echo hauntingly in the night, mingling with the keening moans of the few residents who languish at her desolate gates. Jerusalem's residents (her "children") move sluggishly toward exile, easily apprehended by her pursuers. Emptied of her beloved inhabitants, Jerusalem's painful isolation is the leitmotif of chapter 1, which offers a sketch of a once-pulsating city reduced to a hollow shell.

Isaiah's prophecies stir Jerusalem's residents to return to their city, where joy will surely apprehend them, chasing away all anguished moans (Is. 51:11). Jerusalem no longer recalls her widowhood (Is. 54:4) and her land is no longer desolate (Is. 49:19; 61:3). Jerusalem's population grows so rapidly that the city becomes too small for its residents. The "children of her bereavement" return (seemingly, from the dead!), grumbling at the narrow confines of the teeming city (Is. 49:20), "This place is too narrow for me![5] Move aside so that I can sit!" Jerusalem's astonishment at the rapid influx elicits a pained recollection of recent loneliness (Is. 49:21): "Who bore these for me, and I was bereaved and alone, exiled and cast aside – and these, who raised [them]? I remained alone – these, where are they [from]?"

The following chart illustrates some of the linguistic correlations described above:

ישעיהו	איכה
וּפְדוּיֵי ה' יְשׁוּבוּן וּבָאוּ צִיּוֹן בְּרִנָּה (נ"א, י"א)	וַיֵּצֵא מִבַּת צִיּוֹן כָּל הֲדָרָהּ (א', ו')
שָׂשׂוֹן וְשִׂמְחָה יַשִּׂיגוּן (נ"א, י"א)	כָּל רֹדְפֶיהָ הִשִּׂיגוּהָ (א', ג')
נָסוּ יָגוֹן וַאֲנָחָה (נ"א, י"א)	כֹּהֲנֶיהָ נֶאֱנָחִים בְּתוּלֹתֶיהָ נּוּגוֹת (א', ד')
וְחֶרְפַּת אַלְמְנוּתַיִךְ לֹא תִזְכְּרִי עוֹד (נ"ד, ד)	הָעִיר רַבָּתִי עָם הָיְתָה כְּאַלְמָנָה (א', א')
וּלְאַרְצֵךְ לֹא יֵאָמֵר עוֹד שְׁמָמָה (ס"ב, ד')	כָּל שְׁעָרֶיהָ שׁוֹמֵמִין (א', ד')
הֵן אֲנִי נִשְׁאַרְתִּי לְבַדִּי אֵלֶּה אֵיפֹה הֵם (מ"ט, כ"א)	אֵיכָה יָשְׁבָה בָדָד (א', א')
עוֹד יֹאמְרוּ בְאָזְנַיִךְ בְּנֵי שִׁכֻּלָיִךְ (מ"ט, כ')	מִחוּץ שִׁכְּלָה חֶרֶב (א', כ')
צַר לִי הַמָּקוֹם (מ"ט, כ')	רְאֵה ה' כִּי צַר לִי (א', כ')
גְּשָׁה לִּי וְאֵשֵׁבָה (מ"ט, כ')	אֵיכָה יָשְׁבָה בָדָד (א', א')

---

5. The two words that express the narrow confines of the crowded city (*tzar li*) also appear in Eikha 1:20 to express Jerusalem's anguish.

Jerusalem's enemies prevail in Eikha, leaving a trail of unimaginable cruelty and inconceivable success. Jeers, raucous shouts, and mockery accompany acts of destruction. In Eikha 2:16 we are privy to the blustering boasts of the enemies who shout, "We have swallowed!" in their celebration of Jerusalem's fall.

Isaiah's prophecies of consolation promise an end to the intolerable success of Jerusalem's enemies. God will actively punish the enemies (Is. 49:26) and Jerusalem's "swallowers" will exit the city, making room for the children to return (Is. 49:17, 19). Her status in the world will undergo a remarkable transformation; kings and officers will come to Jerusalem bearing her children, bowing in submission and licking the dust of her feet (Is. 49:23). Jerusalem's tormentors will kowtow and prostrate themselves, calling it "the city of the Lord!" (Is. 60:14) Nations will replenish Jerusalem's plundered wealth along with her populace (Is. 60:5–11). Addressing Jerusalem, Isaiah promises (Is. 60:15): "Instead of being abandoned and hated with none passing through, I will place you as an eternal pride, a joy from generation to generation."

A brief chart illustrates some of the linguistic correlations alluded to above:

ישעיהו	איכה
וְרָחֲקוּ מְבַלְּעָיִךְ (מ"ט, י"ט)	אָמְרוּ בִּלָּעְנוּ (ב', ט"ז)
כִּי לִי אִיִּים יְקַוּוּ (ס', ט')	אַךְ זֶה הַיּוֹם שֶׁקִּוִּינֻהוּ (ב', ט"ז)
וְהָלְכוּ אֵלַיִךְ שְׁחוֹחַ בְּנֵי מְעַנַּיִךְ (ס', י"ד)	נָשִׁים בְּצִיּוֹן עִנּוּ בְּתֻלֹת בְּעָרֵי יְהוּדָה (ה', י"א)

Isaiah devotes a full chapter to Babylon's collapse (chapter 47). Drawing heavily on Eikha's description of Jerusalem's calamity, Isaiah depicts Babylon's downfall in parallel terms. The oppressors become the oppressed; Babylonia's torments return to haunt her. The following chart illustrates the extensive linguistic parallels:

ישעיהו מ"ז	איכה
רְדִי וּשְׁבִי עַל עָפָר (פסוק א')	הֶעֱלוּ עָפָר עַל רֹאשָׁם (ב', י')
בְּתוּלַת בַּת בָּבֶל (א')	לִבְתוּלַת בַּת יְהוּדָה (א', ט"ו)

איכה	ישעיהו מ"ז
יֵשְׁבוּ לָאָרֶץ יִדְּמוּ זִקְנֵי בַּת צִיּוֹן (ב', י')	שְׁבִי לָאָרֶץ אֵין כִּסֵּא בַּת כַּשְׂדִּים (א')
כִּי רָאוּ עֶרְוָתָהּ (א', ח')	תִּגַּל עֶרְוָתֵךְ (ג')
הַבִּיטָה וּרְאֵה אֶת חֶרְפָּתֵנוּ (ה', א')	גַּם תֵּרָאֶה חֶרְפָּתֵךְ (ג')
יֵשְׁבוּ לָאָרֶץ יִדְּמוּ (ב', י')	שְׁבִי דוּמָם (ה')
אוֹתִי נָהַג וַיֹּלַךְ חֹשֶׁךְ וְלֹא אוֹר (ג', ב') בְּמַחֲשַׁכִּים הוֹשִׁיבַנִי כְּמֵתֵי עוֹלָם (ג', ו')	וּבֹאִי בַחֹשֶׁךְ (ה')
לֹא זָכְרָה אַחֲרִיתָהּ (א', ט')	לֹא זָכַרְתְּ אַחֲרִיתָהּ (ז')
מִחוּץ שִׁכְּלָה חֶרֶב (א', כ') הָעִיר רַבָּתִי עָם הָיְתָה כְּאַלְמָנָה (א', א')	וְתָבֹאנָה לָּךְ שְׁתֵּי אֵלֶּה רֶגַע בְּיוֹם אֶחָד שְׁכוֹל וְאַלְמֹן (ט')
תָּבֹא כָל רָעָתָם לְפָנֶיךָ (א', כ"ב)	וַתִּבְטְחִי בְרָעָתֵךְ... וּבָא עָלַיִךְ רָעָה (י-י"א)

God's absence in Eikha is troubling indeed. God never speaks. He does not even respond to the nation's outcries, supporting the sense that God has hidden His face from Israel. Eikha also describes God raising His own hand against them in punishment. Of even greater concern, Eikha raises the possibility that God has permanently rejected Israel. Toward the end of the book, the nation toys with the possibility of God's abandonment of them, framing the frightening idea as a question (5:20): "Why should You forget us forever, forsake us for the length of days?" God offers no response to this question, which trails off without resolution. The conclusion of the book offers no relief from this disquieting notion, closing with a statement of God's utter rejection and excessive wrath.

Isaiah's prophecies of consolation sketch an entirely different portrait of God. God leads the way out of exile, bearing His flock in His bosom (Is. 40:3, 10–11). More to the point, God states unequivocally that He has not rejected His chosen nation (Is. 41:9); on the contrary, God remains alongside His nation, assisting and supporting them with His right hand (Is. 41:10).

As these chapters turn their attention to Jerusalem, promising the restoration of her fortunes, the still-abandoned city repeats Eikha's conclusion. Using the very same verb pair of 5:20, Zion miserably asserts (Is. 49:14): "The Lord has forsaken me and the Lord has forgotten me."[6]

---

6. These parallel verbs, used in tandem about God, appear only in Isaiah 49:14 and Eikha 5:20.

But here, God does not allow this notion to trail off without a reply; without hesitation, God rejects it unequivocally:

> Can a woman forget her child, have no compassion on the child of her womb? Even if they do forget, I will not forget you! (Is. 49:15)

Using the potent metaphor of the mother-child bond, God asserts that His bond with the nation is even stronger, indeed unbreakable. The mention of maternal compassion evokes the horrific portrait of the once-compassionate mothers who consume their children in Eikha 4:10 (cf. 2:20). Even when the moral foundations of humanity have unraveled, and the conditions of famine have obliterated any semblance of compassion, one can still rely upon God to remember and care for His nation.

The following chart illustrates the linguistic correlations noted above:

ישעיהו	איכה
וַיֹּאמֶר לְךָ עַבְדִּי אַתָּה בְּחַרְתִּיךָ וְלֹא מְאַסְתִּיךָ (מ"א, ט')	כִּי אִם מָאֹס מְאַסְתָּנוּ (ה', כ"ב)
אַל תִּירָא כִּי עִמְּךָ אָנִי אַל תִּשְׁתָּע כִּי אֲנִי אֱלֹהֶיךָ אִמַּצְתִּיךָ אַף עֲזַרְתִּיךָ אַף תְּמַכְתִּיךָ בִּימִין צִדְקִי (מ"א, י')	בָּנְפֹל עַמָּה בְּיַד צָר וְאֵין עוֹזֵר לָהּ (א', ז') נִצָּב יְמִינוֹ כְּצָר (ב', ד')
וַתֹּאמֶר צִיּוֹן עֲזָבַנִי ה' וַאדֹנָי שְׁכֵחָנִי: הֲתִשְׁכַּח אִשָּׁה עוּלָהּ מֵרַחֵם בֶּן בִּטְנָהּ גַּם אֵלֶּה תִשְׁכַּחְנָה וְאָנֹכִי לֹא אֶשְׁכָּחֵךְ (מ"ט, י"ד-ט"ו)	לָמָּה לָנֶצַח תִּשְׁכָּחֵנוּ תַּעַזְבֵנוּ לְאֹרֶךְ יָמִים (ה', כ') יְדֵי נָשִׁים רַחֲמָנִיּוֹת בִּשְּׁלוּ יַלְדֵיהֶן (ד', י')

We will now explore the way Isaiah's prophecies of consolation transpose and reverse several specific scenarios and themes of Eikha.

Chapter 2 records the physical collapse of Jerusalem; buildings and people crash onto the ground, depleted of their former stature. The city gates burrow deeply into the earth, entombing Jerusalem's once-bustling portal. Girded with sackcloth, the elders sink onto the ground and place dust on their head. The earthward movement indicates exhaustion and surrender; all relinquish their fate to the pull of the earth, to impending death.

Following this description, Eikha 2:13 questions its ability to offer comfort ("To what can I equate you so that I can comfort you?"), proffering the sea as the symbol of the irreparable brokenness of the city: "For as great as the sea is your brokenness!" This image hints to the copious, salty tears shed by the city, the violent churning of its buildings and populace, and its vast, unbridgeable despair. This hopelessness of this image spawns the narrator's subsequent query, addressed to Jerusalem, evocative in its helpless anguish: "Who can heal you?"

Redemption involves the opposite movement. Isaiah calls to Jerusalem to rise from the ground, to shake off the dust. Awakening Jerusalem from years of dormancy and despondency, Isaiah urges the city to garb herself in clothes of glory, to rise to her restored glory. Responding to the absence of comfort described in Eikha, God's answer is forthcoming: "I, I am your comforter!" (Is. 51:12). Who can facilitate Jerusalem's cure amidst the roiling breakers? Isaiah's answer rings clear: God, the healer (Is. 57:18–19), can cure Israel's woes, as He proclaims: "I am the Lord, your God, who calms the sea and churns up its waves!" (Is. 51:15).

The following chart illustrates the linguistic correlations noted above:

ישעיהו	איכה
עוּרִי עוּרִי לִבְשִׁי עֻזֵּךְ צִיּוֹן לִבְשִׁי בִּגְדֵי תִפְאַרְתֵּךְ יְרוּשָׁלַ͏ִם עִיר הַקֹּדֶשׁ כִּי לֹא יוֹסִיף יָבֹא בָךְ עוֹד עָרֵל וְטָמֵא הִתְנַעֲרִי מֵעָפָר קוּמִי (נ"ב, א'–ב')	יֵשְׁבוּ לָאָרֶץ יִדְּמוּ זִקְנֵי בַת צִיּוֹן הֶעֱלוּ עָפָר עַל רֹאשָׁם חָגְרוּ שַׂקִּים (ב', י')
אָנֹכִי אָנֹכִי הוּא מְנַחֶמְכֶם (נ"א, י"ב) וְאָנֹכִי ה' אֱלֹהֶיךָ רֹגַע הַיָּם וַיֶּהֱמוּ גַּלָּיו (נ"א, ט"ו)	מָה אֲשַׁוֶּה לָךְ וַאֲנַחֲמֵךְ בְּתוּלַת בַּת צִיּוֹן כִּי גָדוֹל כַּיָּם שִׁבְרֵךְ מִי יִרְפָּא לָךְ (ב', י"ג)
דְּרָכָיו רָאִיתִי וְאֶרְפָּאֵהוּ וְאַנְחֵהוּ וַאֲשַׁלֵּם נִחֻמִים לוֹ וְלַאֲבֵלָיו. בּוֹרֵא נוב נִיב שְׂפָתָיִם שָׁלוֹם שָׁלוֹם לָרָחוֹק וְלַקָּרוֹב אָמַר ה' וּרְפָאתִיו (נ"ז, יח-יט)	מָה אֲשַׁוֶּה לָךְ וַאֲנַחֲמֵךְ בְּתוּלַת בַּת צִיּוֹן כִּי גָדוֹל כַּיָּם שִׁבְרֵךְ מִי יִרְפָּא לָךְ (ב', י"ג)

God leads the *gever* of chapter 3 in darkness on a twisted, dangerous path, blocked by animals and stone walls. This journey portrays a convoluted movement toward an uncertain destination. Darkness suggests God's absence, even as God is the one who leads him into this circuitous and perilous route. This sketch also reflects the *gever's* disoriented state of mind, his confusion and uncertainty as he moves through this crisis.

Isaiah's prophecies of consolation open with a different sort of journey. God leads the way; the route is termed "the path of the Lord." God invites Israel to join Him on this route, promising to provide them with water and shade (Is. 41:17–19) and to guide the blind on paths unseen (Is. 42:16). God assures the nation that he will turn the darkness into light and straighten their twisted paths (Is. 42:16). The nation's return from exile contrasts with the *gever's* tortuous journey; a nation that moved confusedly in darkness now proceeds along a steady route, accompanied by God, and filled with purpose and direction.

The following chart illustrates the linguistic correlations noted above:

ישעיהו	איכה
וְהוֹלַכְתִּי עִוְרִים בְּדֶרֶךְ לֹא יָדָעוּ בִּנְתִיבוֹת לֹא יָדְעוּ אַדְרִיכֵם אָשִׂים מַחְשָׁךְ לִפְנֵיהֶם לָאוֹר וּמַעֲקַשִּׁים לְמִישׁוֹר אֵלֶּה הַדְּבָרִים עֲשִׂיתִם וְלֹא עֲזַבְתִּים (מ״ב, ט״ז)	אוֹתִי נָהַג וַיֹּלַךְ חֹשֶׁךְ וְלֹא אוֹר (ג׳, ב׳) גָּדַר דְּרָכַי בְּגָזִית נְתִיבֹתַי עִוָּה (ג׳, ט׳)

The opening verse of chapter 4 reveals a puzzling sight: the streets of Jerusalem are strewn with dimmed gold and holy stones. This image of destruction is puzzling. Why do these jewels lose their worth? Why does no one want these magnificent objects? The sight illustrates Jerusalem's stark misery. Of what worth are dazzling jewels when there is no bread and no hope for the future? The precious stones also function as a metaphor for Jerusalem's children (see 4:2), once valued and precious, and now unwanted and abandoned. Eikha 4:7 continues the portrayal of the wealth and glittering visages of Jerusalem's former residents, who once sparkled like pearls and sapphires. Jerusalem's dignity and prosperity have been erased and her colors have faded; a once-dazzling city is dull and unrecognizable.

Isaiah 54 describes the rebuilding of Jerusalem. It does not restore a makeshift city, rudimentarily rebuilt to accommodate returning refugees. Instead, it portrays a city lined with dazzling and colorful precious stones: sapphires and rubies, beryl and turquoise (Is. 54:11–12). This city is destined to return to her prosperity and regal beauty. The following verse (Is. 54:13) describes learned children, disciples of God, restored to a peace-filled city. In a wordplay between the word for children (*banim*) and the word for builders (*bonim*), a well-known rabbinic passage in Berakhot 64a explains that the children of the city are its builders; their presence restores the city's glory, magnificence, and regality.

The following chart illustrates the linguistic correlations noted above:

ישעיהו	איכה
אָנֹכִי מַרְבִּיץ בַּפּוּךְ אֲבָנַיִךְ וִיסַדְתִּיךְ בַּסַּפִּירִים וְשַׂמְתִּי כַּדְכֹד שִׁמְשֹׁתַיִךְ וּשְׁעָרַיִךְ לְאַבְנֵי אֶקְדָּח וְכָל גְּבוּלֵךְ לְאַבְנֵי חֵפֶץ (נ"ד, י"א-י"ב)	אֵיכָה יוּעַם זָהָב יִשְׁנֶא הַכֶּתֶם הַטּוֹב תִּשְׁתַּפֵּכְנָה אַבְנֵי קֹדֶשׁ בְּרֹאשׁ כָּל חוּצוֹת (ד', א') אָדְמוּ עֶצֶם מִפְּנִינִים סַפִּיר גִּזְרָתָם (ד', ז')
וְכָל בָּנַיִךְ לִמּוּדֵי ה' וְרַב שְׁלוֹם בָּנָיִךְ (נ"ד, י"ג)	בְּנֵי צִיּוֹן הַיְקָרִים הַמְסֻלָּאִים בַּפָּז אֵיכָה נֶחְשְׁבוּ לְנִבְלֵי חֶרֶשׂ מַעֲשֵׂה יְדֵי יוֹצֵר (ד', ב')

Although the description of Jerusalem's destruction in chapter 4 is brief (4:11), its aftermath unfolds in gruesome detail. Blind people wander Jerusalem's streets (4:15), so stained by blood that no one wants to approach them. While Jerusalemites wander in search of a place to reside in exile, nations rebuff them with cries of disgust: "Turn aside, impure one! Turn aside, turn aside, do not touch!" Israel bears the burden of her contamination; she is regarded as sullied and sinful long after her departure from the blood-stained city.

Isaiah follows his proclamation of God's imminent redemption with an urgent call to the exiles to depart the impure land (52:11): "Turn aside, turn aside; depart from there! Do not touch impurity! Depart from her [the land]. Purify – bearers of the vessels of the Lord!" In a superb twist, Isaiah announces that the Judean community is not the source of impurity; instead, it permeates the lands of their exile. The prophet therefore instructs the nation to depart and refrain from touching the pervasive impurity. The Judeans easily reacquire their sanctified status, proudly bearing God's holy vessels as they make their way back to their land.

The following chart illustrates the linguistic correlations noted above:

איכה ד׳, ט״ו	ישעיהו נ״ב, י״א
סוּרוּ סוּרוּ	סוּרוּ סוּרוּ צְאוּ מִשָּׁם
סוּרוּ טָמֵא... אַל תִּגָּעוּ	טָמֵא אַל תִּגָּעוּ

We will conclude this partial examination with one final theme. Body parts play an important role in Eikha; personified Jerusalem decays physically, mirroring the demise of the nation. For example, eyes are referenced ten times in Eikha. Like the other failing body parts, eyes do not fulfill their main function in Eikha, namely, vision. The only occasion in which they endeavor to see in 4:17, it turns out to be a futile ("Our eyes still strain [to see] our futile aid"). In Eikha, eyes stream with tears; a double appearance of the word draws attention to this theme (1:16): "My eyes, my eyes! They flow with water!" It is no wonder that eyes cannot see; they are darkened (5:17), blinded, or worn out by tears (2:11). Although Eikha sometimes describes the inability to cry, this does not mean Jerusalem's eyes are used for sight; rather, the lack of tears suggests paralysis and dejection, eyes kept firmly on the ground. It seems pointless to seek vision in Eikha: the present is too painful and the future unlikely. Absence of sight also figuratively suggests lack of comprehension, a befuddled, cloudy despair.

In an attempt to rouse Jerusalem to prepare for her upcoming redemption, Isaiah twice instructs her to raise her downcast eyes and see her surroundings, to witness the return of her children: "Lift up your eyes and see, all are gathered and coming to you!" (Is. 49:18; 60:4). Clarity has returned and Jerusalem can raise her eyes in joy. Hope is abundant; the present and the future unfold with glorious anticipation. A doubled appearance of the word "eyes" appears in Isaiah as well, as

God promises the salvation and restoration of Jerusalem: "For eye to eye (*ayin be'ayin*) they will see when God returns to Zion."[7]

Alongside the restoration of the well-functioning eyes, the above verse suggests the return of communication between Israel and God, in which they make "eye to eye" contact.[8] Compounded by the loss of communication with God, hopelessness pervades the book of Eikha. God has hidden His face from them; in nearly every chapter of the book, the nation pleads with God to look at them and see (*re'eh vehabita*). Even prayer seems futile. Is God listening? Can prayer penetrate God's veil of anger?

> Even when I cry and plead, He shuts out my prayer. (Eikha 3:8)

> You covered Yourself with a cloud, to prevent prayer from passing through. (Eikha 3:44)

If prayer is not efficacious, then how can Israel reconstruct its relationship with God? Even when the community musters up strength to appeal to God at the end of the book ("Return us to You, Lord, and we will return, renew our days like [days] of old!"), they hastily withdraw, sighing under the weight of despair: "For You have surely rejected us, You have been greatly wrathful against us." Eikha does not conclude with prayer; appealing God's wrathful decree seems futile. God remains inaccessible, the community paralyzed by helplessness and impotence.

Isaiah illustrates how to reacquire belief in prayer. Preceding a description of the destroyed Judean cities and the desecrated and burnt Temple (64:9–10), Isaiah explains that Judah's sins led to this calamity:

---

7. Eikha Rabba 1:57 recognizes the connection between Isaiah 52:8 and Eikha 1:16: "They sinned with the eye…and they were punished with the eye, as it says, 'My eyes, my eyes! They flow with water,' and they will be comforted with the eye, as it says, 'For eye to eye they will see when God returns Zion.'"

8. Radak on Isaiah 52:8 explains that this verse describes the revival of prophecy, namely, direct communication between God and Israel. The other use of this phrase appears in Numbers 14:14, which describes humans having some sort of visual contact with the divine.

You were wrathful and we sinned… We all became impure… And no one called on Your name, [no one] awakened to grab hold of You, for You hid Your face from us and You melted us in the wake of our sins. (Is. 64:4–6)

Unlike Eikha, Isaiah refuses to fall silent in the wake of God's aloofness. Summoning God's parental role, the prophet invokes a reliable avenue for eliciting God's attention:

And now, Lord, You are our father. We are the clay and You are our craftsman; we are all the work of Your hands![9] (Is. 64:7)

No longer do the people writhe in the agony of their alienation from God. God is a dependable parent. He shaped and molded us, and we can trust in an ongoing relationship with Him. This recollection spurs prayer, and in the following verse, the prophet turns to God with a bold request, one that linguistically evokes the open-ended final verse of Eikha:

Do not be greatly wrathful with us (*al tiktzof… ad me'od*), Lord, and do not recall our sin for eternity! Look, please, at Your nation, at all of us! Your holy cities have become a desert, Zion is like a desert, Jerusalem a desolation. Our holy Temple, our glory, where our fathers praised You, was consumed by fire and all our precious things were ruined. Will You restrain Yourself over these, Lord? Will You be silent and afflict us greatly? (Isaiah 64:8–11)

Although the catastrophe initially produces passive despair and the renunciation of prayer, Isaiah's prophecies of restoration educate toward a different approach. These prophecies restore the possibility of prayer and recall God's fidelity and enduring covenant.

---

9. This verse evokes language from Eikha 4:2, where the narrator bemoans Zion's treatment as a disposable earthenware vessel, the work of a craftsman.

The following chart illustrates the linguistic correlations noted above:

ישעיהו	איכה
הֵן אַתָּה קָצַפְתָּ וַנֶּחֱטָא...וַעֲוֹנֵנוּ כָּרוּחַ יִשָּׂאֻנוּ (ס"ד, ד'-ה')	אֲבֹתֵינוּ חָטְאוּ וְאֵינָם אֲנַחְנוּ וַאֲנַחְנוּ עֲוֹנֹתֵיהֶם סָבָלְנוּ (ה', ז')
וְעַתָּה ה' אָבִינוּ אָתָּה אֲנַחְנוּ הַחֹמֶר וְאַתָּה יֹצְרֵנוּ וּמַעֲשֵׂה יָדְךָ כֻּלָּנוּ (ס"ד, ז')	אֵיכָה נֶחְשְׁבוּ לְנִבְלֵי חֶרֶשׂ מַעֲשֵׂה יְדֵי יוֹצֵר (ד', ב')
אַל תִּקְצֹף ה' עַד מְאֹד (ס"ד, ח')	קָצַפְתָּ עָלֵינוּ עַד מְאֹד (ה', כ"ב)
הֵן הַבֶּט נָא עַמְּךָ כֻלָּנוּ (ס"ד, ח')	הַבִּיטָה וּרְאֵה אֶת חֶרְפָּתֵנוּ (ה', א')

Reading Eikha within a wider Tanakh context offers new insights into the way that the Tanakh views the calamitous events of 586 BCE. Despite the agony and despondency produced by the catastrophe, the Tanakh does not leave us hopeless. Isaiah's prophecies of consolation dialogue with the pain-filled book, offering an unmistakable response to Eikha's pain. When read alongside Isaiah's prophecies, it becomes clear that the calamity of Eikha will be rectified; Judah will return from exile, rebuild her city, and reassume its divine destiny. Biblical history continues, illustrating Israel's remarkable fortitude and reaffirming God's ongoing covenantal commitment to His nation.

Eikha Rabba: Filling Eikha's Void

While the book of Eikha laments the destruction of Jerusalem and the First Temple in 586 BCE, early Jewish interpretation of the book takes place within a context of other national catastrophes.[1] First, the Roman destruction of Jerusalem and the Second Temple in 70 CE left the nation dazed. Two unsuccessful uprisings followed, leaving a growing toll of death and suffering.[2] Rabbinic exegesis of Eikha illustrates the way the religious leadership utilized the book to cope with their own contemporary calamities.

A compendium of rabbinic commentaries on the book of Eikha, Eikha Rabba consists of exegesis and supplementary ideas written over the course of several hundred years following the destruction of Jerusalem's Second Temple. Filled with vivid, detailed midrashim, this book offers special insight into Ḥazal's role as educators and counselors seeking to offer their communities guidance in contending with their current situations.[3]

---

1. I am indebted to S. D. J. Cohen, "The Destruction: From Scripture to Midrash," *Prooftexts* 2 (1982), 18–39, for his general approach to the intersection between Eikha and Eikha Rabba.
2. I refer to the uprising of the Jews of Cyrenaica, Egypt, and Cyprus against Rome in 115–117 CE, and the disastrous end of the Bar Kokhba revolt (132–135 CE).
3. The urgent need for a contemporary explanation of the second *ḥurban* may explain why Eikha Rabba is one of the oldest works of midrashic literature. Eikha Rabba (also called *Aggadat Eikha, Megillat Eikha, Midrash Kinot, Eikha Rabbati*) was completed

Ibn Ezra alludes to the rich multiplicity of Eikha's midrashim in the introduction to his commentary on Eikha: "Some [midrashim] contain riddles, secrets, or exalted allegories, some soothe wearied hearts with insightful themes, and some are designed to strengthen those who stumble and fill those who are empty." [4]

In order to apply the book of Eikha to contemporary reality, rabbinic literature presupposes a timeless meaning for the book, in which Eikha's lamentations incorporate all past tragedies and anticipate all future ones.[5] A verse in Eikha can refer to the death of Aaron,[6] the exile of the ten tribes,[7] or to the martyrs of the Tannaitic period.[8] Eikha Rabba 5:9 applies one verse in Eikha to four different time periods: Israel's wanderings in the desert, Daniel's vision, Isaiah's prophecies, and concludes with the contemporary troubles of the rabbinic period, which trumps previous eras in terms of severity.

Rabbinic literature often conflates the two *ḥurban*s, interpreting many verses in Eikha as a forecast of and lament over the second *ḥurban*.[9] Note, for example the following interpretation of the double appearance of the word *apo* (His anger) in Eikha 2:1:[10]

---

approximately in 500 CE, apparently in Israel. For a good overview of Eikha Rabba, see A. Reizel, *Introduction to the Midrashic Literature* (Alon Shevut: Tevunot, 2011), 183–93 [Hebrew]. See also the bibliography on pp. 193–96.

4. Eikha Rabba is not driven solely or even primarily by exegetical interests. Its midrashim use the text of Eikha to supplement or even alter its basic meaning. Maimonides, in his *Guide of the Perplexed* III, 43, maintains that this is generally true about midrashim, which are "not meant to bring out the meaning of the text" (*The Guide of the Perplexed*, trans. S. Pines [Chicago: University of Chicago Press, 1963], 572–73.)

5. The fact that Eikha lacks narrative, dates, or identified persons facilitates this approach. In Ḥazal's view, Eikha may also refer to all pain suffered by all individuals. This is because the book is not about a city or a temple, a religion or a point in history. It is a timeless story of humans who suffer.

6. Eikha Rabba 1:56 explains that Eikha 1:21 refers to Aaron's death.

7. Eikha Rabba 1:23 (explaining 1:2); 4:20; 5:6.

8. Eikha Rabba 2:4 posits that Eikha 2:4 refers to the death of the Ten Martyrs. Eikha Rabba 3:51 explains Eikha 3:51 as a lament over the children who died in the siege of Beitar.

9. A typical formulation interprets a verse first about the Babylonian king, Nebuchadnezzar, and then interprets the same verse as referring to the Roman emperor, Vespasian. See, for example, Eikha Rabba 3:2; 3:4.

10. See similarly the explanation of the double language of Eikha 1:2 in Sanhedrin 104b: "'She shall surely cry (*bakho tivkeh*)' – The [double language of the] two cries – what

"On the day of His anger" (Eikha 2:1). [The word] "His anger" (*apo*) appears twice: once for the First Temple and once regarding the Second Temple. (Eikha Rabba 2:1)

The book of Eikha contains an evocative description of pain. Nevertheless, its approach to dealing with the aftermath of loss proves woefully inadequate. It lacks a well-developed explanation for the nation's suffering, offering instead a laconic portrayal of general sinfulness. Enemies jeer and prosper, prevailing despite their cruelty. God's role (although sometimes justified) is brief and often unpleasant, laced with wrath and hostility. The book's theological grappling appears in a mere nineteen verses at its center (3:21–39), plus an additional two verses toward its end (5:19–20). Eikha offers little by way of rehabilitation, consolation, or hope for the future. Interpreters seeking positive messages for a suffering community find that Eikha falls short of their needs.

Eikha's rabbinic interpreters fill in the void left by the book. Midrashim on Eikha manage to extract from the text messages of rehabilitation, consolation, and hope. This often involves creative interpretation, sometimes even the twisting of the plain meaning in a bid to obtain the required results. For example, Eikha contains no words of consolation. The root *naham* (comfort) appears six times, all framed in a negative or rhetorical context. Instead of surrendering the quest and constructing an uplifting message of its own, Eikha Rabba radically reinterprets a bleak verse:[11]

"She has no (*ein lah*) comforter" (Eikha 1:2) – So says R. Levi: Every place in which it says, "she has none (*ein*)," she will have [what she lacks]. "And Sarai was barren; she had no child" (Gen. 11), and then she had one, as it says, "The Lord remembered Sarah" (Gen. 21). Similarly, "And Hannah had no children" (I Sam. 1), and then

---

is its purpose? Rabba said in the name of R. Yoḥanan: One for the First Temple and one for the Second."

11. I previously cited this midrash in my discussion of Jerusalem's bitterness in Eikha 1:4. Nevertheless, it bears repeating within the context of our examination of Eikha Rabba.

she did, as it says, "For the Lord remembered Hannah" (I Sam. 2). Similarly, "She is Zion, there is none that seeks her" (Jer. 30), and she will have, as it says, "And a redeemer shall come to Zion" (Is. 59). Here too, you say that "she has no comforter." She will have, as it says, "I [God] am your comforter" (Is. 51). (Eikha Rabba 1:26)

Eikha Rabba engages in this sort of bold exegesis in another verse that describes Israel's hopelessness:

"Servants ruled us; there was none to extricate us from their hand" (Eikha 5:8). "Servants ruled us" – this refers to Egypt. "There was none to extricate us from their hand" – were it not for Moses! Another interpretation: "Servants ruled us" – these are the four kingdoms. "There was none to extricate us from their hand" – were it not for God! (Eikha Rabba 5:8)

In a series of interpretive statements, R. Shimon ben Lakish repeatedly declares that although "God despairs of the righteous in this world, He will yet return and have compassion over them [during the time of redemption]" (Eikha Rabba 3:1; 3:6; 3:9; 3:20). While these statements seem to align with the simple meaning of two of Eikha's verses (3:26, 31), they significantly reverse two others (3:2, 18).

Why do *Ḥazal* need to reinterpret the book of Eikha in addressing their calamities? If the book of Eikha does not offer consolation, why go to such lengths to extract messages of comfort from it?

Ironically, Eikha Rabba's disregard for Eikha's textual meaning presupposes *Ḥazal's* respect for the book. In the rabbinic post-prophetic reality, textual exegesis becomes the method for eliciting the word of God. To help their constituents deal with their enormous catastrophes, rabbinic interpreters look to the biblical book of national tragedy for advice and divine messages of consolation. The creativity and energy that underlie this exegesis testify to the importance rabbinic interpreters ascribe to the biblical text.

THE THEOLOGICAL VOID

By not directly addressing the critical questions, Eikha creates a theological vacuum. Why, in fact, does God destroy Jerusalem at this time?

Which specific sins cause this catastrophe, and why is this generation more deserving of punishment than previous ones?

Eikha's refusal to delineate specific sins spawns a lingering sense of disproportionate judgment.[12] The resulting disenchantment with God finds expression in sporadic horrified outbursts, which erupt throughout the book: "The Lord stamped like a winepress on maiden daughter of Judah!" (1:15) and: "You murdered on the day of Your anger, You slaughtered, You did not pity!" (2:21). Despondency laces the following statement: "My endurance is lost and my hope in the Lord" (3:18), while outrage seems to accompany this one: "Look, Lord, and see! To whom have You done this?" (2:20). Although these emotional outbursts often subside in the verses that follow, eruptions continue to flare up, exposing the theological tensions that lie under the book's surface.

For rabbinic interpreters, Eikha does not provide adequate answers, leaving a dangerous void.[13] Without specific sins, the calamity seems unwarranted. This may be the backdrop for the huge variety of sins introduced by Eikha Rabba to explain the *ḥurban*.[14] Midrashim sketch an elaborate portrait of a sin-filled city, presenting an unsystematic panoply of iniquities. Jumbling together sins against God with sins against their fellow man, severe sins along with less serious ones,[15]

---

12. The book of Eikha often acknowledges that general sinfulness caused the *ḥurban*, even if it does not list specific transgressions. Eikha Rabba mirrors this perception, concluding fourteen of its thirty-six proems with the words, "Because they sinned, they were exiled, and because they were exiled, Jeremiah began to lament over them, 'How has the city sat alone!' (Eikha 1:1)." However, Eikha Rabba will provide a more extensive explanation of the sins that lead to the devastating punishment.

13. For more on this topic, see A. Mintz, *Hurban: Responses to Catastrophe in Hebrew Literature* (New York: Columbia University Press, 1984).

14. Midrashim often explain the events as due recompense for the people's sinfulness. Several midrashim begin with the words, "Had you been worthy..." and continue by explaining that their unworthiness led to the undesirable result ("But now, since you were not worthy"). See, for example, Eikha Rabba *Petiḥta* 11; 19; 23. Another refrain in Eikha Rabba 1:57 indicates that Israel's punishment derives directly from its sins ("You will find that that with which Israel sinned, he is struck").

15. In a midrash that is likely meant to admonish his listeners and cause them to reform their behavior, R. Huna opines that people who played ball on Shabbat provoked the punishment (Eikha Rabba 2:4). This does not seem to be a literal attempt to explain the horrific events; indeed, sometimes Eikha Rabba appears to function

the Midrash indicates that the nation's sins are ubiquitous and varied. Jerusalem's inhabitants are morally and religiously untethered, and their lifestyle is unconstrained by social or sacred norms.

To illustrate the breadth of the sinfulness, I offer a partial list of sins mentioned in Eikha Rabba:[16]

- They worshipped idols.
- They refused to listen to prophets.
- There were no righteous people in their midst.
- They did not do good deeds.
- They did not pay their teachers.
- They abandoned the Torah.
- They transgressed the thirty-six sins that are punishable with *karet* (excision).
- They spilled blood.
- They ceased bringing sacrifices.
- They were cruel to the gentiles.
- They took advantage of poor people.
- They stopped learning Torah.
- They profaned God's name.
- They contaminated the Temple.
- They profaned Shabbat and Yom Kippur.
- They were arrogant and vulgar.
- There were false prophets.
- They denied the oneness of God.
- They denied the Ten Commandments.
- They did not believe in circumcision.
- They transgressed the covenant of Sinai.
- They were joyful at the downfall of their fellows.
- They did not turn to God in repentance.

---

less as discourses on events of the past and more as hortatory admonishments for current behavior (see Cohen, "Destruction," 26).

16. My intention is to offer a sense of the wide range of sins mentioned in Eikha Rabba. In order not to make this unwieldy, I have not cited the source for each midrash.

- They ate leavened bread on Passover.
- They held onto the collateral of the poor person.
- They withheld wages from their workers.
- They stole the charity to the poor.
- They ate the tithes for the poor.
- They continued to enslave the indentured Hebrew servant after the sabbatical year.
- They hated their fellow without cause.
- They engaged in improper sexual relations and prostitution.
- They removed from their necks the yoke of heaven.
- They engaged in witchcraft.

Eikha Rabba also cites Israel's perennial sins (the golden calf, the spies), casting blame for the *ḥurban* upon the historical transgressions that accompany Israel in every generation.[17] Eikha Rabba seems to flail about in all directions, frantically searching for explanations that make sense of the terrible calamity.[18]

The point of this catalogue is not to malign the already battered community, but rather to elucidate the *ḥurban* in a way that offers the nation a route to recovery. If the catastrophe occurred because of their sins, then the simplest recourse is to repent and reconcile with God.[19]

A second troubling theological problem of the book relates to God's role in the events. Eikha opens by describing a widowed city, alluding both to the disappearance of Jerusalem's populace and her God.[20] Other verses overtly describe God's desertion, asserting, for example, that, "The Lord's face scattered them – He did not continue to look at them" (Eikha 4:16). The recurring refrain asking God to look and see His nation (e.g., Eikha 1:12; 5:1) implies that God has turned His face away from His people and is no longer interested in a relationship with

---

17. Some of the midrashim in Eikha Rabba elaborate on the sins, offering detailed stories that illustrate how deeply sinfulness had penetrated the psyche of Jerusalem's inhabitants. See, for example, Eikha Rabba 1:36; 4:18.
18. For a similar list, see Shabbat 119b.
19. As we will see, many midrashim in Eikha Rabba describe the efficacy of repentance.
20. See our discussion of the identity of Jerusalem's deceased husband in Eikha 1:1.

them. This state of God's absence leaves a dearth of hope and a profound uncertainty as to how to repair the situation.

The depiction of God becomes more menacing when coupled with His hostile posture in the book. Alarmingly, the principal enemy named in the book is God Himself: "He bent His bow *like an enemy*; steadied His right hand *like an adversary*... The Lord was *like an enemy*, He swallowed Israel. He swallowed all her palaces, He destroyed its fortresses, and He increased in Judah mourning and moaning" (Eikha 2:4–5). God is filled with anger in the book, and He uses it to afflict Israel, with devastating results: "Is there any pain like my pain that has been committed against me, when the Lord made me grieve on the day of His burning anger?" (Eikha 1:12). The book often describes the terrible effects of God's wrath: "I am the man who has seen affliction by the rod of His anger... He walked me in darkness and not light" (Eikha 3:1–2); "The Lord completed His wrath, spilled out the anger of His nostrils. He lit a fire in Zion, and it consumed her foundations" (Eikha 4:11).

For rabbinic educators, this presentation of God is untenable.[21] How can Israel reconcile with God if He is angry and unforgiving? And how can a spiritual leader present God as an adversary to a shattered nation? Where is God and why has He not responded to their misery? God's silence is especially troubling to the rabbis following the second ḥurban, given that their exile shows no signs of ending.

Eikha Rabba frequently reverses Eikha's depiction of God. God may be justifiably incensed at his recalcitrant nation. Nevertheless, the midrashim vividly depict God mourning and lamenting His nation's misfortune:[22]

---

21. I do not mean to suggest that Eikha Rabba fails to recognize God's punitive role and withholds all manner of accusation against God. Like Eikha itself, some midrashim exhibit striking audacity in discussing God's active role in the calamity.

22. For more on these midrashim, see M. Ayali, "The God Who Suffers the Sufferings of Israel," in S. Heller-Willensky and M. Idel (eds.), *Studies in Jewish Thought* (Jerusalem: Magnes, 1989), 29–50 [Hebrew]; Tod Linafelt, "Life in Excess: The Midrash in Lamentations," in *Surviving Lamentations: Catastrophe, Lament and Protest in the Aftermath of a Biblical Book* (Chicago: The University of Chicago Press, 2000), 104–8.

"Over these I weep" (Eikha 1:16). "How I wish that my head were water and my eye a fount of tears so that I could cry day and night for the slain of the daughter of my nation" (Jer. 8:23). Who said this verse? Jeremiah [could not have] said it, for he could not abstain from eating, drinking, and sleeping! It must be that God said this, for He does not sleep. (Eikha Rabba 1:16)

"She surely cries" (*Bakho tivkeh*, Eikha 1:2)... [Jerusalem] cries and causes others to cry with her. She cries and causes God to cry with her, as it says, "And the Lord God of hosts summoned on that day for weeping and lamenting" (Is. 22:12). (Eikha Rabba 1:23)

God said to His ministering angels, "What does a human king who is in mourning do?" They said to Him, "He wears black and covers his head with sackcloth." He [God] said, "So will I do." (Eikha Rabba 3:10)

In Eikha Rabba, God experiences deep empathy for His nation's suffering. In sharing Israel's grief, God becomes a source of consolation. More poignantly, God is presented as a casualty of the catastrophe, in which His chief role is victim rather than perpetrator:

God said to His ministering angels, "Come let us go, you and I, and see what has happened to My house – what the enemies have done to it." Immediately, God and His angels went, with Jeremiah leading the way. When God saw the Temple, He said, "Surely, this is My house, and this is My resting place! Enemies have come and done with it as they please!" At that moment, God wept and said, "Woe to Me for My house! My sons – where are you? My priests – where are you? My beloveds – where are you? What shall I do for you? For I warned you and you did not repent." God said to Jeremiah, "Today I am like a person who had one child and he made for [that child] a wedding canopy, but [the child] died while he was under it." (Eikha Rabba *Petiḥta* 24)

At the moment that the *Shekhina* [God's presence] exited the Temple, she [impulsively] turned back to caress and kiss the walls of the Temple and its pillars. Then she [the *Shekhina*] wept and said, "Be at peace, My Temple! Be at peace, My royal house! Be at peace, My precious house! Be at peace!" (Eikha Rabba *Petiḥta* 25)

"I was watchful, and I am like a lone bird on a roof" (Ps. 102:8). God said, I was watchful so that I could rest my *Shekhina* upon the Temple forever, but I became like a [lone] bird. Just as the bird, when one takes his goslings, she sits alone, so too God said, "I burned My house, and destroyed My city and exiled My children among the nations and now I sit alone [and cry]: *Eikha!*" (Eikha Rabba *Petiḥta* 20)

In these midrashim, God cries with Israel and suffers along with them. God is deeply bereft – suffering the terrible loss of His house, His city, and His children. In the view of the rabbinic interpreters, God certainly has not abandoned Israel. According to some midrashim, God even accompanies Israel into exile:

R. Yehuda the son of R. Simon said: Come and see how precious the children are to God, for the ten tribes were exiled, and the *Shekhina* did not go into exile; Judah and Benjamin were exiled, and the *Shekhina* did not go into exile; the Sanhedrin was exiled, and the *Shekhina* did not go into exile; the watches were exiled, and the *Shekhina* did not go into exile; but when the children were exiled, the *Shekhina* went into exile, as it says, "Her young children went into captivity before the adversary" (Eikha 1:5). And then it says, "Departed from the daughter of Zion is all of her glory" (ibid. 1:6)…. What is this [glory]? This is God. (Eikha Rabba [Buber] 1:3)[23]

"The word that came to Jeremiah from the Lord" (Jer. 40:1). What was that word? [God] said to him: "Jeremiah, if you stay here, I will go with them [into exile], and if you go with them, I will

---

23. An abbreviated version of this midrash appears in Eikha Rabba [Vilna] 1:33.

stay here." [Jeremiah] said to Him: "Master of the Universe, if I go with them, what can I do to help them? Let their King and Creator go with them, for He can help them very much." (Eikha Rabba *Petihta* 34)

God's company is a source of consolation, ensuring that they are not alone in the exile and that God guarantees their future redemption.

In transforming God into a mourner and victim, Eikha Rabba reverses the portrayal of God in Eikha. This indicates both the extraordinary freedom of rabbinic interpretation and the rabbis' resolute determination to utilize Eikha in a manner that is efficacious for their suffering flock.

THE PSYCHOLOGICAL VOID

Eikha does not seek to strengthen the people; it offers little to relieve Israel's bleak psychological state. Alongside the collapse of her city, Eikha describes humiliation at the hands of jeering enemies (Eikha 1:7, 21; 2:16; 3:60–62), resulting in the loss of her self-esteem: "Look Lord and see our shame!" (Eikha 5:1). Eikha refrains from offering overt encouragement, reassurance, or coping devices to restore Israel's ebbing dignity.[24]

Rabbinic leaders cannot sustain this omission, especially given the mockery of the nations following the second *ḥurban*,[25] compounded by the rise of Christianity and the doctrine of supercessionism.[26] Eikha Rabba fills

---

24. Eikha does petition God to take vengeance on the enemies (e.g., 1:22; 3:64–66) and in 4:21–22 expresses certainty that Edom will receive due punishment. There are, moreover, several references to Israel's noble past (1:1; 4:5, 7), although they seem more intent upon highlighting the loss.

25. Cohen, "Destruction," 29 (especially footnote 29), notes that pagans pointed to the Jews' abject state as evidence that their religion is false. This argument first appears in Cicero (who lived prior to the destruction) and was advanced by Celsus in the second century and by Julian in the fourth. Cohen observes that the common biblical motif of "What will the nations say?" (e.g., Ex. 32:12) is developed not by Eikha, but by Eikha Rabba.

26. The following statement by the third-century Christian theologian Origen (in Homily 4 of his *Homilies on Jeremiah*) represents this approach: "For God sent away that people and gave to it a bill of divorce... Where is the ritual, the Temple, the sacrifices? They were driven away from their own place. Hence, He gave to Israel a

the psychological void, tendering a whirlwind of suggestions, anecdotes, and directives designed to boost spirits and navigate Israel toward rehabilitation.[27] Midrashim in Eikha Rabba offer several pathways to buoy the demoralized community. They paint a vivid portrait of Israel's glorious past, drawing attention to its unequalled brilliance. Midrashim also accentuate Israel's evident advantages over her neighbors and enemies, even though in the present reality Israel stands alone, uprooted, unprotected, and shunned.

The book of Eikha occasionally compares the splendid past with a dismal present. The regal city that once teemed with people now sits isolated, a "widowed" city (1:1). Its inhabitants, who ate delicacies and dressed in silken finery, now languish on the streets from starvation and cling to the refuse heap for warmth (4:5). These recollections deepen the sense of loss by highlighting the chasm between Israel's former glory and current abasement.

Midrashim also describe the tragedy of Jerusalem's precipitous fall. However, in a clever twist, instead of focusing on the terrible reversal, they enthusiastically explicate passages that reference Jerusalem's past. In a bid to reinstate the dignity of a wretched people, these midrashim offer fond embellishments of Israel's past wealth and luxurious lifestyle:[28]

> "Precious children of Zion [who were once valued as gold]"
> (Eikha 4:2). What was their value? When a non-Jerusalemite
> man would marry a Jerusalemite woman, he would give her her

---

bill of divorce" (*Origen: Homilies on Jeremiah, Homily on I Kings 28*, trans. J. C. Smith [Washington, DC: Catholic University of America Press, 1998], 33). See also R. Kimelman, "Rabbi Yokhanan and Origen on the Song of Songs: A Third-Century Jewish-Christian Disputation," *Harvard Theological Review* 73 (1980), 588–94.

27. Eikha Rabba certainly presents a fair amount of the pain and grieving that dominate the biblical book. While Eikha Rabba is not primarily a book that consoles and rehabilitates, it has surprisingly positive messages. As Cohen notes ("Destruction," 22), "Although the works have identical interests, they have radically different emphases and conclusions. *Lamentations* is dominated by bitterness and despair, *Lamentations Rabbati* – by consolation and hope."

28. See, for example, the series of midrashim that describe the wealth and pampering of Miriam bat Baitus in Eikha Rabba 1:47–50. While these midrashim end by describing her terrible privations as a result of Jerusalem's capture, they paint a vivid (and apparently uncritical) portrait of Miriam's former lavish lifestyle.

weight in gold. When a Jerusalemite man would marry a non-Jerusalemite woman, they would give him his weight in gold. (Eikha Rabba 4:2)

Midrashim sometimes overtly exaggerate Jerusalem's previous greatness:[29]

"The city that was full of people." R. Shemuel taught: Jerusalem had twenty-four districts. Each district had twenty-four neighborhoods and each neighborhood had twenty-four marketplaces. Each marketplace had twenty-four streets and each street had twenty-four courtyards. Each courtyard had twenty-four houses and each courtyard produced a populace double the number of those who left Egypt.[30] (Eikha Rabba 1:2)

Striking a posture of confidence and even triumph, these midrashim manipulate the contrast between past and present and reverse its primary meaning. It is easy to be swept up in the fantastical depictions of Israel's magnificence, as reconstructed by rabbinic exegesis, and one can almost (but not quite) obliterate the actual context describing the dismal present.

A fascinating, if slightly disturbing, section of Eikha Rabba contains a series of stories in which Israel's cleverness trumps the power, brutality, and riches of the enemy:

---

29. Eikha Rabba 1:2 contains a series of midrashim that attempt to calculate the great numbers of inhabitants of Jerusalem. Eikha Rabba 2:4 records a series of anecdotes that draw special attention to the glory of Jerusalem prior to the destruction.

30. If one computes the number of people who lived in Jerusalem according to this midrash, it emerges that nine and a half trillion people resided in Jerusalem prior to the destruction, an unlikely figure! A similar midrash (Eikha Rabba 3:70) maintains that there were five hundred elementary schools in Beitar prior to its destruction, and that each of these schools had no less than three hundred pupils. Thus, there were no less than 150,000 children in Beitar. While this number is large, it is not inflated to an unrealistic degree, as in the previous midrash. Interestingly, modern day Beitar-Illit has the highest percentage of children in any Israeli city (63%). With a birth rate of 1,800 annually, the modern city mirrors the midrash's depiction of its ancient counterpart.

A man from Athens went to Jerusalem and mocked the inhabitants of Jerusalem.[31] The [Jerusalemites] said, "Who will go and bring him here [so that we can teach him a lesson]?" One man said, "I will go and bring him here with a shaved head."

The Jerusalemite went to Athens and was hosted by that same man. In the morning, they went together to stroll in the marketplace. One of his [the Jerusalemite's] sandals broke. He said to a shoemaker, "Take this trimisa [a gold coin] and fix this sandal."… The next day the two went out to stroll in the marketplace when the other sandal broke. He said to him [the Athenian host]: "Take this trimisa to a shoemaker so that he can fix my sandals."

He [the Athenian] said: "Are sandals so expensive in your [city]?" [The Jerusalemite] said, "Yes!" He said, "How many dinars?" He [the Jerusalemite] responded, "They start at nine or ten dinars; if they are cheap, they can be seven or eight dinar." The Athenian said, "If I come to your [city] with merchandise, could I sell it there?" He said, "Yes, but you will not be permitted to enter the city without contacting me."

He [the Athenian] arranged his affairs, acquired sandals, and came to Jerusalem, sitting at the gates of the city. He sent for him [the Jerusalemite], who arrived and said to him [the Athenian], "We [Jerusalemites] have an agreement that no person may enter to sell his merchandise unless his head is shaved and his face is blackened." He [the Athenian] said to him, "And what do I have to lose if I shave my head and sell my merchandise?" So, he shaved his head and sat in the marketplace.

When a person came to buy sandals from him, he said, "How much is this pair of sandals?" He [the Athenian] replied, "Some for ten dinars, some for nine dinar. But I have nothing for less than eight dinars." When the [buyer] heard that, he struck

---

31. Based on the continuation of the midrash, it seems that the Athenian mocked the Jerusalemites for their unattractive appearance (shaved heads and blackened faces) following the city's destruction. Eikha Rabba 5:5 indicates that the Roman rulers required Judeans to shave their heads and faces as a sign of their servitude. In the same midrash, a blackened face is used as a metaphor for a humiliated person.

him on the head with the sandals and left without purchasing anything.

He [the Athenian returned to the Jerusalemite and] said to him, "Did I treat you so badly when you were a guest in my place?" The Jerusalemite responded, "From now on, you will not insult the residents of Jerusalem!" (Eikha Rabba 1:13)

This story may trouble modern readers, given the Jerusalemite's deception of his Athenian associate. It is therefore important to bear in mind the powerlessness of the once-noble people, who are now subject to incessant mockery.[32] This anecdote illustrates the willingness of the midrash to provide Israel with a psychological boost, even if it entails reneging on the usual directive toward humility and compassionate behavior.[33] It also informs the powerless community that they can easily outmaneuver their enemies, thereby compensating for their weak position and inferior stature.

Evoking Israel's intelligence is good for her self-esteem. More significantly, it reminds the nation that despite their many losses, there is still one thing that no one can take from them – namely, their intelligence, an advantage often highlighted in Eikha Rabba:[34]

"Great among nations" (Eikha 1:1) … Great in intellect. R. Huna said in the name of R. Yosi: Wherever a Jerusalemite went in the provinces, they arranged a seat of honor for him to sit upon in order to listen to his wisdom. (Eikha Rabba 1:4)

---

32. Several midrashim detail the enemies' mockery, underscoring its negative impact. See, for example, Eikha Rabba 3:5. As I noted, this is an important (and distressing) theme in Eikha as well.

33. See Reizel, *Introduction to the Midrashic Literature*, 188, where she summarizes G. Hasan-Rokem's approach to this series of midrashim. See also G. Hasan-Rokem, *Web of Life: Folklore and Midrash in Rabbinic Literature*, trans. B. Stein (Stanford: Stanford University Press, 2000). Eikha Rabba stresses the nation of Israel's wisdom, rather than asserting that the nations are unintelligent: "Should a person tell you there is wisdom among the nations, believe it" (Eikha Rabba 2:13).

34. See Cohen, "Destruction," 17–18.

THE PRAGMATIC VOID

Eikha dwells on the past and the present, offering only brief glimpses into a possible future. When it does look toward the future, it is generally in order to request vengeance upon enemies. Practically, this means that Eikha offers no advice for moving past the dismal present to rebuild the community or reconstitute their relationship with God. This represents a stunning omission, given the dire circumstances facing the community. Can they find a replacement for the canons of Jewish life as it was lived for so many years? How can this community continue to survive, lacking its familiar social and religious institutions? Can the community reconcile with God in the absence of sacrifices, Temple, or priests to conduct the atonement services?[35] Eikha Rabba fills this void as well, proffering pragmatic suggestions for constructing the nation's future following its disaster.

To boost morale, some midrashim assert that the destruction functioned as expiation, wiping away sins in anticipation of a restored future:

> The Rabbis said: The book of Eikha was better for Israel than forty years of Jeremiah's prophecies. Why? Because Israel received full atonement for their sins on the day the Temple was destroyed. (Eikha Rabba 4:25)

Eikha Rabba also reassures the community that God gave them the ability to endure their misfortunes:[36]

> R. Berechya said: [*"Ani hagever"* (Eikha 3:1) – This means that] God strengthened me (*gevarani*) to withstand all [of the misfortunes]. You find in Deuteronomy ninety-eight punitive admonitions, and afterwards it is written, "All of you *stand* here" (Deut.

---

35. Interestingly, Cohen, "Destruction," 27, observes that Eikha Rabba does not express particular concern over the loss of the sacrificial service. This does not mean that there is no mention of the loss of sacrifices – see, for example, Eikha Rabba *Petiḥta* 24, which briefly laments "the place where the children of Abraham would bring offerings to God."

36. See also Eikha Rabba 3:4.

29:9) – this means that you are all strong enough to withstand them all. (Eikha Rabba 3:1)[37]

Another midrash maintains that before God allowed this catastrophe to come upon Israel, He prepared its cure. To illustrate this, the midrash draws on a series of verses from Isaiah, each of which offers a solution to a verse in the first chapter of Eikha. The following citation brings just one example of many:[38]

> You also find that regarding all of the terrible prophecies that Jeremiah prophesied against Israel [in Eikha, chapter 1], Isaiah preceded him with a cure… Jeremiah said, "Judah has been exiled in suffering" (Eikha 1:3), and Isaiah said, "He will gather up the dispersed of Judah" (Is. 11:12). (Eikha Rabba 1:23)

By juxtaposing Eikha and Isaiah, this systematic midrash promises that each calamity will be rectified, and therefore these troubles will not defeat Israel.

Eikha's silence on rebuilding Israel's relationship with God constitutes a risky omission, one that could plunge the people into despair. To make matters worse, the book of Eikha thrusts the nation into further helplessness with its alarming contention that God deflects the nation's prayers (Eikha 3:44). How can Israel continue to function if prayer is no longer effective? Eikha Rabba tackles this problem directly, as we see in the following midrash:

> R. Ḥelbo asked R. Shemuel bar Naḥmani: I have heard that you are successful at homiletic interpretations. What, then, is the explanation for the verse: "You covered Yourself with a cloud to prevent prayer from passing through" (Eikha 3:44)? He replied: Prayer is likened to a *mikve* (ritual bath), while repentance is

---

37. The opening of Eikha 3:1, "*ani hagever*," literally means "I am the man," but the word *gever* etymologically indicates strength.
38. For more examples from this midrash, see the longer citation of it in the chapter above, "Eikha and the Prophecies of Consolation in Isaiah."

likened to a sea. Just as the *mikve* is sometimes open and sometimes locked, so, too, the gates of prayer are sometimes locked and sometimes open. But the sea is always open. So, too, the gates of repentance are always open. R. Ana said: The gates of prayer are never locked! (Eikha Rabba 3:60)

While R. Ana rejects the possibility that God does not accept their prayer (thereby rejecting the simple meaning of the verse), R. Shemuel bar Naḥmani focuses on the power of repentance, which *always* remains efficacious. Repentance is an important theme in Eikha Rabba.[39] In this midrash, it functions as practical advice on how to direct one's spiritual energies when all communication with God appears to have ceased.

Many midrashim stress the ability of repentance to bring about a change for the better. In the following example, even Israel's enemies acknowledge the raw power of repentance. They exert considerable effort to prevent Israel from wielding this valuable tool:

Nebuchadnezzar…commanded [his general] Nevuzaradan: This God of these [Israelites] accepts penitents and His hand is open to accept those who return. Therefore, when you conquer them, do not give them time to pray, so that they will not be able to repent and elicit God's compassion. (Eikha Rabba 5:5)

Repentance returns Israel to God and it also can hasten the advent of the redemption.[40]

Eikha lacks leaders. In Eikha's depiction, Israel's political and religious leaders are corrupt (2:14; 4:13), ineffective (2:10; 5:12), or have vanished into exile (2:9; 4:20). To fill this void, Eikha Rabba directs our attention to the forthcoming arrival of the Messiah, a leader who will

---

39. See also Eikha Rabba *Petiḥta* 25; Eikha Rabba 1:40. Eikha Rabba 2:3 asserts that had Israel repented, God's anger would have abated immediately.

40. Midrashim often assert that repentance has the power to bring about redemption (e.g., *Yalkut Shimoni* Isaiah 484; 498; *Pirkei DeRabbi Eliezer* 42). While Eikha Rabba discusses both redemption and repentance, it does not explicitly connect the two.

extricate the nation from its misfortune, rebuild Jerusalem, and renew Jewish sovereignty, thereby ushering in an eschatological era.

> R. Abba bar Kahana said: If you see benches filled with Babylonians settled in the land of Israel,[41] you should anticipate the arrival of the Messiah... R. Shimon ben Yochai taught: If you see a Persian horse tied up in the land of Israel, you should anticipate the arrival of the Messiah! (Eikha Rabba 1:41)

In spite of the pressing need for promising leadership, Eikha Rabba maintains a cautious ambivalence toward fostering messianic hopes.[42] The book's complex approach to messianism is evident in a lengthy anecdote regarding the birth of a messianic figure, whose task is to deliver Israel from her misfortunes and return her from her exile:

> A man was plowing when his ox bellowed. An Arab passed by and asked him, "What are you?" He answered, "I am a Judean." He [the Arab] said to him, "Release your ox and unfasten your plow." He asked, "Why?" He [the Arab] replied, "Because the Temple of the Judeans has been destroyed." He asked him, "How do you know?" He [the Arab] replied, "From the bellow of your ox." As they were speaking, the ox bellowed again. He [the Arab] said, "Hitch up your ox and your plow, for the savior of the Judeans has been born." He [the Judean] asked, "And what is his name?" "Menachem is his name." "And what is his father's

---

41. *Torah Temima*, Eikha 1:13, note 146, suggests that this refers not to the Babylonian enemies, but rather to the Judeans who return from the Babylonian exile to repopulate the land.

42. The rabbinic bid to prevent messianic hopes from becoming too centrally featured may be partially attributed to the need to distance themselves from the messianic character of Christianity. Moreover, the wariness may be connected to the disappointing failure of the Bar Kokhba revolt (132–135 CE), whose ideological underpinnings included the portrayal of Bar Kokhba as a messianic savior. Eikha Rabba 2:4 records a sharp riposte that R. Yoḥanan ben Torta flings toward R. Akiva, who regards Bar Kokhba as Messiah: "Akiva! Grass will grow between your cheeks and he [the Messiah] will still not have arrived!"

name?" "Hezekiah."[43] "And where can he be found?" "In the city of Bethlehem in Judah." (Eikha Rabba 1:51)

The midrash initially presents an exceedingly hopeful portrait. Immediately following the destruction of the Temple, the messianic savior bursts into the world. Nevertheless, the continuation of this midrash (not cited above) proves less auspicious. In an unsubtle polemic against Christian messianism, the search for this messiah (who is born in Bethlehem) proves futile. The message is both enigmatic and startling: It seems that while the potential for a Messiah exists, one should not devote oneself to a search for this figure. The midrash continues to oscillate between hope for a Messiah and reluctance to focus upon his imminent arrival.[44]

Eikha Rabba strikes a judicious balance in presenting a messianic vision. On the one hand, the promise of a messianic leader enables the nation to nurture hope, faith, and optimism as they confront a grim reality. On the other hand, the book maintains a prudent resistance to focusing on a messianic future. Messianism is often rooted in a negative attitude toward the present, which results in undue focus on the future. Eikha Rabba prefers to focus attention upon the present reality, as we will see shortly. The book is willing to allow messianic hopes to emerge, but it does not encourage the nation to concentrate excessive attention upon future dreams.[45]

---

43. According to Sanhedrin 98b, the Messiah's name is intended to counter the morose verse, "For a comforter (*menaḥem*) is far from me" (Eikha 1:16). Moreover, in naming the Messiah's father, the midrash issues a subtle polemic against the Christian doctrine that their messiah is born to a virgin and is the son of God.

44. In another about-face, Eikha Rabba 1:51 continues with some encouraging messianic statements, bringing proof texts from biblical verses that anticipate a messianic figure. The midrash concludes with a lively debate regarding the name of the coming Messiah.

45. R. J. Z. Werblowsky, "Messianism," in A. A. Cohen and P. Mendes-Flohr (eds.), *Contemporary Jewish Religious Thought* (New York: The Free Press, 1988), 598. As Werblowsky notes (p. 598): "Clearly Judaism was, to begin with, not a messianic religion." And later (p. 599): "Of course, there is no denying that the messianic complex moved from marginality to centrality, and at certain periods even into the very center of Judaism."

The loss of the Temple and political autonomy marked the disappearance of two central components of Israel's national self-definition. Torah study represents a portable way to maintain Israel's spiritual identity, offering the nation a means to maintain a relationship with God even after being exiled from their land.[46] This creative activity can bolster and define the landless community, enabling Israel to retain meaning, dignity, and communal pride.

The prominence of this theme in Eikha Rabba cannot be overstated. The book opens with a call to "raise your voice in words of Torah."[47] Midrashim often direct the community's attention to the importance of Torah study,[48] highlighting the centrality of both synagogues and study houses, which can function as a substitute for the destroyed Temple.[49] Eikha Rabba's focus on Torah study steers Israel to construct a new identity around these transportable activities.[50]

Israel's original decision to embrace the Torah at Sinai also empowers the nation to assert its special privileges before God, fiercely insisting that He forgive their sins:

---

46. Several biblical sources hint at the understanding that Torah study is particularly important during exile, following the loss of Israel's state institutions. This seems to be the intention of Malachi 3:22, which anticipates the impending disaster with the admonition to "remember the Torah of Moses." Following the description in Psalms 89 of the collapse of the Davidic dynasty, Psalms 90 opens with "A prayer of Moses, the man of God"; it is the only psalm attributed to Moses, suggesting that a cure for the exile and loss of the monarchy is to turn to the study of the Torah of Moses.

47. The second midrash in Eikha Rabba (*Petiḥta* 2) also focuses on the centrality of learning and teaching Torah, highlighting the importance of paying proper wages to teachers of Torah.

48. Midrashim express the importance of Torah learning in a negative context as well, by attributing the destruction of Jerusalem to the *absence* of Torah learning in the city (e.g., Eikha Rabba Petiḥta 2; 23; 34; Eikha Rabba 1:33).

49. See Eikha Rabba Petiḥta 1; 2; Eikha Rabba 3:7.

50. To illustrate the rabbinic attempt to replace the losses with Torah study, we recall the story (Gittin 56b) where R. Yoḥanan ben Zakkai petitions Vespasian to give him Yavneh as a place for the Sanhedrin to reconvene so that Torah scholarship may continue. Oddly, while the story of R. Yoḥanan ben Zakkai's encounter with Vespasian appears in Eikha Rabba 1:31, it omits this particular request.

God said to Israel: You have been stubborn [and sinful – why should I forgive you?]. They said to him: Master of the Universe! So it is good for us and so it is proper for us and so it is fair for us [that You return us to You], for no other nation accepted Your Torah except for us. (Eikha Rabba 3:1)

Eikha Rabba recognizes that Torah study is pivotal for Israel's ability to endure the exile. This finds unique expression in a poignant midrash:

"This I shall place upon my heart, therefore, I will hope" (Eikha 3:21). R. Abba bar Kahana said in the name of R. Yoḥanan: A parable. To what is this likened? To a king who married a matron and wrote her a generous marriage document, which read, "The following bridal chambers I am giving you and the following purple garments I am giving you." The king then left her to go to a faraway land and was detained there. Her neighbors would come to her and degrade her, saying, "The king has abandoned you and has gone to a faraway land and will never return to you." She would cry and moan,[51] but when she would come into her house, she would open her marriage document and read it and see [what was written in] her marriage document: "The following bridal chambers I am giving you and the following fine purple garments I am giving you." Immediately she would be comforted.

After many years, the king returned. He said to her, "My dear, I am amazed! How did you wait for me for all those years?" She said to him, "My lord king, had you not written for me such a generous marriage document, my neighbors would surely have caused me to lose hope!"

Similarly, the idolaters mock Israel and say to them, "Your God has hidden His face and removed His presence from you and

---

51. The midrash indicates a repeated exchange between the hostile neighbors and the king's lonely wife. Their routine mockery causes her to cry regularly, which forces her to console herself by reading her marriage document on a regular basis.

He will never return to you."[52] And she [Israel] cries and moans. However, when they enter the synagogues and the houses of study and read the Torah, they find there written, "And I will turn to you, and multiply you, and place My dwelling place among you, and I will walk in your midst" (Lev. 26:9). And then, they are comforted.

Tomorrow, when the redemptive era arrives, God will say to Israel, "My children, I am amazed by you! How did you wait for Me for all these years?" And they will respond to Him, "Master of the Universe! Were it not for the Torah that you gave us, the nations would surely have caused us to lose hope." Therefore, it is written, "*This* I shall place upon my heart [therefore, I will hope]" (Eikha 3:21). "This" always refers to Torah, as it says, "And *this* is the Torah [that Moses placed before the children of Israel]" (Deut. 4:44). (Eikha Rabba 3:7)

Exile is fraught with a sense of alienation from God, leaving Israel uncertain as to the state of their relationship with Him. The envious and hostile nations exacerbate Israel's insecurity, and their jeers echo in the backdrop of Israel's exilic misery. Israel's exilic reality seems intolerable, and it is possible that Israel's only recourse is to have faith in a distant future. Yet, the midrash does not resort to excessive attention upon eschatology. While eschatological hopes remain its ultimate aspiration, the midrash nevertheless proposes a lifestyle that concentrates on routine, daily life. Synagogues and study halls emerge as the prominent institutions, amidst a clear-eyed recognition that Torah study will be the secret of Israel's survival during the period of God's withdrawal.

Ḥazal's perspicacity is nothing short of astonishing. Indeed, Israel's devotion to both prayer and (especially) Torah study unites the exilic community and provides Israel with nobility, purpose, and pride throughout its turbulent history.

---

52. This recalls the writing of some of the early church fathers noted previously, who regard Israel's exile as evidence that God cast off the Jewish nation as His chosen people and does not intend to restore their special status.

Eikha's portrayal of the broken relationship between God and Israel, alongside its lack of attention to Israel's future, leaves gaping voids that are filled by the midrashic imagination. The wise and compassionate messages found in Eikha Rabba support Israel throughout the long and difficult years of exile. Ḥazal's ability to understand Israel's present and future needs facilitated Israel's continued perseverance and ability not simply to survive, but also to flourish in the aftermath of catastrophe.

The Structure of Eikha:
Faith in a Turbulent World

The book of Eikha has a unified, overarching structure. While each chapter stands on its own as an independent composition (as indicated by the acrostics in chapters 1–4),[1] the book is not a random collection of five unconnected laments.[2] The chapters appear woven together intentionally into a unified composition whose form reflects its meaning. Exploring Eikha's structure will reveal the book's broad themes and profound messages.

Eikha demonstrates its literary unity by displaying shared form, linguistic features, themes, and imagery. Three chapters (1, 2, and 4) open with same word (*Eikha*); the unique *kina* meter finds expression in every chapter; and the structural division of chapters 1 and 2 seems to rely on a similar division between speakers. Linguistic connections between chapters include the petition to God to look and see (*re'eh vehabita*), Jerusalem's churning innards (*mei'ai homarmaru*: 1:20 and 2:11), and the

---

1. Chapter 5 lacks an acrostic structure but maintains the twenty-two-verse length.
2. Some scholars consider the book to be a collection of disconnected songs (based on genre and style). See, for example, Westermann, 53–58. In contrast, Dobbs-Allsopp, 23, observes that each chapter connects to other chapters in a multiplicity of overlapping ways.

phrase "affliction and wandering" (*oniya umerudeha*: 1:7 and 3:19). Themes such as the tears that flow from failing eyes, the desperate effects of the famine (such as the mothers' cannibalism), the taunts of the enemies, and Jerusalem's widowed status appear in two or more chapters, thereby displaying the book's cohesion and interconnectedness. The first four chapters appear to end in a similar manner, with a call for vengeance upon the enemy. Sometimes the chapters flow into each other, offering an unfolding reading of the same psalm (Ps. 37) or describing the progression from an inability to cry (2:11, 18–19) to the onslaught of tears (3:48–49).

Eikha does not have an obvious progression of thought.[3] What, then, is the nature of the book's overall structure?[4] Does it progress along a linear continuum, or does it maintain a circular pattern? How would the central chapter fit into a chiastic shape? And most importantly, what is the concept that underlies the book's structure?

A LINEAR APPROACH

Some scholars maintain that a psychological reading of the book can help explain its haphazard structure, which reflects the unsystematic emotional responses that characterize the experience of bereavement.[5]

---

3. Many scholars maintain that the book defies any real order. See, for example, B. S. Childs, *Introduction to the Old Testament as Scripture* (London: SCM, 1979), 594; M. S. Moore, "Human Suffering in Lamentations," *Revue Biblique* 90 (1983); Dobbs-Allsopp, 23.

4. Some scholars have proposed creative explanations for Eikha's structure. For example, Shea, "Qinah," 103–7, suggests that the overall structure of the book is an evocative echo of the *kina* meter often employed in Eikha's binary sentences. Eikha's first three chapters are lengthy ones, while the final two chapters are distinctly shorter, resulting in a 3 + 2 pattern. In another creative theory, Renkema asserts that the letter strophes of the different chapters correspond; J. Renkema, "The Literary Structure of Lamentations (I–IV)," in W. van der Meer and J. C. de Moor (eds.), *The Structural Analysis of Biblical and Canaanite Poetry* (Sheffield Academic Press, 1988), 294–396; J. Renkema, "The Meaning of the Parallel Acrostics in Lamentations," VT 45 (1995), 379–83. Thus, for example, all the verses that open with the letter *alef* (as well as the first verse of chapter 5) address related or interconnected concepts.

5. See P. Joyce, "Lamentations and the Grief Process: A Psychological Reading," *Biblical Interpretation* 1 (1993), 314. Several studies have engaged in psychological analysis of the book of Eikha. See for example, D. L. Smith-Christopher, *A Biblical Theology of*

David Reimar proposes an opposite approach.[6] He suggests that Eikha's chapters progress in a linear fashion, alongside the stages of grief. Using Elisabeth Kübler-Ross's model of five stages of grieving, he detects a dominant perspective in each of the first four chapters that reflects the stages.[7] Kübler-Ross's five stages are:

1. Denial and Isolation
2. Anger
3. Bargaining
4. Depression
5. Acceptance

Reimar correctly notes that isolation is the principal theme of chapter 1, corresponding to Kübler-Ross's initial stage.[8] Anger dominates the second chapter, mirroring the second stage of Kübler-Ross's paradigm. Reimar claims that chapter 3 assumes a bargaining stance, engaging in good behavior (in the form of its reflections on God) in hope of a reprieve. This recalls Kübler-Ross's third stage, in which the patient or grieving person bargains with doctors or with God. Chapter 4, steeped in melancholy and lacking both prayer and hope, reflects a depressed emotional state, which parallels Kübler-Ross's fourth stage. The final stage is acceptance, characterized not by happiness, but by resolution. Reimer does not find this stage in chapter 5, in which he discerns a sustained verbal attack on God and a desire for a future. These attitudes seem to reflect the opposite of Kübler-Ross's acceptance. Still, in Reimar's view,

---

Exile (OBT; Minneapolis: Fortress, 2002), 75–104; H. A. Thomas, "Relating Prayer and Pain: Psychological Analysis and Lamentations Research," *Tyndale Bulletin* 61 (2010), 183–209.

6. D. J. Reimar, "Good Grief? A Psychological Reading of Lamentations," *ZAW* 114 (2002), 542–59.

7. See E. Kübler-Ross, *On Death and Dying* (New York: Macmillan, 1970). Joyce, also utilizes Kübler-Ross's model, arriving at a very different conclusion.

8. Reimar, "Good Greif," 6, admits that there is no denial in chapter 1, although this is the primary idea of Kübler-Ross's first stage. He thus largely bases his theory on the characteristic of isolation, which seems to be a secondary characteristic in Kübler-Ross's model.

the organization of the book revolves around the psychological response of the community to their catastrophe.

Several ideas emerge from this organizational concept. According to this scheme, the book advances in a linear fashion, illustrating how the nation can progress experientially. Small glimmers of forward movement (both in their emotional state and in their relationship with God) may be discernable, especially in chapters 4 and 5.[9] This progression seems to have an ultimate goal of recovery – unlike Kübler-Ross's model, which concludes with the patient's acceptance of impending death. As Reimar notes, this does not occur in the final chapter of Eikha. Instead, the divergence of chapter 5 from Kubler-Ross's model points to a vastly different conclusion reached by the devastated community. Despite its relentless realism and wretched state, Israel maintains an abiding hope in its future. The community never accepts its demise because it continues to believe in life.[10]

A CHIASTIC STRUCTURE

An alternative model proposes that Eikha's chapters are arranged in a chiastic (or concentric) structure.[11] Simply put, this means that the book consists of two concentric circles that revolve around a core center.[12] Chapters 1 and 5 compose the periphery of the book, its outermost circle. The circle inside of that consists of chapters 2 and 4, which correspond thematically and linguistically. All the chapters revolve around chapter 3, which lies at the core of the book and contains its focal theological treatise.

---

9. According to E. Assis, "The Unity of the Book of Lamentations," *CBQ* 71 (2009), 311, 329, this is because the turning point of the book occurs in its middle section, which restores a modicum of hope.

10. One reason for this difference surely lies in the distinction between an individual and the community of Israel. Every individual will die, but the community of Israel has divine assurance that it will always live on.

11. See, for example, Gordis, 127; Assis, "Unity," 306–29.

12. Many scholars maintain that the primary purpose of the concentric structure is to focus attention on its middle (see, e.g., Radday, "Chiasmus," 48–72). However, it seems clear that the fact that the themes of the surrounding chapters correspond to each other is of no less significance in the chiastic design.

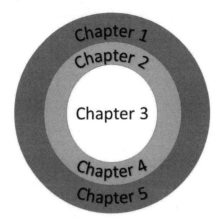

The circular structure indicates that the sufferer's reconciliation with God at the center does not represent a substantive turning point in the book.[13] Instead, the book returns to dwell on the nation's pain and suffering in the following chapters, eclipsing the theological harmony achieved at its center.

In the following section, I will bring evidence for the linguistic and thematic equivalents that create correspondence between the parallel chapters.[14] Following that, I will propose a theological understanding that can account for this chiastic structure, giving it purpose and meaning and underscoring the book's vital idea.

---

13. Assis, "Unity," 310–11, suggests otherwise, although he accepts the concentric structure. As noted above, Assis maintains that chapters 4 and 5 contain guarded hope, even as they mirror the overall themes and tone of their corresponding chapters. He explains that this is because chapter 3 constitutes a turning point, a transition from despair to hope. While one can discern a slight progression in the book after chapter 3, in my opinion, chapter 3 does not constitute a significant turning point in the book. Chapter 4 actually suggests a deterioration, as the chapter lacks any address to God. It seems to me that the circularity of the suffering prevails over any sort of linear progression in the book.

14. Throughout this study, I have pointed out these correspondences. At the summation of chapter 4, I discussed its connection to chapter 2 at length and in the summation of chapter 5, I discussed its connection to chapter 1. In this chapter, I will briefly summarize those correspondences and then I will consider the theological similarities between the chapters, in a bid to understand the book's theology.

Chapters 1 and 5: Emptiness and Mourning

To establish the correspondence between the chapters, we will begin by noting the linguistic similarities between them. Many of these words and phrases are unique to chapters 1 and 5, thereby strengthening the specific linkage between these chapters. The following chart illustrates the extensive linguistic relationship between chapters 1 and 5.[15] Stars indicate that the emphasized words appear only in these two chapters:

איכה, פרק ה׳	איכה, פרק א׳
אִמֹּתֵינוּ כְּאַלְמָנוֹת* (ה׳, ג׳)	הָעִיר רַבָּתִי עָם הָיְתָה כְּאַלְמָנָה* (א׳, א׳)
עַל אֵלֶּה* חָשְׁכוּ עֵינֵינוּ (ה׳, י״ז)	עַל אֵלֶּה* אֲנִי בוֹכִיָּה עֵינִי עֵינִי יֹרְדָה מַּיִם (א׳, ט״ז)
נֶהְפַּךְ לְאֵבֶל מְחֹלֵנוּ (ה׳, ט״ו)	דַּרְכֵי צִיּוֹן אֲבֵלוֹת מִבְּלִי בָּאֵי מוֹעֵד (א׳, ד׳)
נַחֲלָתֵנוּ נֶהֶפְכָה לְזָרִים (ה׳, ב׳) נֶהְפַּךְ לְאֵבֶל מְחֹלֵנוּ (ה׳, ט״ו)	נֶהְפַּךְ לִבִּי בְּקִרְבִּי (א׳, כ׳)
עַל צַוָּארֵנוּ נִרְדָּפְנוּ (ה׳, ה׳)	כָּל רֹדְפֶיהָ הִשִּׂיגוּהָ בֵּין הַמְּצָרִים (א׳, ג׳) וַיֵּלְכוּ בְלֹא כֹחַ לִפְנֵי רוֹדֵף (א׳, ו׳)
עַל זֶה הָיָה דָוֶה* לִבֵּנוּ (ה׳, י״ז)	נְתָנַנִי שֹׁמֵמָה כָּל הַיּוֹם דָּוָה* (א׳, י״ד) כִּי רַבּוֹת אַנְחֹתַי וְלִבִּי דַוָּי* (א׳, כ״ב)
אֲבֹתֵינוּ חָטְאוּ וְאֵינָם (ה׳, ז׳) אוֹי נָא לָנוּ כִּי חָטָאנוּ (ה׳, ט״ז)	חֵטְא חָטְאָה יְרוּשָׁלַ͏ִם (א׳, ח׳)
וְלֹא הוּנַח* לָנוּ (ה׳, ה׳)	הִיא יָשְׁבָה בַגּוֹיִם לֹא מָצְאָה מָנוֹחַ* (א׳, ג׳)
עַל צַוָּארֵנוּ* נִרְדָּפְנוּ (ה׳, ה׳)	עָלוּ עַל צַוָּארִי* הִכְשִׁיל כֹּחִי (א׳, י״ד)
עֲבָדִים* מָשְׁלוּ בָנוּ (ה׳, ח׳)	גָּלְתָה יְהוּדָה מֵעֹנִי וּמֵרֹב עֲבֹדָה* (א׳, ג׳)
בְּנַפְשֵׁנוּ נָבִיא לַחְמֵנוּ (ה׳, ט׳)	כָּל עַמָּהּ נֶאֱנָחִים מְבַקְשִׁים לֶחֶם נָתְנוּ מַחֲמַדֵּיהֶם בְּאֹכֶל לְהָשִׁיב נָפֶשׁ (א׳, י״א)
בַּחוּרִים טְחוֹן נָשָׂאוּ וּנְעָרִים בָּעֵץ כָּשָׁלוּ* (ה׳, י״ג)	הִכְשִׁיל* כֹּחִי...קָרָא עָלַי מוֹעֵד לִשְׁבֹּר בַּחוּרָי (א׳, י״ד–ט״ו)
מִפְּנֵי חֶרֶב הַמִּדְבָּר (ה׳, ט׳)	מִחוּץ שִׁכְּלָה חֶרֶב בַּבַּיִת כַּמָּוֶת (א׳, כ׳)

---

15. This chart appears in English at the conclusion of chapter 5 ("Chapter 5: In Summation").

איכה, פרק ה'	איכה, פרק א'
זְקֵנִים מִשַּׁעַר שָׁבָתוּ (ה', י"ד)	כָּל שְׁעָרֶיהָ שׁוֹמֵמִין (א', ד')
זְקֵנִים מִשַּׁעַר שָׁבָתוּ (ה', י"ד)	רָאוּהָ צָרִים שָׂחֲקוּ עַל מִשְׁבַּתֶּהָ (א', ז')
שָׂרִים בְּיָדָם נִתְלוּ פְּנֵי זְקֵנִים לֹא נֶהְדָּרוּ* (ה', י"ב)	וַיֵּצֵא מִן בַּת צִיּוֹן כָּל הֲדָרָהּ* הָיוּ שָׂרֶיהָ כְּאַיָּלִים (א', ו') ·
עַל הַר צִיּוֹן שֶׁשָּׁמֵם (ה', י"ח)	כָּל שְׁעָרֶיהָ שׁוֹמֵמִין (א', ד') נְתָנַנִי שֹׁמֵמָה כָּל הַיּוֹם דָּוָה (א', י"ג) הָיוּ בָנֶיהָ שׁוֹמֵמִים כִּי גָבַר אוֹיֵב (א', ט"ז)
חַדֵּשׁ יָמֵינוּ כְּקֶדֶם (ה', כ"א)	אֲשֶׁר הָיוּ מִימֵי קֶדֶם (א', ז')
פָּרַק אֵין מִיָּדָם (ה', ח') מִצְרַיִם נָתַנּוּ יָד (ה', ו')	נְתָנַנִי אֲדֹנָי בִּידֵי לֹא אוּכַל קוּם (א', י"ד) פֵּרְשָׂה צִיּוֹן בְּיָדֶיהָ (א', י"ז)
נַחֲלָתֵנוּ נֶהֶפְכָה לְזָרִים בָּתֵּינוּ לְנָכְרִים (ה', ב')	מִחוּץ שִׁכְּלָה חֶרֶב בַּבַּיִת כַּמָּוֶת (א', כ')
יְתוֹמִים הָיִינוּ וְאֵין אָב (ה', ג') אֲבֹתֵינוּ חָטְאוּ וְאֵינָם (ה', ז') פָּרַק אֵין מִיָּדָם (ה', ח')	אֵין לָהּ מְנַחֵם (א', ב') וְאֵין עוֹזֵר לָהּ (א', ז') אֵין מְנַחֵם לָהּ (א', ט') אֵין מְנַחֵם לָהּ (א', י"ז) אֵין מְנַחֵם לִי (א' כ"א)
נָפְלָה עֲטֶרֶת רֹאשֵׁנוּ (ה', ט"ז)	בִּנְפֹּל עַמָּהּ בְּיַד צָר (א', ז')

In addition to their literary similarities, the tone and subject matter of the chapters are also in accord. Chapters 1 and 5 are quiet chapters; they do not concentrate on destruction. Instead, they record the emptiness and loneliness of the devastated city and its bereft community. Concerning themselves with what is no longer, chapters 1 and 5 detail that which is absent from their lives and from their city. These chapters speak longingly of the "days of old."[16] Key words include *ein*, meaning none, and *almana*, indicating a lonely state of widowhood. Israel has no comforter, no help, and no deliverer. These are chapters of hushed grief, which depict tear-filled eyes, desolation (*shomem*), and mourning (*evel*).

---

16. While the phrase "days of old" appears in chapter 2 as well (2:17), there it does not describe the yearning for a glorious past. Instead, that verse describes God bringing about the punishment that He promised in "days of old."

Chapters 2 and 4: Anger and Destruction

Linguistic similarities between chapters 2 and 4 abound, illustrating the correspondence between them.[17] Once again, many of these words and phrases are unique to chapters 2 and 4, thereby strengthening the specific link between them. Stars indicate that the emphasized words appear only in these two chapters in the book:

איכה, פרק ד'	איכה, פרק ב'
שָׁפַךְ חֲרוֹן אַפּוֹ (ד', י"א)	שָׁפַךְ כָּאֵשׁ חֲמָתוֹ (ב', ד')
בְּרֹאשׁ כָּל חוּצוֹת* (ד', א')	בְּרֹאשׁ כָּל חוּצוֹת* (ב', י"ט)
דָּבַק לְשׁוֹן יוֹנֵק אֶל חִכּוֹ בַּצָּמָא עוֹלָלִים שָׁאֲלוּ לֶחֶם (ד', ד')	בֵּעָטֵף עוֹלֵל וְיוֹנֵק בִּרְחֹבוֹת קִרְיָה (ב', י"א)
שִׂישִׂי וְשִׂמְחִי* בַּת אֱדוֹם (ד', כ"א)	וַיְשַׂמַּח* עָלַיִךְ אוֹיֵב (ב', י"ז)
תִּשְׁתַּפֵּכְנָה* אַבְנֵי קֹדֶשׁ (ד', א')	נִשְׁפַּךְ* לָאָרֶץ כְּבֵדִי... בְּהִשְׁתַּפֵּךְ* נַפְשָׁם
הַשֹּׁפְכִים* בְּקִרְבָּהּ דַּם צַדִּיקִים (ד', י"ג)	אֶל חֵיק אִמֹּתָם (ב', י"א-י"ב)
לֹא הֶאֱמִינוּ מַלְכֵי אֶרֶץ (ד', י"ב)	חִלֵּל מַמְלָכָה* וְשָׂרֶיהָ (ב', ב')
	וַיִּנְאַץ בְּזַעַם אַפּוֹ מֶלֶךְ* וְכֹהֵן (ב', ו')
	מַלְכָּהּ* וְשָׂרֶיהָ בַגּוֹיִם אֵין תּוֹרָה (ב', ט')
טוֹבִים הָיוּ חַלְלֵי* חֶרֶב מֵחַלְלֵי* רָעָב (ד', ט')	בְּהִתְעַטְּפָם כֶּחָלָל* בִּרְחֹבוֹת עִיר (ב', י"ב)
רוּחַ אַפֵּינוּ מְשִׁיחַ ה' נִלְכַּד בִּשְׁחִיתוֹתָם (ד', כ')	שִׁחֵת מִבְצָרָיו (ב', ה')
	שִׁחֵת מוֹעֲדוֹ (ב', ו')
	חָשַׁב ה' לְהַשְׁחִית (ב', ח')
בְּשֶׁבֶר בַּת עַמִּי * (ד', י')	עַל שֶׁבֶר בַּת עַמִּי* (ב', י"א)
כִּלָּה ה' אֶת חֲמָתוֹ שָׁפַךְ חֲרוֹן אַפּוֹ (ד', י"א)	אֵיכָה יָעִיב בְּאַפּוֹ... בְּיוֹם אַפּוֹ (ב', א')
	גָּדַע בָּחֳרִי אַף (ב', ג')
	וַיִּנְאַץ בְּזַעַם אַפּוֹ מֶלֶךְ וְכֹהֵן (ב', ו')
כִּלָּה ה' אֶת חֲמָתוֹ שָׁפַךְ חֲרוֹן אַפּוֹ (ד', י"א)	שָׁפַךְ כָּאֵשׁ חֲמָתוֹ* (ב', ד')

---

17. This chart appears in English at the conclusion of chapter 4 ("Chapter 4: In Summation").

איכה, פרק ד'	איכה, פרק ב'
וַיַּצֶּת אֵשׁ בְּצִיּוֹן וַתֹּאכַל יְסוֹדֹתֶיהָ (ד', י"א)	וַיַּבְעֶר בְּיַעֲקֹב כְּאֵשׁ לֶהָבָה אָכְלָה סָבִיב (ב', ג')
מֵחַטֹּאת נְבִיאֶיהָ* עֲוֹנֹת כֹּהֲנֶיהָ (ד', י"ג)	גַּם נְבִיאֶיהָ* לֹא מָצְאוּ חָזוֹן מֵה' (ב', ט') נְבִיאַיִךְ* חָזוּ לָךְ שָׁוְא וְתָפֵל (ב', י"ד) אִם יֵהָרֵג בְּמִקְדַּשׁ אֲדֹנָי כֹּהֵן וְנָבִיא * (ב', כ')
מֵחַטֹּאת נְבִיאֶיהָ עֲוֹנֹת כֹּהֲנֶיהָ (ד', י"ג)	וַיִּנְאַץ בְּזַעַם אַפּוֹ מֶלֶךְ וְכֹהֵן (ב', ו') אִם יֵהָרֵג בְּמִקְדַּשׁ אֲדֹנָי כֹּהֵן וְנָבִיא (ב', כ')
נָעוּ עִוְרִים בַּחוּצוֹת... כִּי נָצוּ גַּם נָעוּ (ד', י"ד-ט"ו)	וַיִּגְעוּ רֹאשָׁם (ב', ט"ו)
צָדוּ צְעָדֵינוּ מִלֶּכֶת בִּרְחֹבֹתֵינוּ (ד', י"ח)	עוֹלֵל וְיוֹנֵק בִּרְחֹבוֹת* קִרְיָה (ב', י"א)
גִּלָּה עַל* חַטֹּאתָיִךְ (ד', כ"ב)	וְלֹא גִלּוּ עַל* עֲוֹנֵךְ* (ב', י"ד)

Chapters 2 and 4 are loud and angry, characterized by depictions of God's wrath, consuming fire, and destruction. The impact of the events reverberates outward, as outsiders react to Jerusalem's fall. Some foreigners express stunned disbelief, pondering their long-held notions of Jerusalem's former status (2:15; 4:11). Israel's hateful enemies speak in strident, arrogant tones, revealing both their delight in Israel's downfall (2:16) and their revulsion at the contamination of the bloodied community (4:15).

A tone of abiding horror prevails in chapters 2 and 4, especially as they display the devastating effects of the famine in all its gruesomeness. Society seems to unravel, as children die on the streets and the adults fail to protect and provide for them. These chapters reach a devastating climax of horror and moral failure when they divulge the unfathomable crime of maternal cannibalism.

THE THEOLOGY OF THE STRUCTURE

The broad range of linguistic and thematic similarities suggests that there is a deeper meaning to the correspondence between these chapters. I propose that they hold the key to unravelling the book's theological approach.[18] As I have noted throughout this study, troubling theological questions simmer beneath the book's surface. These questions relate to God's nature and to the nature of His relationship with Israel. Is God an ally or an enemy? Are the people's sins responsible for this calamity, or is it disproportionate and unjust? This has bearing on how Israel responds to its pain and loss. Is the nation remorseful or defiant? Ashamed or outraged? These represent the critical topics in the book, as they illustrate the intersection between emotions and theology and outline a blueprint for coping with pain and loss.

The structure of the book reflects its theological complexity. It offers two divergent approaches to suffering and God – one that portrays humans coming to terms with God's actions and acknowledging that they are justified, and the other in which humans resist reconciliation, maintaining a defiant posture of incomprehension and outrage.

The peripheral chapters of the book (1 and 5) focus on procuring an admission of guilt, on human recognition of culpability. These chapters struggle with suffering, but they also struggle with sin, with the guilt and shame that accompany a confession. Chapter 1 mentions Israel's sins and rebellion in six different verses (verses 5, 8, 14, 18, 20, 22), and, in the second half of the chapter, Jerusalem moves toward an admission of sinfulness.[19] Initially, the city resists the conclusion that the responsibility for the calamity rests with her, instead focusing on God's great wrath (verse 12). Once Jerusalem acknowledges God's righteousness in verse 18, admission of sin follows (verses 18, 20), and the chapter concludes with Jerusalem's declaration that these events have occurred "because of all of my sins" (verse 22). In chapter 5, the community initially deflects

---

18. Gordis, 126–27, submits that the correspondences between these chapters reflect different historical settings and dates of composition. Chapters 1 and 5 reflect the indignities of national subjection, indicating that their composition takes place long after the destruction. Chapters 2 and 4 offer an eyewitness account, written closer in time to the catastrophe. By contrast, Assis, "Unity," 306–29, utilizes the linguistic and thematic correspondences between chapters 1 and 5, and those between 2 and 4, in order to prove the literary unity of the book. In my opinion, the key to understanding the parallel chapters lies in discerning their theological similarities.

19. The objective narrator (who speaks in verses 1–11b) has little difficulty describing Jerusalem's sins in chapter 1 (see verses 5 and 8–9). It is only once Jerusalem herself begins to speak (at the end of verse 11) that we see her resistance.

responsibility for the calamity, defiantly proclaiming, "Our fathers sinned, and they are no more, and we suffered for their iniquities" (verse 7). The chapter progresses toward an admission of responsibility, and the community concludes with a proclamation, "Woe to us for we have sinned!" (verse 16).[20] Chapters 1 and 5 arrive at a measure of theological equilibrium, regarding sin as the cause of their suffering. These chapters conclude that the world makes sense and God is just.

Chapters 2 and 4 never attain theological tranquility. Guiltless children die alongside righteous leaders (2:20; 4:4–5, 7–8) and the world makes no sense. The general tenor of chapter 4 mirrors the fatalism and confusion of chapter 2. These chapters contain accusation and anger at God, who inflicts His punitive actions disproportionately and indiscriminately ("as an enemy"), perhaps even capriciously, against innocents. Admission of widespread guilt does not appear in these chapters;[21] at best, they point to the culpability (2:14; 4:13) and punishment (2:2, 6, 9; 4:7–8; 16) of their leaders.[22] These chapters depict the incomprehension of people who struggle with God's active role in their suffering. Chapter 2 climaxes by flinging an accusation against God (verse 21): "You murdered on the day of Your anger; You slaughtered, You did not pity!" Chapter 4 never addresses God, whose active role in the chapter is destructive and decisive (verses 11, 16), and whose absence seems final.[23] In these chapters, nothing is resolved. The community continues to struggle with the inexplicable suffering of the righteous and the role of God in an unjust world. If the peripheral chapters of the

---

20. I regard verse 16 as the conclusion of chapter 5. In my opinion, verses 17–22 constitute a general epilogue to the book. See my discussion of this in chapter 5.

21. See the discussion of the phrase *avon bat ammi* (Eikha 4:6), where I explain why this verse remains consistent with my portrayal of chapter 4. In contrast, Gottwald, 67, maintains that all five chapters ("even chapter 2") witness the prophetic concept of sin.

22. This seems to contrast with chapters 1 and 5, which feature the entire nation equally: young and old, men and women, common-folk, priests, and officers.

23. Chapter 4 does conclude by acknowledging the central role that Zion's sinfulness can play in her restoration (Eikha 4:22). However, the main body of the chapter steers away from confession or even prayer, seeming to accept the dissolution of the relationship between Israel and God.

book project some measure of comprehension, the inner circle reflects bewilderment, outrage, and despondency.

How can the book produce two totally different perceptions of God's role in human suffering? What is the *correct* response to God's role in human tragedy, particularly within a national context? The structure of the book indicates that the answer is not simple, and that two opposing approaches co-exist in tension.[24]

On the one hand, chapters 1 and 5 illustrate the need to rely on simple faith, on the belief in divine justice, and on discerning a meaningful pattern in the relationship between God and His nation. Without this type of faith, the world is dark and absurd, incomprehensible and evil. Moreover, by clinging to this approach, Israel can learn to repair its relationship with God and restore order to its world.

On the other hand, Eikha does not rest upon simple formulae or facile answers in confronting preeminent theological quandaries. Chapters 2 and 4 confront the world's absurdities and tragedies with stark frankness. Pat answers cannot explain the death of children or human suffering. Mass tragedy, illness, and suffering are inexplicable. These are also undeniable components of the human struggle to understand God. Chapters 2 and 4 illustrate the anguish and confusion that people experience as they contend with suffering, making room for the complexity of the human condition and the ensuing inability to grasp God's ways fully.

The book's chiastic structure presents a circular manner of contending with God's role in human suffering. Eikha proposes that humans should balance two conflicting approaches, maintaining a perpetual oscillation between contradictory notions: simple, pure faith in God's world, and incensed dismay over its incomprehensibility. This produces a realistic model for those who struggle honestly to balance fidelity to God with a world that can often seem cruel and unfair. How is it possible to maintain a relationship with God within such a disquieting paradox? This ability to navigate an inscrutable world depends upon one's willingness to live with complexity. It also depends upon human tenacity – the steadfast determination to maintain faith in God's goodness and in human resilience, as we see in the middle chapter.

---

24. See Middlemas, "Storm," 94–95.

CHAPTER 3: THE CRITICAL CENTER

The chiastic structure directs our attention to the chapter that lies at its heart. Chapter 3, which portrays a suffering individual who grapples with God's nature, represents the theological center of the book, its ideological crux.[25] The middle section of this chapter (verses 21–39), which constitutes the very epicenter of the book,[26] depicts a righteous God defined by His enduring compassion and allegiance to His nation.

Intriguingly, the subject that lies in the book's innermost core (3:26–30) relates to humans rather than God. In its central axis, Eikha suggests that humans should submit to their suffering in a quest to find meaning in it. The word *"tov"* appears as the opening word of the three *tet* verses (25–27), tantalizing the reader with the optimistic notion that one can find goodness at the heart of the human experience.

Eikha's structure mirrors a whirlwind or a turbulent storm.[27] The middle section of chapter 3 is the placid center, the eye of the storm, around which swirl suffering and misery. This image focuses attention upon the surprisingly calm center but does not ignore the significance of the powerful winds that encircle it.[28]

This design represents the shape of the sufferer's theological experience. Two parallel rings enfold the sufferer, representing the tangled fluctuation between theodicy and outrage. It is critical for the sufferer to move back and forth between these contradictory approaches in order to contend adequately with the theological questions presented by loss. Despite the turbulence that surrounds him, the sufferer can find tranquility and faith in his innermost being. People have the ability to combat the onslaught of hostile forces that swirl around them, because

---

25. Many scholars note the central theological importance of chapter 3. See, for example, Grossberg, *Centripetal*, 85; A. Mintz, "The Rhetoric of Lamentations and the Representation of Catastrophe," *Prooftexts* 2, 1 (1982), 10; Middlemas, "Storm," 88.
26. See Mintz, "Catastrophe," 10; Middlemas, "Storm," 89.
27. For an elaboration of this idea, see Middlemas, "Storm," 84.
28. In the above exploration of Eikha's structure, I have focused only on the center of chapter 3, which illustrates the deep resources of faith at the core of the book. Here, I omit the trajectory of the chapter and its remarkable portrayal of the *gever's* transformation. Chapter 3 charts a linear course, portraying a sufferer who moves from despair to hope, spawned by the faith-filled introspection that appears at its pivotal center.

they draw from the hope and conviction that lie at their core. In this way, *Eikha* weaves a magnificent portrait of the resources and resilience that lie deep within the human soul.

CONCLUSION

Eikha's chiastic structure offers a multifaceted model for the religious person to cope with suffering. The two concentric circles that surround the central chapter reflect the idea that the relationship between God and humans remains a complex affair, filled with circular and contradictory movements that mirror the theological turmoil that envelops humankind. At Eikha's core, we find human tenacity and optimism, fueled by abiding faith in God's righteousness and compassion. God's ways are eternal; they renew themselves daily (3:23). Even if humans do not always comprehend, hope for good prevails.

The experience of loss represents an opportunity to dig deeper into the nature of humankind and its relationship with God. Suffering produces introspection, and an examined life generates purposeful existence. As it turns out, calamity does not necessarily destroy one's convictions; instead, it can enable one to discover them. The experience of adversity can foster faith in a turbulent world.

Acknowledgments

I want to take this opportunity to thank several key people who have been instrumental in producing this book. First, I am grateful to my students at Matan, Midreshet Moriah, and Herzog College, who have been a sounding board for these ideas during the past twenty-seven years of teaching Eikha. It is a great privilege to teach Torah to students of different ages, genders, cultures, and backgrounds. Their variety of life experiences allows for different perspectives, and their comments have deepened and broadened my understanding of the book.

This book began as a series of internet *shiurim* sent out weekly on Yeshivat Har Etzion's Israel Koschitzky Virtual Beit Midrash (VBM). The VBM has contributed greatly to the spread of Torah worldwide, and it provided me a framework within which to write this book. I thank the conscientious editors of that series, Meira Mintz and Yoseif Bloch, for their skilled editing and comments. I am deeply indebted to my dear friend Aviva Aharon, who read every installment of the VBM *Megillat Eikha* series. Despite the somber subject matter, she paid great attention to the details, and with her keen artistic eye she graciously offered me astute suggestions. I thank her for her time and also for her gift of friendship.

I thank the Levene family for their generous support. I am also very grateful to Matan and to Rabbanit Malke Bina not only for supporting this book but also for creating an *ohel shel Torah* for me and for countless other women over the past thirty years. It is an honor to be associated with Matan, which has established the gold standard of women's Torah learning, and I look forward to many years of continued partnership.

I am honored to contribute a second volume to the Maggid Studies in Tanakh series (MST). The staff at Maggid has been unfailingly professional, and it has been a great pleasure to work with them. I especially thank Rachel Miskin for her careful editing and Ita Olesker for her meticulous proofreading and for skillfully shepherding the book to its final stages.

Finally, I thank those whose presence in my life provide abundant love and happiness. My deepest appreciation is for my husband, Rav Reuven Ziegler, who has been involved with this book at every stage. As editor-in-chief of the VBM he set the internet series in motion, and as editorial director of Maggid he facilitated its transformation into a book. Most significantly, I am grateful for his limitless support and encouragement in our shared adventures. My children, Tehilla, Yisrael, Ariel, Yehoshua and Noam – you are my joy and inspiration; may Hashem continue to bless you and watch over you always. Special thanks to my son Yehoshua for preparing the bibliography.

To my father Dr. Allen Zeiger and my stepmother Leah, and my in-laws, Rabbi Zvi and Sandy Ziegler, I offer my love and gratitude for your many kindnesses. I am especially grateful to my father, who called me every time that *daf yomi* mentioned a verse from Eikha. In sharing his insights from his daily learning, my father's wisdom has greatly influenced this book. I keenly feel the loss of my mother, Naomi Ruth Zeiger *z"l*. Her untimely death forced me to grapple personally with some of the darker aspects of Eikha, the theological questions and emotional difficulty of dealing with the death of a loved one. On a more positive note, my mother embedded her love for Jerusalem and for the Jewish people into our family; I have no doubt that her sentiments have made their way into this book.

I have dedicated this book to my dear friend Dr. Avigail Malka Rock *z"l*. Avigail was an exemplary teacher of Tanakh and a person of morality, good humor, and wisdom. Her zest for life and her moral vision were an inspiration for me, and her friendship was a true partnership based on shared values and goals. I am grateful for the many years that we shared life together and for the impact that she left upon me, her family, friends, and *Klal Yisrael*.

With deepest gratitude, I express praise and thanks to the *Ribbono shel Olam*, who has given me *shefa berakhot* and the opportunity to learn Torah and disseminate it. I pray that this book merits *lehagdil Torah ulahaadirah*, to spread the love of Torah and a deeper appreciation for its profound ideas.

יִהְיוּ לְרָצוֹן אִמְרֵי פִי וְהֶגְיוֹן לִבִּי לְפָנֶיךָ ה' צוּרִי וְגֹאֲלִי.

The publication of this book was delayed by the pandemic that swept across the world in early 2020. Since the beginning of the worldwide catastrophe, more than two million people have lost their lives and many more have been affected physically, psychologically, and economically. This has been a challenging time, and I fear that we have yet to see its end or the magnitude of the repercussions of the pandemic. Yet, as is often the case, and as we have seen in this study of Eikha, one can often find a ray of light buried deep within calamity. In times of difficulty, people of faith can turn to God, renewing their devotion through prayer, good deeds, and Torah study. I am privileged to participate in an energetic and uplifting quest for increased Torah study around the world on long distance media such as Zoom, as our community searches for ways to connect to each other and to God. I have also witnessed uplifting examples of people who search deeply within themselves, finding optimism and strength, and faith in the human ability to sustain kindness, humor, and unity during challenging times. I offer my prayers and condolences to those who have been harmed, and my hopes that this pandemic will end soon and that the world community will have a full recovery.

I am grateful for the gift of *talmud Torah*, which has consoled and strengthened the Jewish nation throughout our exile and hardships. I pray that the comfort of *talmud Torah* will continue to help all families dealing with difficulties. In the words of Psalms 119:92: "Were Your Torah not my delight, I would have been lost in my misery."

I conclude by acknowledging my boundless awe and thankfulness that today we are privileged to study Torah in Jerusalem. No longer does the city sit lonely, like a widow. Instead, we witness the fulfillment of the prophecies of consolation of both Isaiah and Zechariah:

> Lift up your eyes and see! They are all gathering and coming back to you [Jerusalem]. Your sons will come from afar and your daughters will be carried tenderly on the hip. (Is. 60:4)

> There shall yet be elderly men and women in the streets of Jerusalem, and each person will hold a staff in his hand because of advanced age. And the streets of the city will be filled with boys and girls playing in the streets. (Zech. 8:4–5)

May we be worthy of this great opportunity, merit the full restoration of Jerusalem's former glory, and continue to reap the blessings of this extraordinary time, as it says:

> May the Lord bless you from Zion and may you see the bounty of Jerusalem all the days of your life. And may you see children of your children, and peace upon Israel. (Ps. 128:5–6)

יְבָרֶכְךָ ה׳ מִצִּיּוֹן וּרְאֵה בְּטוּב יְרוּשָׁלָם כֹּל יְמֵי חַיֶּיךָ.
וּרְאֵה בָנִים לְבָנֶיךָ שָׁלוֹם עַל יִשְׂרָאֵל.

Alon Shevut, Israel
Adar 5781
February 2021

Bibliography

Adeney, W. F. *Songs of Solomon and the Lamentations of Jeremiah*. London: Hodder & Stoughton, 1895.

Albrektson, B. *Studies in the Text and Theology of the Book of Lamentations* in *Studia Theologica Lundensia* 21. Gleerup: Lund, 1963.

Alter, R. *The Art of Biblical Poetry*. New York: Basic Books, 1985.

———. *The Hebrew Bible. A Translation with Commentary*. New York: W. W. Norton & Company, 2019.

Angel, H. *Haggai, Zechariah, and Malachi: Prophecy in an Age of Uncertainty*. Jerusalem: Maggid, 2016.

Assis, E. *Identity in Conflict: The Struggle between Esau and Jacob, Edom and Israel*. Winona Lake, IN: Eisenbrauns, 2016.

———. "The Alphabetic Acrostic in the Book of Lamentations," *CBQ* 69. 2007: 710–24.

———. "The Unity of the Book of Lamentations," *CBQ* 71. 2009: 306–29.

Ayali, M. "The God Who Suffers the Sufferings of Israel," in *Studies in Jewish Thought,* edited by S. O. Heller-Willensky and M. Idel. Jerusalem: Magnes, 1989: 29–50 [Hebrew].

Bar-Efrat, S. "Some Observations on the Analysis of Structure in Biblical Narrative," *Vetus Testamentum* 30. 1980: 154–73.

Bazak, A. *To This Very Day: Fundamental Questions in Bible Study*. Jerusalem: Maggid Books, 2020.

Berkovits, E. *Faith after the Holocaust*. Jerusalem: Maggid Books, 2019.

Berlin, A. *Lamentations*. The Old Testament Library. Louisville: Westminster John Knox Press, 2004.

————. "Reading Biblical Poetry," in *The Jewish Study Bible*, edited by A. Berlin and M. Brettler. New York: Oxford University Press, 2004: 2097–2104.

————. *The Dynamics of Biblical Parallelism*. Bloomington: Indiana University Press, 1985.

Berman, J. "Criteria for Establishing Chiastic Structure: Lamentations 1 and 2 as Test Case," *Maarav* 21, 2014: 57–69.

Black, J. A. et al., eds. *The Electronic Text Corpus of Sumerian Literature*. Oxford, 1998–2006. http://etcsl.orinst.ox.ac.uk/.

Briggs, C. A. *The Book of Psalms*. ICC. Edinburgh: T & T Clark, 1906.

Brown, F., S. R. Driver, and C. A. Briggs. *A Hebrew and English Lexicon of the Old Testament*. Oxford: Clarendon Press, 1951.

Buber, M. *Darko shel Mikra*. Jerusalem: Bialik, 1964 [Hebrew].

Burg, J. F. "Biblical Acrostics and their Relation to Other Ancient Near Eastern Acrostics," in *The Bible in Light of Cuneiform Literature: Scripture in Context*, edited by W. W. Hallo, B. W. Jones, and G. L. Mattingly. ANET Studies 8. Lewiston, NY: Edwin Mellon Press, 1990.

Cassuto, U. *A Commentary on the Book of Exodus*. Jerusalem: Magnes Press, 1967.

Childs, B. S. *Introduction to the Old Testament as Scripture*. London: SCM, 1979.

Clark, G. R. *The Word Hesed in the Hebrew Bible*. Sheffield: JSOT Press, 1993.

Cogan, M. *The Raging Torrent: Historical Inscriptions from Assyria and Babylonia Relating to Ancient Israel*. Jerusalem: Carta, 2015.

Cogan, M., and H. Tadmor, *II Kings*. Anchor Bible; Garden City: Doubleday, 1988.

Cohen, A. *The Psalms*. London: Soncino, 1945.

Cohen, S. D. J. "The Destruction: From Scripture to Midrash," *Prooftexts* 2. 1982: 18–39.

Cohn, G. H. *Textual Tapestries: Explorations of the Five Megillot*. Jerusalem: Maggid, 2016.

Condamin, A. "Symmetrical Repetitions in Lamentations, Chapters I and II," *JTS* 7, 1905: 137–40.

Davis, E. F. "Reading the Song Iconographically," in *Scrolls of Love*. New York: Fordham University, 2006: 84–172.

Demsky, A. "A Proto-Canaanite Abecedary Dating from the Period of the Judges and its Implications for the History of the Alphabet," *Tel Aviv* 4. 1977: 14–27.

———. *Literacy in Ancient Israel*. Jerusalem: Magnes, 2012.

Dobbs-Allsopp, F. W. *Lamentations*. Interpretation. Louisville: Westminster John Knox Press, 2002.

———. "Linguistic Evidence for the Date of Lamentations," *Journal of the Near Eastern Society of Columbia University* 26.1998: 1–36.

Driver, S. R. *An Introduction to the Literature of the Old Testament*. New York: Charles Scribner's Sons, reprinted 1914.

Eissfeldt, O. *The Old Testament: An Introduction*. Translated by Ackroyd P. New York: Harper and Row, 1965.

Elyakim, N. "Connections between R. Yehuda Halevi and R. A. Ibn Ezra in Interpretations of the Bible," *Shemaatin*. 1998: 85–103 [Hebrew].

Engleking, B. *Such a Beautiful Sunny Day... – Jews Seeking Refuge in the Polish Countryside, 1942–1945*. Jerusalem: Yad Vashem Publications, 2016.

First, M. "The *Pe/Ayin* Order in Ancient Israel and Its Implications for the Book of Psalms," in *Esther Unmasked*. New York: Kodesh Press, 2015.

Fishbane, M. "Form and Reformulation of the Biblical Priestly Blessing," JAOS 103. 1983: 115–21.

Freedman, D. N. "Preface," in *Chiasmus in Antiquity: Structures, Analyses, Exegesis*, edited by J. W. Welch. Hildesheim: Gerstenberg Verlag, 1981.

Gerstenberger, Erhard S. *Psalms Part 2 and Lamentations*, FOTL XV. Grand Rapids: Eerdmans, 2001.

Ginsburg, C. D. *Introduction to the Masoretico-Critical Edition of the Hebrew Bible*. London, 1897.

Glueck, N. *Hesed in the Bible*. Cincinnati: Hebrew Union College Press, 1967.

Gordis, R. *The Song of Songs and Lamentations*. New York: Ktav, reprinted 1974.

Gottwald, N. K. *Studies in the Book of Lamentations*. London: SCM Press, 1954.

Granot, T. "That This Song May Answer Before Them Forever." The Israel Koschitzky Virtual Beit Midrash. http://etzion.org.il/en/ song-may-answer-them-forever.

Gray, G. B. *Forms of Hebrew Poetry*. New York: Ktav, 1972.

Gross, J. T. *Neighbors: The Destruction of the Jewish Community in Jedwabne, Poland*. London: Penguin, 2000.

Grossberg, D. *Centripetal and Centrifugal Structures in Biblical Poetry*. SBL Monograph Series. Atlanta: Scholars Press, 1989.

Grossman, V. *Everything Flows*. Translated by R. Chandler, E. Chandler, and E. Aslanyan. New York: New York Review Books, 2009.

Hakham, A. *Daat Mikra: Isaiah*. Jerusalem: Mossad Harav Kook, 1984.

———. *Daat Mikra: Psalms*. Jerusalem: Mossad Harav Kook, 1990.

Hasan-Rokem, G. *Web of Life: Folklore and Midrash in Rabbinic Literature*, trans. B. Stein. Stanford: Stanford University Press, 2000.

Hillers, D. R. *Lamentations*. Anchor Bible. Garden City: Doubleday, 1972.

House, P. R. *Lamentations*. Word Biblical Commentary 23B. Nashville: Thomas Nelson Publishers, 2004.

Israel, A. *I Kings: Torn in Two*. Jerusalem: Maggid Books, 2013.

Joyce, P. "Lamentations and the Grief Process: A Psychological Reading," *Biblical Interpretation* 1. 1993: 304–20.

Kaufmann, Y. *Toldot HaEmuna HaYisraelit*, vol. 7. Jerusalem: Bialik, 1964.

Keil, C. F. *Jeremiah, Lamentations*. Translated by Martin, J. Grand Rapids: Zondervan, 1872, reprinted, 1980.

Kimelman, R. "Rabbi Yokhanan and Origen on the Song of Songs: A Third-Century Jewish-Christian Disputation," *Harvard Theological Review* 73. 1980: 567–95.

Kübler-Ross, E. *On Death and Dying*. New York: Macmillan, 1970.

Kugel, J. L. *The Idea of Biblical Poetry: Parallelism and Its History*. New Haven: Yale University Press, 1981.

Levy, Y. "Jerusalem in the Torah (II): Avram's Encounter with the King of Sodom and with Malki-Tzedek." The Israel Koschitzky Virtual Beit Midrash. https://www.etzion.org.il/en/jerusalem-torah-ii-avrams-encounter-king-sodom-and-malki-tzedek.

Lieberman, S. *Hellenism in Jewish Palestine*. New York, 1950.

Liebreich, L. J. "The Songs of Ascent and the Priestly Blessing," *JBL* 74. 1955: 33–36.

Linafelt, T. "Life in Excess: The Midrash in Lamentations," in *Surviving Lamentations: Catastrophe, Lament and Protest in the Aftermath of a Biblical Book*. Chicago: The University of Chicago Press, 2000.

———. "Living Beyond Lamentations: The Rhetoric of Survival in Second Isaiah," in *Surviving Lamentations: Catastrophe, Lament and Protest in the Afterlife of a Biblical Book*. Chicago: The University of Chicago Press, 2000.

Maimonides, *The Guide of the Perplexed*. Translated by S. Pines. Chicago: University of Chicago Press, 1963.

McDaniel, T. F. "Philological Studies in Lamentations," *Biblica* 49. 1968: 27–53.

Middlemas, J. "The Violent Storm in Lamentations," JSOT 29. 2004: 81–97.

Mintz, A. *Hurban: Responses to Catastrophe in Hebrew Literature*. New York: Columbia University Press, 1984.

———. "The Rhetoric of Lamentations and the Representation of Catastrophe," *Prooftexts* 2. 1982: 1–17.

Moore, M. S. "Human Suffering in *Lamentations*," *Revue Biblique* 90. 1983: 534–55.

Moshkovitz, Y. "*Eikha*," in *Daat Mikra: Five Megillot*. Jerusalem: Mossad Harav Kook, 1990.

O'Conner, K. "Lamentations," in *The New Interpreter's Bible*, vol. 6. Nashville: Abington, 2001.

Origen. *Origen: Homilies on Jeremiah, Homily on I Kings 28*, translated by J. C. Smith. Catholic University of America Press, 1998.

Porteous, N. "Jerusalem: Zion, The Growth of a Symbol," in *Verbannung und Geimkehr, Rudolph Festschrift*, edited by W. Randolph. Tubingen: Mohr, 1961.

Pritchard, J. B. *The Ancient Near East: An Anthology of Texts and Pictures*, vol. 1. Princeton: Princeton University Press, 1953, reprinted 1973.

Provan, I. *Lamentations*. NCBC. Grand Rapids: Eerdmans, 1991.

Radday, Y. "Chiasmus in the Hebrew Biblical Narratives," *Beit Mikra*. 1964: 48–72 [Hebrew].

Reimar, D. J. "Good Grief? A Psychological Reading of Lamentations," *ZAW* 114. 2002: 542–59.

Reizel, A. *Introduction to the Midrashic Literature*. Alon Shevut: Tevunot, 2011 [Hebrew].

Renkema, J. *Lamentations: Historical Commentary on the Old Testament*. Translated by Doyle, B. Leuven: Peeters, 1998.

———. "The Literary Structure of Lamentations (I–IV)," *The Structural Analysis of Biblical and Canaanite Poetry*, edited by M. van de Meer and J. C. de Moor. Sheffield: Sheffield Academic Press, 1988: 294–396.

———. "The Meaning of the Parallel Acrostics in Lamentations," *VT* 45. 1995: 379–83.

———. "Theodicy in Lamentations?" in A. Laato and J. C. de Moor, eds., *Theodicy in the World of the Bible*. Leiden, 2003.

Rosenfeld, A. "Acrostics in Eikha, Chapter 5?" *Sinai* 110. 1992 [Hebrew].

Rozenson, Y. "Divine Providence Over Israel and Over the Nations," *Megadim* 9. 1990: 49–62 [Hebrew].

Ryken, L. *Sweeter than Honey, Richer than Gold: A Guided Study of Biblical Poetry*. Bellingham, WA: Lexham Press, 2015.

Saebø, M. "Who is 'the Man' in Lamentations 3? A Fresh Approach to the Interpretation of the Book of Lamentations," in *Understanding Poets and Prophets*, edited by A. Graeme Auld. Sheffield: Sheffield Academic Press, 1993.

Sakenfeld, K. D. *The Meaning of Hesed in the Hebrew Bible: A New Inquiry*. Missoula: Scholars Press for the Harvard Semitic Museum, 1978.

Sarna, N. *Understanding Genesis*. New York: Schocken Books, 1970.

Shea, W. H. "The Qinah Structure of the Book of Lamentations," *Biblica* 60. 1979: 103–7.

Sherwin, B. L. "Theodicy," in *Contemporary Jewish Religious Thought*, edited by Arthur A. Cohen and Paul Mendes-Flohr. New York: The Free Press, 1987.

Smith-Christopher, D. L. *A Biblical Theology of Exile*. OBT; Minneapolis: Fortress, 2002.

Sommer, B. *A Prophet Reads Isaiah: Allusion in Isaiah 40–66*. Stanford: Stanford University Press, 1998.

Soloveitchik, R. J. B. *Halakhic Man*. Translated by L. Kaplan. Philadelphia: JPS, 1983.

————. *Kol Dodi Dofek.* Translated by D.Z. Gordon. New York: Yeshiva University, 2006.

————. *On Repentance,* edited by P. Peli. Jerusalem: Maggid, 2017.

————. *Out of the Whirlwind: Essays on Mourning, Suffering, and the Human Condition,* edited by David Shatz, Joel B. Wolowelsky, and Reuven Ziegler. Jersey City: Ktav, 2003.

————. "Sacred and Profane." reprinted in *Shiurei HaRav,* edited by Joseph Epstein. Hoboken: Ktav, 1994: 4–32.

Thomas, H. A. "Relating Prayer and Pain: Psychological Analysis and Lamentations Research," *Tyndale Bulletin* 61. 2010: 183–208.

Tov, E. "Recensional Differences Between the Masoretic Text and the Septuagint of Proverbs," in Attridge, H. W. et al., *Of Scribes and Scrolls: Studies on the Hebrew Bible, Intertestamental Judaism, and Christian Origins Presented to John Strugnell.* 1990.

Welch, J. W., ed. *Chiasmus in Antiquity: Structures, Analyses, Exegesis.* Hildesheim: Gerstenberg Verlag, 1981.

Welch, J. W. "Criteria for Identifying and Evaluating the Presence of Chiasmus," *Journal of Book of Mormon Studies* 4. 1995: 1–14.

Werblowsky, R. J. Z. "Messianism," in *Contemporary Jewish Religious Thought,* edited by Cohen, A. A., and P. Mendes-Flohr. New York: The Free Press, 1988: 597–602.

Westermann, C. *Lamentations: Issues and Interpretations.* Minneapolis: Fortress Press, 1993.

Wiesel, E. *Night.* Translation by Wiesel M. London: Penguin, 2006.

Willey, P. T. *Remember the Former Things: The Recollection of Previous Texts in Second Isaiah.* Scholars Press, 1997.

Ziegler, R. *Majesty and Humility: The Thought of Rabbi Joseph B. Soloveitchik.* Jerusalem: Urim, 2012.

Ziegler, Y. "Paradise Regained: *Eretz Yisrael* and the Garden of Eden," in *The Koren Maḥzor for Yom HaAtzma'ut and Yom Yerushalayim.* Jerusalem: Koren, 2015: 101–8.

————. *Promises to Keep: The Oath in Biblical Narrative.* Leiden: Brill, 2008.

————. *Ruth: From Alienation to Monarchy.* Jerusalem: Maggid, 2015.

————. "The Return to Gan Eden in *Shir HaShirim,*" in *BeḤag HaMatzot,* edited by A. Bazak. Alon Shevut: Tevunot, 2015: 329–48 [Hebrew].

Other books in the Maggid Studies in Tanakh series:

The fonts used in this book are from the Arno family

Maggid Books
The best of contemporary Jewish thought from
Koren Publishers Jerusalem Ltd.

—